Handbook of

INTERNET
COMPUTING

INTERNET and COMMUNICATIONS

This new book series presents the latest research and technological developments in the field of internet and multimedia systems and applications. We remain committed to publishing high-quality reference and technical books written by experts in the field.

If you are interested in writing, editing, or contributing to a volume in this series, or if you have suggestions for needed books, please contact Dr. Borko Furht at the following address:

Dr. Borko Furht, Director
Multimedia Laboratory
Department of Computer Science and Engineering
Florida Atlantic University
777 Glades Road
Boca Raton, FL 33431 U.S.A.

E-mail: borko@cse.fau.edu

Handbook of
INTERNET
COMPUTING

Editor-in-Chief and Author Borko Furht
Professor of Computer Science and Engineering
Florida Atlantic University
Boca Raton, Florida

CRC Press
Taylor & Francis Group
Boca Raton London New York

CRC Press is an imprint of the
Taylor & Francis Group, an **informa** business

First published 2000 by CRC Press
Taylor & Francis Group
6000 Broken Sound Parkway NW, Suite 300
Boca Raton, FL 33487-2742

Reissued 2018 by CRC Press

This book contains information obtained from authentic and highly regarded sources. Reasonable efforts have been made to publish reliable data and information, but the author and publisher cannot assume responsibility for the validity of all materials or the consequences of their use. The authors and publishers have attempted to trace the copyright holders of all material reproduced in this publication and apologize to copyright holders if permission to publish in this form has not been obtained. If any copyright material has not been acknowledged please write and let us know so we may rectify in any future reprint.

Library of Congress Cataloging-in-Publication Data

Furht, Borivoje,
Handbook of internet computing / editor-in-chief and author, Borko Furht.
    p. cm. — (Internet and Communications series)
Includes bibliographical references and index.
ISBN 0-8493-0086-X (alk. paper
    1. Internet (Computer network). I. Title. II. Series.

TK5105.875.I57 F88 2000
004.67'8—dc21   00-037850

A Library of Congress record exists under LC control number: 00037850

Publisher's Note
The publisher has gone to great lengths to ensure the quality of this reprint but points out that some imperfections in the original copies may be apparent.

Disclaimer
The publisher has made every effort to trace copyright holders and welcomes correspondence from those they have been unable to contact.

ISBN 13: 978-1-315-89353-2 (hbk)
ISBN 13: 978-1-351-07263-2 (ebk)

Visit the Taylor & Francis Web site at http://www.taylorandfrancis.com and the
CRC Press Web site at http://www.crcpress.com

PREFACE

The Internet is coming of age! A few years ago the Internet was hot, exciting, and wild. Today, the Internet is still hot and exciting, but better structured, well managed, and commercially viable. It became a major information superhighway of the 21st Century and it changed our lives.

Let us remember the history of the Internet. The Internet age can be divided into four time periods, as illustrated in Figure 1:

- Military Development,
- Age of the Arpanet,
- Age of the Internet, and
- Age of the Internet and World Wide Web.

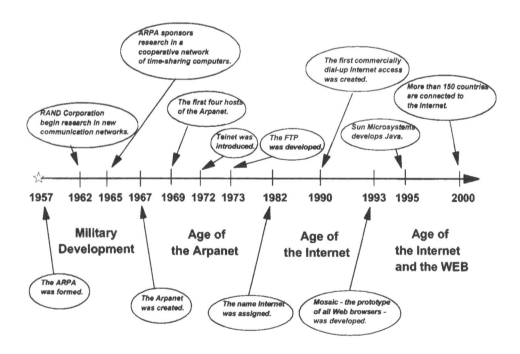

Figure 1. History of the Internet.

The Internet era began in 1957 when the Advanced Research Project Agency (ARPA) was formed. The purpose of ARPA (today known as the Defense Advanced Research Project Agency or DARPA) is to help maintain U.S. technological superiority. In 1962, Rand Corporation began research in new communication networks. In 1965, ARPA sponsored research into a cooperative network of time-sharing computers, and in 1967 the Arpanet was created. The Arpanet was a wide area network of computers developed to link government agencies and universities. In 1969, the first four hosts of the Arpanet were UCLA, UC Santa Barbara, University of Utah, and Stanford Research Institute. In 1972, Ray Tomlinson created the first e-mail program to send personal messages across the Arpanet. Electronic mail helped move the Arpanet beyond its military use. In 1972, *Telnet* standard was introduced, which allows a user to log onto a remote computer. In 1973, *File Transfer Protocol (FTP)* was developed, which allows long-distance transfer of files from one computer to another.

In 1982, officially the Internet was born – the term *Internet* was assigned to a connected set of networks and *TCP/IP* was established as an Internet standard. In 1990, the first commercially available dial-up Internet access was created and the Arpanet was decommissioned.

A major cultural change began in 1993 with the advent of the World Wide Web. Marc Andressen, who would later co-found Netscape Communications Corporation and market Netscape Navigator, developed Mosaic, the prototype of all Web browsers, at the University of Illinois at Urbana-Champaign. In 1995, Sun Microsystems developed Java, which is an object-oriented cross-platform programming language designed to work on network systems like the Internet. Today more than 150 countries are connected to the Internet, and there are more than 20 million host computers.

The purpose of *The Handbook of Internet Computing* is to provide a comprehensive reference on advanced topics in this field. We invited world experts and leading researchers in the field to contribute to this Handbook with their visionary views of the trends in this exciting field. The Handbook is intended for both researchers and practitioners in the field, for scientists and engineers involved in Internet computing and its applications, and for anyone who wants to learn about the field of Internet computing. The Handbook can also be beneficial as the textbook or reference book for graduate courses in the area of Internet computing.

The Handbook is divided into three parts and comprised of 21 chapters. Part I on *"Internet Technologies,"* which consists of 6 chapters, introduces Internet and Web architectures, coding standards, content-based browsing and retrieval techniques, and component technologies for Web-based development. Part II on *"Internet Tools,"* which consists of 7 chapters, covers a variety of advanced Internet tools including tools for building collaborative applications, component Web-search engines, virtual reality systems, mediaspace, and others. Part III on *"Internet Applications"* comprises 8 chapters and covers various contemporary Internet applications including multimedia broadcasting over the Internet, unified messaging systems, geographic information systems, digital libraries, videoconferencing, distance-based learning, and news systems.

I would like to thank all 48 authors who have developed individual chapters for the Handbook. Without their expertise and effort this Handbook would never come true. CRC Press also deserves my sincere recognition for their support throughout the project.

Borko Furht
Boca Raton, Florida

EDITOR-IN-CHIEF

Borko Furht is a professor of computer science and engineering at Florida Atlantic University (FAU) in Boca Raton, Florida. He is the founder and director of the Multimedia Laboratory at FAU, funded by the National Science Foundation. Before joining FAU, he was a vice president of research and a senior director of development at Modcomp, a computer company of Daimler Benz, Germany, a professor at the University of Miami in Coral Gables, Florida, and senior scientist at the Institute "Boris Kidric"-Vinca in Belgrade, Yugoslavia.

Professor Furht received BEEE (Dipl.Eng.), M.Sc. and Ph.D. degrees in electrical and computer engineering from the University of Belgrade. His current research is in multimedia systems, video compression, storage and retrieval, synchronization, and Internet and multimedia applications. He is the author of numerous books and articles in the areas of multimedia, computer architecture, real-time computing, and operating systems. He is a founder and editor-in-chief of the *Journal of Multimedia Tools and Applications* (Kluwer Academic Publishers). He has received several technical and publishing awards, and has consulted for many high-tech companies including IBM, Hewlett-Packard, Xerox, General Electric, JPL, NASA, Honeywell, and RCA. He has also served as a consultant to various colleges and universities. He has given many invited talks, keynote lectures, seminars, and tutorials. He is a senior member of the IEEE and member of the ACM.

EDITOR-IN-CHIEF

CONTRIBUTORS

Krishna Adusumilli
Florida Atlantic University
Boca Raton, Florida, USA

Zijad Aganovic
CyLex Systems
Boca Raton, Florida, USA

Dan Benson
Siemens Technology-to-Business
Center
Berkeley, California, USA

Sandra Brey
Florida Atlantic University
Boca Raton, Florida, USA

Claudio Catania
Hewlett Packard Laboratories
Bristol, United Kingdom

Benjamin Falchuk
University of Ottawa
Ottawa, Canada

Susan Fallon
Florida Atlantic University
Boca Raton, Florida, USA

Eduardo B. Fernandez
Florida Atlantic University
Boca Raton, Florida, USA

Lidia Fuentes
University of Malaga
Malaga, Spain

Borko Furht
Florida Atlantic University
Boca Raton, Florida, USA

Joseph Hardin
University of Michigan
Ann Arbor, Michigan, USA

Scott A. Hissam
Software Engineering Institute
Carnegie Mellon University
Pittsburgh, Pennsylvania, USA

Arding Hsu
Siemens Technology-to-Business
Center
Berkeley, California, USA

Sam Hsu
Florida Atlantic University
Boca Raton, Florida, USA

Jiung-Yao Huang
Tamkang University
Taiwan, ROC

Jeffrey Ice
Pipe Dream, Inc.
West Palm Beach, Florida, USA

Toru Ishida
Kyoto University
Kyoto, Japan

Fernam Jahanian
University of Michigan
Ann Arbor, Michigan, USA

Ahmed Karmouch
University of Ottawa
Ottawa, Canada

Peter Knoop
University of Michigan
Ann Arbor, Michigan, USA

Charles Law
Florida Atlantic University
Boca Raton, Florida, USA

Jang Ho Lee
University of Michigan
Ann Arbor, Michigan, USA

Xiuqi Li
Florida Atlantic University
Boca Raton, Florida, USA

Fernando Lyardet
Universidad Nacional de La Plata
Argentina

G. Robert Malan
University of Michigan
Ann Arbor, Michigan, USA

Oge Marques
Florida Atlantic University
Boca Raton, Florida, USA

Hideyuki Nakanishi
Kyoto University
Kyoto, Japan

Toshikazu Nishimura
Kyoto University
Kyoto, Japan

Chris Phoenix
Cytrix Systems
Fort Lauderdale, Florida, USA

Gilda Pour
San Jose State University
San Jose, California, USA

Atul Prakash
University of Michigan
Ann Arbor, Michigan, USA

Daniele Rizzetto
Hewlett Packard Laboratories
Bristol, United Kingdom

Gustavo Rossi
Universidad Nacional de La Plata
Argentina

Nicolas Roussel
Universite Paris-Sud
Orsay Cedex, France

Daniel Schwabe
PUC-Rio, Brazil

Robert C. Seacord
Software Engineering Institute
Carnegie Mellon University
Pittsburgh, Pennsylvania, USA

Nalin Sharda
Victoria University of Technology
Melbourne, Australia

Hyong Sop Shim
University of Michigan
Ann Arbor, Michigan, USA

Sushila Subramanian
University of Michigan
Ann Arbor, Michigan, USA

Jose M. Troya
University of Malaga
Malaga, Spain

Kurt C. Wallnau
Software Engineering Institute
Carnegie Mellon University
Pittsburgh, Pennsylvania, USA

Fangju Wang
University of Guelph
Guelph, Ontario, Canada

Raymond Westwater
Future Ware
Princeton, New Jersey, USA

Terry Weymouth
University of Michigan
Ann Arbor, Michigan, USA

Michael Wynblatt
Siemens Technology-to-Business
Center
Berkeley, California, USA

Richard Z. Xue
Florida Atlantic University
Boca Raton, Florida, USA

John Yin
Daleen Technologies
Boca Raton, Florida, USA

Chikara Yoshida
Kyoto University
Kyoto, Japan

CONTENTS

PART I

INTERNET TECHNOLOGIES

Chapter 1

THE UARC WEB-BASED COLLABORATORY: SOFTWARE ARCHITECTURE AND EXPERIENCE

Sushila Subramanian, G. Robert Malan, Hyong Sop Shim, Jang Ho Lee, Peter Knoop, Terry Weymouth, Fernam Jahanian, Atul Prakash, and Joseph Hardin

Abstract

*This chapter presents a case study of a web based collaboratory (the **Upper Atmospheric Research Collaboratory** or **UARC**) actively used in the space physics domain over a period of six years. A collaboratory is a system that allows geographically distributed people to work with databases, information sources, and other facilities independent of their location. The UARC software suite is designed as a modular system consisting of an independent set of services that work over a wide area network, a complex array of data suppliers, transformation modules that provide quality of service support in the form of data integration, degradation, filtering and compression, and client groupware applications and data visualization tools. The goal of UARC is to enable space physicists to study space weather phenomena such as magnetic storms and solar winds by consolidating data collected at multiple instrument sites and providing a global view of the system. During the last two years of the project, UARC provided access to over 40 data sources including ground based and satellite based instruments, and predictive model output from supercomputers, in some cases with up to 27 graphing options for data visualization of raw data, to a group of about 10-50 scientists, during operational periods that lasted from 3 days to 2 weeks. We describe the application requirements of a general collaboratory, with details of the specific requirements of the space physics domain. We then present the overall architecture of the system, and details about the services, suppliers, transformation modules, and client tools. The main UARC servers are a data dissemination substrate specifically designed to support push based applications using attribute based routing, and a group management and shared state management server. The servers are scalable, and designed to operate satisfactorily on a wide variety of networking conditions and client resources. Our campaign experiences are presented at the end.*

1. INTRODUCTION

The emergence of the Internet has enabled interactions between people working in the same field across the globe. This has resulted in a number of efforts to solve the problems of supporting group communication, and providing access to information sources that are geographically and administratively scattered. Collaboratories are one way to provide virtual shared workspaces to users. We define a collaboratory as a wide area distributed system supporting a rich set of services and tools that facilitate effective synchronous and asynchronous communication between two or more people who are not co-located [1,2,3,4,5].

The Upper Atmospheric Research Collaboratory is an Internet-based system that gives space scientists a virtual shared workspace for conducting real-time experiments as well as various asynchronous collaborations from geographically dispersed facilities [1]. During the past two years, UARC has integrated a significant fraction of the worldwide observational systems that are devoted to space physics and aeronomy. Moreover, the system now supports real-time outputs from supercomputer-class theoretical models. This has enabled simultaneous comparison of experimental and theoretical data on a global scale. Such comparisons would not be possible without collaboratory technology.

UARC has evolved into a scalable Web-based collaboratory over a period of six years. Since its inception in 1993, UARC has supported more than 10 scientific campaigns, each representing a concerted effort to collect real-time data simultaneously from instruments around the world for several days at a time. The first few campaigns ran on a distributed set of NeXT systems on the NSFNET and could support about a dozen active participants. The current Web-oriented Java-based system supports a more accessible interface by moving away from specific hardware or operating system requirements. This allows UARC to provide sharable multimedia tools across different platforms, support more users, increase the number of sites and instruments feeding data to the collaboratory, and provide access to output from supercomputer-class theoretical models of the thermosphere and ionosphere. The Web-based system continues to evolve, and during the most recent data collection campaign, April 1998, scientists were able to examine data from a suite of 40+ instruments. Some of the instrument sources include the following: Data from ACE, POLAR, JPL GPS, and WIND satellites; Incoherent Scatter Radar arrays in Greenland, Norway, Puerto Rico, Peru, and Massachusetts; magnetometers; riometers; and digisonde arrays.

UARC operates in two modes: *Campaign*, and *Electronic Workshop*. A *campaign* is a concerted effort to simultaneously collect real-time data from instruments around the world. Figure 1 shows a screen snapshot from the April 1998 campaign. In this mode, a scientist is likely to be interested in unfolding phenomena and communicate with other scientists on operational planning or predictive guesses on the state of the system. As an example, during the April 1997 Campaign, radar operators were able to quickly respond to the effects of a solar flare and communicate with other radar operators around the world to keep the instruments going beyond the scheduled time and capture a geomagnetic storm of unusual intensity. An *Electronic Workshop* is a scheduled cyber-gathering with specific goals in mind. Some examples are planning research for the future, collaborating on writing papers, discussing historical phenomena, and classroom presentations with participation by students. This mode relies on access to archived data or preprocessed data presented by participating scientists, as well as shared access to multimedia tools. The workshops bring together the expertise of experimental and theoretical physicists in a common forum.

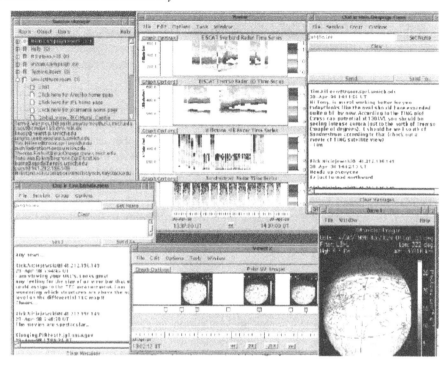

Figure 1. Snapshot of a UARC Campaign in April 1998. At the top left corner is the Room Manager showing the active participants in the highlighted room. The bottom left and top right corners show the Chat application from two different rooms (The Low Latitudes Room and Main Campaign room respectively). The top central data visualizer (Mural) displays time synchronized information from 4 radar sites: EISCAT Tromso and Svalbard in Norway, Millstone Hill near Boston, USA, and Sondrestrom in Greenland. The bottom data visualizer shows data from the UVI instrument on the POLAR satellite, while the bottom right display is a zoomed in view of one of the images from this satellite.

2. APPLICATION REQUIREMENTS

The design of the UARC system was driven by two sets of requirements: those inherent to a scientific collaboratory and the implicit requirements of using the Internet for collaboration. The base unit for space science collaboration is the data. The UARC system had to provide access to remote data sources such as instrument data or model theoretic output from a supercomputer. It had to be possible to record this real-time data for post facto analysis. Moreover, UARC had to provide the ability to annotate this data for future or asynchronous discussions. The system had to provide a coherent system for effective distributed administration and maintenance of the numerous data suppliers and servers. To accommodate the versatility in the scientists' interactions, the UARC system provided tools for seamless transitions between synchronous and asynchronous collaboration. The UARC system provided domain specific data visualizers for the remote data sources. In addition to these custom visualizers, the scientists had to be able to add standard items to the collaboratory workspace including URLs, custom GIFs, and text annotations. This workspace was designed to support both public and private collaboration. Moreover, the level of privacy for this collaboration had to be adjustable based on the needs of the participating scientists. To support dynamic groups of scientists, the tools were aware of the active participants and their locations. Furthermore, the participants' workspaces allowed flexibility in the type and amount of sharing between each other. Finally, for the system as a whole to be useful to the scientists, it had to perform well, and for a long duration - servers needed to be robust to provide the availability needed to support continuous *campaign* style requests for weeks at a time.

The UARC application is an example of a collaboratory where a large amount of information is available for use by its participants. Managing this complexity for presentation to the user places several requirements on the data visualization component. For example, the visualizers must provide a compact representation of multiple graphs in order to overcome screen real estate problems. Additionally for comparison purposes, they also need to be able to display time synchronized views of multiple sources of data simultaneously. These visualizers must be extensible; they need to support the rapid inclusion of new data sources and graph representations. Given a new set of configuration files conforming to the published interface, data visualizers need to be able to incorporate the new choices with limited overhead by an administrator.

The large variation in client bandwidth resources in the heterogeneous Internet environment implicitly imposes additional requirements on the UARC middleware. Its users need the ability to set quality of service parameters on a per graph basis to best utilize their available bandwidth. Servers also need to support an application level quality of service to provide reasonable performance in the face of the large gap in client bandwidth resources. Servers must provide multicast support that is based on the specific semantics of data. Three types of data filtering have been identified and depend on the end user's environment. These include: periodic delivery of data, transformation, such as compression or alternative graph representations, and synchronization such as integration of multiple streams or intervals.

3. ARCHITECTURE

The architecture of UARC consists of five main components:

- The Salamander server: A scalable distributed data dissemination server that supports application level quality of service; persistent data storage; and historical queries for archival data.
- The DistView and Corona Server: A server that manages shared state, event sharing, and group manipulation in terms of creates joins, and deletions.
- Cache and Computation Modules (CCMs): Data transformation modules that convert raw data through filtering, compression, integration or degradation.
- Client tools that include a configurable data visualizer and groupware applications that provide an entry point into a collaborative session.
- Data suppliers that publish data using the data dissemination service to be viewed through graphical data visualizers.

Based on the application requirements discussed above, we describe these components in greater detail. Data dissemination and archival services are provided through the Salamander server. This component is concerned with the distribution of data from remote instruments or transformation modules to client end data visualizers, or archive servers. Salamander also handles variation in bandwidth and network speeds and provides the user the option to explicitly manage input data quality through application layer quality of service controls. The second component is the Corona server which provides support for synchronous sharing of state and events, archiving and replay of actions, group management in terms of joins, leaves, access control and awareness. This is supplemented within UARC by related DistView services that include a registry service, and a Room or Session Manager. The third component is domain specific and deals with transforming raw data from remote instruments into formats the user wants to view the data in. The Cache & Computation Modules (CCM) perform these operations. The output from CCMs is published through Salamander, and subscribed to by client data visualizers. UARC also includes a number of client tools that provide the user interface to access the collaboratory, view the data in a number of available formats, and groupware applications based on the DistView Toolkit such as a multiparty chat or shared whiteboard for annotating interesting data. The last component in the UARC architecture consists of data suppliers that periodically publish data to Salamander from a variety of sources. Data sources include remote instruments such as Incoherent Scatter Radars, satellite images, data published on web pages, or data from predictive models running on supercomputers. Implementation details for all of these pieces are described in Section 5 on the UARC campaign experiences.

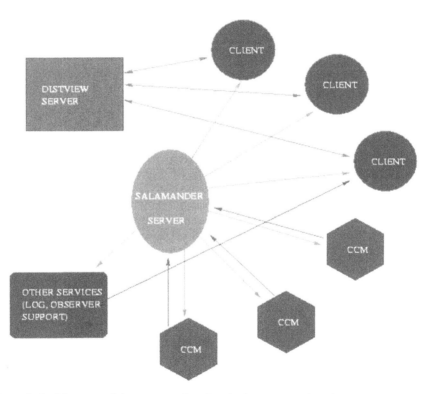

Figure 2. Architecture of the system, showing the interconnections between the Data Dissemination Service (Salamander), Shared State and Event Management Service (DistView and Corona), Cache & Computation Modules (CCM), and Data Suppliers and Client tools.

Figure 2 shows the interconnections between the various servers, client tools, data transformation modules and suppliers. These units are independently administered and maintained. The Corona and Salamander services are completely independent of one another. The data visualizer tool, also known as Mural, relies on both Salamander and Corona to provide full functionality, but will provide limited functionality in the absence of either one. The CCMs rely on Salamander (or some other user configured transport mechanism including a pull based HTTP GET layer) to obtain raw data to run its transformations on. The groupware applications depend on the Corona services to share events and state, in addition to saving persistent state. Data suppliers publish data through the Salamander layer. There are some other servers such as a web server, log server and an observer support server primarily supplied to reach a larger base of users who are interested in merely observing the system as opposed to actively participating in group based activity, as well as to support HCI research.

The overall architecture of the system is designed with a view to being scalable and maintainable. The majority of UARC servers are independent of each other. This approach limits the propagation of any side effects or errors between subsystems. An individual server going down limits the available functionality of a system but does not incapacitate it.

4. TECHNICAL OVERVIEW

The main subsystems of UARC provide support for the following: Group management and communication, and building groupware applications; Scalable data dissemination and application level quality of service; Data visualization and transformation; Data suppliers; and a slew of user support services such as logging user actions, and providing online help. This section provides the technical details underlying each of these aspects of the system.

4.1 ACCESSING THE COLLABORATORY

The collaboration facilities in UARC are supported by Corona and DistView. Entry into the collaboratory is provided through a Session Manager application that relies on the *Corona* server for communication support, and the *DistView Toolkit* for group management and an event sharing mechanism. We describe the Session and Room Manager in greater detail, followed by the services it relies on i.e. Corona and DistView.

Group Management Through Rooms: Users enter UARC through a Session Manager application that uses the Corona server for communication support and the DistView Toolkit for group management and event sharing. To join a UARC session, a user invokes a Session and Room Manager, which is constructed as a coordinated collection of group-aware Java applets[5]. To support dynamic reconfiguration of shared workspaces and allow access over the Internet, the Room Manager uses *rooms* as the high-level grouping mechanism for objects, such as applets, users, and arbitrary data objects. Rooms can be used for asynchronous and synchronous collaboration because their state persists across synchronous sessions. Room participants can perform different roles (such as administrator, member, and observer), with appropriate access rights. Figure 3 gives a snapshot of room activities. The highlighted entry is the room in which the user is currently active. The list in the lower box shows the other people currently in the room. Users have the option of conferring with each other either through the shared applications in the room or directly through email. The number of users in a room is shown in parenthesis beside its name.

The Session Manager provides a common interface to the various applets within rooms. It supports queries on the status of the collaboratory or group membership, and can send commands to applets. When a user enters a room, the Session Manager sends a message to the Room Manager, which checks the user's access control rights and privileges. If the user is allowed entry, the Room Manager updates its data structures and notifies the Session Manager. The user may now instantiate objects within this room.

In the Session Manager, a *room* represents a group activity and has a number of *objects*. An object represents a specific task to be performed as part of a group activity. Example objects within a room include shared tools such as a Chat or data visualization tool or a URL posted by a group member. In order to participate in a group activity, the user enters an appropriate room and runs objects. The Session Manager works in conjunction with the Room Manager, which maintains a database of user whereabouts in the system, e.g., what rooms a user is in and what objects they are running. The Session Manager and Room Manager are both Corona clients and use Corona's inter-group communication and membership notification services to communicate with each other. The Session Manager also communicates with a user registration and authentication server. When a user enters UARC, Session Manager acquires user registration information, i.e., user name and password, and checks with Registry. Only users with a valid name and password may enter UARC.

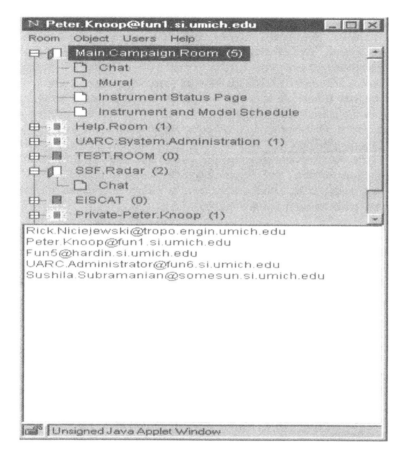

Figure 3. The use of shared workspaces. The upper window of the Session Manager shows a list of 7 visible rooms, the first 6 being public rooms and the last a private room. A private room is automatically created when a user logs in the system. The lower window shows a list of users who are currently in the selected room. An open doorway indicates the current room in use, while highlighted doors indicate rooms in which the user is actively participating. The number in parenthesis following the Room name indicates the number of participants within that room.

The Session and Room Managers feature:

- *User extensibility.* Users can add their own collaborative applets that conform to the published Session Manager interface.
- *Group awareness.* Using the Session Manager API, applets can query about groups, active users, and so on.
- *Link applets.* Users can move among rooms in a hypertext model.
- *Common utility applets.* Tools include shared whiteboards, e-mail support, data

visualizers, and multiparty chat.
* *Asynchronous collaborations*. The Session and Room Managers support persistent rooms and applets that retain state across invocations.

Group Communication Server (Corona): Corona is a group communication service provider to UARC collaboration tools such as the Session Manager, Chat, and DVDraw [7]. The Corona services can be categorized as *stateful*, in that Corona supports communication groups, for which shared application state can be defined, and participates in the management of the groups' shared state. Corona's management is message based and is independent of application semantics. Specifically, Corona models the shared state of a stateful group as a set of arbitrary *objects*, each of which is denoted by client generated identifiers, and allows group broadcast messages to be associated with shared object identifiers. Such messages are called *state update messages*. Corona caches state update messages on disk in order to allow robust state transfer service, in which new members can receive the current state of their groups even in the presence of network failures and client crashes. Corona also supports *persistent groups*. A persistent group outlives its membership and thus supports long group sessions. When the members of a stateful, persistent group re-convene, they can receive the latest group state via Corona's state transfer service and thus do not have to work from scratch. For those members that require exclusive access to shared objects in a stateful group, Corona provides locks. Other Corona services include notification of changes in group membership and client and group properties.

Groupware Applications Toolkit (DistView): DistView provides the interface and libraries to turn a stand-alone application into one that can run in shared mode [8,9]. DistView supports *selective window sharing* in which application windows can be individually exported and imported. Exported and imported windows provide a synchronized view of the shared application state displayed in the windows. At the same time, private work can still be performed on non-shared windows. In order to provide low response times when using shared windows, DistView employs an object replication scheme, in which the application objects associated with shared windows are replicated at import sites. DistView also provides a library of reusable, *group-aware* objects that can be used to design shared windows. These objects are group-aware in that they can be used for private work until shared, at which time they can automatically maintain a synchronized state among their replicas. DistView-based applications are Corona clients and subscribe to Corona services for their communication needs. As such, the toolkit includes an application component, *DVGroup*, that provides Corona client interface.

4.2 CONFIGURABLE DATA VISUALIZERS AND GROUPWARE APPLICATIONS

Mural is a client tool that supports shared, interactive visualization of data from remote instruments distributed via the Salamander server. Mural by itself is not domain specific, but its menus are a reflection of the entries in a set of configuration files and in the case of UARC relate to remote instrument locations, instrument types and available graph types per combination of location and instrument type. Graphs are stacked within a scrollable frame to preserve screen real estate as well as to display data in a time synchronized fashion (with the common X axis being time). Any number of such frames may be opened by the user. Such a stacked model allows the user to scroll back and forth in time through multiple graphs simultaneously as well as to compare data from multiple instruments, or between instrument data and predictive model data. Mural has a published interface with predefined formats for configuration files and methods to add in new locations, instruments and graph types. On startup, Mural reads in the configuration files and creates its menus based on the files. Configurable parameters include Location, Instrument Type, Graph Type, Transport layer (on a per graph basis), and Axes for Graphs. Figure 4 shows two sets of graphs stacked on top of one another in a time synchronized manner. The highlighted icons below the GIF images show the images that are currently displayed. The time axis at the bottoms shows that this currently has a display window of two hours. Notice that the periodicity for the two graph sources is considerably different (shown in the picture by the large number of icons for the first graph versus a smaller number for the second).

Mural can run as an independent application or in shared mode interacting with other UARC applications. It uses the DistView toolkit to make events shareable. As an example, in shared mode, a Mural user would export a set of Mural viewers. Other members of the group working in the same space can import this configuration of graphs. At this point any action taken by any one of the importers or the exporter (such as additions, deletes, resizes) will be visible to all the other users. Features in Mural include: the ability to set data quality on a per graph basis, zoom in and out of images, view a series of images as a movie; options to hide and show pieces of the graph (such as axes) to maximize use of screen real estate, save and restore a favorite configuration of graphs as a single operation, clone graphs and viewers, and the ability to cut and paste images to the shared whiteboard to enable annotations of interesting snapshots.

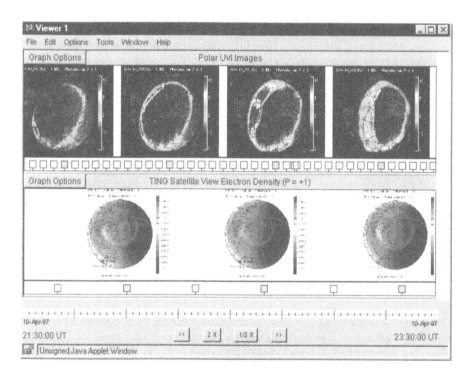

Figure 4. Stacked graphs with a common time axis. This snapshot of Mural shows real-time satellite images from the UVI instrument on the POLAR satellite being compared against images generated by a predictive model (shown in the lower graph) running on parallel computers. The time axis at the bottom shows that the current visible range is for a period of two hours running from 21:30 UT to 23:30 UT on 10 April 1997. The buttons at the bottom allow the user to scroll along the time axis, and reduce or increase the visible time range by clicking the 1/2X and 2 X buttons respectively.

The other client tools supplied by the UARC suite include a multiparty chat tool and a shared whiteboard. Chat is a UARC tool that allows users to exchange text-based messages. It creates a stateful, persistent chat group at Corona and broadcasts chat messages to the group.

Any Chat process that wishes to receive chat messages broadcast to a chat group should join the group. Because a chat group is stateful, any latecomer to the group can download previously broadcast messages to catch up with the current thread of conversation. Chat allows users to specify the number of previous messages to download. Chat also subscribes to Corona's notification services to provide an up-to-date list of participants. In addition, Chat can broadcast messages to other chat groups and support private messages. DVDraw is a shared whiteboard tool for UARC and is used to import images, make annotations, and create shapes and lines. Its canvas contents can be shared by several users at the same time. DVDraw creates a stateful group at Corona and defines the canvas contents as the shared state of the group. When the canvas is updated, DVDraw broadcasts a state update message to the group. To maintain a synchronized state, DVDraw uses Corona's locks to control concurrent accesses to the canvas.

4.3 SCALABLE DATA DISSEMINATION SERVER (SALAMANDER)

The Salamander substrate is one of the UARC system's primary mechanisms for data distribution and archival data retrieval [10]. Specifically, Salamander provides real-time distribution of the atmospheric data collected at remote sites to the experiment's participants distributed throughout the Internet. A Salamander-based system is composed from two basic units: *servers* that act as distribution points that are usually collocated with Web servers; and *clients* that act as both data publishers and subscribers. These units can be connected together in arbitrary topologies to best support a given application.

Salamander provides support for groupware applications by providing virtual distribution channels in an attribute-based data space. In a Salamander system, a tree of distribution nodes (servers) can be dynamically constructed to provide points of service into the data space. Clients can connect to this tree to both publish and subscribe to data channels. The data is *pushed* from suppliers to the clients through this distribution tree. Opaque data objects are constructed by clients that are annotated using text-based attribute lists. Clients provide persistent queries to the Salamander substrate using attribute expressions that represent the data flows they wish to receive, thereby subscribing to a virtual data channel. Salamander connections are first-class objects and are addressable if desired. This addressability allows for feedback from subscribers to data publishers. Additionally, Salamander allows for plug-in modules at any point in the distribution tree for application code to affect the data distribution. These plug-in modules provide the mechanism to support application-level quality of service policies.

Attribute-Based Data Distribution: The Salamander substrate uses flexible *attribute sets* as its addressing mechanism. Opaque data objects are delivered to a group of receivers based on outstanding subscription queries. Applications subscribe to virtual channels based on a stream of data objects' invariant set of attribute values. These attribute sets, or *queries*, are propagated throughout the tree of Salamander servers. The use of text-based attribute key-value tuples for data routing is a flexible and powerful abstraction. In general, it supports a wide and extensible variety of application specific data flows. These flows can be addressed by an arbitrary hierarchy of channels that can be defined and dynamically extended by the application.

The Salamander substrate provides an abstraction for the distribution of data from publishers to subscribers through its channel subscription interface with both anonymous and negotiated push techniques. In *anonymous push*, publisher's package opaque data objects with text-based attribute lists. Subscribers place persistent *queries* to the Salamander substrate using lists of attribute expressions that can be used to match both current and future objects published to the Salamander space as described above. Alternatively, this procedure can be thought of as accessing a distributed database where the queries are persistent. These persistent queries are matched by both the objects archived in Salamander's persistent repositories as well as future updates to the database space. The query aspect of Salamander's attribute-based subscription service differs those in traditional name service and database systems, in that instead of the queries acting once on a static snapshot of the dataspace, they are dynamic entities that act on both the current state of the system and future updates. Publishers may come and go without affecting the connection between the Salamander database and the subscribers.

Application-level Quality of Service: The Salamander architecture provides application-level Quality of Service policies to deliver data to clients as best fits their connectivity and processing resources. Application specific policies are used to allocate the available bandwidth between a client's subscribed flows, providing a client with an effective throughput based on semantic thresholds that only the application and user can specify. These application-level QoS policies are achieved through the use of plug-in policy modules at points in the distribution tree.

The UARC application uses discrete delivery, data degradation, and data conversion plug-in modules. By multiplexing the subscribed flows, discrete delivery modules can be used to prioritize, interleave, and discard discrete data objects. We have constructed a flexible interface that allows the client to both: determine its current performance level with respect to the supply, and to gracefully degrade its quality of service from an application-level standpoint so that it best matches the client connection's service level. The substrate has a set of default policies that can be tuned by parameters taken directly from the user.

In addition to discrete delivery policies, the Salamander substrate provides for on-demand data degradation and conversion of data objects. In general, these mechanisms are used to convert one object into another. In order to support real-time collaboration between heterogeneous clients, some mechanism for graceful data degradation must be made available to provide useful data to the slower participants. At the application level, we understand something about the semantics of the shared data. We can exploit this knowledge, and provide a graceful degradation of the data based upon these semantics. The Salamander substrate uses on-demand (lossless and lossy) compression on semantically typed data, tailoring contents to the specific requirements of the clients. Lossless compression techniques are used for those data that cannot be degraded, such as raw text, binary executables, and interpreted program text. Lossy compression techniques are applied to data that can suffer some loss of fidelity without losing their semantic information, examples of which are: still and moving images; audio; and higher level text like postscript or hypertext markup languages. We give the application layer control over this quality by providing an interface that adjusts the fidelity of the real-time data flow on a per-client basis.

Adding Specialized Services: Salamander's flexible attribute routing provides a mechanism that allows applications to extend the system with specialized services. These services act as publishers to clients with the additional ability to respond to specific queries or commands. They register themselves with Salamander at start up time using the *supply* command. This provides a mechanism for clients to query the Salamander server about the existence of a particular supply or service, and use that information to provide the increased functionality to users. The service queries are routed through the Salamander server, which will return an error if the requested service is not registered. Two general services have been constructed for use with the UARC project: a lightweight temporal database that provides archival support; and a cache and computation module (CCM), described in the next section, that acts as a data filter as well as allows clients to modify the supply characteristics through a feedback loop.

Salamander provides data persistence by incorporating a custom lightweight temporal database. This database supports Salamander's needs by: storing a virtual channel's data as a sequence of write-once updates that are primarily based on time; and satisfying requests for data based on temporal ranges within the update stream. A temporal database generally views a single data record as an ordered sequence of temporally bounded updates. In the Salamander database these records correspond to virtual channels. Salamander's synergy between real-time data dissemination and traditional temporal and relational databases is one of its main contributions. It is taken for granted that queries on a relational or temporal database act as a static atomic action against a snapshot of a system's dynamic data elements. Our model alters this, by providing support for persistent queries that act over both a snapshot of the data elements present in the database and any modifications (real-time updates) to the database elements that may occur in the future.

4.4 CACHE AND COMPUTATION MODULES (CCM)

The Cache and Computation Module (CCM) is a special entity that subscribes to raw data, applies a transformation to it, and then republishes it in a new format. The raw data typically comes from geographically distributed remote instruments, or in some cases from web sites. A CCM uses this data to generate graphs, which are then converted into GIF images and published. Both the raw data and their corresponding images are stored in the Salamander database to support historical queries or time based scrolling. The GIF images are displayed to the client through Mural for active participants or through a web page for casual observers. By converting scientific data into simple image types, the CCMs effectively offload computationally intensive operations from the Java-based clients. The need for the CCMs was quickly realized when we measured Java's performance when calculating FFTs on large floating point data sets. The Cache and Computation Modules provide the mechanisms to trade off network bandwidth for client computational resource.

The CCMs transform input data into several different graphical representations including: line plots, formatted text, a series of independent images, polar plots (Azimuth and Elevation plots), and vector plots (Line of Sight Velocity Vectors). Moreover, the data may be plotted either on a linear or logarithmic scale. As an example of the amount of computation needed, the scientists have the CCMs transform each incoming incoherent scatter radar data set into 27 distinct graphs. This results in periodic bursty traffic due to n graph objects published for every incoming radar data set. However, Salamander utilizes buffering techniques to smooth such bursty trends. CCMs can be very memory and CPU intensive processes depending on the nature of their data transformations. This resource utilization can be balanced through the overall UARC architecture by moving CCMs in response to overloads.

Clients can modify a CCM's behavior by sending them specific messages through the Salamander service. A CCM registers itself with its Salamander server at startup time. The clients can then use this information to remotely start or stop the CCM's data supply or modify its behavior in some manner. Client triggered modifications include: changes in quality of service requirements; domain specific choices of transformation algorithms; time or other bounds on requested data; and control over the data arrival rate. Clients that use CCM services make heavy use of Salamander supported mutable attributes to specify requests and any of their additional parameters. The use of mutable attributes in the header section of a packet speeds up request processing at the CCM end which does not have to touch the data portion of the packet unless necessary.

5. SOFTWARE IMPLEMENTATION AND CAMPAIGN EXPERIENCES

Over the course of the project, UARC has supported more than ten active scientific campaigns. The initial few ran on NeXT systems, and were limited to at most a dozen scientists. This was a relatively simple operation and distributed data from five instruments (Incoherent Scatter Radar, Normal Beam Riometer, Magnetometer, All Sky Camera, and IRIS) located at the Sondrestrom site in Greenland. This was very successful but limited in scalability, which pushed us to move to a Web based system abandoning the NeXT version (although some sites continue to distribute their raw data through the initial installations). Two subsequent campaigns were conducted using a primitive Java-based version of the software. Developers quickly noted that ease of use and a good user interface were critical in keeping electronic collaboration alive between domain scientists. This was in addition to the expectation that the system would be robust, scalable, and provide reasonable performance. The first successful multi-site operation occurred in April 1997, with a peak participation of about 50 scientists. This was also the first time model data from supercomputers and real-time data was displayed simultaneously. Models were created 20 minutes in advance and fed to the system using the same interface as raw data from instruments. Figure 5 displays the entire set of data sources available through UARC in the final campaign held in April 1998.

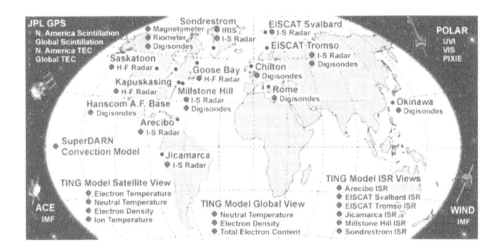

Figure 5. The complete set of available data sources for UARC during the last set of campaigns between April 1997, and April 1998. This includes instruments such as Incoherent Scatter Radars, Magnetometers, Normal Beam Riometers, Digisondes, satellite images from POLAR, JPL, WIND, and ACE, and predictive TING model output.

There was a large variation in the environment in terms of the type of network and CPU used within the entire system. Greenland and Puerto Rico were two sites that connected across a slow 56K line, and periodically published data, as well as occasionally viewed data, while other data sources or clients were on T3 links or on occasion, ATM links. Machine types also ranged from a 486 based PC to high end Pentiums and workstations. The user performance was obviously influenced by their available hardware. The data itself ranged from a few hundred bytes for periodic raw data to 400K GIF images published by the PIXIE instrument on NASA's POLAR satellite. Images generated by the CCMs were in the order of about 80KB and published every 4 minutes or so. The raw data was published from once every 5 seconds in the case of the Sondrestrom ISR (Incoherent Scatter Radar) to about once in 20 minutes from some Digisondes. Average round trip times between most of the servers in Ann Arbor, Michigan and clients or publishers also varied greatly from a few milliseconds within the University of Michigan campus to about 750 ms to Puerto Rico.

All of Mural, CCMs, Corona and DistView code is written in Java. The servers and clients may be connected in arbitrary topologies. There is no requirement for any of these pieces to exist on the same machine, or indeed in the same region. All of the Java subsystems will run on Solaris or Win32 machines. The Salamander server is a POSIX thread implementation on Solaris and is written in "C". Salamander emulates a multicast service in the absence of ubiquitous support for MBone. Most of the data suppliers are written in Java, "C" or run as Perl scripts at the remote instrument sites. Some data suppliers periodically monitor Web pages set up at remote sites and push the data from them as it becomes available through the Salamander interface. The Room Manager and group communication services (i.e. Corona) are implemented as Java applications. The Session Manager runs as a Java applet under a Java enabled browser such as Netscape. Initial communications between the Session and Room Managers assign unique ids to objects within a room. These IDs are used to generate specially tailored HTML documents on the fly by a CGI script which then provide the user with a specialized configuration to work within. Shared workspaces are supported by assigning group ids as well. All of the client end tools including the data visualizers and groupware applications are signed with a Netscape Certificate. Signed tools are primarily used to allow Java applets to access special privileges such as connecting to multiple servers simultaneously.

6. ONGOING WORK

An Internet collaboratory, such as UARC, enables a new paradigm for work that allows domain scientists to work closely while remaining physically distant. This results in several new opportunities including: the ability to obtain a global view of developing phenomena; the ability to contact and discuss issues with scientists having a wide range of expertise; early exposure to real data for students and larger groups of scientists; and finally mentorship opportunities between students and distant scientists. Users like the idea of flexible workspaces and persistence of objects within *Rooms*. Domain scientists favor increased support for utilizing external graphing tools, particularly ones they are more familiar with, such as IDL in the UARC framework. Using an emerging technology such as Java requires us to spend time in ensuring that scientists have access to the latest versions of browsers, and the required support in hardware in terms of available memory and CPU speeds to handle the image intensive applications. We also found that performance and robustness across the Internet's varied network conditions are critical factors in encouraging high user participation. Application level quality of service support was essential in allowing users connected through low bandwidth links to participate.

Ongoing work includes improvement to the current system in terms of robustness, as well as supporting a richer set of collaboration tools. These tools will enable more seamless methods of synchronous and asynchronous collaboration, as well as record and replay support. Workspaces will be more hierarchical allowing for multiple levels of Rooms. Data visualization needs to include sophisticated multimedia support such as audio, video and 3D-simulation support. We will also continue work on networking issues such as support for disconnected operation, mobile clients and increased scalability and Quality of Service support. Finally, we are including access to publishing tools and digital libraries from within the UARC environment to provide support for presentation of results in a *Campaign* or summaries from an *Electronic Workshop*.

7. THE UARC TEAM

The Upper Atmospheric Research Collaboratory is a multi-disciplinary research collaboration supported by the National Science Foundation. UARC studies space phenomena, such as magnetic storms that originate on the sun and can interfere with radio and television reception, disrupt electrical-power transmission, and threaten orbiting spacecraft and astronauts. The UARC team is made up of faculty, researchers, and graduate students from the fields of computer science, social and behavioral sciences, and space physics. The computer scientists work with space physicists to develop the software systems; the space physicists try out prototypes in live collaborative research settings under the eyes of the behavioral scientists; and the behavioral scientists evaluate successes and failures and give guidance to the computer scientists for the next round of prototypes. This iterative feedback loop drove the software design process and resulted in a testbed that is also a successful working collaboratory. The principal investigators at the University of Michigan who were actively involved in the design, deployment, and evaluation of UARC include Daniel Atkins, Robert Clauer, Tom Finholt, Farnam Jahanian, Tim Killeen, Gary Olson, Atul Prakash, Joseph Hardin, and Terry Weymouth. Partnerships with several investigators at other institutions contributed greatly in the creation and evaluation of the testbed. These institutions include SRI International, Danish Meteorological Institute, Millstone Hill Observatory, Arecibo Observatory, EISCAT, NASA JPL, and NASA Goddard Space Flight Center. The home page for the UARC project is at http://www.si.umich.edu/UARC/. A complete list of partner institutions is at http://www.si.umich.edu/UARC/partners.htm.

References

1. G. M. Olson, D.E. Atkins, R. Clauer, T.A. Finholt, F. Jahanian, T.L. Killeen, A. Prakash, and T.Weymouth, "The Upper Atmospheric Research Collaboratory (UARC)," *Interactions,* May-June 1998, Vol.3.
2. T.T. Elvins, S.J. Young, and P.J. Mercurio, "The Distributed Laboratory: An Interactive Visualization Environment for Electron Microscopy and Three Dimensional Imaging," *Communications of the ACM,* 1992, 35(6), pp. 54-63.
3. R.D. Pea, "The Collaborative Visualization Project," *Communications of the ACM,* 1993, 36(5), pp. 60-63.
4. J.C. Tang, E.A. Isaacs, M. Rua, "Supporting Distributed Groups With a Montage of Lightweight Interactions," *CSCW'94: 5th Conference on Computer-Supported Cooperative Work,* 1994, pp. 23-34.
5. A.T. Krantz, I. Rhee, S. E. Chodrow, J. Sult, M. D. Hirsch, and V. S. Sunderam, "Design and Implementation of a Distributed X-Multiplexor," *Proceedings of the IEEE International Conference on Distributed Computing Systems,* Amsterdam, The Netherlands, June 1998.
6. J.H. Lee, A. Prakash, T. Jaeger, and G. Wu, "Supporting Multi-User, Multi-Applet Workspaces in CBE," *Proceedings of the Sixth ACM Conference on Computer-Supported Cooperative Work,* 1996
7. R. Hall, A. Mathur, F. Jahanian, A. Prakash, and C. Rasmussen, "Corona: A Communications Service for Scalable, Reliable Group Collaboration Systems," *Proceedings of CSCW'96, ACM,* 1996, pp. 140-149.
8. A. Prakas and H. Shim, "DistView: Support for Building Efficient Collaborative Applications Using Replicated Objects," *CSCW 1994, ACM Press,* 1994, pp. 153-164.
9. H. Shim, R. Hall, A. Prakash, and F. Jahanian, "Providing Flexible Services for Managing Shared State in Collaborative Systems," *Proceedings of the ECSCW European Conference on Computer Supported Cooperative Work,* 1997, pp. 237-252.

10. G.R. Malan, F. Jahanian, and S. Subramanian, "Attribute-Based Data Dissemination for Internet Applications," *Journal of High Speed Networks (Special Issue on Multimedia Networking),* Vol. 7, No. 3 and 4, 1998, pp. 319-337.

URLs

1. UARC at http://www.crew.umich.edu/UARC/.

2. CCF: Collaborative Computing Frameworks at http://emily.mathcs.emory.edu/ccf/.

3. Collaboratory for Microscopic Digital Anatomy at http://www-ncmir.ucsd.edu/CMDA/.

4. Decisions Systems Group InterMed Collaboratory Project at
    http://dsg.harvard.edu/public/intermed/InterMed_Collab.html.

5. TeamWave Workplace at http://www.teamwave.com/.

Chapter 2

IP SERVICE ARCHITECTURES
FOR CONVERGING NETWORKS

Daniele Rizzetto and Claudio Catania

Abstract

The convergence of the traditional telecommunications world and the Internet has sparked the rapid evolution of Internet Telephony, which has also introduced new implementation paradigms. As a result, the creation of a large variety of new and sophisticated communication services has become possible. This chapter addresses the problem of integrating IP-based telephony with the legacy circuit-switch telephone network and proposes a novel service architecture for their seamless integration. (Portions of this chapter are reprinted with permission, from IEEE Network Magazine, Vol. 13, No. 3, May-June 1999, pp. 34-40; IEEE Internet Computing magazine, Vol. 3, No. 3, May-June 1999, pp. 53-62.)

1. INTRODUCTION

Voice over IP (VoIP) has paved the way for a global approach in designing communication service platforms, but the real driver for this is the convergence between heterogeneous communication network technologies. Articles such as [1] consider some of the problems arising from this integration and describe possible scenarios for the evolution of the current communications world.

The introduction of new technologies and communication tools creates the need to integrate the existing paradigms and therefore leads this convergence to occur more slowly than expected. In order to speed up this process, it is essential to integrate heterogeneous networks at the communication control layer, and this requires the identification of their key control points.

The integration between the Intelligent Network (IN) [2] and IP networks is a key phase in this convergence process. The work presented in this chapter takes a step in the direction of developing a high-level abstraction for integrating IP-based telephony services with legacy circuit-switch telephony IN services. The problem of achieving this integration is also central to the large-scale deployment of VoIP.

This chapter is not aimed at proposing new protocols; it presents a novel service architecture, its components and their subsequent behavior. It focuses mostly on the H.323 ITU recommendation for VoIP [4] and on its central network component: the gatekeeper.

In particular, after an overview of VoIP and the architecture rationale, the chapter describes the architectural design and findings of the experimental prototype; the HPLB gatekeeper developed at HP Laboratories Bristol, and implemented on top of an H.323 platform. Finally, a practical demonstration of inter-working between the Internet and the IN will be described.

2. VOIP OVERVIEW

Since the first days of the Internet, researchers have experimented with real-time communications, such as the transmission of voice and video streams, on top of IP. The explosion of the Internet has made it abundantly clear that packet-switched networks have a lot of benefits in comparison with the traditional circuit-switched networks, most notably a more efficient and cheaper way of using and managing bandwidth.

Next generation telecom operators (called NextGen Telcos) are building backbones entirely based on IP. They are also leveraging opportunities generated by the telecom deregulation, enforced by the telecommunication ACT of 1996, in order to offer the first commercial application of VoIP: toll by-pass (http://www.technologylaw.com/telecom_bill.html). This application consists of avoiding the expensive circuit-switched PSTN backbones by "moving" telephone calls to inexpensive packet-switched data connections.

The technical problems that all these new operators have to solve are related firstly to the unreliability of IP networks that have not been designed to provide reliable and manageable QOS and secondly, to the difficulties of integration with the other more established communication networks.

Implementing real-time voice communications over packet-switched networks requires the packetization of voice streams at the sender end, their delivery and subsequent unpacketization at the receiver end. This process presents issues such as packet delay, jitter and packet loss that are not present in the traditional PSTN (Public Switched Telephone Network). The problem of defining a standardized way of implementing QOS on packet-switched networks has been debated for years but the Internet community is still far from reaching a widely agreed-upon solution. The interconnection between packet-switched and circuit-switched networks also requires the deployment of inter-working devices to integrate different signaling protocols. In particular, gateway functionality is required to interoperate with SS7 (ITU recommendation Signaling System #7 [13]), the PSTN signaling protocol. Once the integration at the signaling level is achieved, there is still a need to integrate the two networks at the control level where communication services are actually executed.

The current opportunity exploited by emerging NextGen Telcos is only the first step towards integrated communications. In the future, IP is expected to take over the entire network infrastructure and more sophisticated services will be offered, especially in the light of their seamless integration with other existing IP applications, such as the Web. Traditional telecom operators are getting on this wave and most of them have already announced substantial reductions of their investments in the circuit-switched network infrastructure and are ready to switch to more flexible packet-based networks.

This "race to IP" has generated different standards for VoIP communication protocols. In the following sections we will describe the most important of them, SIP and H.323, and give a general overview of the gateway control protocols. Our description is based on the assumption that all these new communication technologies face the problem of integrating with the PSTN legacy, which is already widely deployed and will not disappear overnight.

2.1 H.323

H.323 is an umbrella recommendation of the International Telecommunications Union (ITU-T) for multimedia communications over Local Area Networks (LANs) that do not provide a guaranteed Quality of Service (QoS) [4] (for a concise and introductory tutorial see [8]). The scope of this standard is point-to-point communications as well as multi-point conferences. It addresses call control, multimedia management, bandwidth management and interfaces between LANs and other networks. H.323 is part of the H.32X series of communications standards for videoconferencing across a variety of networks. This series includes H.320 and H.324, which address ISDN and PSTN analog communications, respectively.

The recommendations are still under development (Version 2 of the standard, H.323v2, was approved in January 1998) but some basic concepts are widely accepted. The architecture elements are **user terminals**, **gateways** (GW, for the integration with the PSTN), **multi-point control units** (MCU, for conferencing) and entities called **gatekeepers** (GK). Terminals, gateways and MCUs are generically addressed as **endpoints** (Figure 1).

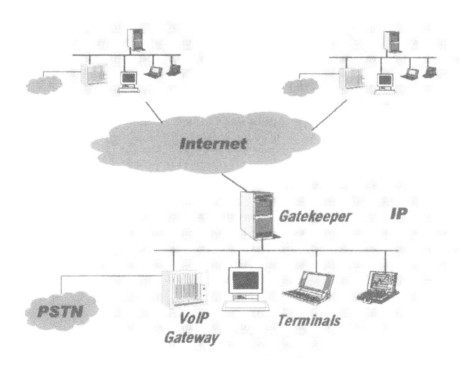

Figure 1. H.323 architecture.

Terminals are the LAN client endpoints that provide real-time, two-way communications. Gateways perform the conversion of signaling and media streaming exchanged between H.323 endpoints and PSTN endpoints.

Gatekeepers are responsible for call authorization, address resolution and bandwidth management. Gatekeepers can intercept all the call signaling between endpoints and can use it in order to provide "signaling-based" advanced services. They can provide all those services that cannot be decentralized and implemented by endpoints.

When an endpoint is switched on, it performs a multicast discovery for a GK and registers with it; therefore, the GK knows how many users are connected and where they are located. The collection of a GK and its registered endpoints is called a zone; an H.323 VoIP network is a collection of zones.

The Registration Admission Status (RAS) protocol is the key gatekeeper protocol. RAS messages are carried in User Datagram Protocol (UDP) packets exchanged between an endpoint and its gatekeeper. For instance, when an endpoint comes up, it sends a RAS Registration Request (RRQ) to the gatekeeper. This message contains information such as terminal transport address, alias (the user identification), E.164 telephone number and other data. If the GK accepts the registration, it sends a Registration Confirm message (RCF); otherwise it sends a Registration Reject (RRJ) message.

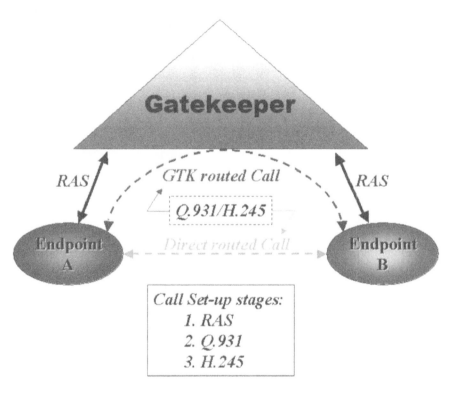

Figure 2. H.323 Call set-up.

The H.323 call setup life-cycle can be split into the three following phases (named according to the protocol used):

RAS: Anytime an H.323 endpoint wants to make a call, it asks for permission from the gatekeeper by sending a RAS Admission Request (ARQ) message. This message contains, amongst its parameters, the destination alias, name or phone number of the user the calling party wants to contact. The GK may grant the permission for the call by sending back an Admission Confirm (ACF) message containing the actual transport address associated with the called party alias sent along with the ARQ. The GK may also reject the request with an Admission Reject (ARJ) message giving a variety of reasons such as "not enough bandwidth" or "security violated". Therefore, during this phase the GK accomplishes three different functions: address translation, call authorization and bandwidth management.

Q.931: This phase is derived from ISDN end-to-end call-setup signaling (SETUP, PROCEEDING, ALERTING, CONNECT) and provides the logical connection between the two endpoints, the calling party and the called party. In H.323, Q.931 is implemented on top of TCP.

H.245: As soon as the Q.931 phase is finished, the two endpoints exchange their capabilities. During this stage they agree on the nature of the information that will be exchanged through the media channel (audio, video or data) and its format (compression, encryption etc.). H.245 is implemented on top of TCP.

After these three stages, the RTP/RTCP (the IETF Real Time Protocol/Real Time Control Protocol, running on top of UDP) media channels between the two endpoints are opened according to the capabilities just exchanged and the actual media communication can start. Data communications are based on the T.120 specification. During the call, DTMF "touch tones" are transmitted over the LAN through the H.245 User Input Indication message.

Call signaling can be GK-routed (i.e., it goes through the gatekeeper) or direct-routed between the endpoints. RAS is, by nature, GK-routed. It is a GK's choice to decide whether to route Q.931 and H.245 through the gatekeeper, so that it could act as a proxy between endpoints. If the GK intercepts the signaling it can perform call management, maintaining a list of ongoing H.323 calls in order to keep endpoints state or to provide information for the bandwidth management function. In any case, the media flows directly between endpoints because the GK is just a signaling entity that is not callable (in the H.323 terminology).

H.323v2 has introduced new features:

- Security: the H.235 standard addresses authentication, integrity, privacy and non-repudiation.

- Fast Connect procedure: this allows endpoints to expedite the exchange of terminal capabilities during the signaling phase by encapsulating them in Q.931 messages. By doing that, RTP channels can be opened just after this phase, avoiding the slow H.245 negotiation.

- Supplementary Services have been defined by the H.450 series. H.450.1 is the signaling protocol between endpoints for the control of supplementary services. H.450.2 defines call transfer of an established call; H.450.3 defines call diversion for implementing call forwarding unconditional, call forwarding busy, call forwarding no reply and call deflection. New services can be introduced through the standardization of new H.450.X series. In any case, the series puts in place signaling mechanisms to control services but they do not define the way in which the logic behind them should be implemented.

2.2 SIP

Coming from a completely different approach to information transmission and service creation, the Internet community has proposed a set of protocols to establish interactive communication between networked terminals. This is substantially different and by far much more flexible than the one proposed by the ITU-T.

This set of protocols is organised in a different way from ITU-T and was designed to satisfy communication requirements that had a larger scope than pure voice transmission. However, the advent and the commercial success of Voice over IP has raised the importance of some of these protocols and created momentum around them. A good comparison between this set of protocols and H.323 can be found in [10].

The most important of all these protocols is SIP (Session Initiation Protocol, [9]). Its role is to deal with user location, session establishment and, partially, conference management. As the name suggests, it does not deal with call signalling directly. In this respect, it is less rich than ITU-T signalling protocols, but its strengths lie in its simplicity and flexibility.

SIP separates the session establishment phase from the channel allocation phase and the media transmission. It is a client/server transaction-based protocol similar in several ways to the HyperText Transfer Protocol (HTTP). Apart from the terminal entities (agents in the SIP terminology) that initiate communication sessions, there are three other components (See Figure 3). Registration servers receive agents' location registrations and status updates. Proxy servers and redirection servers are used to resolve requests to locate called parties, coming from agents or other servers. The difference between them is in their behavior when they are not able to resolve the request themselves. The first type of servers (proxies) keeps the request and forwards it on behalf of the requester, the other type (redirect) determines the next server that may satisfy the request and sends them back to the requestors. The definition of the algorithms by which proxies and redirect servers resolve the queries and determine the call routing is outside the scope of SIP. These two behaviors reflect, in the H.323 world, the difference between GK-routed and direct-routed calls, respectively.

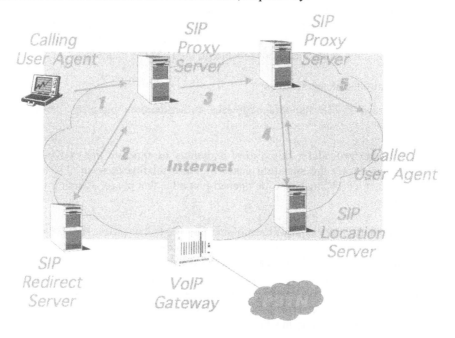

Figure 3. SIP architecture.

Another essential component in the IETF set is SDP (Session Description Protocol). Rather than being a fully-fledged protocol, SDP is a description format. It specifies the way of describing session parameters and conveys information related to the characteristics of the audio/video streams, to the parties involved in the session and the capability set used to establish connection. SDP describes only the capabilities of the two clients and does not contain negotiation methods. In this respect a complete capability exchange protocol has yet to be devised by IETF.

The last protocol that we want to mention in this paragraph is RTP, the Real Time Protocol and its companion RTCP. RTP is used to establish the transport layer between all the agents. RTP packets are wrapped up in UDP packets and contain the encoded media in different formats. RTR is extremely important for Internet communication since it is the widely accepted standard for the physical transmission of packetized real-time streams over IP networks. As mentioned in section 3, the packetization and transmission of voice and other communication media over such networks has very different characteristics from the dedicated channels used in PSTN. Packets can be lost, delayed, or arrive at the recipient in the wrong order. RTP takes into account all these characteristics and makes sure that the sequencing is preserved and packets are delivered and rebuilt properly at the other end, respecting the real-time characteristics of the communication. RTCP works jointly with RTP monitoring its packets. It provides additional information about the sessions such as QOS feedback and media synchronisation.

2.3 GATEWAY CONTROL PROTOCOL

The critical point of the integration between the PSTN and IP networks is represented by the VoIP gateway component. Gateways perform the media conversion from PCM (Pulse Code Modulation) telephone channels to connections over IP and vice versa. They are also responsible for terminating the call signaling on both networks and converting it from PSTN to VoIP and vice versa. VoIP signaling can be based on SIP or H.323. PSTN signaling can be either ISDN or based on SS7; if a gateway supports SS7 connectivity then the PSTN/VoIP integration becomes seamless because no two-stage dialing is required. In fact, if the gateway has an ISDN interface then calling users must dial the gateway number and then provide the VoIP number of the user they intend to reach, this is the two-stage dialing. If the SS7-based Intelligent Network and the VoIP Network are integrated then PSTN calling users can dial directly the VoIP number, the Intelligent Network will intercept the call and the location of the called party on the IP Network will happen "behind the scenes", transparently to the calling user. Similarly, this seamless integration will happen for calls originated from IP and terminated over PSTN.

Uncoupling the gateway's media part (called media gateway, MG) from the gateway's signaling and switching control part (called media gateway controller, MGC) can make this integration more effective (Figure 4).

The main rationale behind this separation is that the signaling access points are likely to be much less than the media access points. Therefore, one MGC can control more than one MG and the overall architecture becomes easily extensible. Furthermore, the components that implement the two functionalities can be developed independently.

Less sophisticated players such as ISPs (Internet Service Providers) can also take advantage of this separation, because they do not have the capability to run a signaling interconnection or traditional telecom operators do not trust them sufficiently to allow this interconnection. In fact, if the signaling interconnection is an SS7 link this imposes strict carrier-grade requirements in terms of high-availability and security. If the two functionalities were separated in two different components then telecom operators would deploy the MGC and ISPs would deploy only the MGs. Finally, keeping the call-processing engine as a separate entity from the media processing would also allow more powerful management system policies.

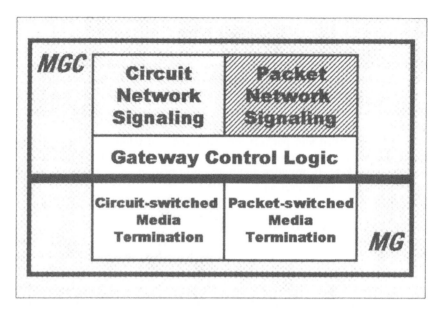

Figure 4. Gateway decomposition.

As soon as these two functionalities are separated a protocol is necessary to interconnect the components that implement them, and within this area a lot of proposals have been made. Initially Bellcore (now Telcordia) proposed SGCP (Simple Gateway Control Protocol, http://www.argreenhouse.com/SGCP/), a SIP-like protocol. Then a consortium led by Level3 Communications (a next generation telecom operator) proposed IPDC (IP Device Control Protocol), a series of protocols based on DIAMETER. SGCP and IPDC merged together into a new proposal called MGCP (Media Gateway Control Protocol). Now the IETF MEGACO (MEdia GAteway COntrol, http://www.ietf.org/html.charters/megacocharter.html) working group is working on the standardization of such a protocol and a new working group (SIGTRAN, SIGnaling TRANsport, http://www.ietf.org/html.charters/sigtran-charter.html) has been established to study a new protocol for transporting signaling over IP in a way that meets the stringent requirements imposed by the traditional telephone network.

Essentially every proposal in this area refers to the following diagram, shown in Figure 5.

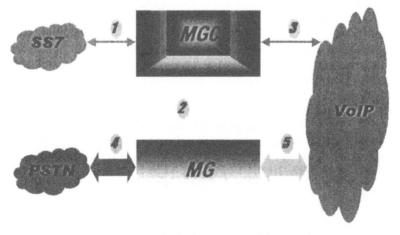

Figure 5. VoIP and telephone network integration.

The MGC exports three interfaces:

- To the SS7 network via its call control protocol ISUP (ISDN User Part).
- To the Media Gateway (MG) via a protocol that is the subject of the proposals described above.
- To the VoIP network via H.323 or SIP.

The MG is the component that carries out the media conversion from packet-switched channels to circuit-switched connections and vice versa. Current proposals assume that MG is connected to the telephone network through a trunk connection (marked "4" in the picture) and each bearer channel can be opened either as an audio one (for voice streaming) or as an unrestricted digital one (for data connections, like PPP). The MG's IP interface (marked as "5") is either RTP, in case of real time connections, or simply TCP/IP for data connections.

Essentially, gateway control protocols allow the logic implemented by the MGC to control the MG. The MGC can instruct the MG, through these protocols, to connect an incoming PSTN call to and RTP connection and vice versa, to monitor a connection, to tear down a connection, to detect DTMF (Dual Tone Multiple Frequency) tones or other events and notify back the MG. The first interesting application of these kinds of protocol has been developed for controlling cable set-top-boxes that can be considered as "residential" gateways [14].

3. SERVICES IN THE CONVERGED SPACE

The convergence between heterogeneous networks poses the problem of creating and deploying services that span multiple communication protocols and are accessed by different types of terminals. The difficulties of integrating all these technologies originate from the need to accommodate extremely different design philosophies. In our approach, the level of abstraction for the integration of different platforms is located at the control level where network and communication control takes place.

Traditional communication services such as call forwarding and call waiting are built on voice call signaling protocols and do not exploit the accessibility offered by the Internet to allow the creation of services and applications unimaginable in the traditional telecom world. The importance and the potential of these approaches can already be seen in areas like customer relationship management and voice-enabled Web information services. However, traditional problems such as technical support, application ownership and charging methods still have to be solved [12].

One of the main design principles behind the standardization of H.323 was its interoperability with existing protocols like H.320 and ISDN. To comply with this requirement, H.323 services have been specified as they were in PSTN [4]. H.450, the set of protocols that contains the specifications of the basic voice services such as call forwarding and call signaling, are directly derived from Q.SIG, a widely used standard to specify PBX (Private Branch eXchange) services. ITU-T has tackled the problem by reducing the integration complexity and limiting the scope of the services to the traditional PBX-like ones. By doing so, H.450 can be easily integrated with legacy PBX platforms but it does not exploit the innovation potential of the new technology. H.450 services are supposed to be invoked by clicking a series of buttons in a standardized order on a graphical panel. By doing so, flexible software phones, with powerful GUI capabilities, are used as if they were desktop handsets. Moreover, considering the new domain as a simple extension of the traditional telephony requires going through long standardization processes to introduce new services.

It has often been observed that, with the advent of VoIP, communications services would more logically be implemented in the terminals rather than in centralized service components [7]. The reason behind this is that VoIP software communication devices are far more powerful and smarter than traditional dumb telephones, they offer much better user interfaces, can be installed on any desktop anywhere in the IP network and offer a high degree of programmability. Without any doubt, migration to IP terminals will eventually happen, and more and more services will be implemented in devices that sit at the edge of the network.

On the other hand, this migration will not occur to every service. There is a large group of services that, due to the functionality they implement, cannot be logically placed in the end systems and require a server-based approach. All of them have the common characteristic of not being usable when software phones are unavailable. Among them there are call routing, directories and services that suffer from the "always-on"[1] problem of end client terminals [15]. One of the main requirements generated by the availability of different communication networks that offer the same type of functionality is a high level of abstraction to execute the services independently from the network the user is connected to. In order to meet such a requirement it is necessary to define a network-independent service environment into which different communication stacks can be plugged. Uncoupling the protocols from the platform, one of the main principles behind the introduction of the Intelligent Network concept, is the first step towards the convergence at the control layer [18].

This separation introduces the problem of defining an appropriate language to create, develop and deploy services for server-based services. The H.323 community has not decided to adopt a specific language. However, gatekeeper-routed calls are based on a Call State Model, therefore any existing service creation environment based on such an approach could be used. For example, Microsoft TAPI, SDL (http://www.sdl-forum.org) or ECTF (*http://www*.ectf. org).

The Internet community has taken a far more advanced approach and made two different proposals in this area: SIP-CGI [16] and CPL (Call Processing language [17]), both under development in the IPTel IETF Working Group (http://www.ietf.org/html.charters/iptel-charter.html). The first one relies on the fact that SIP is derived from HTTP and therefore the typical properties of CGI such as language independence, extensibility and transaction handling can be reused. CGI could be an appropriate technology to develop stateless services like address translation or redirection but may not be appropriate in implementing stateful services. Concepts like Web cookies are being developed by IETF [16] to keep the status between transactions, but the effectiveness of this solution is still to be proven. The other proposal is CPL, a Call Processing Language for Internet Telephony, an entirely new scripting language based on XML (eXtensible Mark-up Language, http://www.w3c.org) and non-cyclic graphs to describe the service. The main advantage of this approach is that the language is less flexible and therefore less likely to introduce problems that may disrupt the service provision, giving untrusted users the opportunity to develop their own services.

Another requirement for integrated service platforms is to provide end-users access to the services and their configuration [3]. This functionality was very difficult to offer in the PSTN where access to service resource was mediated by the switches. The fact that on the Internet the same protocol (IP) is used both in the backbone and at the access level makes this requirement a much easier one to fulfil. However, letting end-users configure their own services requires a careful analysis of the language used to create them, because a badly programmed logic can harm the overall functionality of the network. This is a well-known problem that, in the past, has prevented a wide acceptance of user-configurable services. A

---

[1] *It is the problem that stems from the fact that VoIP terminals are not always switched on and connected to a network.*

well thought-out paradigm for a user-friendly language that can handle complex and advanced services and offers the appropriate reliability features required by communication networks still has to be devised. See [11] for some of the most recent approaches to the problem.

4. SERVICE ARCHITECTURE

The architecture we propose and describe in this chapter takes advantage of the flexibility offered by VoIP and defines the means for convergence at the communication control layer rather than at the transport layer, in which the actual media communication takes place. As it has been outlined in the previous paragraph the main requirements for a service platform in the converged communication space are independence from the network element and autonomy of the platform, ability to support different communication stacks and networks, support of distributed intelligence residing in the end systems and user access to service configuration.

Independence from the underlying layer is implemented using an agent-based approach to the provisioning of communication services. The service platform implements service objects that react to events coming from the network and dialogues with other entities involved in the communication session. Similar approaches are the CMA (Call Management Agent) [5], and the architecture described in [6]. This solution provides seamless integration with different communication stacks as it relies only on the delivery of platform events. It also implements a peer-to-peer negotiation in the service platform among all the service objects of the parties involved in the communication session.

This approach offers a simple rule-based language to program the service logic and allows users to modify the logic of their services and to define the behavior of their personal services. It implements a peer-to-peer service negotiation, taking a step beyond the traditional telephony world service model, in which the called party plays a dominant role in triggering and executing services.

Finally, our solution, though essentially server-based, acknowledges the "intelligence at the edge" vision and supports it by offering an entirely IP-based platform easily accessible to smart terminals.

The main components of the architecture are shown in Figure 6. The gatekeeper platform provides a high-level Application Programming Interface (API) that implements an abstraction layer for executing services independently from the underlying networks. Each gatekeeper platform has a local service platform in which service objects are executed. A service object implements services for a particular user that can modify and configure them at any time. For each user there is a service object stored in a particular home server, which is a shared repository for service objects belonging to several users. The server can be located anywhere in the network, not necessarily near to a gatekeeper/service platform. When a user changes location, the local gatekeepers/service platform accepts the registration and downloads the user's service object from the home server in which the object is stored.

4.1 HOME SERVER

The Home Server contains the service objects and provides them when requested by a service platform. It is more than a simple repository because it plays an essential role in supporting user and service mobility, synchronizing multiple instances of the service objects and providing access to service creation environments.

A service object is located by using the alias address of the user it belongs to. The alias is structured according to the addressing scheme adopted by SIP [9], in which users are identified by an email-like formatted alias: userName@HomeServer. When a service platform needs to download a service object of a particular user, it uses that structure to locate the HomeServer and to download the service object of userName.

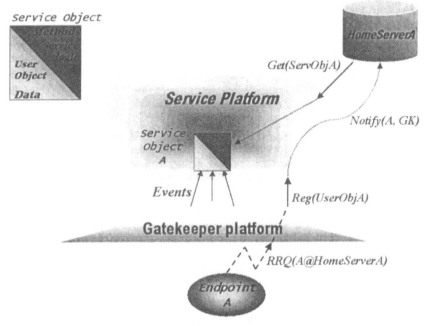

Figure 6. Service architecture (Registration time).

Obviously, this location mechanism is not valid when the service platform is given a user's alias address that is outside the adopted addressing scheme. This is the case for E.164 telephone numbers that in the Internet do not belong to any domain; therefore they have to be translated into the meaningful structured aliases defined above. This is very a well-known PSTN/IP integration issue and we expect to be able to use the results from the standard bodies that are working on it. In particular the ETSI TIPHON (Telecommunications and Internet Protocol Harmonization Over Networks) technical body and its working group IV (http://www.etsi.org/tiphon).

The Home Server is also responsible for synchronizing multiple requests for the same service object. For example when there is more than one call attempt to the same user. This problem stems from the fact that the same service object can be accessed by different service platforms. It can be solved using a centralized approach (the Home Server itself is responsible for the synchronization) or a distributed one (the service objects communicate between themselves in order to avoid inconsistencies).

The Home Server is also where the service object creation takes place. In the traditional telephony network, terminals provide a very poor interface (an alphanumeric keypad with some extra buttons) and the only way of configuring services is by typing cumbersome sequences of digits. In our solution, Web-based Service Creation Environment (SCE) can offer a user-friendly GUI-based service configuration. A similar approach is described in [11].

4.2 SERVICE PLATFORM

The service platform controls the life cycle of service objects execution. Once downloaded from the home server, the objects are executed locally and receive events coming from the underlying communication stacks.

In Figure 6, the GK platform provides the abstraction layer for events coming from a generic network, therefore seamless service provision for different communication networks is a natural consequence. This abstraction requires the identification of commonalities between existing and emerging communication paradigms adopted by protocols used in wireless, fixed and VoIP networks. This can be achieved by observing that the functionality of virtually all of them can be grouped in three main areas: a registration phase during which terminals communicate their presence and related data, an admission phase during which they ask for the called party's number translation and a call signaling phase during which entities exchange messages to control the actual communication. This distinction allows us to define a level of abstraction that provides the ability to plug different communication stacks into a single platform.

The user objects, encapsulated in service objects (Figure 1), are the recipient of fast changing user information such as the address of the current user location, the user status (busy, free, in a call setup etc.) or the status of the calls the user is involved in.

Before describing the behavior of the service platform, we will categorize service objects according to the following three classes:

- Installed service objects, downloaded at registration time. They live in the platform until the user unregisters (Figure 6).
- Downloaded service objects, downloaded during a call attempt. They live until the call terminates.
- Replica service objects are downloaded when there are already other instances of the same service object, which are installed into or downloaded to some other service platforms. They live in the service platform in which they are downloaded until the call terminates.

When a user registers with a local gatekeeper, communicating presence and location, the service platform sends a "Notify" message to the Home Server, downloads the appropriate service object and installs it. The Installed service object gets a copy of the user object, created by the gatekeeper as soon as the user registers, and initiates it to receive events from the network, via the gatekeeper and the service platform. The service logic behavior is driven by such events, which carry information about the user status and status of the possible calls the user is involved in. This information can vary swiftly and this is the reason for downloading the whole service object; in fact, this updating process is inefficient, if it is not done locally.

Examples of services that can take advantage of it are:

- International Call Barring: When a user tries to place a call, the "call request" is passed to his service object that can use its logic and the data stored in the user object to do a pre-checking and decide whether the call can progress.
- Presence Services: Once the user registers, the service object can notify his/her location to other applications that can start prescheduled calls or deliver messages waiting for the user to be available.

When a registered user (user A@HomerServerA in Figure 7) wants to place a call, the gatekeeper the individual is registered with alerts the associated service platform. This platform then checks whether the called party service object is installed locally; if it is not, then the appropriate service object is downloaded from the called party Home Server. At this stage, two scenarios are possible:

- The called party is registered with a different gatekeeper (GK Y, Figure 7). In this case the Home Server of the user B (the called party) creates a called party Replica service object, which contains a reference to the Installed called party service object running in the service platform associated to the gatekeeper Y. The replica gets downloaded into the service platform X and retrieves an updated user object from the Installed service object, which is also responsible for the synchronization between itself and its replica.

- If the called party is not registered with any other gatekeeper, then its downloaded service object does not need any updated user object. The called party status indicates that the user is disconnected. This is the typical case when the service logic would route the call to a voice-mail system (Figure 2). The synchronization between possible replica service objects, due to simultaneous call attempts, is left to the Home Server B.

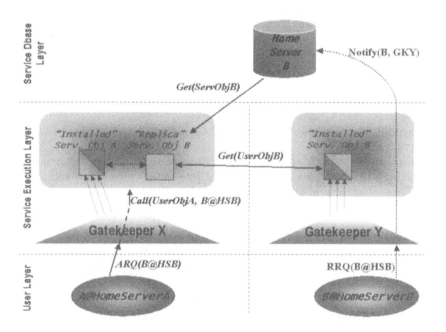

Figure 7. Call placing (from A to B).

To summarize, the goal is to have all service objects involved in a call in the same service platform, which is the one associated with the gatekeeper that the calling party is registered with. The calling party service object is already installed in that service platform. The called party service object, when it is not already there, is downloaded from a Home Server.

An interesting evolution of the proposed architecture is intelligent edge devices running a lightweight version of the service platform. This implies moving it from the Service Execution Layer to the User Layer (see Figure 7) and removing the gatekeeper platform between the device itself and its service platform. In this way, such devices may directly access other service platforms without going through gatekeeper mediation.

4.3 SERVICE OBJECTS BEHAVIOR

Once the service platform has all the service objects involved in the call, the peer-to-peer call negotiation between them can start. The calling party's service object asks the other service object for the called party's location. This is carried out by invoking a "locate" method, part of the interface of every service object, which chooses the right destination transport address. This process could use the user object's fast changing data.

The service logic implemented by the "locate" method consists of a set of if <conditions> then <actions>. The <condition> field contains different types of information: time-of-the-day, call-originator ID, devices the user is currently using, etc. Possible <actions> include return <transport address>, reject, ask the other service object for further information.

The called party service object can return a single response or a list of possible options. For example, when the user is unavailable the calling party's service object has the choice to either stop the call or proceed, leaving a message with a voice mail system. When the calling party service object gets the response, it executes some more logic (address post-checking, availability...) and then passes it to the calling party's terminal through the service platform.

For privacy and security reasons, the called party service object does not have direct access to the calling party's user object. However, it can ask the calling party's service object for information about its user such as current terminal capabilities or preferences on the media. During this negotiation phase, the two parties agree on the media communication type and its format. As we will point out later in the chapter, this feature could be useful in particular for H.323v2.

As described above, the negotiation phase requires more than a single invocation of the "locate" method, therefore it is more reasonable not to call the method remotely on the Home Server but to transport the whole object through the network. If $T_{download}$ is the service object downloading time, T_{remote} is the transmission delay for a single message, T_{local} the transmission delay within the platform and n the number of message exchanged between the two service objects, the negotiation phase overall delay is $T_1=T_{download}+2*n*T_{local}$, if the whole object is downloaded and $T_2=2*n*T_{remote}$, if it is not. Assuming T_{local} negligible and $T_{remote} \cong T_{download}$ then $T_1 << T_2$, when n is significantly large. This is the main reason for downloading the called party's service object, even if this could have an impact on post-dial delay.

In addition, service mobility has some security implications. Since service objects are downloaded into a foreign service platform, their internal data and methods should not be completely exposed. To overcome this problem, service objects could be implemented as "empty" proxies and their methods executed via remote calls. This could be a feature that Home Server providers can make available. Obviously, security advantages are obtained at the expenses of the performance benefits that were gained by downloading the service objects.

Alternatively, host service platforms have to shield local resources in order to prevent malicious service objects from accessing local information and communicating relevant data back to the Home Server or to other applications. This goal can be achieved by using authentication and signed code techniques prior to the execution, i.e., every service object is checked by the platform when downloaded and it is executed only if its code complies with some specific guidelines. Obviously, interoperability between service platforms and home server providers requires well-defined communication interfaces and service level agreements between them.

5. PRACTICAL IMPLEMENTATION

The implementation of the architecture is shown in Figure 3. VoIP is central to the prototype and we wanted it to interoperate with the currently available VoIP clients, the most popular of which is Microsoft® NetMeeting™; therefore we chose H.323 as the VoIP protocol.

The H.323 stack handles messages coming from the IP network. The gatekeeper core logic stores information about ongoing calls (Call Objects) and registered users (user objects) into the respective databases (see Figure 3). The components located above the dashed line have been implemented using Java taking advantage of the built-in Remote Method Invocation (RMI) for the communication between these components.

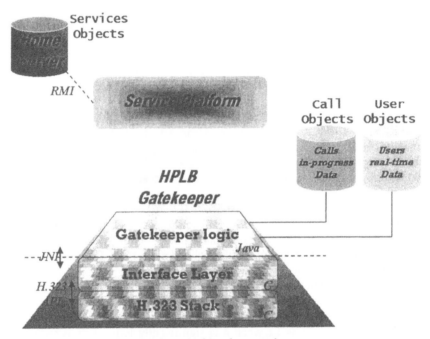

Figure 8. Practical implementation.

5.1 HPLB GATEKEEPER

The HPLB Gatekeeper implements the functionality described by the H.323 standard except bandwidth management (Figure 9). Its internal architecture is composed of three different functional blocks: the H.323 stack, the interface layer and the gatekeeper itself divided in the Java communication API and the core logic.

The Java communication API, which sits in between the core logic and the interface layer, has been designed to be independent from the underlying communication protocols. This creates an additional level of abstraction for RAS (registration and call admission) and Q.931 (call signaling). Thanks to this abstraction a variety of protocols can be plugged into the platform, allowing a seamless integration between different networks.

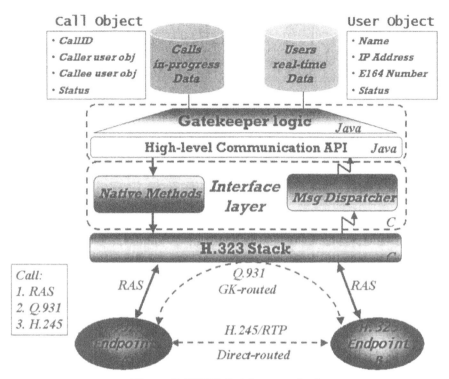

Figure 9. HPLB Gatekeeper platform.

The interface layer between the C API of the H.323 stack, which has an API written in C, and the Java communication API has been based on the standard Java JNI (Java Native Interface) mechanism. This layer can be split into two major functions: the message dispatcher and the native methods. The message dispatcher is triggered by callback functions coming from the stack API. It instantiates Java objects with the parameters contained in the received messages and invokes the appropriate communication API methods to pass these objects. Native methods simply map requests from the Java gatekeeper logic into H.323 stack API method invocations.

The gatekeeper core logic has access to the user and call databases (Figure 9) that contain data related to registered users and to ongoing calls respectively. The user database contains user objects. They contain user's status and basic properties such as their user's alias, E.164 telephone number and IP address. The status can be DISCONNECTED, REGISTERED, BUSY or SETUP (if the user is in the call setup phase). The call database contains Call Objects, consisting of a call-ID, the references of the user objects of all the parties involved in the call and the call status. The call status reflects the Q.931 messages exchanged between the two endpoints through the gatekeeper.

When the gatekeeper receives an Admission Request (ARQ), the service platform is invoked to start the service objects negotiation. After the response is sent back by the service platform and the permission for the call is granted, the Q.931 signaling starts to flow through the Gatekeeper updating the related users and call objects. We have chosen to have H.245 routed directly between the endpoints because it involves a large amount of information to be exchanged that is of little interest to the gatekeeper itself.

The HPLB Gatekeeper core logic implements a simple internal admission policy based on resource availability. Two parameters, based on network capacity, can be set-up at launch time: the maximum number of registered users and the maximum number of ongoing calls.

Registrations or call requests that could cause the network to exceed these parameters are rejected. Future admission policies can be based upon more complex interactions with firewalls or bandwidth management servers. These policies could require the interception of the H.245 flow. In fact, if the GK must allocate resources for guaranteeing QoS for a particular media connection, it should know the UDP port where the stream takes place. The GK can get this parameter intercepting H.245 messages. This parameter is also useful for monitoring and measurement purposes.

5.2 SERVICE OBJECTS

Service objects are stored and provided by the Home Server through the following simple RMI interface:

```
getServiceObject().
releaseServiceObject().
```

The mechanism for synchronizing multiple instances of the same service object is implemented internally in the home Server.

The service object Java interface is composed of the following methods:

`locate()`, this method is invoked by the calling party service object, onto the called party one, in order to start the call negotiation. In the current implementation, this method has one parameter: the calling party ID (E.164 number or preferably the structured alias whenever is available, i.e., the call comes from an IP terminal).

`die()`, this method is used to terminate the object life cycle. Normally, it is invoked by the service platform when the user unregisters or by the calling party object to force the stop of the call negotiation. In the first case the object is released and the Home Server is notified about this. In the second case the behavior is more complicated and it depends on whether the object is "installed", "downloaded" or a "replica".

`freeze()`, this method is invoked by an installed service object, located in the service platform associated to the GK the user is registered to, onto a replica of it (Figure 7). This method is used to freeze temporarily the replica, located in the service platform associated to the GK that has originated the call for the same user, in order to avoid conflicts between the decisions taken by the two objects that may affect the same user.

`unfreeze()`.

`release()`, invoked by a replica service object onto the original installed one to notify that it no longer exists.

`getUserStatus()`.

`getServiceStatus()`, the service status can be NORMAL or FROZEN. If a service object is in the latter state it is likely that the other party service object will stop the call.

`updateUserStatus()`, `updateCallStatus()`, invoked by the service platform.

H.323v2 can really benefit from the service object negotiation. In fact, its Fast Connect procedure coupled with the prior service objects call negotiation makes sure that media channels with the optimal characteristics, chosen during this call negotiation, can be always opened just after the call setup. This requires passing terminal capabilities to the GK at registration time instead of exchanging them during the H.245 phase, after the service objects negotiation. While this feature is already part of the SIP protocol, H.323 will provide it in future versions. This is one of the problems that have to be solved when designing a service architecture that must support a variety of underlying protocols. It is also worth pointing out the relationship between H.450 and our proposal. The former is a signaling mechanism to control services implementation, the latter is the logic behind it.

Since service objects are essentially Java objects, we use Java as Service Logic Language; service logic scripts are interpreted by the Java Virtual Machine. One advantage of this choice is that it does not require a new virtual machine for interpreting a new scripting language. There are several proposals for a scripting language that handle calls. The most interesting of them, from a VoIP point of view, is CPL [12], a Call Processing Language for Internet Telephony, under development by the IPTel IETF Working Group (http://www.ietf.org/ html.charters/iptel-charter.html).

The two main objections to using a normal programming language like Java for service setup by end-users are that service creation could be difficult and that common languages are too complex for this scope (handling calls). This complexity can easily generate service misbehaviors. These drawbacks can be overcome using controlled and simple service creation environments. In this context, we are exploring JavaBeans™ as a valuable option to address these issues. In particular they can be useful as JavaBeans™ can be manipulated graphically. This can generate an interesting evolution of service creation environment. In fact, Home Server providers may make available different classes that can be directly customized by end users using JavaBeans™. Different classes of Services may be offered, from a simple static call redirection (to a number decided by the user) to the provision of the whole service object by a end user with good programming skills (that actually implements the whole logic).

5.3 DEMONSTRATION

The practical demonstration is aimed at showing the ease of deploying personalized user services and the potential interaction with IN components, in particular with the Service Control Point (SCP), which is the platform currently used by telecom operators to offer value added services [2]. The architecture, depicted in Figure 10, provides Internet Call Waiting. This service allows users to receive incoming calls, through a VoIP gateway, when they are connected in dial-up and their telephone line is engaged. The demonstration was presented at the HP Laboratories review in Bristol.

The SCP is simulated by a Java application running on a machine connected to a PBX, through specialized cards supporting the British signaling standard DPNSS. This "virtual SCP" communicates with the gatekeeper through Java RMI, but call requests reach the gatekeeper through the same high level communication API used by the H.323 stack. A plug-in has been written to make the Virtual SCP inter-operate with the gatekeeper through this API. The H.323 gateway runs on a different machine connected to the same PBX. The range of telephone numbers served by the PBX, connected to the normal PSTN, has been split: a sub-range for the GW and another sub-range for the virtual SCP. Each extension in the SCP sub-range corresponds to an Internet Call Waiting subscriber.

When there is a call attempt for a subscriber the PBX tries to contact the user telephone number. When the number is engaged the virtual SCP is alerted, which contacts the gatekeeper to find out if the user, corresponding to the dialed E.164 number, is registered (note that the user must have registered him providing the same E.164 number). If so, the process goes on as described before: the service platform is invoked and the personalized user service is executed. The demonstration is limited to Internet Call Waiting, so we assume that whenever called users are connected in dial-up to an ISP, they are also registered to the particular GK associated to the SCP (there is a well-known fixed binding between them). If the called party is not registered to that particular GK, it means the user is busy in a PSTN call and the calling party will get the busy tone (alternatively, the normal IN call waiting service can be activated).

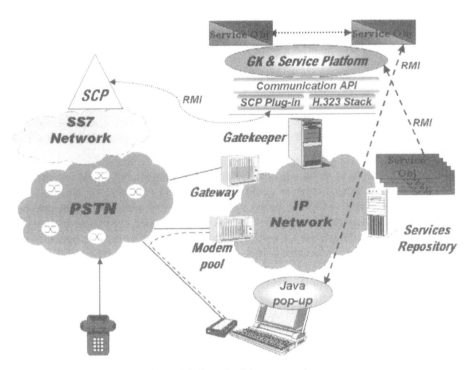

Figure 10. Practical demonstration.

In our demonstration, the logic in the called party service object is programmed for examining its own user status. If the user is not busy in a VoIP call then its IP address is returned. Otherwise, the service contacts a small Java application launched at registration time running on the current user machine and delivers a pop-up window, asking the user if he/she wants to take the call (leaving to the client the responsibility to manage multiple calls), divert it to another IP address, divert it to a telephone number or reject it.

In order to do this the service platform security manager implements a dynamic policy that allows a service object to open a remote connection to the current machine where the registered user is located.

If the user returns an IP address then the gatekeeper allocates a "phantom" number on the range associated with the gateway. The gatekeeper gets this range from the gateway at registration time, through H.323. The gatekeeper returns the number to the SCP, keeping the association between the phantom number and the IP address. The virtual SCP communicates with the PBX to divert the incoming call to the gateway "phantom" number. When the gateway receives the call it sends a RAS ARQ message to the GK with the phantom number as destination; the GK knows the IP address associated to that phantom number and connects the H.323 call.

In our demonstration we have assumed that there is a static relationship between the SCP and the gatekeeper/service platform and every time a user is connected in dial-up to the Internet he registers with that particular gatekeeper. If the called party can be registered with a GK other than the one associated with the SCP then there are some consequences related to E.164 numbers translation. In particular, the gatekeeper associated with the SCP receives, from the SCP itself, call requests containing just two parameters: Caller-ID and dialed number. It is important to stress that, in this context, the dialed number is a user identification and not a classic E.164 number that gives information on call routing. If there are no users registered locally with the E.164 numbers provided by the SCP then the GK must translate E.164

numbers into the structured e-mail-like aliases in order to locate the Home Servers and then download the user objects and the service objects. The GK can perform this translation in several ways: by performing a look-up in a central database or by asking other GKs through IGCP (the Inter-GK Communication Protocol, see H.323 Annex G [4]).

- If the GK is able to translate these E.164 numbers and locate the called party and calling party's Home Servers then service execution proceeds as usual. Otherwise, there are two possible scenarios:
- If either the called party Home Server is not located or the called party is not registered to any GK then, as far as the service platform is concerned, the call is rejected.
- If either the calling party Home Server is not located or the calling party is not registered to any GK then a dummy service object is created to interact with the called party service object.

6. CONCLUSIONS

VoIP networks have now come of age, with significant investment from key industry players, in particular the carriers. New network and communications technologies are dramatically changing the way services are deployed. There is now a critical need for services that span heterogeneous networks and VoIP, with its extreme openness, will be a key factor in enabling the communication control convergence. In the VoIP context, the use of this type of "active networking", through objects downloadable into gatekeeper-like servers, seems to be a reasonable way to address the problem.

The architecture presented in this chapter is a first step in this direction and a lot more work is expected to be done in this area in the future. Users, carriers and equipment vendors must map future service requirements and opportunities into an architecture, from which the rest (e.g., protocols, technologies, and specific products) will be determined. The transition from a closed, circuit switched, usually monopoly (or oligopoly) owned telephone network to a packet network that is much more open to and configurable by users poses many difficulties. This chapter brings up some of the problems that will be encountered in this transition, and introduces our perspective on them.

Our experience shows that the integration between all the control elements of traditional and emerging networks gives a powerful tool to rapidly deploy and offer new services. We believe that approaches like the one we propose are suitable for the so-called next-generation service providers and will replace the existing closed solutions.

Acknowledgments

The material presented is a summary of experiences acquired from extensive discussion and joint development with people from the Crescent Project of the Internet Communications Services Department at Hewlett-Packard Laboratories in Bristol (UK). In particular, we owe a debt of gratitude to Steve Hinde who shepherded us through this work and contributed superb ideas. Special thanks also go to Hans Daanen and Lawrence Wilcock for their intellectual companionship. They provided invaluable help to clarify our thoughts.

References

1. H. Schulzrinne, "Re-engineering the Telephone System," *Proc. of IEEE Singapore International Conference on Networks (SICON)*, Singapore, April 1997.
2. J. Garrahan et al., "Intelligent Network Overview," *IEEE Communication Magazine*, Vol. 31, No.3, March 1993.

3. C. Low, "Integrating Communication Services," *IEEE Communications Magazine*, Vol. 35, No. 6, June 1997.

4. International Telecommunication Union, "Visual Telephone Systems and Equipment for Local Area Networks Which Provide a Non-Guaranteed Quality of Service," Recommendation H.323, Telecommunication Standardization Sector of ITU, Geneva, Switzerland.

5. O. Kahane and S. Petrack, "Call Management Agent System Requirements Function Architecture and Protocol," IMTC VoIP Forum Contribution, Seattle, January 1997. Work in progress. ftp://ftp.imtc-files.org/imtc-site/VoIP-AG/VoIP97-010.doc.

6. H. Schulzrinne, "Personal Mobility for Multimedia Services in the Internet," *European Workshop on Interactive Distributed Multimedia Systems and Services*, Berlin, Germany, March 1996.

7. D. Isenberg, "The Dawn of the Stupid Network," *ACM netWorker*, Vol. 2, No. 1, February-March 1998, pp. 24-31.

8. DataBeam Corp., "A Primer on the H.323 Series Standard," http://www.databeam.com/h323/h323primer.html.

9. M. Handley, H. Schulzrinne, E. Schooler, and J. Rosenberg, "SIP: Session Initiation Protocol, RFC 2543," Internet Engineering Task Force, March 1999. ftp://ftp.isi.edu/in-notes/rfc2543.txt.

10. H. Schulzrinne and J. Rosenberg, "A Comparison of SIP and H.323 for Internet Telephony," *Proc. of Network and Operating System Support for Digital Audio and Video (NOSSDAV)*, Cambridge, England, July 1998.

11. O. Mizuno et al., "Advanced Intelligent Network and the Internet Combination Service and its Customization," *IEICE Trans. on Communications*, Vol. E81B, No. 8, August 1998.

12. J. Rosenberg, J. Lennox, and H. Schulzrinne, "Programming Internet Telephony Services," *IEEE Network*, Vol.13, No. 3, May/June 1999

13. T. Russel, "Signaling System #7," McGraw-Hill, 1995.

14. C. Huitema et al., "An Architecture for Residential Internet Telephony Service," *IEEE Network*, Vol.13, No. 3, May/June 1999

15. J. Lennox, H. Schulzrinne, and T.F. La Porta, "Implementing Intelligent Network Services with the Session Initiation Protocol," Technical Report CUCS-002-99, Columbia University, New York, January 1999.

16. J. Lennox, J. Rosenberg, and H. Schulzrinne, "Common Gateway Interface for SIP," Internet Draft, Internet Engineering Task Force, May 1999. Work in progress.

17. J. Lennox and H. Schulzrinne, "CPL: A Language for User Control of Internet Telephony Services," Internet Draft, Internet Engineering Task Force, February 1999. Work in progress.

18. D. Rizzetto and C. Catania, "A Voice Over IP Service Architecture for Integrated Communications," *IEEE Network*, Vol. 13, No. 3, May/June 1999.

Chapter 3

THE MPEG-4 STANDARD FOR INTERNET-BASED MULTIMEDIA APPLICATIONS

Charles Law and Borko Furht

Abstract

With the development of the MPEG-4 standard in 1998, a new way of creating and interacting with audio-visual media was conceived. This chapter provides an overview of this new standard. Topics covered in the chapter include a description of visual and audio objects, both natural and computer generated, and a description of how scenes are put together in MPEG-4. We also present an overview of the systems necessary for MPEG-4 operation and insight into possible Internet-based multimedia applications. We briefly discuss some research issues in MPEG-2 design and implementations.

1. INTRODUCTION

In the last several years, a number of standards for representation and coding of audio-visual data have been proposed and adopted. Video coding standards, their format, compressed bit rates, and applications are summarized in Table 1, adapted from [13].

The Moving Picture Experts Group (MPEG) was established in January 1988 with the mandate to develop standards for coded representation of moving pictures, audio, and their combination. The first standard, MPEG-1, specified coding of audio-visual data for bit rates of 1.5 Mbps, while the second standard MPEG-2 is more generic standard intended for a variety of audio-video applications at the bit rate in range of 3-40 Mbps.

A new generation of multimedia and video applications requires new functionalities that are not supported by previous MPEG-1 and MPEG-2 standards. Therefore, a request for proposal concerning the MPEG-4 standard was made in July 1995. This new standard (MPEG-4) is designed to provide an object-oriented and content-based methodology for producing, delivering, and consuming audio-visual content. MPEG-4 was finalized in October 1998. Currently, MPEG is working on a fully backward compatible extension titled "MPEG-4 Version 2." This extension should be finalized by January 2000.

Table 1. Video Coding Standards and Their Characteristics.

STANDARD	FORMATS	COMPRESSED BIT RATE	APPLICATIONS
H.261	QCIF CIF	p x 64 Kbps p=1,2,...30	Videophone and videoconferencing via ISDN.
H.263	SQCIF 16CIF	Flexible	From low bit rate videophone to high quality videoconferencing.
MPEG-1	SIF	1.5 Mbps	Interactive multimedia, storage and retrieval of VCR quality video on CD-ROM.
MPEG-2	Flexible	3-40 Mbps	Digital TV, HDTV, broadcasting satellite services, electronic cinema, home television theatre.
MPEG-4	Flexible	Flexible	Interactive multimedia, mobile multimedia, content-based storage and retrieval, video games, video broadcast, collaborative scene visualization.

MPEG-4 combines elements from three fields: digital television, interactive graphics, and the World Wide Web [14]. Unlike previous MPEG standards, MPEG-4 allows for separately coding and describing each content-based object comprising a scene. This means that objects such as background music, foreground speech, a graphically generated globe, a specific video object (such as a person), and scene background, can be individually defined and manipulated. In previous standards, the scene would have to be created as a singular audio-visual entity such as an MPEG-2 clip. Furthermore, because each item is separate, it can be individually removed from the scene. This means that applications, which are unable to compose an entire MPEG-4 scene, may scale the scene down to only critical aspects.

Additional functionality provided by MPEG-4 includes:

- Intellectual property rights management.
- Synchronization of audio-visual objects.
- User interaction with audio-visual objects (change viewing coordinates, enlarge or shrink an object, modify pitch, select object enhancements if offered, replace scene, etc.)
- Scaling of audio-visual objects.
- Error robustness.
- Transparent delivery of information either locally or remotely.

MPEG-4 provides some powerful tools in which to create scenes. To control composition of these scenes, MPEG-4 uses a binary language to specify scene description rather than imbed the information into the compressed objects. This makes MPEG-4 objects highly reusable. All of this gives the user much more control over the presentation of a scene than was available with the earlier standards. Figure 1, which illustrates typical MPEG-4 scene composition, shows several objects (desk, globe, blackboard, instructor, and audio) placed into a 3-D coordinate system relative to the supposed viewer [4].

1.1 OVERVIEW OF MPEG-4 VIDEO CODEC

A general architecture of MPEG-4 video codec (encoder and decoder), shown in Figure 2, is based on the concept of video objects [13,16]. Both video encoder and video decoder are composed of a number of video object encoders and decoders, which apply the same coding scheme to each video object separately. The user can interact with the objects at the encoder or decoder side – operations include scaling, dragging, and linking objects.

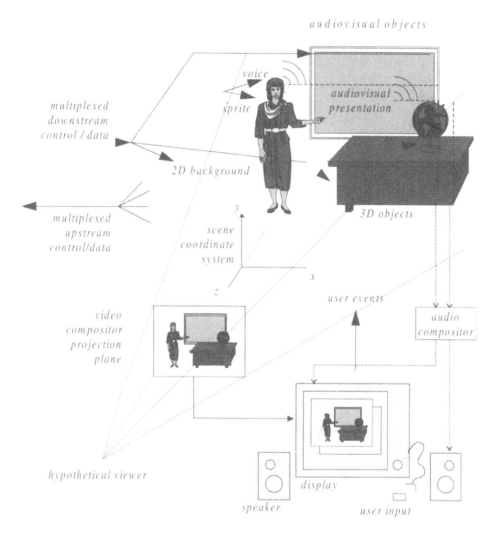

Figure 1. MPEG-4 scene (from [4]).

Figure 3, adopted from [13], illustrates an example of video coding and composition using MPEG-4. Several objects, such as *Man*, *Car*, and *House*, are separated from the original input video. Each video object is then encoded separately by video object (VO) encoder and then transmitted through the network. At the receiving side, these objects are decoded separately using VO decoder and sent to the compositor. The user can interact with the compositor to reconstruct the original scene (a), or to manipulate objects and create different scenes (b). In addition, the user can request from the composer to download new objects from a local or remote database libraries, and insert or replace objects in the scene (c).

The main components of a MPEG-4 video coder include [13]:

- Shape coder,
- Motion estimation and composition, and
- Texture coder.

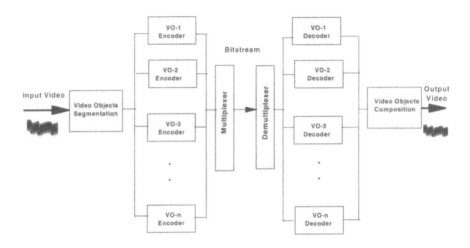

Figure 2. The architecture of MPEG-4 video codec.

The shape coder is used to compress the segmentation information, which specifies the object region and contour within the scene. Motion estimation and composition is used to reduce temporal redundancies. The texture coder is applied to intra and residual data after motion compensation.

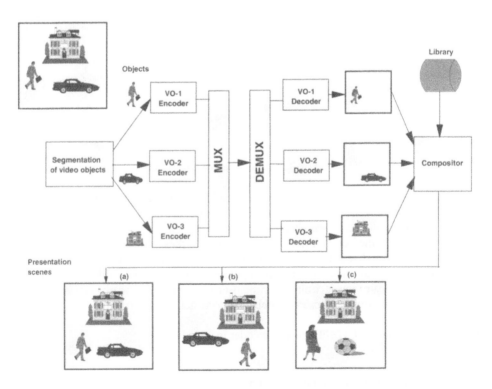

Figure 3. An example of video scene and composition in MPEG-4.

2. VISUAL OBJECTS

Visual objects in MPEG-4 may be composed of natural objects, synthetic objects, or both. Natural objects are pixel based images and video, while synthetic objects are computer-generated images and animations.

2.1 NATURAL VISUAL OBJECTS

The elementary units of a natural visual object are called video objects (VOs). An example of a VO could be a tennis player (without background) or the crowd watching the tennis player. VOs such as a tennis player, where the object is in motion and the background is masked out, are known as Video Object Planes (VOPs). Because the background is omitted, VOPs are essentially irregularly shaped videos as opposed to the full rectangular video images we get with MPEG-1 and MPEG-2. The background image may be further broken down into other VOPs, or a static sprite. A static sprite is a large still image, describing panoramic background [4]. By using it as a sprite, the background only needs to be fully encoded once. Afterwards, the background can be repositioned through eight global motion parameters encoded for each subsequent frame. The decoder will combine VOPs and sprites to recreate the original video. In this way, the amount of data needed to reproduce a scene is reduced (effectively compressing the scene).

Figure 4 shows how VOPs and sprites may be used to construct a single scene [4]. The tennis player in the foreground is segmented from the background as a VOP. The background is then extracted as a sprite prior to encoding. The sprite image is transmitted only once and is stored in a sprite buffer. In each subsequent frame, only the eight camera parameters relevant to the background are transmitted. The VOP is transmitted separately as an arbitrary-shape video object. The receiver can now reconstruct the background for each frame in proper sequence based on the sprite, and can overlay the VOP onto the background to correctly recreate the original scene.

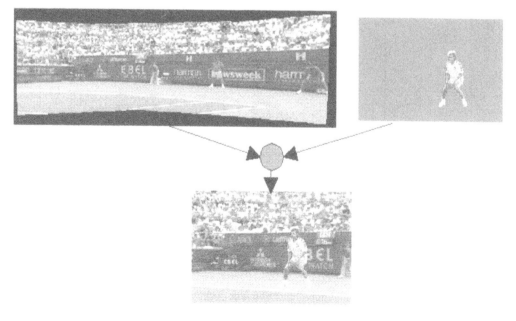

Figure 4. VOP and sprite coding of a video sequence (from [4]).

Multiple VOPs comprising a higher level video object are each coded as a separate layer of the video object, each with its own shape, motion, and texture components. The arbitrary shape comprising an individual layer may be described in two ways. First, for lower quality content or low bit rate environments, binary shape coding may be used. In binary shape coding, a map is used to define whether or not a pixel is part of the object (a pixel is either 'on' or 'off'). The second method of describing a shape is gray scale or alpha shape coding. In this type of coding, each pixel is not merely 'on' or 'off', but is assigned a transparency value. With the added transparency information, VOP layers can be blended more smoothly and will give higher quality content than with binary shape coding.

The ability to blend multiple VOP layers is part of the content-based feature of the MPEG-4 video model. Being content-based, video objects can be separated and separately decoded. This enables scaling of information both spatially (reduction of the size of objects) and temporally (reduction in the amount of information received per unit time). In this way, low bandwidth applications may still be able to obtain meaningful information by scaling back the less important aspects of the information being received.

Coding of each VOP sequence (whether rectangular size or not) is based on the same method already used in the previous MPEG standards [5]. The MPEG-4 coding algorithm encodes the first frame of a VOP as an intra-frame (I-VOP). Subsequent frames are coded using Inter-frame prediction (P-VOPs). Bi-directionally predicted frames (B-VOPs) are also supported and may be used. Each frame is broken into 16x16 pixel macroblocks, which are in turn related to six 8x8 YUV blocks (four luminance – Y1, Y2, Y3, Y4; two chrominance – U, V). This is illustrated by Figure 5.

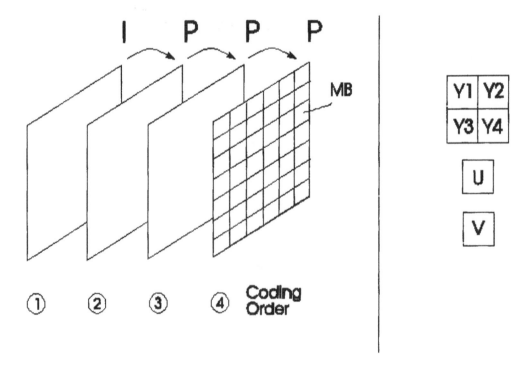

Figure 5. VOP frame coding.

In order to code shape, texture, and motion information for arbitrarily shaped VOPs, a constant size reference window (a multiple of 16x16 pixel blocks) is used as a container for each VOP comprising a scene. The VOP is positioned within the reference window so it is in correct spatial position relative to all the other VOPs comprising the same scene at that same time. Each VOP will use a similar reference window. The VOP shape is mapped onto a shape-adaptive macroblock grid within the reference window. The border of the VOP shape defines the VOP window. A shift parameter is coded to show the position of the VOP window within the reference window. This is illustrated by Figure 6.

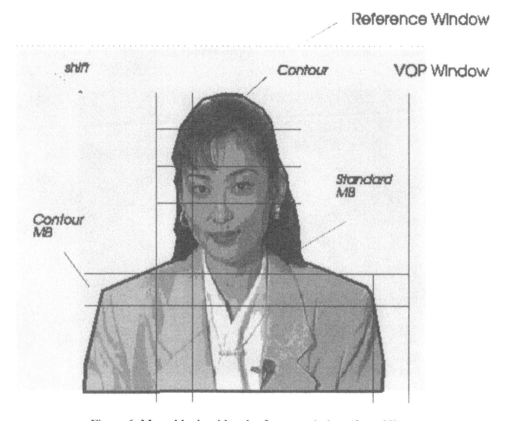

Figure 6. Macroblock grid and reference window (from [5]).

An alternative, more revolutionary way to object-based image coding is to consider the complete image object as the smallest possible entity. The texture, contour, and motion of this object are separately coded [17].

In order to support a wide range of natural video applications, the MPEG-4 standard provides algorithms and tools for very low bit rate applications (typically between 5 and 64 kbit/s), as well as high bit rate applications (typically 64 kbit/s to 10 Mbit/s). Either tool set provides the content-based functionalities (scalability and object manipulation).

2.2 SYNTHETIC VISUAL OBJECTS

Synthetic objects in the MPEG-4 standard may be either two-dimensional or three-dimensional. Two-dimensional objects consist of rectangles, circles, lines, polygons, curves, and 2-D meshes [6]. Three-dimensional objects consist of boxes, cones, cylinders, spheres, and 3-D facial meshes [6]. These objects, both 2-D and 3-D, have the general properties of transparency, color, and texture. Furthermore, other video objects such as still images or moving video may be mapped onto meshes as texture.

A 2-D mesh is a partition of a 2-D planar region into triangular patches. Animation of the mesh is done by updating motion vectors for the patch vertices, thus giving the image the appearance of motion. Since the motion vectors of the vertices of a triangular patch will most likely be different, the triangle formed by those vertices will be 'warped'. Likewise, any texture mapped onto that patch will be 'warped'. Thus, by moving the vertices of the triangles, the patches, as well as their mapped textures, will be 'warped'. This can be used to create video-like objects which are, in reality, still images mapped to an animated 2-D mesh (e.g., a flag mapped onto a rectangular mesh can be animated to appear as if waving in the breeze). Figure 7 shows an example of a fish mesh [4]. By deforming the mesh, the fish can be made to 'swim'. Additionally, any texture can be mapped to the mesh (fish, corporate logo, etc.).

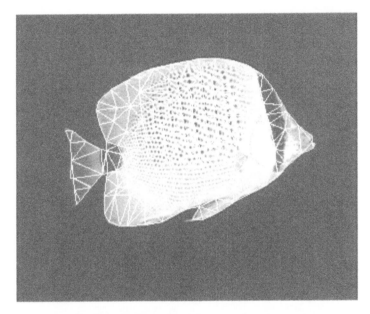

Figure 7. 2-D mesh modeling of a fish (from [4]).

Using 2-D mesh animation will provide a large bit rate saving over using motion video since only the motion vector updates are transmitted on a regular basis (the original mesh and texture are only transmitted once).

Currently, the only 3-D mesh supported by MPEG-4 is the 3-D facial mesh. A 3-D mesh is constructed using Face Definition Parameters (FDP). Once constructed, the face is generic with a neutral expression. Now, using Facial Animation Parameters (FAP), the face can be animated. FDPs and FAPs are part of Binary Format for Scenes (BIFS, see section 4.1); the binary scene description language used in MPEG-4. FAPs control animation through a Face Animation Table within the FDPs and through the Face Interpolation Technique. A Face Animation Table provides functional mapping of FAP commands to control points on the mesh. The Face Interpolation Technique determines the effect of multiple FAPs on common control points before applying the animation.

Like 2-D meshes, any texture can be mapped onto the 3-D facial mesh. Usually, however, a facial image is mapped onto the mesh. This is illustrated by Figure 8.

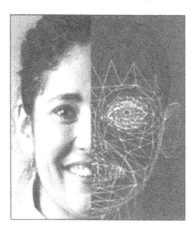

Figure 8. Facial mesh (from [3]).

Synthetic visual objects have view-dependent scalability. This means that the viewing position in a 3-D world is taken into account when determining what data to send. Only that information relevant to objects visible at the viewing position is sent. This may scale down the amount of encoded and decoded data considerably.

2.3 ERROR ROBUSTNESS

To accommodate a wider range of applications, some of which may be more prone to error (such as wireless networks), MPEG-4 provides for robust error recovery through three general mechanisms: resynchronization, data recovery, and error concealment.

Resynchronization allows for the detection of synchronization fields in the bit stream. When an error occurs, only the data from the previous synchronization point to the next synchronization point is considered suspect. The decoder can then discard all of the suspect data or use data recovery techniques to retain part of the data.

Data recovery is used after synchronization has been reestablished so data that might otherwise be lost can be recovered. Generally, the data is encoded in such a way as to make it more resilient to error. One particular method uses the Reversible Variable Length Codes tool to encode the information so that it can be read in both the forward and reverse directions. In this way, data occurring before or after the error can be recovered. Figure 9 illustrates this method of data recovery [4].

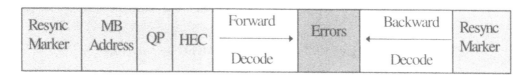

Figure 9. Data recovery using Reversible Variable Length Codes.

Error concealment is used to 'cover' for lost data. If lost information can be adequately localized in resynchronization, then lost data may be concealed by using data from previous frames (problem areas will be essentially invisible to the human eye). For enhanced concealment capabilities, texture and motion information could be separated (with an additional resynchronization marker placed between the motion and texture data). Now, if texture data is lost, it can be recreated using previous texture data along with the current motion data.

3. AUDIO OBJECTS

Audio objects in MPEG-4, like visual objects, may be composed of natural objects, synthetic objects, or both. Natural objects are composed of sounds which naturally occur (are based on analog sound waves). Some natural objects are human speech and orchestral music. Synthetic objects are composed of sounds that are generated (synthesized) based on structured descriptions such as MIDI. MPEG-4 also provides for a more advanced form of synthesized sound with the structured audio format. This format is not itself a method of synthesis, but a way of describing methods of synthesis. This will enable MPEG-4 to accommodate any current or future type of synthesis. Figure 10 illustrates the types of sound handled by the MPEG-4 standard [3]. Natural sound sampling requires a high bit rate, while synthesized sound (whether the simple type used today, or the more complex and higher quality type promised through structured audio) requires a lower bit rate.

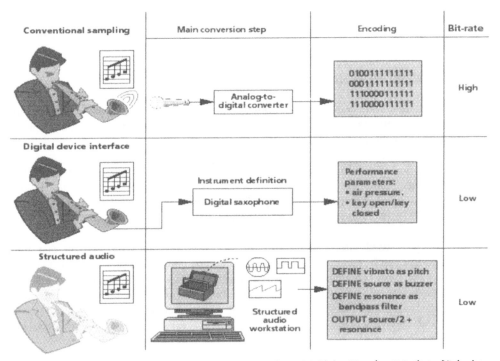

Source: Eric Scheirer, Massachusetts Institute of Technology

Figure 10. Types of sound in MPEG-4.

3.1 NATURAL AUDIO

Natural audio encompasses a range of frequencies covering both speech and general audio (music, etc.). In order to achieve high audio quality within this spectrum, the MPEG-4 standard integrates both speech coding techniques and general audio coding techniques into one framework.

MPEG-4 provides tools for coding speech that can work for bit rates from 2 kbit/s to 24 kbit/s (even lower bit rates can be accommodated in variable bit rate mode) [4]. Speech is coded by two algorithms. One, Harmonic Vector eXcitation Coding (HVXC), is a parametric method used for operations at or below 4 kbit/s [4]. The other, Code Excited Linear Predictive (CELP), is used for operating bit rates between 4 kbit/s and 24 kbit/s [4]. CELP uses sampling at 8 kHz and 16 kHz to support narrowband and wideband speech respectively.

General audio is coded at bit rates from 6 kbit/s to beyond 128 kbit/s [3]. This range encompasses everything from a mono signal to high quality stereo. Coding techniques used for general audio include TwinVQ as well as the advanced audio coding (AAC) algorithm from the MPEG-2 standard. AAC provides for efficient compression of audio in the upper bit rate range and provides very high quality audio at effective bit rates which are considerably lower than the MP3 audio format currently used throughout the internet today [3].

Figure 11 shows the general framework of MPEG-4 audio. This framework was defined to allow for scalability (see Section 3.3) while maintaining optimal coverage of the bit rates.

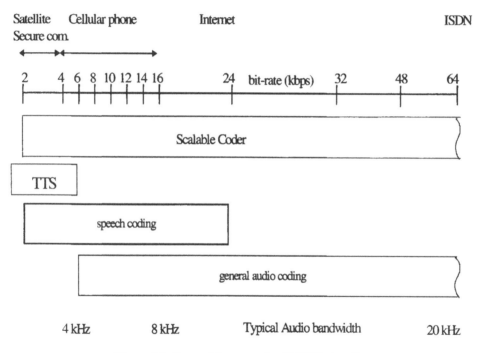

Figure 11. General framework of MPEG-4 audio.

3.2 SYNTHESIZED AUDIO

The MPEG-4 standard provides for several types of input from which to generate synthesized audio. In addition to general sounds, such as music, text input can be converted to speech using the Text-To-Speech (TTS) decoder. Using structured audio tools will allow the delivery of synthesized audio at extremely low bit rates.

TTS coders operate at bit rates between 200 bit/s and 1.2 kbit/s [4]. The generated speech may be synchronized to a facial mesh animation to give the appearance of a talking head. Furthermore, the speech generator can be supplied with prosodic parameters (information about vocal stress, tone, pitch, accent, cadence, etc.) to facilitate the generation of intelligible, human-like speech, as opposed to flat, droning mechanical speech.

Structured audio uses a synthesis language called SAOL (Structured Audio Orchestra Language) to drive its coding/decoding process. Rather than refer to a specific synthesis process, SAOL describes methods of sound synthesis. Within this method description, instruments can be defined and downloaded. Control over the instruments described in SAOL is handled by a language called SASL (Structured Audio Score Language). With SASL, a musical score can be created using the instrument definition. Since structured audio provides for such detailed sound descriptors for the synthesis (oscillators, filters, etc.), the quality of audio produced through structured audio is very high. For applications that do not require or can not handle the sophisticated synthesis of structured audio, MPEG-4 allows for wavetable bank synthesis (already in use on many PC sound cards).

3.3 ADDITIONAL AUDIO FUNCTIONALITY

The use of objects in MPEG-4 allows audio elements to be considered separately (i.e., each audio object is considered a separate channel). Audio objects can be background music (natural or synthesized), speech, a stereo channel, etc. With multiple audio objects, various channels can be mixed in various ways to produce a different output for each listening situation. Additionally, each object can be manipulated independently of any other object (e.g., an echo can be added to background music without modifying foreground speech).

In order to facilitate a variety of applications pertaining to audio objects, additional audio functionality is provided through the MPEG-4 standard. This functionality pertains to the scalability and manipulation of audio objects as follows [4]:

- *Bit rate scalability* – allows a bitstream to be parsed (either during transmission or in the decoder) into a lower bit rate stream so that meaningful data is not lost.
- *Bandwidth scalability* – a particular case of bit rate scalability where a portion of the frequency spectrum is removed from a bitstream.
- *Encoder complexity scalability* – allows encoders of differing complexity to generate valid, meaningful bitstreams.
- *Decoder complexity scalability* – allows decoders of differing complexity to decode a bitstream. In general, higher quality audio is obtained with more complex encoders and decoders.
- *Speed change* – allows, while in the decoding process, a time scale change without altering pitch.
- *Pitch change* – allows, while in the decoding process, a pitch change without altering the time scale. This can only be done when using parametric or structured audio coding methods.
- *Audio effects* – allows for the processing of decoded audio signals so that functions such as mixing, reverberation, and 3-D spatial positioning of sound can be performed.

4. SCENE COMPOSITION AND MANIPULATION

Once a set of audio-visual objects has been formed, they must be grouped together and synchronized to form a scene. This grouping entails the composition of a scene which, due to the object structure in MPEG-4, can be further manipulated by a user. Creation and manipulation of scenes is accomplished through a special language called BIFS.

4.1 BINARY FORMAT FOR SCENES

The language used by MPEG-4 to describe and dynamically change a scene is specified by a compact binary format known as Binary Format for Scenes (BIFS). With BIFS, objects may be added to a scene, removed from a scene, or modified within a scene. Scene modifications (audio or visual) may be made either in response to a set of pre-defined commands, or in response to user interaction.

BIFS, designed with many of the same concepts used in the Virtual Reality Modeling Language (VRML), has the ability to define 3-D objects (sphere, cube, tube, etc.). Unlike VRML, however, BIFS also has the ability to define 2-D objects (lines, rectangles, etc.), and can be used for real-time streaming. Since BIFS code is binary, its data stream is typically 10 to 15 times shorter than a VRML stream with the same content [3].

BIFS is comprised of four components:

- Semantic elements (scene nodes)
- Binary syntax
- BIFS-Update protocol (control scene changes)
- BIFS-Anim protocol (control animation streams)

BIFS scene nodes contain four types of information:

- Media object attributes (define audio-visual properties)
- Structure of scene graph (layout of media objects in 3-D space)
- Pre-defined animation behavior of the objects
- Animation behavior due to user interaction

The benefits of using BIFS are as follows:

- Integration of 2-D and 3-D media using a single format. Scenes will not need to be designed, encoded, and decoded using multiple formats and associated tools. This makes for greater ease of use, and lower resource utilization.
- Streaming of scene information. Scene components do not have to be completely downloaded before scene presentation can begin.
- Improved compression. Compression is improved since a binary format is used rather than a text format. Typically, a 12 to 1 reduction in needed bandwidth can be obtained by using BIFS to stream animation (as opposed to uncompressed text streaming) [1].

As illustrated by Figure 12, BIFS scenes represent visual and audio objects in 3-D space, with the BIFS scene descriptions falling into sub-categories such as [2]:

- 2-D only primitives
- 3-D only primitives
- 2-D and 3-D scenes layered in a 2-D space
- 2-D and 3-D scenes used a texture maps for 2-D or 3-D primitives
- 2-D scenes drawn in a local two-dimensional plane within a 3-D scene.

4.2 SCENE DESCRIPTION

Audio-visual objects in MPEG-4 require additional information in order to be combined into a cohesive scene. This information, called scene description, is used to determine the placement of the objects both spatially and temporally. Illustrated in Figure 13, the description follows a hierarchical structure that provides a 'script' needed for scene composition. Each node represents either an individual audio-visual object, or a group of such objects. The top node represents the scene, and groups all of the objects together. These nodes expose a set of parameters through which aspects of their behavior (pitch, tempo, frame speed, color, etc.) can be controlled.

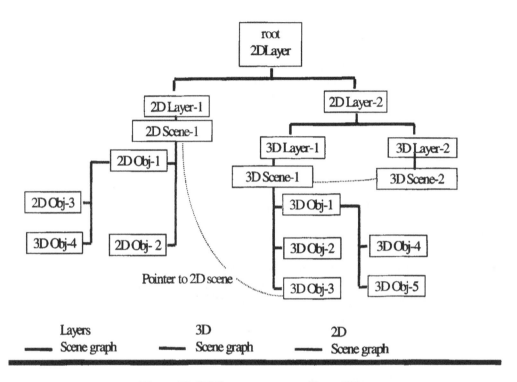

Figure 12. BIFS scene structure (from [2]).

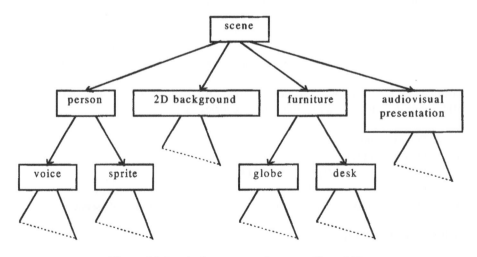

Figure 13. Logical structure of a scene (from [4]).

The information in the scene description is used to place the scene's objects into a common representation space in preparation for rendering to the appropriate media device. This is done through use of local and global coordinate systems. Each media object (node) in the scene description has a local, coordinate system. A local coordinate system is one in which the media object has a fixed spatio-temporal location and scale (orientation and size). Media objects are positioned in a scene by specifying a coordinate transformation from the object's local coordinate system into another coordinate system (global coordinate system) defined by one or more parent nodes in the scene description tree. This is called composition and rendering and is illustrated in Figure 14.

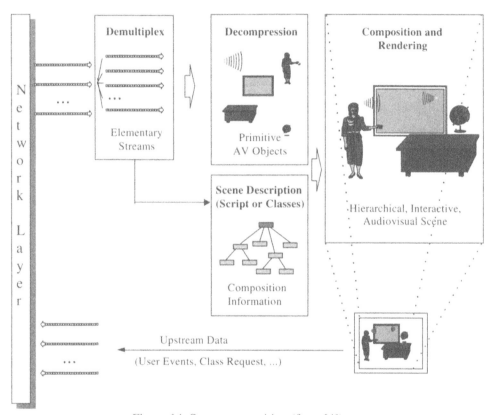

Figure 14. Scene composition (from [4]).

The logical construct used in MPEG-4 to facilitate the transport of media objects is the elementary stream (ES). Elementary streams are produced and consumed by the encoder and decoder respectively, and represent the streaming data between two systems. Some objects, such as background music, may have a single ES. Other objects may have one ES for the basic information and several more for a series of enhancement layers, thus providing scalability. BIFS information used to describe the scene is conveyed in its own ES. This separation of the media object from its scene description provides for reusability of the object (reuse same object with different description) and easy manipulation of the object (modify the description and attributes of the object without having to decode the object's bitstream and change its contents – editing a BIFS bitstream is easy since it is a binary format and not compressed, whereas media object are usually compressed entities).

In order to associate elementary streams to each other and to media objects used in a scene description, object descriptors are used. An object descriptor is a collection of descriptors describing the elementary stream or streams comprising a single media object or scene description. The descriptors comprising an object descriptor are called elementary stream descriptors. An ES descriptor contains information telling the system how to decode the stream as well as intellectual property identification. Object descriptors, like scene description, are conveyed in a dedicated elementary stream. This allows for the dynamic update and removal of object descriptors or their components as a scene changes. To associate media objects in a scene description to a particular object descriptor, a unique numeric identifier (object descriptor ID) is assigned to each object descriptor. Likewise, an ES descriptor identifies a single stream with a numeric identifier (ES ID), and an optional URL pointing to a remote source for the stream. Access to content is gained through an initial object descriptor made available at session setup. This descriptor points into the scene description and object descriptor elementary streams as illustrated in Figure 15.

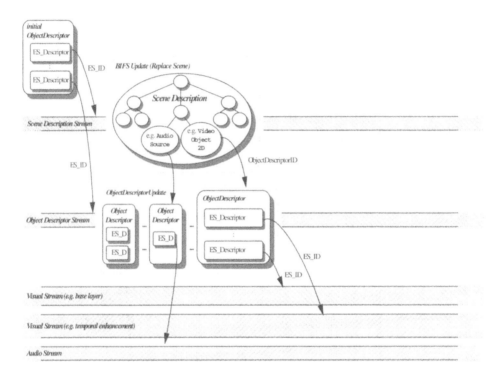

Figure 15. Object descriptor framework (from [2]).

4.3 TIMING

Synchronization of media objects conveyed by one or more elementary streams is dependent upon clock references and time stamps. While time at a receiving terminal is with reference to the terminal's own system time base (STB), each media object has its own reference known as the object time base (OTB). A special time stamp, the object clock reference (OCR), is used to convey the OTB to the decoder. In this way, timing information may be translated from the OTB to the STB for scene synchronization.

To facilitate the synchronization process, data comprising an elementary stream is partitioned into access units. An access unit (AU) is the smallest entity to which timing information can be attributed. Each individually accessible portion of decoder output produced from access units is called a composition unit (CU) – an access unit corresponds to one or more composition units. Composition units reside in a buffered area known as composition memory. The time at which an access unit must be available for decoding is given by the decoding time stamp (DTS), while the time at which a composition unit must be available for composition is given by the composition time stamp (CTS). At DTS, an AU is instantly decoded with the resulting CUs being placed in composition memory. This is illustrated in Figure 16.

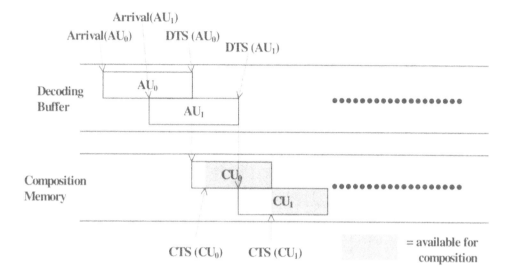

Figure 16. Timing in MPEG-4 (from [2]).

4.4 USER INTERACTION

The content-based and object-oriented nature of the MPEG-4 standard gives way to a high degree of user interaction. Separation of scene description information from media objects allows for manipulation of content attributes at the bitstream without touching the actual object content. Likewise, programmed scene changes can be attached to events associated with objects in a scene (e.g., a mouse click on a spinning globe will cause it to stop spinning).

Some of the possible object manipulations include:

- Change of spatial position
- Change of size
- Change of motion speed
- Addition of optional objects available in composition memory (scaling up)
- Object removal (scaling down)
- Modification of displayed scene area
- Change of pitch
- Change of tempo
- Replacement of scene

Interactivity in MPEG-4 is separated into two major categories: client side and server side. Client side interaction involves content manipulation locally at the user terminal, and is usually performed in response to a user event (mouse click or keyboard stroke). Server side interaction is performed at the transmitting source, and requires additional communication between the sender and receiver. Figure 17 shows an example of scene transformation at the client side [7].

Scene before transformation

Scene after transformation

Figure 17. Scene transformation at the client side [7].

5. INTELLECTUAL PROPERTY RIGHTS MANAGEMENT

Intellectual property represents, among others, the ideas, information, and inventions created by an individual or individuals. The legal authority granted designated owners of intellectual property through national and international copyright protection is an intellectual property right. Because of the ability to easily copy electronic information over global networks, a set of tools to ensure intellectual property management and protection (IPMP) is desirable. Although MPEG-4 can not of itself adequately perform IPMP, it does provide for a generic interface to external IPMP tools.

Within MPEG-4, an intellectual property identification is contained within ES descriptors. This identification is dependent upon the content providers. It may be similar to the international standard book number (ISBN) used on books, or it may use a number of key value pairs, such as "Composer/Johann Strauss." The actions performed in carrying out intellectual property protection are in the hands of applications developers. An IPMP framework must be built to take advantage of a standardized MPEG-4 IPMP interface which links MPEG-4 constructs to domain-specific IPMP systems (not standardized in MPEG-4). This interface consists of IPMP descriptors (IPMP-D) and IPMP elementary streams (IPMP-ES). An IPMP-D is an extension of the MPEG-4 object descriptors while an IPMP-ES is an ordinary elementary stream.

IPMP-Ds and IPMP-ESs provide communication between the MPEG-4 terminal and the IPMP system or systems. IPMP-Ds are associated with MPEG-4 objects requiring management and protection. These IPMP-Ds specify which IPMP systems will protect the associated MPEG-4 objects while providing information to these systems about how to protect and manage the objects. Figure 18 illustrates an IPMP framework.

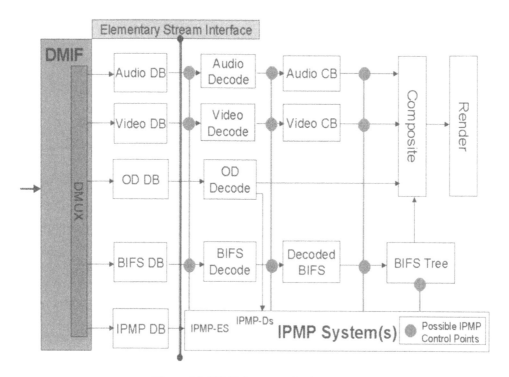

Figure 18. IPMP framework (from [10]).

6. SYSTEMS ARCHITECTURE

The architecture defined by the MPEG-4 standard provides a framework in which the MPEG-4 functionality can be accomplished. That is, it provides the means by which audio-visual information is transported, synchronized, and compressed or decompressed. This is done through a layered approach. First, the TransMux layer provides an interface to the transport medium. Second, the Sync layer handles the synchronization of the streams. Finally, the Compression layer handles the encoding/decoding of the streams. This structure is shown in Figure 19.

To support this architecture, MPEG-4 includes the FlexMux tool and an interface to the DMIF protocol framework. FlexMux (a tool for low delay, low overhead multiplexing of data) can be used to facilitate data transport, while DMIF (Delivery Multimedia Integration Framework) is used to create connections between MPEG-4 sources and destination so that delivery of the necessary information may be accomplished.

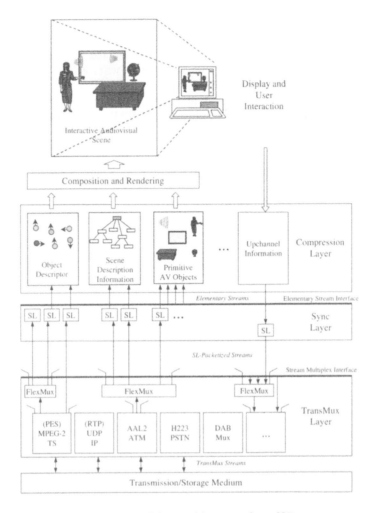

Figure 19. MPEG-4 architecture (from [2]).

6.1 DELIVERY MULTIMEDIA INTEGRATION FRAMEWORK

DMIF is both a protocol and a framework by which multimedia information is delivered. Although DMIF is defined separately (not part of MPEG-4), MPEG-4 does specify an interface to DMIF. DMIF and its interfaces provide the delivery layer. This layer provides transparent information access and delivery irrespective of the technology used. The portion of the TransMux layer dealing with FlexMux channels is considered the DMIF layer. The DMIF layer along with the rest of the TransMux layer encompasses the delivery layer. DMIF works as a session protocol similar to FTP. The essential difference is that FTP returns data while DMIF returns pointers to where information may be obtained.

The DMIF functionality needed for establishing MPEG-4 sessions and access to transport channels is expressed by the DMIF-Application Interface (DAI). This interface lies between the Sync layer and the DMIF layer. When remote communication is necessary, the DMIF Network Interface (DNI) is used. The DNI emphasizes the kind of information DMIF peers need to exchange and requires an additional module to map DNI primitives into corresponding native network signaling messages. Figure 20 illustrates the structure of the delivery layer and its DMIF interfaces.

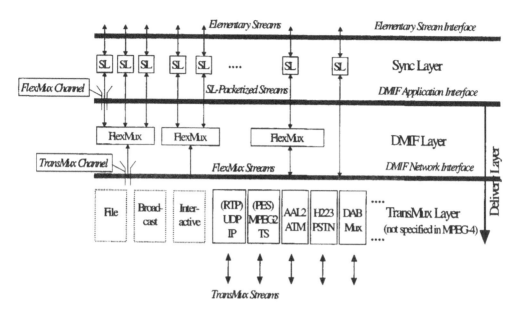

Figure 20. Delivery layer and DMIF interfaces (from [4]).

DMIF takes care of delivery technology details and presents only a simple interface to the MPEG-4 application. The application only interacts with the DAI and is not concerned with the type of transport technology (network, broadcast, and disk or local storage) used. Figure 21 shows how DMIF can be set up to handle the three types of transport technology while leaving all the transport details transparent to the applications.

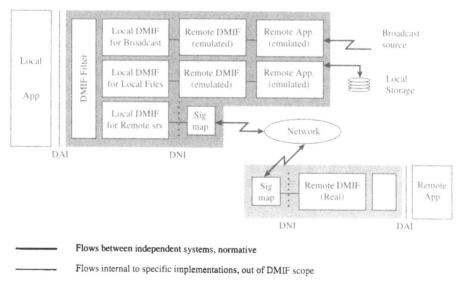

Flows between independent systems, normative

Flows internal to specific implementations, out of DMIF scope

Figure 21. DMIF communication architecture (from [4]).

Establishment of remote connections using DMIF is done by first creating local and remote peer DMIF sessions. Then, using these sessions, a connection between the local and peer application can be made. This is illustrated by Figure 22 as follows [4]:

- The originating application requests the activation of a service to its local DMIF Layer -- a communication path between the application and its local DMIF peer is established in the control plane (connection 1).
- The originating DMIF peer establishes a network session with the target DMIF peer -- a communication path between the originating DMIF peer and the target DMIF peer is established in the control plane (connection 2).
- The target DMIF peer identifies the target application and forwards the service activation request -- a communication path between the target DMIF peer and the target application is established in the control plane (connection 3).
- The peer applications create channels (requests flowing through communication paths 1, 2 and 3). The resulting channels in the user plane (connection 4) will carry the actual data exchanged by the applications.

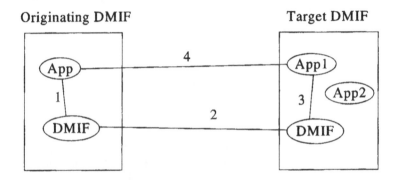

Figure 22. DMIF computational model (from [4]).

6.2 DEMULTIPLEXING, SYNCHRONIZATION, AND DECOMPRESSION

In order to obtain MPEG-4 elementary streams, the information must be extracted from the transmission medium. To do this, the physical data must be demultiplexed as specified by the transport protocol being used. This is outside the scope of MPEG-4 and any multiplexing functionality suitable for MPEG-4 data streams (e.g., ATM, IP, MPEG-2 Transport Stream) may be used. The TransMux layer is a generic term used to abstract this multiplexing functionality. All demultiplexing occurs at the delivery layer (DMIF and TransMux layers). When the transport facility can not sufficiently multiplex MPEG-4 streams, the FlexMux tool is used to provide additional interleaving of data at the transmitter and demultiplexing of the data at the receiver. Data stream interface and use of the FlexMux tool is supported through DMIF.

Once the information is demultiplexed, the delivery layer will pass Sync layer packetized streams to the Sync layer. Sync layer packetized streams are composed of one access unit or a fragment of an access unit. The Sync layer extracts the timing information associated with the access units to enable synchronized decoding and, subsequently, composition of the elementary stream data.

The compression layer reads the elementary streams so that in can form a scene description and decode compressed media objects in preparation for composition and rendering.

7. MPEG-4 VERSION 2

Although the MPEG-4 standard was frozen in October 1998, work has continued for version 2 of the MPEG-4 standard. Version 2 is not meant to replace the current MPEG-4 standard. Rather, it is meant as an enhancement to the standard and is to be fully backward compatible with version 1. This section summarizes the planned enhancements.

The following enhancements to visual aspects are planned for MPEG-4 Version 2:

- Increased flexibility in object-based scalable coding of natural video.
- Improved coding efficiency of natural video.
- Improved error robustness in natural video.
- Coding of multiple views in natural video.
- Addition of 3-D body meshes (extension to facial meshes).
- Coding of generic 3-D meshes.
- Improved 3-D mesh scalability (allow change in the level of detail and allow spatial reduction)

The following enhancements to audio aspects are planned for MPEG-4 Version 2:

- Improved error resilience.
- Improved parameterization of acoustical properties to provide environmental spatialization.
- Reduction in coding/decoding delay.
- Backchannel syntax.
- Small step scalability – allows scalable coding with very fine granularity.
- Parametric audio coding.

The following enhancements to BIFS are planned for MPEG-4 Version 2:

- Multiuser functionality – allows several users to interact with a scene.
- Advanced audio BIFS – enables more natural sound source and environment modeling.
- Added support for 3-D body animation.
- Added VRML compatibility

Other enhancements planned for MPEG-4 Version 2 are:
- Improved delivery capabilities through an expanded DMIF.
- Formalization of an MPEG-4 file format (MP4).
- MPEG-J – Java programming interface

8. INTERNET APPLICATIONS

The ability to scale and separate scenes into component objects makes MPEG-4 a useful tool in the facilitation of applications over the Internet. These applications, which may also apply to other network environments (LANs, WANs, Intranet, etc.) include:

- *Streaming media* – streamed audio and video will be improved through the ability to remove unneeded aspects from the stream (scaling) and the synchronization information imbedded in the stream. In addition, MPEG-4 will allow user interaction with the stream (e.g., fast forward, fast reverse, pause, and clickable actions to activate video and audio options).

- *Remote content-based storage and retrieval* – because MPEG-4 divides scenes into objects, content-based libraries using MPEG-4 are easier to construct and access than non-MPEG-4 libraries. In other words, identification of desired content is more easily done using the more compact, less cluttered MPEG-4 objects. Thus, Internet applications requiring the retrieval or storage of content-based information are better facilitated through the MPEG-4 standard.

- *Multimedia messaging* – unlike typical text email, multimedia messaging uses audio and video as well. Messages constructed through MPEG-4 will require less bandwidth and may be scaled at the decoder if necessary.

- *Infotainment* – interactive audio-visual presentations (virtual worlds, interactive games, etc.) can be constructed and streamed using MPEG-4. Presentations built using VRML can not be streamed. Also, VRML is a text based language, whereas MPEG-4 uses a binary language (BIFS). Since VRML is a more powerful 3-D presentation tool, complex forms of infotainment will probably use both VRML and MPEG-4 together (the whole VRML construct is itself an object).

- *Interpersonal communications* – MPEG-4 allows for presentation control and scalability of such interpersonal communications as videoconferencing and videotelephony. Using MPEG-4, an additional stream can be added to provide augmented reality. Using augmented reality, a video stream can be added to the audio-video stream used for conferencing so that synthetic video objects can be included in the scene (e.g., synthetic furniture added to an empty office).

9. CONCLUSIONS

In summary, MPEG-4 integrates most of capabilities and features of multimedia into one standard, including live audio and video, synthetic objects, and text, all of which can be combined in real-time and interactively. The content-based, object-oriented nature of the MPEG-4 standard, along with its ability to provide intellectual property rights management and to deploy along a transparent delivery interface should make the standard appealing to a variety of applications. These applications (in addition to those previously listed in Section 8) include:

- Broadcast media
- Interactive storage media – DVD, etc.
- Local content-based storage and retrieval
- Wireless multimedia

Although some reactions to the MPEG-4 standard have been somewhat hostile, in the belief that the standard is meant to supercede MPEG-2 (especially with the HDTV work already done using MPEG-2), MPEG-4 was never meant to replace MPEG-2 [3]. Instead, it has been created to enable new applications (such as good wireless multimedia) and new content types. With its ability to reduce the amount of information needed to create a scene through the use of BIFS, static sprites, VOPs, animations etc., along with its user interactivity and scalability, the MPEG-4 standard should find many uses for a long while.

There are a number of issues in MPEG-4 that are currently under the investigation by researchers in this field. One of the critical issues deals with efficient implementations of the MPEG-4 coder. A real-time interactive MPEG-4 encoder has been proposed in [13,16], which uses a cluster of workstations. Authors also described three scheduling schemes for assigning the encoding tasks to the workstations in order to achieve proper load balancing.

Another important topic includes the development of new methods for texture coding for MPEG-4. Some methods for object-based texture coding have been investigated in [17].

An interesting research topic deals with rate control techniques when transmitting MPEG-4 video over the communication networks. Rate control techniques have been intensively investigated for other video coding standards (such as H.261, H.263, MPEG-1, and MPEG-2), and recently for MPEG-4. A new rate control algorithm for multiple video objects in MPEG-4 has been proposed in [18].

References

1. MPEG, "MPEG Systems (1-2-4-7) FAQ, Version 7.0a," Document ISO/IEC JTCI/SC29/WG11 N2527, October 1998.
2. ISO/IEC 14496-1 Systems, "Information Technology – Generic Coding of Audio-Visual Objects," 21 April 1999.
3. R. Koenen, "MPEG-4: Multimedia for Our Time," *IEEE Spectrum*, Vol. 36, No. 1, February 1999.
4. MPEG, "Overview of the MPEG-4 Standard," Document ISO/IEC JTCI/SC29/WG11 N2725, Seoul meeting, March 1999.
5. T. Sikora, Internet Document, "The Structure of the MPEG-4 Video Coding Algorithm," URL: (http://wwwam.hhi.de/mpeg-video/papers/sikora/fmpeg4vm.htm).
6. MPEG, "MPEG Requirements," Document ISO/IEC JTCI/SC29/WG11 N2456, Rome Meeting, December 1998.
7. Internet document, "MPEG 4: Coding of Audio-visual Objects," URL: (http://www.stud.ee.ethz.ch/~rggrandi/mpeg4.html).
8. MPEG, "DMIF FAQ", Document ISO/IEC JTCI/SC29/WG11 N2313, July 1998.
9. L. Chiariglione, MPEG Internet document, "MPEG-4 FAQs," URL: (http://drogo.cselt.stet.it/mpeg/faq/faq_mpeg-4.htm), July 1997.
10. MPEG, "MPEG-4 Intellectual Property Management & Protection (IPMP) Overview & Applications", Document ISO/IEC JTCI/SC29/WG11 N2614, December 1998.
11. L. Chiariglione, MPEG Internet Document, "About MPEG," URL: (http://drogo.cselt.stet.it/mpeg/about_mpeg.htm), September 1998.
12. MPEG, "MPEG-4 Applications," Document ISO/IEC JTCI/SC29/WG11 N2724, Seoul Meeting, March 1999.
13. Y. He, I. Ahmad, and M.L. Liou, "Real-Time Interactive MPEG-4 System Encoder Using a Cluster of Workstations," *IEEE Transactions on Multimedia*, Vol. 1, No. 2, June 1999, pp. 217-233.
14. B.H. Haskel, P.G. Howard, Y.A. LeCun, A. Puri, J. Ostermann, M.R. Civanlar, L. Rabiner, L. Bottou, and P. Haffner, "Image and Video Coding – Emerging Standards and Beyond," *IEEE Transactions on Circuits and Systems for Video Technology*, Vol. 8, No. 7, November 1998, pp. 814-837.
15. T. Sikora, "The MPEG-4 Video Standard Verification Model," *IEEE Transactions on Circuits and Systems for Video Technology*, Vol. 7, No. 1, February 1997, pp. 19-31.

16. Y. He, I. Ahmad, and M.L. Liou, "A Software-Based MPEG-4 Video Encoder Using Parallel Processing," *IEEE Transactions on Circuits and Systems for Video Technology*, Vol. 8, No. 7, November 1998, pp. 909-920.
17. A. Kaup, "Object-Based Texture Coding of Moving Video in MPEG-4," *IEEE Transactions on Circuits and Systems for Video Technology*, Vol. 9, No. 1, February 1999, pp. 5-15.
18. A. Vetro, H. Sun, and Y. Wang, "MPEG-4 Rate Control for Multiple Video Objects," *IEEE Transactions on Circuits and Systems for Video Technology*, Vol. 9, No. 1, February 1999, pp. 186-199.

Chapter 4

INTERNET ARCHITECTURES FOR APPLICATION SERVICE PROVIDERS

Borko Furht, Chris Phoenix, John Yin, and Zijad Aganovic

Abstract

In recent years, business on the Internet has increased exponentially. Consequently, the deployment and management of business applications on the Internet is becoming more and more complex, which requires the development of new Internet architectures suitable to efficiently run these business applications. In this chapter we present and evaluate several computing models and related Internet architectures for application service providers. We also introduce the server-based model and the corresponding Internet architecture and two case studies, which use the proposed architecture for application deployment.

1. INTRODUCTION

1.1 COMPUTING MODELS FOR INTERNET-BASED ARCHITECTURES

The increasingly competitive global marketplace puts pressure on companies to create and deliver their products faster, with high quality and greater performance. To get the new products and technologies to consumers is through a new industry called Application Service Providers (ASPs). Similar to Internet Service Providers, that linked businesses and consumers up to the Internet, ASPs lease software applications to businesses and consumers via the Internet. These applications range from word processing programs to payroll management software, document management systems, and many others. The major challenge is to develop an efficient Internet-based architecture, which will efficiently provide access to these software applications over the Internet.

Application architectures have traditionally followed software development architectures. The software development architectures can be classified into:

- Traditional desktop computing model

- Client-server computing model

- Network computing model

- Server-based computing model

Traditional desktop computing model assumes that the whole application is on the client and the application is executed locally. The client must be a fat client.

Client-server computing model assumes that clients are powerful and processing is centered around local execution on clients. Computer resources were split between a server and one or several clients. This architecture allowed for larger, more scalable applications to be brought to a larger number of clients. However, the key for this architecture was to successfully partition the complexity of overall application and determine correctly which part should reside on the server and which part should run on the client. As more and more functionality migrated to the client, it became harder for applications to be maintained and updated.

Network computing model, supported by Sun, Oracle, Netscape, IBM, and Apple, assumes that software applications are dynamically downloaded from the network into the client for execution by the client. This architecture requires that the clients are fat.

Server-based computing model, supported by Citrix, assumes that business applications reside on the servers and can be accessed by users without requiring them to be downloaded to the client. The client can be either thin or fat.

In the proposed Internet-based architecture we selected server-based computing model, which is described in detail in the following section.

1.2 SERVER-BASED COMPUTING MODEL

The fundamental three elements of the server-based computing model are [1]:

- Multi-user operating system
- Efficient computing technology
- Centralized application and client management

Multi-user operating system allows multiple concurrent users to run applications in separate, protected sessions on a single server.

Efficient computing technology separates the application from its user interface, so only simple user's commands, received through keystrokes, mouse clicks, and screen updates are sent via the network. As a result, application performance does not depend on network bandwidth.

Centralized application and client management allows efficient solution of application management, access, performance, and security.

A server-based computing model is very efficient for enterprise-wide application deployment, including cross-platform computing, Web computing, remote computing, thin-client device computing, and branch-office computing, as illustrated in Figure 1 [1].

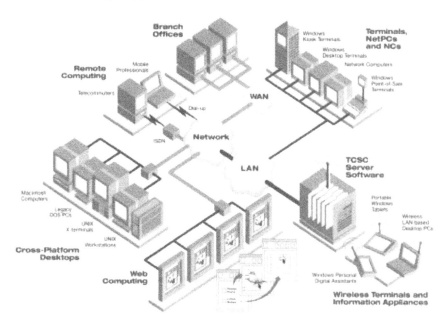

Figure 1. Server-based computing models can be used for enterprise-wide application deployment.

2. EVOLUTION OF INTERNET-BASED APPLICATION SERVICE ARCHITECTURES

Similarly to software development architectures, applications service architectures have emerged from the traditional client-server architectures to three-tier and multi-tier architectures.

The first generation of Internet-based application service architecture was based on delivery of information via public Web sites. This technology, sometimes referred to as the "first wave" Internet [2] employs the Web to present the information to the user and then allows the user to give some relevant information back. The primary focus of this architectural model is mass distribution of public information over the Internet. This architecture, which focuses on accessing information, consists of three levels (or three tiers) – presentation level, content level, and data and service level, as shown in Figure 2 [2].

At the presentation level, there is the client system, which is used to view Web page information. The client contains both presentation and application logic components. At the content level, there is a Web server that provides interactive view of information from a relational database. Finally, at the data and service level, there is a relational database system, which provides data for the Web server. This architecture is also called three-tier architecture consisting of client tier, Web server tier, and database tier.

With the advancements of the Internet, the Web, and related technologies (such as Java and HTML), as well as acceptance of standard communication protocols (such as TCP/IP and HTTP), a new architecture has emerged. In this architecture, sometimes referred as to the "second wave" Internet [2] or network-based application architecture [3], focus is on highly targeted, private distribution of software services over Intranets and Extranets. In this architecture, the Web page is not only the agent for providing information, but it also offers a variety of application services to speed up business transactions and offer additional services. This architecture consists of n-tiers and offers maximum functionality and flexibility in a heterogeneous, Web-based environment. An example of four-tier architecture is shown in Figure 3.

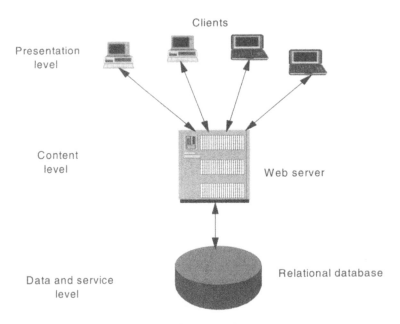

Figure 2. The three-tier architecture for application service providers is focused on accessing information.

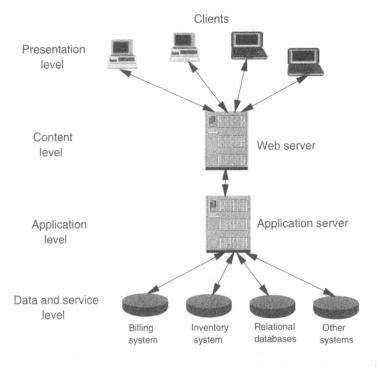

Figure 3. The multitier Internet-based architecture for application service providers is focused on accessing application services.

At the presentation level, the client views Web pages for information as well as for a variety of application services. At the second, content level, the Web server provides an interactive view of information and supports client-initiated transactions. At the third, application level, there is an application server, which is used to find requested data and services, makes them available for viewing, and carries out transactions. At the fourth, data and service level, there is a variety of data and services accessible by the application server. This architecture, also called multitier architecture, consists of client tier, Web server tier, application server tier, and database tier.

Two-tier Internet architecture is typically limited for systems with a small number of users, a single database, and non-secure network environments.

3. APPLICATION SERVER

In the second generation of Internet architectures, the focus has shifted to access to business services rather than to information only. The main component of the system is an application server, which searches for services and data – this is done in the background without involving the user.

The main challenges in developing the first generation of Internet architectures and application services were related to user interfaces and cross-platform interoperability. In developing the second generation of Internet architectures, the main challenge for service developers is to deliver their services seamlessly via the Internet, which in turn requires innovations in many areas. The following challenges need to be addressed in developing the second generation of Internet architectures:

Standards. There are many standards for developing Web pages, which causes difficulties for developers.

Increased programming complexity. The implementation of business services on the Internet is a very complex programming task.

Network performance. Business applications over Intranets and Extranets require very reliable and high performance networks.

Security. Business applications on the Internet require a very high level of security.

Web access to legacy applications. As mentioned earlier, the new Internet architectures are focused on accessing various business applications rather than just information.

Database connection support across Web-based requestors. Users should be able to access a variety of databases connected to the application server.

The majority of these functions, sometimes called *middleware*, are implemented in application servers that provide support for developing and deploying business applications located on the server or partitioned across client and server.

Application server offers support for developing and deploying business logic that may be located on the server or, more often, partitioned across client and server. Running business applications on the server provides many benefits [4].

3.1 KEY TECHNOLOGIES FOR APPLICATION SERVERS

Key technologies for developing contemporary application servers include:

- Java programming language and environment,
- JavaBeans – the Java based component technology, which allows the development of new applications more rapidly and economically,
- ActiveX – the competing technology to JavaBeans, which is Windows platform-dependent and language-independent,
- Java Database Connectivity (JDBC) – the Java SQL that provides cross-platform database access for Java programs,
- Java servlets – small Java routines that service HTTP requests and dynamically generate HTML,
- CORBA – provides a standard architecture for distributed computing and interoperability on the Internet

The key technologies are described in detail in Chapter 10.

Java application servers have recently emerged as an efficient solution for the application server tier. A Java application server provides the following features:

- Makes it easy to develop and deploy distributed Java applications.
- Provides scalability, so hundreds to thousands of cooperative servers can be accessed from ten of thousands clients. Therefore, Java must be fully multithreaded and have no architectural bottlenecks that prevent scaling.
- Provides an integrated management environment for comprehensive view of application resources (for example, Java Beans, objects, events, etc.), network resources (databases), system resources (ACLs, threads, sockets, etc.), and diagnostic information.
- Provides transaction semantics to protect the integrity of corporate data even as it is accessed by distributed business components.
- Provides secure communications.

CORBA (Common Object Request Broker Architecture) and JavaBeans are open standards for component software development and deployment that allow writing small code objects that can be reused in multiple applications and updated quickly. They also allow developers to expose legacy system data and functionality as services available over the Web, and therefore most application servers are based on these technologies.

For example, the CORBA architecture makes it possible to find and use services over the Internet. Similarly, Enterprise JavaBeans is a standard server component model for Java application servers that provides services to network-enable applications, so that they may be easily deployed on Intranets, Extranets, and the Internet [5].

CORBA provides universal connectivity in broadly distributed environments as well as cross-platform interoperation of both infrastructures and applications. The object Web model based on CORBA and other standards is shown in Figure 4 [7].

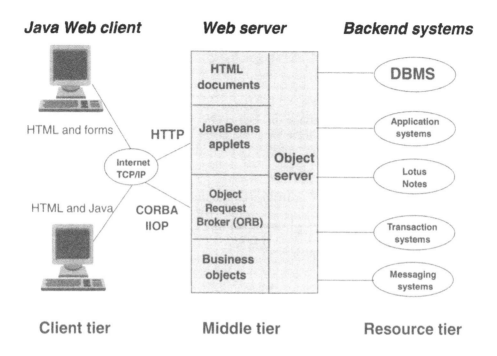

Figure 4. The object Web-model based on CORBA and other standards provides universal connectivity in distributed environments.

CORBA currently provides many services including naming, security, transactions, and persistence, as illustrated in Figure 5 [7].

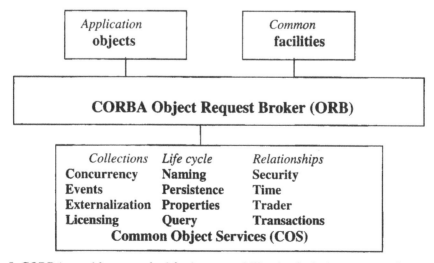

Figure 5. CORBA provides a standard for interoperability that includes many services required by object applications.

4. IMPLEMENTATIONS OF INTERNET ARCHITECTURES FOR APPLICATION SERVICE PROVIDERS

In this section we present four popular architectures for application service providers (ASP) developed by Sun, Netscape, IBM, and Microsoft.

4.1 SUN'S ARCHITECTURE

Initially, Sun Microsystems defined in Fall 1996 Java-based application development architecture, which consisted of three tiers: the client tier that provided user interface, the middle tier for business logic and database access, and the database tier, as illustrated in Figure 6 [8].

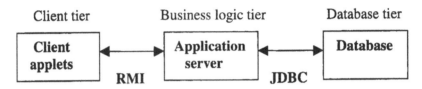

Figure 6. The Sun's Java-based three-tier architecture for ASP.

Sun selected Java language for the client tier, which provided more sophisticated GUI capabilities than HTML implementation. Client applets did not perform significant business logic functions in order to keep clients as thin as possible. Java technology was also used for the middle tier and the middle-tier servers were implemented as standalone Java applications.

Because both client and middle tiers are implemented using Java, client-middle tier communication was performed using Remote Method Invocation (RMI), where the middle-tier servers created the necessary RMI objects and made them available to clients via the RMI object registry. The middle tier communicated with the database via the JDBC API. This architecture is based on client/server computing model, in which client resides on the user's desktop, and the middle and database tiers reside on one or more of five data centers around the company.

Recently Sun has developed an enhanced multitier architecture, which includes an additional tier – the WebTop server tier, as shown in Figure 7 [8].

In the three-tier architecture (Figure 6), applets were dynamically downloaded at runtime to the users' locations from an application server. For remote locations and modem connections with constrained bandwidth, applet download time was a few minutes, which was unacceptable.

Another issue related to three-tier architecture was the access to network resources such as files and printers. Java prohibits applets from accessing any local or network resources. In addition, Java does not allow communications with any machine other than the one from which the applet was downloaded. As a result of these limitations, file access occurred at the middle tier. This meant that information might be sent from the client to the middle tier and then back to a file server near the client.

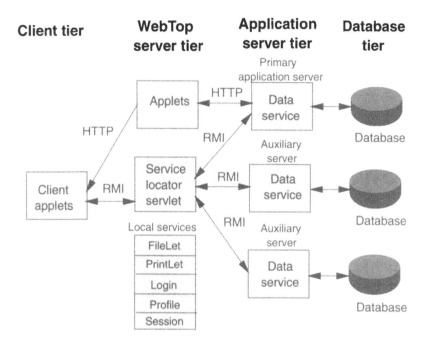

Figure 7. The Sun's Java-based multitier architecture for ASP.

Introducing a new tier, WebTop server tier, has resolved the issues related to the three-tier architecture. The WebTop server runs the Java Web server and is located near the users it serves. This server is used as a cache for applets and static application data, so the first problem was resolved. The server also supports services that access network resources such as user files and printers, which are typically located near the users. Finally, the WebTop server is used to find the services that users need.

In the architecture in Figure 7 the client is thin and typically includes a graphical user interface written as an applet that runs from a Web browser. The application server tier provides access to data and implements business logic and data validation. The application server is responsible for all database transaction handling.

For the communication between the client and WebTop server tier and between the WebTop server and the application server tier, HTTP and RMI are used. Communication between application servers and databases is performed via JDBC.

One of the main benefits of the multitier architecture is that it increases application scalability and performance by enabling clients to be connected concurrently. In a client-server model clients are directly connected to databases, while in a multitier architecture only application servers connect directly to databases. In this way, the application server can process multiple requests from many clients through a pool of preallocated database connections, thus reducing the database server load. Load on the application server tier can be balanced by using multiple application servers.

Another benefit of the multitier architecture is that it supports thinner clients, because most of the logic runs in the application server and database tiers. Thus broad range of client platforms can run the applications.

4.2 NETSCAPE'S ARCHITECTURE

Similarly to Sun's architecture, Netscape recently developed multitier architecture for application service providers, which is based on the separation of presentation logic from application logic, as illustrated in Figure 8 [2].

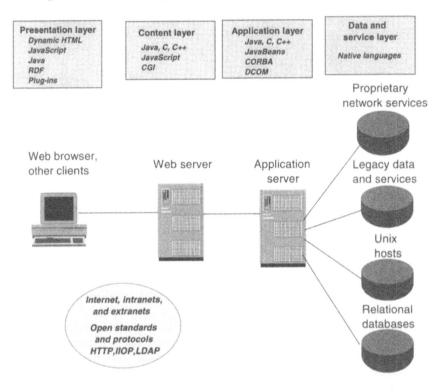

Figure 8. Netscape's multitier architecture for ASP.

In the Netscape's multitier architecture, the client tier is typically based on an open-standard browser such as Netscape Navigator. The presentation logic and GUI is built using HTML pages that include Java applets. At the content level, a Web server primarily uses HTTP. It provides base-level information and content services as well as simple database information access via Java, JavaScript, and other high-level CGI scripting languages like Perl.

The application server uses CORBA and JavaBeans components or objects. Transaction services enable access to relational databases and other legacy systems.

The first three levels in the multitier architecture in Figure 8 are provided by Netscape technologies and products, while the last level – back-end services and other legacy systems – are accessed through standard Internet interfaces.

4.3 IBM's ARCHITECTURE

IBM has developed the Component Broker, which is Internet middleware for distributed objects [7]. Component Broker is a software system that allows developers to build, run, and manage Web-enabled business objects, components, and applications. Component Broker consists of:

- Tools for building distributed and business objects, and applications,
- A runtime that provides a distributed-object infrastructure on the middle tier, and
- A system management functions for the distributed object runtime and its resources.

Component Broker architecture, shown in Figure 9, accepts inputs from any clients (Java or C++) transported via Internet InterORB Protocol, and ActiveX transported via a bridge. The object server consists of components that provide control, services, context, and connection resources.

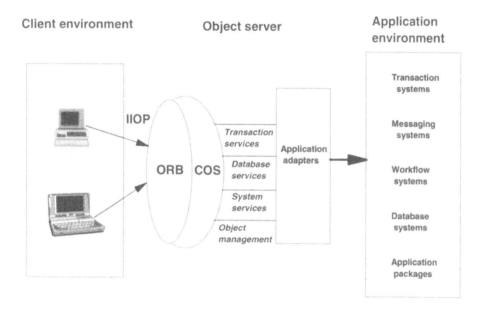

Figure 9. Architecture of the IBM's Component Broker at the middleware tier.

The Component Broker receives client requests through the CORBA-compliant Object Request Broker (ORB). Object services are supplied through the CORBA Common Object Services (COS). These services provide object transaction services, database services, system services, and object management functions, as illustrated in Figure 9.

Application adapters connect Component Broker object applications with existing software systems and applications.

4.4 MICROSOFT'S ARCHITECTURE

Microsoft Internet architecture is a component-based architecture based on Windows DNA [14]. The heart of Windows DNA is the Component Object Model (COM) that allows developers to build applications from binary software components at any tier of the application architecture. These components provide support for packaging, partitioning, and distributing application functionality [14]. Distributed COM (DCOM) enables communications between COM components that reside on different machines. DCOM is a competing model for distributed object computing to CORBA, described in Section 3.

5. A CONTEMPORARY ARCHITECTURE FOR ASP

In this section, we propose ASP computing architecture using server-based computing model and ASP application architecture.

5.1 ASP COMPUTING ARCHITECTURE

Our computing architecture for application service providers is based on the server-based computing model, described in Section 1.1. As we indicated earlier, in server-based computing all applications and data are managed, supported, and executed on the server. This architecture provides the following benefits:

- Single-point management
- Predictable ownership costs
- High reliability
- Bandwidth-independent performance
- Universal application access
- Use of thousands of off-the-shelf applications
- Low-cost and fast application development
- Use of open standards
- Graphical and rich user interface
- Wide choice of client devices

The proposed server-based architecture uses two technologies developed by Citrix:

- Independent Computing Architecture (ICA), and
- Windows-based terminal (WBT)

Independent Computing Architecture is a Windows presentation services protocol that turns any client device (thin or fat) into the thin client. The ICA consists of three components: server software, client software, and network protocol. On the server, ICA separates applications from the user interface, while on the client users see and work with applications' interface. The application logic executes on the server. The ICA protocol transports keystrokes, mouse clicks, and screen updates over standard protocols requiring less than 20 Kbps of network bandwidth.

A *Windows-based terminal* is a thin-client hardware device that connects to Citrix server-based system software. The WBT does not require downloading of the operating system or applications and there is no local processing of applications at the client, as in the case of other thin clients such as network computers or NetPCs. A WBT has the following features:

- An embedded operating system such as DOS, Windows CE, or any real-time OS
- ICA protocol to transport keystrokes, mouse clicks, and screen updates between the client and the server
- Absolute (100%) execution of application logic on the server
- No local execution of application at the client device

The proposed architecture also allows consumers and business to access software applications from their Internet browsers. This is provided using Citrix's software *Charlotte*. In addition, software component *Vertigo* allows more interactive applications on the Web. This software allows customized Web pages such as electronic trading accounts to be updated automatically without hitting the refresh button on the computer.

The proposed architecture for ASP using server-based model and Citrix technologies is shown in Figure 10.

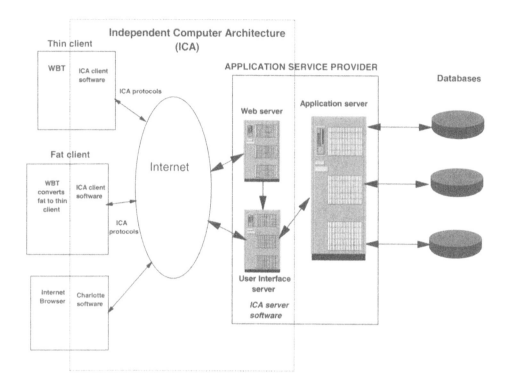

Figure 10. The proposed architecture for ASP uses server-based model. All applications are executed at the server or cluster of servers.

The proposed architecture is platform independent and allows non-Windows and specialized ICA devises to run Windows applications residing and executing on application server farm. Application server farm is a group of application servers that are linked together as a single system to provide centralized administration and scalability.

The architecture in Figure 10 allows application service providers to rapidly develop and deploy applications across complex computing environments. It also provides application access to all users, regardless of the their location, type of client device, or form of network connectivity. The architecture can be applied to any type of client hardware, and therefore requires no change in client hardware. The system significantly reduces requirements for network bandwidth compared to other architectures. Finally, the proposed architecture reduces the total cost of application, as analyzed in Section 6.

5.2 ASP APPLICATION ARCHITECTURE

To take maximum advantage of ASP computing architecture, a new breed of applications needs to be developed. The key drivers of new distributed application architecture is a need for wide spectrum of thin clients, bandwidth usage optimization, application multi identity shared back end computing, reliable data flow management, security, legacy application integration, and long list of service operation requirements. The diagram shown in Figure 11 can depict a desired architecture of an ASP application.

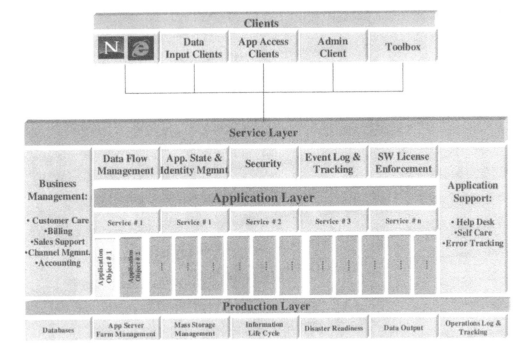

Figure 11. Architecture of an ASP application.

5.2.1 Client Software

ASP application client software is in general very different from types of client software provided as part of traditional client server applications available on the market today. To support ASP business model, client software must be "thin" requiring minimum computing power, installation and support effort, minimum communication bandwidth, and minimum version upgrade. Highly distributed nature of ASP service requires from client software ability to support versatile data inputs, highest level of user's security, and ability to support multiple communication protocols.

Data Input
ASP service architecture is in essence remote computing architecture, which requires capabilities to generate and import application data into the remote application. Data can be generated as part of specialized batch program or as by-product of third party software. Data input clients can be stand alone or integrated within other clients or legacy applications. Multi step data flow requires advanced information security, tracking, reporting, and above all ability to restore data in case that any stage system failure results in data loss. Data input clients may or may not be "thin." Footprint of these clients is primarily defined by local functionality necessary to create the data at optimum cost.

Application Access
Application access clients are characterized by limited local computation capability and remote command capability to the server side application concentrated at service back end. These clients are the ones that should be as generic and as "thin" as possible. Smaller and simpler the client lesser the operational cost at the front end. The ideal application access client is plain Web browser. However, browser access is limited to very low level of functionality provided by HTML protocol. Function rich application computing requires specialized client software or plug-ins providing access to remote application at the back end.

Toolbox
To bridge the existing legacy applications with ASP service, an ASP application software requires a comprehensive set of APIs or application enabling tools providing the system integration capabilities and customizations.

Administration
This client should provide the end user with the ability to completely control its own application. Desired functions are: adding new users, setting up security profiles, managing application specific variables, usage tracking and reporting, and billing presentments and reporting.

Security
Client software security capability must include ability to authenticate users on the front end and to create virtual private channel of communication with the service back end.

5.2.2 Service Layer

Server side application is characterized by concentration of all computing and data intensive processes at back end, application multi-identity, sophisticated data flow management, and by its ability to integrate with business management, application support, and service production components. The ultimate goal of such application engineering is to create the fastest computing environment, economy of scale through all customers' sharing of common computing and data management infrastructure, and maximum operational readiness.

Application Layer
At the core of service layer is the application layer of software providing actual computing application packaged as specific service, for example: Service #1. This service application can be either stand alone application or user interface into integrated solution based on several other independent third party applications.

Data Flow Management
Data generated through data input clients is managed by data flow management software. One can consider this software component as a data switch capable of accepting data input, decompressing and decoding data, identifying the owner of data and target data base, importing data in the target data base, cashing and mirroring data at each stage for disaster readiness reasons, and creating logs for data input tracking and reporting.

Application State and Identity Management
An ASP provider will have many different applications for many different customers simultaneously. Also, each individual application will have many different users requiring different application set-up and profile. Application state and identity management software acts as an application switch identifying individual users and applications and then assigning the appropriate user's profile. Therefore, ASP applications must support multiple identity capability. Ability to share the same computing and data management resources between many different users and applications is essential for reliable service delivery and economy of scale.

Business Management
The ASP application should also integrate into business management software enabling automatic account creation, and usage data feed into billing solution.

Application Support
The ASP application should also integrate with application support solution that consists from customer self support site.

6. EVALUATION OF VARIOUS ASP ARCHITECTURES

Analysts and IT professionals have developed numerous models for estimating the total cost of IT services, sometimes called "total cost of ownership" (TCO). In the past, these models had the hardware-centric view because they analyzed the costs of owning and maintaining desktop computer hardware. In the age of the Internet, Web-based computing, and E-commerce, applications must be accessible across a wide variety of connectivity options, from low-speed dial-up connections to wireless, WAN- and Internet connections. A contemporary cost analysis should consider the total cost of application ownership (TCA), rather than the total cost associated with specific computing devices. The Tolly Group has developed a model for comparing the TCA of different computing models, discussed earlier [9]. We present and discuss their results in this section.

In order to determine the cost of application deployment, four computing models introduced in Section 1 can be analyzed from the following points of views:

- Physical location of the application
- Execution location of the application
- Physical location of data, and
- Location of the user and means of connectivity

The cost of complexity of deploying and managing an application strongly depends on physical location of the application. The cost of application distribution, installation, and managing of updates must be considered.

The choice of where an application is executed determines the hardware, network, and connectivity costs. An application can run on the server, on the client, or in a distributed server/client environment. In some cases, the application must be downloaded from a server to a client, which has an impact on performance and productivity.

The location of stored data determines the speed at which information is available. It also has an impact on the cost related to protecting and backing up critical corporate data.

Location of the user and the means of connectivity also have an impact on the cost and complexity of deploying an application.

Table 1 summarizes the application deployment characteristics for four computing models introduced in Section 1 [9].

Table 1. Computing Models and Application Deployment Characteristics

	APPLICATION LOCATION	APPLICATION EXECUTION	DATA LOCATION	USER ACCESS	NETWORK REQUIRE-MENTS
Traditional desktop	Client	Client	Client	Local	None
Client-server	Client and server	Client and server	Client and server	Lan, WAN, Internet	High bandwidth
Network-based	Server	Client and server	Server or client	LAN, WAN, Internet	High bandwidth
Server-based	Server	Server	Server	LAN, WAN, Internet	Low bandwidth

Tolly Group has analyzed and calculated the total cost of application ownership for a medium-size enterprise of 2,500 users, with 175 mobile users working on the road. The calculated costs were divided into (a) Initial (first-year) cost (which includes hardware, software, network infrastructure, and user training) and (b) annual recurring costs (which includes technical support and application maintenance). The results of analysis are presented in Figure 12.

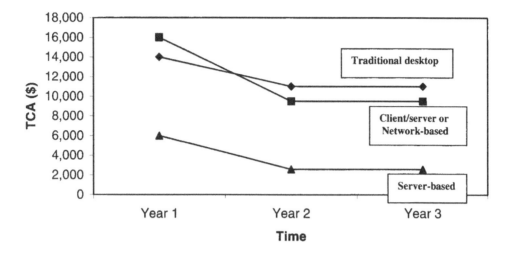

Figure 12. Analysis of total cost of application (TCA) for various computing approaches [9].

Traditional desktop computing approach requires relatively high initial cost for hardware, software, network infrastructure, and training ($14,000) as well as very high annual recurring costs for technical support and application maintenance ($11,000 annually).

Client/server and network computing approaches require slightly higher initial investment ($16,000) in order to replace existing client hardware, however annual recurring costs are reduced ($9,500). This model becomes less expensive than the traditional desktop model from the third year forward.

The server-based approach gives the best TCA both in terms of initial costs and annual recurring costs ($6,000 and $2,600, respectively). The reason for it is that this model allows any type of client to access any application across any type of connection. This model also provides single point for the deployment and management of applications.

In summary, the server-based model, which was applied in our architecture, is the most efficient and cost-effective solution to application deployment and management.

7. OVERVIEW OF INTERNET BUSINESSES AND ASPs

In this section we present the Internet business model, adopted from [10], and present two case studies of application service providers based on the proposed server-based ASP architecture.

7.1 INTERNET BUSINESS MODEL

In the Internet business model proposed in [10], Internet businesses are categorized as (a) horizontal businesses (or industries) and (b) vertical businesses (or industries), as illustrated in Figure 13.

Vertical Businesses

Horizontal Businesses

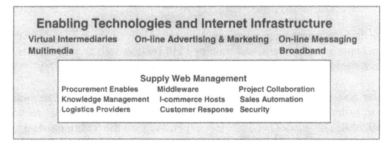

Figure 13. Internet business model consists of horizontal and vertical businesses
(Source: Stephens Inc. [10]).

Horizontal industries are further divided into: (i) portal and community sites, and (ii) enabling technologies and Internet infrastructure. Some leading companies from both categories, vertical and horizontal, are presented in Tables 2 and 3 [10].

In 1998 there were approximately 28 million households in U.S. that used the Internet. According to Forester Research, this number will double in year 2003 and reach about 53 million households. Percentage of total households using E-commerce in 1998 was 29% (or 8.7 million households), and the projected growth is that this percentage would reach 35% (or 40 million households) in year 2003. Business-to-business Internet commerce in 1998 was $43 billions, and projected market for 2002 is $1,330 billions.

Table 2. A Sample of Vertical Internet Business Leaders [10]

VERTICAL INDUSTRY	BUSINESS LEADERS
Healthcare services	WebMD, Healtheon, Prescription.com, Soma.com
Financial services	E*Trade, Ameritrade, Knight/Trimark, NetBank, Telebank, InsureMarket, Quotesmith
Human Capital Management	Monster.com, Taps.com, NetStaff, Jones Intl
Transportation and Logistics	National Transportation Exchange, Cargo Finder, Eurotrans
Retail	Amazon.com, Buy.com, Onsale.com, CDNow, Reel.com
Manufacturing	VerticalNet, Chemdex, ProcureNet, PartNet
Energy	Altra Energy, Silicon Energy, Southern California Gas
Travel	Amadeus, Galileo, Sabre, Preview Travel, Travelocity
Media	CMP Media, CNet, EarthWeb, Thestreet.com, Sportsline

Table 3. A Sample of Horizontal Internet Business Leaders [10]

HORIZONTAL INDUSTRY	BUSINESS LEADERS
Portals & Community Sites	AOL, Yahoo!, Excite, Netcenter, Koz, Lycos
Enabling Technologies and Internet infrastructure	
Virtual Intermediaries	EBay, uBid, Island
On-line Advertising and Marketing	DoubleClick, Flycast, NetGravity
On-line Messaging	Message Media, USA.net, Critical Path, Bigfoot
Multimedia	Real Networks
Supply Web Management	
Procurement Enablers	Ariba, Commerce One, Dynamic Web, Supply Works
Middleware	Iona, Bea Systems, Inprise
Knowledge Management	BroadVision, OpenText, Momentum, CyLex
Project Collaboration	Microsoft, IBM
i-commerce Hosts	Globix, Exodus, Psinet
Sales Automation	Open Market, Digital River, BroadVision
Customer Response	Edify, Acuity, Aptex, netDialog
Security	Check Point, Entrust, Network Associates
Payment	Checkfree, Cybercash, Wave Systems
Logistics Solution Providers	I2 Technologies, Manugistics, Logility
Broadband	Aware, AtHome

7.2 CASE STUDIES

We describe two case studies of using the proposed architecture for ASPs:

(a) An online document management system created by CyLex Systems and Pride Enterprises and applied for collection and management of motor vehicle applications in State of Florida, and

(b) A billing and customer care system developed by Daleen Technologies.

7.2.1 Online Document Management System – CyLex Systems

The Department of Highway Safety and Motor Vehicles (DHSMV) serves as the central point of collection and management for all motor vehicle title applications generated throughout the state. DHSMV needed to replace its existing title microfilming operation. The current system was costly, slow, and did not provide the level of service expected by the state's citizens. Filling simple requests for title applications could take up to three weeks.

CyLex Systems, Inc. has teamed up with its business partner, Pride Enterprises, to propose a totally outsourced solution. Pride Enterprises performs all document conversion and indexing, while CyLex Systems, Inc. provides a complete on-line document information management system. This solution reduces title retrieval time to 15 seconds once the documents have been processed.

The CyLex Systems, Inc. outsourcing solution provides the following benefits:

- Reduces the cost of document management
- Reduces document retrieval time from days and weeks to minutes or seconds
- Requires no up-front investment in technology or hardware
- Requires no on-going cost of maintaining and updating technology
- Is quickly implemented
- Is complementary to the existing computing infrastructure

Overview
Located in Tallahassee, Florida, the State of Florida Department of Highway Safety and Motor Vehicles is one of the four largest motor vehicle agencies in the country. The DHSMV receives approximately 18,000 title applications per day consisting of 4.5 pages each for a total of 81,000 documents. This represents a yearly total of approximately 20 Million documents. In such a vast, diverse and demanding environment, the ability to provide consistently high quality administrative services while containing costs presents an ongoing challenge.

The Micrographics Section of the Division of Administrative Services of the DHSMV was performing these tasks with a staff of 48 full-time employees. Staying up to date with such a consistently high volume was impossible; backlogs often approximated 17 days. For example, document retrieval was stretched beyond an acceptable time frame, taking anywhere from days to weeks to retrieve a title.

The CyLex Express® Solution
The DHSMV issued a Request for Proposal (RFP) for document image management services to replace the department's existing microfilming process. The DHSMV challenged contractors to provide a turnkey solution that would effectively manage the millions of

documents generated every year. Contractors were also evaluated based on the quality of their technical proposals, implementation and administrative costs. To meet the needs of DHSMV's RFP, CyLex Systems, Inc. and Pride Enterprises proposed a document image management system with four functional pieces consisting of document preparation, image capture, image administration and image review and retrieval, as shown in Figure 14.

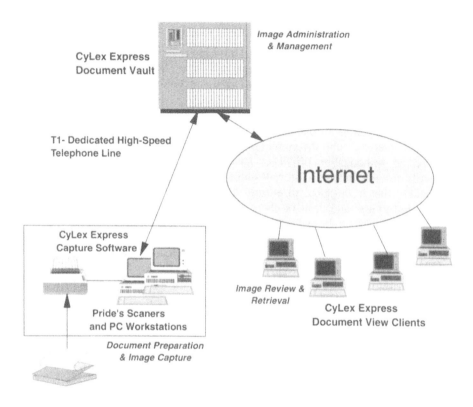

Figure 14. Document on-demand image management system applied at DHSMV.

The CyLex Express Service provides a centralized and secure document vault for storing and managing electronic images of paper files. The *CyLex Express Capture Software* provides all the functions needed to scan, index, and upload the documents. *CyLex Express View Software* allows remote viewing of documents as well as printing.

The DHSMV project consists of high volume document scanning and indexing. Pride Enterprises performs daily document pick-ups from the DHSMV headquarters in Tallahassee, Florida, and transports them to one of Pride's two secure document conversion facilities to prepare for scanning and indexing. To ensure the highest level of quality control, all indexes are double-keyed and images are examined for quality control.

Pride uses a network of high-speed scanners and document-imaging workstations to provide image capture of both fronts and backs of documents. Pride Enterprises' equipment includes: two Kodak 9500D machines, capable of scanning 180 pages per minute; one Kodak 3500 capable of scanning 175 pages per minute, and 12 indexing quality control PC workstations. In addition, Pride Enterprises maintains file servers and communication gear with a T1 dedicated high-speed telephone line for the fastest possible data transmission to the *CyLex*

Express Document Vault. The T1 line is capable of handling 1.54 megabits of data per second.

All document content is managed by the CyLex Document Vault, a state-of-the-art server facility, maintained by EMC Corporation, the world's leading supplier of intelligent enterprise storage and retrieval technology, located in Hopkinton, Mass. On-line documents are managed on RAID media and near-line in tape libraries. Document access is enabled only to authorized DHSMV employees.

The DHSMV uses the CyLex Express Software for on-line electronic retrieval of documents. Scanned images are stored and managed by the CyLex Express Document Vault. The DHSMV accesses the CyLex Express Document Vault through direct dial up or an Internet connection.

An important feature to the DHSMV is the built-in layers of security that CyLex Express Software integrates into the system to protect documents and to ensure that only users with the proper authorization privileges have access to the CyLex Express Document Vault. Security features include a firewall preventing illegal entry; a multi-tier log-in ID/password procedure that is designed to ensure that each user can access only documents they are authorized to use; and positive client authentication. Optionally, CyLex Express allows all scanned documents to be encrypted at the client site and then stored.

Currently, the DHSMV maintains 25 computer workstations that are authorized for users of CyLex Express with direct access to the Document Vault. The vault also provides real-time document retrieval of on-line stored images within the 15-second-per-image retrieval time required, anytime, 7 days a week.

Phase II of the DHSMV project will provide direct on-line access to the vault from more than 200 local tax collector offices statewide. On-line access will enable them to view 4.5 million title applications filed each year in Florida, as well as 18 million additional images of documents. This will translate into a reduction of administrative time from present 2-3 weeks using a microfilm system to 15 seconds with CyLex Express.

7.2.2 Billing and Customer Care (Daleen Technologies)

The growth of E-commerce, emergence of ASP, and ever increasing competition among the Internet-based service providers significantly complicated the Internet business models and raised the end users' expectation. Internet business models widely used include:

- Free
- Advertisement based
- Transaction based
- Utility based (usage + recurring fee).

At the same time, end users no longer want to be treated as a mass. Instead, they want to be treated as individuals and communities [17]. These new requirements and challenges helped to push billing and customer care (BACC) to the top of the prioritization list of any serious Internet-based service provider such as an ASP and to propel BACC vendors such as Daleen Technologies to stardom. H. Adams put it very well: "Without Billing, It's Just a Hobby." [18].

The BACC functions required by a typical ASP include:

Billing
- Pricing
- Service bundling and discounting
- Usage collection
- Usage rating
- Taxing (future)
- Payment processing
- Treatment and collection
- Settlement and commission processing
- Service Level Agreement (SLA) penalty processing

Customer Care
- Customer management
- Help desk
- Service ordering
- Electronic bill presentment and payment
- Online self-care

As we can see, the BACC components hold critical information (customer data, service data, and usage data) for a service provider. Using such data, a service provider can determine its most valuable customers from the rest, offer superior personalized customer service/support, tailor its services to an individual or a community, and conduct revenue planning and assurance.

On the other hand, BACC is only one of many business support systems (BSS) and operation support systems (OSS) that an ASP may need to have. Other systems include network management, security, accounting, asset management, and decision support systems. Therefore, a BACC must have necessary interfaces (such as APIs) to support interoperability with other BSS/OSS systems so that they can access BACC data and functions. Figure 15. shows how Daleen Technologies' BillPlex™ uses an N-tier architecture to satisfy such requirements.

In addition to such an advanced architecture, the next generation ASP BACC solution must include the following capabilities:

1. Ability to collect (possibly through a usage mediation product) and rate usage data related to applications and services offered by the ASP.

2. Ability to "personalize" billing for an individual user of a community of users so that the pricing and billing are value- rather than usage oriented.

Several companies have shipped products that help to collect usage data for ASPs. XACCT, Narus, and Softblox have products that can collect IP and application (such as Microsoft Word) usage data. An industry workgroup (http://www.ipdr.org) is also working on a standard for IPDR (IP Detail Record Format). One of the objectives for this standard is to uniformly represent usage data for both IP and ASP services.

In a customer-centric environment pricing and billing need to be "personalized" for each customer based on the value provided to the customer and NOT on the resource used. Because value is perceived differently by each customer, value-based pricing/billing requires thorough understanding of the customer. Such understanding not only helps pricing and billing for existing services but also enables a service provider to define new tailored services for the customer. This positive feedback cycle will continue to push customer satisfaction and service provider revenue higher. Only a right BACC system can make this happen.

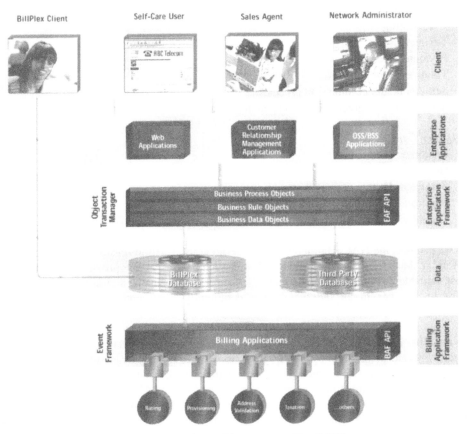

Figure 15. The N-tier architecture used by BillPlex.

Interestingly, not only ASPs need BACC functions, BACC functions can also be provided through an ASP (i.e. *BACC ASP*). In fact, billing service bureaus have long been in existence. Some of these billing service bureaus used mainframe and remote terminals to provide billing services to telephone and utility companies. However, a new generation of BACC ASPs will emerge to offer far superior BACC services through the ASP model. Using Internet and leading BACC products such as BillPlex, these BACC ASPs will be able to bring the best BACC solution to their customers at the least cost.

8. CONCLUSIONS

In this chapter we presented and evaluated contemporary multi-tier Internet architectures, which are well suited for application service providers. We evaluated several computing models for Internet-based architectures and proposed a server-based computing model, which has a number of advantages over the other models. We also presented two case studies of Internet applications that use the proposed ASP architecture.

References

1. "Server-Based Computing," Citrix Systems, white paper, *www.citrix.com*, 1999.
2. P. Dreyfus, "The Second Wave: Netscape on Usability in the Services-Based Internet," *IEEE Internet Computing*, Vol. 2, No. 2, March/April 1998, pp. 36-40.
3. "Software Development for the Web-Enabled Enterprise," Sun Microsystems, white paper, 1999.
4. "What is a Java Application Server," BEA WebLogic, *weblogic.beasys.com*, 1999.
5. A. Thomas, "Selecting Enterprise JavaBeans Technology," WebLogic, Inc., Boston, MA, July 1998.
6. R. Orfali, D. Harkey, and J. Edwards, "Instant CORBA," John Wiley & Sons, 1997.
7. C. McFall, "An Object Infrastructure for Internet Middleware: IBM on Component Broker," *IEEE Internet Computing*, Vol. 2, No. 2, March/April 1998, pp. 46-51.
8. Gupta, C. Ferris, Y. Wilson, and K. Venkatassubramanian, "Implementing Java Computing: Sun on Architecture and Application Development," *IEEE Internet Computing*, Vol. 2, No. 2, March/April 1998, pp. 60-64.
9. "Total Cost of Application Ownership," The Tolly Group, Manasquan, NJ, White paper No. 199503, June 1999.
10. J.B. Eichler, R.Y. Roberts, K.W. Evans, and A.L. Carter, "The Internet: Redefining Traditional Business and Giving Rise to New Ones," Report, Stephens Inc., Little Rock, AR, May 1999.
11. D. Rosenberg, "Bringing Java to the Enterprise: Oracle on Its Java Server Strategy," *IEEE Internet Computing*, Vol. 2, No. 2, March/April 1998, pp. 52-59.
12. M. Benda, "Internet Architecture: Its Evolution from an Industry Perspective," *IEEE Internet Computing*, Vol. 2, No. 2, March/April 1998, pp. 32-35.
13. "Enterprise JavaBeans Technology: Server Component Model for the Java Platform," Sun Microsystems, white paper, java.sun.com, 1999.
14. G.R. Voth, C. Kindel, and J. Fujioka, "Distributed Application Development for Three-Tier Architectures: Microsoft on Windows DNA," *IEEE Internet Computing*, Vol. 2, No. 2, March/April 1998, pp. 41-45.
15. C.J. Woodard and S. Dietzen, "Beyond the Distributed Object Decision: Using Components and Java Application Servers as a Platform for Enterprise Information Systems," *Distributed Computing*, 1998.
16. G. Pour and J. Xu, "Developing 3-Tier Web-Based Enterprise Applications: Integrating CORBA with JavaBeans and Java Servlets," *Proceedings of the 3rd International Conference on Internet and Multimedia Systems and Applications*, Nassau, Bahamas, October 1999.
17. L. Downes and Chunka Mui, "Unleashing the Killer App," Harvard Business School Press, 1998.
18. H. Adams, "Communications Billing & Customer Care: Time to Think Outside the BOCs," *Impact!*, August 1999.

Chapter 5

CONTENT-BASED MULTIMEDIA RETRIEVAL ON THE INTERNET

Oge Marques, Susan Fallon, and Borko Furht

Abstract

In this chapter we first discuss the motivation behind content-based multimedia retrieval systems. A complete overview of a Content-Based Visual Information Retrieval (CBVIR) system follows, from the user's perspective to the complex calculations that take place behind the scenes. The specifics of Web-based CBVIR systems are discussed next. Finally, we compile a list of currently available commercial systems and prototypes that illustrate the concepts and applications discussed in this chapter.

1. INTRODUCTION

In this section we describe the motivation and main challenges behind multimedia retrieval on the Internet.

1.1 THE GROWTH OF MULTIMEDIA AND THE NEED FOR BETTER SEARCH AND RETRIEVAL TECHNIQUES

The amount of audiovisual information available in digital format has grown exponentially in recent years. Gigabytes of new images, audio and video clips are generated and stored everyday, helping to build up a huge, distributed, mostly unstructured repository of multimedia information, much of which can be accessed through the Internet.

Digitization, compression, and archival of multimedia information has become popular, inexpensive and straightforward, and there is a broad range of available hardware and software to support these tasks. Subsequent retrieval of the stored information, however, might require considerable additional work in order to be effective and efficient.

There are basically three ways of retrieving previously stored multimedia data:

1. **Free browsing**: the user browses through a collection of images, audio, and video files, and stops when she finds the desired information.

2. **Text-based retrieval**: the user adds textual information (metadata) to the audiovisual files during the cataloguing stage. In the retrieval phase, this additional information is used to guide conventional, text-based query and search engines to find the desired data.

3. **Content-based retrieval**: the user searches the multimedia repository providing information about the actual contents of the image, audio, or video clip. A content-based search engine translates this information in some way as to query the database and retrieve the candidates that are more likely to satisfy the user's request.

The first two methods have serious limitations and scalability problems. Free browsing is only acceptable for the occasional user and cannot be extended to users who frequently need to retrieve specific multimedia information for professional applications. It is a tedious, inefficient, and time-consuming process and it becomes completely impractical for large databases.

Text-based retrieval has two big problems associated with the cataloguing phase:

(a) the considerable amount of time and effort needed to manually annotate each individual image or clip; and
(b) the imprecision associated with the subjective human perception of the contents being annotated.

These two problems are aggravated when the multimedia collection gets bigger and may be the cause of unrecoverable errors in later retrieval.

In order to overcome the inefficiencies and limitations of text-based retrieval of previously annotated multimedia data, many researchers, mostly from the Image Processing and Computer Vision community, started to investigate possible ways of retrieving multimedia information – particularly images and video clips – based solely on its contents. In other words, instead of being manually annotated using keywords, images and video clips would be indexed by their own visual content, such as color, texture, objects' shape and movement, among others. Research in the field of Content-Based Visual Information Retrieval (CBVIR) started in the early 1990's and is likely to continue during the next decade. Many research groups in leading universities and companies are actively working in the area and a fairly large number of prototypes and commercial products are already available.

In this chapter we examine the state of the art, ongoing research, examples, and open issues in designing Content-Based Visual Information Retrieval (CBVIR) systems to access multimedia information distributed over the Internet.

1.2 RESEARCH CHALLENGES BEHIND THE DESIGN OF CBVIR SYSTEMS

The design of CBVIR systems brings up many interesting problems and challenges, some of which are summarized in [1]. An important subset of these problems is related to the way human beings perceive visual information and how much the knowledge of the human visual perception can help translating it into a set of features, rules, and criteria for comparing and selecting images. An example of a problem that falls into this category is the understanding of how human beings express their (subjective) understanding of the contents of an image using words, drawings, sketches, or similar images. A closely related problem is to understand how human beings perceive visual similarities. These and other similar problems have a great impact on the design of contemporary CBVIR systems.

A good CBVIR system will be one whose design is guided by the following open questions:

(1) How to minimize the "semantic gap" between the low-level features that are automatically extracted from the visual contents of an image and the human interpretation of such contents?

(2) How to make it possible to users to express their queries in a way that allows them to clearly specify which image or type of image they are interested in?

(3) How to minimize the impact of human subjectivity in the performance of the system?

(4) How to measure the similarity between two images?

Attempting to provide meaningful and satisfactory answers to the questions above will possibly impact the design of almost every functional block of a CBVIR system. Some of the major decisions that might be influenced by these questions include:

(a) The choice of image features and their mapping into semantic contents.

(b) The decision on which type of query and retrieval will be supported: visual-based, text-based, or both.

(c) The inclusion of user feedback to improve the system's performance.

2. ANATOMY OF CBVIR SYSTEMS

In this section we describe the main aspects of CBVIR systems, from the user interface to the feature extraction and similarity measurement stages.

2.1 A TYPICAL CBVIR SYSTEM ARCHITECTURE

Figure 1 shows a block diagram of a generic CBVIR system, whose main blocks are:

- **User interface**: friendly GUI that allows the user to interactively query the database, browse the results, and view the selected images / video clips.
- **Query / search engine**: responsible for searching the database according to the parameters provided by the user.
- **Digital image and video archive**: repository of digitized, compressed images and video clips.
- **Visual summaries**: representation of image and video contents in a concise way, such as thumbnails for images or keyframes for video sequences.
- **Indexes**: pointers to images or video segments.
- **Digitization and compression**: hardware and software necessary to convert images and videos into digital compressed format.
- **Cataloguing**: process of extracting features from the raw images and videos and building the corresponding indexes.

Digitization and compression have become fairly simple tasks thanks to the wide range of hardware and software available. In many cases, images and videos are generated and stored directly in digital compressed format. The cataloguing stage is responsible for extracting features from the visual contents of the images and video clips. In the particular case of video, the original video segment is broken down into smaller pieces, called scenes, which are further subdivided into shots. Each meaningful video unit is indexed and a corresponding visual summary, typically a key frame, is stored. In the case of images the equivalent process could be object segmentation, which just a few systems implement. In either case, the cataloguing stage is also where metadata gets added to the visual contents. Manually adding metadata to image and video files is mandatory for text-based visual information retrieval systems. CBVIR systems, however, typically rely on minimum amount of metadata or none at all.

Digitization, compression, and cataloguing typically happen off-line. Once these three steps have been performed, the database contains the images and videos themselves, possible simplified representations of each file or segment, and a collection of indexes that act as pointers to the corresponding images or video segments.

The online interaction between a user and a CBVIR system is represented on the upper half of the diagram in Figure 1. The user expresses her query using a GUI. That query is translated and a search engine looks for the index that corresponds to the desired image or video. The results are sent back to the user in a way that allows easy browsing, viewing, and possible refinement of the query based on the partial results.

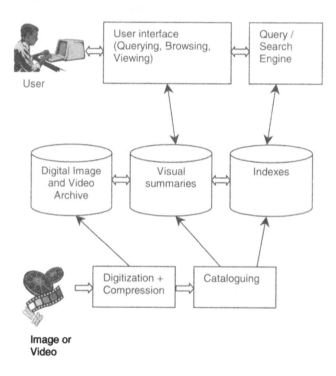

Figure 1. Block diagram of a CBVIR system.

2.2 THE USER'S PERSPECTIVE

The user interface is a crucial component of a CBVIR system. Ideally such interface should be simple, easy, friendly, functional, and customizable. It should provide integrated browsing, viewing, searching, and querying capabilities in a clear and intuitive way. This integration is extremely important, since it is very likely that the user will not always stick to the best match found by the query/search engine. More often than not the user will want to check the first few best matches, browse through them, preview their contents, refine her query, and eventually retrieve the desired video segment.

Searching the visual database contents should be made possible in several different ways, either alone or combined. For instance a user should be able to perform a pictorial query, e.g. querying by similarity (using another video clip or a static image as a reference) and a query by keyword simultaneously.

Query options should be made as simple, intuitive and close to human perception of similarity as possible. Users are more likely to prefer a system that offers the "Show me more video clips that look similar to this (image or video)" option, rather than a sophisticated interactive tool to edit that video shot key-frame's histogram and perform a new search. While the latter approach might be useful for experienced technical users with image processing knowledge, it does not apply to the average user and therefore has limited usefulness. An ideal CBVIR system query stage would hide the technical complexity of the query process from the end user. A search through visual media should be as imprecise as "I know it when I see it." [3]

2.3 FEATURE EXTRACTION

CBVIR systems should be able to automatically extract visual features that are used to describe the contents of an image or video clip. Examples of such features include color, texture, size, shape, and motion information. In specific contexts the process of feature extraction can be enhanced and/or adapted to detect other, specialized attributes, such as human faces or objects. Because of perception subjectivity, there is no best representation for a given feature [4]. The color information, for instance, can be represented using different color models (e.g., RGB, HSV, YCbCr) and mathematical constructs, such as color histograms [5], color moments [6], color sets [7, 8], color coherence vectors [9], or color correlograms [10]. In a similar way, texture can be represented using co-occurrence matrix [11], Tamura texture features [12] or Wavelets [13-15], to name just a few.

2.4 HIGH-DIMENSIONAL INDEXING AND SIMILARITY MEASUREMENTS

The extracted features are grouped into some suitable data structure or mathematical construct (e.g., a normalized feature vector), and suitable metrics (e.g., Euclidean distance) are used to measure the similarity between an image and any other image. At this stage, the main challenges are the high dimensionality of the feature vectors (typically of the order of 10^2) and the limitations of Euclidean similarity measure, which although mathematically elegant might not effectively simulate human visual perception [4].

Solutions to the high dimensional indexing problem include reducing the dimension of the feature vectors and the use of efficient multi-dimensional indexing techniques. Dimension reduction is typically obtained using either the Karhunen-Loeve Transform or clustering techniques. Examples of multi-dimensional indexing techniques include specialized data structures (e.g., k-d tree, R-tree and its variants). To overcome the limitations of Euclidean similarity measures, researchers have proposed the use of clustering and neural networks.

2.5 THE SEMANTIC GAP

The human perception of visual contents is strongly associated to high-level, semantic information about the scene. Current Computer Vision techniques work at a lower level (as low as individual pixels). CBVIR systems that rely on low-level features only can answer queries such as:

- Find all images that have 30% of red, 10% of orange and 60% of white pixels, where orange is defined as having a mean value of red = 255, green = 130, and blue = 0.
- Find all images that have a blue sky above a green grass.
- Find all images that are rotated versions of this particular image.

In general case, the user is looking for higher-level semantic features of the desired image, such as "a beautiful rose garden", "a batter hitting a baseball", or "an expensive sports car". There is no easy or direct mapping between the low-level features and the high-level concepts. The distance between these two worlds is normally known as "semantic gap."

There are basically two ways of minimizing the semantic gap. The first consists of adding as much metadata as possible to the images, which was already discussed and shown to be impractical. The second suggests the use of rich user interaction with relevance feedback combined with learning algorithms to make the system understand and learn the semantic context of a query operation.

2.6 USER'S RELEVANCE FEEDBACK

Early attempts in the field of CBVIR aimed at fully automated, open-loop systems. It was hoped that current Computer Vision and Image Processing techniques would be enough for image search and retrieval. The modest success rates experienced by such systems encouraged researchers to try a different approach, emphasizing interactivity and explicitly including the human user in the loop. A clear example of this shift can be seen in the work of MIT Media Lab researchers in this field, when they moved from the "automated" Photobook [16] to the "interactive" FourEyes [17].

The expression "relevance feedback" has been used to describe the process by which a system gathers information from its users about the relevance of features, images, image regions, or partial retrieval results obtained so far. Such feedback might be provided in many different ways and each system might use it in a particular manner to improve its performance. The effect of relevance feedback is to "move" the query in the direction of relevant images and away from the non-relevant ones [18]. Relevance feedback has been used in contemporary CBVIR systems, such as MIT's FourEyes [17], UIUC's MARS [19-24], and NEC's PicHunter [25-29], among many others.

In CBVIR systems that support relevance feedback a search typically consists of a query followed by repeated user feedback, where the user comments on the items that were retrieved. The use of relevance feedback makes the user interactions with the system simpler and more natural. By selecting images, image regions, and/or image features, the user is in one way or another telling the system what she wants without the burden of having to describe it using sketches or keywords, for instance.

There are many ways of using the information provided by the user interactions and refining the subsequent retrieval results of a CBVIR system. One approach concentrates on the query phase and attempts to use the information provided by relevance feedback to refine the queries. Another option is to use relevance feedback information to modify feature weights, such as in the MARS project [19-24]. A third idea is to use relevance feedback to construct new features on the fly, as exemplified by [30]. A fourth possibility is to use the relevance feedback information to update the probability of each image in a database being the target image, in other words, to predict the goal image given the user's interactions with the system. The latter is the approach taken by Cox et al. [25-29] in the PicHunter project.

3. WEB-BASED CBVIR SYSTEMS

In this section we describe research and design issues specific of Web-based CBVIR systems and present a case study on a particular image metasearch engine, MetaSEEk.

3.1 ISSUES IN DESIGNING A WEB-BASED CBVIR SYSTEM

Making a CBVIR system accessible through the Internet, particularly on the Web, extends its usefulness to users anywhere in the world at the expense of new design constraints, which are summarized below [2]:

- Visual information on the Web is highly distributed, minimally indexed, and schema-less. Internet-based CBVIR systems lack a well-defined schema or consistent metadata.
- The query and retrieval stages have no control over the cataloguing process and must rely on possible metadata stored in HTML tags associated with the images and video clips.
- In order to keep the query response time below a tolerable limit (typically two seconds), the number of visual features used for comparison and matching has to be kept low.
- The user interface should work with reduced-size images and videos until the final stage, when the user issues an explicit request.
- The use of content-based query methods may be deferred until a stage where the scope of the search has been reduced to a specific semantic category, selected by the user.

3.2 A CASE STUDY: COLUMBIA UNIVERSITY'S METASEEK

Researchers at Columbia University have a developed a prototype content-based metasearch engine for images, MetaSEEk (available at **http://www.ctr.columbia.edu/metaseek/**). The system contains three main components:

- the *query dispatcher*, which selects target search engines for each query;
- the *query translator*, which translates the user-specified query into a format understood by the target search engine; and
- the *display interface*, which merges the query results from all the target search engines and displays the best candidates on the screen.

MetaSEEk currently works with four target search engines, whose internal characteristics are hidden from the end user: IBM's QBIC, Columbia's VisualSEEk and WebSEEk, and Virage.

The user interface supports random browsing, content-based retrieval, or keyword-based retrieval. Content-based retrieval is possible either selecting a sample image from one of the supported databases or typing in the URL to an external image. MetaSEEk uses two visual features for content-based retrieval: color and/or texture. Several other parameters can be specified by the user, e.g., the number of search options to be searched simultaneously, the maximum waiting time (in seconds), the number of images to be displayed, and the category the user is interested in (the default category is "All").

Once a query has been received, MetaSEEk's dispatcher selects the target engines and search options to be used. For content-based visual queries the selection of target engines is based on past performance of each target search engine for each query image. Performance data is stored in form of scores in a performance database. If the user selects a query image that has never been used before, MetaSEEk downloads the image and matches it to the corresponding clustering structure to obtain a list of the most similar clusters. Images from the closest clusters are selected and presented to the user. Based on the average performance scores of the cluster selected by the user, MetaSEEk will then choose a suitable search engine. Moreover, the new query image is added to the performance database for future queries.

MetaSEEk uses the K-means clustering algorithm for grouping visually similar images into clusters, Tamura algorithm for detection of texture-related features, and color histograms for detection of color-related attributes. Two feature vectors are compared using Euclidean distance.

MetaSEEk allows users to search for images under a specific semantic category, e.g., flowers, people, or animals. Each category has its own performance database and clustering structure. MetaSEEk's database is hierarchical: images are first classified according to their semantic meaning (specified by the user), then grouped according to the visual features used (color, texture, or both), and finally clustered in classes for each particular visual feature.

Once the results are returned from each individual search engine, the MetaSEEk display component selects, organizes, and presents them back to the user. For random or keyword-based queries the results are presented in random order. For content-based queries, the results are sorted according to a combination of the relevance score informed by the target search engine and the performance metrics of the search engines themselves, stored in MetaSEEK's database.

The system also incorporates user relevance feedback. Once the best candidates have been displayed, the user can click on checkboxes indicating whether they like or dislike a particular result image. This information is used to update the performance metric of the corresponding search engine.

Ongoing work on MetaSEEk has been focusing on the following research issues [2]:

- More sophisticated approaches to user feedback and performance monitoring
- Support for customized search, e.g., color layout, and color percentages.
- Increase on the number of visual features and automatic or semiautomatic visual feature selection based on user preferences
- Faster clustering techniques
- Use of machine learning techniques to boost performance

4. EXAMPLES OF CBVIR SYSTEMS

Numerous CBVIR systems, both commercial and research, have been developed in recent years. From the point of view of the end user, most systems support one or more of the following options:

- Random browsing
- Query by example
- Query by sketch
- Text-based query
- Navigation with customized categories

Systematic studies involving actual users in practical applications still need to be done to explore the tradeoffs among the different options listed above [4]. Some of the currently available CBVIR systems are described below. Several of them are surveyed and explored in more detail in Section 5.

QBIC
QBIC (Query By Image Content) [32-34] was the first commercial CBVIR system. It was developed by IBM Almaden Research Center. Its framework and techniques have influenced many later systems. QBIC supports queries based on example images, user-constructed sketches, and selected colors and texture patterns. In its most recent version, it allows text-based keyword search to be combined with content-based similarity search. The online QBIC demo can be found at: **http://wwwqbic.almaden.ibm.com.**

Photobook
Photobook [16] is a set of interactive tools for browsing and searching images developed at MIT Media Lab. Photobook consists of three sub-books, from which shape, texture, and face features are extracted respectively. Users can query the system based on features from each of

the three sub-blocks. Additional information about Photobook can be found at: **http://www-white.media.mit.edu/vismod/demos/photobook/index.html.**

FourEyes

FourEyes [17] is an improved version of Photobook that includes user relevance feedback. Given a set of positive and negative examples, it decides upon which models or combinations of models to use and learns which combinations work best for solving particular types of problems. When presented with a new problem similar to one it has solved before, FourEyes can solve it more quickly than it could the first time. More details about the system can be found at: **http://www-white.media.mit.edu/vismod/demos/photobook/foureyes/.**

Netra

Netra is a prototype CBVIR system developed in the UCSB Alexandria Digital Library (ADL) project [35]. It uses color, shape, texture, and spatial location information in the segmented image regions to search and retrieve similar images from the database. An online demo is available at **http://vivaldi.ece.ucsb.edu/Netra/.**

MARS

MARS (Multimedia Analysis and Retrieval System) [19-24] was originally developed at University of Illinois at Urbana-Champaign. The main focus of MARS is not on finding a single "best" feature representation, but rather on how to organize the various visual features into a meaningful retrieval architecture, which can dynamically adapt to different applications and different users. MARS formally proposes a relevance feedback architecture in Image Retrieval and integrates such technique at various levels during retrieval, including query vector refinement, automatic matching tool selection, and automatic feature adaptation. More information about MARS can be obtained at: **http://www-db.ics.uci.edu/pages/research/mars.shtml.**

PicToSeek

PicToSeek [18] is an image search engine developed at University of Amsterdam. PicToSeek uses autonomous Web crawlers to collect images on the Web. Then, the collected images are automatically catalogued and classified into predefined classes and their relevant features are extracted. The users can query PicToSeek using image features, an example image, or simply browsing the precomputed image catalog. A demo version of PicToSeek is available at: **http://www.wins.uva.nl/research/isis/zomax/.**

VisualSEEk

VisualSEEk [36,37] is part of a family of CBVIR systems developed at Columbia University. It supports queries based on both visual features and their spatial relationships. An online demo is available at: **http://www.ctr.columbia.edu/VisualSEEk/.**

PicHunter

PicHunter [25-29] is a CBVIR system developed at NEC Research Institute, New Jersey. PicHunter uses relevance feedback and Bayes's rule to predict the goal image given the users' actions.

Virage

Virage [38] is a commercial content-based image search engine developed at Virage, Inc. Virage supports queries based on color, composition (color layout), texture, and structure (object boundary information) in any arbitrary combination. The users inform the system which weight should be associated with each atomic feature according to their own emphasis. More information about Virage products can be found at: **http://www.virage.com.**

Visual RetrievalWare

Visual RetrievalWare is a CBVIR engine developed by Excalibur Technologies Corp. [39]. Similarly to Virage, it allows combinations of several visual query features, whose weights are specified by the users. More information about Excalibur products can be found at: **http://www.excalib.com.**

Other systems

There are several other CBVIR systems available on the Web, such as Blobworld [40], Webseer [41], and ImageRover [42], among many others. Some of them are examined in more detail in the next Section.

5. SURVEY OF CBVIR SYSTEMS

In this section we explore some specifics of selected CBVIR systems.

ImageRover

ImageRover [42,48] is a CBVIR system developed by Boston University that is currently available as an online demo version. This is a Web-based tool, which gathers information about HTML pages via a fleet of automated robots. These robots gather, process, and store the image metadata in a vector format that is searched when a user queries the system. The user then receives relevance feedback with thumbnail images, and by selecting the relevant images to their search, can utilize the content-based searching capabilities of the system until they find their desired target image. The demo is located at **http://www.cs.bu.edu/groups/ivc/ImageRover/demo.html/.**

Figure 2 shows the basic setup of the HTML collection system utilized by ImageRover. There are two types of "modules" or robots, which gather and process the metadata: the gathering and digestion modules. The gathering modules recursively parse and traverse WWW documents, collecting the images as they go. The digestion modules compute image metadata over 6 subimages of the given image. Submodules compute the following data for each subimage:

- Color analysis via color histograms
- Texture orientation analysis using steerable pyramids and orientation histograms
- Text analysis via weighted word frequency histograms.

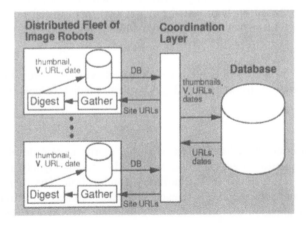

Figure 2. Diagram of the HTML document collection subsystem.

Figure 3 shows the query subsystem for the program, based on a client-server architecture. The system gives relevance feedback that selects L-m Minkowski distance metrics on the fly, allowing the user to perform queries by example on more than one image and successive iteration produces the desired result.

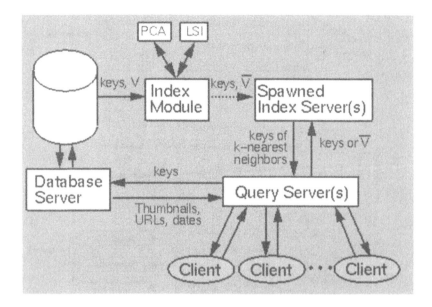

Figure 3. Diagram of the query server subsystem.

WebSeek

WebSeek [50] is similar to ImageRover in its HTML collection processes through Web robots, though it has the advantage of video search and collection as well. It was developed at Columbia University, and currently has a working demo available on the Web at **http://www.ctr.columbia.edu/webseek/**. The user receives relevance feedback in the form of thumbnail images and motion icons or spatially and temporally reduced video forms given as short *gif* files to the user.

Figure 4 illustrates the process of gathering of images and videos. Three types of Web robots utilized by the system are (a) the traversal spider, which assembles lists of candidate Web documents that may include images, videos, or hyperlinks to them, (b) the hyperlink parser, which extracts the Web addresses or URLs of the images and videos, and (c) the content spider, which retrieves, analyzes, and iconifies the images and videos.

Figure 5 shows how the images and videos are detected, and Figure 6 shows how each image or video is processed. WebSeek classifies the images/videos by their URLs and HTML tags with term extraction, directory name extraction, automated key-term to subject mapping using the key-term dictionary and semi-automated directory name to subject mapping. It then places these classifications in unique categories to be searched through textually, along with the image metadata for its content based searching which utilizes color histogram similarity. The user can even adjust the color histograms of the images to reiterate a search for a better match as shown in Figure 10.

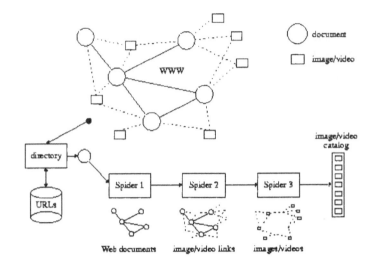

Figure 4. Image and video gathering process in WebSeek.

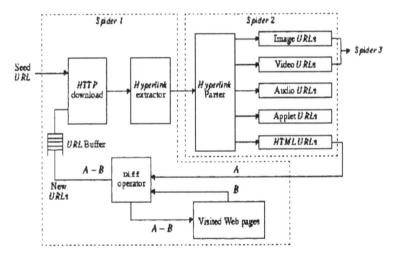

Figure 5. List assembly process of URLs of the images and videos.

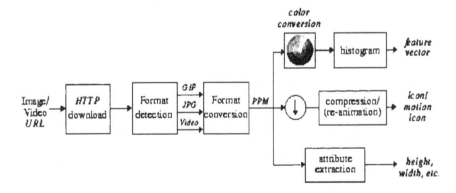

Figure 6. Processing of images and videos in WebSeek.

The user can navigate through the options shown in Figure 7 to perform a textual search. Search and retrieval process consists of record extraction, manipulation, search and ranking, and viewing, as shown in Figure 8. Figure 9 illustrates search results for a textual search for "*nature*" and a content-based search for images/videos of an image of a "*red race car.*" Finally, Figure 10 shows relevance feedback to the user, along with the color histogram manipulations available to use.

Figure 7. WebSeek - main user screen.

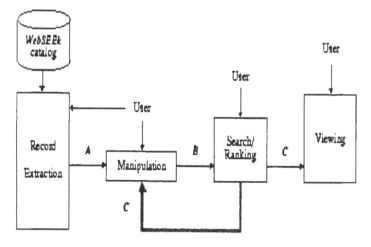

Figure 8. WebSeek - search and retrieval process.

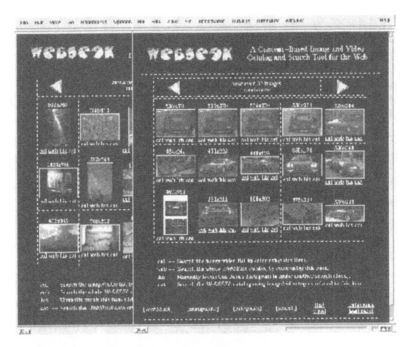

Figure 9. WebSeek - search results for text based query "*nature*" and
a content-based query for a "*red sports car.*"

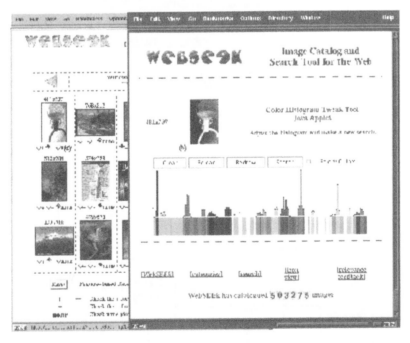

Figure 10. Relevance feedback search for user and color histogram manipulation.

QBIC

QBIC is a system created by IBM, which allows the user to search through an already existing
database and find images by textual searches, as well as content-based searches. This system
also allows the user to utilize a sketching program to find a similar image to the given sketch

drawn. This system assumes an already existing database and does not allow for full Web searching through automated robots. A demo version is available at: **http://www.qbic. almaden.ibm.com/stage/.**

The user can search for images based on color percentages, texture, shape, color layout, and object position. Users can enter a textual description, browse through a given set of thumbnails, or enter a content-based description through an image or sketch. It now includes a standalone Java application providing a GUI front end for use with any database of images.

Figures 11 through 15 show some examples of sample searches one can perform on QBIC system. The sample images were extracted from: **http://www.almaden.ibm.com/cs/showtell/ qic/Initpage.html/.**

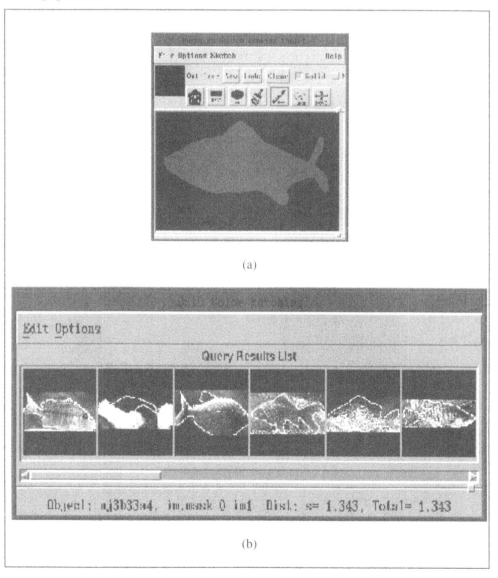

Figure 11. (a) Sketch entry to QBIC, (b) results of search.

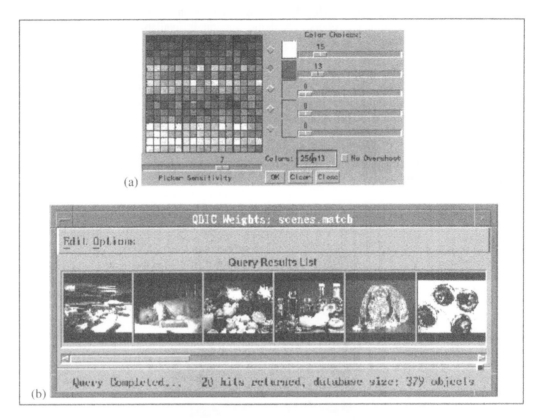

Figure 12. (a) QBIC: Search by color percentages: 15% yellow and 13% blue, (b) search results.

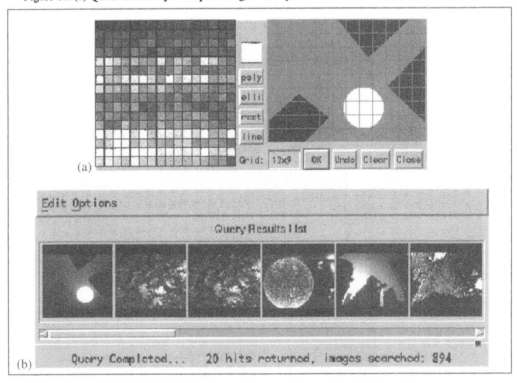

Figure 13. QBIC: Search by user drawn pattern, (b) search results.

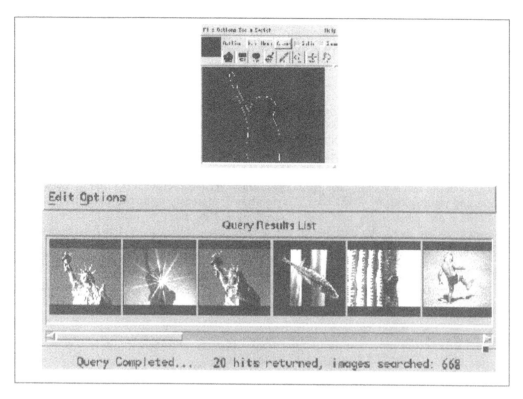

Figure 14. QBIC: Search for sketch created by the user, (b) results for sketch search.

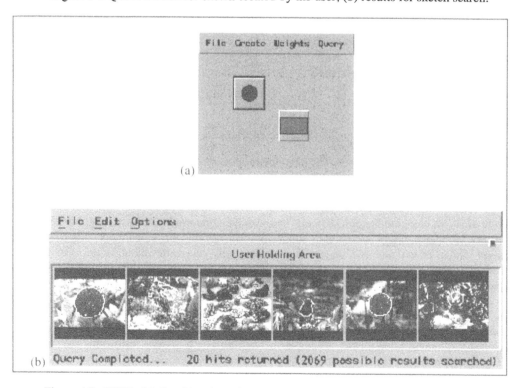

Figure 15. QBIC: (a) Combination of search properties: color (red), shape (round) and background color (green), (b) results from combination search.

QBIC is currently available as a demo form on the Web, as well as in use by the U.C. Davis Art History Department at **http://www.qbic.almaden.ibm.com/stage/**.

AMORE

AMORE is a search engine that also has a Web demo available to try at: **http://www.ccrl.com/amore**. This search engine only has image retrieval capabilities and does not have the ability to search the entire Web via automated robots, but it does have an automated robot (or harvest gatherer as they call it) which can scour and classify images from user specified URLs. The system uses the Harvest Information Discovery and Access System for text indexing and searching, and the content-oriented image retrieval (COIR) to index the images and retrieve them. COIR uses a region-based approach, using attributes like color, texture, size and position for indexing. Everything but the entry of the URL addresses is automated for the user. An example of the indexing mechanism in AMORE is shown in Figure 16.

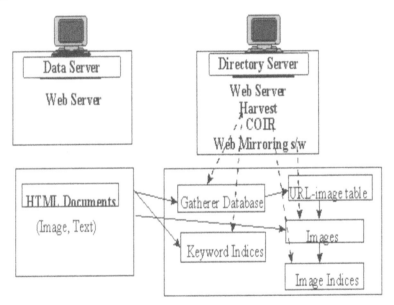

Figure 16. The indexing process in AMORE.

The user can query the system textually or content-based, by entering either a textual keyword image search (i.e. "sailboat"), a content-based search (entering a picture of a sailboat or a sketch of such), or a combination of both. The search engine used is known as "glimpse" and the retrieval engine, COIR, determines similarity of images by shape and color, indexing the images with a match rate and determining compatibility via a threshold value. Both the threshold value and color-shape ratio can be altered by the user for increased match capability. Figure 17 illustrates the querying mechanism.

The user can search for a particular document, search for a class of documents, perform media-based navigation by specifying an image to find a similar image, or enter a rough sketch input, much like in QBIC. Examples of various search queries and results are shown in Figures 18 through 21.

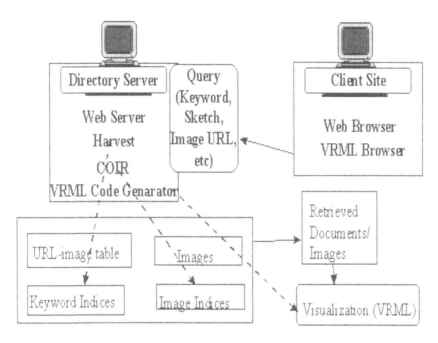

Figure 17. AMORE querying mechanism.

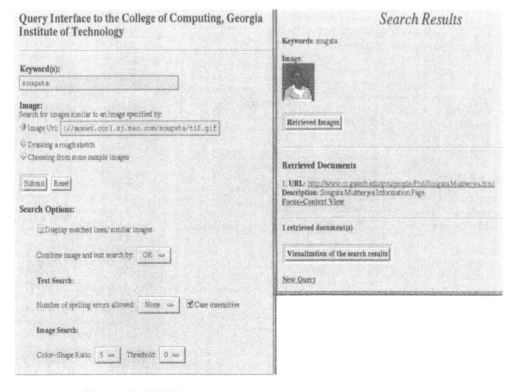

Figure 18. AMORE: Search by text and image to find a Web page.

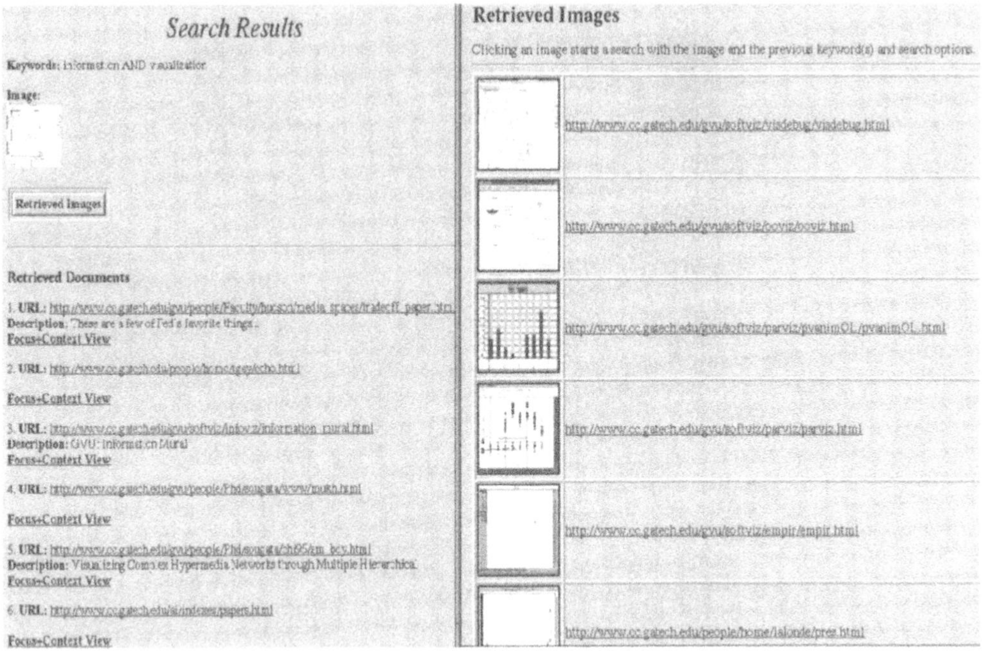

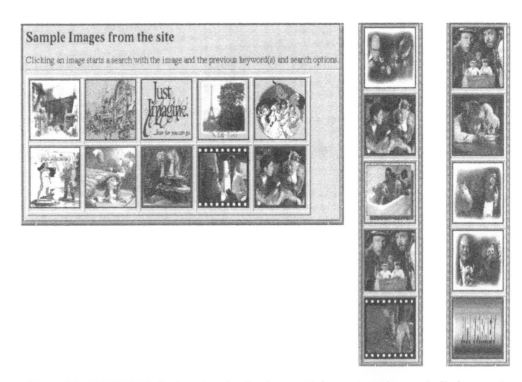

Figure 19. AMORE: Keyword search combined by "or" with an image search of an image of a window dump from an information visualization project. Search results are shown on right.

Figure 20. AMORE: Media-based navigation by combining text and image similarity search for movie clips from the Walt Disney Web site.

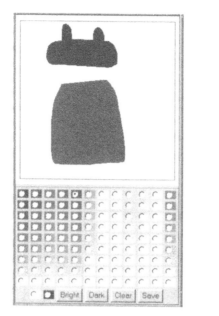

Figure 21. AMORE: Rough sketch input and results.

The user can visualize results in a number of ways. As shown above, the user can view thumbnail images, Web pages, etc., as a normal view. The user can also view a scatterplot visualization, perspective wall visualization, or a "focus + context" view of Web nodes. These types of visualizations give the user a better understanding of the search results, why they happened, and for the "focus + context" view, the user can also be given the actual location of a particular image in the scheme of a Web page. Examples of the scatterplot view, the perspective wall visualization, and the "focus + context" view are shown in Figures 22, 23, and 24, respectively.

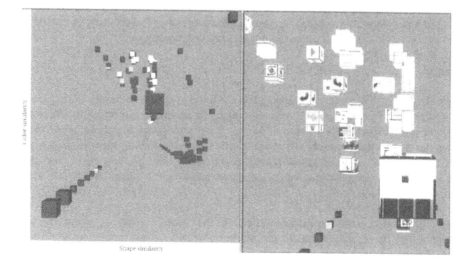

Figure 22. Scatter-plot view of search results plotted by color similarity and shape similarity. The left part shows an overview, and the right part shows the user zoomed into the document with the maximum keywords.

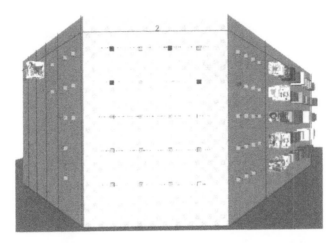

Figure 23. Perspective wall visualization, with each "wall" containing documents with similar number of keywords and the sizes of the cubes representing the similarity of the images in the documents to the user specified image.

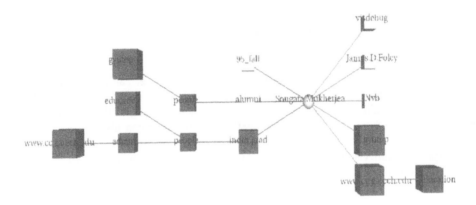

Figure 24. "Focus + context" view of a homepage of one of the authors of [53]. It maps out documents' positioning.

Blobworld

Blobworld [40] is a system, developed at U.C. Berkeley, which allows for content-based image retrieval. The program automatically segments an image into regions, which roughly correspond to object or parts of objects allowing users to query for photographs or images based on the objects they contain. Their approach is useful in finding specific objects and not, as they put it, "stuff" as most systems which concentrate only on "low level" features with little regard for the spatial organization of those features. It allows for both textual and content-based searching.

This system is also useful in its feedback to the user, in that it shows the internal representation of the submitted image and the query results. Thus, unlike some of the other systems, which allow for color histogram similarity metrics, which can be adjusted, this can help the user understand why they are getting certain results.

Images are segmented by modeling the joint distribution of the color, texture, and position features of each pixel in the image. The Expectation-Maximization (EM) algorithm is used to fit a mixture of Gaussian models to the data. The resulting pixel-cluster memberships provide the segmentation of the image. After the segmentation is performed, the description of each region's color, texture, and spatial characteristics is produced.

Figure 25 shows a picture of a wolf and its "blobworld" representation. User screens for content-based and/or text-based image search are shown in Figure 26 and 27. Sample query results from **http://www.cs.berkeley.edu/~carson/blobworld** are shown in Figure 28.

(a)

(b)

Figure 25. (a) Picture of a wolf, (b) blobworld representation of the image.

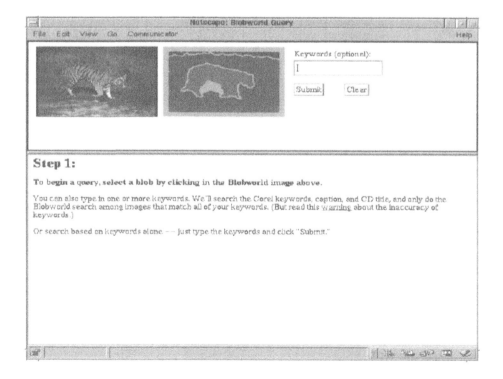

Figure 26. Blobworld: User screen for content-based and/or text based image search.

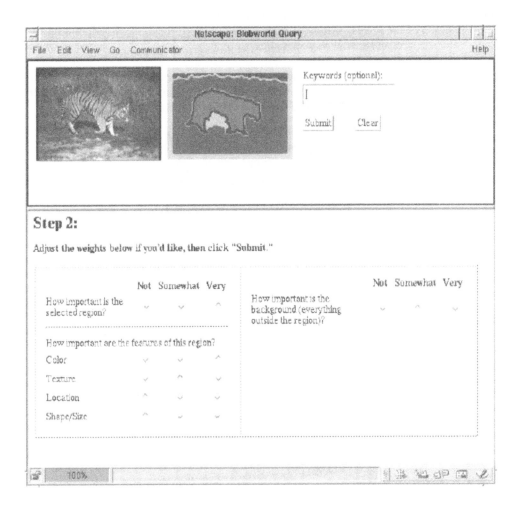

Figure 27. After highlighting the Blobworld region to be looked for, the user can rank the importance of features such as color, texture, location, size/shape and background.

Blobworld is currently available in online demo form at: **http://galaxy.cs.berkeley.edu/ photos/blobworld/.**

The UC Berkeley Digital Library Project

The UC Berkeley Digital Library Project is similar in some ways to the Blobworld program. It assumes an existing database of images and bases its queries on "high-level" content of the images. It begins with low level color and texture processing to find coherent regions, and then it uses these properties and their relationship with one another to group them at progressively higher levels.

First, the system locates isolated regions of color in the images for classification by looking for 13 specified colors in each image. The image's hue, saturation, and value (HSV) channels are mapped into the 13 color channels, it is filtered to isolate "dots" and ignore uniformly colored regions, and the output of these filters is then compared to a threshold value. This system is known as "color dots."

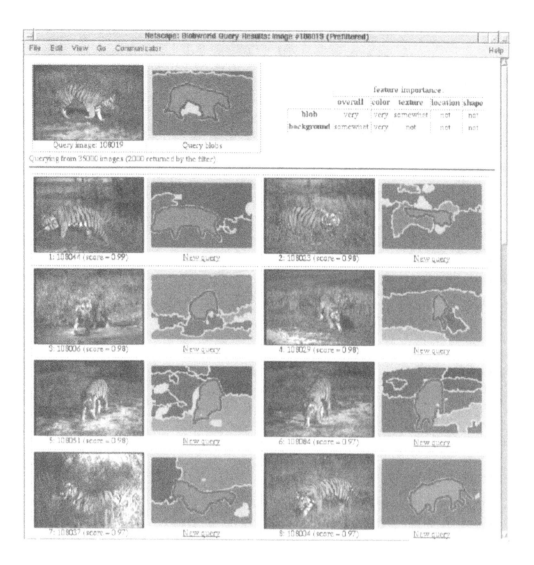

Figure 28. Results from Blobworld query looking for a tiger, which illustrates similar images, their "blobworld" representations, and the chance to perform another query.

Each image is stored only as image metadata in the database available for textual and content-based searching. Each image has 24 textual attributes, including a brief description, a category, subject and internal identification number, as well as some keywords. All of the image's information is stored as text for speed of searching.

This system was designed to handle images that are basically heterogeneous in nature, thus hard to distinguish by most searching means. Figure 29 shows a sample user interface from **http://elib.cs.berkeley.edu/papers/db/**, while results of various searches are presented in Figures 30 through 33.

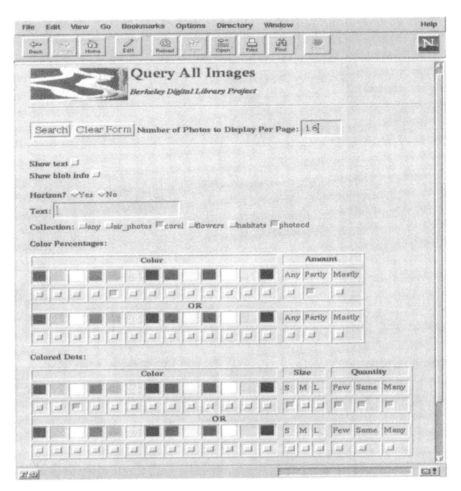

Figure 29. Sample user query interface for The Berkeley Digital Library Project. The user can adjust color, colored dots, database info, or enter text information as well.

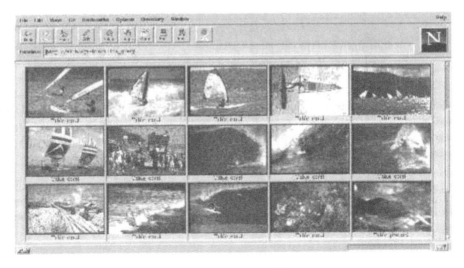

Figure 30. The Berkeley Digital Library Project:
Sample results from "sailing and surfing" textual query.

Figure 31. The Berkeley Digital Library Project: Sample query results for "pastoral" query.

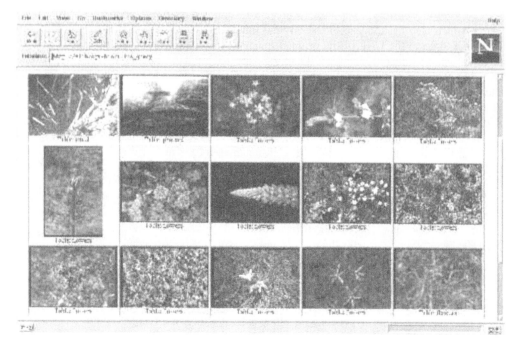

Figure 32. The Berkeley Digital Library Project: Sample results for "purple flowers" query.

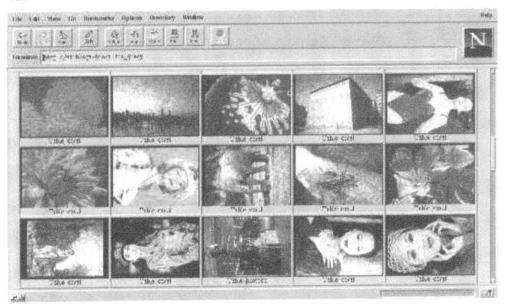

Figure 33. The Berkeley Digital Library Project: Sample results for "people" query.

WebSeer

WebSeer [41] was developed by the University of Chicago and is completely automated in all aspects of its searching capabilities. This system only searches for images and allows for only text-based queries. It allows for a user to enter dimensions of an image, a file size range, relevant colors, type of image (photograph, sketch, graphic, etc.) and even the number of faces or size of a portrait. The user receives a resulting selection of thumbnails from their search, which also list the size of the original image. The user can then either click on the thumbnail to go to the URL of the original image or they can click on the page icon next to the image and be transferred to the URL of the page that contains the image.

The system is composed of five major executables and, with the exception of the URL Server, which is written in Java, all executables are written in C++ and run on a Windows NT 3.51 platform. WebSeer works in five steps:

1) The WebSeer Crawler searches the Web for images by scanning for them in the HTML code,
2) The URL Server receives requests to download URLs from the Crawler,
3) The WebSeer Indexer creates the searchable index of images for the user to search,
4) When a user posts a query from the WebSeer form, the CGI script opens a connection to the WebSeer Search Server and formats the results for the user, and
5) The Search Server accepts the request and the search is performed.

Images are indexed and classified by their surrounding HTML information, much the same as WebSeek and ImageRover. This means that the text on the page containing the image is examined, such as the image file name, the captions, the textual description of the image (if any), the document title, hyperlinks, or other text. Further, the image content is looked at (such as size, file type, color/grayscale, and date) in order to further categorize the image in the database. Tests such as the band difference test, the farthest neighbor test, the color test, the most common color test and the narrowness test each are used to decide if the image is a photograph or drawing. Face matching techniques, developed by MIT and Carnegie Mellon University, are used to detect faces in the images.

Virage

Virage [51] was developed by Virage Inc. and it allows for query by text and by example. This system also allows for both video and image retrieval, as well as query by sketch. This system is now available through AltaVista and snap.com, greatly improving these companies' search engines' capabilities. Virage, Inc. has an online demo of its search engine in which images/videos can be searched based on color, texture, color distribution in the image, and general structure. Searches can be based on various weighted characteristics of the images/videos. This system runs on an existing database (no auto searching).

This system works with four layers of information abstraction, the raw image or Image Representation Layer, the process image or Image Object Layer, the user's feature of interest or Domain Object Layer, and the user's events of interest for videos or the Domain Event Layer. Virage features three primitives to calculate image metadata, namely, color, texture and shape, which the user has the power to adjust the weights of during a search. Information such as scene breaks, cuts, dissolves or fades are taken into account for videos. Image metadata is stored in vector form for videos and images, much like the other systems.

Virage includes image processing tools to normalize, scale, or crop images, as well as perform more advanced operations such as color histograms. Users can insert images for comparison or perform textual searches. Also, users can enter a sketch to compare and find similar images/videos too.

Figure 34 shows an example of Virage's technology on snap.com, which runs textual searches of videos (in this case for the presidential election 2000 and "education") and presents results to the user who can then click on the icons to play the video or view the text of the video.

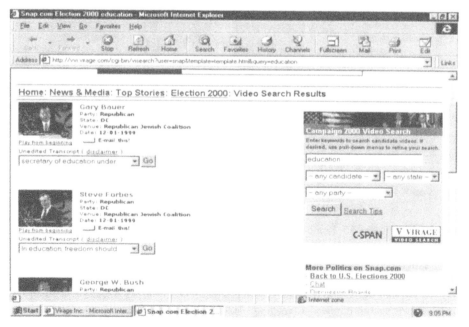

Figure 34. Example of Virage technology with snap.com. The user can query the system for video clips of presidential candidates by entering text.

VisualSEEk

VisualSEEk is a part of the Columbia University projects such as WebSeek and WebClip. The system enhances the search capability by integrating the spatial query (like those used in geographic information systems) and the visual feature query. Users ask the system to find images/video that include regions of matched features and spatial relationships. Figure 35 shows a query example in which two spatially arranged color patches were issued to find images with blue sky and open grass fields.

Figure 35. Sample query for color patches using VisualSEEk.

Yahoo's Isurf

Yahoo is a popular commercial based search engine, which utilizes Excalibur technologies in its image-based search engine. Images are searched in a text-based only method and Web addresses must be entered manually by the user for categorization. The system is similar to AMORE, only the images are added to a global database for all users and image classification is manually dependent on user descriptions/keywords. Figure 36 illustrates an example of text-based search for "cats" using Yahoo's Isurf.

Figure 36. Yahoo's Isurf: Results for "cats" search.

The results in Figure 36 are in thumbnail form and the user can click on the images to go to the Web page of origination of the image. Namely, an image cannot be retrieved and is not stored on Yahoo's database.

AltaVista

As mentioned before, AltaVista has acquired image and video searching capabilities through Virage, Inc. This search engine, like Yahoo, is only text-based currently, allowing the user to enter textual data to locate images or videos categorized textually via keywords/categories in the system. The user cannot add pages to this database as in Yahoo. Once a set of images is returned to the user, the user can click on the text below the image or video to find out more information about it, and then can refine the search by "finding similar pages to that page."

Figure 37 illustrates an example of text-based search for "cats." By clicking on one of the images the user can get additional information about the particular image, as illustrated in Figure 38. The results for video searches are the same and cannot be performed in conjunction with image searches.

Netra

NETRA is a prototype image retrieval system that is currently being developed within the UCSB Alexandria Digital Library project. NETRA uses color, texture, shape and spatial location information in segmented image regions to search and retrieve similar regions from a database. This is a region-based program (much like Blobworld), so the user can choose a region and find similar image regions to the submitted one, thus being a content-based system only. Also, the user can choose multiple region attributes for a search.

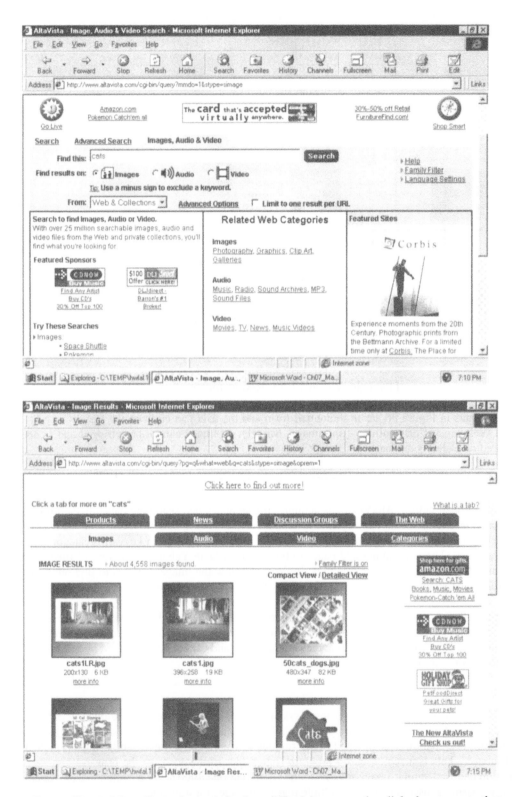

Figure 37. AltaVista: Textual search for "cats." Each image can be clicked on to go to that page, or find out more information about the image.

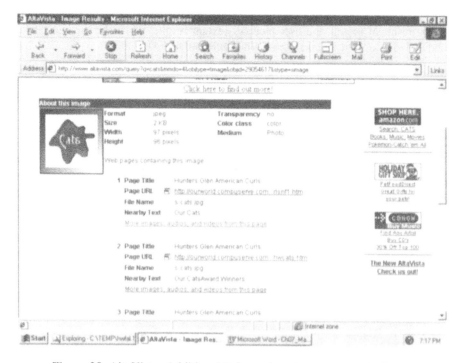

Figure 38. AltaVista: Additional information about a particular image.

PicToSeek

Much like ImageRover, WebSeek and WebSeer, PicToSeek automatically scans the Web for images and allows the user to search by content-based techniques of image matching. Figure 39 shows a sample search of the image on the left, with results on the right. When the user clicks on the small images on the left, that image is loaded and the Web address is given to the user.

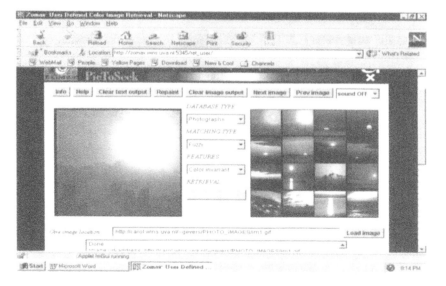

Figure 39. PickToSeek: Results of picture-based query.

VideoSeeker

As part of snap.com, VideoSeeker search engine lets the user enter a textual search for a video clip. As the result of search, the user receives textual results, which he/she can click on to download and view a short video as shown in Figures 40 and 41.

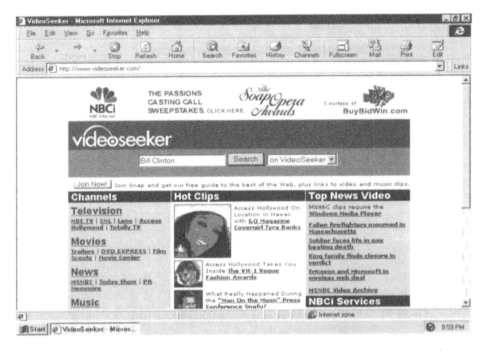

Figure 40. VideoSeeker: Search engine interface to locate videos based on textual query, say "Friends".

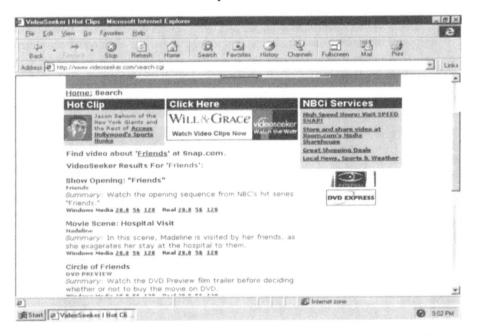

Figure 41. VideoSeeker: Results of search for "Friends," which the user can click on to download and view video clips from the NBC show.

FourEyes

FourEyes is a tool, which segments and annotates images and it is included in the Photobook-6 interface. It was developed by MIT; more information can be found at **http://www-white.media.mit.edu/vismode/demos/photobook/foureyes/**. With this program, the user can click on certain regions of an image and label them. Depending on the type of feature the user is looking for, FourEyes will choose a labeling model among its "society of models" or combine models in order to label the user's image. Figure 42 shows an example of FourEyes extrapolating the labels of "building," "car," and "street" from an image. In this way, this search engine can intelligently search for various regions on an image.

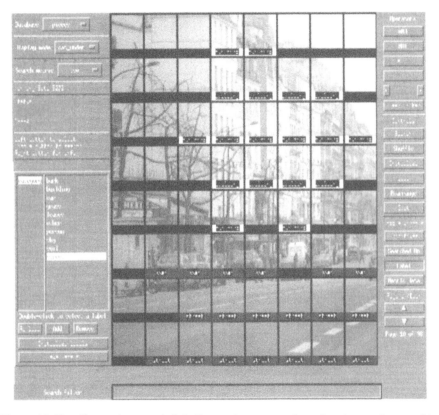

Figure 42. FourEyes: Automatic labeling and segmentation of an image for searching based on regions.

6. SUMMARY

In this chapter we discussed the main issues and challenges in designing multimedia search and retrieval systems with the focus on the Web-based CBVIR systems, which provide search and retrieval on the Internet. We presented the system architecture of a CBVIR system and addressed open issues in designing and developing these systems. We also presented a number of commercial and prototype image and video retrieval systems, which are both text-based and content-based. Table 1 summarizes the features of these systems.

Table 1. Characteristics of Commercial Multimedia Retrieval Systems

SYSTEM	SEARCHES BY	SEARCHES FOR	DATABASE Where it searches	MAIN USE
AltaVista	Text	Images/Videos	Separately created collection	To find images/videos on the Web easily
Lycos	Text	Images/Videos	Entire Web With Web Robots (FAST)	To find images/videos on the Web easily
Yahoo	Text	Images/Videos	Collection of URLs manually entered by all Web users	To find images/videos on the Web easily
VideoSeeker	Text	Videos	Separate collection of video clips	To find video clips to download online
ImageRover	Text/Content	Images	Entire Web With Web Robots	To find images on the Web and be able to refine searches through image comparison
AMORE	Text/Content	Images	URLs specified by the user	To find images on specific Web pages and have adjustable values to refine search
WebSeek	Text/Content	Images/Videos	Entire Web With Web Robots	To find images/videos on the Web and have adjustable values to refine search
WebSeer	Text/Content	Images	Entire Web With Web Robots	To find images and have adjustable values to find images or specific people/number of faces
The Berkeley Digital Library Project	Text/Content	Images	Separately created	To find images in a database of heterogeneous images
PicToSeek	Text/Content	Images	Entire Web With Web Robots	To find images with adjustable values/ refineable search means
Netra		Images	Separately created	To find by region matching via content-based retrieval
PhotoBook/F oureyes	Text/Content	Images	Separately created	To find specific regions of images or automatically label regions of images
VisualSeek	Text/Content	Images	Separately created	To search a specific URL or through a database of images to find by content or by region
Blobworld	Text/Content	Images	Separately created	To find specific objects through "blob" or object comparisons
Virage	Text/Content	Images/Video	Separately created	To find images/videos in an online collection with adjustable values to refine search
QBIC	Text/Content	Images	Separately created	To find images in an online collection with adjustable values to refine search

References

1. O. Marques and B. Furht, "Issues in Designing Contemporary Video Database Systems," *Proc. IASTED Conference on Internet and Multimedia Systems and Applications*, Nassau, Bahamas, October 1999.
2. S.-F. Chang, J. R. Smith, M. Beigi, and A. Benitez, "Visual Information Retrieval from Large Distributed Online Repositories," *Communications of the ACM*, Vol. 40, No. 12, December 1997.
3. Gupta, S. Santini, and R. Jain, "In Search of Information in Visual Media," *Communications of the ACM*, Vol. 40, No. 12, 1997.
4. Y. Rui, T.S. Huang, and S.-F. Chang, "Image Retrieval: Past, Present, and Future,"
5. M. J. Swain and D. H. Ballard, "Indexing via Color Histograms", *Proc. Third International Conference on Computer Vision*, 1990.
6. M. Stricker and M. Orengo, "Similarity of Color Images," *Proc. SPIE Storage and Retrieval for Image and Video Databases*, 1995.
7. J. R. Smith and S.-F.Chang, "Tools and Techniques for Color Image Retrieval," *Proc. SPIE Conference on Storage and Retrieval for Image and Video Database IV, 2670*, San Jose, CA, February 1996.
8. J. R. Smith and S.-F.Chang, S.-F., "Single Color Extraction and Image Query," *Proc. IEEE International Conference on Image Processing*, 1995.
9. G. Pass, R. Zabih, and J. Miller, "Comparing Images Using Color Coherence Vectors," Proc. ACM Conference on Multimedia, 1996.
10. J. Huang, S. Kumar, M. Mitra, W.-J. Zhu, R. and Zabih, "Image Indexing Using Color Correlogram," *Proc. IEEE International Conference on Computer Vision and Pattern Recognition*, 1997.
11. R. Haralick, K. Shanmugam, and I. Dinstein, "Texture Features for Image Classification," *IEEE Transactions on Systems, Man, and Cybernetics*, Vol. 3, No. 6, 1973.
12. H. Tamura, S. Mori, and T. Yamawaki, "Texture Features Corresponding to Visual Perception", *IEEE Transactions on Systems, Man, and Cybernetics*, Vol. 8, No. 6, 1978.
13. T. Chang and C.-C. Jay Kuo, "Texture Analysis and Classification with Tree-Structured Wavelet Transform," *IEEE Transactions on Image Processing*, Vol. 2, No. 4, 1993.
14. A. Laine and J. Fan, "Texture Classification by Wavelet Packet Signatures," *IEEE Transactions on Pattern Recognition and Machine Intelligence*, Vol. 15, No. 11, 1993.
15. M. H. Gross, R. Koch, L. Lippert, and A. Dreger, "Multiscale Image Texture Analysis in Wavelet Spaces," *Proc. IEEE International Conference on Image Processing*, 1994.
16. A. Pentland, R.W. Picard, and S. Sclaroff, "Photobook: Content-Based Manipulation of Image Databases," Chapter 2 in *Multimedia Tools and Applications*, Furht, B., Ed., Kluwer Academic Publishers, Boston, 1996,
17. T. Minka, "An Image Database Browser that Learns from User Interaction," MEng Thesis, MIT, 1996.
18. T. Gevers and A. W. M. Smeulders, "The PicToSeek WWW Image Search System," *Proceedings of the International Conference on Multimedia Computing and Systems*, Florence, Italy, 1999.
19. Y. Rui, T. S. Huang, M. Ortega, and S. Mehrotra, "Relevance Feedback: A Power Tool for Interactive Content-Based Image Retrieval," *IEEE Transactions on Circuits and Systems for Video Technology*, Vol. 8, No. 5, pp. 644-655, 1998.
20. Y. Rui, T. S. Huang, S. Mehrotra, and M. Ortega, "A Relevance Feedback Architecture for Content-Based Multimedia Information Retrieval Systems," 1997.
21. Y. Rui, T. S. Huang, and S. Mehrotra, "Content-Based Image Retrieval with Relevance Feedback in MARS," *Proc. IEEE Int. Conf. Image Processing*, 1997.
22. Y. Rui, T. S. Huang, S. Mehrotra, and M. Ortega, "Automatic Matching Tool Selection Using Relevance Feedback in MARS", Proc. 2nd Int. Conf. Visual Information Systems, 1997.

23. Y. Rui, T. S. Huang, and S. Mehrotra, "Relevance Feedback Techniques in Interactive Content-Based Image Retrieval," *Proc. S&T SPIE Storage and Retrieval of Images/ Video Databases VI, EI'98*, 1998.

24. M. Ortega, Y. Rui, K. Chakrabarti, A. Warshavsky, S. Mehrotra, and T.S. Huang, "Supporting Ranked Boolean Similarity Queries in MARS,"

25. I.J. Cox, M.L. Miller, T.P. Minka, T. Papathomas, and P.N. Yianilos, "The Bayesian Image Retrieval System, PicHunter: Theory, Implementation and Psychophysical Experiments," *IEEE Transactions on Image Processing*, 2000 (to appear).

26. I.J. Cox, M.L. Miller, S.M. Omohundro, and P.N. Yianilos, "PicHunter: Bayesian Relevance Feedback for Image Retrieval," *Proc. Int. Conference on Pattern Recognition*, Vienna, Austria, 1996.

27. I.J. Cox, M.L. Miller, S.M. Omohundro, and P.N. Yianilos, "Target Testing and the PicHunter Bayesian Multimedia Retrieval System", Advanced Digital Libraries ADL'96 Forum, Washington D.C., 1996.

28. I.J. Cox, M.L. Miller, T. Papathomas, J. Ghosn, and P.N. Yianilos, "Hidden Annotation in Content Based Image Retrieval," *Proc. IEEE Workshop on Content-Based Access of Image and Video Libraries*, 1997.

29. I.J. Cox, M.L. Miller, T.P. Minka, T. Papathomas, and P.N. Yianilos, "An Optimized Interaction Strategy for Bayesian Relevance Feedback," CVPR, 1998.

30. T.P. Minka and R. Picard, "Interactive learning using a 'society of models," MIT Media Laboratory Perceptual Computing Section Technical Report No. 349, 1995.

31. A. Benitez, M. Beigi, and S.-F. Chang, "Using Relevance Feedback in Content-Based Image Search", *IEEE Internet Computing*, Vol. 2, No. 4, pp. 59-69, 1998.

32. M. Flickner, H. Sawhney, W. Niblack, J. Ashley, Q. Huang, B. Dom, M. Gorkani, J. Hafner, D. Lee, D. Petkovic, D. Steele, and P. Yanker, "Query by Image and Video Content: The QBIC System," in *Intelligent Multimedia Information Retrieval*, Maybury, M. T., Ed., American Association for Artificial Intelligence (AAAI), Menlo Park, CA: 1997.

33. W. Niblack, R. Barber, W. Equitz, M. Flickner, E. Glasman, D. Petkovic, P. Yanker, C. Faloutsos, and G. Taubin, "The QBIC Project: Querying Images By Content Using Color, Texture and Shape," 1993.

34. J. Ashley, R. Barber, M. Flickner, J. Hafner, D. Lee, W. Niblack, and D. Petkovic, "Automatic and Semi-Automatic Methods for Image Annotation and Retrieval in QBIC," Research Report RJ 9951 (87910), IBM Research Division, Almaden Research Center, 1995.

35. Y. Deng and B.S. Manjunath, "NeTra-V: Toward an Object-Based Video Representation," *IEEE Transactions on Circuits and Systems for Video Technology*, Vol. 8, No. 5, 1998.

36. J. R. Smith and S.-F.Chang, "VisualSEEk: A Fully Automated Content-Based Image Query System," *Proc. ACM Multimedia '96*, Boston, MA, November, 1996.

37. J. R. Smith and S.-F.Chang, "Querying by Color Regions Using the Visual SEEk Content-Based Visual Query System," in *Intelligent Multimedia Information Retrieval*, Maybury, M. T., Ed., American Association for Artificial Intelligence (AAAI), Menlo Park, CA, 1997.

38. J.R. Bach, C. Fuller, A. Gupta, A. Hampapur, B. Horowitz, R. Humphrey, R. Jain, and C. Shu, "The Virage Image Search Engine: An Open Framework for Image Management," *Proc. SPIE Conference on Storage and Retrieval for Image and Video Databases*,

39. J. Dowe, "Content-Based Retrieval in Multimedia Imaging," *Proc. SPIE Conference on Storage and Retrieval for Image and Video Databases*, 1993.

40. Blobworld home page. http://www.cs.berkeley.edu/~carson/blobworld/.

41. Webseer home page. http://infolab.cs.uchicago.edu/webseer/.

42. ImageRover home page. http://www.cs.bu.edu/groups/ivc/ImageRover/Home.html.

43. W.-Y. Ying Ma and H.J. Zhang, "Content-Based Image Indexing and Retrieval," Chapter 11 in the Handbook of Multimedia Computing, B. Furht, Ed., CRC Press, Boca Raton, Florida, 1999.

44. H.J. Zhang, "Content-Based Video Browsing and Retrieval," Chapter 12 in the Handbook of Multimedia Computing, B. Furht, Ed., CRC Press, Boca Raton, Florida, 1999.

45. G. Ahanger and T.D.C. Little, "A Survey of Technologies for Parsing and Indexing Digital Video," *Journal of Visual Communication and Image Representation*, Special Issue on Digital Libraries.

46. S.-F. Chang, Q. Huang, T. Huang, A. Puri, and B. Shahraray, "Multimedia Search and Retrieval," Chapter in Advances in Multimedia: Systems, Standards, and Network, A. Puri and T. Chen, Eds., Marcel Dekker, New York, 1999.

47. B.-L. Yeo and M.M. Yeung, "Retrieving and Visualizing Video," *Communications of the ACM*, Vol. 40, No. 12, December 1997, pp. 43-52.

48. S. Sclaroff, L. Taycher, and M. La Cascia, "ImageRover: A Content-based Image browser for the World Wide Web," *Proc. IEEE Workshop on Content-based Access of Image and Video Libraries*, June 1997.

49. J. R. Smith and S. Chang, "Searching for Images and Videos on the World-Wide Web,"*Center for Telecommunications Research Technical Report #459-96-25*, http://www.ctr.columbia.edu/webseek/paper/.

50. C. Frankel, M. J. Swain, and V. Athitsos, "WebSeer: An Image Search Engine for the World Wide Web," *University of Chicago Technical Report # 96-14*, August 1996.

51. A. Gupta, "Visual Information Retrieval: A Virage Perspective," *Virage, Inc.*, formerly available at http://www.virage.com/papers/.

52. C. Carson, S. Belongie, H. Greenspan, and J. Malik, "Blobworld: Image Segmentation Using Expectation-Maximization and its Application to Image Querying", from http://www.cs.berkeley.edu/~carson/papers/pami.html/.

53. S. Mukherjea, K. Hirata, and Y. Hara, "Towards a Multimedia World Wide Web Information Retrieval Engine", http://www.decweb.ethz.ch/.

54. V. Ogle and C. Carson, "Storage and retrieval of Feature Data for a Very Large Online Image collection", http://elib.cs.berkeley.edu/pepers/db/.

55. K. Hirata, S. Mukherjea, W. Li, and Y. Hara, "Integrating Image Matching and Classification for Multimedia Retrieval on the Web," *Proceedings of the International Conference on Multimedia Computing and Systems*, Florence, Italy, 1999.

56. J. R. Smith and S. Chang, "Visually Searching the Web for Content," *IEEE Multimedia*, Vol. 4, No. 3, July - September, 1997.

57. G. Raik-Allen, "Virage Unleashes Video-Search on Clinton Testimony," *Red Herring Online*, September 29, 1998. Available at http://www.herring.com/insider/1998/0929/virage.html/.

Chapter 6

COMPONENT TECHNOLOGIES: EXPANDING THE POSSIBILITIES FOR DEVELOPMENT OF WEB-BASED ENTERPRISE APPLICATIONS

Gilda Pour

Abstract

In this chapter we first provide an overview of component-based enterprise software development and multi-tier client/server application architectures for Web-based enterprise applications. Then we discuss the use of leading component technologies for development of multi-tier Web-based enterprise applications. The discussion is focused on the key features that Java-based component model (Enterprise JavaBeans (EJB) and JavaBeans) and COM-based component model (Microsoft Transaction Server (MTS) and ActiveX) each offers for Web-based enterprise application development.

1. INTRODUCTION

This section provides an overview of component-based enterprise software development, multi-tier client/server application architectures for Web-based enterprise applications, and component-based approach to developing multi-tier Web-based enterprise applications.

1.1 COMPONENT-BASED ENTERPRISE SOFTWARE DEVELOPMENT

Component-based enterprise software development (CBESD), which is rapidly emerging trend in industrial software engineering, is indeed the natural evolution of distributed object technology. CBESD has the potential to:

- Reduce significantly the cost and time-to-market of enterprise applications by delivering the promise of large-scale software reuse and allowing the applications to be built through assembling reusable components rather than from scratch.

- Enhance the reliability of enterprise applications by allowing the applications to be developed through assembling the pre-tested reusable software components.

- Improve the maintainability and flexibility of enterprise applications by allowing replacement of old components with quality components.

- Enhance the quality of enterprise applications by allowing application-domain experts to develop reusable components and software engineers to build enterprise applications by assembling the components.

CBESD approach is used for building enterprise software systems including Web-based enterprise applications. CBESD is based on the concept of building software systems by selecting a set of pre-engineered and pre-tested reusable software components, customizing the components, and integrating them within appropriate software architectures.

There is no generally accepted definition of components. We define a component as an encapsulated and distributable piece of software with well-defined interfaces that are separated from the component's implementation. The primary objective of developing a component is reuse of the component in various software systems. Judith Hurwitz identifies the major characteristics of components that make them ideal modules for software development: they are large grained, self-contained, and standard-based.

There are major differences between a component-based enterprise software system development lifecycle and the traditional software development lifecycle. For instance, design of a component-based software system includes new activities such as selection, analysis, and creation of software architectures; as well as evaluation, selection, and customization of software components. In addition, implementation of a component-based software system is based on the integration of a set of reusable software components within appropriate software architecture, no more extensive coding to build the software from scratch. Indeed the coding required in the implementation phase is mainly for developing software components (including wrappers) that glue reusable components together to build the system.

1.2 MULTI-TIER ARCHITECTURES FOR WEB APPLICATIONS

The architecture of a software system defines the system in terms of computational components and interactions among the components. Three groups of components are identified in Web-based enterprise applications: (1) presentation, (2) application logic, and (3) data management components.

Presentation components are primarily used for interaction of software system with users. Application logic components perform calculations and determine the flow of the application. More specifically, application logic components read data from the server, perform application logic and send data back to the server. Data management components manage information that should persist across sessions, planned shutdowns, and systems failures. The components interact through client/server protocols and database-accessing protocols.

The idea of placing each component group in a different layer has motivated the use of multi-tier client/server application architectures for Web-based enterprise applications. The most commonly used architectures for Web applications are 2-tier and 3-tier client/server application architectures.

1.2.1 2-Tier Client/Server Application Architectures for Web Applications
In 2-tier client/server application architectures, presentation and application logic components run together on the client side in tier 1 and data management components on the server side in tier 2. This is illustrated in Figure 1.

2-tier architectures have several drawbacks affecting their scalability, maintainability and performance. The integration of presentation and application logic components in tier 1 lowers the degree of the maintainability of these components, because evolution of one aspect cannot be performed independent of the other. In addition, a user of a 2-tier system is allowed to access only one data source at a time; access to other data sources must be done via gateways, raising serious performance issues for enterprise systems. Furthermore, due to lock contention, scalability of 2-tier applications is limited. Moreover, lock resolution is independent of the server's speed; therefore, installing more powerful Data Base Management System (DBMS) servers does not provide significantly greater performance.

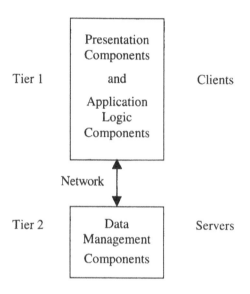

Figure 1. 2-tier client/server application architecture.

A large number of users and databases in a secure distributed enterprise network environment should be able to communicate on the Web. This requires databases to maintain connections to each active client while the connections consume machine resources. In addition, the security model does not work well outside of trusted Local Area Network (LAN) environments. That is why 2-tier architecture should be used only for departmental-scale Web applications with small numbers of users, a single database, and secure and fast networking.

1.2.2 3-Tier Client/Server Application Architecture for Web Applications
In 3-tier client/server application architectures, each component group (i.e. presentation, application logic, and data management components) forms a distinct unit. As shown in Figure 2, presentation components operate in tier 1, application logic components in tier 2 (middle tier), and data management components in tier 3.

Each tier provides a different set of services: tier 1, presentation services; tiers 2, processing services; and tier 3, data services. Presentation components of a software system provide presentation services by managing the interaction between users and the software system. Clients place their requests for application services with the presentation components. Then presentation components send clients' requests to application logic components in tier 2.

Application logic components manage the clients' requests for application services including the requests for connections to the data management components in tier 3. A client may request connections to multiple heterogeneous servers including back-end servers, DBMS servers, and legacy applications. The connection is made possible through the use of some native interfaces such as SQL for relational databases. Furthermore, the middle tier resolves many difficult infrastructure issues such as naming, location, security and authentication.

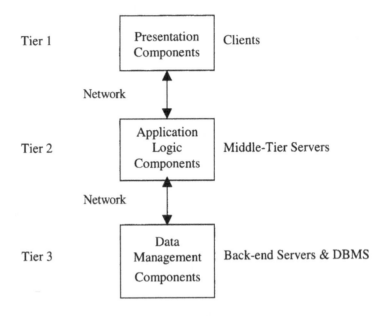

Figure 2. 3-tier client/server application architecture.

The separation of the three component groups and their services into three layers promotes interoperability, reuse, and manageability of Web-based enterprise applications. Furthermore, 3-tier architectures allow application components to run on middle-tier servers, independent of presentation and database implementation. This provides application developers with more choices for enhancement of application scalability, performance, reliability, security, and load balancing. 3-tier architectures have additional major benefits including the following:

- System administrators can replicate application components and run them on different machines simultaneously. This enhances the software availability, scalability, and performance.

- Application logic components can share database connections. This improves software performance by lowering the number of total sessions that a database server in a distributed computing environment must support.

- Access to other sources is provided through native protocols & application interfaces rather than data gateways. This improves the software performance and allows users to control the data access.

- Software developers are allowed to make the most of various reusable application logic components. This will improve the process of software development and maintenance.

1.3 COMPONENT-BASED DEVELOPMENT OF 3-TIER WEB APPLICATIONS

There is fast growing demand for rapid and cost-effective development of scalable, maintainable, extensible, flexible, and secure Web-based enterprise applications for heterogeneous distributed computing environments. Such Web applications should cross the boundaries of different hardware platforms, different networking and operating systems, different software applications, and different programming languages. This has motivated the use of component-based enterprise software development approach to building multi-tier Web-based enterprise applications.

As shown in Figure 3, a 3-tier Web-based enterprise application consists of Web browsers in tier 1, Web application servers in tier 2, and DBMS servers, back-end information/data sources, back-end corporate servers, and legacy applications in tier 3.

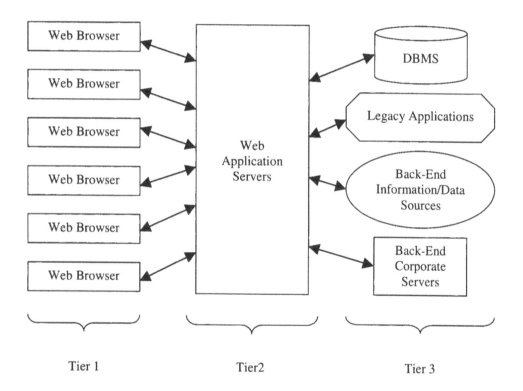

Figure 3. 3-tier Web-based enterprise applications.

Web application servers in middle tier combine various aspects of middleware, Web servers, development toolkits, and sometimes more. As a result, application servers provide scalability in addition to the access to resources that is required for Web-based enterprise applications. A variety of commercial Web application servers have recently been introduced.

2. COMPONENT MODELS

A component model refers to a set of standard specifications that delineate the APIs, encapsulation boundaries, binding and bridging mechanisms, such services as event handling and persistence storage that a software component should support to interoperate with other software components.

A component model provides the standardized way to build, manage, and maintain components. As a result, a component model allows software developers to focus on the core logic behind the components, and the components' relationships rather than the infrastructure and low-level systems programming.

A component model consists of both client and server component models. The idea of using client-side components such as graphical user interfaces (GUIs) (i.e. spreadsheet and table components) has been around for some time. However, development of server-side components for enterprise systems has been challenging due to the complexity of server-side issues.

A server component model adds a server component environment, which is a transparent layer between client and server. This layer monitors the client/server communications, and modifies the communications to ensure that the correct thread, security, transaction, and persistence semantics are used. Consequently, server logic does not require any transaction-specific code. In this new setting, all application developers need to do is to configure the environment to use the correct transaction rules.

One of the key challenges in component-based development of Web-based enterprise applications is the selection of the component model that fits the project at hand. Two major component models are available: (1) Java-based component model and (2) COM-based component model. Enterprise JavaBeans (EJB) is the Java-based server component model and JavaBeans is the Java-based client component model. Microsoft Transaction Server (MTS) is the COM-based server component model and ActiveX is the COM-based client component model. Furthermore, the Object Management Group (OMG) is working on CORBA Components Specification.

2.1 JAVA-BASED COMPONENT MODEL

Java advantages including Web enablement and platform-independent deployment have been the key to the extensive use of Java and Java-based technologies for development of Web-based enterprise applications. Java-based component model comprises Enterprise JavaBeans (EJB) specification for server-side component development and JavaBeans specification for client-side component development. JavaBeans and EJB together provide a universal integration and enabling technology for multi-tier Web-based enterprise application development.

Java platform for Web application development is extensible and flexible to adapt to rapid and enormous changes in the requirements and computing environment. The widespread use of Web and the need for a solid approach to providing interactivity of heterogeneous and distributed computing environments created the perfect climate for an innovative technology like Java. Java mission statement is "Write once and run anywhere."

Java is intrinsically object-oriented (OO). As a result, Java has all OO attractive features including higher level of maintainability, flexibility and extensibility. Furthermore, Java offers an elegant and efficient approach to address major issues in Web-based enterprise application development, namely, portability and security. JavaBeans and EJB extend all native strengths of Java including portability and security to component-based development of Web-based enterprise applications.

2.1.1 Portability

Java is portable to any platform as long as it has a Java Virtual Machine (VM). This practically covers any platform. The use of the pair of Java bytecodes and Java VM has made Java cross-platform independent. A Java program is an applet or an application. A Java application runs under the operating system of the computer while Java applets can run inside Web browsers.

As illustrated in Figure 4, the Java compiler located on the server side compiles Java programs (Java source code files) into platform-independent (portable) bytecodes. Java bytecodes can be downloaded from Web servers to Web browsers on the client side that has a Java VM. Java bytecodes will then be verified, dynamically linked in any needed Java classes, and executed by the Java run-time interpreter on the client side. Therefore, compiled bytecodes can run on any platform supporting Java VM, making Java codes platform-independent.

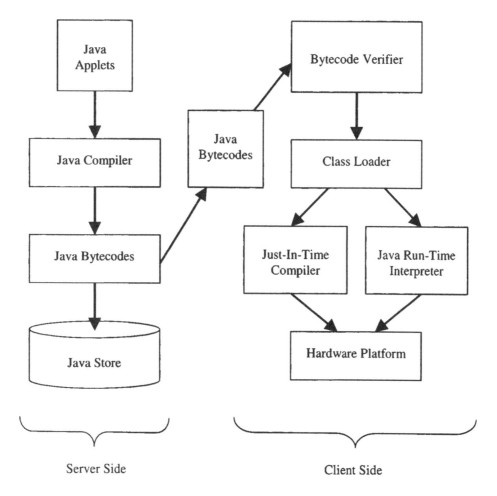

Figure 4. Java bytecodes from production to execution.

For the pair of Java VM and bytecodes to work, Java creators have made data formats and size to be independent of both platform and compiler. For instance, an integer in Java is always 32 bits regardless of the word size of the platform on which Java code runs.

2.1.2 Security
Java 2 provides the ability to create and manage security policies that treat a Java program according to its trust level (i.e. trusted, partially trusted, and untrusted). A set of security

algorithms such as digest algorithms, signing algorithms, and encryption algorithms can be plugged in the Java security architecture using the security Provider interface.

The Java security feature is made possible through the pair of Java VM and portable bytecodes and the extensive security features of the standard and extended Java APIs. To ensure that the compiler follow Java language rules, Java VM analyzes the symbolic data/information stored inside of the downloaded Java bytecodes before the bytecodes being executed on the client side.

Furthermore, a Java VM memory manager automatically allocates new memory and frees unused memory; precluding risks of data corruption that arise if a user's program steps over memory bounds--a common problem in applications written in other languages including C/C++.

To ensure that downloaded bytecodes do not put the client side at risk (e.g. corrupt the hard drive, read the private files, etc.), Java has adopted the combination of the following three different approaches:

- Code signing
- Sandboxing
- Trusted servers

Code Signing
The capability to digitally sign Java bytecodes is a major part of Java approach to addressing security issues. Java bytecodes carry digital signature, which has special mathematical properties that is difficult to forge. Bytecode verifier in the client side (shown in Figure 4) checks the digital signature of the downloaded bytecodes to determine the trust level. The browser or non-browser-based VM on the client side can be set to accept Java applets signed by trusted parties, and to reject applets signed by the parties that are not trusted.

Sandboxing
Downloaded Java bytecodes are given different levels of access to resources outside the sandbox on the client side. The level of access depends upon the level of trust that is determined by the bytecode verifier on the client side (shown in Figure 4). Untrusted Java bytecodes are not allowed to access the resources outside the sandbox, partially trusted bytecodes are placed in specially constructed custom sandbox, and fully trusted bytecodes are allowed to access all resources on the client side.

Trusted Servers
Some corporate servers are considered trusted not to deliver Java code that contains viruses and damages the system on which it is downloaded and executed.

Java and all Java-based technologies combine code signing (using digital signature), sandboxing, and trusted servers to provide different levels of trust. This has provided higher level of security in Java and all Java-based technologies. Furthermore, these technologies are robust in the case of accidental bugs in the code because of integrating sandboxing and different levels of trust.

2.1.3 Multi-Threading and Performance
Java has built-in support for multi-threading that is required for building high performance multi-threading applications.

2.1.4 Garbage Collection

Java offers automatic garbage collection for memory management. The system keeps track of memory usage. When an item is no longer needed, the memory allocated to the item is made available to other users. Java memory management approach prevents the problems that arise with dangling pointers; making the Java security model work even better.

2.2 JAVABEANS

JavaBeans is a leading component technology for development of client-side components for Web-based enterprise applications. The JavaBeans mission statement is "Write once, run anywhere, reuse everywhere."

Creators of JavaBeans from JavaSoft/Sun Microsystems Inc. define bean as "a reusable software component that can be manipulated visually in a builder tool." A Java bean is a special kind of Java class or set of classes designed as a reusable component that can be created, customized, reused, and assembled with other components to create robust enterprise systems.

A software developer can use a Java builder tool to customize a bean through its property table or customization methods. Multiple beans can be combined and interrelated to build Java applets or applications, or to create new, more comprehensive, and specialized Java beans.

2.2.1 An Overview of Beans

Beans are platform-independent and reusable Java-based components that are used as the emerging foundation of all Java application frameworks. The primary use of JavaBeans is to develop building blocks of software for heterogeneous and distributed computing environments--Internet and Intranets. Beans address important issues related to client-side components; for example, application packaging, reusability, and customization.

The characteristics of a bean are represented by the bean's properties. Beans can register and listen for a set of different events that are triggered by other beans (called event sources). Event mechanism is used to provide the communications and collaboration of Java beans. JavaBeans specification defines a standard API for beans' properties and events, standard naming conventions, and coding standards for developing beans.

2.2.2 Bean Construction

Bean construction involved questions such as what the bean must do, how the bean will be used, and what changes to the beans might be needed in the future. The major activities involved in bean construction are as follow:

- Design
- Implementation
- Customization
- Testing
- Packaging

Bean Design

The design of a bean consists of the following major activities:

- Laying out the bean's properties
- Defining the bean's public methods
- Determining the events used by the bean for communicating with other beans and programs

Bean Implementation

For the bean implementation, Beans Development Kit (BDK) can be used. It is available at http://www.javasoft.com.

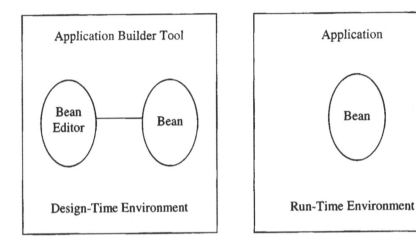

Figure 5. JavaBeans design-time environment versus run-time environment.

Bean Customization

Customization of beans is required to adapt beans to the environment of a new application. As shown in Figure 5, a bean editor is used for bean customization that is done through visual application builder tools.

For keeping beans as compact as possible, bean editor is physically stored apart from the bean itself, and does not have to be shipped with the bean. In other words, a Java bean can be shipped with or without the bean editor. This is an important feature for a mobile code.

For bean customization, Java supports the following:

- Property editors
- Property sheets
- Customizers

Property editors provide visual interfaces for editing a particular type of bean property, one property editor for each property type. JavaBeans provides property editors for built-in Java data types such as integers, strings, etc. Bean developers should provide a suitable editor for their custom properties if they want those properties to be available for bean development. Furthermore, JavaBeans provides property sheets for bean customization. Property sheets are visual interfaces that consist of all the property editors necessary to edit the public properties of a bean.

Customizers provide more elaborate visual interfaces for editing complex beans. They typically provide editing facilities within the context of a series of questions. JavaBeans supports the use of customizers; however, developers should design and implement customizers.

Bean Testing

A test container called the BeanBox, which comes with the BDK, can be used for testing beans. BeanBox provides a simple test-bed for trying out the bean (i.e. helps to lay out, edit, and interconnect beans visually). Other tools are also available.

Bean Packaging

The standard method of distributing beans involves packaging beans into compressed archives called JAR (Java ARchives) files. JAR files use a compression scheme based on the one used in ZIP files.

2.3 COM-BASED COMPONENT MODEL

COM-based component model uses ActiveX for development of client-side components and Microsoft Transaction Server (MTS) for development of server-side components.

2.3.1 From OLE to COM/DCOM and ActiveX

Object Linking and Embedding (OLE) 1 from Microsoft was a mechanism for creating and working with compound documents. OLE 1 was based on the idea that a component document could be created either by linking two separate documents together or by completely embedding one document in another.

For the second release, the architects of OLE developed a set of technologies that were not just for compound documents. One of such technologies was the Component Object Model (COM), which provided a foundation for OLE 2. COM establishes a common paradigm for interaction of a variety of software such as libraries, applications, system software, etc. With COM, a new architecture for component reuse was introduced; allowing dynamic and efficient composition of systems from independently developed binary components. OLE became a label for any COM-based technology.

Objects are the central idea behind all these technologies. The creators of COM have defined and used objects differently from other popular object technologies. For instance, COM supports only interface inheritance, not implementation inheritance. The COM creators have described that their approach prevents exposing the implementation of COM objects to the objects inherited from those COM objects. The approach taken by COM to reuse object code is based on containment and aggregation. With containment, one object delegates another object to carry out its functions. With aggregation, an object presents one or more of another object's interfaces as its own; therefore, a client sees a group of interfaces of two or more aggregated objects as one single object.

COM objects are classes that advertise their services through their interfaces. COM, like JavaBeans, supports multiple interfaces, each interface with a different set of methods. An authorized client component or program must first acquire a pointer to the interface that provides the services it needs. Then the client can use the pointer to invoke methods on the object and access the COM object's services.

COM has its own Interface Definition Language (IDL) that is an extension of the IDL used in Microsoft's Remote Procedure Call (RPC). COM defines a standard binary format for interfaces to allow a client to invoke an object's method regardless of the programming language that the object and client are written in. As a result, COM/DCOM and ActiveX are language-dependent.

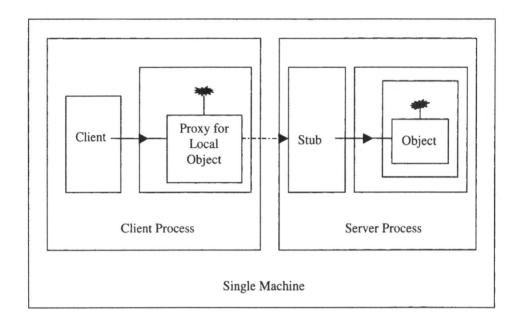

Figure 6. Accessing a COM object on a local server.

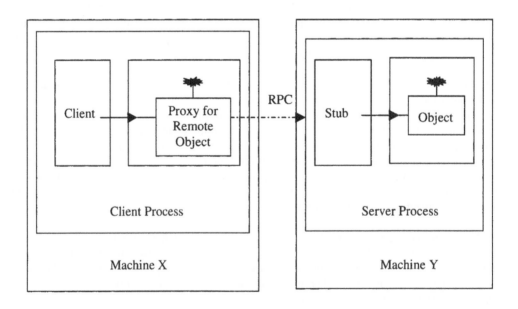

Figure 7. Accessing a COM object on a remote server.

Distributed Component Object Model (DCOM) is the Object Request Broker (ORB) for ActiveX. DCOM serves as a core technology for remote communications between ActiveX components. In March 1996, Microsoft introduced ActiveX as the company's main strategy for the Web. Understanding COM/DCOM is required for understanding ActiveX.

2.3.2 Portability
COM/DCOM and ActiveX are Windows-platform-dependent.

2.3.3 Security
To address security issues, ActiveX makes use of digital signatures--a kind of encryption technology that relies on signing arbitrary binary files by the developers, distributing and certifying those files. ActiveX offers two levels of trust: trusted or untrusted.

When a signed ActiveX control is downloaded, the browser detaches the signature block and checks the identity of the signer using Authenticode. It is a two-step process:
1. Examining the identity of the certificate authority
2. Checking the one-way hash to ensure that the downloaded code is the same code that has been signed.
 In this approach, only the identity of the signer is checked and that the code has not changed since signing.

Furthermore, Microsoft Internet Explorer with its fourth release has implemented a "security zone" concept, which organizes Web sites into four zones of trust:

*   Local Intranet zone
*   Trusted sites zone
*   Internet zone
*   Restricted sites zone.

Each zone can be configured with different levels of security: high (most secure), medium (more secure), low, or custom. A user is allowed to manage Authenticode security zones. Despite the security zones, ActiveX practically provides two levels of trust.

2.4 COMPONENT MODEL EVALUATION

Both JavaBeans and ActiveX are used for developing Web applications. However, they have major differences. In this section, we discuss their differences in terms of portability, security, and existing code base as it relates to Web-based enterprise application development.

JavaBeans is portable and language-dependent while ActiveX is Windows-platform-dependent and language independent. The Internet market share of Java-based technologies has significantly expanded due to portability of these technologies. Furthermore, language-dependency of JavaBeans does not seem to be a problem because Java can run on any platform with Java VM (practically all platforms).

JavaBeans and ActiveX address security issues differently. JavaBeans approach is based on the combination of sandboxing, code signing, and trusted servers while ActiveX approach is based on code signing.

ActiveX has large existing code base due to its widespread use of its underlying OLE Controls (OCX) technology by the Windows software community. The use of Java-based component technologies is expanding especially with the emergence of JavaBeans and EJB.

2.5 INTEROPERABILITY

JavaBeans and ActiveX are evolving to become more powerful technologies as they continue to compete for market share. JavaSoft has built JavaBeans/ActiveX Bridge that provides interoperability between applications using the two competing technologies. This has expanded the possibilities for developing Web-based enterprise applications that make use of both competing component technologies.

3. SERVER COMPONENT MODELS

The two leading server component models are Enterprise JavaBeans (EJB) and Microsoft Transaction Server (MTS). The Object Management Group (OMG) is working on the CORBA Components Specification. We first provide an overview of EJB and MTS in this section. Then we compare the key features of these component technologies.

3.1 AN OVERVIEW OF ENTERPRISE JAVABEANS

Enterprise JavaBeans (EJB), designed by a consortium of companies led by Sun Microsystems Inc., is the Java-based server component model. EJB inherits all Java attractive features including portability, security, and reliability features. This contributes significantly to making EJB suitable for developing portable server-side components that are robust.

EJB specification defines an architecture for the development and deployment of reusable platform and application independent sever-side components--called enterprise beans. An enterprise bean is a specialized non-visual JavaBeans component (a Java class with transactional properties) that runs in a container in an application server, transaction server, and DBMS server. An EJB class can be manipulated and customized through its property table and customization methods.

Enterprise beans can be assembled with Java beans to create a wide variety of enterprise applications. Enterprise beans can use CORBA IIOP for the following purposes: (1) interoperating across multi-vendor servers, (2) propagating transaction and security contexts, (3) servicing clients using software written in different programming languages, and (4) supporting ActiveX via DCOM/CORBA bridges.

3.1.1 EJB Advantages
EJB specification provides a server component environment, which is a transparent layer between clients and servers in multi-tier Web-based enterprise applications. This layer monitors all the communications between clients and servers, and modifies the communications to ensure the use of correct thread, security, transaction, and persistence semantics. Application developers are no longer responsible for writing transaction-specific code, low-level system programming, etc. Therefore, they can concentrate on the application logic and configuration environment.

EJB provides additional major advantages for Web-based enterprise application development including the following:

- Efficient data access across heterogeneous servers
- Faster Java client connections, transaction state management, caching, and queuing
- Connection multiplexing
- Transaction load balancing across server

3.1.2 Interfaces of Enterprise Beans
The EJB specification defines an interface of an enterprise bean as a standard Java RMI[1] interface. However, the actual communication is independent of RMI. An enterprise bean has two interfaces: home interface and remote interface

---

[1] RMI is the acronym for Remote Method Invocations. Java RMI is used for communications between Java objects.

3.1.3 EJB Architecture

As shown in Figure 8, an enterprise bean resides inside an EJB container. The type of container associated with an enterprise bean depends on the enterprise bean's class. This is determined at deployment. EJB specification describes the types of services that a bean can expect. As long as the bean conforms to the specification, it will run in any compliant EJB container or any platform

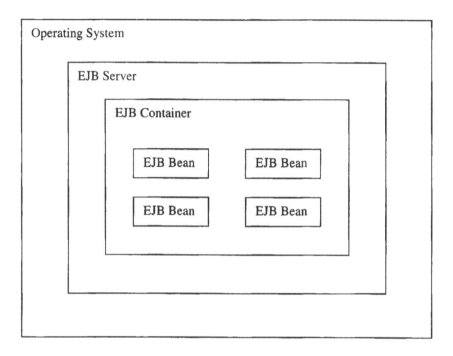

Figure 8. High-level view of EJB architecture.

A client never communicates directly with an enterprise bean. Instead, the client uses the enterprise bean's home and remote interfaces that are provided by the EJB container. This is illustrated in Figure 9. An EJB container is in charge of implementing the management and control services that are required for the lifecycle of enterprise beans residing in the container. For example, an EJB container supports the management and control services for transaction, security, multiple instances, transparent distribution, persistence, and concurrency.

An EJB container communicates with enterprise beans residing in the container via callback interfaces. An EJB container intercedes between client calls on remote interface and the corresponding methods in a bean to enforce transaction and security constraints. EJB specification provides declarative transaction and security management; an application developer should simply specify the bean's transactional and security attributes declaratively through deployment descriptor. This significantly simplifies the process of developing transactional applications using EJB, and provides a level of abstraction that makes it possible to run enterprise beans across EJB servers. When the enterprise bean is deployed, the container reads the bean's deployment descriptor and automatically provides the necessary transaction support.

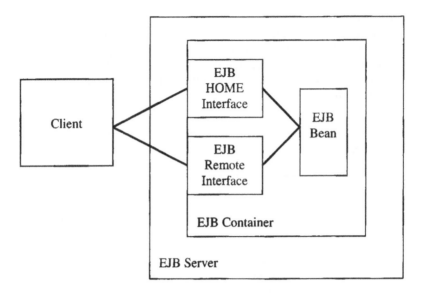

Figure 9. Communication between an enterprise bean and its client.

EJB container also provides notification at the start and end of each transaction involving a bean instance. An EJB container provides enterprise beans with the ACID properties of transactions:

- Atomicity: The set of actions that constitute one transaction must be either executed as one logical unit or not executed at all.
- Consistency: The changes in the state of database must be undone if the transaction is not executed.
- Isolation: The state is not visible from outside until a transaction is committed.
- Durability: The changes are stored permanently once the transaction is completed.

In addition, an EJB container enforces policies and restrictions on bean instances such as reentrance rules, security policies, etc. EJB container provides support for EJB security by requiring a deployer to specify the Access Control List (ACL) for an enterprise bean as a whole or for any one of the bean's methods. The ACL of a bean determines which users can access the ACL-protected bean.

Furthermore, an EJB container provides support for persistence to enterprise beans by storing the state of an enterprise bean to a file or a database rather than requiring developers to implement database calls to save and restore the bean's state. For instance, an application developer should simply specify the fields that should be persistent for an entity enterprise bean with container-manged persistence. EJB container will then take the responsibility for saving and restoring these fields.

To improve the performance, an EJB container also provides support for management of multiple instances such as the following:

- Database connection pooling. Instead of creating a new database connection, a database connection from the pool of available database connections may be used. This avoids unnecessary overhead, which is critical particularly for enterprise applications.

- Instance passivation. When the container needs other resources, it may deactivate the enterprise bean temporarily and swap it out to storage.

- Instance polling. An EJB container creates a pool of beans instances (excluding the session stateful beans) and uses that pool as needed rather than creating a new instance for each client connection.

- Precached instances. To accelerate the initial creation of enterprise beans the state information that the EJB needs to load from a database, are precached and stored in memory or a highly indexed database table.

As shown in Figure 8, an EJB server is the container of EJB containers. The EJB server provides the EJB container with lower-level services such as network connectivity, various facilities including threading information, resource management, and distributed transaction management service. Currently, the choice of the interface between the EJB server and EJB containers living on the server are up to the individual server and container vendors.

3.1.4 Types of Enterprise Beans
An EJB specification describes two types of enterprise beans: (1) Session enterprise beans, and (2) Entity enterprise beans. A session enterprise bean is a transient object and an entity enterprise bean is persistent.

A session enterprise bean is developed by a client, is typically only for the use of that particular client. Hence, a session enterprise bean is anonymous. Session enterprise beans represent application functionality, and usually exist for the duration of a single client-server session. A session enterprise bean, on the behalf of its client, performs operations such as accessing and updating data in an underlying database or performing calculations. If the server crashes, all session beans running on the server are lost. A session enterprise bean is destroyed when the EJB server is restarted or crashes, or when the client's connection to the bean times out.

There are two kinds of session beans:

- Stateless session beans
- Stateful session beans

A stateful session bean maintains conservational state across methods and transactions while a stateless session bean does not. A stateful session bean has its own state. After a client creates or finds a stateful session bean, it starts a session that uses the same bean from that point on. When a client does not need the session enterprise bean any more, it ends the session. While the session is open, the stateful session bean may use its instance variables to store information about its interaction with the client.

A stateless session bean does not maintain conservational state across methods and transactions. That is why it has no instance variables, and is used only by one client at a time. Several clients can use the stateless session bean on a message-by-message basis because message calls do not share any data. Furthermore, the server may use pools of stateless session beans to minimize the total number of beans created.

An entity enterprise bean has a persistent object reference that generally survives the crash and restart of the EJB server on which the EJB container lives. An entity bean is intrinsically tied to an underlying database interface. The internal state of an active Entity EJB should always be synchronized with its underlying data after a transaction concludes.

There are two kinds of entity beans:

- Entity beans with bean-managed persistence
- Entity beans with container-managed persistence

The bean developer of an entity bean with bean-managed persistence is responsible for managing the bean's persistence though the use of a piece of code that updates the underlying databases. However, an entity bean with container-managed persistence does not have such a code, and it relies on its container to update the underlying database when necessary.

3.1.5 Roles in EJB

To simplify development of complex enterprise software systems, EJB specification defines six roles associated with different tasks in the system development. The following is the list of those tasks. The roles are illustrated in Figure 10.

- Developing enterprise beans
- Implementing a platform for both development and execution of distributed enterprise applications
- Providing EJB containers for connecting enterprise beans with EJB server
- Assembling enterprise beans to build applications
- Deploying applications
- Managing and administering the execution of applications

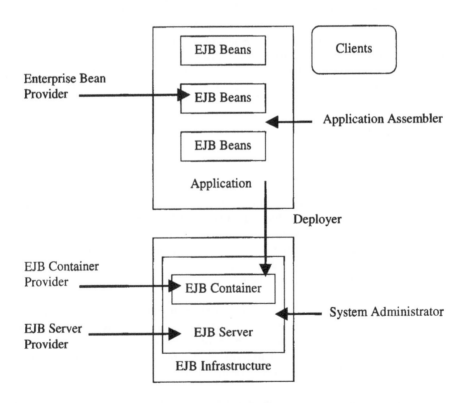

Figure 10. Roles in EJB.

Enterprise Bean Provider

An enterprise bean provider, the expert in the application domain, implements and packages enterprise beans. As described earlier, an EJB container provides all the transaction and network communication support for enterprise beans living in the container. Therefore, the enterprise bean provider does not need to be engaged in any low-level programming, networking, or transaction processing. Instead, the enterprise bean provider can focus on the application logic that should be implemented.

EJB Server Provider

EJB server provider is in charge of providing an EJB server that will contain EJB containers and provide services to the containers. The EJB server provider implements a platform, which facilitates the development of distributed enterprise applications and provides a run-time environment for those applications. An EJB server provider is required to have expertise in such areas as transaction processing, network communications, and concurrent programming.

Enterprise Container Provider

An EJB container provider, an expert in distributed enterprise systems, provides an EJB container in which enterprise beans live. The EJB container provider is required to provide transaction support, security, and persistence.

Application Assembler

An application assembler integrates EJB classes (i.e. building blocks of the application) with Java applets, servlets, and GUI clients to build an EJB application. The assembly of enterprise beans involves the enterprise beans' interfaces rather than the beans' implementations. The application assembler might need to provide a GUI for the Web application.

Deployer

A deployer is primarily in charge of installing ejb-jar file into an EJB container, and adapting an EJB application to the target operation environment. The latter task involves modifying the properties of the enterprise beans, setting transaction and security policies by modifying the appropriate properties in the deployment descriptor, and integrating with enterprise management software.

System Administrator

A system administrator monitors the execution of the EJB application (e.g. keeping security information up-to-date, monitoring the performance of the server, etc.), and takes appropriate actions in the case of abnormal behavior of the application.

3.2 ENTERPRISE BEAN CONSTRUCTION

A primary objective of the EJB specification is to free application developers of enterprise applications from the infrastructure and system-level issues so they can focus on the application logic. To achieve this objective, EJB specification saves application developers from system-level programming, and separates the development of actual bean objects from development of their clients. The client of an enterprise bean may or may not exist in the same application.

Enterprise bean construction involves three major phases:

- Building enterprise beans
- Deploying enterprise beans
- Connecting to enterprise beans

3.2.1 Building Enterprise Beans
Each EJB provides three required classes:

- EJB implementation class
- EJB home interface
- EJB remote interface

There are two types of deployment descriptors: SessionDescriptors for Session EJBs and EntityDescriptors for Entity EJBs. An EJB deployment descriptor is a Java serialized object that extends the base deployment descriptor class. A deployment descriptor contains the following:

- Name of the EJB class
- Name of the EJB home interface
- Name of the EJB remote interface
- ACLs of entities authorized to use each class or method
- A list of container-managed fields (applies to entity beans)
- A value denoting whether the bean is stateless or stateful (applies to session beans)

Furthermore, a ".properties" file, which contains any environment properties that the bean expects to have at run-time, should be created. Another file called .manifest should also be created. The Java Archive (Jar) packager will add new entries to update the list of files in the directories in the manifest file automatically. For distribution of EJBs, a file called "ejb-jar" should be used.

3.2.2 Deploying the Enterprise Beans
For each EJB in an "ejb-jar" file, application developer should insert an entry in the "manifest" file. At deployment time, the EJB container reads ejb-jar file, creates implementations for the EJB home and remote interfaces, reads the deployment descriptor and ensures that bean has what it needs, and add the beans' property settings to the environment so that they are available to the bean at run-time.

3.2.3 Connecting to the Enterprise Beans
Clients can communicate with EJB through CORBA or RMI. In either approach, the client should find the EJB home interface in one of the following ways: (1) using Java Naming and Directory Interface (JNDI) to look up the EJB, or (2) Using CORBA Common Object Services (COS) naming service directly or via JNDI. The naming service returns to the client a reference to an object that implements the enterprise bean's home interface. The client uses the EJB object just like other objects.

That object serves as a factory of enterprise beans; creating the enterprise beans for the client and removing them when the client does not need those beans any more. The object is constructed at the time of deployment by the EJB host. The interface or proxy forwards messages to the enterprise bean as needed. The object implementing the EJB home interface works with the bean to initialize it.

The client invokes a method on the bean's interface home to get a reference to the bean's remote interface. The client contacts the bean's home interface to call the bean's lifecycle services for creating, finding, and destroying the bean's instances. The client obtains a reference to an object implementing the object's remote interface. Then the client invokes the methods that the EJB object makes public in the remote interface. The remote interface specifies the business methods provided by the enterprise bean, and lists the entire enterprise bean's methods or public interfaces that clients can call. The "class implementation" implements the functionality defined in both home and remote interfaces. When the client does not need the bean any more, it can call the remove() method on the home interface or on the remote interface.

3.3 AN OVERVIEW OF MICROSOFT TRANSACTION SERVER (MTS)

Microsoft Transaction Server (MTS) is the COM/DCOM-based server component model. MTS was introduced in 1996. It provides a language-independent in Windows-only computing environment for components to run in multi-tier client/server application architectures. MTS provides a framework that data management products can be plugged into. In addition, it provides a general description of a resource manager. Product vendors provide resource managers for their specific products. Any of the resource mangers will then be able to play within the distributed two-phase commit protocol. Furthermore, MTS also the ability to manage a database connection pool.

The next generation of MTS, called COM+, is delivered as a part of Windows 2000. COM+ combines MTS, COM and DCOM. COM+ promises to provide significant functionalities such as asynchronous components and an advanced event technology, and to improve load balancing in MTS.

3.4 EJB VERSUS MTS AND CORBA COMPONENTS

EJB and MTS are designed for developing server-side components. They both provide support for component-oriented transactions, declarative authorization, resource pooling, state management, and some other related services. The OMG CORBA Components (currently under development) will have the advantage of language neutrality over EJB, and the advantage of portability over MTS. However, EJB offers additional attractive features including the following:

- EJB is portable. The EJB transaction server concept allows scalability, reliability, load balancing, and atomic transactions of enterprise applications on various platforms. However, MTS is Windows-platform-dependent.

- EJB inherits attractive features of Java. As a result, EJB leads MTS in addressing security issues, which are critical in development of Web-based enterprise application.

- Development of applications using EJB does not involve creating and using Interface Definition Language (IDL) files. Consequently, applications using JavaBeans and EJB are easier to modify and maintain than those using CORBA, MTS, or other COM-based technologies are.

- Development of applications using EJB does not deal with transactional and security semantics in the bean implementation because the transaction and security rules for an EJB can be defined at assembly and deployment phases. The transaction semantics are defined declaratively through a bean's deployment descriptor rather than programmatically. The EJB server, on the behalf of its enterprise beans, manages the start, commit, and rollback of transactions. It does so according to a transaction attribute specified in the EJB deployment descriptor. Therefore, development of applications using EJB does not involve low-level system programming such as thread-aware programming. This will allow application developers to focus on the application logic and configuration environment rather than low-level system programming.

4. FINAL REMARKS

As described in this chapter, the adoption of component-based enterprise software development and component technologies expands the possibilities for component-based development of multi-tier Web-based enterprise applications.

All major component technologies are rapidly evolving to become more powerful. Each component technology offers a different set of features. For instance, ActiveX and MTS are Windows-platform-dependent and language-independent. Furthermore, ActiveX and MTS still lag JavaBeans and EJB in terms of security support. Considering the platform-dependency and security features of ActiveX and MTS, the COM-based component model is the most suitable for component-based development of Web-based applications that run over Intranet with a network of only Microsoft Windows-platforms.

On the other hand, JavaBeans and EJB together extend the power and benefits of Java attractive features to component-based development of Web-based enterprise applications that are portable, scalable, maintainable, extensible, flexible, and more secure. Furthermore, JavaBeans and EJB can be integrated with Jini, JavaSpaces, Java servlets, other Java-based technologies, and eXtensible Markup Language (XML) to develop a wide variety of Web-based enterprise applications.

The key to development of robust Web-based enterprise applications is to make the most of all the leading component technologies (i.e. JavaBeans, EJB, ActiveX, and MTS), and to properly integrate these component technologies to build multi-tier robust Web-based enterprise applications. This requires a good understanding of all these component technologies and experience in combining them to develop enterprise solutions.

References

1. P. Allen and S. Frost, "Component-Based Development for Enterprise Systems," Cambridge University Press, 1998.
2. S. Asbury and S. Weiner, "Developing Java Enterprise Applications," Wiley, 1999.
3. L. Bass, P. Clements, and R. Kazman, "Software Architecture in Practice," Addison-Wesley, 1998.
4. C. Berg, "Advanced Java Development for Enterprise Applications," Prentice Hall, 1999.
5. D. Box, "Essential COM," Addison Wesley, 1998.
6. D. Callaway, "Inside Servlets," Addison Wesley, 1999.
7. D. Chappell, "ActiveX and OLE," Microsoft Press, 1996.
8. A. Denning, "ActiveX Controls Inside Out," Microsoft Press, 1997.
9. R. Englander, "Developing Java Beans," O'Reilly, 1997.
10. A. Ghosh, "E-Commerce Security: Weak Links, Best Defenses," Wiley, 1999.
11. D. Govoni, "Java Application Frameworks," Wiley, 1999.
12. T. Jell, "Component-Based Software Engineering," Cambridge University Press, 1998.
13. H. Jubin, "JavaBeans by Example," Prentice Hall, 1998.
14. H. Kern, R. Johnson, S. Galup, D. Horgan, and M. Cappel, "Building the New Enterprise," Prentice-Hall, 1998.
15. G. McGraw and E. Felten, "Securing Java," Wiley, 1999.
16. G. McGraw and E. Felten, "Java Security," Wiley, 1997.
17. B. Meyer, "On To Components," *IEEE Computer*, Vol. 32, No.1, January 1999, pp. 139-140.
18. B. Meyer, "The Significance of Components," *Software Development*, Vol. 7, No. 11, November 1999, pp. 56-57.

19. B. Meyer, "Reusable Software: The Best Object-Oriented Component Libraries," Prentice Hall, 1998.

20. B. Meyer, "Object-Oriented Software Construction, Second Edition," Prentice Hall, 1997.

21. B. Orfali and D. Harkey, Client/Server Programming with Java and CORBA, Wiley, 1998.

22. J. Penix, B. Fischer, J. Whittle, G. Pour, and J. VanBaalen, "Automating Component Integration for Web-Based Data Analysis Applications," *IEEE Aerospace Conference: Gateway to 21st Century Technology*, IEEE CS Press, to appear, March 2000.

23. D. Platt, "Essence of COM with ActiveX," Prentice Hall, 1998.

24. A. Pope, "The CORBA Reference Guide," Addison-Wesley, 1998.

25. G. Pour, "Component-Based Development of 3-Tier Web-Based Enterprise Applications for Manufacturing," *World Automation Conference (WAC) 2000*, Maui, Hawaii, to appear, June 2000.

26. G. Pour, "EJB Server Component Model: New Opportunity for Development of Distributed Enterprise Applications," *Software Development*, to appear, January-February 2000.

27. G. Pour, "Integrating Component-Based Enterprise Application Development into Software and Information Engineering Curriculum," *Frontiers in Education (FIE) Conference*, ASEE, San Juan, Puerto Rico, to appear, November 1999.

28. G. Pour, G. and J. Xu, "JavaBeans, Java, Java Servlets, and CORBA Revolutionizing Web-Based Enterprise Application Development," *Proc. World Conference of the WWW, Internet, and Intranet (WebNet)*, Honolulu, Hawaii, October 1999.

29. G. Pour, "Enterprise JavaBeans, JavaBeans and XML Expanding Possibilities for Web-Based Enterprise Application Development," *31st International Conference on Technology of Object-Oriented Languages and Systems*, IEEE CS Press, Nanjing, China, September 1999.

30. G. Pour, "Java-Based Component Model for Enterprise Application Development," *Proc. 30th International Conference on Technology of Object-Oriented Languages and Systems (TOOLS USA)*, IEEE CS Press, August 1999.

31. G. Pour, "Quality Component Development: Making the Most of JavaBeans and Enterprise JavaBeans Features," *Proc. 30th International Conference on Technology of Object-Oriented Languages and Systems*, IEEE CS Press, Santa Barbara, CA, August 1999.

32. G. Pour, M. Griss and J. Favaro, "Making the Transition to Component-Based Enterprise Software Development: Overcoming the Obstacles - Patterns for Success," *Proc. 29th International Conference on Technology of Object-Oriented Languages and Systems (TOOLS EUROPE)*, IEEE CS Press, Nancy, France, June 1999.

33. G. Pour, "Developing Web-Based Enterprise Applications with Java, JavaBeans, and CORBA," *Proc. World Conference of the WWW, Internet, and Intranet (WebNet)*, Orlando, FL, November 1998.

34. G. Pour, "Moving Toward Component-Based Software Development Approach," *Proc. 27th International Conference on Technology of Object-Oriented Languages and Systems (TOOLS ASIA)*, Beijing, China, IEEE CS Press, September 1998.

35. G. Pour, "Towards Component-Based Software Engineering," *Proc. 22nd International Computer Software & Applications Conference (COMPSAC)*, IEEE CS Press, Vienna, Austria, August 1998.

36. G. Pour, "Component-Based Software Development: New Opportunities and Challenges," *Proc. 26th International Conference on Technology of Object-Oriented Systems and Languages (TOOLS USA)*, IEEE CS Press, Santa Barbara, CA, August 1998.

37. G. Pour, "Component-Based Software Development: Is It the Next Silver Bullet?," *Workshop, Proc. 26th International Conference on Technology of Object-Oriented Systems and Languages (TOOLS USA)*, IEEE CS Press, Santa Barbara, CA, August 1998.

38. G. Pour, "JavaBeans, Java, and CORBA Expanding Web-Based Enterprise Application Development," *Proc. International Workshop on Advanced Software Technology in the 21st Century*, IEEE CS Press, Santa Clara, CA, March 1998.

39. J. Savit, S. Wilcox and B. Jayaraman, *Enterprise Java*, McGraw Hill, 1998.

40. M. Shaw and D. Garlan, "Software Architecture: Perspectives on an Emerging Discipline," Prentice Hall, 1996.

41. R. Sessions, "COM and DCOM: Microsoft's Vision for Distributed Objects," Wiley, 1998.

42. E. Roman, "Mastering Enterprise JavaBeans and the Java 2 Platform," Enterprise Edition, Wiley, 1999.

43. A. Thomas, "Enterprise JavaBeans Technology: Server Component Model for Java Platform," *http://java.sun.com/products/ejb/white_paper.html*, December 1998.

44. T. Valesky, "Enterprise JavaBeans: Developing Component-Based Distributed Applications," Addison Wesley, 1999.

45. A. Vogel and M. Rangarao, "Programming with Enterprise JavaBeans, JTS and OTS: Building Distributed Transactions with Java and C++," Wiley, 1999.

PART II

INTERNET TOOLS

Chapter 7

BUILDING INTERNET-BASED COLLABORATIVE MULTIMEDIA APPLICATIONS WITH PLUG-AND-PLAY COMPONENTS

Lidia Fuentes and Jose M. Troya

Abstract

MultiTEL is a compositional framework for developing collaborative multimedia applications, and also designates a Web-based distributed platform that supports inter-component communication. In this chapter, we show how compositional and coordination paradigms can be successfully applied to design cooperative Java applications with multimedia data exchange. We focus on multimedia and network architectures, which define generic and specific components coordinated by connectors for resolving the resource management needs of distributed and collaborative applications. MultiTEL platform performs the dynamic composition of application components providing mechanisms for building services with plug-and-play transport and multimedia resources. We illustrate our proposal with a case study.

1. INTRODUCTION

The World Wide Web and private Intranets are increasingly perceived as the natural way for accessing Internet services, specially multimedia and cooperative services. This kind of applications requires distributed access and processing which is not directly supported by Web technologies. Recent works tries to overcome this deficit by developing distributed component platforms supporting the coordination of distributed components.

Therefore, multimedia and cooperative services might be supported by an open distributed platform that must solve component communication, isolating applications from multimedia and network management issues. Consequently, an important development aim for collaborative multimedia applications is the integration of them into a Web-based distributed platform. Currently, there are several approaches that aid the design of multimedia applications over the Web, but most of them only address the integration of moving images into Web pages [1].

The Sun proposal is the Java Media Framework (JMF) API as a collection of classes that enable the synchronization, display and capture of time-based data within Java applications and applets [2]. JMF offers a multi-platform framework for multimedia programming, although hardware device control and predefined classes for multiparty collaboration are lacking in this API.

Furthermore, the most important project concerning the definition of distributed software architecture is the Telecommunication Intelligent Network Architecture (TINA) [3]. Although implementations of TINA complying with CORBA specifications exist, providing a complete environment for the design and development of multimedia telecommunication services remains an open issue [4]. The TINA second phase started recently in 1998 with the goal of achieving development of dynamic TINA components and TINA applications, which will enable TINA service offerings to fully benefit from by the TINA architectural framework [5].

On the other hand, the coordination paradigm has been applied widely to collaborative multimedia programming with several benefits [6]. By separating communication and computation into different entities we enable the linkage of components, like multimedia devices, in a dynamic and external manner without requiring changes to the components' code. However, the application of coordination and compositional paradigms is usually restricted to the synchronization and compression/decompression of multimedia data [7]. Thus, applying composition and coordination paradigms to collaborative applications could still be considered an open issue.

In this chapter, we will focus on the multimedia and the networking issues concerning a framework for multimedia services that we have called MultiTEL [8]. We also describe a distributed and compositional platform in Java that manages multimedia and networking resources used to help in the design of complete multimedia collaborative services [9]. It is an Internet-based infrastructure, which provides a mechanism that abstracts the details of communication and collaboration between components and their deployment sites, allowing the runtime composition of different multimedia products, chats or GUIs [10]. This echanism includes support for various network protocols, component location, and so forth.

The application level of a multimedia service is composed at runtime by service, multimedia and network components, which are retrieved as part of an applet class. The kernel of MultiTEL is an extensible platform that supports, the creation, deployment and management of multimedia applications in the Web and mechanisms for resource allocation (e.g., connection management, admission control, multimedia devices plugging, QoS mapping, etc.).

We consider that the main benefits of this approach are: (i) shorter system development time by using a complete multimedia collaborative framework; (ii) services can be built from components supplied by different vendors; (iii) services can be customized in accordance with user preferences and local resources; (iv) dynamic composition of collaborative applications, allowing transport and multimedia resources plug-and-play; (v) services can be executed in heterogeneous networks, since they are implemented in Java.

This chapter is organized as follows. In Section 2 we will describe the compositional technology used in the development of the MultiTEL framework. In Section 3 we then describe the Service, Multimedia and Network architectures of MultiTEL, showing the functionality of the base components and connectors that define the skeleton of a multimedia application. In Section 4 we show the common services offered by the MultiTEL kernel, that is, application configuration and execution and the dynamic plug-and-play of multimedia devices. Finally, in Section 5 we explain how to construct multimedia services with MultiTEL and also how to extend a service with new functionality without modifying service components. The example we present is *TeleUni* an educational service for teaching and learning.

2. MULTITEL COMPOSITIONAL TECHNOLOGY

Recent advances in distributed software engineering lead to platform independent distributed component-based software. Component platforms like DCOM [11] or JavaBeans allow the construction of independent software components which can further be assembled via application-level frameworks. They provide an excellent infrastructure for dealing with multimedia and collaborative applications problems like the programmability, portability, maintainability and reusability, important issues that could determine the success of a product. For instance, the World Wide Web and Java have successfully demonstrated how current technology can support sharing information and applications among large dispersed groups.

In this section, we present an overview of MultiTEL compositional framework implemented in the Java language. Components, implemented as Java objects, will run on a distributed platform that uses Java/RMI and Web services for inter-component communication. In the beginning, we attempted to develop an open service model that reflected, at the design level, the collaboration and synchronization that must take place between service components. We have found that compositional models that place coordination and data processing in different components, are a good approach. Perhaps the main benefits of component-oriented technology for multimedia programming are the dynamic composition of multimedia devices as components developed by different manufacturers. In addition, this reuse technology provides components with standard interfaces that can be easily connected to make a new multimedia application.

2.1 COMPOSITIONAL MODEL

The MultiTEL framework includes the implementation of a compositional model in Java, which is the basis of the architecture of the derived multimedia applications. This model is described more fully elsewhere [8]. The first level entities are the components which model real entities like multimedia devices and the connectors which implement communication protocols between two or more components, for instance the reproduction of multimedia data. Since the main goal of this model is the integration of heterogeneous and distributed components as part of the same multimedia application components do not contain components/connectors references, they report the status changes by the propagation of an event. Composition of components and connectors is performed dynamically by a global configuration object called USP. We are going to describe these three aspects of our model in the following subsections.

2.1.1 Components

Components are passive entities characterized by the complete ignorance of how propagated events influence the execution of a particular multimedia service. In our approach we provide collaboration transparency through event selective broadcasting in which a conference connector □ by catching events □ can synchronize independent instances of components according to the application coordination protocol. In fact, those events that are not considered relevant to the service are discarded by the platform, allowing the plugging of legacy code into applications.

The implementation of a component (the *Component* base class) encapsulates the *event()* method, which is invoked by the descendant component classes for the throwing of events. This method delegates an event to a global configuration class (USP described later), thus components' code does not contain method invocations of any external entity (in our model the connectors). Since components do not contain references to other system entities, they might be reused in any context like COTS. The target application only has to provide the appropriate connectors for event handling.

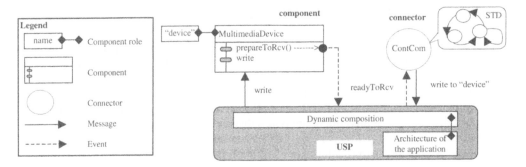

Figure 1. Components and connectors model. Dynamic composition.

2.1.2 Connectors

Alternatively, connectors are abstractions of coordination patterns which implement coordination protocols. By handling the events propagated by external components a connector can control the execution of any component. Connectors encapsulate the state transition diagram (STD) of a protocol that is triggered by component's events. The implementation of the connectors' protocols follows the *State* design pattern [12]. Since connectors control the execution of a group of components they may create or delete components or connectors, altering dynamically the application architecture.

The connector base class implements the *catchEvent()* method which uses the Reflect packet of Java for event method invocation. The inspection requirement for Internet components is easily achieve by the reflection capability provided by the Java language.

In Figure 1 the *readyToRcv* event propagated by a *MultimediaDevice* component is caught by the *ContCom* connector which responds by sending the *write* message to the component identified inside the application architecture by the name *"device"*. Events and messages are sent in independent threads allowing the concurrent manipulation of components (like GUIs) and connectors.

2.1.3 Dynamic Composition

The third and most important class defined by the middleware platform is the USP (User-Service Part) class. The USP class is the core of the middleware framework performing the application dynamic composition and providing useful application services. As shown in Figure 1, the USP intercepts both events and messages and gives them to the corresponding target entities. USP's methods and its internal attributes can be classified in the following categories:

- *Service parameters.* This class contains the initial values of global parameters and components/connectors parameters. These values are assigned in the configuration phase (explained later) and stored in USP's local structures. In this way, connectors can create components or other connectors without knowing constructor's parameters. After creation components/connectors will look for their attribute's initial values at the USP.

- *Service architecture.* One of the main problems in application frameworks is that the framework architecture disappears in the large number of framework classes. MultiTEL separates the framework architecture from the reusable components and connectors and explicitly specifies the component-connector connections inside this global configuration class. The service architecture (SA) defines the links that may be established during application execution. It is implemented as USP data structures that store information about how to plug components into connectors. The designer has to set up the SA by supplying information for event handling and message passing.

- *Application Context.* The application context (AC) is formed by the components and connectors, which were bound for a particular distributed application. The role of the AC is to delimit the binding region in which components and connectors are searched during the object selection process — target components for messages and connectors for events. AC members are spread all over the MultiTEL platform, so the references placed in it may be local or remote. Initially, the USP creates the components and connectors that initiate the application execution.

- *USP-USP communication.* Users of the same distributed application (e.g. a videoconference) collaborate and share information through their USP objects. USPs can communicate themselves by Java/RMI. RMI enables the programmer to create distributed Java-to-Java applications, in which the methods of remote Java objects can be invoked from another Java virtual machine. A USP has to collect both local and remote component messages and connector events, so it is implemented as a remote object identified by a unique URL.

- *USP-Kernel communication.* MultiTEL kernel encapsulates the application development tools and manages user local resources (i.e. multimedia and network resources). MultiTEL applications reside in a home machine which acts as a nexus for discovering the global list of application participants (the sites where AC's components and connectors reside). The USP needs the global list of participants — to locate components and connectors — which is held by the kernel of the application home machine. Since this information is dynamically updated with new users, the USP has to interchange information with the kernel periodically. The USP retrieves this information from the home kernel through its local kernel by RMI.

- *Event handling.* Dynamic composition is performed according to the propagation of events. This class encapsulates the *event()* method invoked by local components. When a USP object receives a request to catch an event, it looks up in the SA and in the current AC, which connector is supposed to handle the propagated event. Lastly, the USP calls the *catchEvent()* method of the target connector by a simple or RMI call.

- *Message delivery.* The USP also implements methods for message passing from connectors to components as well as for message broadcasting. Connectors may send messages to components by using three different versions of the USP's *sendMessage()* method. With the first version a connector has to provide the class name of the target components, the second one requires a component role name and the last one is used when the connector knows the component object reference.

MultiTEL platform not only supports the dynamic creation and composition of reusable components, it also acts as a distributed framework for integrating new components into itself. In addition, the USP is able to modify its internal structures for adding external components created inside the local kernel, making possible the component plug-and-play. Another consequence of this is that developers can mix and match components from different vendors wrapped with MultiTEL components or connectors. We will go deeply into this feature in Section 4.2.

2.2 MULTITEL PLATFORM ARCHITECTURE

The MultiTEL platform is structured in two different levels: application components that are dynamically composed at runtime; and a middleware platform that provides common services for controlling multimedia data delivery (see Figure 2). The first one is divided in the following two parts:

- *Application Level (AL)*. Multimedia service execution is performed by the dynamic composition of service, multimedia and network components, which are retrieved from the network. Service components model the user interactions, that is, the service logic. These kinds of components are application dependent, therefore they are not considered part of the middleware platform. On the other hand, Multimedia and Network components mainly model multimedia devices and multicast connections. Since these components model the user's real resources, the local kernel must bind them. The USP object described above supports the mechanisms for the interactions between service, multimedia and network components that enable the basic communication process.

- *User-Service Part (USP)*. The USP object is an agent that represents a user inside a distribute application. Users join a collaborative application by running the corresponding USP applet class from a browser. By loading USP applets embedded in HTML documents across the network, we also retrieve all the required classes from the net. Users interact with the application through a USP component, which represents the local service access point. This object encapsulates the application architecture, which drives the dynamic composition of the distributed components. Besides this, it is able to modify its internal structures for adding external components, making possible the component plug-and-play.

The third level is the kernel of the middleware platform:

- *Kernel*. It includes tools for sharing and running applications over the Web. One of its components is the *Resource Manager,* which acts as a mediator between application components and users' local resources. The *Application Directory* is a common service component that shows and manages the list of registered applications.

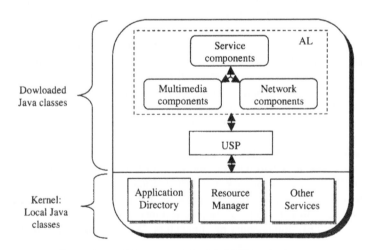

Figure 2. Architecture of the MultiTEL platform.

Figure 2 shows the architecture of a running application inside a computer for one participant of a collaborative service.

3. APPLICATION COMPONENTS

We present an MTS architecture that is based on component orientation and distributed computing, which provides flexibility for designing and operating services over a wide variety of network and multimedia technologies. This vision implies a software architecture that offers reusable software components, eases service construction and hides from the service designer the details of underlying technologies and the complexity of collaboration patterns. Similar to other approaches like TINA-C [3] we have divided the architecture into three main subsystems: Service, Multimedia and Network.

3.1 SERVICE COMPONENTS

Service architecture defines the "service logic", that is, the definition of the user interaction models which are specialized for specific services. However, in this work, we only present Multimedia and Network subsystems, which are closely related to the management of resources.

The principal actors involved in the service provisioning process are the *Organizer*, the *Manager* and the *Participant* of a service, which are modeled as service components. They constitute the main part of the Service subsystem.

- *Organizer.* When an operator wants to resell a service to her/his customers, she must join the service as organizer. The organization service of MultiTEL allows the customization of generic multimedia applications according to the organizer's preferences and to her/his own resources. The organizer may specify component or connector parameters for resource reservation, name and resource mapping or media stream protocol selection.

- *Participant.* A simple participant can receive video and audio from the service provider (centralized applications) or from other participants (collaborative applications). The participant component is composed by subcomponents (*InComponents*) that are dynamically added according to the service logic. Each subcomponent encapsulates a specific GUI for user interaction like an audio or video control panel. However, she/he will only send multimedia data when the service logic allows it. This control is performed by a specific connector which catches user input events and reports them to the other users.

- *Manager.* The manager is a specialization of a participant component and is in charge of starting and managing organized services. In multi-party services, the manager component includes *InComponents* with control panels for access control, service scheduling or resource renegotiations.

Base components and connectors that constitute the Service architecture of the framework are not included here, but we will illustrate how to use them for the development of a videoconference service in Section 5.

3.2 MULTIMEDIA COMPONENTS

The compositional Multimedia architecture has to deal with several evolutionary processes like changes in the hardware for multimedia applications, performance evolution, or new data representations for image, audio, video and other media types. Developers want to create applications that can adapt to and take advantage of changes in platform functionality, new compression formats and so on, and also that can be executed in heterogeneous environments.

Compositional frameworks offer mechanisms for incorporating these changes into the programming environment in a quick and secure way. Moreover, the dynamic binding of our compositional model makes it possible for these changes to be incorporated into applications at runtime.

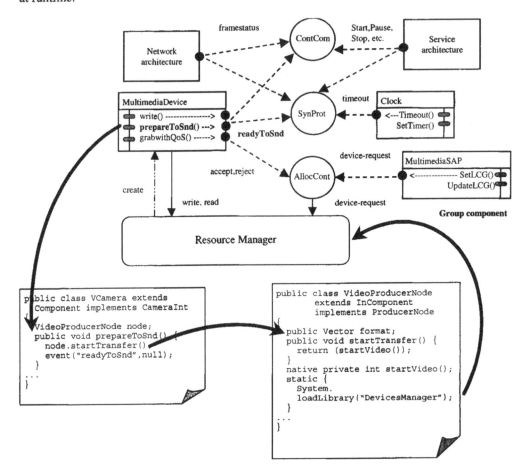

Figure 3. Multimedia architecture and implementation issues.

The full Multimedia architecture appears in Figure 3, but shows only the event throwing. Multimedia devices are modeled as components while connectors encapsulate the coordination protocols that specify the dynamic relationships among them. A multimedia device (*MultimediaDevice*) has many nodes, where each node contains a set of format components that represent the media that the component understands. Multimedia devices are arranged in a component hierarchy of 'producers', 'consumers' and 'files devices' where each one encapsulates a control panel as an *InComponent*. During operation, device components generate a variety of events that could be of application interest or not. In fact, connecting components to connectors implies that the application is registering relevant events that will be caught by the appropriate event handlers (connectors).

Components and connectors are transferred as Java applets, since they are platform independent, except for those whose implementation depends strongly on the client system. For instance, the implementation of a multimedia device component changes with the platform but it always throws the same events. The architecture dynamically reconfigures its multimedia devices according to the kernel of clients' environments. Furthermore, nodes are

InComponents that encapsulate the native code, that is, kernel dependent programs, for controlling data reading or writing.

Native components and connectors are managed by the *Resource Manager* (RM), which offers a standard common interface to collaborative services. A partial implementation of a camera device (*VCamera* class) is shown in Figure 3. Following the arrows you can see how the *prepareToSnd()* method causes the invocation of the native method *startVideo()* defined inside the RM for camera initialization. After that, the *VCamera* component propagates the *readyToSnd* event by calling the *event()* method of the *Component* base class.

The organizer of a service specifies multimedia device requirements by providing a logic connection graph (LCG) as a parameter of the service. In Section 4 we illustrate a LCG example showed in Figure 10. Then, during the resource allocation process, the local kernel translates the global parameters into specific hardware or software device parameters. The *AllocCont* connector, in accordance the local user's resources and QoS requirements, controls the allocation of devices, which is negotiated for each participant. The *AllocCont* extracts the connection information of a participant from the global LCG initiating the resource allocation phase. It negotiates the device's format and tries to allocate all the requested devices.

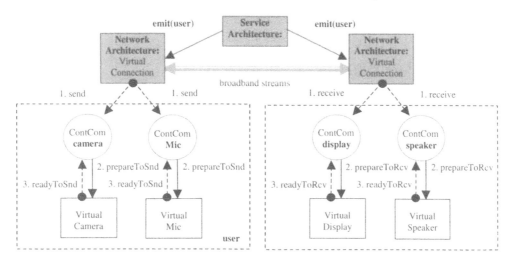

Figure 4. Preparing devices for data transmission.

However, there are some situations in which is desirable to get together service users with different levels of resource and access. For those situations we have defined three versions of this connector. The first version rejects the admission of participants that do not have the required devices. A weak version of it accepts any participant independently of their resources. Finally, we have an intermediate version that accepts participants that only have a predefined subset of devices (e.g., microphone and loudspeaker). In consequence, designers may include participants with heterogeneous multimedia devices in the same collaborative application.

A *MultimediaDevice* is plugged, at architectural level, into a *ContCom* connector that encapsulates data control commands (Start, Pause, etc.). Connections between multimedia devices are established by the *Network* architecture that will be explained below. The *ContCom* connector contains the STD for sender (e.g. microphone), receiver (e.g. speaklouder) and sender/receiver (e.g. textual chat) devices.

Figure 4 shows the sequence of actions (events and messages) for preparing user participation. The emission process begins as soon as the *Service* architecture broadcasts an *emit* message to all the *VirtualConnection* components. The devices of the speaker's machine are prepared for emission and the rest of the conference audience has to be prepared for data receiving. The *ContCom* connectors of a participant catch the *send* event and initiate the corresponding protocol actions for device preparation. This connector is also created by the RM according to the type of the multimedia device component.

On the other hand, components that are subject to real-time constraints are plugged into a *SynProt* connector type instead of into a *ContCom* one. It encapsulates the synchronization of frames that are delivered concurrently, by two or more *MultimediaDevice* components.

The *MultimediaSAP* is a global component that encapsulates all the multimedia resources of one service session. Usually it is located in the service manager machine since it initiates and finalizes the service. For collaborative services, in which subsets of participants maintain private side-band conference sessions, the application creates a *MultimediaSAP* component for representing each subsession. For instance, in an education service (*TeleUni* service presented in Section 5) the lecturer might form discussion groups which are private conferences represented by *MultimediaSAP* components which encapsulate the LCG of the private subsessions.

3.3 NETWORK COMPONENTS

The Network architecture defines a set of components and connectors for the management and reservation of broadband multimedia channels (see Figure 5). Apart from inter-component communication, which is resolved by MultiTEL platform, media transport is required for the distribution of media streams. Since different services may require different transport protocols we separate the transport function from the general logic of the service which affords us the flexibility of building services with plug-and-play transport.

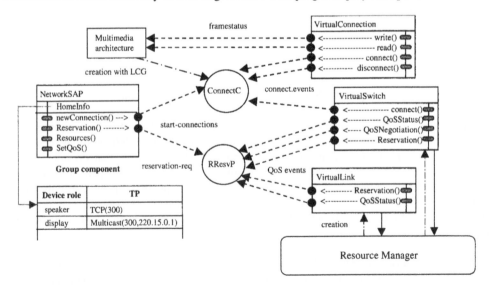

Figure 5. Network architecture.

VirtualSwitch and *VirtualLink* base components define a common interface for making broadband stream reservations with QoS requirements. They access user local resources by invoking the appropriate primitives implemented at the RM. For instance, services may use the RTP/RSVP protocols by only adding the *VirtualSwitch* and *VirtualLink* components that perform RSVP [13] reservations and create RTP [14] sessions. The control information about RTP packet transmission rate collected by the RTCP protocol is sent to the *RResvP* connector who may modify the initial reservation of network resources. This connector encapsulates the resource re-negotiation politics for each participant.

Multicast and unicast connections are modeled by specific components inheriting the *VirtualConnection* base component type. We have implemented different versions of the *VirtualConnection* component; one of them uses the Multicast classes defined in the java.net packet of the Java language. These components define a common standard interface for setup and release transport connections.

An external connector (*ConnectC*) controls the *VirtualConnection* components, that is, mediates between multimedia components and the network platform. The role of the *ConnectC* connector is controlling the connection setup procedures between local devices and the rest of participants and it also handles disconnections initiated by the network.

The *NetworkSAP* component provides a single point of access for the Service architecture handling the join requests of new participants and coordinating the creation/reservation of network resource components. *VirtualConnection* components publish the media transport information of producer devices like the transport protocol and port. This information is stored in a generic structure (*HomeInfo*) that may hold any kind of media stream protocol (e.g., Figure 5 shows the *HomeInfo* information for a loudspeaker that used TCP connections and a display software device which receives video data through a multicast stream).

Figure 6 shows the sequence of adding a new participant. The joining process begins when the Multimedia architecture orders the *ConnectC* creation. Following this, an instance of the corresponding *VirtualConnection* component is created and plugged into the downloaded service by adding it to the user's USP. The *ConnectC* connector provides the *VirtualConnection* component with the necessary information for initiating the connection setup process and waits for the *connectReady* event. At this point in time, the rest of service participants must be told to add or modify their connections. Since the *NetworkSAP* component encapsulates all the network resources of one service, it will propagate an *addUser* event to every instance of the *ConnectC* connector, which will control its local connection setup process.

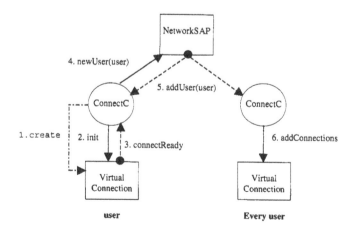

Figure 6. A new user joining a videoconference.

4. MULTITEL KERNEL

Common services related to component-connector communication, network and multimedia resource management and application execution are part of a middleware platform (see Figure 2). This platform includes common services for looking up and downloading components, connectors and applications across the network. With MultiTEL, service providers may offer generic services to service operators instead of to final users. Operators can adapt a multimedia application by configuring some service parameters, by using the Application Directory (AD) tool. The AD is a common service that provides an application searching engine over the Web. Besides, the Resource Manager (RM) provides a standard interface for the allocation and control of local resources from generic services. This object links multimedia device components to a running application by applying a plug-and-play mechanism.

4.1 APPLICATION CONFIGURATION

Access to and execution of MultiTEL collaborative applications is performed through the AD tool, which stores and displays the list of local and remote applications that are being offered by the entire platform. MultiTEL applications and machines may be distributed throughout the platform by hierarchical domains following the Internet principle. Each machine inside a domain is responsible for its local components, connectors and applications.

Besides this, there is one machine per domain that is defined as a gateway to other domains. Thereby, we imitate the subnetting internetworking of the Internet. For a gateway, a "routing table" exists that instructs the gateway as to which other domains it has to forward the requests. Thus, the distribution structure can be statically or dynamically configured, the same as in the IP protocol of the Internet (see Figure 7). This tool stores and displays the name of each available application, a string describing the service it offers, and a miscellany field. The latter stores general information that is relevant to a specific application, for instance, the date and time scheduled to initiate this service.

```
Service = { Name, Description, Miscellany, state, URL, AdvanceInformation }
```

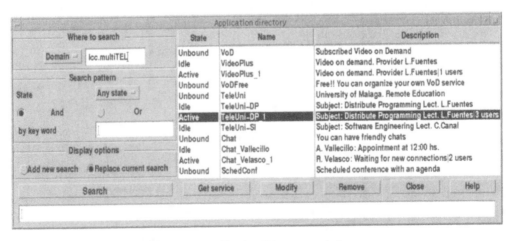

Figure 7. Application Directory window.

The state field values can be *unbound*, *idle* or *active*. Unbound services are incomplete applications that will be configured by an operator customer for re-selling purposes; idle services are ready to be executed; active services are those currently running on one or several machines. The AD also implements a search engine that accepts queries about application services based in any of these fields.

4.1.1 Generic service configuration

An organizer is a potential operator who buys a generic service, adapts it to her/his resources and preferences, and finally offers it to final customers. The configuration of generic services involves mapping logical names to physical names, and setting parameter values.

We have defined the script language LCF for describing the configuration of generic services. The organization connector interprets this input configuration file and asks a customer for parameter values. When a service configuration has finished we obtain an output file with all the parameters bound to a concrete value. The USP will load this file which will be consulted by connectors for component-connector creation purposes. The following example corresponds to the configuration of the educational TeleUni service for Distributed Programming subject. These configuration parameters are stored in the TeleUni-DP.cnf file.

```
set parties multicast
set manager, conference_program "http://sgi9.lcc.uma.es/TeleUni"
set conference_program local
set NetworkSAP remote
...
put text "Logic connections" parname multimediaSAP::lcg
                           value="http://sgi10.lcc.uma.es/vc.lcg"
if role=manager
     put text "Network Quality of Service" parname networkSAP::qos
     value="best-effort"
     default "best-effort" in "best-effort", "guaranteed"
...
```

First, the *set parties* sentence states that a videoconference is a multi-party application. After that, the organizer uses the *set* statement to map component and connector logical names to physical names. A component may be searched at runtime by the USP in a location identified with an URL or in a local or remote machine. The purpose of the *put* statement is to set values to component parameters. In the example we show the configuration of the *lcg* parameter of the *multimediaSAP* component with a filename and the *qos* parameter of the *networkSAP* component with the *best-effort* value. The organizer may use the *if* sentence for specifying different levels of application users according to their roles allowing heterogeneous configuration of participants.

```
<HTML>
<applet code=java.apps.TeleUni width=640 height=480
<param name=file value=TeleUni-DP.cnf>
<param name=role value=manager>
<param name=manager value=lidia_fuentes>
</applet>
</HTML>
```

Figure 8. HTML file for running a configured service (TeleUni).

Finally, we are going to illustrate the configuration and execution of a collaborative multimedia application for the TeleUni service. The first step for launching the TeleUni service, is to publish it in the Web, using the AD. The initial state of the service is unbound. The organization or configuration phase will start when someone picks its entry in the AD. After that, it must be configured by an organizer, the lecturer in this example, which registers it in the idle state (see entry TeleUni-DP in Figure 7). After the execution of the organization service MultiTEL kernel generates the HTML file TeleUni-DP.html that users will run from a browser (Figure 8). See that the TeleUni-DP.cnf configuration file appears as one of the parameters of the HTML file. The java.apps.TeleUni applet is the USP class of the generic service TeleUni personalized by the TeleUni-DP.cnf parameters.

Then, the application, a virtual classroom about Distributed Programming, is ready for execution. The lecturer initiates a session, which provokes the addition of an active entry (see entry *TeleUni-DP_1* in Figure 7). Then, students can enter the classroom by clicking in the active entry. The execution of the application implies the download of the TeleUni USP class and the initial components and connectors code.

4.2 DEVICES PLUG-AND-PLAY

The role of the *Resource Manager* (RM) is the management of multimedia and network resources in MultiTEL. Multimedia devices and switching components are local to the client machine therefore they can not be shared or downloaded from the network, like other service components. In addition, it is also desirable that multimedia groupware applications adapt to performance differences on a given platform, such as different hardware devices, device access times, display capabilities and resource reservation protocols. In consequence, we designate the RM for creating these kinds of components instead of using the USP. The RM behaves as a resource allocator because it mediates and arbitrates conflicting requests for resources made by various parties in the system.

Because the RM creates resource components following a common interface, a generic application is able to dynamically adapt its components to each participant's local resources, taking into account general constraints. It creates software and hardware devices' components with a requested data format where the hardware ones are associated with a hardware device.

The RM is implemented as a Java remote object accessed by RMI. Communication between the components of the application level and RM is performed through the USP object, which knows RM's remote reference. Although the RM is considered part of the MultiTEL platform, it is the only one that is machine dependent. However, adding only the native code of resource components, a version for each operating system can be produced.

There are a wide variety of multimedia devices from different vendors that can produce their own list of data formats. However, from the service designer's point of view there is a list of typical devices that could be part of a multimedia service architecture (e.g. camera, speaker, moviefile, etc.).

Bearing in mind the designer's viewpoint, MultiTEL tries to overcome the diversity of multimedia devices by defining standard interfaces and universally identifying the devices that could be part of a multimedia service. In order to plug a device component into a new multimedia application, designers only have to know the identifier and the corresponding Java interface, that is common to all MultiTEL users.

RM has a device database (*ResourceInfo*) containing MultiTEL hardware or software device information, which could be easily extended by adding new entries (see Figure 9). Each device identified by a name has an associated implementation class that implements a MultiTEL standard interface, which contains the native code for device manipulation.

Figure 9 shows information about a camera, identifying it as the hardware device class java.mm.VirtualCamera which is implementing the java.mm.CameraInterface interface. Usually, this implementation class calls a standard dynamic library of the service customer machine. For the Silicon Graphics the implementation class defines Java native methods that calls the corresponding "C" programs of SG Digital Media library.

Coming back to Figure 9, it shows how the RM plugs a camera, a speaker and a display window into an application controlled by a local USP. The Multimedia subsystem captures the list of the required devices by invoking the *captureDevices()* method of the RM through the USP indicating the global identifier of the devices (e.g. "camera"). The RM finds the implementation class of this device in the *ResourceInfo* table (e.g. "java.mm. CameraInterface"). After that, the RM invokes the *createDevComponent()* method of the local USP for setting the implementation class name that this object needs for component creation.

Afterwards, the device component is added to the USP application context of the client machine, that is, RM completes the device component plug-and-play. In consequence, MultiTEL designers do not need to know the implementation class of this component, which is dynamically bound by the local RM. *VirtualDisplay, Virtual Speaker* or *VirtualCamera* components have nodes which encapsulate the native methods (like vlOpenVideo() in Figure 9), but externally are considered as common components.

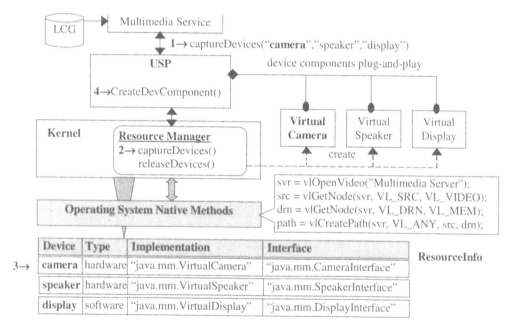

Figure 9. Resource Manager implementation.
Sequence of actions for device component plug-and-play.

MultiTEL defines a standard hierarchy of multimedia device interfaces that must be implemented by all the devices of the same type (device identifier). We use the reflective package of Java for checking whether a Java implementation class provides the desired service and propagates the correct events.

Device reservation is configured as a logic connection graph (LCG) that is provided by the service organizer as a *MultimediaSAP* parameter in the LCF script. The LCG defines the devices and connections that will be established for each participant role or name. There are some typical interaction models such as the Star or Fully-connected patterns. Figure 10 shows the list of devices with a QoS that may be allocated to the user having the *lff@lcc.uma.es* e-mail.

```
user = "1ff@lcc.uma.es"
role = "S/R"
devices = { ("camera",("size","xy","320,240")),
        ("screen",("size","xy","320,240")),
        ("speaker",("channels","integer","2"),
        ("samplingrate","integer","44100")),
        ("microphone,("channels","integer","2"),
        ("samplingrate","integer","44100"),
        ("chat",null)}
#Fully-connected pattern
connectTo = "all"
```

Figure 10. A logical connection graph example defining how to connect multimedia devices.

Network components are modeled, created and managed by the RM in a very similar way to multimedia components, therefore their description is not included in this article.

5. DESIGNING AND EXTENDING A VIDEOCONFERENCE SERVICE : A CASE STUDY

In this section we are going to show how to design a videoconference service and afterwards we are going to extend it with new features. We come back to the TeleUni example, which can be considered a videoconference service, since they allow multiple users to interact remotely and collaborate to do the same task. We start defining the roles of the service customers: the lecturer will act as the service manager and the students will be simple participants. We will focus our discussion on the design of the Service architecture, since the Multimedia and Network ones do not need to be extended for this service.

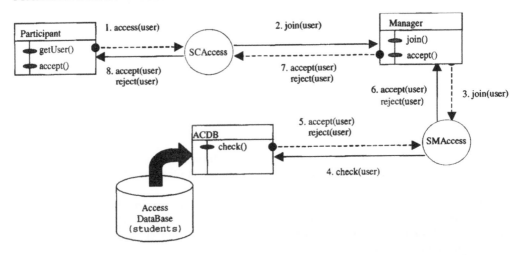

Figure 11. Component and connector architecture of the database access protocol.

5.1 DESIGNING THE TELEUNI SERVICE

First, we have to decide which kind of access protocol for restricting user admission will be used. MultiTEL offers several possibilities like *manager access protocol*, in which the manager decides whether a user can join the service, the *database access protocol*, where there is an access control database containing the users subscribed to a service. In TeleUni we will apply the latter, using the students database for access validation (the ACDB component encapsulates the list of subscribed students).

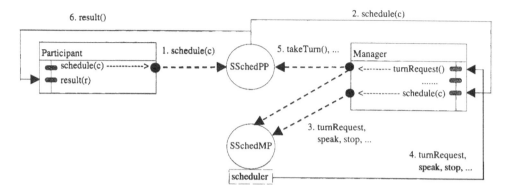

Figure 12. Component and connector architecture of the scheduling protocol.

The *SCAccess* connector processes the access parameters propagated from the participants inside events and asks the lecturer about her/his opinion. However, the decision is taken by the *SMAccess* connector, which encapsulates the decision criteria associated to the manager. Figure 11 shows the access architecture of TeleUni where the *SMAccess* connector's protocol handles the *join* event by consulting a component that models the access database inside the architecture. Accordingly, service provisioning begins with an access phase that controls the students who join TeleUni. The result of this phase will be acceptance or rejection.

```
public class VCManager extends Component {

    public void showSchedControl(){
        if(sched==null){
            try{
                    sched=new ScheduleFrame(usp,this);
                    sched.show();
            }catch(Exception e){
            System.out.println("Exception"+e);
            e.printStackTrace();
            }
        }
    }
    public void schedule(String command,String user){
        Object args[]={command,user};
        switch (command)  {
            case "turnRequest": event("turnRequest",args);
                                break;}
            ...
        }
    }
    public void turnRequest(String user){
        message("User "+user+" has requested the turn");
        Object args[]={user};
        if (/* Manager decision */)
            event("takeTurn",args);
        ...
    }
    ...
}
```

Figure 13. Implementation class of the Manager component.

Secondly, we have to choose the scheduling protocol. TeleUni involves a large number of participants with a model of interpersonal communication which determines the utility of the service. The scheduling says that the lecturer is speaking all the time, and the rest are simply listening until somebody makes or answers a question.

Figure 12 shows the service architecture of TeleUni with the scheduling components and connectors, and the sequence of actions (events and messages) for requesting a scheduling command. The *SSchedMP* connector knows which component has to make the decision about giving or not giving the turn to a participant. As shown in Figure 12, the manager component is the one who makes this decision, although this information is provided as the external parameter "scheduler". Later we will modify this architecture by adding an agenda for making scheduling decisions automatically.

The implementation of components and connectors are achieved by inheriting the corresponding Component and Connector classes. Figure 13 shows a partial implementation of the Manager component used in TeleUni. For components, user designers only have to define the input messages and the corresponding output events. Usually, components have a GUI which is controlled by the corresponding connector. The *showSchedControl()* method displays the schedule control panel (an *InComponent*) that is controlled by the *SSchedMP* connector which enables and disables the buttons, which represents manager commands, according to its internal protocol. Methods of components that provoke the propagation of an event end with a call to the *event()* method.

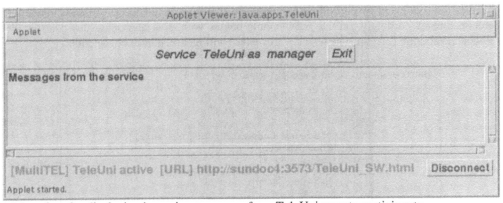

(a) Interface for displaying incoming messages from TeleUni remote participants.

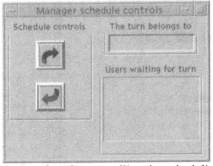

(b) Interface for controlling the scheduling

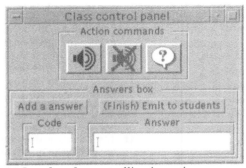

(c) Interface for controlling incoming answers

Figure 14. Manager interface in TeleUni service.

The Manager component can have up to three *InComponent* each one encapsulating a separated window (Figure 14).

The implementation of the connectors' protocols follows the State pattern [12], where each state is implemented as a class with a method for each input event. These methods are directly invoked by the *catchEvent()* method by using the Reflective package of Java. Figure 15 shows the Idle state implementation of the scheduling protocol used by the manager in TeleUni. At the beginning, this connector catches the start event ordering the creation of the remaining *InComponents* ((b) and (c) of Figure 14) by the Manager component.

Now, let's take the *turnRequest* event handled by this connector under the Idle state. The implementation of this method illustrates the use of the *sendMessage()* method of the USP. When somebody asks for speaking, the *SSchedMPTU1* connector sends a message to the **scheduler** component, which in this case is the lecturer who acts as a manager. Since **scheduler** is a service parameter that represents the target component that is in charge of making scheduling decisions, we will be able to change this component by only altering the value of this parameter.

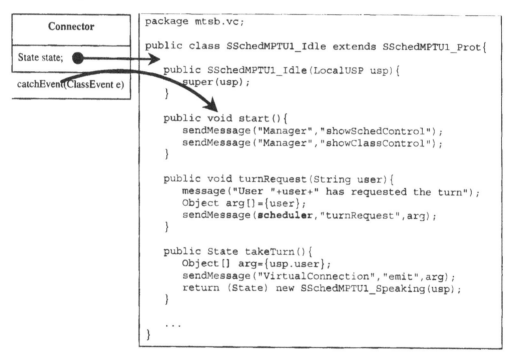

```
package mtsb.vc;

public class SSchedMPTU1_Idle extends SSchedMPTU1_Prot{
    public SSchedMPTU1_Idle(LocalUSP usp){
        super(usp);
    }

    public void start(){
        sendMessage("Manager","showSchedControl");
        sendMessage("Manager","showClassControl");
    }

    public void turnRequest(String user){
        message("User "+user+" has requested the turn");
        Object arg[]={user};
        sendMessage(scheduler,"turnRequest",arg);
    }

    public State takeTurn(){
        Object[] arg={usp.user};
        sendMessage("VirtualConnection","emit",arg);
        return (State) new SSchedMPTU1_Speaking(usp);
    }
    . . .
}
```

Figure 15. Implementation class of the Idle state of the SSchedMP connector protocol for the TeleUni service.

As soon as the manager decides to give the turn to a user by propagating the *takeTurn* event, this connector initiates the data transmission phase, by sending the emit message to the VirtualConnection components, as shown previously in Figure 4, and after that the connector's protocol changes to the Speaking state.

After gathering all the components and connectors needed to construct the TeleUni service, the designer has to compose the application with them, that is, she/he has to define and implement the USP class of the service. Figure 16 shows the main methods of a USP descendant class. First, TeleUni components are defined under the *defComponents()* method that is used to introduce component information needed by the USP classes. Relevant component information is the role name, localization information extracted from the configuration file included in Section 4.1 and the name of the implementation class.

```
package java.apps;

public class TeleUni extends ServiceUSP{

    public void defComponents(){
        component("Participant",{"participant,local","manager,remote"},
                                "mtsb.vc.TUParticipant");
        component("Manager",{"participant,remote","manager,local"},
                                "mtsb.vc.TUManager");
        component("ACDB",{"participant,local","manager,remote"},
                                "mtsb.vc.VCACDB");
        ...
    }
    public void defConnectors(){
        connector("SCAccess",{"participant,local","manager,remote"},
                                "mtsb.vc.SCAccess1");
        connector("SMAccess",{"participant,remote","manager,local"},
                                "mtsb.vc.SMAccess1");
        connector("SSchedPP",{"participant,local","manager,remote"},
                                "mtsb.vc.SSchedPP1");
        connector("SSchedMP",{"participant,remote","manager,local"},
                                "mtsb.vc.SSchedMPTU1");
        ...
    }
    public void loadConnections(){
        String[] events1={"join"};
        handlesEventsFrom("SMAccess",events1,"Manager");
        String[] events2={"access"};
        handlesEventsFrom("SCAccess",events2,"Participant");
        String[] events3={"accept","reject"};
        handlesEventsFrom("SCAccess",events3,"Manager");
        handlesEventsFrom("SMAccess",events3,"ACDB");
        String[] events6={"schedule"};
        handlesEventsFrom("SSchedPP",events6,"Participant");
        String[] events7={"missTurn","takeTurn","leftOverTime","goodbye"};
        handlesEventsFrom("SSchedPP",events7,"Manager");
        handlesEventsFrom("SSchedMP",events7,"Manager");
        String[] events8={"turnRequest","speak","stop","service","ask"};
        handlesEventsFrom("SSchedMP",events8,"Manager");
        String[] events10={"bye"};
        handlesEventsFrom("SSchedPP",events10,"Participant");
        handlesEventsFrom("SSchedMP",events10,"Manager");
        ...
    }
    public void participantInitialContext(){
        try{
            createComponent("Participant,SCAccess");
        }catch(Exception e){ System.out.println("InitialContext Error"); }
    }
    public void managerInitialContext(){
        try{
            createComponent("Manager, ACDB, SMAccess, SSchedMP, ...");

        } catch(Exception e){
            System.out.println("InitialContext Error ");e.printStackTrace();}
    }
    public void loadOrganizationParameters(){
        // Load value for the "scheduler" parameter of SSchedMP connector
    }
...
}
```

Figure 16. Partial implementation of the TeleUni service architecture.

For example, a component that plays the Participant role is considered as local for students' USP but remote from the manager point of view, and the implementation class is *mtsb.vc.TUParticipant*. We designate MultiTEL classes with universal identifiers, but if MultiTEL users have the component classes installed locally the browser will use local components instead of downloading the code from the home machine, making the loading and execution of the service more efficient. Likewise components, the *defConnectors()* method is used to introduce connector information.

Architectural connections are defined in the *loadConnections()* method, by specifying the list of events that a connector may catch and the role of the source component. The definition of the initial context for participants and the manager, event and method renaming and parameters initialization complete the implementation of the USP descendant class. According to the service architecture presented in Figure 12 we set the scheduler parameter with the "Manager" value. Figure 16 shows a partial implementation of the USP class including the access and the scheduling architecture.

5.2 EXTENDING THE TELEUNI SERVICE

Now, suppose that the lecturer demands new functionality to the TeleUni service. For instance, the lecturer wants to make questions to the students at the end of each lesson, but the students have to answer in a previously configured order. The solution adopted should be to design a new component that models an event agenda. The component *EventAgenda* is designed to store data structures with temporal scheduling events. Then, this component will automatically decide which student has the turn to speak.

```
package java.apps;

public class TeleUni_New extends TeleUni{

    public void defComponents(){
        ...
        component("EventAgenda",{"participant,remote","manager,local"},
                                "mtsb.vc.Agenda");
    }

    public void loadConnections(){
        ...
        String[] events1={"missTurn","takeTurn","leftOverTime","goodbye"};
        handlesEventsFrom("SSchedPP",events1,"EventAgenda");
    }

    public void managerInitialContext(){
        try{
            ...
            createComponent("EventAgenda");

        } catch(Exception e){
            System.out.println("InitialContext Error");e.printStackTrace();}
    }

    public void loadOrganizationParameters(){
        /* Load value EventAgenda for the "scheduler" parameter of
        SSchedMP connector */
    }
}
```

Figure 17. Extending the TeleUni service with an event agenda.

Our goal is to extend the functionality of the TeleUni service reusing all the components and connectors, that is, without changing components' or connectors' code. MultiTEL framework supports the black box mechanism extensibility by defining interfaces for components that can be plugged into the framework via object composition, which is achieved in MultiTEL by redefining architectural methods of the USP class.

Therefore, in this example we can achieve these changes by defining a new USP class and redefining the *defComponents()*, *loadConnections()*, *managerInitialContext()* and *loadOrganizationParameters()* methods. We reconfigure the architecture by introducing a new component *EventAgenda*, connecting it to the *SSchedPP* connector and setting the scheduler parameter of this connector with the *EventAgenda* role name.

We have derived different versions of multi-player games, VoD, collaborative games (*Pictionary*) and videoconference services, including Lectures like TeleUni, Conferences, and Business Meetings, and the time and effort spent in developing these services was significantly reduced compared with traditional approaches.

6. CONCLUSIONS

The design of multimedia cooperative applications requires an understanding of multimedia, network and collaboration issues. In this chapter, we have shown how compositional and coordination technologies facilitate to non expert users the building of multimedia collaborative applications, shortening the development time. Resulting applications will run over a Web-based platform, which resolves component-connector communication and transparently manages local user resources for applications. MultiTEL services support the coordination of users with heterogeneous multimedia or network resources, dynamically plugging in the adequate components and adapting them to user profiles.

The novel characteristics of the Java language, such as the reflective programming and RMI, have facilitated the implementation of MultiTEL, but unfortunately this language presents important drawbacks related to efficiency. This problem gets even worse when using native methods, slowing down the capture and presentation of audio/video frames. Nevertheless, with the new versions of JDK this problem tends to disappear.

The MultiTEL framework has been implemented in the Java language JVM 1.2.2 version and the native code in Digital Media Library (DM). The base platform has been ported to Solaris, Windows95/98 and IRIX-SG. The complete framework and platform stands at roughly 60,000 lines of Java code, including multimedia application code but excluding C native code of local resources components. The software is available freeware at *http://www.lcc.uma.es/~lff/ MultiTEL/* for researching and testing purposes.

References

1. K.H. Wolf, K. Froitzheim, and M. Weber, "Interactive Video and Remote Control via the World Wide Web," Lecture Notes in Computer Science No. 1045: Interactive Distributed Multimedia Systems and Services, March 1996, Berlin, Multimedia Systems and Services, March 1996.
2. Sun Microsystem, White Book of Java Media Framework. 1998.
3. TINA-C, "Overall Concepts and Principles of TINA," Deliverable TINA-C, February 1995.

4. T. Saridakis, C. Bidan, and V. Issarny, "A Programming System for the Development of TINA Services," *Proceedings. of the Open Distributed Processing and Distributed Platforms*, Chapman & Hall, May 1997, pp. 3-14.

5. H. Berndt and T. Hamada, "TINA: Present and Future," *IEEE Communications Surveys*, 1999.

6. K. Goldman et al., "The Programmer's Playground: I/O Abstraction for User-Configurable Distributed Applications," *IEEE Trans. Software Eng. J.*, Vol. 21, No. 9, 1995, pp. 735-746.

7. S. Gibbs, "Multimedia Component Frameworks," Object-Oriented Software Composition, Prentice Hall, Chapter 11, 1995, pp. 306-319.

8 . L. Fuentes and J.M. Troya, "MultiTEL : A Component-Oriented Framework in the Domain of Multimedia Telecommunication Services," A Chapter in the book *Object-Oriented Application Frameworks*, Wiley & Sons, 1999.

9. L. Fuentes and J.M. Troya, "Towards an Open Multimedia Service Framework," *Symposium on Object-Oriented Application Frameworks, ACM Computing Surveys*, December 1998.

10. L. Fuentes and J.M. Troya, "A Java Framework for Web-Based Multimedia and Collaborative Applications," *IEEE Internet Computing*, Vol. 3, No. 2, March/April 1999, pp. 52-61.

11. R. Sessions, "COM and DCOM: Microsoft Vision for Distributed Objects," John Wiley & Sons, 1997.

12. E. Gamma et al., "Design Patterns," Addison Wesley, Reading, Mass. 1995.

13. B. White, "RSVP and Integrated Services in the Internet: A Tutorial," *IEEE Communications Magazine*, pp. 100-106. May 1997.

14. H. Schulzrinne, "RTP. A Transport Protocol for Real-Time Applications," Request for Comments 1889, January 1996.

Chapter 8

COMPONENT WEB SEARCH ENGINES

Robert C. Seacord, Scott A. Hissam, and Kurt C. Wallnau

Abstract

Traditional, large-scale software repositories have historically failed, principally as a result of their conception as centralized systems. New and emerging technologies such as traders, brokers, location services and search engines have yet to be proven effective in the location and adoption of reusable software components. The COTS-Based Systems (CBS) Initiative at the Software Engineering Institute (SEI) developed the Agora software prototype to investigate the integration of search technology with component introspection to create a distributed, component repository. This chapter describes the objectives of this work, the features and capabilities of Agora, and the design and implementation of the prototype. Agora is positioned relative to existing products that provide similar services and the issues, tradeoffs and future evolution of the approach are discussed.

1. INTRODUCTION

Software developers welcome the emergence of a robust marketplace of software components, as a highly competitive marketplace works to the advantage of both producers and consumers of software components. However, two essential requirements for a component marketplace have been slow to emerge: standard, interchangeable parts, and the consumers' ability to find the right parts for the job at hand. Fortunately, recent advances in component and Web technology are, at last, providing the means for satisfying these requirements. Component technology, such as JavaBeans and ActiveX, provides a basis for interchangeable parts, while the Web provides a means for consumers to locate available components.

1.1 WEB SEARCH AND COMPONENTS

Agora is a prototype developed by the Software Engineering Institute at Carnegie Mellon University. The object of this work is to create an automatically generated, indexed, database of software products classified by component type (e.g., JavaBean or ActiveX control). Agora combines introspection[1] with Web search engines to reduce the costs of bringing software components to, and finding components in, the global software marketplace.

Until recently, surfing was a typical approach for finding information on the Web. Search engines, such as Webcrawler, Lycos [3], AltaVista, and InfoSeek, enable users to search for and locate information published on the Web more effectively. Search engines use indexes that are automatically compiled by computer programs (such as robots and spiders) and that go out over the Internet to discover and collect Internet resources. Searchers can connect to a search engine site and enter keywords to query the index. Web pages and other Internet resources that satisfy the query are then identified and listed [7].

Even modest steps towards integrating component technology and Web search can have an impact on the emergence of an online component marketplace by

- providing developers with a worldwide distribution channel for software components
- providing consumers with a flexible search capability over a large base of available components
- providing a basis for the emergence of value-added component qualification and certification services, within and across specific business sectors

1.2 COMPONENT LIBRARIES

The benefits of developing an effective component library are readily apparent: by allowing system integrators to fabricate software systems from pre-existing components rather than laboriously develop each system from scratch, enormous time and energy can be saved in the development of new software systems. The President's Information Technology Advisory Committee (PITAC) interim report [11] to the President, for example, states that "The construction and availability of libraries of certifiably robust, specified, modeled and tested software components would greatly aid the development of new software. However beneficial a component library might be, a useful and effective repository has turned out to be an elusive goal."

URLs in this chapter

Agora • agora.sei.cmu.edu/agora
Gamelan • www.gamelan.com
JavaBeans Directory •
    www.javasoft.com/beans/index.html
jCentral • www.ibm.com/java

2. FEATURES AND CAPABILITIES

Agora supports two basic processes: the location and indexing of components and the search and retrieval of a component. The location and indexing of components is primarily an automated background task, while a human typically performs search and retrieval. Agora also provides an interface for vendors to add their own components to the index.

2.1 LOCATION AND INDEXING

Agora uses a variety of agents for locating and indexing component information. Currently a JavaBeans agent and a CORBA agent have been developed, each able to locate and index components of their respective type.

---

[1] Introspection is a term, primarily associated with JavaBeans, which describes the ability of components to provide information about its interfaces. CORBA provides a similar capability of divulging information about interfaces, although these data are maintained external to the CORBA server in an implementation repository.

Components are introspected during the indexing phase to discover their interfaces. Introspection of JavaBeans is accomplished using the mechanism provided by JavaBeans Introspector class. In CORBA, interface information is maintained separately in an interface repository (IR). As a result, this information may not be available because it is not in the IR, the IR is not running, or the IR cannot be located. In each of these cases, the interface information cannot be successfully retrieved and indexed.

Once a component has been identified, the interface information is decomposed into a set of tokens. A document is created in the index that includes these tokens. Unlike a text document, component interface information can be differentiated into different fields. Examples of fields may be methods, attributes, or events. This information is also maintained for each component to enable specialized searches to be performed. The component name and type are also preserved as fields to enable searches by name and component type. Meta-information about each component is also maintained with the document, including the Uniform Resource Locator (URL) for each component. Maintaining the component URL allows detailed interface information to be re-collected during the search and retrieval process and allows the user to examine, in the case of hypertext transfer protocol (HTTP)-based URLs, the Web page containing the component.

2.2 SEARCH AND RETRIEVAL

Search and retrieval in Agora is a two-step process. A searcher initially enters query terms and optionally specifies the type of component. These terms and other criteria are searched against the index collected by the search agents. It is also possible to issue a *field* search to find a term in a particular context (for example, to find components of a given name or components that implement a given component model). The result set for the query is sent back to the user for inspection. Each result includes meta-information including the URL of the component. The searcher can then refine or broaden the search criteria based on the number and quality of the matches.

Figure 1. Agora query interface. (From *IEEE Internet Computing*, Vol. 2, No. 6, Nov./Dec., 1998. With permission.)

Once the searcher has completed this broad search to identify candidate components, individual components can be examined in detail. The component is re-introspected whenever detailed information about the interface is requested. This approach reduces the amount of information that must be maintained in the index for each indexed component, ensures that the component is still available at the specified location (URL), and guarantees that an up-to-date interface description is retrieved. The disadvantage of this approach is that it depends on the availability of the remote server.

Figure 1 shows the results from a JavaBeans search. In this case, the search criterion specifies that the JavaBean must contain methods `color` and `draw` and property `color` but must not contain the term `funscroll`. This search resulted in two documents being found—each with relatively low relevancy ranking. The word count indicates how many occurrences of each term were found in the database.

Once a suitable result list has been returned, the searcher can select the link to the component's URL. This normally allows the searcher to see what the component looks like when it is operational and possibly collect additional information about the component. Selecting the component name causes the component's interface description to be displayed.

2.3 ADVANCED SEARCH FEATURES

Agora supports the basic operators '+' and '-': these operators indicate words or phrases that are required or prohibited in the search results. Agora also allows advanced search capabilities that support the Boolean logic operators AND, OR, NOT, and NEAR, as well as the ability to specify ranking words that are different from the words in the search.

Agora also supports a number of special functions that allow the user to narrow the search criteria using specific characteristics of the component. Table 1 shows special functions that operate across all component types.

Table 1. Generic Component Special Functions

Keyword	Function
component:type	Finds components of this type. Each type corresponds to some agent.
name:name	Finds components with this name. This is equivalent to the applet function in AltaVista.

For, example, the user may restrict a query to search for components implemented as JavaBeans by using the component function to specify the component type with the following query:

```
component:JavaBeans
```

In addition to special functions such as components that operate across all component types, there are also component model-specific special functions. These functions are specific to each component type, supporting component-specific capabilities and the use of domain-specific terms.

For example, Agora supports the special functions shown in Table 2 for CORBA interfaces. The CORBA special functions for *operation* and *attribute* map to the Java special functions for *method* and *property*, shown in Table 3. Different names are used for these functions to match more precisely to the corresponding component model's nomenclature. There is no mapping between the JavaBeans event function and CORBA. Special functions for *exception* and *parameter* in CORBA derive naturally from the capabilities of the interface repository.

Table 2. JavaBean Special Functions

Keyword	Function
property:name	Finds components that define a specific property. Use *property*:color to find components that define a property called color.
event:name	Finds components that define specific event sets. Use *event*:propertyChange to find components that define an event set called propertyChange.
method:name	Finds components that define specific methods. Use *method*:createAnimation to find components that define a method called createAnimation.

Table 3. CORBA Special Functions

Keyword	Function
operation:name	Finds CORBA interfaces that include specific operations. Use *operation*:selectDrill to find a CORBA interface that defines an operation called selectDrill.
parameter:name	Finds CORBA interfaces that include parameters of a given name or type. Use *parameter*:long to find a CORBA interface that contains an operation that takes a long as a parameter.
exception:name	Finds CORBA interfaces that define specific exceptions. Use *exception* :InvalidName to find CORBA interfaces that define an exception called InvalidName.
attribute:name	Finds CORBA interfaces that define specific attributes. Use *attribute*:color to find CORBA interfaces that define an attribute called color.

2.4 INDUSTRY DOMAIN

Application-specific lexicons are being developed that can be used to facilitate searches by application domains such as manufacturing, medical, and finance. In theory, these lexicons will help identify components in these domains and simplify the process of identifying suitable components. Lexicon terms may be distilled from existing component interfaces that are representative of a given domain. However, it is insufficient to parse these interfaces in a similar manner to the Agora indexer, as selected terms should be indigenous to a given domain and are not easily found outside it.

During the search process, specifying a domain causes the lexicon of domain-specific terms to be attached to the query. This allows the search engine to perform a relevancy ranking on components that match the query terms. Query terms are best given by using the "+" operator when searching a specific domain, as this ensures that these terms are found in components included in the result set.

Lexicon terms are currently selected manually in Agora due to the intelligence required to identify domain-unique terms.

3. IMPLEMENTATION

Agora is designed to be extensible to different component technologies, provide good performance to searchers accessing the Web site, and provide advanced searching capabilities. The implementation strategy adopted required the use of existing components as leverage since the project had to be completed in a relatively short period of time with limited resources. For example, the basic functionality of the AltaVista Internet service was incorporated into Agora. This service is used to identify Web pages containing Java applets. This basic functionality was extended to identify and introspect JavaBeans. Introspected interfaces are then used to build a searchable index of terms.

In addition to the AltaVista Internet service, Agora incorporates the AltaVista Search Developer's Kit (SDK). This allows Agora to provide advanced search capabilities at considerably lower cost than possible by custom development.

The overall Agora architecture is shown in Figure 2. Independent agents are used for each component class, making the design extensible to other components models. An agent in Agora is simply an independent process that understands a specific domain and component class. Two agents have been developed so far: a JavaBeans agent that harvests URLs from the AltaVista Internet service and a CORBA interface agent. The JavaBeans agent searches for hypertext markup language (HTML) pages containing applet tags using the AltaVista Internet service, loads and introspects these applets, and indexes the interfaces of any JavaBeans that are discovered. The CORBA interface agent uses the CORBA naming service to find CORBA interfaces and the implementation repository to discover their interfaces. We believe that ActiveX controls are amenable to discovery and introspection using an approach similar to that used by the JavaBeans agent.

The query client is implemented using Java Server Pages (JSP) on Sun's Java Web server. The use of Java Server Pages allows Java code to execute on the server to generate HTML pages that are then downloaded to the client.

Java Server pages can be extended using JavaBeans to which both explicit and implicit calls are made. Implicit calls are made to set properties within the JavaBean corresponding to input fields in the HTML form. For example, the main text input field for entering the search criteria in the Agora query interface is named criteria. When a POST method occurs, either because the enter key was pressed or because an input field of type submit was selected, the Java Web Server calls the `setCriteria()` member function on the imported JavaBean.

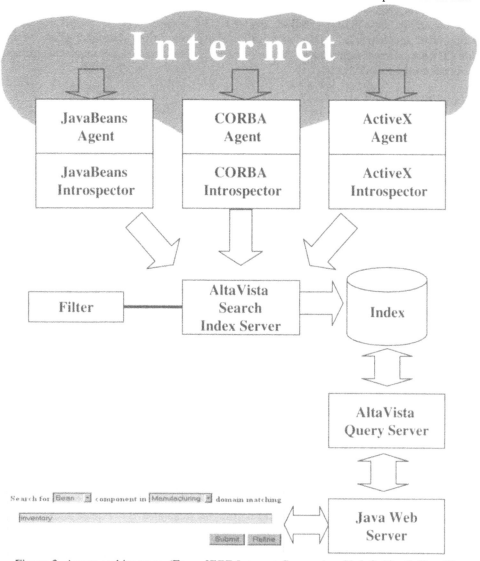

Figure 2. Agora architecture. (From *IEEE Internet Computing*, Vol. 2, No. 6, Nov./Dec., 1998. With permission.)

The existing implementation of Agora has been used to identify and catalog JavaBeans over the Internet and installed on a publicly accessible server where these results can be examined. This version of Agora is also capable of indexing CORBA interfaces, although an effective CORBA search algorithm has not yet been implemented. In addition to these component types, it is possible to develop agents that search, introspect, and catalog ActiveX controls, remote method invocation (RMI) servers, and other reusable software components. In fact, multiple agents may be developed per component class to implement different search strategies (for example, a traditional spider to search intranets for JavaBeans).

3.1 ALTAVISTA SEARCH DEVELOPER'S KIT (SDK)

Digital's AltaVista SDK is used by Agora for indexing and retrieving component data. The AltaVista SDK provided advanced search capabilities that would have required substantial effort to develop. Although the AltaVista SDK had many advantages, it also introduced design constraints in that the AltaVista SDK is composed of C language interfaces and libraries that are only available on Windows NT and DEC Alpha platforms. Rather than resort to the use of the Java Native Interface (JNI), a C++ wrapper was developed around the existing SDK functionality. SDK functionality is exported to the remainder of the system using CORBA. This design isolated the C++ code from the Java-based components, making the overall design more robust.

3.2 JAVABEANS AGENT

We implemented the Internet JavaBeans agent as a *metasearch engine* to harvest candidate URLs from the AltaVista Internet service. The AltaVista service was selected because of its special functions for Web searches. In particular, searches of the format: `applet:class` can locate HTML pages containing applet tags where the code parameter is equal to specified Java applet class. For example, a search for `applet:sine` can be used to find applets where the code parameter is specified as `sine` or `sine.class`.

The harvest algorithm we implemented queries the AltaVista search engine to find pages containing applets the `applet` special function. At the time of writing, there exist a total of 1,530,275 documents matching the query: `applet:*`. AltaVista responds by generating an HTML page containing the first 10 hits from the resulting set. After parsing the page to extract the URL for these Web pages, the string `&navig` is appended to the end of the command sent to AltaVista along with the number of hits. This command is sent to the AltaVista Internet service that returns the subsequent 10 hits.

One problem with this approach is that the AltaVista service, either by design or by flaw, does not provide matching documents beyond the first thousand for a given query. This required that a mechanism be developed to distribute the estimated 1.5 million documents across multiple queries so that each query (or most of the queries) returns less than 1000 documents.

The mechanism we implemented for distributing documents across multiple queries uses the date field. Advanced searches in AltaVista can be restricted to find documents last modified during a specific date range. The advanced search capability of the AltaVista Internet service provides a function that can be used to find the exact number of matches for this that can be invoked by passing `&fmt=n` to AltaVista's query common gateway interface (CGI) executable file. The exact number of matches from the generated HTTP page is examined to see if it is between 0 and 1000. If the number of matching documents is greater than 1000, we reduce the date range by half and resubmit the query. Alternatively, if we find 0 matches, we expand the date range. Once a date range that contains between 0 and 1000 hits has been identified, we harvest these documents by reissuing the search query without the `&fmt=n` parameter, bringing up the actual search results. This query distribution mechanism was generally successful in finding queries that contain between 1 and 1000 entries. However, there have been cases when a single day contains more than 1000 entries. Since a single day is the limit of granularity for these queries, we must harvest the first 1000 entries and discard the remainder.

Another approach for distributing these documents across multiple queries that we did not implement is to segment the documents according to the first three characters in the name of each applet. The AltaVista service supports the use of wildcards such as an asterisk (*) to broaden a search. The wildcard, however, must be proceeded by at least three characters. The number of combinations of N alphanumeric characters taken M ways can be calculated using the following formula:

$$C_{NM} = \frac{N!}{M!(N-M)!}$$

AltaVista defines a word as any string of letters and digits separated by white space or special characters and punctuation. These 36 alphanumeric characters can be combined into 7,140 unique, 3-character strings. If distributed evenly across the 1.5 million documents, this would result in approximately 210 documents per query. Actual applet names are, of course, not evenly distributed across these groupings. This query distribution mechanism may in fact provide better results than the mechanism we implemented.

Another defect in the AltaVista Internet service is that the "exact" number of matches returned by the &fmt=n parameter is not always accurate. This is primarily a concern when the number returned is greater than the actual number of matching documents, since the JavaBeans agent will continue to loop in an attempt to harvest these results. This made it necessary to add a timeout mechanism so that the algorithm would terminate after a fixed number of attempts to retrieve these matching documents from AltaVista.

3.2.1 Indexing

One of Agora's key features is the way it indexes the component information collected through introspection.

Agora introspects JavaBeans by means of the JavaBeans Introspector class, then organizes the retrieved interface information into five fields associated with the corresponding document: *component, name, property, method,* and *event.* The component field is always assigned the value "JavaBean." This field lets users search for components of a particular type. The name field, common to all component types and supporting index-wide searches by name, contains the fully qualified name of the class or interface represented by the JavaBean. The fully qualified name relates to the class name appearing in the applet tag.

The property field contains a list of *property descriptors,* obtained from each *JavaBean's bean info.* Each descriptor describes a property exported by a JavaBean via a pair of accessor methods, which allow a component user to get or set property values. The bean info contains information about a JavaBean, supplied by the developer or obtained by automatic analysis using low-level reflection of the bean classes' methods. Agora processes the property descriptors to get the property name, type, and the names of any read or write methods defined for the property.

The property descriptor can also be an *indexed property descriptor,* which describes a property that acts like an array and has an indexed read and/or indexed write method to access specific array elements. If these methods are defined, they are recorded in the property field for each JavaBean. Event sets are handled like properties. An *event set descriptor* describes a group of events that a given JavaBean fires. The events are delivered as method calls on a single event listener interface, and an event listener object is registered via a call on a registration method supplied by the event source.

Agora retrieves the name, adds listener method and removes listener method for each event set and adds them to the tokens associated with the event field. The list of target methods within the target listener interface is retrieved, and the method names are added to the event field.

The JavaBean agent inspects JavaBean methods after processing properties and event sets. Methods are less complex than either properties or event sets. *Method descriptors* for each JavaBean, retrieved from the bean info, describe a particular method that a JavaBean supports for external access from other components. The JavaBean agent invokes the JDK getMethod() call on each method to obtain the method's low-level description, then parses this description to retrieve the tokens. These tokens are then added to the method field for this document.

To limit redundant information, Agora also maintains exclusion tables that exclude the names of properties, event sets, and methods common to all JavaBeans.

3.2.2 Performance
Considerable effort was spent optimizing the speed at which components could be collected. Initially, we found that the JavaBeans agent was discovering JavaBeans at low rate, and even this performance would drop off quickly.

The JavaBeans agent is implemented using the beta2 version of Java Development Kit (JDK) 1.2 (Figure 3). This version of the JDK contains classes, such as the URL class loader, that are not available in JDK 1.1. Initially, the agent was implemented using a single thread of control. We discovered that this agent might run well for several minutes, but would hang in calls to the URL class loader. A typical run might retrieve in the vicinity of 20 JavaBeans before grinding to a halt. We attempted to solve this problem by specifying a time-out. However, the URL class loader available with the beta2 JDK 1.2 release did not provide a mechanism for specifying a time-out or a means to access the underlying socket layer.

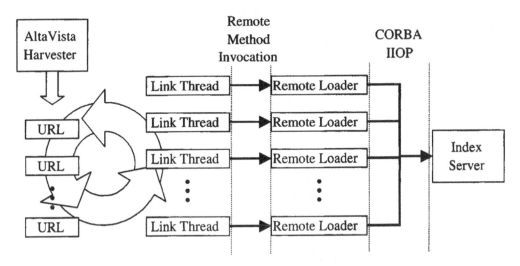

Figure 3. JavaBeans agent. (From *IEEE Internet Computing*, Vol. 2, No. 6, Nov./Dec., 1998. With permission.)

To address this problem, we decided to introduce multiple threads for examining the URLs harvested from AltaVista, loading the classes with the URL class loader and performing the introspection on the resultant class. The main program would harvest URLs from the AltaVista site and add them to a synchronized queue. Approximately 20 independent threads would then retrieve these URLs from the queue for introspection.

Since loading and introspecting classes is the most central processing unit (CPU)-intensive portion of the overall component collection process, we further decided to separate this functionality out into a collection of identical RMI servers. This arrangement allows us to provide load balancing by distributing the work of loading and introspecting classes across multiple processors. Each of these remote loaders, in turn, connected to the index CORBA server running on the NT platform. The resultant architecture is shown in Figure 4. Although the index server might appear to be the bottleneck in the system, it was, in actuality, never severely taxed and no data was lost due to time-outs from the server.

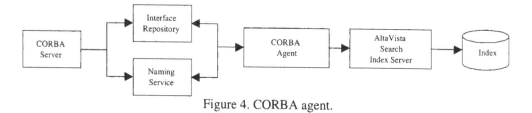

Figure 4. CORBA agent.

This more sophisticated arrangement helped, but we found that after retrieving an average of 40-60 JavaBeans the JavaBeans agent again began to bog down in calls to the URL class loader. We tried using the Sun supplied sunwjit compiler at this time, which provided an order of magnitude better runtime performance of the JavaBeans agent. However, this improved performance only served to decrease the time required to collect the components and did not affect the total number of JavaBeans retrieved.

At this point we looked at other options for achieving continual operation of the JavaBeans agent and optimizing the number of components indexed. One option was to provide some level of internal thread management to kill and restart threads that were hung. We eventually decided to implement a crude but effective solution. The JavaBeans agent was modified to check point its work by recording its progress through the AltaVista database: the JavaBeans agent recorded the current date range being examined and the number of hits in that data range processed so far. The JavaBeans agent is restarted each hour (using cron under UNIX or the service Schedule under Windows NT) using the preserved state data. A similar approach was used in IBM's jCentral [1] and appears to be an effective means of improving performance. In Agora we were able to retrieve over 800 JavaBeans in a 24-hour period, and an additional 1400 JavaBeans over a 48-hour period.

We expect these numbers to improve as we address other deficiencies in the implementation and integrate newer, more robust versions of the JDK.

3.3 CORBA AGENT

In addition to the JavaBeans agent, a CORBA agent was implemented, although this agent is more experimental due to the lack of a CORBA infrastructure necessary to fully support the location of CORBA-based components.

3.3.1 CORBA Background

To understand the implementation of the CORBA agent, it is necessary to understand some details about CORBA itself. In CORBA, servers are implemented as distributed objects. Each of these objects is represented by an object reference. Object interfaces are defined using the Object Management Group Interface Definition Language (OMG IDL). This language is used to define the operations that may be performed on objects and the parameters to those operations. IDL is compiled into stubs that can be statically linked at compile time. It may also be translated into an interface repository that can be dynamically accessed at runtime.

CORBA servers can implement any number of interfaces and any number of objects can be created that implement a given interface. The object request broker (ORB) maintains objects in a vendor-specific manner in an implementation repository. Objects may be located in an implementation-independent fashion using the naming service.

The naming service is defined by the OMG as part of the Common Object Services or CORBA Services. The naming service allows one or more logical names to be associated with an object reference. A server that holds an object reference can register it with the naming service, giving it a name that can be subsequently used by clients of that server to find the object. Client applications can use the naming service to obtain the object reference using the logical name assigned to that object.

3.3.2 Application Bridge

The naming service provides a standard mechanism for locating CORBA objects, allowing Agora to dynamically locate objects at runtime. This is a necessary but insufficient mechanism since Agora must also be able to dynamically determine component interfaces at runtime. This problem is partially addressed by the CORBA interface repository. An interface repository contains descriptions of CORBA object interfaces. The data in an interface repository are the same as in IDL files, but the information is organized for runtime access by clients. A client can browse an interface repository or look up the interface for any object for which it has a reference.

Figure 4 illustrates the architecture of Agora's CORBA agent. The CORBA agent binds to a CORBA naming service and iterates through the values using the BindingIterator naming service interface. The binding name of each object is then resolved to a CORBA object. The CORBA object can be used to access interface information directly using the `get_interface()` call or indirectly using the repository identifier.

For each CORBA interface discovered in this fashion, we extract attribute and operation names (including associated return value, parameter names, and defined exceptions) and index the terms. As discussed previously, CORBA interfaces can be searched for using special functions to find components that define a particular operation, attribute, parameter, or exception.

The AltaVista index server was developed using version 2.3 of Iona's Orbix. The JavaBeans agent, for example, establishes a connection with the index server using the `bind()` function. The CORBA agent was implemented to work with the Visigenics' VisiBroker implementation repository and Naming Service. VisiBroker was selected in this case due to some vendor unique services, such as the location service, that we wished to investigate.

The use of VisiBroker introduced a design problem in that the CORBA agent could not be both a VisiBroker and an Orbix client at the same time, as these libraries would clash. It is possible, but difficult, to get an Orbix client to communicate with a VisiBroker naming service, since a call to resolve_initial_references() to resolve the "NameService" can only be used to connect to the naming service supplied by the same vendor. This requires that the interoperable object reference (IOR) for the naming service be obtained independently and converted in an object reference and narrowed to the naming service.

Rather than deal with these interoperability problems, we used an application bridge to connect the index server with the CORBA agent by introducing an additional RMI server between the two processes as shown in Figure 5.

Like the JavaBeans agent, the ORB bridge is implemented as an Orbix client; however, it also functions as an RMI server. The CORBA agent can now be freely implemented as a VisiBroker client and communicate with the ORB Bridge via RMI calls over the Java Remote

Method Protocol (JRMP). This solution was simple to implement and does not introduce any significant runtime overhead.

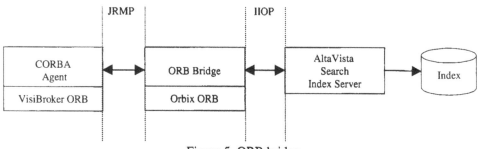

Figure 5. ORB bridge.

4. COMPARISON OF AGORA TO RELATED TECHNOLOGIES

Agora can be compared and contrasted with two different technologies: Web search technology and software repository technology. There are also some interesting comparisons that can be made between developing agents for JavaBeans and CORBA interfaces.

4.1 AGORA AND EXISTING SEARCH ENGINES

Existing search engines provide convenient support for different kinds of Web content. Different search capabilities are provided for different types of content. For example, text content can be searched by simple but effective pattern matching, while images can be searched only by image name.

Leaders in the Internet development community are voicing concerns about the growing ineffectiveness of monolithic search engines used for a specific purpose [1]. As the Internet grows, information associated with any given keyword grows accordingly, causing general-purpose search engines to become clogged with massive amounts of often irrelevant data.

The Agora search engine enhances existing but rudimentary search capabilities for Java applets. By using Java introspection, the Agora search engine can maintain a more structured and descriptive index that is targeted to the type of content (the component model) and the intended audience (application developers) than is supported by existing search engines. For example, information about component properties, events, and methods can be retrieved from Agora.

Developers of search engines such as AltaVista might decide to incorporate this kind of search capability; this would be a welcome indication of Agora's success. However, it is also possible that capabilities such as the Agora search engine will occupy a value-added market niche in the overall World Wide Web. For example, capabilities such as domain-specific searches may be too narrow for broad-based search engines to support profitably.

4.2 AGORA AND SOFTWARE REPOSITORIES

A traditional approach has been to develop large-scale software repositories as large central databases containing information about components and, often, the components themselves. Examples of such systems include the Center for Computer Systems Engineering's Defense System Repository, the JavaBeans Directory, and the Gamelan Java directory. Software libraries have traditionally been conceived as large central databases containing information about components and, often, the components themselves. Examples of such systems include the Center for Computer Systems Engineering's Defense System Repository, the JavaBeans Directory, and the Gamelan Java directory.

While the JavaBeans and Gamelan directories are still going concerns, similar systems have failed in the past largely as a result of their conception as centralized systems. Problems with this approach include limited accessibility and scalability of the repository, exclusive control over cataloged components, oppressive bureaucracy, and poor economy of scale (few users, low per-user benefits, and high cost of repository mechanisms and operations).

Agora replaces old-fashioned and costly software repositories. Agora automatically compiles indexes by going out over the Internet and discovering and collecting information about software components. Agora does this in a nonjudgmental manner, so the problem of having a sole arbiter decide what does and does not belong in the repository is eliminated. Quality assurance in the Agora model is not guaranteed—we believe that component databases need to be, at first, free and inclusive. Value-added industries such as consumer reports and underwriter labs can add value by providing independent quality assurance of popular components. This will help ensure that candidate components are identified and not simply eliminated based on the criteria of the company maintaining the repository.

4.3 LOCATION SERVICES

All CORBA implementations must provide a mechanism for clients to locate and bind to an object implementation. These mechanisms are generally used for locating servers in a local subnet and generally are not applicable to discovering servers over the Internet. Inprise's VisiBroker's Smart Agent, a particularly aggressive location service, is a distributed directory that locates specific implementations so that a connection can be established between the client and the implementation. VisiBroker locates a Smart Agent for use by a client program or object implementation on a local network using a User Datagram Protocol (UDP) broadcast message. The VisiBroker Smart Agent configures the scope of UDP broadcast messages using the Internet Protocol subnet mask. Instead of considering an IP address as just a network ID and host ID, a network administrator divides the host ID portion into a subnet ID and a host ID. In addition to the IP address, a host must also know how many bits are used for the subnet ID and how many for the host ID. This is specified using a subnet mask.

As subnet-directed broadcasts are restricted to all hosts within a specified subnet, it is not possible to use this form of broadcast to locate Smart Agents over the Internet. For a Smart Agent on one network to contact a Smart Agent on another local network, the remote agent's IP address must be made available to the local agent using an environmental variable. Candidate IP addresses must be identified by some other means and provided to the Smart Agent.

VisiBroker's Smart Agent cannot be used to locate servers implemented with CORBA products other than VisiBroker, which is an additional limitation. Binding services in other ORBs are at least as restrictive. The binding service in Orbix 2.3 first attempts to contact an Orbix daemon process at the local host. If there is no such process, the location attempt fails. The locator then invokes the `lookUp()` method, which contacts the local Orbix daemon and requests the host name list for the specified server name. Orbix returns the first host at which the desired service is registered. If the server is not registered at any of these hosts, Orbix attempts to locate the server at the local host, and if it does not find it registered, the location attempt fails.

Instead of using a broadcast method, as the VisiBroker Smart Agent does, the Orbix 2.3 locator mechanism uses the names of hosts registered with a local Orbix daemon. Although each of these approaches has advantages and disadvantages for locating servers in a local subnet, neither location approach can be effectively used to discover CORBA servers over the Internet.

4.4 OBJECT TRADER SERVICE

Another, higher level service for locating CORBA object implementations is the OMG Object Trader Service, which provides a matchmaking service for objects. A trader object can be viewed as an object through which other objects advertise their capabilities and match their needs against advertised capabilities. Advertising a capability or offering a service is called export; matching against needs or discovering services is called import. Export and import facilitate dynamic discovery of, and late binding to, services.

The CORBA Service Provider registers a service availability by invoking an export operation on the trader passing information about the offered service as parameters. The export operation includes

- an object reference for use by a client to invoke operations on the advertised services
- a description of the type of the offered service (that is, the names of the operations to which it will respond, along with their parameter and result types)
- information on the distinguishing attributes of the offered service

To import, an object asks the trader for a service having certain characteristics. The trader checks against the service descriptions it holds and responds to the importer with the location of the selected service's interface. Unlike existing CORBA trading services, components in Agora are collected automatically, with no requirements for registration or restrictions due to fees.

5. ISSUES, TRADEOFFS & FUTURE DIRECTIONS

Agora was designed and implemented to demonstrate the feasibility of a component repository using existing infrastructures and available information. Agora demonstrates the extent to which an automatically indexed, database of software components can be implemented given the current state of commercial technology. Agora does not address all the issues that need to be resolved before such an approach can be effectively used on a broad scale. Some of the tradeoffs between the approach taken by Agora and more traditional repositories are discussed in this section. Areas in which component-based software engineering may evolve to more effectively support component repositories are identified.

5.1 MODELED

The PITAC report stipulates that components available in a repository must be fully modeled. This may mean that a behavioral model of the component has been developed. Alternately, it could mean that the component adheres to a predefined component model.

A component model describes the coordination model used by subscribing components so that they may be seamlessly integrated into a system that applies the model. The most prominent component technologies, including Enterprise JavaBeans and ActiveX, all impose constraints on components [8]. Existing CORBA servers do not fully meet the requirements of being a component model, but are still of interest as the OMG is planning on adopting a component model as part of the CORBA 3.0 specification.

Agora was designed to support search and retrieval of multiple component models, but only JavaBeans were fully developed. Some experimentation with CORBA was attempted, but results were not promising due to the difficulty in locating and introspecting CORBA servers. A component repository should be able to locate, index and retrieve a broad variety of components.

Traditional repositories often collected software products, language specific subroutines, or link-able libraries. In removing sources of architectural mismatch [9], evolving component models should improve the effectiveness of the software repository concept.

5.2 INTERFACE DESCRIPTIONS

An obvious limitation of Agora is the lack of descriptive information about the component's interface. In the case of JavaBeans, for example, information gathered through introspection is restricted to method signatures including function names, return and parameter types. In other component models, such as CORBA servers, interface information is maintained externally to the component and may not be available at all. In all cases, descriptive information about the overall purpose of each component and the various APIs is lacking. In addition, information about functional semantics is completely absent.

The lack of information concerning functional semantics in Agora could be addressed if component models provided a well-defined mechanism for accessing this information. In JavaBeans, for example, the semantics of the API calls is normally described in structured comments in the source code. The javadoc tool is can extract these structured comments to produce a corresponding set of HTML pages describing public and protected classes, inner classes, interfaces, constructors, methods, and fields. This information could also be converted by a doclet[2] into a runtime accessible format. If the JavaBean specification were extended to include a reference from a JavaBean component to the associated doclet, Agora and other component-based software development tools could provide information about the component semantics to the component-based system developer.

As demonstrated in WaterBeans [10], component models could also provide a means of including contact information so that the original author(s) may be contacted.

Traditional repositories are better positioned to provide interface descriptions than Agora. Interfaces are typically documented using a repository standard format or by making the original component documentation available within the repository.

5.3 QUALITY ASSURANCE

The quality of components in traditional software repositories is often assured by the organization that maintains the repository. There are number of problems with this approach:

1. Timeliness – having a single organization responsible for providing quality assurance for every version of very component created is an impossible goal. Taking this approach instantly creates a bottleneck, restricting the number of components that can be incorporated into the amount of time it takes to get a component reviewed and incorporated into the repository.
2. Lack of context – components must be qualified as being able to perform a specific task. A component that is qualified to perform a certain function may not be suitable, for example, for a real time application.

---

[2] Doclets are programs written in the Java programming language that use the doclet API to specify the content and format of the output of the Javadoc tool.

3. Bias – it is highly unlikely that the organization maintaining the component repository is completely unbiased. Most organizations that might be capable of providing this service have their own products, customers, and strategic relationships and partnerships. It would be naïve to assume these relationships would not impact, at the very least, the components that are included in the repository.

The Agora model is based on the premise that component databases need to be free and inclusive. Value-added industries such as consumer reports and underwriter labs can add value by providing independent quality assurance of popular components. The existing Agora prototype would be extended to allow underwriter labs to link product evaluations to specific components maintained within the repository. Again, this process will be handled in a completely decentralized fashion. Potential consumers can review these reports and form their own opinions as to the reputation of the organization providing the information and the value of the report. It may be also possible to automatically generate mailing lists on a per component basis to let consumers of that component directly exchange experiences.

Components in the repository (or elsewhere) can be digitally signed to indicate that they provide specific quality of service attributes, for example that they are guaranteed to execute in a specified period of time (for use in real time systems) or that the component has completed some battery of tests. The objects can be signed directly by some certifying agency, or by the developer. Providing tamper-proof packaging will increase the level of trust of consumers that the component being evaluated does in fact have the certified qualities.

5.4 OPEN SYSTEM

Traditional component repositories were conceived as centrally managed systems. This allowed the group or organization maintaining the repository to certify the degree to which components in the repository were robust, specified, modeled and tested. Without central management, it is very difficult to ensure the quality of the components in the repository.

In contrast, we believe that component repositories need to be, at first, free and inclusive. Agora automatically compiles indexes by going out over the Internet and discovering and collecting information about software components. Component collection is performed in a nonjudgmental manner, so the problem of having a sole arbiter decide what does and does not belong in the repository is eliminated.

The traditional, centralized approach is analogous to a centrally planned economy in that both are slow to respond to market changes and often succeed only when the investment outweighs the benefits. The free and inclusive approach can be compared to a market driven economy that is more responsive to market realities but does not provide the safeguards of the more rigidly planned system.

5.5 COMPONENT UNIQUENESS

A goal of a component repository is to incorporate each component once and only once, but this is easier said than done. There are a number of different ways to determine if a component is unique. Here are a sample of methods that can be used to determine uniqueness and the associated drawbacks:

1. The component has a unique URL. Unfortunately, multiple identical copies of a component often appear at multiple locations so this approach does not guarantee a component only appears once in the database.
2. The component has the same application programming interface (API). Since the API can be introspected, it can be compared with other APIs as a test for uniqueness.

However, multiple different versions of a component could easily have identical interfaces. Another potential issue is if different versions of the same component should be considered to be different components or not.

3. The component matches byte for byte with an existing component. This is a relatively restrictive test for uniqueness although there are still potential problems. For example, an Enterprise JavaBean may be modified at deployment time to support specific characteristics defined in the deployment descriptor. It is therefore possible that the same Enterprise JavaBean deployed in one environment will not match the same Enterprise JavaBean deployed elsewhere.

Component models should have a means of specifying a major and minor version number in the component. This could provide a useful mechanism for differentiating two components that otherwise have the same API.

5.6 DATA RIGHTS AND PRIVACY

Agora automatically collects components discovered over the Internet using a spider. This raises some interesting questions regarding data rights and privacy.

Spiders follow HTML links in existing documents. Most of these documents have been placed in locations where they are accessible to the public. There are probably some cases where confidential or proprietary documents have inadvertently been made accessible to the public but this is an exceptional occurrence.

Java classes are often included on web pages to increase the dynamic content of the page. In most cases the components are not provided for the express means of collection and integration by other system integrators.

Although the source code used to generate these components can be protected under copyright laws, there is no defined mechanism for protecting the binary copies of a program other than preventing copies from being distributed or integrating some manner of licensing software. ActiveX controls, for example, can be built to work only at design time, runtime or in either situation using LPK files.

Automatic collection of components also requires that an agent, such as a spider, establish communication with a computer. In the case of Web spiders, this communication is on a well-defined port number and protocols exist [8] to restrict access by these agents. Locating CORBA servers, however, is more problematic. One possibility is to examine IIOP ports that are set up by default for a particular vendor's ORB. This assumes that the developer has not changed the port number. If this is true, the only way to locate these services is to systematically examine each port —a process that can be easily determined as an attack.

5.7 ELECTRONIC COMMERCE IN COMPONENTS

Closely related to the problem of data rights and privacy of components is electronic commerce in components. Most publicly accessible components are freely available, non-proprietary, and non-commercial. However, because of the degree of investment required, many types of components may only be available commercially. However, vendors of commercial components are very unlikely to make these components publicly available unless they have some means of protecting their investments.

There are a number of potential solutions for this problem. One solution would require the development of an electronic commerce model where components could be "rented". An initialization call could, in fact, provide a credit card number that can be electronically authorized (in a similar fashion to any retail store). Subsequent calls to the component could be charged against the credit card. Depending on the expected calling frequency, this might require the use of nano-bucks – extremely small measures of currency.

Another solution would be that commercial companies make skeleton versions of components publicly available as a means of advertising the features of the component. The system integrator would then need to contact the vendor to license the component prior to employing it. ActiveX controls, for example, could be built to work only at design time. This would allow the controls to be indexed by an automated component repository while the development organization retained control of component distribution. It is easy to imagine other schemes that could also be employed to achieve similar results.

5.8 SOFTWARE ENGINEERING

Introspection, as defined by the JavaBeans specification, provides a means for development tools, such as the BeanBox, Borland's JbuilderTM, IBM's Visual Age® for Java and Symantec's Visual Cafe to discover component interfaces at runtime. This allows developers to integrate components within a development environment without having to "teach" the development tool about the component.

This same introspection capability made possible the indexing of interface information by Agora. A Component repository can be thought of as a software engineering tool used by system integrators to develop component-based systems. This is relevant because any enhancement to existing component models to support component repositories will generally benefit the broader class of development tools.

For example, extending the JavaBean component model to support the description of the API would allow development tools such as the BeanBox to provide on-line documentation for API calls at run-time to assist the developer in the integration of the component.

5.9 LOCATION SERVICES

JavaBean components found by Agora are typically used to add dynamic behavior to static HTML-based Web pages. While this is a potentially useful area of components to be made available in a component repository, it does not represent the full range of JavaBeans that may be available. While it is expected that this Web-based method could also be used to successively retrieve ActiveX components, it may be less effective in finding CORBA servers, Enterprise JavaBeans, or other component types.

CORBA defines multiple, competing mechanisms for locating CORBA servers including implementation repositories, location services, naming services and Object Trader Services. Implementation repositories and location services are not generally useful outside of specific subnet. Object Trader Services require that components be registered, a process that often requires fees. Locating CORBA objects in a naming service turned out to be problematic for several reasons. First, the majority of CORBA servers do not store their object references in a naming service. Second, even if they did, there is no good bootstrapping process for finding an initial object reference for the naming service. This problem could be addressed by having naming services respond to queries on a well-known standard port number or providing some sort of meta-naming service. The best opportunity to discover a naming service is to look for them at vendor-supplied default port numbers.

Agora currently provides a means for component developers to register their components at the Agora web site. This allows components that cannot be located using existing location techniques to be included in the repository.

6. SUMMARY AND CONCLUSIONS

Agora is designed to make it easier for system integrators to discover components that meet the requirements of their systems and provide a means for component producers to advertise their products. With Agora, components can be quickly located and evaluated as candidates for integration, eliminating an inhibitor for component-based software development. Although more work must be done to support a true commerce in software components, Agora represents a useful integration of Web search engines and component introspection.

In general, we had considerably more success locating and introspecting JavaBeans than CORBA interfaces. Locating CORBA services turned out to be problematic for several reasons. First, the majority of CORBA servers do not store their object references in a naming service. Second, even if they did, there is no good bootstrapping process for finding an initial object reference for the naming service. This problem could be addressed by having naming services respond to queries on a well-known standard port number or providing some sort of meta-naming service. The best opportunity to discover a naming service is to look for them at vendor-supplied default port numbers. Third, unlike Java applets, CORBA services are not integrated into Web pages directly, but through intermediate languages such as Java. This makes it difficult to use existing search services such as AltaVista to discover CORBA services on the Internet.

Once a CORBA server is located, it is also difficult to extract interface information since this information is not inherently part of the component, as in JavaBeans. Instead, CORBA relies on an external interface repository. Use of the interface repository is optional, and the majority of CORBA servers do not use it. Although it is apparent that CORBA servers have some understanding of operations (without resorting to the interface repository) to support Dynamic Invocation, there is no interface that provides access to this information.

Further, the necessity of establishing communication with a naming service, interface repository, and object decreases the likelihood of finding and introspecting a CORBA interface.

Agora demonstrates that it is feasible to create an automated tool for locating, introspecting, and indexing JavaBeans on the Internet. Although not yet implemented, we hypothesize that an ActiveX agent is equally plausible. For a CORBA Agora agent to be successful, the Object Management Group (OMG) must adopt a component model comparable to JavaBeans, an integrated interface repository, and a means of locating the naming service by means of a well-known port or other mechanism.

References

1. M.H. Aviram, "Code-Centric Search Tool Strives to Reduce Java Development Time," *JavaWorld*, http://www.javaworld.com/jw-06-1998/jw-06-jcentral.html, June 1998.
2. M. Maudlin, "Lycos: Design Choices in an Internet Search Service," *IEEE Expert*, Vol. 12, No. 1, January-February 1997.
3. K. Webster and K. Paul, "Beyond Surfing: Tools and Techniques for Searching the Web," *Information Technology*, January 1996.
4. A. Brown and K. Wallnau, "The Current State of Component-Based, Software Engineering (CBSE)," *IEEE Software*, September 1998, pp. 37-47.
5. D. Garlan, R. Allen, and J. Ockerbloom, "Architectural Mismatch: Why Reuse is So Hard," *IEEE Software*, November 1995.

6. D. Plakosh, D. Smith, and K. Wallnau, "Water Beans Component Builders Guide," CMU/SEI-99-TR-024, August 1999.
7. President's Information Technology Advisory Committee Interim Report to the President, National Coordination Center for Computing, Information, and Communications, Arlington, VA, August 1998.
8. J. Karl, "Protocol Gives Sites Way To Keep Out The 'Bots," *Web Week*, Vol. 1, Issue 7, November 1995.

Chapter 9

WEB-BASED MEDIASPACE

Nicolas Roussel

Abstract

This chapter addresses the use of the Web as a platform for developing mediaspaces; environments that combine audio, video and computing to support distributed groups in their daily tasks. It does not focus on transmission quality, latency, or packet losses. Instead, it shows how Web standards and protocols can be used to create a software infrastructure and user interfaces that offer accessibility as well as privacy. Building on previous work on the social and technical issues of mediaspaces, we introduce three important design principles: integrability, flexibility and privacy. We show how Web standards and protocols can be used to create a software platform consistent with these principles. We present Mediascape, a Web-controlled analog audio/video mediaspace and videoServer, a Web server dedicated to digital video communication. Finally, we introduce videoSpace, a toolkit that allows building Web-based video applications.

1. INTRODUCTION

Stults coined the term "Media Space" at Xerox PARC in the mid 1980's [1]. In order to link two related laboratories located in Palo Alto, California and Portland, Oregon, Stults and his colleagues developed one of the first systems that combined audio and video with computers to support coordination, communication and collaboration among distributed groups. For more than 10 years, research has explored the social and technical issues raised by these environments, including privacy concerns, long-term use, and appliance and service design [2, 3].

Many systems have focused on using video to support formal distributed meetings among groups of people. Experiences with mediaspaces have demonstrated the ability of these environments to support informal communication. This form of communication has proved to be essential for distant people to coordinate and develop relationships despite the lack of physical proximity. It can be described by the following properties [4]: frequent, brief, unscheduled, often dyadic, frequently supported by shared objects, intermittent and lacking formal openings or closings.

The Web is constantly evolving, becoming more dynamic, more interactive and more tailorable. It has already changed many of our habits. But although we might use it sometimes to communicate with distant people by exchanging text or images, the Web is still mostly used as a ubiquitous access point to information, as a link between people and knowledge.

This chapter focuses on the combined use of audio, video and the Web to link people with other people. Building on previous work on the social and technical issues of mediaspaces, we identify three important design principles for such systems: *integrability*, *flexibility* and *privacy*. We show how Web standards and protocols can be used to create a software infrastructure and user interfaces consistent with these principles. We present Mediascape, a Web-controlled analog audio/video mediaspace. We then present videoServer, a Web server dedicated to digital video communication. Finally, we introduce videoSpace, a toolkit that allows building Web-based video applications.

2. LEARNING FROM PREVIOUS MEDIASPACES

Technically, a mediaspace consists of a group of offices and public spaces connected through an audio/video network. Early mediaspaces used an analog network: standard cameras and monitors connected to a computer-controlled crossbar switch [5,6,7,8]. A typical office "node" had a video camera with a microphone, a monitor with speakers, and a workstation to run the connection management software (Figure 1). These early systems were developed on analog infrastructures because computers and digital networks could not handle live video in real-time with an adequate image quality. Although digital video is still pushing the limits of the technology, this is less and less true, and more recent mediaspaces rely on a digital network such as Integrated Services Digital Network (ISDN), local area network (LAN), or asynchronous transfer mode (ATM) [9,10,11].

Figure 1. Typical configuration for an analog mediaspace node.
(From IEEE MultiMedia, 6:2, 1999. © IEEE.1999. With permission.)

Mediaspaces provide users with different kinds of services, including:

- *Awareness view* [12]: a window displaying a series of small digitized images of the different nodes, grabbed at regular intervals;
- *Background connection*: a public source, instead of having a black screen when there is no connection (for example, a view of the campus or a TV channel);
- *Office share*: a background connection used to "share" an office with someone for a long period of time;

- *Videophone*: an audio and video link between two nodes, used like a traditional phone call;
- *Glance*: a one-way video connection lasting a few seconds, to see if someone is there.

The introduction and use of a mediaspace raise a lot of issues concerning the protection of individual privacy and access control. In all the existing systems, different technical solutions have been designed, along with the services, from a strict reciprocity rule ("I can see you if you can see me") to explicit negotiation or dynamic user-defined mechanisms for access control and notification. The cultural context around the mediaspace is also important. In addition to the technological solutions, social protocols and a sense of culture emerges when "living" in a mediaspace [13].

Gaver's analysis of the affordances of mediaspaces shows that the physical characteristics of devices modify the way users perceive and act in such spaces [14]. Following this approach and building on our own experience using these environments, we have identified three important principles for the design of a mediaspace:

- *Integrability*: the integrability of a mediaspace is the degree to which it supports existing practices and tools, rather than impose new ones on the user;
- *Flexibility*: the flexibility of a mediaspace is the degree to which its components can be repurposed to support new uses with little effort;
- *Privacy*: a mediaspace supports privacy when users can easily understand, operate and trust the mechanisms that control information available about them and others' access to it.

In this section, we detail these three principles and explain how they can be applied to the design of a mediaspace software infrastructure and user interfaces.

2.1 INTEGRABILITY

Bly et al. [2] emphasize the importance of placement and physical access to communication devices (such as cameras and monitors) and their integration into work practices. For example, videoconference rooms require users to go in a dedicated room, explicitly switching between personal and group activities. On the contrary, mediaspaces tend to augment physical space by integrating devices in the real world and making them instantly and permanently accessible. This approach eliminates the notion of a call, with a beginning and an end, and fosters smooth transitions between peripheral awareness (hearing and seeing) and more focused communication (listening and looking). In this sense, mediaspaces are related to Ubiquitous Computing [15] and Augmented Reality [16], two research directions that aim to integrate computers into the real world.

Grudin [17] suggests integrating groupware features with features that support individual activities and, if possible, adding them to already successful applications. In traditional desktop videoconferencing, which resemble videoconference rooms, users have to switch between the video application and the other ones until they find the optimal layout for the multiple windows on the screen. The telephone model implemented by these applications requires explicit actions for placing and accepting calls, making the interface even more cumbersome. In contrast, using a mediaspace is not a primary activity in itself. It is a peripheral activity that supports spontaneous interactions. However, this also makes mediaspace interfaces difficult to design, because the frequency and variety of uses are hardly compatible with a task-centered design approach.

Several mediaspace systems are able to manage existing applications or documents [9,10,11]. However, they tend to integrate them into their own framework, contrary to the idea of interacting with the mediaspace in the background of other activities. A mediaspace interface should be integrated into the software environment in the same way its physical devices are integrated in the real world. The ubiquitous/augmented approach should be used here: interactions with the mediaspace should not be available through a single workstation and/or application. Instead, we should integrate the digital media and the interface into any existing document or application, whether individual or collective. When designing the software infrastructure of a mediaspace, we must think in terms of components to integrate into existing practices, not in terms of new applications.

2.2 FLEXIBILITY

The affordances of analog mediaspaces depend not only on the physical properties of the devices, but also on how people can use them. Suchman points out [18] that people commonly improvise and repurpose their actions. Mediaspace hardware configurations can easily be tailored by moving devices, adjusting them (for example, the sound volume or the image brightness), replacing them, or combining them (adding a wide-angle lens or an audio mixer). Again, this contrasts with dedicated videoconference rooms where users cannot change complex preset setups.

A large variety of services can be created by changing the duration (very short, intermittent, or persistent) and the nature of media (small digitized image, video only or audio/video) of a connection. These services support different activities, from formal to informal and from scheduled to spontaneous. Like hardware configurations, mediaspace software should be tailorable. Instead of providing users with rigid predefined communication services, we should try to create a "medium" that users can adapt to suit their needs.

Bentley and Dourish [19] show that the notion of medium, as opposed to mechanisms, arises from systems openness and flexibility. Open protocols [20] and component architectures [21, 22] can serve to implement a set of basic mediaspace software parts for developers and users. Each of these parts would correspond to a well-defined set of system requirements: connection management, access control and notification, session management, digital media services, etc. Users could then define their own policies or patterns of use by configuring, replacing or combining these parts, like they do with physical devices. In many existing systems, this flexibility tends to be accessible only to developers or expert users. Care must be taken to bring tailorability to the large majority of non-programming users as well.

2.3 PRIVACY

Asymmetric connections such as awareness views and glances are essential for providing nonobtrusive awareness of the presence and activity of other mediaspace users. Since these services break the strict reciprocity rule of the real world, mechanisms become necessary to ensure users' privacy and, at the same time, keep the system as open and accessible as possible.

Privacy in a mediaspace is important because of the highly dynamic nature of access control to live media. Whereas access rights on documents are usually simple to specify by using read/write permissions granted by the owner, access rights on live video or audio sources are much more complex because of the multiple uses these media might serve. A short glance into an office, a slowly updated view or a live video feed correspond to different intentions by the caller although they have the same basic requirement (a video link). The identity of the person requesting live media is also important: relatives, friends, colleagues or strangers should not have the same access to a user's camera and microphone. Mediaspace software should provide users with notification mechanisms that help determine the identity and intention of the remote person. It should also provide users with simple mechanisms to control available information about themselves, based on this knowledge.

Another important issue is the extent to which users trust the system. When users turn off or unplug a physical device, they know the effects on the device and the system as a whole, they can easily check these effects, and they know they can always go back to the previous state. Ideally, the same should be true of software access control. Notification and control mechanisms should be simple so that people can trust them like physical mechanisms. Flexibility again offers the key to a successful compromise between unobtrusive spontaneous interactions and explicit access control. Users should not be restricted to binary choices (that is, accept or deny the service) but should be able to describe complex behavior such as changing the request before execution (for example, switching to a lower resolution). Graphical or auditory notification should also be available before, during and after the execution of a request, so that the state of the system is always known. Every modification of the access policy should be easily checked and reversible. All these elements contribute to Dourish's notion of selective accessibility [13].

3.   WEB SUPPORT FOR MEDIASPACES

HTTP is an application-level protocol for transferring resources across the Internet. A resource is "a network data object or service" [23] and is specified by a URL (Uniform Resource Locator). HTML is a simple data format used to create hypertext documents [24]. Together, these standards contributed to create the Web: a globally accessible and platform-independent hypermedia information system. The Web is one of the most successful systems for communication between people, and in many ways, it is becoming a central access point to applications and services: more and more applications and programming toolkits are able to use HTML for content description or HTTP as a transfer protocol.

This section investigates the use of these standards to support the implementation of a mediaspace software infrastructure. It presents several features of HTTP that make it suitable for connection management and digital video streaming services. It also shows how HTTP clients and HTML documents help create interfaces to these services consistent with the three principles introduced above.

3.1 INTEGRABILITY USING HTTP AND HTML

HTTP is a request/response protocol between a client and a server. It provides both parties with a set of methods and status codes to express different semantics. Client methods include retrieval and posting of data (GET and POST), which are the two basic actions performed when browsing the Web. Status codes allow servers to describe the success of a request (for example, 200 OK, followed by the requested document, image or sound), and also authorization or payment requirements, redirection to another resource, and server or client errors (including the famous 404 Not Found). Another code, rarely used in existing applications, indicates that the request succeeded but didn't generate any output for the client (204 No content). This feature of HTTP makes it possible to issue commands that do not retrieve data from the server. In a mediaspace server, these commands can control the switching of analog audio and video connections, or the movement of a remote camera. Access to the mediaspace is then achieved by including links such as `<a href="http://mediascape/connect_X_to_Y"> X-Y </a>` in any HTML document.

HTTP servers usually respond to each client independently of previous requests by the same client. A state management mechanism known as cookies [25] lets clients and servers place requests and responses within a larger context. A cookie set by the server in a response contains information that the client should transmit back in subsequent requests to that server. Generally, this information is a unique ID that lets the server restore the client's context. This notion of context simplifies the naming of the mediaspace's resources (services). A mediaspace server based on HTTP can use cookies to store the identity and location of users. This way, a unique resource `/connectWith.Y` can be used instead of multiple `/connect_X_to_Y` as mentioned previously. This lets different users use the same HTML document containing the appropriate URLs as an interface to the mediaspace services.

When an HTTP server receives a `GET` request, it usually sends back the corresponding resource and then closes the connection. A mechanism known as "server push" [26] can take advantage of a connection held open over multiple responses, so the server can send more data when available, every new piece of data replacing the previous one. This mechanism can be used to send a series of images instead of a single image. With this feature, HTTP can transmit live pictures and video streams from a mediaspace server to existing clients without modifying them or adding a plug-in. This makes digital video sources available to nearly everyone connected to the Internet.

The integrability of a mediaspace requires easy access to its services over time and space. By implementing the mediaspace software as HTTP servers, we can make analog connection management and digital video services available to any existing Web-aware application. By embedding HTML commands —URLs pointing to the servers—, we can make these services accessible from any Web document. These are two important steps towards the integration of the mediaspace interface into existing work environments.

3.2 FLEXIBILITY USING HTTP AND HTML

An HTTP URL usually has the following form:

```
http://host:port/path?querystring#fragment
```

The optional query string specifies parameters that control how the server handles the request, whereas the optional fragment consists of additional reference information to be interpreted by the client after the retrieval action has been successfully completed. For example, the query string parameters can control the duration of a connection (`http://mediascape/glance.nicolas?duration=3`) or request an image with a given resolution by specifying a zoom factor (`http://mediascape/glance.nicolas?zoom=4`).

In addition to letting users specialize requests, HTTP offers three types of intermediaries between a server and a client for composing a request/response chain:

- *Proxies* are forwarding agents. They receive requests, rewrite all or part of the message, and forward the reformatted request to the original server.
- *Tunnels* act as a relay point between two connections without changing the messages.
- *Gateways* act as a layer above some other server, translating the requests to the underlying server's protocol.

These intermediaries let developers customize an HTTP-based system. They can compose them to create new services from existing ones, for example adding a proxy to implement an access policy or a gateway to an ISDN videoconferencing system. They can configure or replace each element at any time without affecting the others. This lets developers share their experience by exchanging these elements. They can also benefit from existing clients and servers, and overcome possible incompatibilities by inserting intermediaries, for example, creating a tunnel to go through a security firewall.

The interface of EuroPARC's RAVE mediaspace used Buttons [27], a system based on end-user tailorable objects. Some of this systems characteristics are found in the way people create and edit HTML documents: different classes of users (worker, tinkerer, handyman, programmer) share their experience by begging, borrowing or stealing pieces of HTML from others. The current architecture of the Web encourages such forms of reuse, since anyone can view the source of an HTML document and copy and paste parts of it without understanding the details of how it works. The tolerant use of HTML tags by current browsers supports this reuse. The use of HTML-based interfaces to mediaspace services supports a tailoring culture based on existing skills and work practices, rather than the development of new ones. Thus, we can have interfaces that are easier to start, learn, operate and customize.

Using HTTP as a transfer and command protocol and HTML to describe the interface offers some level of tailorability to the users. Although perhaps insufficient in the long term, it allows quick creation of easily tested and modified prototypes.

3.3 PRIVACY USING HTTP AND HTML

Publishing information on the Web is like putting documents in the middle of the street, hoping that someone will see them. But it is hard to tell if anyone sees them and if so, who they are. Users need two things to communicate efficiently on the Web without exposing their privacy: they need to know who is retrieving the information they publish and to be able to deny access or adapt the information according to that knowledge.

Despite the saying that "On the Internet, nobody knows you're a dog", some information about the client always goes along with an HTTP request, often without the user's consent or knowledge. HTTP communication usually takes place over TCP/IP connections. Even before the client sends the first byte, an HTTP server already knows the name or IP address of the remote host from the underlying TCP connection. It can use this name or address to query the login name of the remote user (for example, through the Ident [28] daemon). This login name can then be used to inquire further details about the user, such as his or her real name and email address, through SMTP [29] or the Finger [30] protocol (Figure 2).

The HTTP server also gets information from the request sent by the client. This includes the name of the client software (possibly including operating system name and version), the types of media or encoding it can handle, the URL of the last resource accessed by the client, a cookie obtained from a previous request, or authentication information (Figure 3).

Most of the Web servers employed today do not use this information. At best, they record it into log files. Users usually don't know where these log files are stored, and getting the useful data out of them often requires running scripts. However, having all or part of this information, it is usually easy to guess the identity of the person or process that made the request, or at least to know whether it comes from a known source. An HTTP server specifically designed to ensure users' privacy could trigger notification and control mechanisms before handling requests. These mechanisms would let users decide of the reply, based on the identity or location of the requester and the description of the request itself.

```
Remote host      : sgi5.lri.fr
Remote TCP port  : 7832

Login name       : roussel

Real name        : Nicolas Roussel
Email address    : roussel@sgi5.lri.fr

Finger info      :

  Login name: roussel        In real life: Nicolas Roussel
  Directory: /u/roussel      Shell: /bin/sh

  On since Sep  7 10:12:11 on ttyq0 from :0.0
  4 minutes 3 seconds Idle Time

  No unread mail

  Plan:
    See my web page (http://www-ihm.lri.fr/~roussel/)
```

Figure 2. Sample information gathered from a TCP connection.

```
User-Agent : Mozilla/4.61C-SGI [en] (X11; I; IRIX64 6.5 IP30)
Accept : image/gif, image/x-xbitmap, image/jpeg, image/pjpeg,
image/png, */*
Accept-Encoding : gzip
Accept-Charset : iso-8859-1,*,utf-8
Accept-Language : en
Referer : http://www-ihm.lri.fr/
Cookie : LOCATION="office228"
Authorization: Basic bWJsOndlbmR4
```

Figure 3. Sample information sent by an HTTP client.

4. MEDIASCAPE

Since 1993, our group at LRI Université Paris-Sud has been working in a mediaspace that connects our offices with audio/video links. Over these years, we have developed several software prototypes for low-level analog switching, digital video transmission, abstract services and collaborative session management, access control and notification. Mediascape is one of the prototypes we have developed to explore the ideas described in the previous section. It is a mediaspace based on an analog audio/video network connecting six workspaces (or nodes), several public spaces, a VCR and one of our workstations used to digitize analog images.

Figure 4 shows Mediascape hardware configuration. For simplicity, it shows only three nodes and does not include audio equipment. Node A is an analog node with the camera and monitor connected to the switch. Node B, a digital node, uses a digital camera and displays video on the computer screen. It also sends and receives analog video through a video digitizing board. Node C is an analog node where the workstation can control the orientation and zoom of the camera through a serial line. The public nodes consist of a window camera and a VCR. SwC marks the workstation that controls the switch through a serial line. It runs the connection server used by other nodes to establish connections.

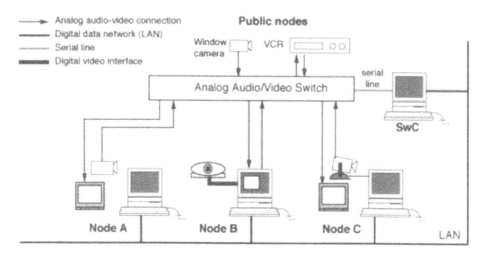

Figure 4. Mediascape hardware configuration.
(From IEEE MultiMedia, 6:2, 1999. © IEEE.1999. With permission.)

Mediascape offers the following services to our group:

- register, to inform the system of the user's current location;
- glance, a bi-directional analog video-only connection lasting a few seconds;
- call, a bi-directional analog audio/video connection, lasting an unknown duration (like video phone);
- authlevel, to choose between three levels of accessibility (everything, glance only, or nothing).

In addition to these services available to local people only, three other services are publicly available:

- postit, to allow other users to leave messages on our computer screens;
- grab, to get a frame-grabbed still image from one of our nodes.

The current implementation of Mediascape consists of two custom HTTP servers: one for analog connection management and image digitizing, the other for driving a computer-controlled video camera. Digital images are captured on a per-request basis. They are available in different sizes, from 80x60 to 640x480 pixels, and can be gamma corrected (specifying these with a query string). PostIt messages composition employs an HTML form sent by the connection server and can contain HTML code. Commands automatically added to the message include the sender's name and a snapshot that can be used to call back the sender (Figure 5).

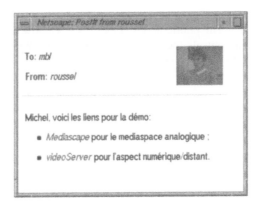

Figure 5. PostIt sample.
(From <u>IEEE MultiMedia</u>, 6:2, 1999. © IEEE.1999. With permission.)

4.1 MEDIASCAPE INTEGRABILITY

The connection server uses resource names containing only the service and the callee names (for example, /call.nicolas). People must identify themselves with their name and location the first time they use the mediaspace. The server stores their location and sets a cookie in their client containing the user's name, which accompanies any subsequent request. Thus, when the server receives a request for /call.nicolas, it also contains a cookie such as NAME=Paul, telling who wants to call Nicolas. If the request does not contain the cookie, the server returns a user identification form to the client. Users can change their location by issuing a register command (such as /register.office228). The connection server also permits requesting several resources at once: /glance.paul/glance.michel.

An HTML document can contain references to other resources in a number of ways, such as images, hypertext anchors or embedded objects. We can use existing Web browsers to build a mediaspace interface by including the appropriate code in an HTML document. For example:

- Include a snapshot grabbed upon retrieval of the document

```
<img src="http://mediascape/grab.nicolas">
```

- Add links to allow people to call me or my officemate

```
Call <a href="http://mediascape/call.nicolas"> me </a>
or <a href="http://mediascape/call.paul"> Paul </a>
to know where is office 228
```

- Combine the two previous examples to include a snapshot that people can click on to call me

```
<a href="http://mediascape/call.nicolas">
<img src="http://mediascape/grab.nicolas">
</a>
```

- Add JavaScript code to a text link that will execute a glance when the mouse passes over it

```
<a
href=http://www-ihm.lri.fr/~roussel/
onMouseOver="window.location='http://mediascape/glance.nicolas"
> N. Roussel </a>
```

- Add a link to compose a postit for Paul

```
<a href="/postit.paul"> Note for Paul </a>
```

- Add a command that executes several glances in sequence

```
<embed
src="http://mediascape/glance.michel/glance.stephane">
```

The default interface to Mediascape is an HTML document that displays still images of the different users (Figure 6). The server alters these images to reflect users' accessibility. Three icons represent door states, as in CAVECAT [8]. Each door state (open, ajar or closed) corresponds to an authorization level (`authlevel` service) controlled by the user. A user can glance at others by moving the mouse over their name or call them by clicking on the snapshot. Two other icons provide access to the PostIt service and a mail gateway. The document also contains metainformation that tells the browser to reload it after a few minutes to keep it up to date. As explained previously, the use of cookies in the connection server and the naming of resources (for example `/call.nicolas` instead of `/X.call.nicolas`) allow everyone to use the same document.

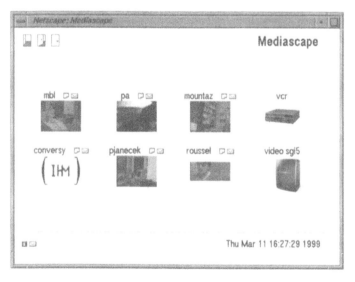

Figure 6. Basic interface to Mediascape.
Conversy has closed his door and Roussel's is ajar.
The two rightmost icons give access to public nodes (a VCR and a digital video source).
(From IEEE MultiMedia, 6:2, 1999. © IEEE.1999. With permission.)

4.2 MEDIASCAPE FLEXIBILITY

Since Mediascape's basic interface is an ordinary HTML document, users familiar with HTML authoring can save a copy and modify it to create their own personal interface. Users could for example select a subset of the users, remove icons to save screen space, or add icons that allow panning, tilting and zooming with the remote camera. This type of adaptation — described as surface customization of the interface [19]— lets users choose between a number of predefined options, determined by the capabilities of HTML and other related languages such as JavaScript or VRML.

So far, we have only seen *dedicated* HTML documents used to interface our mediaspace. However, HTML code requesting Mediascape resources can also be added to *existing* documents. When collaborating on a project, people can add snapshots and Mediascape commands to the project description. This allows any project member to know who is around and easily make connections every time he checks the current state of the project. This assists coordination: in a co-authoring situation, the authors can include a connect command in the document (Figure 7). Each time one of the authors reads or works on the document, the connection with the other author is automatically established. As an increasing number of email applications understand HTML and HTTP, mediaspace commands can also be included in a message and executed when the receiver reads it, again providing implicit coordination between users.

Figure 7. Coordination between co-authors through a Mediascape-aware document. Here, we can see that both authors are present at the same time. (From IEEE MultiMedia, 6:2, 1999. © IEEE.1999. With permission.)

4.3 MEDIASCAPE PRIVACY

The Mediascape servers log all requests. Users can check the log files to see if someone called in their absence. They can also use applications that monitor these files and deliver feedback when someone requests a connection or an image from the Web. For example, they could use nonspeech audio to differentiate between callers.

For privacy purposes, a request for a still image grabbed by the video digitizer is treated like a glance, because these requests usually come from distant users who do not have access to our analog audio/video network. Whereas analog services are based on a strict reciprocity rule, image digitizing uses a relaxed version of this relationship because remote users can see us but we can't see them. We use the information gathered from the HTTP connection to identify the caller and forward this information to the callee. If someone repeatedly asks for images, it is usually easy to let them know we are aware of their presence by gesturing, showing a message on a piece of paper, or sending an email.

5. VIDEOSERVER

Mediascape supports local audio/video connections as well as remote access to live pictures, but not remote live video or audio. To support video communication over long distance with colleagues, friends or relatives, we have designed and implemented videoServer, a software component for both interpersonal and interprocess digital video transmission.

The first videoServer prototype was an extension of our Web server (a CGI script). The current implementation is a custom HTTP server written in C++ that can run efficiently on SGI workstations —ports are underway on Macintosh, MS-Windows and Linux platforms. It encodes live or prerecorded video as a series of JPEG images (also known as Motion-JPEG or MJPEG) and sends them using the server push mechanism described earlier.

VideoServer offers the following services:

- `/photo` captures a single live image;
- `/video` produces a series of live images;
- `/file/test` sends a video file named "test" in the directory from which videoServer was launched.

5.1 VIDEOSERVER INTEGRABILITY

Since most Web browsers can display a server-pushed sequence of images in place of an ordinary image without any plug-in, videoServer allows a large number of users to get live video. The frame rate depends on the available bandwidth. A typical 160x120 JPEG image is about 3 Kbytes and we routinely get 10 to 15 frames per seconds, even over long distances. A snapshot image, live or recorded video can be included in place of any image in an HTML document simply by using links of the following types:

```
<img src="http://videoserver/photo">
<img src="http://videoserver/video">
<img src="http://videoserver/file/test">
```

We have distributed videoServer outside the lab to experiment with bi-directional connections with friends and colleagues. We often use these long distance digital video links in conjunction with third-party applications such as text chat or audio broadcasting, or with regular phone calls.

5.2 VIDEOSERVER FLEXIBILITY

Clients can use a query string to specify the compression ratio and zoom factor of live images (for example `/photo?zoom=4&cratio=20.0`). These two parameters let clients adapt their requests to the available bandwidth by reducing the resolution or augmenting the compression ratio. For live video, two extra parameters are available to specify the number of images requested and the time to wait between two subsequent images. The former can be used to create a glance connection, the latter to create awareness views updated at a slow rate.

More sophisticated HTML code can be used. For example, the following code uses JavaScript to insert a snapshot that turns into live video when the cursor is over it and turns back to a snapshot when the cursor leaves it:

```
<a
href=http://www-ihm.lri.fr/
onMouseOver='document.img1.src="http://videoserver/video"'
onMouseOut='document.img1.src="http://videoserver/photo"'>
<img name="img1" src="http://videoserver/photo" >
</a>
```

This code can be used to create an awareness view from several videoServers (**Figure 8**). This document differs from traditional awareness views in two ways. First, users can freely modify the set of images, which is not restricted to a list of registered people. Second, the JavaScript code allows two-degree awareness by switching between still and live images.

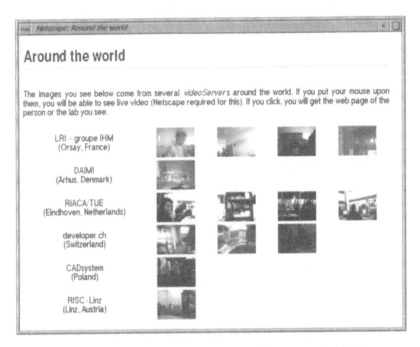

Figure 8. HTML document presenting images from several videoServers. (From IEEE MultiMedia, 6:2, 1999. © IEEE.1999. With permission.)

5.3 VIDEOSERVER PRIVACY

For every request it receives, videoServer executes an external notifier program with arguments indicating the name of the client's machine, possibly the sender's login name, the requested service and the values of the query string arguments. The notifier sends back the description of the service to execute, which can differ from the one the client requested. This simple mechanism lets people control the available information about themselves and how other users can access it.

The default notifier, a UNIX shell script, allows users to easily define different access policies. For example, different sounds can reflect the requested service or the address of the remote client, implementing a form of caller ID. The notifier program can also control image access. Since the notifier can redefine the service to execute, it lets users change the resolution, quality, number of images and refresh rate. In particular, a very high compression factor generates a highly degraded image that still provides useful information, such as the number of people present (Figure 9). Such degraded images can be used for example for requests issued by unidentified users. Another interesting use of service redefinition for privacy is the ability to send a prerecorded sequence instead of live video, for example, a short clip showing that the person is away or busy.

Figure 9. Degrading image quality by increasing compression.

When the request does not specify the number of images for live video, videoServer limits it to 5000 (that is, up to three minutes). This ensures that constant monitoring cannot take place without periodically asking permission. Thus, when every service has an associated auditory notification, repeated requests quickly gain notice, as if someone stood watching through the window while leaving a finger on a doorbell.

6. VIDEOSPACE

To access Mediascape and videoServer, end-users can create dedicated HTML documents or modify existing ones. This approach supports quick prototyping of high-level services by cutting and pasting HTML code or exchanging files and emails. However, browsers' capabilities and the description languages they use limit this document-centric approach. In some cases, we may want to use complex data and input/output techniques —for example, touchpad, sound or shaped windows— not available in HTML browsers. We may also want to access or control the mediaspace from within other existing applications, such as a shared editor.

In order to extend the accessibility of mediaspace services, we have developed videoSpace, a software toolkit designed to facilitate the integration of live video into existing or new applications for the purpose of supporting collaborative activities. The first goal of videoSpace is to promote the development of collaborative environments where communication facilities are embedded in the applications rather than provided as separate applications. The second goal of videoSpace is to support novel uses of video by supporting real-time filtering of live video images.

6.1 TOOLKIT OVERVIEW

The videoSpace toolkit is implemented in C++, with Tcl/Tk [31] and Python [32] bindings also available. The design of the toolkit has been driven by the principle that simple things should be simple and complex things should be possible. Creating a video connection requires a few lines of code; managing multiple sources and including video processing is not much more complicated. For a detailed description of the toolkit, see [33].

VideoSpace is organized around the following basic concepts:

- Images: rectangular pixmaps in various formats;
- Image sources: objects that generate images;
- Image filters: algorithms that transform or analyze images;
- Image sinks: visible representations of images;

- Multiplexers: control objects that can wait on several sources and sinks simultaneously to multiplex several streams.

Two kinds of image sources are available: local sources (local files and digitizing hardware) and network sources. Network sources are servers generating series of JPEG images. Naturally, videoServers are the most common network sources we use. However, we also use anonymous WebCams available on the Internet that also use the server push protocol.

In addition to the server push streaming mechanism, two alternative protocols have been added to videoServer. Instead of sending the images over the TCP connection associated with the HTTP request, videoServer can send them as unicast or multicast UDP datagrams, using the TCP connection as a signaling channel. UDP can be more efficient than TCP over long distance and is well adapted to live video: lost packets are not retransmitted, therefore achieving the best possible frame rate and lag according to the available network bandwidth. However, these two UDP-based protocols are available only to videoSpace applications, not to traditional Web browsers.

Image sources are described by an encoding —a pixel format— and a URL. Image source objects are created from their URL by a factory object. When a new source type is added to the toolkit (for example, if a new protocol is implemented in videoServer), the factory object is modified to handle the corresponding URLs and all applications benefit from it without any other change. In addition to standard HTTP URLs used to access server push sources, two new URL schemes have been introduced for UDP unicast and multicast protocols (vstp and vsmp). When given one of these URLs, the image source factory is responsible for sending the appropriate HTTP request to the videoServer, adding information to describe the UDP protocol to use as well as the host (or group) address and port number. For example, the URL

```
vstp://sgi5.lri.fr/video?zoom=2
```

accessed from the machine sgi3 would result in an HTTP request like

```
GET /video/udp?zoom=2&host=sgi3.lri.fr&port=8965 HTTP/1.0
```

sent to the videoServer running on machine sgi5.

Every videoSpace application can be seen as a custom HTTP client able to retrieve video images from several network servers and local sources at the same time and display or process these images in an arbitrary way. These applications supplement the document-centric approach described in the previous two sections in a consistent way: the same HTTP URLs can be used in HTML documents and videoSpace applications to access videoServers, which will use the same notification and control mechanisms, regardless of the origin of the request.

6.2 SAMPLE APPLICATIONS

Several applications have been developed with videoSpace to allow users to display video streams outside HTML documents. The simplest client, videoClient, displays a single stream in a window on the computer screen that the user can resize. This application can be used for focused forms of communication, for example accompanying a phone call (Figure 10).

Several other applications take advantage of the analog video output capability of some workstations to display one or more video streams on a TV monitor. One such application has been used to install a mediaspace between two common spaces at Aarhus University (Figure 11).

Figure 10. videoClient.

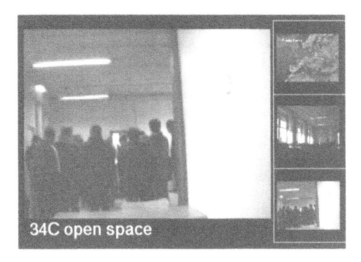

34C open space

Figure 11. Snapshot of an analog video output showing a weather map updated from CNN's web site and live video from two common spaces.

VideoClient can take advantage of the architecture of the X Window system to display video in a new subwindow of a running application, rather than in a new window. With a few lines of Unix shell commands, it is possible to add video to any running application. Figure 12 shows an *xterm* window running the Unix *talk* program with an embedded videoClient. Since the video window is a child of the xterm window, it is moved, raised, lowered and iconified with it. In addition, interaction with the video window (for example, clicking in it) is handled by videoClient, not the host application.

This approach can also be used in conjunction with user interface toolkits that explicitly support widgets that host external applications. For example, the frame widget of the Tcl/Tk toolkit can host a separate application by setting the widget's 'container' property to true. We have developed a series of simple Tcl/Tk applications based on that feature.

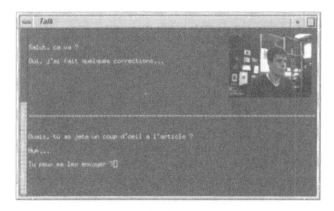

Figure 12. Vtalk, a video "augmented" talk.

One such application provides a lightweight awareness view showing local Mediascape users and remote videoServers. It consists only of a title bar that reveals recent snapshots of the users when the cursor passes over it (Figure 13). We also have integrated videoClient with GroupKit [34], a Tcl/Tk-based toolkit for developing groupware applications. With a few lines of code, any GroupKit application such as a shared drawing editor can be "augmented" with video links between the participants.

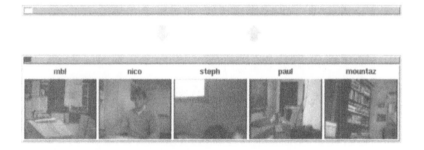

Figure 13. Lightweight awareness view.
(From IEEE MultiMedia, 6:2, 1999. © IEEE.1999. With permission.)

Developers can also use the C++ API of videoSpace to implement their own video-enabled client applications. In particular, with the advent of digital video and the increasing CPU power of computers, the images of a video stream can be analyzed in real-time to extract useful information. VideoSpace supports video filters that can transform or analyze the video frames as they go through the application. Previous work on mediaspaces shows that such video filters can enhance their services. Examples include remote camera control by local movement detection [35], addition of recent activity representation to digitized images [36], and to support privacy, substitution of a shadow for a person [37], or eigen-space filtering [38]. VideoSpace supports several techniques based on simple image difference and partition algorithms to extend collaborative applications (including Mediascape). These extensions include context capture —knowing whether a user is present or absent—, motion detection, and image segmentation to support natural annotation and gesturing [33].

VideoServer is an HTTP server. The videoSpace applications presented so far are HTTP clients. Other applications can be implemented that correspond to other roles in the HTTP request/response chain. For example, a proxy could compose several image sources and make the resulting composition available as a single video stream. A gateway could translate between the UDP-based protocol and the server-push protocol, so that video displayed in HTML documents would also benefit from the faster frame rate provided by UDP.

7. SUMMARY

We have introduced three important principles for the design of a mediaspace: integrability, flexibility and privacy. We have described how to use the Web standards and protocols to implement the software infrastructure and the user interfaces of a mediaspace with respect to these principles. We have presented Mediascape, our Web-controlled analog mediaspace, videoServer, a Web server dedicated to digital video communication, and videoSpace, a toolkit based on videoServer to integrate live video into applications.

We have described how Mediascape supports a document-centric approach through the design and use of different interfaces. Commands for the mediaspace services can be integrated into any HTML document, making it easily accessible, intuitive to use and easy to adapt and customize. We have described how videoServer expands our local mediaspace to distant people, again using a document-centric approach, by taking advantage of the simple server push mechanism to bring live video into Web browsers. We have shown how the notification and control mechanisms of videoServer provide a good balance between this high degree of accessibility and the need for privacy. VideoSpace is an example of an application-centric approach of the Web: by developing applications as a set of custom HTTP clients, servers or intermediaries, it is possible to overcome the limitations of Web browsers but still be compatible with them.

The document-centric approach has proved useful for informal communication between distant people. This is not surprising. The properties we might choose to describe daily Web usage in a workplace would probably be close to the ones that describe informal communication: frequent, brief, intermittent, unscheduled, lacking formal openings or closings. The application-centric approach offered by videoSpace allows to move towards more complex or focused forms of communication, such as traditional videoconferencing tools or collaborative applications.

The notification and control mechanisms implemented in videoServer are rather unusual for an HTTP server. Most traditional servers are designed to bring generic information online, regardless of who is making it available or who is retrieving it. In order to communicate through the Web, people have to make trade-offs: when you put a picture of your house, your dog or your children on the Web, it is accessible to your friends and relatives, but also to perfect strangers. People usually accept this, sometimes naively thinking that if the picture is not referenced anywhere, it will be accessible only to those who have the exact URL. We believe that simple content negotiation and access notification based on the user or process that made the request could lead to more subtle forms of communication between individuals. Our current work investigates the generalization of such mechanisms to other media than video (text documents for example) and to evaluate the impact of these mechanisms on client and server architectures as well as Web protocols.

Detailed information about videoSpace and its availability can be obtained from `http://www-ihm.lri.fr/~roussel/videoSpace/`

Acknowledgments

Thanks are due to Michel Beaudouin-Lafon for the inspiration and motivation for the development of Mediascape, videoServer and videoSpace. I thank Stéphane Conversy for the many discussions we had about the implementation of HTTP clients and servers. I also want to acknowledge the different people around the world who have used videoServer and thank them for their enthusiasm and collaboration. This work was partially funded by CNET-France Telecom.

References

1. R. Stults, "Media Space," Technical Report, Xerox PARC, 1986.
2. S.A. Bly, S.R. Harrison, and S. Irwin, "Mediaspaces: Bringing people together in a video, audio and computing environment," *Communications of the ACM*, 36(1), January 1993, pp. 28-47.
3. W. E. Mackay, "Media Spaces: Environments for Informal Multimedia Interaction," In M. Beaudouin-Lafon, Editor, "Computer-Supported Co-operative Work," Trends in Software Series, John Wiley & Sons Ltd., 1999.
4. E. A. Isaacs, S. Whittaker, D. Frohlich, and B. O'Conaill. "Informal Communication Re-examined: New Functions for Video in Supporting Opportunistic Encounters," In K. E. Finn, A. J. Sellen, and S. B. Wilbur, Editors, Video-Mediated Communication, Lawrence Erlbaum Associates, 1997.
5. C. Cool, R.S. Fish, R.E. Kraut, and C.M. Lowery, "Iterative Design of Video Communication Systems," *Proceedings of ACM CSCW'92 Conference on Computer-Supported Cooperative Work*, Toronto, Ontario, ACM, New York, November 1992, pp. 25-32.
6. W. Buxton and T. Moran, "EuroPARC's Integrated Interactive Intermedia Facility (IIIF): Early Experiences," In Multi-User Interfaces and Applications, S. Gibbs and A.A. Verrijn-Stuart, North-Holland, September 1990, *Proceedings of IFIP WG8.4 Conference*, Heraklion, Greece, pp. 11-34.
7. W.W. Gaver, T. Moran, A. MacLean, L. Lövstrand, P. Dourish, K. Carter, and W. Buxton, "Realizing a Video Environment: EuroPARC's RAVE System," *Proceedings of ACM CHI'92 Conference on Human Factors in Computing Systems*, ACM, New York, 1992, pp. 27-35.
8. M.M. Mantei, R.M. Baecker, A.J. Sellen, W.A.S. Buxton, and T. Milligan, "Experiences in the Use of a Media Space," *Proceedings of ACM CHI'91 Conference on Human Factors in Computing Systems*, ACM, New York, 1991, pp. 203-308.
9. K. Watabe, S. Sakata, K. Maeno, H. Fukuoka, and T. Ohmori, "Distributed Multiparty Desktop Conferencing System: MERMAID," *Proceedings of ACM CSCW'90 Conference on Computer-Supported Cooperative Work*, ACM, New York, October 1990, pp. 27-38.
10. H. Gajewska, J. Kistler, M.S. Manasse, and D.D.Redell, "Argo: A System for Distributed Collaboration," *Proceedings of Multimedia 94*, ACM, New York, October 1994, pp. 433-440.
11. J.C. Tang and M. Rua, "Montage: Providing Teleproximity for Distributed Groups," *Proceedings of ACM CHI'94 Conference on Human Factors in Computing Systems*, ACM, New York, April 1994, pp. 37-43.
12. P. Dourish and S. Bly, "Portholes: Supporting Awareness in a Distributed Work Group," *Proceedings of ACM CHI'92 Conference on Human Factors in Computing Systems*, ACM, New York, 1992, pp. 541-547.
13. P. Dourish, "Culture and Control in a Media Space," *Proceedings of European Conference on Computer-Supported Cooperative Work ECSCW'93*, Milano, Kluwer Academic Publishers, September 1993, pp. 335-341.
14. W.W. Gaver, "The Affordances of Media Spaces for Collaboration," *Proceedings of ACM CSCW'92 Conference on Computer-Supported Cooperative Work*, Toronto, Ontario, ACM, New York, November 1992, pp. 17-24.

15. W. Buxton, "Living in Augmented Reality: Ubiquitous Media and Reactive Environments," In K. Finn, A. Sellen, and S. Wilber, editors, Video Mediated Communication, Lawrence Erlbaum Associates, 1997.
16. M. Beaudouin-Lafon, "Beyond the Workstation, Media Spaces and Augmented Reality," In People and Computers IX, Cambridge University Press, August 1994. Opening plenary session at HCI'94 (Glasgow, UK), pp. 9-18.
17. J. Grudin, "Groupware and Social Dynamics: Eight Challenges for Developers," *Communications of the ACM*, 37(1), January 1994, pp. 92-105.
18. L. Suchman, "Office Procedures as Practical Action: Models of Work and System Design," *ACM Transactions on Office Information Systems*, Vol. 1, 1983, pp. 320-328.
19. R. Bentley and P. Dourish, "Medium Versus Mechanism: Supporting Collaboration Through Customization," *Proceedings of European Conference on Computer-Supported Cooperative Work ECSCW'95*, Stockholm, Kluwer Academic Publishers, September 1995, pp. 133-148.
20. M. Roseman and S. Greenberg, "Building Flexible Groupware Through Open Protocols," *Proceedings of ACM Conference on Organizational Computing Systems*, California, ACM Press, October 1993, pp. 279-288.
21. O. Stiemerling, "Supporting Tailorability in Groupware through Component Architectures," *Proceedings of the ECSCW '97 Workshop on Object Oriented Groupware Platforms*, Lancaster, GB, September 1997, pp. 53-57.
22. G.H. ter Hofte, "Working Apart Together : Foundations for Component Groupware," Number 001 in Telematica Instituut Fundamental Research Series, Telematica Instituut, Enschede, the Netherlands, 1998.
23. R. Fielding, J. Gettys, J. Mogul, H. Frystyk, L. Masinter, P. Leach, and T. Berners-Lee, "Hypertext Transfer Protocol - HTTP/1.1," Standards Track, RFC 2616, IETF Network Working Group, June 1999.
24. D. Raggett, A. Le Hors, and I. Jacobs, "HyperText Markup Language - HTML/4.0," Technical Report, W3C User Interface Domain, April 1998, http://www.w3.org/TR/REC-html40/.
25. D. Kristol and L. Montulli, "HTTP State Management Mechanism," Proposed Standard, RFC 2109, IETF Network Working Group, February 1997.
26. "An Exploration of Dynamic Documents," Technical Report, Netscape Communications, 1995, http://home.netscape.com/assist/net_sites/pushpull.html.
27. A. Maclean, K. Carter, L. Lövstrand, and T. Moran, "User Tailorable Systems: Pressing the Issues with Buttons," *Proceedings of ACM CHI'90 Conference on Human Factors in Computing Systems*, Seattle, ACM, New York, April 1990, pp. 175-182.
28. M. St Johns, "Authentication Server," RFC 931, IETF Network Working Group, January 1985.
29. J. Postel, "Simple Mail Transfer Protocol," RFC 821, IETF Network Working Group, August 1982.
30. D. Zimmerman, "The Finger User Information Protocol," RFC 1288, IETF Network Working Group, December 1991.
31. Tcl/Tk Home Page, Scriptics Corporation, http://www.scriptics.com/.
32. Python Language Home Page. http://www.python.org/.
33. N. Roussel and M. Beaudouin-Lafon, "VideoSpace: A Toolkit for Building Mediaspaces," Research Report 1216, LRI, Université Paris-Sud, France, May 1999.
34. M. Roseman and S. Greenberg, "Building Real Time Groupware with GroupKit, A Groupware Toolkit," *ACM Transactions on Computer-Human Interaction*, 3(1), March 1996, pp. 66-106.
35. W.W. Gaver, G. Smets, and K. Overbeeke, "A Virtual Window On Media Space," *Proceedings of ACM CHI'95 Conference on Human Factors in Computing Systems*, Denver, ACM, New York, May 1995, pp. 257-264.

36. A. Lee, A. Girgensohn, and K. Schlueter, "NYNEX Portholes: Initial User Reactions and Redesign Implications," *Proceedings of GROUP'97*, Phoenix, ACM, 1997, pp. 385-394.
37. S. E. Hudson and I. Smith, "Techniques for Addressing Fundamental Privacy and Disruption Tradeoffs in Awareness Support Systems," *Proceedings of ACM CSCW'96 Conference on Computer-Supported Cooperative Work*, Boston, Mass., ACM, New York, November 1996, pp. 248-257.
38. J. Coutaz, F. Bérard, E. Carraux, and J. Crowley, "Early Experience with the Mediaspace CoMedi," *Proceedings of IFIP Working Conference on Engineering for Human-Computer Interaction*, Heraklion, Crete, 1998.

Chapter 10

FreeWalk: SHARED VIRTUAL SPACE FOR CASUAL MEETINGS

Hideyuki Nakanishi, Chikara Yoshida, Toshikazu Nishimura, and Toru Ishida

Abstract

In this chapter we present FreeWalk, a meeting environment for casual communication in a networked community, which provides a 3D common area where everyone can meet and talk freely. FreeWalk represents participants as 3D polygon pyramids, on which their live video is mapped. Voice volume remains proportional to the distance between sender and receiver. For evaluation, we compared communications in FreeWalk to a conventional desktop videoconferencing system and a face-to-face meeting.

1. INTRODUCTION

Most computer systems for collaborative work provide desktop videoconferencing tools for business meetings. However, meetings aren't always formal or business related. Casual meetings such as chatting during a coffee break or in a hallway occur daily. They maintain human relationships, and also play an important role in collaboration. We believe that conventional desktop videoconferencing systems, which multicast pictures and voices, can't support casual meetings.

We aim to support everyday activities by forming a community through computer networks. Our product FreeWalk [1, 2], a social environment for communication lets people meet casually in shared three-dimensional (3D) virtual spaces such as a park or a lobby. The following list describes the inherent features of casual meetings and how FreeWalk can support them.

1. *Casual meetings*

    In conventional desktop videoconferencing systems such as Office Mermaid [3], participants turn on the system when they start a meeting. When in operation, the system displays the faces of all participants on their workstations, which hinders free conversation. The system lists the participants before the meeting starts, thereby prohibiting accidental encounters with other participants.

Several desktop videoconferencing systems have tried to extend their functions to support casual meetings. Cruiser [4] randomly selects some of the participants and displays their faces to other participants to simulate accidental encounters. In contrast, FreeWalk's approach provides a common virtual space for casual meetings wherein participants can move and meet by themselves. It doesn't promote any system-directed encounters. The participants' faces display on screen only when the bodies of their avatars meet.

2.   *Meetings with many people*

In meetings such as parties, several tens of participants simultaneously exist in the same space. In such cases, it's almost impossible to use desktop videoconferencing systems, since they try to display the faces of all participants at once. Plus, even if it were possible, it would be very hard for users to comprehend the situation.

In FreeWalk, participants can freely change their locations and view directions. For example, they can wander around before they talk to someone else. They can also watch other participants.

Many systems realize a 3D shared virtual space. The Distributed Interactive Virtual Environment (DIVE) [5], a multiuser platform, lets people create, modify, and remove objects dynamically. This system has a script language to define autonomic behaviors of objects. Another multiuser virtual environment, Diamond Park [6], has a park, a village, and an open-air cafe. In addition, Community Place [7] integrates Virtual Reality Modeling Language (VRML) and has an online chat forum. InterSpace [8] supports audio and video communication for the experimental service CyberCampus, which features distance learning and online shopping. These systems aim to construct realistic virtual worlds containing many kinds of virtual objects such as mountains, oceans, buildings, artifacts, and so on.

We implemented a basic system to support casual meetings in a 3D virtual space that represents dynamic changes in people's locations during casual meetings. The role of 3D space in our system resembles the spatial model of interaction in Massive [9], a VR-based conferencing system with text and audio communication.

Since researchers have not sufficiently investigated social interactions in 3D virtual space, we conducted an experiment to determine the characteristics of interactions in FreeWalk.

2. INTERACTION DESIGN

In this section we describe FreeWalk's design for interaction of the 3D community common area. We also discuss how FreeWalk supports casual group meetings.

2.1 3D COMMUNITY COMMON AREA

Figure 1 shows an image of a FreeWalk window. FreeWalk provides a 3D community common area where people can meet. Participants move and turn freely in the space using their mouse (just as in a video game). Locations and view directions of participants in the space determine which pictures and voices get transmitted.

Figure 1. FreeWalk window.

In this 3D space, a pyramid of 3D polygons represents each participant. The system maps live video of each participant on one rectangular plane of the pyramid, and the participant's viewpoint lies at the center of this rectangle. The view of the community common area from a participant's particular viewpoint appears in the FreeWalk window. Figure 2a shows participant A's view when participants B and C are located as shown in Figure 2b.

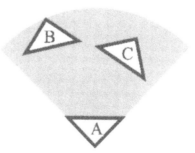

(a) Participant A's view   (b) Map of B and C's locations

Figure 2. Participant's view of community common area.

Participants standing far away in the 3D environment appear smaller and those closer appear larger. FreeWalk does not display participants located beyond a predefined distance. The system also transfers voices under the same policy—that is, voice volume changes in proportion to the distance between sender and receiver (see Figure 3).

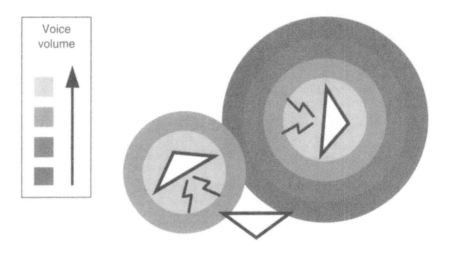

Figure 3. Voice transfer.

2.2 SIMULATING CASUAL MEETINGS

In FreeWalk, meetings can start with an accidental encounter. Figure 4 shows an example of an accidental encounter, where the user finds others on the radar screen displayed at the right bottom corner of the window (Figure 4a), watches them to find out what they are talking about (Figure 4b), and then joins them (Figure 4c).

(a) Finding others on the radar screen   (b) Watching a talking pair

(c) Joining their conversation

Figure 4. Accidental encounter.

Since distance attenuates voice, a participant must approach the others in order to talk to them. On the other hand, not only can the participants in the conversation hear the speaker's voice, but anyone in the neighborhood can listen. This mechanism forces people to combine actions and conversations in the space. People can smoothly join the conversation that attracts their interest, since they can guess the subject by listening to the conversation beforehand. People can exit a conversation by leaving a group and join a conversation by approaching another group.

2.3 ORGANIZING MEETING GROUPS

Desktop videoconferencing systems provide various functions to support the organizational behavior of participants, such as speaker selection. Although these functions let participants manage multiple conversation threads in parallel, they also damage the freedom we're aiming for. FreeWalk doesn't take this approach. Instead, it uses a common 3D space that promotes a casual feeling in communication.

People form a group by standing close to each other to engage in conversation. Figure 5 shows this situation. Since voice volume attenuates in proportion to the distance between sender and receiver, people can have a confidential conversation by keeping away from others. If groups have enough distance between them, people in one group can't hear people in other groups. Therefore, participants can form separate meeting groups and not bother each other. This feature makes FreeWalk an effective tool for holding a party.

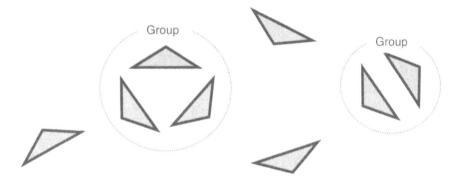

Figure 5. Meeting organization.

2.4 USING NONVERBAL SIGNALS

Space provides a context for interaction [10]. Spatial positioning is a nonverbal cue, which serves to communicate liking and disliking and attraction to a relationship. The orientation of a body and eye contact are used to start, sustain, and end interactions. These nonverbal signals are important in casual meetings since they smooth out and regulate social behavior. In the virtual space of FreeWalk, users can partially use these signals.

Interaction is controlled by a behavior that is changing body orientation, and communication becomes easy to do if this behavior is judged correctly [11]. The behavior that is turning directions of eyes, a head and a body is based on the structure of a human body. Turning behavior reflects emotional attitude toward others. The orientation of a pyramid represents the body orientation of a user in FreeWalk.

Since the participants' locations and view directions reflect a pyramid orientation, each participant can observe the distances or directions of other participants and what other people are doing from a distance. Participants can also observe others around them by turning their body. Figure 6 shows the view changes of participants A and B as participant B changes his direction in front of A.

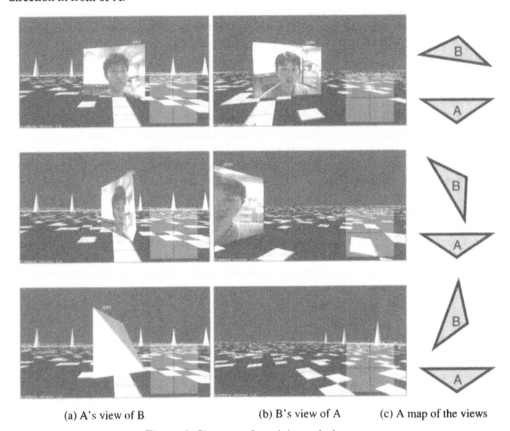

(a) A's view of B   (b) B's view of A   (c) A map of the views

Figure 6. Changes of participants' views.

3. SYSTEM DESIGN

In this section we discuss FreeWalk's system design and implementation.

3.1 SYSTEM CONFIGURATION

The FreeWalk system consists of a community server and clients, each of which includes vision and voice processes. Figure 7 illustrates the interaction between the community server and clients.

When participants move in the 3D space using their mouse, the corresponding client calculates the new location and orientation, and sends them to the community server. The server then compiles this information into a list of client locations in the 3D community common area. The server finally sends the list back to each client for screen updating. Since only control information transfers between the server and the clients, the community server can efficiently maintain a global view of the ongoing activities in the community common area.

When a client receives the list of other clients, the client's vision system sends its owner's picture to the other clients. On receiving pictures from other clients, the vision system redraws the display based on the information in the list and the pictures received.

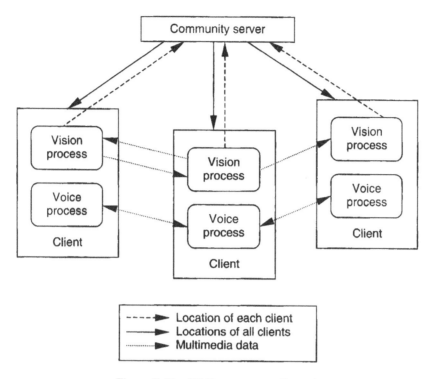

Figure 7. FreeWalk system configuration.

Because each client can't see all clients, it's not necessary for each one to send its picture to all others. Similarly, each client doesn't have to send full-size pictures to clients far away. FreeWalk uses these facts to optimize the bandwidth of video communication as follows:

- The sender adjusts the picture's size to the size the receiver needs.

- The client sends its picture to others who can see the client.

Figure 8 shows an example of a video transfer in FreeWalk. Since client A lies near client C, client C sends a large picture to client A. In contrast, client C sends a small picture to client B, because it's located far away.

Voice communication occurs in the same manner. FreeWalk clients don't send voice data to those clients located too far away to hear the participants' voices.

3.2 APPLYING VIDEOGAME USER-INTERFACE

Some videogames provide multiuser environments where users can control their *characters*. After investigating the similarities and differences between the two areas, we reach to conclude that videogames and videoconferencing systems can share user-interface design.

It is worthwhile to point out that videogames utilize the 3D presentation. Most of them realize virtual spaces so that players can control their characters freely. We believe that the following features of videogames can be introduced into videoconferencing systems.

- *Displaying global situations in a 3D space*

In videogames, since the movement of characters is fast, and they are often time-bounded, most of them provide facilities for users to grasp global situations.

- *Running on low cost machines*

  Though some of arcade games need special expensive input devices, most of videogames, especially game machines for home use (known as ``nintendo'' machines) or personal computers, do not. People can play them only with the low-priced general-purpose machines with a joy-pad, joystick, mouse or keyboard. Moreover, most of these devices are the standard attachments to such machines.

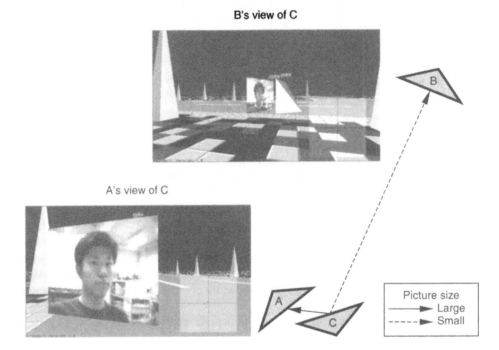

Figure 8. Video transfer among clients.

We applied the user-interface such as action, shooting and racing games to the design and implement FreeWalk for realizing casual meetings in a network. FreeWalk imitates the user-interface of a videogame in controlling the user's character and in grasping the surrounding situation.

3.2.1 Freely Walking in the 3D Space

Since the standard input device for a home game machine is joystick with several buttons, almost all videogames are designed for this device. Since one of the standard devices of workstations is a mouse, the motion of users' pyramids is controlled by X and Y valuators of a mouse pointer when its left button is down. A user controls the orientation of the pyramid by a mouse so that the moving/turning speed is proportional to the distance between the mouse pointer and the center of the FreeWalk window. Since users can easily control the speed of moving/turning, they can run when the target is in the distance and slow down as the target becomes closer.

3.2.2 Grasping Situations in the 3D Space

Since the view angle in CRT is much narrower than that of human eyes, it is hard to grasp surrounding situations. Moreover, a human in the real world can easily look around by turning his/her head, but cannot do the same thing in the 3D space. Though virtual reality systems can simulate this by a head-mounted display (HMD), widely used machines do not equip it. In videogames, therefore, additional auxiliary indicators and viewpoint switching functions are introduced to help users to grasp their situations. From this observation, we implemented the following functions in FreeWalk.

• *Radar Screen*

A radar-like screen indicates the simplified view of surroundings, including locations of characters. Figure 9 shows the FreeWalk radar screen. The radar screen can also indicate the volume of people's voice so that user can roughly know the activities within the groups.

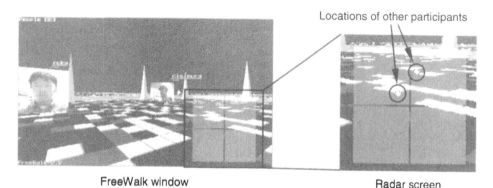

FreeWalk window   Radar screen

Figure 9. Radar screen.

• *Viewpoint Switching*

In some situations, the bird's-eye view is more suitable for grasping the situation. The viewpoint switching function allows users to use multiple viewpoints to select an appropriate view. Figure 10 shows the bird's-eye view from the back of the user's character. This view enables the user to watch both the user's character and his/her surroundings. As a result, the user can have a better view of geometric relations among participants, and thus move more easily than when using the normal view.

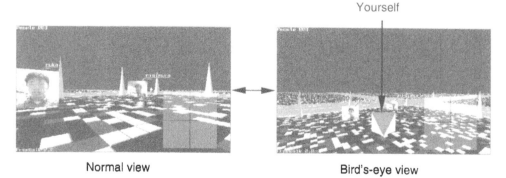

Normal view   Bird's-eye view

Figure 10. Switched viewpoint.

3.3 SHARING WWW DOCUMENTS

In real life, people often talk while reading magazines or watching TV together to make their conversation richer in topics. FreeWalk has a function which enables participants to generate topics by watching common information sources. A participant uses this function to make Web browsers of others displaying the same WWW document by transferring URL of his/her Web browser to others. Participants can watch the same WWW document to have a conversation in 3D virtual space with a rich stock of topics.

Figure 11 shows the route of URL transfer. In this figure, user A transfers the URL, which indicates the document in the user A's browser, to user B by pointing to user B drawn in user A's FreeWalk window. As a result, user B's browser displays the same document as user A's browser displays. Another possible way is to set up 3D objects corresponding to blackboards or bulletin boards in a 3D virtual space. But, by reducing the number of 3D objects to a minimum, the speed of 3D drawing is kept high in FreeWalk so that participants can move smoothly in a 3D virtual space. Therefore, we did not choose this approach.

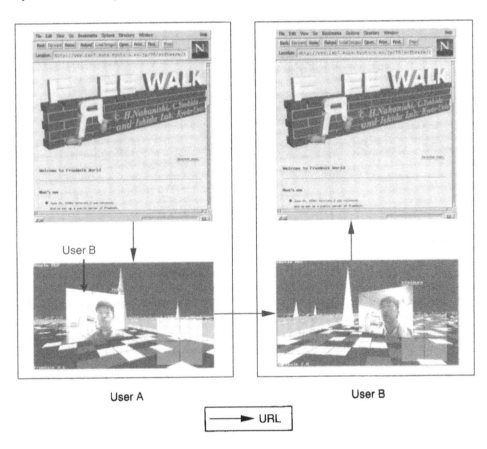

Figure 11. URL transfer.

3.4 USING A LARGE SCREEN

We implemented the FreeWalk system on an immersive environment as well as on a desktop environment. We used a special room with a large-scale projector screen connected to a graphics workstation. Figure 12 shows a virtual space displayed on the large screen in the room.

Figure 12. Virtual space on a large screen.

Several people can simultaneously view the large virtual space displayed on the screen and talk to other people moving within that space. People using a desktop environment see the room represented as a larger pyramid. A large live video of the room visible in the space makes it easy to include the room and its participants in the virtual space.

4. PRELIMINARY EXPERIMENTS

4.1 EXPERIMENTS IN LABORATORIES

We organized six clients in different rooms of our department and validated our implementation policy. The major results we have obtained are as follows.

- Each participant could move according to his/her own will. The six people formed several groups from time to time. People reported that they could share the same space without confusion. Various behaviors have been noted so far, such as approaching a pair of participants talking to each other from a distance to secretly listen to their conversation, and chasing a moving participant while calling him/her to stop. Most of the participants enjoyed the experience due in part to its relaxed atmosphere.

- Most users felt that its user-interface is similar to videogames, intuitively understandable, and easier than other videoconferencing systems. There were a few people who found it difficult to control the moving speed using the distance between the mouse pointer and the center of the FreeWalk window. For this type of user, we added a mode where a user specifies only the direction of movement by the keyboard while the speed is set constant. Since the radar screen covers a wide area, it is not easy to distinguish adjacent participants. We are planning to make the range variable and customizable by users.

4.2 INTRANET EXPERIMENTS

We experienced an intranet meeting with FreeWalk in the event called *Open Campus* (the campus was open to public) held in Tohwa University. The visitors of the event joined FreeWalk meetings without any scheduling beforehand. The meeting continued about six hours and a maximum of 13 users participated simultaneously. As a result of investigating the log data, interesting behaviors of users in the virtual space were found as follows.

- *Most people move around the center landmark of the space*

All the participants did not try to go far from the center. As population density around the center became high, network traffic exploded. This is because multimedia data of many participants are transferred to each client though he/she does not talk to most of them.

- *A group of people moved together*

It was often observed that a couple of people moved together to a long distance, but seldom more than three. Some users reported that they wanted to ride a bus, because it is hard to move together.

- *Some people wandered from a group to group*

In the latter half of the meeting, a number of participants who moved around decreased. Moving participants then wander from a group to group. It is very often observed that a couple of people face each other.

4.3 INTERNET EXPERIMENTS

We also conducted a preliminary experiment to verify whether our implementation of FreeWalk is competent to communicate through Internet. In this experiment, four users at Kyoto University in Japan and one user at University of Michigan in the United States joined the community server of FreeWalk at Kyoto University.

The frame rate of 3D drawing was about 10 frames per second, the same as in the previous intranet experiments. Though the delay of the live video was longer than that of an intranet, it was inconspicuous and did not affect the control of the player's character much. The users reported they could hold a meeting as good as through an intranet. Sometimes the bandwidth between Japan and the United States forced us to lower the video frame rate to 4 frames per second. However, the users were still able to find others smiling through the live video.

The delay of audio was inconspicuous, too. However, the audio of the user in the United States sometimes became intermittent and the other users were unable to catch what he said while he could clearly hear the voice from Japan. Farther experiments found that the loss of UDP (Internet User Datagram Protocol) packet transmitting audio data caused the intermittent audio. The market-based approach to control quality-of –service [12] can be one solution.

Table 1. Functional Comparison

	FreeWalk	InPerson
Process of Joining	Enter a 3D virtual space voluntarily	Called by someone who has already joined
Maximum number of participants	Unspecified (practically, 20 or so)	7
Occurrence of conversation	Caused by participants' approach of their own accord	Caused by turning on the system by a coordinator
Meeting group	Multiple groups	Single group

5. COMPARISON OF COMMUNICATION ENVIRONMENT

There are many functional differences between shared virtual spaces and conventional videoconferencing systems. We compare these two kinds of communication environments to show the inherent advantages of shared virtual spaces for casual meetings. We took Silicon Graphics' *InPerson* (see http://www.sgi.com/software/inperson/) as the example of a conventional videoconferencing system and FreeWalk as the example of a shared virtual space. Table 1 shows the functional differences between these two environments.

• *Process of joining*

In FreeWalk, the process used to join a meeting is just to enter the 3D virtual space provided. Each user selects which virtual space to enter when he/she starts up the system. The conversation protocol of InPerson inherits that of telephones: in order to hold a meeting between two persons, one should call the other via InPerson. If one wants to join the meeting, he/she needs to be called by someone who has already joined it. A newcomer cannot join an InPerson meeting freely.

• *Maximum number of participants*

The maximum number of participants is seven in InPerson. This limitation is from the size of workstation displays. On the other hand, FreeWalk does not limit the number of participants, though if the number exceeds 20, the performance of the system becomes intolerable given the current condition of computer networks.

• *Occurrence of conversation*

In FreeWalk, a conversation may be started by an accidental encounter while the participants are walking around the 3D virtual space. A conversation is started by participants' contact of their own accord. In the case of InPerson, conversation is started when the coordinator of a meeting turns on the system and contacts all participants.

• *Meeting group*

In FreeWalk, participants approach one another to organize a meeting group. Participants can form multiple meeting groups simultaneously. In the case of InPerson, however, participants always form a single meeting group since everyone faces the others and hears the voices of the others.

6. INTERACTION ANALYSIS

Some earlier studies tried to compare communication aided by desktop videoconferencing systems to face-to-face (FTF) communication. Various characteristics of conventional video communication became clear through those studies[13]. However, the characteristics of the communication aided by a desktop videoconferencing system with a 3D shared virtual space remained unclear. In this section we show the characteristics of 3D communication compared to FTF and conventional video communications. We used InPerson as the conventional video environment and FreeWalk as the desktop videoconferencing system with a 3D shared virtual space.

6.1 HYPOTHESES ON CONVERSATION ENVIRONMENTS

We believe that 3D environments are more effective for casual communication than conventional video environment due to the following reasons:

- Participants using a conventional videoconferencing system tend to be strained and their conversations do not smoothly. This is because all their faces are always displayed and the system keeps everyone facing the others. A 3D virtual space eliminates this strain by giving them locations and view directions.

- It is impossible to reproduce communication with moves like real life communication in a conventional video environment. A 3D virtual space reproduces communication with moves by enabling participants to move freely.

Sellen compared communication in two video conferencing systems, Hydra and Picture-in-a-Picture (PIP), and in the FTF environment[14]. She found no differences among the three environments for conversation in terms of turns (transferring the initiative of speech), even though previous studies showed that more turns occurred in the FTF environment than in the videoconferencing environment. We expected that the number of turns might increase in casual meetings, so we analyzed the number of turns in our experiment.

In another study, Bowers investigated how the movement of avatars coordinated with conversation in a virtual environment[15]. Results showed that the avatars' moves transferred the initiative of conversation. In 3D and FTF environments, the moves of people relate to their communication skills. In our experiment, we analyzed the moves of people in meetings.

Additionally, we counted the number of occurrences of chat and calculated the standard deviation of utterance. We thought a casual atmosphere might stimulate the occurrence of chat and change the amount of utterance of each participant.

6.2 DESIGN OF EXPERIMENT

Twenty-one undergraduate students participated in our one-day experiment. We prepared three environments for conversation to compare FTF, conventional video, and 3D communications (see Figure 13). We set up seven SGI O2 workstations connected by a 100-Mbps Ethernet for the video environment (InPerson) and the 3D environment (FreeWalk). The meetings in the three environments consisted of three tasks as follows.

FTF

InPerson

FreeWalk

Figure 13. Three different environments for conversation.

1. *Agreeing on a group travel destination (Task 1)*

    This was a decision-making task. We made the participants decide where they would travel a month later. They were asked to pretend to be friends from high school days. Also, they did not have many chances to meet after they left the high school.

2. *Discussing social problem (Task 2)*

    This task was to shape ideas. They were asked to pretend that they attend the same lecture and had to hand in reports.

3. *Conversing freely (Task 3)*

    Participants had conversation without any guidelines.

We chose these tasks to examine various types of communication comprehensively. For each task, we told participants to organize three groups of seven people. Thus nine types of meetings took place. Each meeting lasted for 20 minutes. We didn't choose any chairpersons of the meetings in advance. Before performing the three tasks, the participants introduced themselves in each group so that they could memorize each other's faces and voices. They also practiced operating FreeWalk. The independent variables of this experiment were the differences between the environments and the tasks.

We collected experimental data using videotape recordings. During the FreeWalk and InPerson meetings, we recorded the screen images of the workstations on videotape recorders. In FTF meetings, we recorded the scenes on 8-mm video. We reviewed the videotape pictures to record the start and end times of participants' utterances to create conversation records.

In addition, we collected the system logs of FreeWalk to find the pattern of moves in the 3D virtual space during meetings. The FreeWalk community server stores system logs in which it records locations and orientations of participants in a 3D virtual space. We made a tool called *SimWalk* to analyze participants' moves. SimWalk draws lines along the participants' moves and connecting their locations in sequence. It also can reproduce participants' behavior. Triangles corresponding to participants move to reproduce participants' moves in meetings. The triangles blink to indicate utterances of participants.

6.3 RESULTS

In this section we present the results of analysis of participants' conversations and moves.

6.3.1 Conversation

We organized the analysis results of the conversations into number of turns, standard deviation of utterance, and occurrence of chat.

1.   *Number of turns*

This value represents the number of events. Each event transfers the initiative of talking from one person to another. The turn occurs when someone starts talking immediately after or while another talks. We didn't count cases in which someone stopped talking and started talking again after a brief silence.

Figure 14 shows the relation between the frequency of turns and environments.

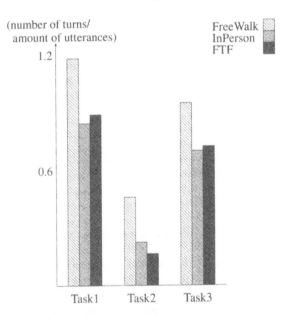

Figure 14. Frequency of turns.

The frequency of turns equals the number of turns divided by the amount of utterances. The rankings of contributions of environments to the number of turns is characterized as:

FreeWalk > FTF ≈ InPerson

The effect of the difference in environments showed that FreeWalk activated turns more often than InPerson and FTF.

2. *Standard deviation of utterance*

This value represents the standard deviation of the ratio of the total time of utterances of each participant to the total time of all utterances of all participants. Table 2 summarizes the standard deviations of utterance. It also provides the following ranking of environments for each task:

Task 1 FTF > InPerson > FreeWalk
Task 2 FTF > InPerson ≈ FreeWalk
Task 3 InPerson > FTF ≈ FreeWalk

Interestingly, the deviation remained the smallest in FreeWalk for all tasks. This means that the amount of utterances of each participant became equalized in FreeWalk.

Table 2. Standard Deviation of Utterance

	Task 1	Task 2	Task 3
FTF	13.93	19.19	14.07
InPerson	12.31	15.97	17.25
FreeWalk	9.28	15.45	13.45

3. *Occurrence of chat*

This value represents starting a conversation that doesn't contribute to accomplishing the task. Figure 15 shows the occurrence of chat in Task 1 and Task 2 in each environment.

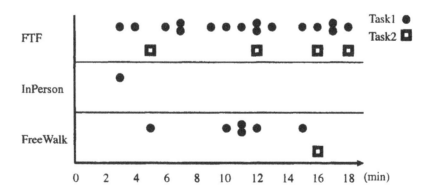

Figure 15. Occurrence of chat.

In Figure 15, the horizontal axis represents time, and each mark represents the occurrence of chat. Figure 15 shows that chat occurred more actively in FTF than in

FreeWalk, while it seldom occurred in InPerson. The rankings of the contributions of environments to the occurrence of chat follow:

FTF > FreeWalk > InPerson

In FreeWalk, the atmosphere among participants might have been relaxed since they formed a circle to have a conversation, while in InPerson everyone faced the others.

6.3.2 Participants' Moves

In FTF meetings, participants seldom moved after forming a circle to have a conversation. During InPerson meetings, everyone faced the others on the screen.

Figure 16 shows participants' moves during a 15-minute period in FreeWalk meetings. In Task 1 and Task 2, they seldom moved after forming a circle as in FTF. Unlike the other two tasks, they moved actively around the 3D virtual space in Task 3, as Figure 16 shows. In Task 3—free conversation—we observed the following behaviors:

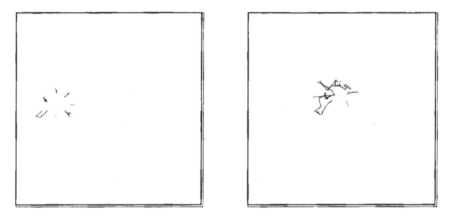

Task 1   Task 2

Task 3
Figure 16. Pattern of moves in a 3D virtual space.

1. Moving in a 3D virtual space

At the beginning of the task, participants moved actively. For example, they moved to the edge of the 3D virtual space and rushed toward others. The occurrence of conversation was scarce. Figure 17a presents snapshots of SimWalk, which reproduces the participant's moves.

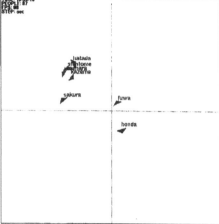

(a) Moving in a 3D virtual space   (b) Facing each other to greet

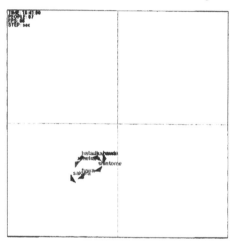

(c) Gathering to start conversation

Figure 17. Participants' moves in Task 3.

2. Facing each other to greet

In the middle of the task, participants faced one another frequently to greet. The lengths of conversations were short. We noted that some participants blamed others for approaching them when they tried to whisper to each other. You can see the participants greeting each other in Figure 17b.

3.   *Gathering to start conversation*

Toward the end of the task, all participants gathered to converse. We noted that a certain participant ran about trying to escape from the meeting place since he was unwilling to talk, while another participant looked for someone else who had gone elsewhere. This situation is represented in Figure 17c.

6.4 DISCUSSION

As a result of our analysis, we categorized the effects of a 3D virtual space into two types. In the first type, we observed that 3D communication resembles FTF communication. Two primary characteristics exist: frequency of chat and behavior of participants. The second category, however, remains peculiar to 3D virtual spaces. These environments equalize the amount of utterances for each participant more than the other environments, increase the number of turns, and sometimes stimulate participants to move around to converse freely.

The results show the effectiveness of a 3D virtual space in casual meetings. The freedom of 3D virtual space lets participants enjoy their conversation, and its relaxed atmosphere stimulates participants into initiating conversations. On the other hand, participants having a meeting in a 3D virtual space tend to concentrate less than in the other environments.

7. CONCLUSIONS

FreeWalk supports casual meetings among many people. This system provides a three-dimensional (3D) community common area wherein participants can behave just as they do in real life. FreeWalk imitates the user-interface of videogames in operation and display.

We have conducted preliminary experiments by establishing FreeWalk on an intranet and the Internet. From the intranet experiments, we have verified that FreeWalk runs at practical speed with a large number of users. The Internet experiment showed that the implementation enables users to communicate through the Internet.

We have performed an interaction analysis to investigate the communication via FreeWalk, in comparison with that in a conventional videoconferencing system and face-to-face environment. The results show the effectiveness of a 3D shared virtual space in videoconferencing systems.

Acknowledgments

We would like to thank the members of the Media Center of Tohwa University and Edmund H. Durfee of the University of Michigan for their help in conducting the intranet/Internet experiments. Also many thanks to the members of Ishida laboratory at Kyoto University.

References

1.   H. Nakanishi, C. Yoshida, T. Nishimura, and T. Ishida, "FreeWalk: Supporting Casual Meetings in a Network," *Proceedings of International Conference on Computer Supported Cooperative Work (CSCW 96)*, ACM Press, New York, pp. 308-314, 1996.
2.   H. Nakanishi, C. Yoshida, T. Nishimura, and T. Ishida, "FreeWalk: A 3D Virtual Space for Casual Meetings," *IEEE MultiMedia*, Vol. 6, No. 2, pp. 20-28, April-June 1999.

3. K. Watabe, S. Sakata, K. Maeno, H. Fukuoka, and T. Ohmori, "Distributed Multiparty Desktop Conference System Mermaid: Platform for Groupware," *Proceedings of International Conference on Computer Supported Cooperative Work (CSCW 90)*, ACM Press, New York, pp. 27-38, 1990.
4. R. W. Root, "Design of a Multimedia Vehicle for Social Browsing," *Proceedings of International Conference on Computer Supported Cooperative Work (CSCW 88)*, ACM Press, New York, pp. 25-38, 1988.
5. O. Hagsand, "Interactive Multiuser VEs in the DIVE System," *IEEE MultiMedia*, Vol. 3, No. 1, pp. 30-39, Spring 1996.
6. R. C. Waters and J. W. Barrus, "The Rise of Shared Virtual Environments," *IEEE Spectrum*, Vol. 34, No. 3, pp. 20-25, 1997.
7. R. Lea, Y. Honda, K. Matsuda, and S. Matsuda, "Community Place: Architecture and Performance," *Proceedings of Symposium on Virtual Reality Modeling Language (VRML 97)*, ACM Press, New York, pp. 41-50, 1997.
8. S. Sugawara, G. Suzuki, Y. Nagashima, M. Matsuura, H. Tanigawa, and M. Moriuchi, "InterSpace: Networked Virtual World for Visual Communication," *IEICE (The Institute of Electronics, Information, and Communication Engineers) Transactions on Information and Systems*, Vol. E77-D, No. 12, pp. 1344-1349, 1994.
9. C. Greenhalgh and S. Benford, "Massive: A Collaborative Virtual Environment for Teleconferencing," *ACM Transactions on Computer-Human Interaction*, Vol. 2, No. 3, pp. 239-261, September 1995.
10. S. Duck, "Human Relationships," SAGE Publications, London, Third Edition, 1998.
11. M. V. Cranch, "The Role of Orienting Behavior in Human Interaction," *Behavior and Environment*, Proceedings of International Symposium held at the 1968 Meeting of the American Association for the Advancement of Science in Dallas, Texas, pp. 217-237, 1971.
12. H. Yamaki, P. W. Michael, and T. Ishida, "A Market-Based Approach to Allocating QoS for Multimedia Applications," *Proceedings of International Conference on Multi-Agent Systems (ICMAS 96)*, pp. 385-392, 1996.
13. J. Galegher and R. E. Kraut, "Computer-Mediated Communication and Collaborative Writing: Media Influence and Adaptation to Communication Constraints," *Proceedings of International Conference on Computer Supported Cooperative Work (CSCW 92)*, ACM Press, New York, pp. 155-162, 1992.
14. A. J. Sellen, "Speech Patterns in Video-Mediated Conversations," *Proceedings of International Conference on Human Factors in Computing Systems (CHI 92)*, ACM Press, New York, pp. 49-59, 1992.
15. J. Bowers, J. Pycock, and J. O'Brien, "Talk and Embodiment in Collaborative Virtual Environments," *Proceedings of International Conference on Human Factors in Computing Systems (CHI 96)*, ACM Press, New York, pp. 58-65, 1996.

Chapter 11

CAPTURING AND USING DESIGN EXPERIENCE IN WEB INFORMATION SYSTEMS

Fernando Lyardet, Gustavo Rossi, and Daniel Schwabe

Abstract

In this chapter we introduce Navigation and Interface patterns, and show why they are useful for capturing, recording and reusing design experience in Web Information Systems. We first introduce Web Information Systems, and show the need to profit from experienced designers' expertise. Then we give a framework to reason about hypermedia design structures, and describe design patterns. Next we present some simple but effective patterns, with examples from the WWW. We finally discuss how patterns can be integrated into the development process.

1. INTRODUCTION

A working definition of a Web Information System can be as a set of WWW documents, in one or more sites, under the same administration, storing information to be used – created, accessed, and modified – by some identified community of users.

At least part of the phenomenal success of the WWW, and the increasing integration of "traditional" information systems into it, is the recognition that it actually provides a richer communications channel between human beings that make up institutions, companies, schools, interest groups, or, more generally, society.

From its inception, the WWW was meant to be a way to help people access and use information, as stated by Tim Berners-Lee [1] - "In fact the thing that drove me to do it (which is one of the frequently asked questions I get from the press or whoever) was partly that I needed something to organize myself. I needed to be able to keep track of things, and nothing out there, none of the computer programs that you could get, the spreadsheets and the databases, would really let you make this random association between absolutely anything and absolutely anything, you are always constrained. For example, if you have a person, they have several properties, and you could link them to a room of their office, and you could link them to a list of documents they have written, but that's it. You can't link them to the car database when you find out what car they own without taking two databases and joining them together and going into a lot of work. So I needed something like that."

A WIS can be seen then as an example of a "hybrid" system, a system conceived to be part of a man-machine team in solving a problem. This means that part of the task will be executed by the computer and part by the human being. Since the human being will be performing part of the task, information must be presented to him in the most appropriate way - hence, multimedia and hypertext. This definition is quite flexible and can accommodate most existing WISs, since the boundary between the part performed by the computer and the part performed by the human being is movable. In one extreme one falls into traditional systems, where the computer does all the processing, and in the other extreme one falls into many current websites, where the computer just stores information and presents it to the human being, who then does the task.

"Universal access means that you put it on the Web and you can access it from anywhere; it doesn't matter what computer system you are running, it's independent of where you are, what platform you are running, or what operating system you've bought and to have this unconstrained topology, which because hypertext is unconstrained it means you can map any existing structures, whether you happen to have trees of information or whatever. As people have found, it is very easy to make a service which will put information onto the Web which has already got some structure to it, which comes from some big database which you don't want to change, because hypertext is flexible, you can map that structure into it." (Tim Berners-Lee, [1])

The WWW is based on the hypertext paradigm, inasmuch as it is composed of pages (in HTML) which can be linked to each other through URLs (links). Regardless of how a reader has reached a page, he will normally have the option of accessing the pages linked to the current page; by choosing a particular link, he will cause the page pointed to by the link to be exhibited; this process can repeat itself indefinitely. This succession of steps is know as "navigation", and is intrinsic to hypertext, and hence to the WWW.

Designing this kind of hypermedia applications is not easy, as we have to solve many different problems such as: specifying which are the atomic units the user will navigate (nodes); deciding the connections among those units (links); the different starting points for navigation; the possible sequences of information units the user may navigate through, etc.

Moreover, since Web applications are highly interactive, we also have to address many issues related with the user interface such as defining meaningful perceivable objects, deciding which interface objects will trigger navigation, and so on.

To make matters worse, as more corporations re-design their information systems to make them accessible by web browsers, and as new application areas such as electronic commerce appear, we face new design and implementation problems. First, applications are no longer static, since:

• the underlying information base grows quickly, and we have to keep users informed of new information items available (e.g., new products and services),

• users navigate to perform certain tasks that affect the information base; e.g. they buy, sell or even exchange products (see auction sites, for example),

• the information system is integrated with other "internal" systems; e.g.: in an electronic commerce system, the client's orders initiate some actions such as getting the item, sending it by mail, etc.

Finally, implementing Web Information Systems involves a combination of different technologies, from databases to scripting and mark-up languages. We clearly need a way to organize the development process; we need to improve documentation and use solid software engineering practices.

In this chapter we address the problem of capturing and reusing design experience in the development of Web Information Systems. We first introduce the OOHDM design approach, to give a framework for the following discussion; then we introduce design patterns and show why they are useful in the WWW. We next give some examples of navigation and interface patterns, and show how they have been used in the development of Web applications. We then discuss how they can be integrated into the development of new applications. Some further work is finally presented.

2. THE OOHDM DESIGN FRAMEWORK

As previously said, when we design Web applications, there are conflicting requirements that must be satisfied in a unifying framework. On one hand, in the final application, navigation and functional behavior must be seamlessly integrated; i.e. it should be obvious for a regular user how he can act on the system while browsing information.

On the other hand, during the design process we should be able to decouple design decisions related with the application's navigational structure from those related with the domain model itself. While the navigational architecture is strongly related with the user tasks and profiles, the domain model and their behaviors should be more comprehensive.

The Object-Oriented Hypermedia Design Method (OOHDM) is a rigorous approach for designing and implementing applications involving navigational behavior such as Web Information Systems.

According to OOHDM, the development of Web applications occurs as a four activities process – Conceptual Design, Navigation Design, Abstract Interface Design, and Implementation – that are performed in a mix of iterative and incremental styles of development; in each step a model is built or enriched. The reader can refer to [15,16] for a comprehensive discussion on OOHDM. In this section we just mention the most relevant features of OOHDM that are related with design reuse.

OOHDM clearly separates navigation design from conceptual design by defining navigation objects as views (in the database sense) of conceptual objects. It also provides appropriate abstractions to organize the navigation space. In this sense, OOHDM generalizes state-of-the-art modeling approaches such as UML [18] by introducing indexes and navigational contexts, as well as InContext classes, a primitive that is a kind of Decorator [4]. Finally, user interface design is addressed as a different activity using a customized notation that emphasizes interface objects, events and behaviors [8].

During the Conceptual Design phase we define the domain model, using well-known object-oriented modeling principles [13]. The product of this activity is a set of classes and relationships. These classes implement the desired application behavior.

One distinguishing feature of Web applications is the notion of navigation, in which the user of an application in this domain navigates in a space composed of navigation objects. These objects are not the same as the conceptual objects, but rather objects customized to the user's profile and tasks. This customization is achieved using the view mechanism between objects, analogously to views in databases. Navigation objects are not directly perceived by the user; rather, they are themselves accessed via interface objects. Accordingly, the Abstract Interface Design specifies interface objects that are responsible for mediating user interaction with navigation objects.

Finally, during the implementation activity we map conceptual, navigation and interface objects onto the particular runtime environment being targeted. This may involve defining HTML pages (or, for example, Toolbook or Director objects in non Web-based environments), scripts in some language, queries to a relational database, etc; in this way the author produces the actual Web application to be run.

The OOHDM approach has provided us with a framework for reasoning on design concerns and design problems. We have found that, while building Web applications, developers usually face similar problems. Moreover, they use similar solutions even though their applications may belong to quite different and disparate domains.

In the rest of this chapter we introduce navigation and interface patterns as tools to encapsulate and convey designers' expertise.

3. DESIGNING SOFTWARE WITH PATTERNS

Design patterns are used in software design [3,4] as a way to record design experience. They describe problems that occur repeatedly, and specify the core of the solution to those problem, in such a way that we can (re)use this solution many times in different contexts and applications.

In the object-oriented field, patterns show micro-architectures that go beyond naive solutions to recurrent design problems. In this area the important elements of a pattern are the responsibilities that must be assigned to each component (or class), and the thread of collaborations among them.

For example, the Strategy design pattern shows when it is necessary to decouple objects from the algorithms operating on them. When using Strategy designers do not apply the basic object-oriented principles (encapsulating algorithms inside objects that need them), but go a step further by defining a separate class hierarchy.

The importance of knowing these patterns, i.e.: problem-solution pairs, is that we get to know what experienced designers do when facing a non-trivial problem.

Using patterns in object-oriented design is a key approach for maximizing reuse, as summarized in [4]:

-*Patterns enable widespread reuse of software architectures.* Reusing architectures is more valuable than reusing algorithms or data structures.

-*Patterns improve communication within and across software development teams as they provide a shared concise vocabulary.* Using patterns, the level of discourse among team members has a higher level of abstraction.

-*Patterns explicitly capture knowledge that designers use implicitly.* Though expert designers usually make good decisions, they do not document what problem they are solving and the rationale for that solution.

The Patterns movement began in the area of architecture almost 20 years ago with the work of Christopher Alexander [1]. More recently, the object-oriented community has embraced this subject and there is a good corpus of work already developed [4]. There are many patterns and pattern languages that are specific to specific domains such as communication, organizational computing, etc. As we show in this chapter, this is also true for Web patterns.

There is no fixed format to describe patterns, although the essential elements must always appear: name, problem, solution, consequences. Design patterns are usually found in the format proposed by [4]. More abstract patterns, i.e., those that encompass more abstract solutions that can be implemented in many different ways usually appear in the "Alexandrian" format. It contains name, context, problem, solution, and related patterns [1].

Design Patterns complement methods in that they address problems at a higher level of abstraction. Many design decisions that cannot be recorded through the use of the primitives of a method can be described using patterns. We claim that using design patterns, Web application designers can profit from existing design knowledge in several communities such as hypermedia or user interface design. However, as the www is a completely new applications environment, new recurrent problems will appear and it is possible that a whole patterns' catalogue should be developed in this field. In the following sections we introduce navigation and interface patterns and show examples in the WWW.

4. DISCOVERING PATTERNS IN THE WWW

We have been mining and using patterns in the field of hypermedia for the past three years and have studied how to use them to record the experience of hypermedia designers [9,10,11]. Patterns in our catalogue are organized in a taxonomy that includes architectural patterns, navigational patterns and user interface patterns. Architectural patterns address the problem of decomposing a Web application in components, i.e.: how to connect databases with other components, how to relate objects in a client with server functionality, etc. Navigational patterns help to organize the hyperspace in such a way that it can be easily navigated. Finally, interface patterns give guidelines to define meaningful interface objects that simplify user interaction, and help in the use of the application.

While architectural patterns are similar to those in [4], navigational and interface patterns are more like the original urban architecture Alexandrian patterns. They describe the organization of a navigable space, the roads you can follow to reach different homes, the kind of orientation signs you will find, the short cuts, etc.

A good source for discovering new patterns is the Web itself. By analyzing sites and applications, and framing them into the OOHDM model, we have found many commonalties and have described them using the pattern notation. We have then used those patterns while developing new applications, and have obtained new feedback on them. In this paper we have chosen to illustrate our patterns with successful commercial applications, instead of using applications we have developed, since these applications are more likely to be known by the general public.

Since Web applications are a particular kind of hypermedia application, most of our navigational and interface patterns apply directly to this field. However, we have also found many patterns that are particular to the Web environment (as for example Web search patterns in Section 7). We next present some patterns, grouped in different categories for the sake of comprehension. Those patterns that have been published elsewhere are summarized with an indication of the source.

5. NAVIGATIONS PATTERNS

5.1 NODE AS A NAVIGATIONAL VIEW

Intent:
How to provide navigation capabilities to database applications? How to customize those applications for different user profiles?

Motivation: In many situations, existing applications can benefit from a hypermedia interface, such as when making them accessible via the WWW. Moreover, it may be valuable to give each user a "personal" view of the application, taking into account his interests and needs.

Solution: Define a navigational layer between the application to be enhanced and its graphical interface, build up of object's observers that are called nodes, Implement the navigational behavior in nodes.

Examples:

Many Internet News sources use this pattern for providing personalized views of their news database. In figure 1, for example the user can configure different views of the same information base according to his/her preferences.

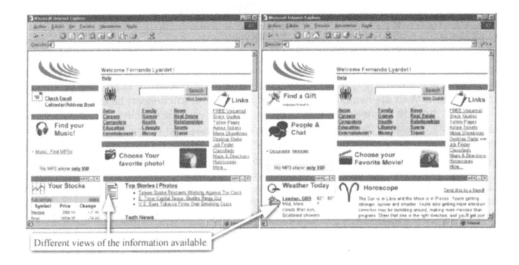

Figure 1. Example of a node as a navigational view.

5.2 SET-BASED NAVIGATION

Intent:
Provide the user with closed navigational sub-sets that can be navigated sequentially.

Motivation:
WISs usually involve dealing with collections of objects (e.g., Paintings, Cities, Books, CDs etc.). In an electronic shop we may want to explore all Books about Painting in France. We could also want to navigate to all Books about impressionist painters (including French ones). This is a recurring situation that appears in different domains, such as institutional or entertainment sites. Identifying these sets may help the user to navigate through them easily.

Solution:
The usual naive strategy followed by designers consists in providing an index to set members (see for example the results of a query in Amazon); users must then go back to the index to navigate to the next member of the set. There is no way to navigate directly from one node to the next or previous one.

The solution is to consider set-based navigation as a "first-class" navigation strategy. We group nodes into meaningful sets, and provide inter and intra-set navigation facilities. These facilities include indexes and links for letting the user navigate to the "next" and "previous" elements of the current one in his traversal. Notice that a node may belong to more than one set, so it is often useful to allow the user to "switch sets". Navigation inside contexts complements conventional semantic links, such as, for example, those connecting a node about a Book with the node about its author, or books to reviews about them. In other words, the reader can browse through the set or leave it to explore other nodes (or eventually other sets). [See 12]

Examples:
"Sets" appear in almost all web-sites, though not always set-based navigation is provided. An interesting exception can be found in http://www.netgrocer.com/. See Figure 2.

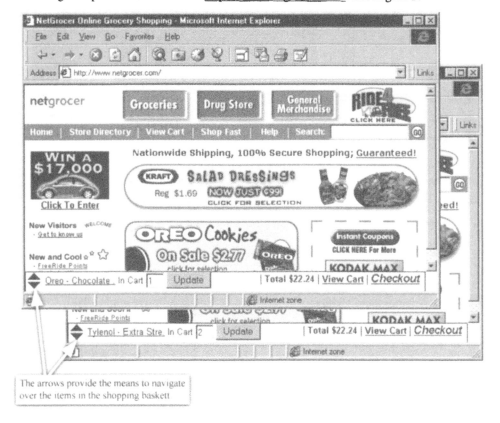

Figure 2. Set-based navigation in NetGrocer's shopping basket.

5.3 BASKET

Intent:
How to keep track of user selections during navigation, making these selections persistent to process them when the user decides it.

Motivation:
When users go shopping in the Web they want to navigate through the e-market to decide what they will buy and when. We may ask the user to proceed to buy each product he selects, although in this way he will have to complete forms for each product and he will feel that he is wasting time.

Solution:
Provide the user with a metaphor similar to bookmarking, by allowing him to select the products he wants to buy as they are traversed. Provide a "persistent" store for those items (a basket) that can be accessed as another navigation object and associate processing operations to the basket such as eliminate an item, change quantities, check-out, etc. [See 12]

Examples:
An interesting and original use of the Basket concept can be found in http://www.compare.net. You can choose products to compare, and then process them afterwards. The site provides two different views of the shopping basket (which is not actually used for shopping!), one with a summary and a second view, used for comparisons. In Figure 3, we can see a basic model of a generic basket, where all selected items are listed.

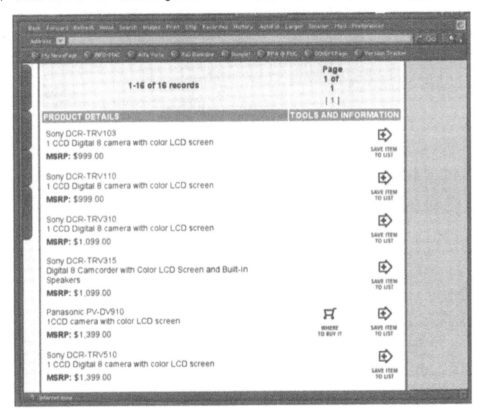

Figure 3. A model of a typical basket browsing.

5.4 NEWS

Intent:
Provide the user with timely information regarding new products or services in a Web site.

Problem:
Most Web applications are in constant growth. How can we be sure that users will know about new products or services we are offering as the applications evolve? Trying to solve this problem poses a design challenge for Web designers, who must balance between a well-

structured web-site where information is organized in items with sub-items, etc. and, a star-shaped navigational structure where all information is reachable from the home page.

Solution

Structure the home page in such a way that a space is devoted to the newest additions, including a summary and a link to the information object. This approach allows the designer to preserve a good organization of the information, while giving users feedback of the changes that take place within the site. "News" implement shortcuts to information that may be located in the leaves of a tree-structured site, without compromising the underlying structure.

Examples:

"News" is used in hundreds of web-sites and applications such as where it is used to announce new collections and the current tours available (see Figure 4).

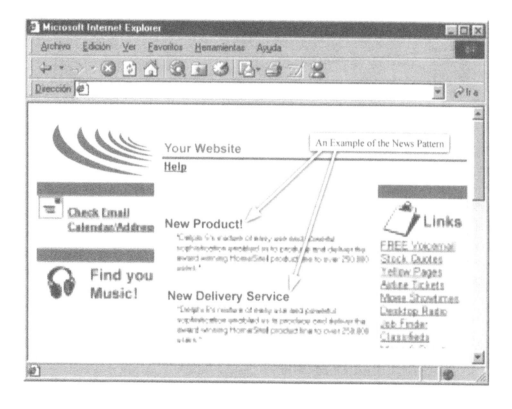

Figure 4. An example of a website applying News in its homepage.

5.5 LANDMARK

Intent:

Indicate outstanding entry points in the application, so that the user can move easily to them.

Problem:

Many times our application has many distinguished places that we want the user to recognize and reach easily. However they may be unrelated with each other. Building a domain model and making navigation reflect that domain model is a key approach for achieving a solid navigation architecture. However, these singular "entry-points" should be easy to reach.

Again, we have to struggle between structure, usability and maintaining the design documents concise. How do we make those places perceivable to the user without compromising structure?

Solution
Define a set of landmarks and make them easy to access from every node in the network. Make the interface of links to a landmark look uniform. In this way users will have a consistent visual cue about the landmark.

Examples:
Landmarks can be found in different Web applications such as http://www.amazon.com where they indicate each different sub-store (Books, Audio, Video, etc.). In Figure 5 we show an example of Landmarks in http://www.hotmail.com.

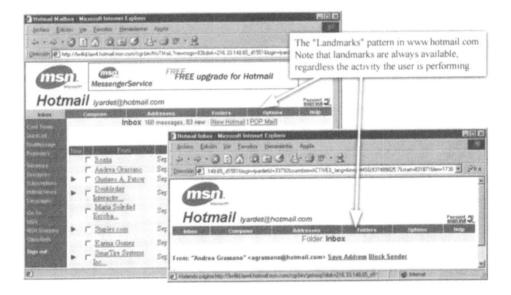

Figure 5. Landmarks in www.hotmail.com.

6.   INTERFACE PATTERNS

6.1 INFORMATION ON DEMAND

Intent:
Help to accommodate many items in the interface when perceivable space is scarce.

Problem:
We usually find ourselves struggling to decide how to show the attributes and anchors of a node. Unfortunately, the screen is usually smaller than what we need, and many times we cannot make use of other media (such as simultaneously playing an audio tape and showing an image), either for technological or cognitive reasons.

Solution:
Present only a subset of the most important ones, and let the user control which further information is presented in the screen, by providing him with active interface objects (e.g. buttons). The activation of those buttons does not produce navigation; it just causes different

information of the same node to be shown. This just follows the "What you see is what you need" principle.

Examples:
Figure 6 shows an example of obtaining information on demand.

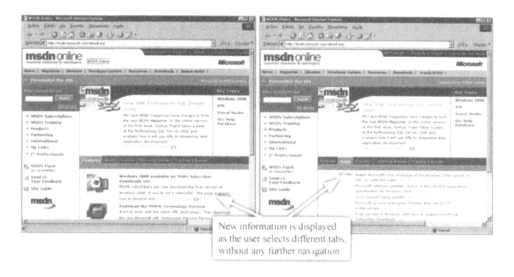

Figure 6. Information on demand in msdn.microsoft.com.

6.2 BEHAVIORAL GROUPING

Intent:
To organize the different types of controls in the interface so the user can easily understand them.

Motivation:
A problem we usually face when building the interface of web application is how to organize interface objects (such as anchors, buttons, etc.) to produce a meaningful interface. We must take into account that the same kind of object (e.g. a hot-word) may be used to navigate, to trigger a specific functionality or just to implement an information on demand effect (See Section 6.1). So, how do we provide the user with a consistent interface?

Solution:
Group control interface objects according to their functionality in global, contextual, structural and application objects, so that each group enhances comprehension.

Examples:
There are many websites that could be cited as examples. In Figure 7 we show a generic example of behavioral grouping.

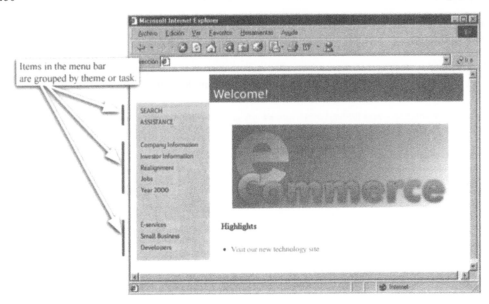

Figure 7. A generic example of behavioral grouping.

6.3 BEHAVIOUR ANTICIPATION

Intent:
Indicate to the user the effect or consequences of activating an interface object?

Problem:
Many times, when building an interface, it is necessary to combine different interface elements such as buttons, hotwords, media controls or even custom-designed elements. It is usual to find readers wondering what happened after they activated a control, and the exact consequences of the action performed. How do we give him a cue about what will happen?

Solution:
Provide feedback about the effect of activating each interface element. Choose the kind of feedback to be non-ambiguous and complete: different cursor shapes, highlighting, small text-based explanations called "tool tips". In addition, these elements can be combined with sound and animations.

Examples:
In Figure 8, we show an example of behavior anticipation in www.inprise.com. Notice the combination of the Landmark pattern [11] with the information about the contents of that Landmark (described using Behavioral Anticipation).

7. WEB SEARCH PATTERNS

Though the navigational metaphor has proved to be quite effective to give access to huge information spaces, it has to be complemented with other computational facilities such as querying and searching. In this context, Web search engines are the most well known tools to find information on the WWW.

Previously presented patterns show ways to organize the navigational space in a Web application. However, designing the search functionality of a Web application is also difficult, and it is also a common source of widely spread misconceptions.

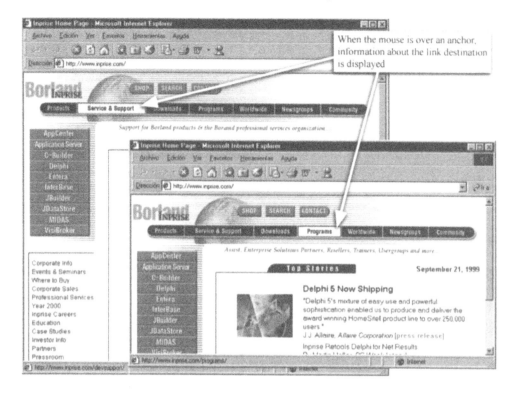

Figure 8. Behavior anticipation in www.inprise.com.

We next discuss some design issues that a designer must be aware of while improving a Web application with search functionality. We also present them in the pattern format, as they have been discovered studying successful Web applications.

The solutions in these patterns can be often implemented using either standard technology or reusing existing search tools.

7.1 SELECTABLE SEARCH SPACE

Intent:
Specify a category in which the search should be made or restricted to.

Motivation:
As the information spaces become bigger, users are not always successful searching for the desired information. When the user begins searching, there will be certain information in the information space which will be highly relevant to its information needs, some of which will be useful, some marginally relevant and some not relevant at all. A search engine will return only some of this relevant information. How can we improve the effectiveness of the search?

Solution:
Provide the user with a mechanism to select a category (sub-space) within which he is going to search. The requirement to implement this solution is very simple: it should be possible to

split the information space into disjoint sub-spaces. The same piece of information should not belong to more that one group at a time.

Examples:
Almost all search engines provide some kind of facility for refining the search space. In Figure 9 we show an example in http://www.search.microsoft.com.

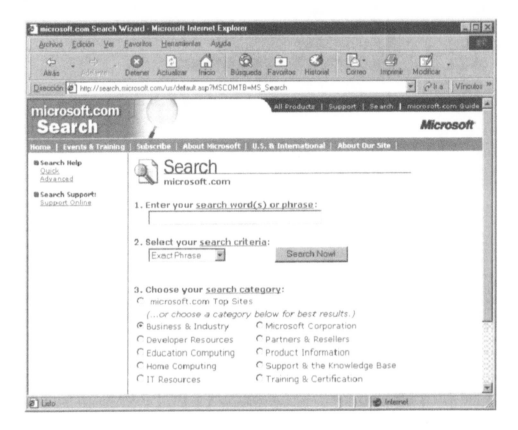

Figure 9. Selectable search spaces in www.search.microsoft.com.

7.2 SELECTABLE KEY WORDS

Intent:
Suggest a set of keywords that are relevant to the results of previous searches, in order to improve the quality of subsequent search results.

Motivation:
The most common interaction that users have with search engines is by typing relevant keywords about the topic of search. Nevertheless, since the web search space is very large, there may be several possible matches for a given word, thus a more sophisticated search must be specified, which almost always requires further keywords in order to reduce the search space and allow a better matching.

Solution:
Provide the user with a list of the possible keywords, according to the search already performed and let him refine his search.

Examples:

In Figures 10 and 11 we show how an example of a site that gives the possibility of refining the first search. Figure 10 shows an initial search on databases, while in Figure 11 we can choose some keywords to make our search more "specific".

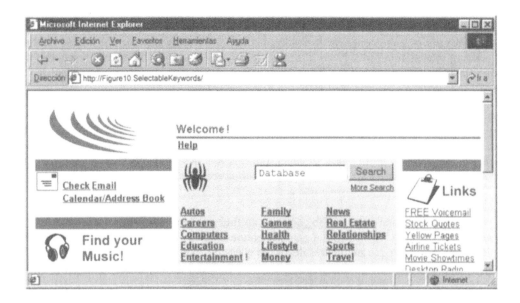

Figure 10. An initial query.

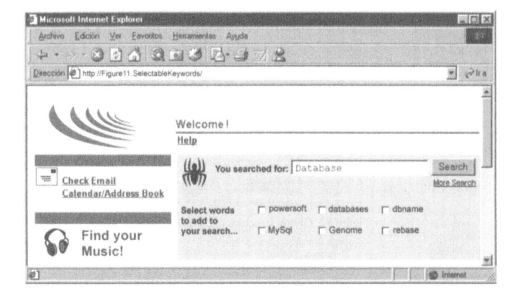

Figure 11. Refining the previous search with keywords.

7.3 STRUCTURED ANSWER

Intent:
Provide the user an organized information report as the result of a query.

Motivation:
The vast extent of the web space is a problem when specific information must be located, through the use of search engines. In this context, search results may include a huge number of relevant information links. Even if we use *Selectable Keywords* the search result may be rather flat. The point here is that a list of links is not enough. Further information is needed to assist a user deciding on the right link.

Solution:
Provide the user with a more structured result that organizes the information in order to help him decide which choice is the most suitable. We can include a brief abstract of the target page, or information about links to other information that may be related, a taxonomy organizing the information space in meaningful sub-spaces, etc.

Examples:
In www.excite.com, and www.yahoo.com we can find good examples of Structured Answer. In www.altavista.com we also find a graphical representation of the result space, and related topics. In Figure 12 we present the results of the query on "components".

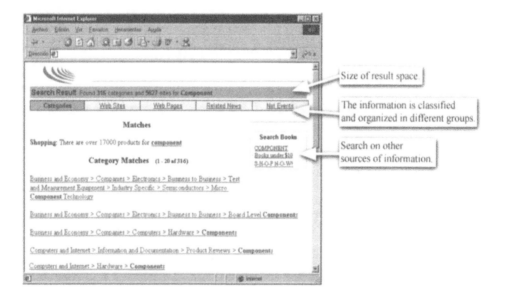

Figure 12. Giving structure to the answer.

Related Patterns:
Structured Answer plays a dual role with respect to Selectable Keywords. While Selectable Keywords allows to reduce the search space, Structured Answer gives more information about the result space, by organizing results in different categories.

8. PATTERNS IN SPECIFIC DOMAINS

Many times specific domains have problems that do not appear in other areas. In this way pattern languages have arisen in domains such as telecommunications, organizational computing, etc. (see for example, [14]).

Thus, it is not strange that particular Web application areas may also have their own design issues and problems. We have discovered many patterns that appear in domains such as newsgroups or electronic commerce. We next give an example of a simple but effective pattern in the electronic commerce domain.

8.1 OPPORTUNISTIC LINKING

Problem:
How to keep the user interested in the site? How to engage him to keep navigating in the site even when he has already found what he was looking for?

Motivation:
Suppose we are building a Web-Information System for an electronic shopping such as www.amazon.com. By entering the site we can buy many different products such as videos, books or CDs. We can explore the products, and besides we provide links to recommendations, comments about the products, news, etc. However, many users navigate with a specific target: for example buying one particular book. Once they have bought that book, there the risk that he leaves the site.

One possibility is to add links to each product page to motivate the reader to navigate. In a well-structured site, however, we must try to provide links with strong semantics to reduce the risk of disorientation. So, how do we reconcile these two requirements?

Solution:
Improve the linking topology by suggesting new products to explore from a given one. Take into account that many of these links may change from day to day so that the interface is defined accordingly. Notice that this pattern can also be used at the conceptual level to derive new relationships. However the intent is clearly navigational: keep the user navigating in a pleasant way.

Examples:
Opportunistic Linking can be found in many electronic stores. For example in http://www.cdnow.com you may jump to an Album advisor that manages the new references. One extreme example can be found in Amazon.com: Once the user has chosen a book and put it in the shopping cart, he receives a suggestion of another book he might be interested in.

9. FROM PATTERNS TO WEB APPLICATIONS

Although the description of patterns very often look obvious, it is still hard to determine how and when to use them in the design process. In other words, while patterns help in solving particular design problems, there is still a need to integrate their use in the overall design process. One way this can be achieved is in the context of a scenario-based process for synthesizing navigation designs [6]. According to this process, navigation design proceeds in the following steps:

1. Determination of user profiles (types of users); identification of user tasks

2. Scenario collection

3. Analysis of scenarios, producing a simple diagrammatic representation of the navigation path described in the scenario. In most cases, in this step the designer has to fill in incomplete information such as implied indexes, missing orderings, exception handling, etc... The designer also uses design patterns to help in this step. A second result of this step is a revision of the preliminary navigation class diagram, as well as a description of how each class used in the scenario is viewed in it.

4. Synthesis of a partial context diagram, specifying navigation in contexts that support the task described in the scenario. Again, design patterns describing known navigation solutions are often employed in this step.

5. Synthesis of final context diagram, through a process of union and amalgamation of partial schemas produced in the analysis of each scenario in step 4. Once this final context diagram has been defined, it also possible to define the navigation class and its InContext classes (decorators). Eventually, a revision of the navigation class schema may be done.

From the process outlined above, it should be clear that the use of patterns fits into various steps. Even though we have stressed navigation design, a similar line of reasoning can be applied for the other phases, such as interface design and implementation.

10. CONCLUDING REMARKS

In this chapter we have shown how to use navigation and interface patterns to capture designers' experience in the context of Web Information Systems development. We presented several simple patterns that we discovered and used in the last years. There is also a growing number of authors who are collecting such patterns, and a public repository is being made available online, under the auspices of ACM SIGWEB (see http://www.designpattern. lu.unisi.ch).

If one carries the design pattern approach to its extreme, one ends up with entire applications in specific domains as giant patterns. In a way, this has already become true with the increasing use of frameworks [7]. A natural outgrowth of this approach has been the definition of hypermedia application frameworks [17], which can be defined as "a reusable design of a complete (or partial) hypermedia application, represented by a set of objects the user may navigate, and a set of possible navigation structures." The goal is to capture in the framework the common design decisions in a set of application in a given domain, in order to facilitate development of new hypermedia applications for that domain. One way to look at one such framework is as an architectural "mega-pattern" for a particular application domain.

In conclusion, one should not forget that designing information systems in the Web is a hard and time consuming task; we must find ways to record and convey good practices in order to improve the development of new applications.

References

1. B. Alexander, S. Ishikawa, M. Silverstein, M. Jacobson, I. Fiksdahl-King, and S. Angel, "A Pattern Language," Oxford University Press, New York 1977.
2. T. Berners-Lee, "The World Wide Web - Past, Present and Future," *Journal of Digital Information* Vol. 1, No. 1, http://journals.ecs.soton.ac.uk/jodi/Articles/timbl.htm.
3. J. Coplien, "A Generative Development-Process Pattern Language," Pattern Languages of Programs 1, Johnson and Cunningham Eds., Addison Wesley, 1995.
4. R. Gamma, R. Helm, R. Johnson, and J. Vlissides "Design Patterns: Elements of Reusable Object-Oriented Software," Addison Wesley, 1995.

5. A. Garrido, G. Rossi, and D. Schwabe, "Patterns Systems for Hypermedia," *Proceedings of PLoP'97, Pattern Language of Program*, 1997. In http://st-www.cs.uiuc.edu/~hanmer/PLoP-97.
6. B.N. Güell, "User Centered Design of Hypermedia Applications," MSc Thesis, Dept. of Informatics, PUC-Rio, 1998 (in Portuguese).
7. W. Pree, "Framework Patterns," SIGS Books & Multimedia, 1996.
8. G. Rossi, D. Schwabe, C.J.P.L. Lucena, and D.D. Cowan, "An Object-Oriented Model for Designing the Human-Computer Interface of Hypermedia Applications," in Fraisse S., Garzotto F., Isakowitz T., Nanard J., Nanard M., (Eds.) *Hypermedia Design*, ISBN 3-540 19985-3, Springer, November 1995, pp. 131-152.
9. G. Rossi, A. Garrido, and S. Carvalho, "Design Patterns for Object-Oriented Hypermedia Applications," Pattern Languages of Programs 2, Vlissides, Coplien and Kerth Eds. Addison Wesley, 1996.
10. G. Rossi, D. Schwabe, and A. Garrido, "Design Reuse in Hypermedia Applications Development," *Proceedings of ACM International Conference on Hypertext (Hypertext'97)*, Southampton, April 7-11, 1997, ACM Press.
11. G. Rossi, F. Lyardet, and D. Schwabe, "Patterns for Defining navigable Spaces," In Pattern Languages of Program Design, Addison Wesley, 1999.
12. G. Rossi, F. Lyardet, and D. Schwabe, "Integrating Hypermedia Patterns into the Development Process," *New Review of Hypermedia and Multimedia*, 1999.
13. S. Rumbaugh, M. Blaha, W. Premerlani, F. Eddy, and W.Lorensen, "Object Oriented Modeling and Design," Prentice Hall, 1991.
14. D. Schmidt, "Using Design Patterns to Develop Reusable Object-Oriented Communication Software," *Communications of the ACM*, Vol. 38, No. 10, October 1995, pp. 65-74.
15. D. Schwabe, G. Rossi, and S. Barbosa, "Systematic Hypermedia Design with OOHDM," *Proceedings of the ACM International Conference on Hypertext (Hypertext'96)*, Washington, March 1996.
16. D. Schwabe and G. Rossi, "An Object-Oriented Model for Building Web Applications," TAPOS (Theory and Practice of Object Systems), Wiley and Sons, October 1998.
17. D. Schwabe, "Just Add Water" Applications: Hypermedia Application Frameworks," *Proceedings of the 2nd Workshop on Hypermedia Development*, Darmstadt, February 1999. Available at: http://ise.ee.uts.edu.au/hypdev/ht99w/submissions/ SchwabeHT99 Workshop.pdf.
18. Rational Inc., "The UML Notation Guide," September 1, 1997, http://www.rational.com/uml/documentation.html.

Chapter 12

A COLLABORATIVE VIRTUAL REALITY SYSTEM ON THE WEB

Jiung-Yao Huang

Abstract

Studies of the multi-user virtual reality system have become a popular topic in the computer graphics community in the recent years. World Wide Web (WWW) provides a seamless, browsable and boundless way for the user to view and retrieve information from the Internet. Integration of the multi-user virtual reality environment into the Web environment provides a richer way for the user to access the network resource, such as video or sound clip, and to build a virtual society over the Internet.

This chapter presents the architecture and the implementation of a multiple user 3D Web browsing system, called the SharedWeb system. The SharedWeb system successfully integrates the DIS technique into the existent Web server to provide a natural solution for the multiple user interactions over the Web environment. Problems of providing the multi-user interaction on the Web and the solutions from the SharedWeb system are fully elaborated here. Some experimental results are also presented to show the effects of different frame rates and threshold values on system performance. And at the end, this chapter will be concluded with the demonstration of supported virtual worlds.

1. INTRODUCTION

Virtual reality is a technique to immerse the user in a synthetic world built by the computer or a remote environment electronically transmitted to the computer for the purpose of training, simulation, prototyping, design, or data acquisition. The multiple user virtual environment is a computer-generated synthetic world on the network where users can navigate and interact with each other. Due to the rapid evolvement of Internet technology, researches on the multi-user virtual environment have become popular in the computer graphics community over the past years.

The World Wide Web (WWW) is a project to bring a global information universe into existence [1]. The Virtual Reality Modeling Language (VRML) is an attempt to deliver a virtual reality world into the WWW environment [2]. The VRML standard enables the user to design 3D multimedia and shared virtual worlds, which are interconnected together via hyperlinks, on the Internet. After the introduction of the VRML language, many VRML-supported browsers were developed, including the WebSpace from SGI, WebOOGL from the Geometry Center, AmberGL from DIVE Lab., WorldView for Intervista Software, Inc. With these browsers, you can view and walk through a virtual world described by the retrieved VRML file.

The original goal of designing the VRML standard is to allow multiple participants to interact over the Web environment. However, even for version 2.0 that was published in August 1996, this design goal was not fulfilled. In addition, none of the above browsers provide multiple-user interaction capability. The development of VRML has nevertheless spurred broad research on distributed multi-user virtual reality systems.

The following sections begin with a survey of related works on the multiple user virtual reality system, and then followed by the methodology and mechanism to design a seamlessly integrated multiple user virtual reality system on the Web. The implementation and experiments of the SharedWeb system based upon the principle of seamless integration will be discussed, along with some experimental results that show the effects of different frame rates and threshold values on system performance. Finally, this chapter will be concluded with the demonstration of supported virtual worlds along with conclusions and future works.

2. RELATED WORK

The researches on the multiple user virtual environments can be classified into two categories: network-based and web-based virtual reality systems. The first category of the multiple user virtual reality system does not necessarily comply with the architecture of the Web environment. This type of virtual reality system generally focuses on providing a large-scale multiple user virtual environment with every available network technique. On the other hand, the web-based multiple user virtual reality system emphasizes providing collaborative virtual environments on top of the existent Web environment. Although this chapter is concentrated on designing a multiple user virtual reality system on the existent Web environment, the techniques from the network-based multiple user system also provides partial solutions to our work. Hence, the techniques used by the network-based virtual reality system will be discussed first.

2.1 NETWORK-BASED MULTIUSER SYSTEMS

There are two issues to be solved when a multi-user virtual environment over the Internet is built: One is the spatial consistency problem and the other is the time coherency problem. Due to the intrinsic network latency, time coherency is almost an insolvable problem for the researchers. Hence, most of the researches of the networked virtual environment have focused on the spatial consistency problem. Various methods have been proposed to maintain the consistency of the synthetic world among distributed players. These methods include communication protocols to log in an existent virtual world and to share the status of objects among distributed participants.

In addition, these communication protocols are tightly related to the database models used by the networked virtual reality systems. According to the distribution of the virtual world database, Macedonia and Zyda [3] classified the networked virtual environments into four types:

- **Replicated homogeneous world database.** SIMNET [4] and NPSNET [5] are two delegations of the replicated homogeneous world model. The NPSNET system uses the DIS (Distributive Interactive Simulation) standard [6], which is descended from the

SIMNET, to communicate the entity status changes among distributed players. The DIS is an IEEE standard for multi-user interaction over the Internet, which will be discussed in the following subsection.

- **Shared and centralized database**. RING [7] and VLNET [8] are two systems that employ the shared and centralized database model. VLNET focuses on providing realistic virtual human characters inside the virtual world. To achieve such a goal, different protocols were designed for the object behavior, navigation, body posture, and facial expression.

- **Shared and distributed database with peer-to-peer updates**. Similar to SIMNET, DIVE [9] system has fully duplicated homogeneous and distributed databases. However, the entire databases are dynamic and a reliable multicast protocol is used to actively replicate new objects.

- **Shared, distributed and client-server databases**. In order to scale up the number of participants without compensating the shared object consistency, BRICKNET [10] and MASSIVE [11] systems employ shared, distributed and client-server databases to achieve the goal. In addition, BRICKNET took one step further to allow objects' dynamic behaviors to be shared among distributed players. MASSIVE uses a spatial model for database partition among clients. These features require complex protocols to ensure strict harmony among distributed sites.

Although the above systems were proven to provide effective distributed virtual worlds, none of them worked on integrating the multi-user system with the Web environment. With the emergence of the VRML standard that brings the virtual world into the Web environment, researches on supporting the multi-user interaction on the Web environment have become a popular topic. Hence, a survey of the previous works on providing multiple user interactions on the Web environment will be discussed next.

2.2 WEB-BASED MULTIUSER SYSTEMS

The Web environment is client/server architecture, and it is widely used to share information over the Internet. Due to the intrinsic characteristic of the HTTP that is used by the Web architecture, the traditional Web system is a "one way street". In other words, it is impossible to achieve the interactivity among users under the existent Web architecture. Hence, mechanisms and protocols have to be designed to support the multiple user interactions on the Web environment. The VRML standard is an attempt to deliver the virtual world on the Web, and its original goal is to support the interaction of multiple participants. However, even the VRML version 2.0[2], which was released in August 1996, failed to define the standard to meet the goal. Hence, several researches on the web-based collaborative systems have their own proprietary methods to support the multiple user interaction [12, 13].

The Virtual Society (VS) is a research project of Sony Computer Science Laboratory [12]. This project is an attempt to define a global architecture and a set of protocols to realize a multi-user interactive 3D environment in a WWW setting. The VS project was originally based on the DIVE platform from the Swedish Institute of Computer Science [9], and a so-called Community Place browsing system [14] was designed for this project. Different from the DIVE system, the Community Place browsing system is a VRML-standard virtual reality system on the Web environment

In order to support large-scale shared 3D spaces using the VRML, the Virtual Society proposed a so-called Virtual Society Server Client Protocol (VSCP) to extend the function of the existing VRML standard. In addition, a scripting architecture is also designed for different levels of consistency for the shared objects. However, the Virtual Society architecture is not seamlessly integrated with the Web environment. For example, the VS client can not enter a virtual world from a Web server form which the scene file was downloaded. Instead, after a scene file is successfully downloaded, the VS client must send a URL to that Web server to query the information of the VS server. The Web server then returns an HTML document to the browser associated with that VS client. The answering HTML document contains the IP address and port number of a VS server that will handle that particular scene. The Web browser then forwards the received server information to the VS client.

According to the Virtual Society architecture, the VS server is an independent program from the WWW server. Consequently, the Virtual Society does not support information exchange between the data on an HTML document and the objects inside a virtual world. Hence, the Virtual Society is an extension of the networked virtual reality system to the Web environment rather than merges the networked virtual reality system into the Web architecture.

German National Research Center for Information Technology (GMD) proposed another type of web-based multi-user system by defining new nodes for VRML standard [13]. Different from the Virtual Society project, the multi-user system of GMD does not require a multi-user server to maintain the consistency among distributed objects. Instead, after a VRML scene file has been downloaded from a Web server, the browser introduces itself as a user to the server. The Web server responds to this new user with an embodiment file of all existing players, along with a multicast address and a port number. The multicast address refers to the IP address of the Web server, and the port number denotes an existing virtual world. Hence, during the course of interaction, each participant sends its status change to the specified port on the Web server and listens to the update information of other users from another port representing a multicast channel.

Since each individual client sends the update messages to the specified port and the Web server redistributes the messages through a multicast channel, an extended HTTPD server is designed to receive update information to monitor the status of the virtual world. If the HTTPD server does not receive an update message from a client for a designated period of time, a time-out mechanism on the HPPD server will issue a *quit* message to the multicast channel for that client.

To achieve the consistency control of shared objects, GMD proposed a so-called Active Lock mechanism and two extension nodes, Interaction node and Behavior node, for the VRML standard. Although the research of GMD was concentrated on extending the VRML standard for the multi-user interaction, issues of seamless integration discussed in the next subsection still require further studies.

The Scalable Platform for Large Interactive Networked Environment (Spline) from Mitsubishi Electric Research Lab (MERL) used yet other approach to integrate the multi-user virtual environment with the Web [15]. Spline is essentially a network-based multi-user virtual reality system that uses Interactive Sharing Transfer Protocol (ISTP) as its communication protocol [16]. ISTP incorporated several simple HTTP protocols to enable the HTTP server to participate the multi-user interaction. With the help of ISTP, the Spline system provides a Web-like virtual environment. However, it is not a web-based multi-user system.

Other web-based multi-user systems that are commercially available include OnLive! Community browser [17] from OnLive! Technologies Inc., OZ Virtual [18] from OZ

Interactive Inc., Ccpro [19] from Blaxxun interactive Corp. and V*Realm Multi-User browser [20] from Integrated Data Systems. All of the above browsers adapt the VRML standard as their virtual scene file format, and each system uses its proprietary technique to provide interactivity among distributed users. In addition, none of the above browsers is fully integrated with the traditional HTML browser. Active World browser [21] from Worlds Inc. is another kind of multi-user browser that is not a VRML browser, but instead, it merges the traditional HTML browser into its own 3D VR browser.

2.3 CHARACTERISTICS OF THE SEAMLESS INTEGRATION

A multiple user virtual reality system on the Web architecture must provide mechanisms for the multi-user server to "remember" the information of the registered participants and to process the messages communicated among them [12, 13]. However, in order to take full advantage of the Web environment, the supported multi-user virtual reality system must be seamlessly integrated with the Web architecture. For a distributed multi-user system to be seamlessly integrated with the Web environment, it must have the following characteristics:

1. The user can download a scene file from any Web server with the HyperText Transfer Protocol (HTTP). That is, the user can select a scene file from any supported HTML document and access that virtual world by double clicking the mouse button.

2. The multi-user system must provide the hyperlink feature to retrieve various media resources that are supported by the Web environment. With the help of this feature, the user of the network-based virtual environment can easily access any media resource, such as a video, sound or image file, hyperlinked by objects inside the virtual world.

3. The multi-user system must be able to handle information exchange between the data on an HTML document and an object inside a virtual world. That is, the user can easily control an object inside the virtual world by filling data into forms on an HTML document. Similarly, the contents of an HTML document can be modified by the status change of an object inside the virtual world. Since an HTML document provides a more convenient way to display information, this feature is very important for a multi-user system to be completely integrated into the Web architecture. The most obvious application is to support a distributed 3D wargaming environment [22].

4. The multi-user server itself is an add-on function of an existent Web server. This characteristic makes the multi-user interaction a part of the WWW services and allows the multi-user server to easily access the database provided by the Web server.

5. The user can directly enter a virtual world from a Web server of which the scene file is downloaded. With this feature, since the Web server takes the role of the user's login process, the multi-user server can be easily replaced and upgraded. In addition, the fault tolerance and the load balance features among the servers of the multi-user virtual reality system can also be easily implemented.

In summary, the seamless integration implies that the user can download a virtual scene file from any supporting Web server and navigate to other virtual world which is managed by other Web server without the awareness of the user. At the same time, the user can fully explore the services provided by the Web environment.

2.4 DISTRIBUTIVE INTERACTIVE SIMULATION

Although VRML brought virtual worlds into the Web environment, the only standardized communication protocol for multi-user interaction over the Internet is the Distributive

Interactive Simulation (DIS) standard [6]. The DIS standard is originally designed for peer-to-peer simulation and aims at military training simulation, however, its concept has been adapted by other distributed virtual reality systems [9, 11]. In addition, the PDU and the Dead Reckoning model have been proven to be two useful techniques to support the web-based virtual reality system [23]. Hence, an overview of the DIS standard is given here before further discussion.

The goal of the DIS standard is to link the interactive, free play activities of people in an operational exercise to form a time- and space- coherent synthetic world. This synthetic environment is created through the low latency (100 to 300 milliseconds) exchange of data units between distributed, computationally autonomous simulation applications. These computational simulation applications may be presented in one location or distributed geographically. Two important techniques have been defined in the DIS standard: the Protocol Data Unit (PDU) and the Dead Reckoning (DR) model.

Since the DIS standard requires each participating host to have the replicated homogeneous world database, the PDU is the data unit that defines the information exchanged among simulation hosts through the network. The PDU contains the information of simulated entity status and the type of interaction that took place in an operational exercise. It also defines the data format for the simulation management to monitor the simulation process. The DIS defines 27 types of PDUs, which are organized into six protocol families: entity information/interaction, warfare, logistics, simulation management, distributed emission regeneration and radio communication. The Entity State PDU, that defines the information required to communicate an entity's state to other entities, is the most important PDU among them.

Furthermore, since the purpose of the DIS technique is to link the simulated entities distributed over geographically separated sites, a so called Dead Reckon model is used to estimate each entity's position and orientation based upon the pervious information. The objective of this Dead Reckon model is to reduce traffic load on the network when maintaining the spatial consistency among simulated entities [24]. For each simulated entity, the Dead Reckoning model uses its previous updated information to predict its next position and orientation called Dead Reckon values. A host uses the Dead Reckon values to move distributive simulated entities before their actual postures are received from the network. In addition, for the simulated entity that is controlled by a host, its Dead Reckon value is calculated along with its actual position and orientation. With the Dead Reckoning technique, it is not necessary for a host to send an Entity State PDU of a simulated entity about every change in position and orientation that occurs over the time. Only when the Dead Reckon value of an entity is different from its actual posture by a predetermined threshold, a new Entity State PDU for that entity is actually sent onto the network. When other hosts in the same simulation receive this Entity State PDU, they will correct the posture of this entity to the updated value and resume its Dead Reckoning calculation from this new posture.

In other words, this approach specifies when the status change of an entity must be transmitted by a host to other participants. It also specifies how the state of an entity is estimated by each host before a status change information of that entity arrives. Thus, a participant can send less information to the network with the Dead Reckoning model.

3. DESIGN OF A COLLABORATIVE 3D WEB BROWSING SYSTEM

The SharedWeb system is a collaborative 3D web browsing system that was designed and implemented in Multimedia and Virtual Reality Lab., Department of Computer Science and Information Engineering, Tamkang University [25]. The goal of the SharedWeb system is to support interaction among clients over the existing Web environment. By the seamless integration of the network-based virtual reality system with the Web architecture, the SharedWeb system provides a boundless way to retrieve information over the Web environment while the users are interacting with each other.

In the following subsections, mechanisms to support the multi-user interaction on the existent Web environment are discussed first, followed by introduction of the infrastructure of the SharedWeb system. And finally, the communication protocol for the SharedWeb system will be presented.

3.1 MECANISMS TO SUPPORT THE MULTIPLE USER INTERACTION ON THE WEB

Because of the distinct characteristics of the HTTP protocol, the existent Web server uses the request-and-response technique for its clients to retrieve information. Thus, the link between the server and the client is established only when a client issues a request to the server. This link is broken and "forgotten" immediately by the server after the requested information is sent to that client. Hence, the Web architecture imposes four intrinsic problems on the support of the multiple user interactions: they are Client-Information Recording, Server-to-Client Callback, Excessive Network Loading, and Virtual World Entrance.

3.1.1 Client Information Records

Since the link is broken immediately after the server has sent the requested information to the client, the server generally does not keep the records of the clients who have requested information from it. This is called the **Client Information Recording** problem.

To solve this problem, each browser must be able to provide a sequence number, called Unique Identification (UID), to uniquely identify itself to the server. Modified from Chin's proposal [23], the SharedWeb browser uses the combination of LTP, which stands for Login name, Time stamp and listen Port number, as the UID to identify itself. The login name is the nickname of the user who logins to a virtual world. Whereas, the time stamp is the time when the browser is first activated and the listen port number is the port number that the browser uses to receive messages. With this UID number, the SharedWeb server can easily identify a new registered player and assign a User ID to that browser. Moreover, this UID number will be recorded by the SharedWeb server for future reference.

3.1.2 Server-to-Client Callback

The HTTP link between the server and the client is established only when a specific request is raised by a client, and the Web server does not have any information to actively set up a connection to its client. Therefore, if a client intends to send information to other clients in the same virtual world, the server does not have the ability to forward this information to those clients. This is referred as the **Server-to-Client Callback** problem.

To solve this problem, the server has to "remember" the browsers that were registered to a virtual scene. In addition, each browser must also provide its information, such as IP address and port number, to the server, so that the server can actively send information to the registered browser. With the Client Information Recording method discussed in the previous sub-section, the SharedWeb browser sends the UID information to the SharedWeb server after a user has logged in. When the SharedWeb server receives the registration information from a browser, it saves this registration message and replies the registered browser with its IP address and port number. Therefore, during the course of the multi-user interaction, each registered browser sends its status change to the SharedWeb server and the SharedWeb server then actively forwards the received message to the appropriate participants.

Another technique being widely discussed recently is "Cookies" [26, 27]. The Cookie technique is based on a two-stage process. First, a "cookie", or a small piece of information, is sent by the Web server and stored in the user's computer without its consent or knowledge. Second, the cookie clandestinely and automatically establishes connection to the Web server. In its current form, Cookies can not be used as the Callback mechanism from Web server.

3.1.3 Excessive Network Loading

Because the HTTP link establishes only when a request is issued, a linking delay is added on top of the intrinsic network latency. Although a web-based multi-user virtual reality system does not necessarily require a multi-user server to maintain the spatial consistency of a virtual world, still, a central server is required to mediate communication among the clients [13]. The network bandwidth will be overloaded very quickly, as the number of players increases, and the server will rapidly become an input/output bottleneck as well. This situation is described as an **Excessive Network Loading** problem.

Since the DIS standard is a fully distributed simulation method, the DIS concept is adapted by the SharedWeb system to reduce this problem. That is, like the DIS standard, each SharedWeb browser has the entire virtual world information. The status change information of an entity is also encapsulated into a self-contained data package, called protocol data unit (PDU), which is forwarded to each participating browser through the SharedWeb server. With the PDU, the frequency of data transmission is reduced. In addition, with the help of the Dead Reckoning model from the DIS standard, the status change information needs not to be transmitted so often. As guided by the Dead Reckoning model, the status change of an entity is sent to the server when this change exceeds a predefined threshold. Hence, the bandwidth requirement is further reduced. However, since the DIS technique was originally designed for the military training purpose, the SharedWeb system extends the PDU format of the DIS standard for a more general utilization.

3.1.4 Virtual World Entrance

An important issue of designing a collaborative 3D web browsing system is that the Web server must be able to send the IP address and the port number of a multi-user server to its clients. However, since the Web architecture employs the request-and-response method of HTTP, the Web server is not aware of the client who has downloaded a scene file. Consequently, the Web server can not automatically forward the information of the multi-user server to that client. The problem is referred as **Virtual World Entrance**.

To solve this problem, we can either embed the multi-user server information into the downloaded scene file or allow the client to issue a query message to the WWW server for the information of the multi-user server. Although the first option is simpler, this method will cause trouble when a multi-user server is crashed and a replacement server is activated. As to the second option, the client has to wait until the replied HTML document is received before it then can connect to the virtual world as Virtual Society from Sony SCL did. Both methods fail to satisfy the criteria of the seamless integration as the outline in Section 2.3.

For a networked VR system to be seamlessly integrated into the Web environment, the Web server has to treat the multi-user server as an add-on application. In the Web architecture, the Web server uses the Common Gateway Interface (CGI) program to communicate with its add-on application. Hence, a CGI program can be used to forward the login information from the Web server to the multi-user server, and, thus, the client does not care if the multi-user server and the Web server reside in the same host.

In addition, a hierarchy structure of the multi-user servers can be implemented so that the Web server can pass client login information to a load-monitor program, which can forward the client transparently to another multi-user server. This allows load balancing and the fault-tolerance features to be implemented for the multi-user server.

3.2 THE INFRASTRUCTURE OF THE SharedWeb SYSTEM

With the mechanisms presented in the previous subsection, the SharedWeb system provides a natural extension of the Web environment into a multi-user virtual environment. The infrastructure of the SharedWeb system is shown in Figure 1. The nodes of the SharedWeb system can be classified into two types: the server site and the browser site. The browser site is composed of four modules: Multiple Participants Interface, 3D Render Engine, Chat Phase, and WWW Homepage Viewer modules. The server site is designed as an add-on application of the existing Web server with two modules: a CGI program and the SharedWeb server. The server and the browser communicate through the SharedWeb Communication Protocol (SWCP), which will be fully explored in the next subsection. Each of these modules is responsible for the tasks described below.

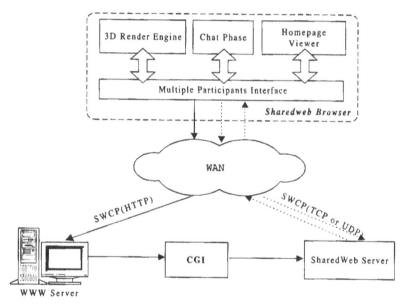

Figure 1. An infrastructure for the SharedWeb system.
(From IEEE Internet Computing, Sept. 1998. © IEEE 1998. With permission.)

3.2.1 The Browser Site
The Multiple Participant Interface module runs on top of Winsock to manipulate the interaction between the browser and other players. This module is the kernel of a SharedWeb browser. Its main functions are to calculate browser's UID, encapsulate and de-capsulate the PDUs, transmit/receive data to/from the network, and coordinate messages among 3D Render Engine, Chat Phase, and WWW Homepage Viewer modules.

The 3D Render Engine module provides a visual window for the user to explore the virtual world. When a browser retrieves a scene file from the Web server, it is an ASCII file. The scene file is then translated into a virtual world database recognized by the 3D Render Engine module.

The Chat Phase module is designed to support text communication among distributed players. This module enhances the interactions among distributed participants and, hence, broadens the applicability of the SharedWeb system. Without this module, the shared virtual world will be a wordless world that makes the user bored easily when playing with the SharedWeb browser.

The WWW Homepage Viewer module is a standard HTML browser. By seamlessly integrating this module into the SharedWeb browser, a user can enter another virtual world by double clicking a hyperlink provided on a homepage or inside the virtual world. Further, the user can exchange information with each other by using a homepage and the HTTP protocol.

3.2.2 The server site

The Web server is a gateway for a SharedWeb user to enter a virtual world. A user only needs to download a scene file from this Web server and logs in a nickname to enter a virtual world. After the Web server receives the login information from a browser, it passes the received user information to the SharedWeb server through the CGI program.

The SharedWeb server module is the kernel of the entire SharedWeb system. This program is responsible for mediating the information exchange among the browsers in the same virtual world. All the client information is sent to the server and the server routes the received information to the browsers in the same virtual world, with the exception of the Chat function among users.

3.3 SharedWeb COMMUNICATION PROTOCOL

Up until now, there is no standardized communication protocol for the web-based multi-user virtual reality system and different protocols have been proposed by various systems over the years [12,13,16]. The communication protocol includes steps to join an existent virtual world, to forward messages among distributed users, and to leave the virtual world. On the other hand, the DIS standard is so far the most successful technique that enables a fully distributed virtual environment to be built on the Internet.

The DIS standard, even though it was not designed for the Web, has been proven to effectively support the networked multi-user virtual environment on the Internet. Inspired by the success of the DIS technique [28], the SharedWeb communication protocol (SWCP) extends the DIS to support the multi-user interaction in the Web environment. The extensions focus on the methods to fully integrate the networked virtual reality system into the existing Web architecture. For example, an HTTP PDU is designed for a user to pass URL address to other users. With this function, a user can send his/her homepage or any network resource to other users. In addition, the HTTP PDU enables the user to use the data on an HTML document to control the objects inside the virtual world. To demonstrate this feature, a 3D wargaming environment was constructed and fully elaborated in Section 5.3.

3.3.1 Common Portions of the SharedWeb PDUs

Seven PDUs are defined for the SharedWeb system, and most of them are composed of two common portions and other related fields. The first common portion is called **PDU Header**. Since the SharedWeb system supports more than one scenario at a time, each PDU contains a PDU Header to identify a user in different scenes. The PDU header is composed of the following five fields:

{Protocol Version, PDU Type, Time Stamp, Scene Name, Scene ID}

Among the above five fields, the Protocol Version field is used to identify the SWCP version. The PDU Type field tells the receiver what kind of PDU it is, such as Initial PDU, Object State PDU, End PDU, Acknowledge PDU, Chat PDU, HTTP PDU, or Error PDU. The Time Stamp field records the time when this PDU was sent and it can be used to justify the validation of the user's message. Notice that the Time Stamp field is ignored by the conventional "real-time" simulation, and it is used to ensure that the proper order of the simulation events for some time-critical simulations, such as wargaming, is enforced. For example, two tanks are firing at each other in a wargame simulation. If a tank is observed to be hit when it is moving away, the Time Stamp is used to determine which event occurs first. The Scene Name stores the file name of the downloaded virtual scene, and the Scene ID is the unique identification number of the downloaded virtual scene. The SharedWeb server uses the Scene Name and Scene ID fields to recognize the virtual world in which the browser issuing the PDU resides.

The second common portion for most PDUs is the **User Information**. It contains the information for a user to identify himself/herself, and is comprised by the following three fields:

{User ID, IP Address, Avatar Type}

The User ID field stores the unique identification number of a browser inside a virtual world, and it is assigned by the SharedWeb server when the user logs in to a virtual world. The IP Address field records the browser's network address. The Avatar Type field gives the user an option to choose his/her represented shape, usually a human figure, inside the virtual world.

With the PDU Header and the User Information portions discussed above, the SharedWeb PDUs and protocols are introduced as follows:

3.3.2 Entering and Exiting a Virtual World

The SharedWeb uses two PDUs, the Initial PDU and the Acknowledge PDU, to control the process of a SharedWeb browser to enter a virtual world. Similarly, the End PDU and the Acknowledge PDU are used to communicate the event of a SharedWeb browser leaving a virtual world. Since these three PDUs have exactly the same format, they will be discussed together here.

In addition to the PDU Header and the User Information portions, all of these three PDUs have another important portion, called UID. That is, all three PDUs are compounded by three portions: **(PDU Header)(User Information)(UID)**. This UID is calculated by the browser when the browser is activated. The SharedWeb server saves this UID number in its client table, and uses this information to communicate with that specific browser. Unlike the User ID field of the User Information, which is unique within a virtual world only, the UID uniquely identifies a user from others at all times even if they do not reside in the same virtual world. In other word, if two users are in two distinct virtual worlds, they may have the same User ID number, but they must have different UID numbers. The UID field contains the following three fields, which were fully introduced in Client Information Recording method on Section 3.1.

{Login User Name, Time, Port number}

The Initial PDU allows a browser to submit the information to the SharedWeb server to log into a virtual world. After a browser has downloaded a scene file from a Web server, an Initial PDU is created when the user keys in a login nickname. However, the SharedWeb browser is not aware of the existence of the SharedWeb server when it downloads a scene file from a Web server. In order to provide a seamless way to support multi-user interaction on the Web environment, the SharedWeb browser sends the Initial PDU as an HTTP string directly to the Web server. When the Web server receives this HTTP string, it activates a CGI program to forward this Initial PDU to the SharedWeb server. Using this methodology, the SharedWeb server acts as an add-on function to the existing Web server. Another benefit of this method is the possibility of providing the load balance and the fault tolerance features on the multi-user server site. Since the CGI program is used to mediate the login process, the Web server can easily transfer a new login user to a different SharedWeb server if the previous server is overloaded or crashed.

When the SharedWeb server receives the Initial PDU from a browser, it responds with an Acknowledge PDU to the browser. This Acknowledge PDU has the same fields and contents as the Initial PDU except the PDU Type and Time Stamp. This Acknowledge PDU is used by the SharedWeb server to verify that an Initial PDU has been received and to send the assigned unique User ID back to the browser.

When a user wants to exit a virtual world, the browser sends an End PDU to notify the SharedWeb server. The End PDU contains the same data format, except the PDU Type and Time Stamp, as the Initial PDU. When the SharedWeb server receives the End PDU, it first removes the corresponding avatar information from its client table and responds to this event by issuing an Acknowledge PDU to that browser. The SharedWeb sever also forwards the End PDU to other browsers so that they can remove its represented avatars from their respective virtual world.

3.3.3 Exchange of Status Information Inside a Virtual World

The Entity State PDU is the most important PDU for the DIS protocol because it is used to exchange the status information among the distributed entities. Similarly, the SWCP defines an Object State PDU to mirror the Entity State PDU. However, from the perspective of the SharedWeb system design goal, the definition of the Object State PDU is not as complicated as that of the Entity State PDU. Therefore, in addition to the PDU Header and User Information portions, the Object State PDU contains four fields:

(PDU Header)(User Information){Location, Linear Velocity, Orientation, DR Parameter}

The Location, Linear Velocity and Orientation fields define the postures of an avatar, which represents the user inside a virtual world. The DR Parameter field is set by the browser to specify the parameter for the Dead Reckoning model that controls the movement of an avatar.

After successfully logging in to the virtual world, the browser uses the Object State PDU to send the status information of an avatar to the SharedWeb server. Based upon the Dead Reckoning model being used, the Object State PDU is issued only when the actual position of its represented avatar exceeds its Dead Reckon value by a predefined threshold. This mechanism reduces the number of messages flowing on the network and thus bandwidth requirement. When the SharedWeb server receives an Object State PDU from a browser, it forwards this PDU to all the other browsers residing in the same virtual world.

3.3.4 Chat Phase

The chatting function is an important feature to enhance collaboration among the distributed users. The SharedWeb system adopts a widely accepted chatting protocol called the Internet Relay Protocol (IRP) [29] to design the Chat PDU. Since the IRP is a peer-to-peer chatting protocol, Chat PDU is the only PDU that bypasses the SharedWeb server. The Chat PDU includes the PDU Header portion for the receiver to verify that the sender is within the same virtual world and two additional fields: Sender ID and Text Massage.

(PDU Header){Sender ID, Text Message}

Although a chat server can be designed to support group chatting, it can generate a bottleneck on the SharedWeb server site as the number of players increases. Hence, SharedWeb supports only the peer-to-peer chatting protocol at this time.

3.3.5 Resource Integration with WWW Environment

The design goal of the SharedWeb system is not only to provide a seamless way to support multiple user interactions on the Web environment, but also to furnish a method to integrate the Web resources. An HTTP PDU is implemented to achieve this goal. The HTTP PDU allows the user to send a URL address of a web resource, such as an HTML document or sound, to other users. After a browser receives an HTTP PDU, it downloads the specific web resource from the specified URL location. Particularly, the HTTP PDU enables the user to control the objects in the virtual world from an HTML document. Whenever the forms of an HTML document on the SharedWeb browser are filled and sent, these data are sent to the Web server. The Web server forwards the received information to the SharedWeb server through the CGI program. Hence, the HTTP PDU has the following format:

(PDU Header){Receiver ID, URL Address, Events}

The Receiver ID field contains the User ID that is going to receive this PDU. The URL Address field is the network location of the specified web resource, and the Events field is a string of data that were filled in the forms of the HTML document. With this particular PDU, a user can easily send his/her HTML document or other resource to the other users in the same virtual world. Moreover, the HTTP PDU allows the users to play an interactive wargame over the Web environment as demonstrated in Section 5.3.

4. IMPLEMENTATION AND EXPERIMENTS OF THE SharedWeb SYSTEM

4.1 IMPLEMENTATION

The SharedWeb system was implemented on Microsoft Windows platform using Visual C++ ver 4.0. The SharedWeb server is run on Windows NT Server ver 4.0 with an embedded WWW server. In addition, for the sake of flexibility and extendibility, the SharedWeb browser was implemented as a standalone browser at this moment. The SharedWeb browser will be implemented as a plug-in application for the Netscape Communicator or the Internet Explorer in the near future. The interface of the SharedWeb browser is as shown in Figure 2.

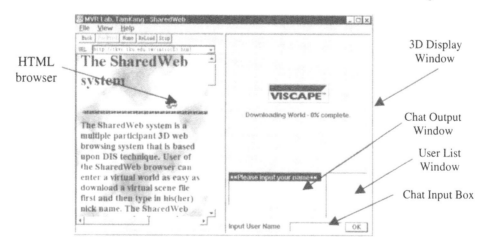

Figure 2. Interface of the SharedWeb browser.
(From <u>IEEE</u> Internet Computing, Sept. 1998. © IEEE 1998. With permission.)

As displayed on the upper-right window of Figure 2, Viscape software from Superscape [30] is used as the 3D Render Engine. The lower-right window is the Chat Output Window that will display the text messages that are communicated among distributed users, and the user can type in his message from the Chat Input Box. When the browser is initiated, the Chat Input Box is originally labeled as "Input User Name" and is used for the user to type in his nickname to login the downloaded virtual world. Before the user logins a virtual world, the chat function and the multi-user interaction feature are disabled. After the user has successfully logged in a virtual world, the Chat Input Box will be activated automatically and all of the users' names residing in the virtual world will be listed in the User List Window. Furthermore, a "Send URL" button will emerge at the same time, as shown in Figure 3. The "Send URL" button is a special function for the user to send a hyperlinked resource, such as an HTML document or audio clip, to other users. This function is another feature for the SharedWeb system to be seamlessly integrated into the WWW environment.

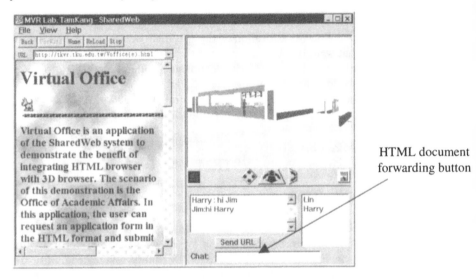

Figure 3. URL button for forwarding HTML document.
(From IEEE Internet Computing, Sept. 1998. © IEEE 1998. With permission.)

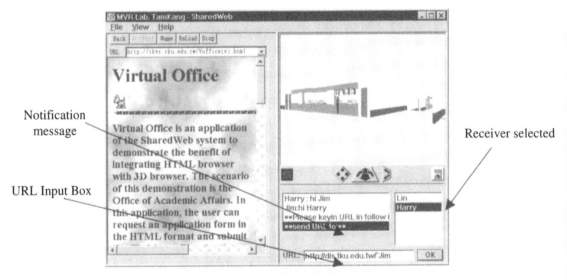

Figure 4. Snapshot after the "Send URL" button is pressed.
(From IEEE Internet Computing, Sept. 1998. © IEEE 1998. With permission.)

After the "Send URL" button is pressed, it will disappear again and a highlighted message will be displayed in Chat Output Window to notify the user. In the meantime, as shown in Figure 4, the label of the Chat Input Box is changed to "URL:" for the user to input the URL address of a web resource, such as an HTML document or audio clip. The sender selects the receiver(s) by clicking one or more names from the User List Window. By clicking the OK button, the specified network resource will then be automatically forwarded to the receiver(s).

4.2 EXPERIMENTS AND RESULTS

According to the mechanisms designed for the SharedWeb system, four factors will affect the interaction among the distributed users.

- The bandwidth required by the SharedWeb browser to reflect the status change of an avatar;
- The network latency between the SharedWeb server and browser;
- The network bandwidth provided by the network structure, such as the Internet;
- The computational load of the SharedWeb server in forwarding the received PDUs;

The second and third factors completely depend upon the network structure, such as a local area network or a wide area network that is used. In addition, with the help of the Dead Reckoning model, the second and third factors have little influence on the interaction among the distributed users. The fourth factor is a constant time since the SharedWeb server simply records and forwards the received PDUs according to the information saved on its Client Table. As to the first factor, it depends upon the size of the Object State PDU and how often this PDU is sent by the SharedWeb browser. By multiplying the size of the Object State PDU by the number of the PDU that is sent by a browser per second, the bandwidth required by a single user can be easily decided. Significantly, this factor will decide not only the network bandwidth required for the SharedWeb system but also the number of players that can be interacting simultaneously. Hence, in the rest of this subsection, the experiments will focus on analyzing this factor.

One important mechanism adopted by the SharedWeb system is the Dead Reckoning model. With the Dead Reckoning model, the number of the Object State PDUs sent to the network is minimized. The equation of Dead Reckoning model used by the SharedWeb system is a linear equation, $P=P_0+V*t$. In this equation, P stands for Dead Reckon (DR) value and P_0 is the last updated actual position. The velocity V is the speed of movement of an avatar. The most important factor of this equation is the definition of the time t. Instead of using the host clock, t is defined as the logical time of the virtual world. This definition will ensure that the movement of avatars will not be affected by the computational power of each host, and the computation of the Dead Reckoning model is simplified consequently. Since the target frame rate for a virtual reality system is 30 frames per second, the experiments project a logical time unit as 1/30 second of local clock on the host.

The essential point of the Dead Reckon model is how to set the threshold value appropriately. The greater DR threshold value is used, the larger jerky motion may be perceived. On the other hand, if the DR threshold value is too small, more PDUs will be sent to the network. Consequently, the choice of threshold value will significantly affect the simulation fidelity as well as the network bandwidth [21]. Hence, the experiments were concentrated on deciding an appropriate threshold value under different frame rates. In the experiments, the number of PDUs for different frame rates under different threshold values is collected. Moreover, the experiments were based on the following assumptions:

- Each pace of an avatar is the width of this avatar. Since, for the SharedWeb system, the size of an avatar depends on the scale of the virtual world and the distance of each pace may change as well.

- The threshold value is measured by the number of paces between the actual position and the DR value. That is, if a value 3 is adopted as the threshold value, an Object State PDU is sent out whenever the difference between the actual position and DR value is 3 times greater than the pace size.

- The worst case is assumed. That is, the experiments aim to find a moving trajectory for an avatar that the browser will send out the Object State PDUs as frequently as possible. After a careful investigation, the experiments found out that a circular movement will cause the actual position of an avatar different from its DR value on its every movement. In Figure 5, point P_i' represents the DR value and point P_i is the actual position. An Object State PDU will be sent out when the difference between P_i' and P_i is greater than the threshold value. By carefully setting the radius r of the circular trajectory, the experiments force the number of the Object State PDU generated per logical time equal to the value of the threshold. This is believed to be the closest situation to the worst case.

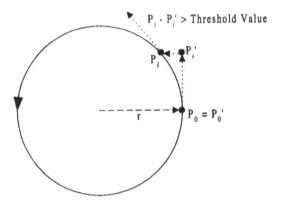

Figure 5. The trajectory of our experiment.

- Finally, the velocity V is a constant value. That is, the avatar moves at a constant speed. Although the SharedWeb system allows each avatar to move with different velocities, this assumption will simplify our simulation and produce a result that is close to the real case.

4.3 DISCUSSION OF THE EXPERIMENTAL RESULTS

The result of the experiment is shown in Table 1 and Figure 6. During this experiment, the radius of trajectory is set to be 10 times of an avatar's pace. In addition, the trajectory in Figure 5 is simulated by rotating the avatar 10-degree pre frame while it is moving forward. In Table 1, the first column represents different threshold values that are used and the first row represents the frame rates tested during the experiment. The table shows that, at the threshold value 10, a PDU is generated every 1.98727 frames (that is, frame rate 8 divided by 4.02562 PDUs per second). Similarly, a PDU is generated every 2.977165 frames when the threshold value is 20 and so on. The graph in Figure 6 is a comparison of the number of PDUs generated per second versus different Frame rates under different threshold values.

Table 1. The Number of PDUs Generated per Second at Different Frame Rates and Dead-reckoning Threshold Values

Frame rate Threshold	8	12	24	36	52
10	4.02562	6.21677	12.4024	18.2287	26.1428
20	2.68712	4.16112	8.49192	11.8745	17.6048
30	2.02458	3.15029	6.32563	9.12651	12.9868
40	1.62442	2.50606	5.02114	7.29393	10.3976
50	1.34774	2.09612	4.17452	5.98301	8.62408

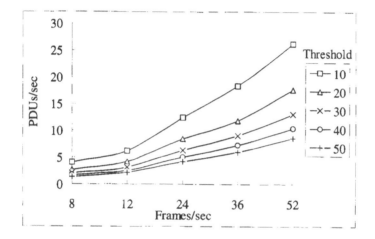

Figure 6. The PDU number generated per second versus frame rates under different dead-reckoning threshold values.
(From IEEE Internet Computing, Sept. 1998. © IEEE 1998. With permission.)

Based upon the above result, a threshold 30 is chosen for the SharedWeb system. That is, for each virtual world, three times of an avatar width is selected as our Dead Reckoning threshold value. With this threshold value, an Object State PDU will be sent every four frames in the worst case. Since the size of the Object State PDU is 528 bits, in the worst case, the network bandwidth required by a SharedWeb browser is 528 * 6.32563 ≅ 3,340 bits per second at 24Hz display rate. Hence, the SharedWeb system can theoretically support more than 300 simultaneous players (that is, 314 roughly equal to 1 Mbits divided by 3,340 bits per second) in the network environment with 1 Mbits of bandwidth.

5. DEMONSTRATED VIRTUAL SCENES

To fully explore the features provided by the SharedWeb system, different virtual worlds were constructed. The following scenarios are part of the virtual worlds currently supported in the SharedWeb environment.

5.1 VIRTUAL CAMPUS

The virtual campus is a scaled-down duplication of the main campus of Tamkang University, Taiwan. The purpose of this virtual campus application is to investigate the possibility of designing a virtual University over the Web environment. This application provides a new way for the students to visit the campus without leaving their desks. Inside this virtual campus, the students can chat with each other while navigating the virtual campus. In addition, each building inside this virtual campus has a hyperlink to another virtual world that models the interior of that building. If a building has many storeys, it will contain hyperlinks to more than one virtual world and each floor is modeled as a virtual world. Figure 7 shows the snapshot when the user downloads the scene file of the virtual campus. In addition, a brief introduction of this virtual world will also be automatically downloaded as an HTML document at the same time. However, before the user logins a virtual world, he is alone.

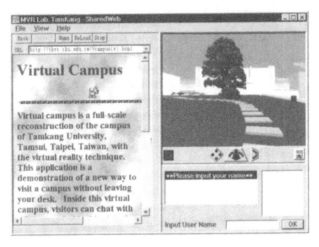

Figure 7. Snapshot of the virtual campus after it is downloaded.

Figure 8 is an illustration of the virtual campus from the view of user **"Jim"**. When the user logins to the virtual campus, the names of all users that are already inside this virtual world will be displayed on the User List window. This particular scene includes three users with their names, except the observer **"Jim"**, are displayed on the User List window. Each user can navigate the virtual campus by clicking and dragging the control panel provided by the Viscape software, and the other user inside the virtual campus will observe the movement of his represented avatar. Figure 8 also shows the result of the user **"Jim"** greeting to another player **"Pony"** through the Chat Phase module.

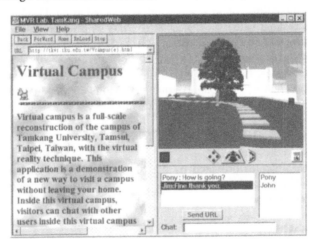

Figure 8. Snapshot of the virtual campus after the user, **"Jim"**, has logged in.

When a user wants to chat with other participants, he can input his message into the Chat Input window and this message will be displayed on the Chat Output Window of each participant's browser. Notice that, before the user enters a virtual world, the Chat Input Box is labeled as "Input User Name" as shown in Figure 2. After the user has successfully logged in the virtual campus, the label of the Chat Input Box will automatically change to "Chat."

5.2 VIRTUAL OFFICE

The virtual office is a hyperlinked virtual world when the user clicks on the Administrative Building of the virtual campus. The virtual office application is an effort to study the possibility of performing some of the university's administrative tasks online. Since the SharedWeb system is an integration of the virtual reality system with the HTML browser, a user can use the HTML document to fill the application form, say, for a new student ID. As shown in Figure 9, various application forms are hyperlinked by pictures on the wall inside this virtual office. The user can click one of the pictures to download an application form to the HTML browser. Since the application form is implemented as an HTML document, different types of the application form can be easily designed and modified. Hence, a virtual shopping mall can be easily implemented with the help of this integrated HTML browser as well.

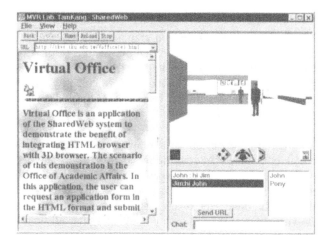

Figure 9. Pictures on the wall of the virtual office representing various application forms.

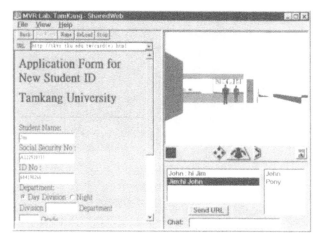

Figure 10. Snapshot after the user has downloaded and filled an application form.
(From IEEE Internet Computing, Sept. 1998. © IEEE 1998. With permission.)

Figure 10 shows that, when the student has filled the application form and clicked the "Send" button on the HTML document, the filled information will be sent to the WWW server for processing. After the server has successfully received this information, the server will reply with an acknowledgement message to the client.

5.3 3D WARGAMING ENVIRONMENT

The 3D tank wargaming simulation is a prototype of a wargaming system in the Web environment. This application is a 3D version of a Role Playing Game (RPG) simulation, where the player can choose his role inside the game. The character of the game is controlled by the user's command rather than being directly manipulated by the input device, such as joysticks. That is, after the player issues his command, the movement of the character is controlled by certain pre-defined rules according to the user's command. For example, assume that you are playing an RPG of Fleet War and you are a captain of a warship. You can issue a command to move the warship to a new location. Whether that ship will reach that location will depend upon whether an enemy attack occurs on route. If an enemy attack is engaged, the system will prompt you for defense. Therefore, it is a strategy training software instead of a motor-skill exercising game.

The RPG is traditionally using a two-dimension graphical layout. In addition, it requires an interactive dialogue box, or command sheet, for the player to control his character inside the game. Since the SharedWeb system fully integrates the HTML browser with the virtual reality navigator, the command sheet can be easily implemented by an HTML document. In addition, a game master, which is required for an RPG to control the game rules, was implemented in the SharedWeb server.

This prototype 3D wargaming system allows three users to enter a virtual battlefield. One user plays the blue tank commander by logging in as "**bluetank**", another plays the red tank commander by typing in **"redtank"** as his user name, and the third player is the referee of this combat exercise. Blue tank and red tank commanders can use forms and check boxes that are available on the HTML document to control two tanks inside the virtual battlefield. Figure 11 shows the viewpoint of the red tank commander after all three users have entered this virtual battlefield.

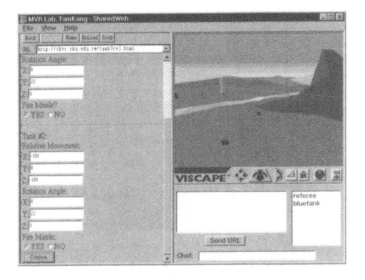

Figure 11. Snapshot of the user "**redtank**" after entering a virtual battlefield.
(From <u>IEEE Internet Computing</u>, Sept. 1998. © IEEE 1998. With permission.)

Figure 11 also shows that, after the user has successfully logged in this virtual battlefield, the user command sheet will be automatically downloaded into the HTML browser. The title of command sheet will specify if the user is a red tank or a blue tank commander, and the user can input data to control his tanks movement. In addition, check buttons are also provided for the user to issue the firing ammunition command.

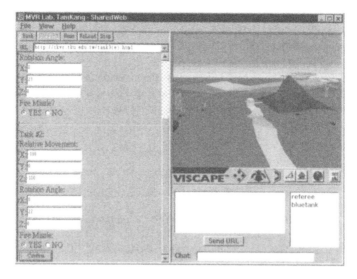

Figure 12. Viewing the ongoing battle from a different perspective.

After the user inputs his command and presses the "Confirm" button, the user commands will be sent to the SharedWeb server. The server will then forward these commands to all participants to "modify" the status of each tank, such as fire or destroy. Figure 12 shows a different view of observing the combat exercise. With the help of the virtual reality technique, the trainee can have a different view to observe the exercise.

6. CONCLUSIONS AND FUTURE WORK

This chapter presents the concept of seamlessly integrating the multi-user system with the Web environment. With this seamless integration, the multi-user interaction can be easily supported by an existing Web server, and a shared virtual world can thus be easily constructed. The infrastructure and the communication protocol of this concept are fully elaborated in this paper. In addition, the architecture of a web-based multi-user system, called the SharedWeb system, is also presented. Under the architecture of the SharedWeb system, the existing Web server remains intact while supporting the multiple participant interactions. In addition, the SharedWeb environment is transparent to the users. Each user only needs to download a scene file from a WWW server and logins his nickname, and the WWW server will then gracefully transfer the user to an appropriate SharedWeb server.

Although the current SharedWeb implementation successfully demonstrates the concept of seamless integration with the Web environment, more research is required to improve the multi-user interaction. For example, the consistency control of the shared objects is an important function for computer-supported cooperative work (CSCW) type of applications.

Moreover, due to the "broadcast" mechanism used by the SharedWeb server, a large number of PDUs flowing inside the network may flood the bandwidth. Whenever an avatar of a virtual environment with N avatars changes state, the SharedWeb server has to "broadcast" this information to each of the $N-1$ browsers. Thus, in the worst case, a total of N^2-N PDUs must be sent to the network with N users. This approach yields $O(N^2)$ complexity on updating messages and could exhaust the computation power of a host even before the network gets saturated. To overcome this shortcoming, the concept of spatial culling [11] is currently under investigation for the SharedWeb server. This would allows the server to send out PDUs selectively during the course of interaction. For example, the SharedWeb server can forward the received PDU only to the browsers residing in the same virtual room as the browser who issues this PDU.

A multi-server function, that would organize the world database into a client-server architecture and thus scales up the number of participants, is another investing topic. This function would also provide fault tolerance on the server site.

References

1. T. Berners-Lee, et al., "The World-Wide Web," *Communication of the ACM*, Vol. 37, No. 8, August 1994, pp.76-82.
2. "The Virtual Reality Modeling Language Specification Ver. 2.0," August 1996, available on line at http://vrml.sgi.com/moving-worlds/spec.
3. M. R. Macedonia and M. J. Zyda, "A Taxonomy for Networked Virtual Environments," *IEEE Multimedia*, Vol. 4, No. 1, January-March 1997, pp.48-56.
4. J. Calvin et al., "The SIMNET Virtual World Architecture," *Proceedings of the IEEE Virtual Reality Annual International Symposium*, September 1993, pp. 450-455.
5. M.R. Macedonia et al., "NPSNET: A Multi-Player 3D Virtual Environment Over The Internet," *ACM SIGGRAPH Special Issue on 1992 Symposium on Interactive 3D Graphics*, Cambridge, MA, 1995, pp. 93-94.
6. ANSI/IEEE Std. 1278-1993, "Standard for Distributed Interactive Simulation (DIS) – Application Protocols," March 1993.
7. T. A. Funkhouser, "RING: A Client-Server System for Multi-User Virtual Environments," *ACM SIGGRAPH Special Issue on 1992 Symposium on Interactive 3D Graphics*, Cambridge, MA, 1995, pp. 85-92.
8. T. Capin, et al., "Virtual Human Representation and Communication in VLNET," *IEEE Computer Graphics and Applications*, Vol. 17, No. 2, 1997, pp. 42-53.
9. O. Hagsand, "Interactive Multi-user VEs in the DIVE System," *IEEE Multimedia*, Vol. 3, No. 1, Spring 1996, pp. 30-39.
10. G. Singh, et al., "BRICKNET: Sharing Object Behaviors on the Net," *Proceedings of VRAIS'95*, IEEE Computer Society Press, March 1995, pp. 19-25.
11. C. Greenhalgh and S. Benford, "Massive, A Collaborative Virtual Environment for Teleconference," *ACM Transactions on Computer-Human Interaction*, Vol. 2, No. 3, 1995, pp.239-261.
12. Y. Honda, K. Matsuda, J. Rekimoto, and R. Lea, "Virtual Society: Extending the WWW to Support a Multi-user Interactive Shared 3D Environment," *Proc. of VRML'95*, San Diego, CA, August 1995. Also available at http://www.csl.sony.co.jp/person/roger.html.
13. W. Broll, "VRML: From the Web to Interactive Multi-User Virtual Reality," *Proceedings of the GI Workshop on Modeling - Virtual Worlds - Distributed Graphics*, Bad Honnef/Bonn, Germany, November 1995. Also available at http://orgwis.gmd.de/projects/VR/vrml/papers/MVD95.ps.

14. "Community Place Browser," available on line at <http://www.sonypic.com/vs>.
15. R.C. Waters, et al., "Diamond Part and Spline: Social Virtual Reality with 3D Animation, Spoken Interaction, and Runtime Extendibility," *Presence,* Vol. 6, No. 4, August 1997, pp. 461-481.
16. R. C. Waters, D. B. Anderson, and D. L. Schwenke, "The Interactive Sharing Transfer Protocol Version 1.0", Available on line at http://ww.merl.com/reports/index.html/TR97-10.
17. "OnLive! Community Browser," available on line at <http://www.onlive.com>.
18. "OZ Virtual," available on line at <http://www.oz-inc.com/ov>.
19. "Blaxxun Community Client," available on line at < http://ww3.blacksun.com/ >.
20. "V*Realm Multi-User Browser," available on line at http://www.ids-net.com/ids/vrealm.
21. "Active Worlds," available on line at <http://www.activeworlds.com/>.
22. J. Y. Huang, J. L. Chang, C. W. Li, and K. C. Lin, "Design of a Multiple Participant 3D War Game Environment over WWW," *SPIE's 12ᵗʰ Annual International Symposium on Aerospace/Defense Sensing, Simulation, and Control*, Orlando, FL, April 1998.
23. J.Y. Huang, F.B. Wang, W.H. Hsu, and J.F. Chen, "Usage of DIS Technique to Create an Interactive WWW Environment," *14ᵗʰ DIS Workshop*, Orlando, Florida, March 1996, pp. 201-210.
24. K.C. Lin and D. E. Schab, "The Performance Assessment of the Dead Reckoning Algorithms in DIS," *Simulation*, November 1994, pp. 318-325.
25. J. Y. Huang, C. T. Fang-Tson, J. C. Chen, and F. B. Wang, "SharedWeb – A Shared Virtual Environment Over World Wide Web," *Pacific Graphics'97*, Korea, October 1997, pp. 178-189.
26. R. Sikorski and R. Peters, "A privacy Primer for the Web: Spam, Bread Crumbs, and Cookise," *JAMA - The Journal of the American Medical Association*, April 1998, Vol. 279, No. 15, pp. 1219.
27. R. Schwarz, "Manage Your Cookies With VB6 WebClasses," *Visual Basic Programmer's Journal*, October 1998, Vol. 8, No. 12, pp. 88.
28. D. Rogers, "STOW-E Lessons Learned, Focus on the 3 Primary Army STOW-E Sites," *12ᵗʰ Workshop on Standards for the Interoperability of Distributive Simulation*, Vol. I, Position Papers, IST-CF-95-01.1, Orlando, FL, February 1995. Available on line at ftp://ftp.sc.ist.ucf.edu/public/STDS/workshop/12th/papers/026.doc.
29. J. Oikarinen and D. Reed, "Internet Relay Chat Protocol," Internet RFC #1459, May 1993.
30. "VRT for Windows - User Guide," Superscape Inc., UK, 1996.

Chapter 13

ACCESSING LEGACY DATABASES FROM THE WEB USING CORBA

Richard Z. Xue and Eduardo B. Fernandez

Abstract

After comparing general architectures for accessing business databases from the Web a platform-independent, language-independent, object-oriented, four-tier CORBA-based architecture is proposed. A Web Reservation System (WRS) was created to test this architecture. Starting from an analysis pattern, a design model for the WRS was developed using the CORBA Object Request Broker (ORB); this was a Virtual Car Reservation System (VCRS). In the VCRS system, a user can get a reservation number when necessary information is entered from a Web browser. The user can also retrieve the reservation information by using the reservation number. All reservation information is stored in a distributed database system at a remote site. Security controls for the WRS were also considered.

1. INTRODUCTION

Dynamic communications via Internet/Intranet has begun to emerge over the past few years. Traditional static HTML-based communications cannot meet today's high demands for dynamic and distributed computing [1]. Distributed database systems that can be accessed by remote users across the network are very important to centralize entire information into a single database management system. This centralized distributed system creates less vulnerability and greater reliability and increases data security, consistency, and integrity [2]. Most of existing corporate information is stored in relational database management systems and their associated client/server application programs are written in C, C++, Ada, Smalltalk, or COBOL while the majority of Internet application programs are coded in Java [3]. Accessing the distributed database from different computer systems using different computer languages across a network appears very difficult.

Several approaches to provide this type of access have been proposed; we survey some of them in the next section. Peng et al. [4] presented a pure middleware approach for accessing existing business databases, which delivers the data between the Web server and applications or Database Management Systems (DBMS), without modifying either. The middleware gateway includes DB2 World Wide Web Connection and Net.Data. This approach can only be used to access IBM DB2 databases. Other commercial DBMS and Web server vendors provide other approaches to enable DBMS from Web servers or enhance Web servers for DBMS support. In general, those approaches lack flexibility and portability.

The Common Object Request Broker Architecture (CORBA) provides a very good solution for accessing distributed databases via Internet/Intranet. CORBA objects can be written in any computer language and are supported on any platform. With its scalable nature and broad industry support, CORBA is a good choice for distributed database applications that serve a wide range of users on different platforms over internetworking systems [5]. CORBA programs create objects and make invocations on objects elsewhere in the network. Direct remote accessing of Relational Database Management Systems (RDBMS) can be performed with small additions.

In this chapter, a four-tier CORBA architecture is presented to access legacy databases from the Web. The architecture allows remote access/invocation to any existing legacy application programming interfaces (APIs) and DBMS, including RDBMS. To test these ideas, a Web Reservation System (WRS) was created using the proposed architecture. An object-oriented design model for the WRS was developed using the CORBA Object Request Broker (ORB). This design model was based on a previous analysis pattern. A virtual car reservation system (VCRS), a client/server object-oriented application, was developed to study the CORBA objects' communications via an ORB over the TCP/IP network protocol. A Java applet was developed as the client program while a Java program was written as a server. An IBM/DB2 database was used as a relational database for the VCRS. Several operations were implemented in the client/server program to demonstrate the CORBA objects communication over the Internet. Section 2 discusses current approaches, while Section 3 presents the proposed architecture. Section 4 shows the implementation of a test application. We end in Section 5 with some conclusions.

2. OVERVIEW OF ARCHITECTURES FOR ACCESSING DATABASES FROM THE WEB

2.1 HTML FORMS AND CGI

Traditionally, dynamic Web applications have been designed using HyperText Markup Language (HTML) forms and Common Gateway Interface (CGI) programming. HTML forms allow user to enter data from a browser and then post the entered form to the Web server. A CGI program then starts in the server to query data from a database, formats the data into an HTML page, and sends the HTML page back to the browser [6]. This traditional approach has been successful; most Web applications still use it to retrieve less complex data from existing database. However, HTML forms do not support sophisticated user interfaces and CGI programs are slow and not platform independent.

2.2 DB2 WWW CONNECTION OR NET.DATA

There are three basic approaches for dynamic Web applications: (1) modify the Web server to support DBMS functions; (2) modify the DBMS to enhance Web connectivity; and (3) pure middleware to deliver data between the Web server and applications. The first two approaches require changes of legacy database applications and lack flexibility and portability. The third approach can seamlessly and transparently deliver the data between the Web server and applications or DBMS without modifying either [4]. The IBM solutions of middleware gateways include DB2 World Wide Web (WWW) Connection and Net.Data. DB2 WWW Connection enables connections of applications that access relational DBMS data (DB2) by using a macro file. The macro file allows developers to define cross-language variables between HTML inputs/outputs and SQL query/result strings. The variables can also be defined through the uniform resource locator (URL). Macros are platform independent and portable to different Web servers. Net.Data is a successor to DB2 WWW Connection that expands its macro language features, supports multiple language environments, and improves performance [4]. However, both approaches can only access IBM DB2 databases.

2.3 DCOM

Microsoft's Distributed Component Object Model (DCOM) is the distributed extension of the Component Object Model (COM), and defines an application- level protocol for object-oriented remote procedure call (RPC) [7]. COM specifies a binary standard to build applications from components with well-defined interfaces. DCOM extends the capabilities of COM to a network environment [8]. It layers on the distributed computing environment (DCE) RPC specification and acts as a framework to facilitate the construction of task-specific communication paths between distributed applications [9]. DCOM provides several features for distributed computing: (1) platform independence; (2) multiple interfaces; (3) interface-level versioning scheme; (4) authenticated connections; (5) security channels; and (6) references (including by-value) to objects. Due to these features, DCOM, part of the Windows NT 4.0 operating system, has become a Microsoft standard for remote access to applications through Microsoft and non-Microsoft database products. DCOM objects communicate through Microsoft's Object Description Language (ODL). However, DCOM application programming interfaces (APIs) are not structured for distributed client/server applications [8]. DCOM programmers need to know COM component architectures that only run on Microsoft's Windows operating systems.

2.4 JAVA ENTERPRISE APIs

Java Enterprise APIs include Java Database Connectivity (JDBC), Remote Method Invocation (RMI), and Java Security. JDBC supports Java application and applets to send SQL queries to database servers and provides a bridge to connect to the existing Object Database Connectivity (ODBC) database servers [10]. It lets applications access relational database systems without system-specific knowledge [3]. RMI is an interface that allows distributed Java applications to invoke methods of Java objects over the network. Java Security provides digital signatures, message digests, key management, and access control lists [10]. The main drawback for using Java Enterprise APIs is that both client and server programs must be implemented in Java (language dependence). Most legacy database applications were not written in Java.

2.5 CORBA

CORBA automatically performs many common network programming tasks such as object registration, location, and activation; request demultiplexing; framing and error-handling; parameter marshalling and demarshalling; and operation dispatching [11]. CORBA is a scalable distributed computing architecture that supports distributed/network objects, local/remote objects, and single/multi-process objects.

The key component of the CORBA standard is the Interface Definition Language (IDL). IDL allows mappings for many languages (such as C/C++, COBOL, Java, Ada, or Smalltalk), is independent of the operating system, provides multiple-inheritance, and is a public interface-structured specification language [12]. IDL also supports interoperability between static and dynamic request mechanisms. IDL is used only to define the interface to the underlying objects instead of specifying actual implementation of classes or the operations within them. IDL compilers can generate client-side object interfaces (stubs) and server-side implementation interfaces (skeletons).

The main components of the CORBA architecture can be divided into three specific groups: client side, server side, and object request broker (ORB) core. CORBA objects use the ORB as an intermediary to communicate with each other over many popular networking protocols (such as TCP/IP or IPX/SPX). As a part of CORBA 2.0 standard, the Internet Inter-Orb Protocol (IIOP) is used to communicate ORBs from different vendors over TCP/IP [10]. ORB job for managing the interaction between client and server objects includes all the responsibilities of a distributed computing system, from location and referencing of objects to the marshalling of request parameters and results between machines, processes and address spaces [13].

Clients may issue requests through Client Stubs (static) or Dynamic Invocation Interface (DII) while Object Implementations receive requests through Implementation Skeletons (static) or Dynamic Skeleton Interface (DSI) without knowledge of the invocation approach. The Object Adapter associates object implementation with the ORB. An object adapter provides management of references, method invocation, authentication, implementation registration, activation, and deactivation [12].

3. A FOUR-TIER CORBA ARCHITECTURE

Basic requirements for accessing legacy databases from the Web are platform independence, language independence, high-performance, and scalability. CORBA provides a very good solution for accessing the distributed database via Internet/Intranet. As described above, CORBA objects can be written in any computer language and are supported on any platform. Compared with DCOM, CORBA has three advantages [14]: (1) multiple vendors, which greatly increase the options the CORBA developer can choose from; (2) better scalability and flexibility; and (3) mature technology [3].

The Sun's Java-only solution – Java Enterprise API, is good for legacy server applications already written in Java. Compared with CORBA, Java RMI has two limitations: (1) poor performance, and (2) no object activation policy. CORBA also provides rich and comprehensive distribution services such as naming, events, trading, security, externalization, licensing, concurrency, transactions, persistence, and time [13].

We propose a four-tier client/server architecture for accessing legacy database applications from the Web (Figure 1). This approach adapts the three-tier client/server architecture [15] and combines it with the standard CORBA ORB architecture. On the client side (the first tier of the architecture), clients request data objects through traditional Web browsers (HTML pages) with embedded Java Applet programs. A Java applet program simply makes a method call on its connected client object and returns a Java object containing the requested data.

The second tier consists of a Web HTTP server and CORBA servers. An implementation object waits for requests on the server side. When a remote method call arrives, CORBA automatically identifies the correspond method to call on the server object that implements the method to fetch the required data and returns a business data object. The Web HTTP server is needed for clients to download Web pages documents and images while the CORBA server is used to communicate objects between the Java applet clients and application servers.

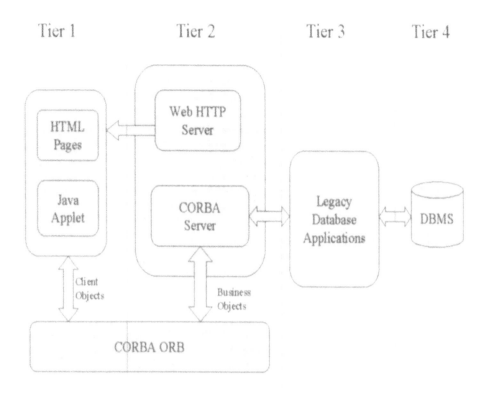

Figure 1. Four-tier CORBA architecture.

The third tier is made up by existing legacy database applications that connect to the DBMS (the forth tier). The legacy database applications written in any object-oriented language implement all existing business requests and return business data objects. The database application programs and the DBMS can reside on any platform system under any operating system as long as a CORBA object can have access to them.

4. IMPLEMENTATION OF THE FOUR-TIER CORBA ARCHITECTURE

4.1 WEB RESERVATION SYSTEM

To test the proposed architecture, a Web Reservation System (WRS) was developed. A Java applet was used for the client program. The legacy database applications can be any existing database application programs that connect to a DBMS and perform necessary corporate business requests on the databases. In the WRS, clients use CORBA static stubs to invoke a method on a reservation object to either (1) enter reservation information and get a reservation number; or (2) enter a reservation number and retrieve/display reservation information. CORBA server implementations use IDL-generated skeletons to manage the CORBA reservation object.

Netscape Enterprise Server 3.5.1 was used for the Web HTTP Server. The Netscape Enterprise Server uses the Internet Service Broker (ISB) for Java/C++, that is an ORB for developing distributed object-based applications. ISB for Java/C++ provides a complete implementation of the CORBA 2.0 specification. ISB for Java has five important features: (1) support for Java programming; (2) object lookup by name or by URL; (3) ability to distribute objects across a network; (4) support for persistent object references; and (5) interoperability with other ORB implementation [16]. ISB for C++ has similar features. The Netscape Enterprise Server supports the CORBA ORB using IIOP and includes the IDL compiler.

As one of the CORBA services, the Naming Service allows components on the object bus to locate other components on the bus by a user defined name [17]. Both Netscape Enterprise Web Servers and Netscape Communicators support the Naming Service that let you to associate a URL with an object. Any client of the Web server can access the object reference through the URL. As a security feature, the Naming Service is one of the Web resources that can be controlled by Enterprise Server's Access Control Lists [17].

4.2 WRS OOA/OOD MODELS

An entity reservation analysis pattern, developed by Fernandez and Yuan [18], was used for the WRS OOA model. From that pattern, an object-oriented design (OOD) model was developed for the WRS (Figure 2). This UML model is a subset of the analysis model plus some new architectural classes. A CORBA ORB is used to communicate between the Client Applet and the CORBA Server via CORBA portable Stubs (ObjectImpl) and Skeletons. The ORB provides a variety of client/server middleware services that let objects discover each other at run time and invoke each other's services [19]. The model uses three CORBA objects: Reservation, ReservationManager, and ReservationInfo. The ReservationManager is a factory object that creates and returns instances of other objects. The ReservationManager manages all Reservation and ReservationInfo objects with two basic methods: *getResNum()* and *getResInfo()*.

The ClientApplet performs two tasks: (1) gets a reservation number and (2) gets reservation information by using the above two methods via ORB. The first task takes reservation information for a given customer such as name, address, phone number, and particular requests for the reservation from a Java-enabled Web browser, acquires the Reservation object for that customer through the ReservationManager, and displays a reservation number. For the second task, the ClientApplet uses the ReservationManager to obtain a new reference to the specific ReservationInfo object for a customer to enter a reservation number and then prints all related information about his/her reservation through a browser.

The Reservation object represents the Web reservation information for a particular customer and provides a reservation number for the customer when all related reservation information is entered through a browser. The ReservationInfo object can later query and display the reservation information through a browser based on a given reservation number.

The Legacy Application Server represents existing corporate business application servers. The application server connects to the DBMS via an Adapter and provides all necessary APIs for business applications. The legacy application APIs should include at least two methods: (1) to save reservation information to a database and generate a reservation number; and (2) to query the legacy database and retrieve/return reservation information from a given reservation number. The two methods in the ReservationManager can invoke these APIs to implement the ClientApplet's requests to get a reservation number and/or get reservation information.

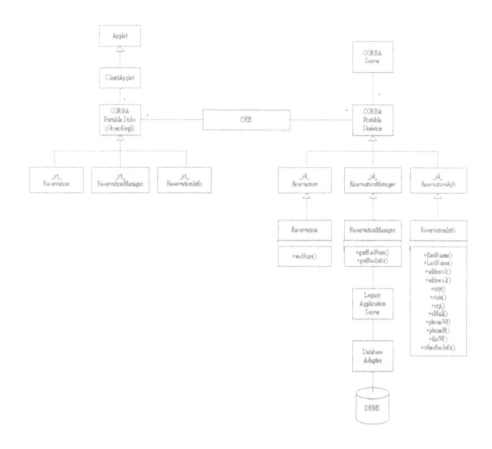

Figure 2. Class diagram for the WRS design model.

4.3 SECURITY CONTROLS

Security is a very important issue for accessing distributed databases. In the WRS, four layers of security controls were considered. In the ClientApplet side, Java Security Framework within the JDK can be used to control network security. The Java Security Framework supports cryptography with message digests, digital signatures, encryption, decryption, and authentication. The Java Cryptography Extension (JCE) package will be added to the JDK in a future release [21]. In the second layer, the CORBA ORB includes a built-in security feature that provides context information in its messages to handle security.

In the HTTP Web Server side, most commercial Web servers provide security controls on file accesses. The Netscape Enterprise Server 3.x provides a Restrict Access control for the CORBA IIOP Naming Service. It allows a Web server administrator to enable access control and set permissions to the Naming Service. The access control and permissions lists should be set up in such way that (1) any machine running a CORBA server in order to register a name should have write/delete access and (2) any machine running a CORBA client to resolve a name should have read access. The fourth layer of security controls is the use of security features implemented in the commercial DBMS. Many commercial DBMSs provide security features including (1) password or external service authentication for users and roles, (2) login packet encryption for client-to-server and server-to-server connections, and (3) authorization systems. Some DBMSs also use network data encryption and check summing so that data cannot be viewed or modified by unauthorized users [21]. As discussed in [22], security at different levels requires coordination, not well performed in current systems.

4.4 APPLICATION OF WRS OOA/OOD MODEL

To demonstrate the applicability of the four-tier CORBA architecture and the Web Reservation System concept, the WRS OOA/OOD models were applied to a virtual car reservation system (VCRS). The VCRS allows customers to make car reservations from a Web browser and obtain a reservation number without talking to any reservation representative. Customers can also check and query their car reservation information by entering the reservation number through the browser.

For simplicity, both the CORBA server program and the application (a legacy database application), were implemented in Java. The IBM DB2 database used is a relational DBMS. A customer can enter renter-related information from a Java-enabled browser (Figure 3a) and then enter car-related information including special options (Figure 3b). After all this information is entered, the customer can click on the Reservation Number button to receive a reservation number from the browser. At this point, all entered car reservation information will be stored in the relational DBMS at a remote site.

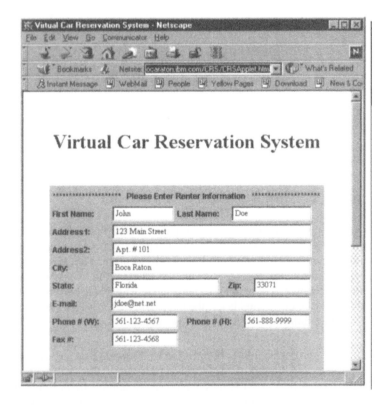

Figure 3a. Virtual car reservation system (Entering renter information).

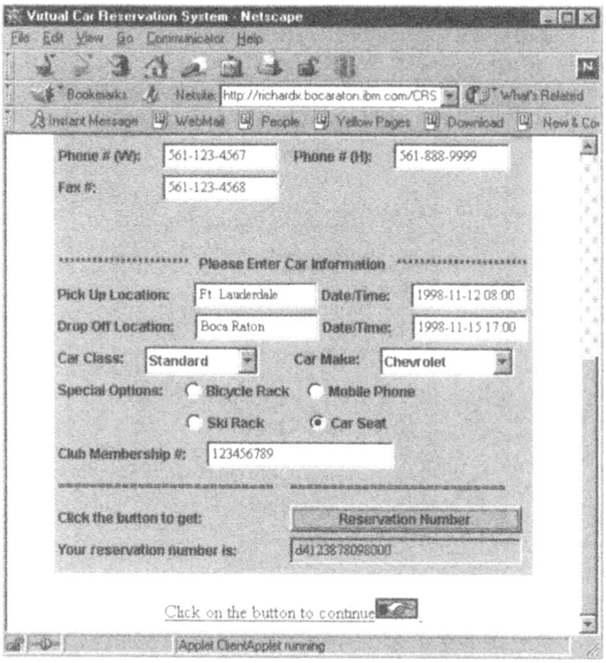

Figure 3b. Virtual car reservation system (Entering car information).

The customer can then click on the Continue button on the bottom of the page to continue. The customer will be now prompted to enter a reservation number (Figure 4a). After the Get Reservation Info button is clicked, all car reservation information in the DB2 database for that reservation number will be queried and displayed on the Web page (Figures 4a and 4b). For reasons of space, we don't show here the actual Java code; this can be found in the original report [24].

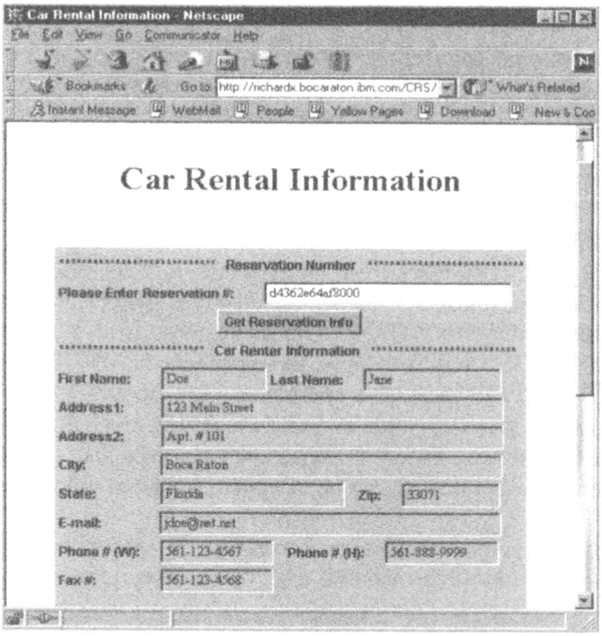

Figure 4a. Query car reservation information (Car renter information).

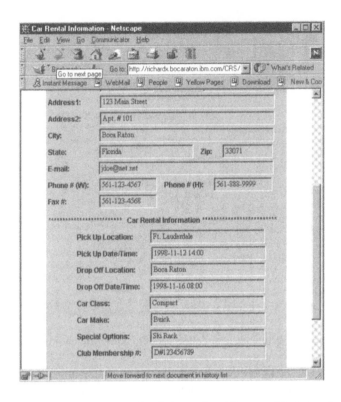

Figure 4b. Query car reservation information (Car rental information).

5. CONCLUSIONS

The rapid growth of Internet/Intranet technologies is attracting more and more applications to the network. There is a strong demand to access existing corporate business applications from the Web to enhance the efficiency and productivity of a company. It is surely not cost effective to abandon or convert these legacy database application systems to new architectures. In this chapter, general architectures for accessing business databases from the Web were discussed and compared. A platform-independent, language-independent, object-oriented, distributed database approach, a four-tier CORBA client/server architecture, was presented to access legacy databases from the network. A Web Reservation System (WRS) was created based on this four-tier CORBA architecture. An object-oriented model for the WRS was developed using the CORBA Object Request Broker (ORB). A Virtual Car Reservation System (VCRS) was developed to implement the WRS object-oriented model. Security controls in the WRS were also considered. This application demonstrates that the four-tier CORBA architecture is flexible and scalable. Using an ORB, clients at a remote site can easily request and access objects in the CORBA server that connect them to legacy database applications. The application can be extended to support other functions.

Future work includes security extensions to coordinate the different security mechanisms at each level, as proposed in [22], and the use of analysis patterns to build distributed applications.

References

1. Duan, N. N., "Distributed Database Access in a Corporate Environment Using Java," *Proceedings Fifth International World Wide Web Conference*, May 6-10, 1996, France. http://www5conf.inria.fr/fich_html/papers/P23/Overview.html

2. DOODBMS, *"Distributed Object-Oriented Database Management Systems,"* http://www.isc.rit.edu/~jam3198/doodbms.htm

3. Morgan B., "CORBA Meets Java," *JavaWorld*, October, 1997. http://www.javaworld.com/javaworld/jw-10-1997/jw-10-corbajava.html

4. Peng, C. S., S. K. Chen, J. K. Chung, A. Roy-Chowdhury and V. Srinivasan, "Accessing Existing Business Data from the World Wide Web," *IBM Systems Journal*, Vol. 37. No. 1, pp. 115-132.

5. Betz, M., "OMG's CORBA," *Dr. Dobb's Special Report*, Winter 1994/95, pp. 8-12.

6. Bayeh, E., "The WebSphere Application Server Architecture and Programming Model," *IBM Systems Journal*, Vol. 37. No. 3, pp. 336-348.

7. Wang, Y. M., *Introduction to COM/DCOM*, Tutorial Slides, 1997. http://www.research.att.com/~ymwang/slides/DCOMHTML/ppframe.htm

8. Wang, Y. M., O. P. Damani, and W. J. Lee, "Reliability and availability Issues in Distributed Component Object Model (DCOM)," Position Paper, 1997. http://www.research.att.com/~ymwang

9. Brown, N. and C. Kindel, "Distributed Component Object Model Protocol – DCOM/1.0," Internet Draft, 1996. http://www.microsoft.com/oledev/olecom/draft-brown-dcom-v1-spec-01.txt

10. Flanagan, D., "Java in a Nutshell – A Desktop Quick Reference," 2nd Edition, O'Reilly & Associates, Inc., Sebastopol, CA, 1997.

11. "Overview of CORBA," 1998, http://siesta.cs.wustl.edu/~schmidt/corba-overview.html

12. Object Management Group, "A Tour of CORBA," 1994. http://www.omg.org .

13. Resnick, R. I., "Bringing Distributed Objects to the World Wide Web," 1996, http://www.interlog.com/~resnick/javacorb.html

14. Chung, P. E., Y. Huang, S. Yajnik, D. Liang, J. C. Shih, C. Y. Wang, and Y. M. Wang, "DCOM and CORBA Side by Side, Step by Step, and Layer by Layer," 1997, http://www.research.att.com/~ymwang/papers/HTML/DCOMnCORBA/S.html

15. Orfali, R., D. Harkey, and J. Edwards, "CORBA, Java, and the Object Web," *BYTE*, October 1997, pp. 95-100.

16. Netscape Corp., "Programmer's Guide – Netscape Internet Service Broker for Java," 1998, http://developer.netscape.com/docs/manuals/enterprise/javapg/basics.htm

17. Lee, M. S., "Using Naming Service: Accessing CORBA Objects," 1998. http://developer.netscape.com/docs/technote/components/corba/naming.htm

18. Fernandez, E. B. and X. Yuan, "An Analysis Pattern for Reservation and Use of Reusable Entities," *Proceedings Of Patterns of Programming Languages Conference* (PloP99), http://st-www.cs.uiuc.edu/~plop/plop99

19. Orfali, R. and D. Harkey, *Client/Server Programming with JAVA and CORBA*, John Wiley & Sons, Inc. New York, NY, 1997.

20. Flanagan, D., *Java Examples in a Nutshell – A tutorial Companion to Java in a Nutshell*, O'Reilly & Associates, Inc., Sebastopol, CA, 1997.

21. Oracle Corporation, *Distributed Database* Concepts - *Oracle8 Server Distributed Database Systems, Release 8.0*, Oracle Corporation, 1997.

22. E.B.Fernandez, *"Coordination of security levels for Internet architectures,"* *Proceedings 10th Int. Workshop on Database and Expert Systems Applications* (DEXA99), IEEE 1999, pp. 837-841.

23. R.Z.Xue and E.B.Fernandez, "Accessing Legacy Databases Using Java and CORBA," Florida Atlantic University, Report TR-CSE-99-18, March 1999.

PART III

INTERNET APPLICATIONS

Chapter 14

MULTIMEDIA APPLICATIONS ON THE INTERNET

Michael Wynblatt, Dan Benson, and Arding Hsu

Abstract

Recently maturing technologies for digital multimedia and the Internet exhibit a powerful synergy with the potential to provide a whole range of new applications and tools. Multimedia and Internet technologies not only offer enhancements to one another, but their combination suggests entirely new communication paradigms. This chapter reviews the state of the art in Internet multimedia from the perspectives of the developer, the network administrator, the content provider, and the user, and then investigates some of the up-and-coming application areas: participatory publishing, enriched multimedia databases, integration of the WWW with broadcast media, and universal messaging systems. Remaining challenges, such as authoring in the large, multimedia information management, network latency, and browsing issues are then discussed.

1. INTRODUCTION

Among the most exciting technological developments of the last decade was the maturation of digital multimedia and of the Internet's World Wide Web into consumer-ready technologies. Digital multimedia, the ability to create and include images, audio, and animated content in digital compositions, promises to fundamentally change the way in which people communicate and chronicle their lives. The World Wide Web offers the most powerful and wide reaching new publishing medium since television, and will likely surpass all previous media in its scope and importance.

One of the most interesting aspects of these two technologies is that they are complementary. The Internet promises to enhance multimedia by making it more widely available and practical, while multimedia is responsible for bringing the Internet into the mainstream. Moreover, the synergy between the two technologies promises entirely new metaphors in publishing, communication and commerce.

The Internet impacts multimedia computing in three important ways. First, it allows content vendors virtually unlimited storage capability for their applications and data. Traditional software distribution on CD-ROMs is quite restrictive to multimedia developers, due to the high storage demands of digital audio and video. The Digital Versatile Disc (DVD) offers an improvement, but still bounds the quantity of media that can be included. The Internet gives the user direct access to the author's possibly vast storage facilities, albeit with a restricted transfer rate. In this way, the quantity and quality of the audio, video and image data that a developer may include within a multimedia presentation is significantly increased. It also allows for more interactive and customizable applications, since large amounts of media make it possible to offer the user more choices.

The second major impact of the Internet on multimedia is the addition of an important new multimedia application domain: real-time communication. Without networks, multimedia is generally limited to prefabricated presentations of one author's ideas. User interaction in such presentations is mostly limited to navigating through the presentation. When attached to a network, especially the Internet, multimedia can be used for real multi-way applications, unlocking the great power of audio and video for transferring live information. The promise of truly interactive television and radio is one of the more exciting prospects of the near future. Internet-based multimedia collaboration tools have already found application in a few specialized fields, such as medicine and academics, and we expect to see such tools used for a wider variety of applications in the future.

A final important impact of the Internet is that it gives the general public broad access to sources of digital audio, video and images. If digital multimedia is to become commonplace in everyday communication, everyday people must have access to digital content. The Internet not only provides vast collections of free media, but also allows users to access the collections provided by commercial content developers. In a sense, the Internet acts as a huge shared database of content. With such a database, it is no longer necessary to have expensive digitizing hardware and software in order to include non-text media in a document.

Multimedia's impact on the Internet is clear: without multimedia, the World Wide Web would not exist as it does today. The text-only WWW, and its pre-cursor, gopher, predated NCSA's graphical Mosaic browser [39] by several years, but it wasn't until Mosaic added images and graphics that the Web gained consumer acceptance. Today, the Web is adorned with media of all kinds, including animated graphics, images, and audio content. It is fair to say that a great deal of the Web's initial popularity stemmed from these compelling presentations.

One important example of this is the integration of the mainstream mass media into the Web. Traditional mass media, such as television networks and magazines, have always used non-text media extensively, especially in their advertisements. Before such services were available on the Web, there was essentially no mainstream media presence on the Web. With the addition of images, graphics, audio, and video and other types of animation, we have seen nearly all major national magazines, newspapers, and television networks create a significant presence on the Web. Their presence has, in turn, improved the breadth and timeliness, and thus the utility, of the Web's information content.

The impact of multimedia on the Internet is not entirely positive. Non-text data is much more resource intensive than text, especially in terms of bandwidth requirements. On the WWW, load-time latency is significantly increased due to the much larger size of individual pages. On the USENET, groups for distributing binary images account for a large percentage of the total bandwidth used, despite producing a comparably small number of articles.

Multimedia also exacerbates an existing problem. The Internet has long suffered from information overload: there is so much information present that it can be difficult to find what you want, even when it is available. Non-text data makes this worse, since such data is particularly difficult to index or search. Overall, providing content in non-text formats makes finding it more difficult and retrieving it slower.

In general, however, both multimedia and the Internet are enhanced by their combination. Section 2 of this chapter describes the current state of the art, the technologies, which make this combination possible. Moreover, the convergence of the Internet and multimedia yields more than just the sum of the two parts. There is a synergy between the two that opens up a wide range of new possibilities: new applications and entirely new paradigms of communication and information management. Section 3 of this chapter discusses some of these potentially exciting new uses for multimedia. Section 4 looks at what challenges await the designers of these applications, how these challenges might be met, and the future of multimedia on the Internet.

2. STATE OF THE ART

In this section we present the current state of the art of multimedia on the Internet, at the time of our writing. This technology is evolving so quickly that some of our discussion may have become dated just in the time it took to publish this book, but hopefully not too much of it. After a brief overview of architecture of the Internet, the discussion is divided into sections by task, featuring the tales of the developer, the content provider, the network, and the user.

2.1 GENERAL ARCHITECTURE OF THE INTERNET

Figure 1 shows a representation of the Internet from the perspective of a corporate user. The user is part of a proprietary network of computers called an *Intranet*, which may consist of one or more LANs or WANs. Access to the Intranet from the outside is restricted to a few local gateways, which support communications services but otherwise provide a *firewall* against unauthorized use. A *proxy* machine allows the Intranet user to take part in two-way protocols, by providing a trusted host outside the firewall. Beyond the firewall, thousands of other LANs and WANs are connected by the Internet backbone, as well as millions of single users connecting through Internet Service Providers. The user may access information or run programs stored on remote servers, and communicate with remote users, using dozens of protocols for data transfer.

2.2 THE DEVELOPER'S TALE

The primary language for authoring on the Web is HTML [68]. As the 'T' implies, HTML is a text-oriented language, and most of the features it provides are for representing text. Additionally, HTML offers support for two-dimensional layout specifications, including the layout of still images. Most WWW browsers support several image formats, notably GIF and JPEG. Support for images includes "image maps" defined at either the client or server side, which allow the designation of hot spots within an image. HTML also allows access to some HTTP commands, such as automatic timed refreshes, which can be used to do simple animation. The widely supported GIF89a image format allows "flip book" style animations to be encoded, and the majority of web page animations are created in this way.

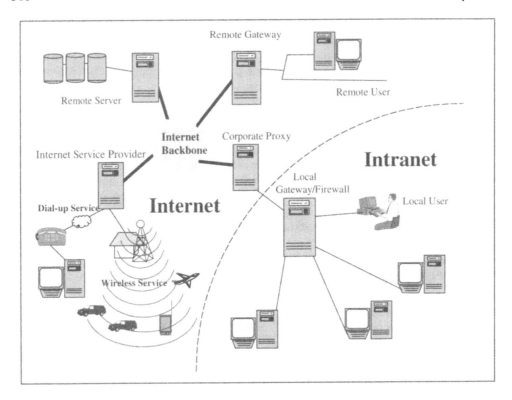

Figure 1. A corporate user's perspective of the Internet.

Dozens of WWW page design applications, which output HTML code, are available in the marketplace. Such programs feature graphical layout spaces and generate the HTML code automatically. These tools save a lot of time, and allow less technically inclined developers to get involved with the web design process. The WebStyler and SilkWeb research projects even allow developers to author web documents through informal sketching techniques [19]. Fine-tuning truly custom pages, however, is still in the domain of the text editor.

As a multimedia specification language, the original HTML was quite limited. Except for the features mentioned above, it generally did not support dynamic presentations, nor did it offer much support for audio. Moreover, since HTML does not describe how to render any given data format, each individual browser must be equipped to handle each data format that it encounters, or fail to render its content. Finally, although HTML did support form-based interaction, more sophisticated types of direct manipulations are not supported. To address these needs, HTML was extended with new dynamic properties, and most WWW browsers have added support for several additional technologies, the most notable being scripting, applets, plugins, and helper applications.

A widely available WWW authoring technology is *scripting*. Scripts are programs that are distributed on web pages as source code and interpreted by the client side browser. The term "scripts" might suggest ease-of-use compared with traditional programming languages, but this is somewhat misleading. The two most popular WWW scripting languages, *JavaScript* [44] and *VBScript* [32], are not particularly approachable for non-programmers, but rather are subsets of popular programming languages, Java and Visual Basic.

Scripting languages integrate easily with HTML forms, and so most client-side form-based processing is done with scripts. This allows for simple interactivity on a Web page. WWW scripts can actually generate new HTML code on the fly, which allows a certain amount of customization of a document's contents at loading time. Since scripts are included directly in a web page, they can be created or changed dynamically whenever HTML can be generated, such as by other scripts, or by CGI programs (discussed below).

Even with scripting, HTML is quite limited as a multimedia specification language, lacking support both for dynamic presentation and for direct manipulation of a page's component objects. These limitations have been addressed by the *Dynamic HTML* [31,43] standard, which evolved from Microsoft and Netscape in cooperation with W3C. Dynamic HTML, based on the Document Object Model [66], offers additional flexibility to developers in several ways. Most importantly, Dynamic HTML allows the contents of a page to vary dynamically, without requiring an access to a remote server. Second, individual components of a document can be addressed individually from WWW scripts. Third, the coordinates of a component can be set absolutely.

From a multimedia standpoint, these capabilities allow the user to have much finer grained interactivity with animated effects. For example, an image might grow, change color, or change its content as a result of a user's actions. Similarly, a part of a web page might change its position as a result of a user's action. This essentially allows a user to directly manipulate the objects on a web page. When these capabilities are combined with a script that accesses a clock, traditional timeline-based animations can be defined. For example, a ball can be made to bounce around a web page, or an animated character could walk a pre-determined path.

Another limitation of HTML is that all documents must be specified using a fixed set of presentation specifications: the tags defined in the HTML definition. For developers, it would often be useful to define their own tags so as to allow more customized presentation. For this reason, there is growing support the *XML* [67] mark-up language. XML is a subset of SGML [8], which allows a developer to define new tags, attributes, and the relationships between them, so that WWW documents can be specified in a custom language appropriate to the developer's needs.

Applets are small programs stored in a platform-independent byte-code, which can be included by reference in a WWW page. The client-side browser downloads and executes the applet upon accessing the page. An applet occupies a fixed rectangle of space on the web page, and can render output to that space and accept mouse and keyboard input focused within it. Since applets are arbitrarily complex programs, they can generate sophisticated output including all manner of multimedia. Indeed, the term "applet" seems to have become synonymous with the small animations that adorn many web pages. A significant limitation on the complexity of applets is that the playback environment varies widely from user to user, and as is discussed in section 4, more demanding applets may have to be scaled back to allow access to a broad base of users. Sun Microsystems' Java Media Framework [56] offers a standard method for including video, waveform audio, and MIDI within Java applets.

Currently, the most popular and widely supported language for building applets is Java [22]. A wide range of Java classes is available to support animation and audio capture, processing, and playback of digital waveforms as well as MIDI data.

An alternative technology is Microsoft's ActiveX, with which web-page controls can be built with the full functionality possible in a regular Windows program. This is both an advantage and a disadvantage, since as a result, ActiveX applets can commit many security violations that Java applets cannot.

Although they may seem similar, there are several practical differences between precompiled WWW applets and uncompiled WWW scripts. Applets are generally self-contained within a web page, while scripts may be tightly woven into the HTML code. Applets are essentially fixed, while scripts can be generated on the fly. Finally, applets are written in complete programming languages while scripts are written in language subsets. As a result, the scripts do not have the entire functionality of applets; for example, although Java offers a variety of classes to support audio, JavaScript does not include those classes.

From the developer's perspective, the major drawback of applets is that they are designed with programmer's languages, rather than multimedia developer's languages. Java programming, only a few skips away from C++ programming, is very unlike the drag-drop-and-script multimedia specification systems found with most modern authoring tools. ActiveX controls are typically built in C++ itself. But developers who would prefer visual and 4GL environments to hard core programming have an excellent alternative: content developed from such programs may be accessible using plugins.

Plugins are code libraries, dynamically linked to a WWW browser at runtime. The plugin API, developed by Netscape and also supported by several other browsers, is intended to allow a WWW browser to support a new data format without requiring a modification or re-release of the browser itself. The browser recognizes a particular data format by its filename extension, and then passes the data to the plugin module for rendering. The plugin may be assigned a rectangular region on the page in which to render the data, or may be given the entire page. Plugins can be built for any data type, making browsers extremely extensible in terms of the data that they can represent, and in turn allowing developers a great flexibility in the types and formats of media they can employ.

A *helper application* is an alternative to a plugin, in which the browser invokes an independent application to render an unknown data format. In the case of helper applications, the rendering is always separate from the browser window, and thus is not integrated into the presentation of the rest of the web page.

The rendering process used by a plugin can be much more sophisticated than simply drawing a bitmap on the screen. The plugin can capture user events, create separate threads, and generally act as an independent program from the browser. This flexibility allows that very complex data formats can be rendered faithfully. Notably, the *Shockwave* [24] plugin can render output files from Macromedia's popular multimedia authoring tools, Director and Authorware. Multimedia developers can therefore build presentations using high level tools such as these, and have the results be immediately accessible on the Internet.

Another data format for which plugins are available is *Virtual Reality Markup Language (VRML)* [63]. VRML allows the description of three dimensional objects and scenes, and VRML plugins like *Contact* [4] and *Cortona* [49] allow the user to navigate within these scenes. Three-dimensional environments, as discussed in section 5, are a promising area for new kinds of information representation and computer-aided and human-computer interfaces on the Net. Thanks to plugins, they can be incorporated directly in any web document.

Other popular data formats for which plugins have already been built include MPEG, AVI, MP3, MIDI, WAV, AU, AIFF, AutoCAD, Corel, TIFF, PDF, Astound and PowerPoint.

Netscape's *LiveConnect* [46] technology allows a closer interaction between scripting languages and plugins. One of the fruits of such interaction is the Beatnik plugin and scripting API from Beatnik [13]. Beatnik allows playback of several audio formats, notably

MIDI and Beatnik's own Rich Music Format. The API between the plugin and JavaScript allows a developer to build highly interactive music into a web page, for example, allowing a musical composition to vary depending the motion of a user's mouse around the document. Hybrid systems like Beatnik promise a very rich, interactive, multimedia future for the Web.

Microsoft has integrated its *DirectAnimation* [27] technology into its browser. DirectAnimation provides the browser native support for such diverse media types as 2-D vector graphics, 3-D graphics, sprites, audio, and video, obviating the need for plugins for many common data types. DirectAnimation capabilities are accessible from both scripts and applets, which in turn allow a good deal of interactivity with the user. Unlike applets, DirectAnimation animations with Dynamic HTML are not restricted to a rectangular region in the browser. All elements on the page may be manipulated and the various media types may be rendered anywhere on the page. This technology opens up many new possibilities for authors. The major drawback of DirectAnimation is that is not supported in browsers other than Microsoft's.

Overall, the technologies for authoring multimedia on the Web are maturing, and are nearing the level of authoring multimedia for CD-ROMs. Some of the difficulties still encountered are described in Section 4.

2.3 THE CONTENT PROVIDER'S TALE

Once a multimedia presentation has been authored, the next question is how can it be organized and made available to Internet users. Once again, the emphasis of this section will be on the WWW.

One simple way to provide multimedia content on the Internet is through a remote access file system like *WebNFS* [57]. WebNFS allows traditional file sharing, in the UNIX style, across the Internet. The World Wide Web has not followed this model, but has instead been built around a browsing-oriented model in which accesses are by *document* rather than by file, and where accessing a document is equivalent to rendering it. To this end, WWW servers have been developed which deliver a single document at a time, where a document may consist of several files. Making use of both the HTTP and FTP transfer protocols, WWW servers can transfer all of the data types described in the developer's tale: HTML, applets, WWW scripts, and plugin data. WWW servers make use of Universal Resource Locators (URLs) to index files of various types. The URL identifies a server, a file within that server's file system, and possibly a marker within the file.

The major limitation of URL-based indexing is that it requires a file system-like storage model, and does not allow the structured organization and query-style access of a more traditional database. This restriction quickly led to the development of the *CGI* [38], which allows web clients to launch independent programs on the server side. These programs can be used for many purposes, but are often query engines for server-side databases. The CGI protocol allows the programs to accept text parameters, and to return HTML files, (which, in turn, may include references to non-text, applet, and plugin data, as well as WWW scripts). Thus, interactive multimedia presentations are possible in which content is generated on the fly from database stores as a result of user actions. The CGI paradigm is extended by the *BGI* [55] protocol which allows the client to send binary data through the interface as well as text, but BGI is not widely supported at this writing.

CGI-based multimedia applications are limited primarily in the granularity of interactivity that they allow. Since a full web page is transmitted as the result of each CGI request, and the latency of a client-server communication must be endured, very fine-grained interactivity is not possible. Another limitation of CGI is that a separate process is generated by each client request. This overhead is not reasonable if a server is expected to handle large numbers of simultaneous requests. This drawback is addressed in BGI, as well as in several built-in web-server APIs like *ISAPI* [28], *NSAPI* [45], and *Apache* [58], which use only a light-weighted thread for each request.

Another limitation of CGI applications is that they are completely transaction based, and do not maintain state information about clients. This limitation has been remedied to some extent with through the use of *cookies*. Cookies are data stored on a client's machine, which are sent and retrieved by the server side. They allow the server to note the previous transactions of the client and use this information during current transactions, in effect maintaining some state information.

Server-side scripting is a method of generating customized web pages on-demand. It has the advantage over client-side scripting, from the provider's point of view, of hiding the script source code from the users. As far as the user is concerned, the received document appears to be a static HTML document, but in reality it was generated dynamically at the time it was accessed. For example, based on a user's history profile maintained by the server, a server-side script might pull together information from a database specific to that user's interests, and format it in the way most suitable for the target browser.

Given these technologies, the major problem for accessing multimedia content over the Internet is not retrieving known content but finding the content to begin with. In this regard, Internet multimedia is limited by the more general problem of indexing non-text media. There are two primary indexing schemes used on the Web today, variations of the *Wide Area Information System (WAIS)* protocol [37], which allows keyword indices of a site's contents to be queried remotely, and web-crawling third party search engines. The latter use a number of indexing techniques to build proprietary databases of WWW URLs, also indexed by keyword. Both techniques are optimized for text based information and usually involve such measures as the number of occurrences of a keyword on a page, or the relative position of several keywords on a page. None of these systems are particularly effective at recovering non-text objects, as they are successful only when those objects appear with extensive text information which categorize them.

One popular alternative to keyword search is search by progressive refinement. Some vendors have built hierarchical catalogs of WWW pages that are organized by category [74]. A user may navigate down through the hierarchy by choosing progressively more refined categories until eventually a leaf category is reached. The leaves are URLs, which may then be loaded. This kind of catalog can be equally useful for finding text or non-text information. Unfortunately, such catalogs must be built manually, so they do not offer an improvement over keyword searches in terms of the effort required to index non-text information.

Another way in which content providers can make their content more accessible is through the use of "channels." Microsoft's *Channel Definition Format* (CDF) [9] allows content providers to cluster certain documents on their site as channels. Once a user selects a channel of interest, so-called "push-enabled" browsers use this channel information to regularly pull the relevant documents from these sites. The major advantage of such a configuration is that the content provider can specify, in a user-transparent way, which documents are likely to vary regularly, and on what schedule. Thus, the end-users need not make the effort to determine it themselves. Starburst's *Multicast File Transfer Protocol* (MFTP) [33] supports this approach by making the transfer of multiple simultaneous files fast and efficient.

CDF is currently useful with HTML data, rather than the streamed media data discussed in the next section. Since the purpose of media streaming is to avoid downloading an entire media object ahead of time, the push/channel concept does not make much sense in this context.

2.4 THE NETWORK'S TALE: DELIVERY TECHNIQUES AND PROTOCOLS

Between a server and a client, a protocol is needed to transfer data across the network. In 1993, the *MIME* [5] format was developed so that Internet e-mail messages could include an arbitrary variety of data formats. Foreshadowing the emergence of plugins on the WWW, MIME could transfer any data format but left the responsibility of rendering the data to the receiver's local software. MIME was the first widely used multimedia transfer mechanism on the Internet.

The development of the WWW was encouraged by the wide acceptance of the HTTP protocol [47], which optimizes the transfer of text, and also can communicate with servers of other protocols including FTP, SMTP, WAIS, and gopher. This was the first step in supporting on-demand multimedia transport over the WWW. Since WWW documents are expected to be re-accessed by the same user, HTTP also includes facilities for determining the last modified date of a document, so that caching schemes can be used.

Although HTTP allows on-demand access to arbitrary data formats, early browsers had the limitation that an entire file must be downloaded before it could be rendered. This led to a very long latency period for storage-intensive media like audio and video. For dynamic media, this latency was unwarranted: since the medium's samples are typically sent in chronological order, the client could begin playback immediately upon receiving the first few samples. Playback of this kind requires a moderately consistent delivery rate and a buffering scheme, otherwise quality of service is unacceptable; these features are not present in HTTP.

To meet this challenge, several continuous stream delivery protocols have been developed, such as *RealMedia* [51]. On the client-side, RealMedia works in conjunction with a WWW browser as a helper application (see Section 2.2), so that hyperlinks to audio files can be provided within WWW pages. RealMedia works by bypassing the HTTP server, and connecting directly to a dedicated server. Since individual packets are not critical in audio, UDP is used as the underlying transport protocol, which improves the transfer rate at the risk of lost packets. RealMedia also uses a custom compression format to help reconstruct lost data, filling in the gaps due to lost packets. Current versions of RealMedia use the *Real-Time Streaming Protocol (RTSP)* [21], a proposed standard for Internet transport suitable for audio or video over either UDP or IP-multicast.

RealMedia, and other protocols like *NetShow* [30], allow several types of media to be streamed and synchronized, including audio, video, still images, animations, and URLs for hyperlinks. These protocols require a plugin or helper application if the media is to be included within an HTML document. A useful alternative offered by the *Emblaze* [10] protocol allows the media to be streamed through an applet, so that neither the client nor server requires the installation of custom software.

While RealMedia is designed primarily for client-initiated media-on-demand, the *Internet Multicast Backbone (MBONE)* [48] is a set of protocols designed for server-initiated multicasting. The MBONE is often used for audio or video presentations, sometimes live, which are sent to a large number of clients at the same time. Like RealMedia, the MBONE uses unreliable service in order to gain a performance benefit, providing an UDP-like protocol built on top of IP-multicast.

RealMedia and the MBONE are *best effort* protocols, in the sense that the quality of the output may vary widely as a result of the current network traffic. For higher quality presentations, it is desirable to reserve network bandwidth to guarantee a certain quality of service. The *Resource Reservation Protocol (RSVP)* [6] is designed to allow applications to request a certain amount of dedicated bandwidth between the client and server. This protocol is obviously useful for stream oriented multimedia presentations and one of its first applications will be in the MBONE.

2.5 THE USER'S TALE

From the user's perspective, there are basically two ways in which to use multimedia over the Internet today. The first is to use a WWW browser to view, and possibly interact with, the multimedia content. The second is to use a multimedia communications tool to interact directly with other people.

At a minimum, WWW browsers are expected to support the standard WWW browsing environment, first introduced with NCSA's *Mosaic* [39]. This environment provides a two-dimensional rendering of structured text and graphics, which the user manipulates through a windows/menus/pushbuttons GUI. It is desirable that browsers support all of the specification methods described in section 2.2: HTML, animated GIF, applets, WWW scripting, and plugins. Several commercial browsers do. Additionally, many browsers can play audio files that are attached by links, and the *background audio* tag specifies an audio file to be played automatically while the page is being viewed. The *Lynx* browser [60] is still maintained as the standard bearer for text-only browsers.

In the constantly changing WWW, browsers are expected to be extensible to new data types, and plugins provide this extensibility. HTML is also constantly being extended with new custom tags, which eventually become official or *de facto* standards. Since the extension of HTML is driven by competition among the browser companies themselves, the latest browsers support a wide variety of the latest tags.

Several techniques have been developed for browsing the Web based around the idea of using audio for input or output. Work at Texas Instruments has investigated applying speech recognition technology to a browser interface so that a user can follow WWW links simply by speaking the text of the link anchor [14]. This work also offers an alternative to graphical forms, by allowing web pages to offer a set of speech-based inputs. Speech-based input for forms was generalized by Motorola in *VoxML* [35]. VoxML is a language for specifying speech-based interactions, such as those found at telephone call-centers.

Systems like *WebOnCall* [41] from NetPhonic, allow access to participating web sites over a normal telephone. Using WebOnCall, a user browses the web using touch tone keys to select from lists of links, and listens to audio versions of a page's content provided by text-to-speech conversion or pre-recorded narration. A fax-back service is provided so that purely visual information can still be made available if necessary, or to obviate the need for an extended phone call in order to browse long documents. A drawback of systems like

WebOnCall is that they require server-side preparation. Thus, a user with a telephone can browse sites which have retooled for WebOnCall, but not other sites. The *WIRE* (Web-based Interactive Radio Environment) system [70] from Siemens Corporate Research, allows audio browsing of any HTML based web site, with no server-side preparation. WIRE renders HTML as audio through a document analysis that preserves the context that would be found in a visual representation of a document, and rendering the document text using text-to-speech synthesis. WIRE also supports audio data such as WAV files and RealMedia audio streams.

WebTV [64] technology, licensed recently by several hardware manufacturers, allows users to browse the WWW using their television sets. The system renders HTML and image formats for the low resolution of television and provides a custom input device used like a remote control. Although WebTV does not itself offer new multimedia features, it does hint at a future direction for Internet multimedia: integration with traditional television.

Multimedia has also been important in Internet communication applications. In the asynchronous world, the MIME protocol has been very successful in allowing the transmission of non-text data. The idea behind MIME is that each message only has the responsibility of identifying the boundaries and types of its content. The receiving system is responsible for understanding how to render any particular content "part". In a heterogeneous environment like the Internet, with dozens of data formats, this approach was critical to encourage widespread use of the protocol. Many e-mail programs also allow the inclusion of formatting instructions for text, so that text fonts, styles, and colors may be rendered in a message. Since these instructions are contained in a separate MIME part, mail readers that only handle ASCII text are not inconvenienced.

Multimedia has also been useful in the new "near synchronous" communications methods offered on the WWW. Web servers equipped with appropriate CGI programs have been turned into IRC-like chat-servers, in which a user reads other people's comments on a "chat page", enters their own comments using a form, and a CGI program recreates the chat page with the new comments appended at the bottom. The new twist here is that the posted comments can include any HTML instructions that the browser understands. Not only can text be formatted, but also non-text media and scripts can be included directly into the posted message.

But multimedia's most prominent impact on Internet communications has been in synchronous communications. Internet conferencing tools like Microsoft's NetMeeting [29] make use of audio and video channels and graphical whiteboards for information transfer. Some, like Vocaltec's *Internet Conference* [62], actually include a shared WWW browser. Video conferencing tools, like Connectix's *VideoPhone* [7], can also run across the Internet, although their frame rate over the Internet is not as high as their LAN performance. Internet telephony applications, which allow users to make phone calls without paying long distance charges, have been immediate hits, and after an early explosion of small service providers, this industry has begun to consolidate [34]. Since 8KHz, 16-bit playback is well within the capability of modern PCs, telephone quality audio can be realized.

3. FUTURE MULTIMEDIA APPLICATIONS FOR THE INTERNET

The synergy between the Internet and multimedia promises to bring about an explosion in application possibilities. Over the years, technologies such as the graphical user interface, the mouse, and plug-and-play peripherals have made computers easier to use and have greatly increased the number and variety of people who use them. In turn, new kinds of users have created new demands on the technology while adding new creative input to applications. With the tremendous growth of the Internet, we expect a similar burst of creativity and technological demands for multimedia applications. The most important trend will likely be toward more personalized and interactive applications through which the user can make more productive use of the Internet. The future offers unlimited possibilities, so in this section we give just a few examples of what we might expect to see.

3.1 PARTICIPATORY PUBLISHING

Web pages are currently the most common form of publishing on the Internet. When compared with other traditional forms of mass media, such as print and broadcasts, Internet publishing has the unique properties of interactivity and data sharing. With this in mind, we envision a new form of publishing that we call "participatory publishing" in which readers are able to contribute to and influence the content along with authors. This might range from individual requests for specific topics to personalized novels to live commentaries on top of web pages. With more direct reader participation, writers and editors of multimedia publications will begin to create and deliver documents that can be customized and modified according to individual readers. We envision several potential applications illustrated below.

One of the early services, promised first with video-on-demand and now made possible on the Internet, is personalized news. This differs from traditional services from the major news organizations, which is to provide all "worthy" news, from which subscribers choose the stories that they are most interested in, the format and degree of detail they desire, and at what time to receive the stories. With participatory publishing, one can imagine subscribers taking a more active role such as making requests for specific stories they would like to have covered or investigative inquiry into topics that may otherwise go unnoticed. This would be a major step toward providing news that people really want.

Another form of participatory publishing involves advertisers. We will undoubtedly see increasingly innovative ways of introducing advertising on the WWW, as it seems to be one of the easiest ways of producing revenue on the Internet. One of the best forms of advertising is word-of-mouth: letting others do your advertising for you. We already see this in many ways, such as conspicuous labels on clothing or brand names on T-shirts where, in effect, people actually pay money to advertise for companies! In the future, companies on the web might offer not T-shirts, but entertaining and compelling multimedia presentations like videos or cartoons. These presentations could be customizable and personalized. For example, you might send in a picture of your face and get back a professionally produced animation in which you star as an avatar in a cartoon, who just happens to be drinking a can of a well-known soft drink. You could place this animation on your own home page or send it to others as a sort of web-postcard.

A third form of participatory publishing is adding dynamic annotations to web pages. Other than email links and input forms, current web pages are essentially one-way communication from publisher to reader. There have been some attempts at adding text or link annotations to web pages [35,69] perhaps the most notable example coming from Third Voice [59] which offers the ability to capture comments and discussions related to the contents of web pages, store these comments, and share them with others. Users wishing to add comments to any web page or users wanting to view annotations left by others must first download and install the free client-side software. Annotations are actually stored on the Third Voice server and are rendered as essentially a transparent overlay on top of the web page, leaving the original untouched. While this form of participatory publishing can greatly enhance information exchange through the web, it should be noted that there has been strong concerns expressed that it may also lead to abuses in terms of privacy, security, graffiti, and copyright infringement [52,54].

3.2 ENRICHED MULTIMEDIA DATABASES

Databases already play a significant role on the web, but we believe the uses and demands of databases on the Internet and Intranet will increase dramatically, particularly when it comes to managing multimedia. If we consider the WWW as an enormous collection of loosely organized multimedia, one of the most fundamental and difficult problems is finding what you want. It is no surprise that some of the first Internet applications to become so popular were searching services. Unfortunately, these initial search engines are vastly limited when it comes to multimedia, particularly content-based searching.

Suppose you would like to find an audio recording of a dog barking. Certainly, with all the multimedia that people have made available on the web, there must be an audio clip of a dog barking somewhere. Better yet, what about a video clip or an animation of a barking dog? The best current services are hierarchical collections of media, which allow keyword searches, such as that offered by Lycos. These systems are limited because they must either be constructed manually, which severely limits their scope on the massive WWW, or they must rely on text associated with the images on web documents, either within meta-tags or simply located nearby. Going beyond the use of text to formulate queries, advanced media search engines will be capable of accepting various types of media as input to do similarity searches. For example, queries like "Find pictures that look like this picture," [2,17,18] or "Find audio clips of music where the melody goes like this..." [11] may be possible.

Databases will deliver everything from HTML text documents to full-blown multimedia presentations. A user querying a database will not know, or care, about the actual source of the information. Some queries will be invisibly dispatched across the web to multiple databases, merging the results from each to form a coherent result. Just as many WWW documents today are generated on the fly from local databases, future multimedia presentations will be generated on the fly from remote databases. Internet multimedia databases will be capable of *constructing* multimedia to match the query request. A simple example of this is an animation database that returns an animated GIF file consisting of several small pictures that are selected according to the query criteria. A weather report web page might construct dynamic icons on-the-fly based on current forecast models, and so might traffic report web sites, or other sites offering animated rendering of dynamic data. A more complex database might construct a video sequence by mixing together certain actors, backgrounds, or sound tracks. Negroponte has suggested entire television shows based on objects and scripts rather than raster images [40].

Given the cost and effort it often takes to create significant multimedia compositions, many authors will want to reuse data whenever possible. In addition to the data itself, there may be links to associated information that goes along with it. Internet multimedia databases will store *wrapped media* that encapsulate multimedia objects to include additional inherent information about that object such as alternative renderings, URLs, or other related documents. In this way, a wrapped media object inserted in any web document automatically inherits its own *content-links* (See Section 4.2). For example, a picture of the Mona Lisa might be wrapped along with a URL pointing to a page about Leonardo Di Vinci, or text giving a brief history of the painting. Any web document that includes the wrapped picture also gets the link and history text. In a sense, the wrapped media becomes an independent document or composition in and of itself.

3.3 INTEGRATION OF THE WWW WITH TRADITIONAL BROADCAST MEDIA

One of the first metaphors to catch hold on the WWW was publishing. The Web was seen as an alternative to printed material, not only for companies to distribute product information and colleges to post their course offerings, but also for mass-market magazines and technical journals as well. Not only have dozens of "webzines" been created, available only on the Internet, but nearly all major print magazines and newspapers have a significant web presence as well.

Just as non-text media has become more integrated into the WWW, the Internet has also received similar attention from the non-print mass media. A tremendous amount of live and near-live radio content is available over the WWW (Over 430 stations are listed on Yahoo! [72]). With the maturation of streamed video protocols, television stations have followed suit, and several networks and local stations now provide streamed video [73]. Since broadcast media stations earn money almost exclusively from advertising, unlike the more subscription-oriented print media, the WWW is an even more natural fit. With the emergence of technologies like WebTV and WIRE (see Section 2.5), the distinction between WWW content and broadcast content will become even more blurred in the mind of the user.

As WWW and broadcast media become more coupled, they will likely become more integrated. WWW URLs will appear regularly on TV feeds and both TV and computer interfaces will allow users to follow them immediately with their integrated browsers. Broadcast media will absorb some of the interactivity of the WWW, sending multiple simultaneous streams that the user can navigate between, depending on their personal interests. Advertisers will welcome the chance to market toward more specific audiences. Moreover, just as many web pages today are generated with advertisements based on a user's profile and history, so too will broadcast streamed commercials be targeted towards specific demographic populations.

Perhaps the biggest change in mass media will come from the explosion of small audience, WWW-based audio and video "stations". The capital required to start a conventional broadcast station, or even a cable TV station, puts it out of the range of the small businesses or hobbyists. Starting a WWW-based station requires more modest costs. Just as broadcast stations can attach their feed to the Internet, so eventually will small business ventures and amateurs. These endeavors, using either advertising or subscription fees to cover their costs, will produce a huge variety of radio- and TV-like programs for both broad and narrow audiences. The worldwide reach of the WWW offers to provide a reasonable audience base for even the most esoteric subjects. Some programs will support active user feedback or even participation, and in some cases the line between video-conferencing and television programming may itself become blurred.

3.4 WEBSPACE IN THREE DIMENSIONS

The current metaphor for the content of the WWW is "documents". When users access a remote site, they view the content much like they would read a magazine. Unlike a magazine, WWW documents may be created on the fly, customized to a particular user, and can include time-based or interactive content. Like a magazine however, the Web has adopted a metaphor of viewing "pages", which is both a familiar and a useful concept for structuring information.

An alternative metaphor that has gained some support is that WWW content represents "spaces" [69]. Support for the *VRML* in WWW browsers allows developers to present their content as places rather than documents. Rather than flipping through the pages of a document, users "fly" through the virtual space, exploring it as they might explore a real room or building. "Doors" encountered in these spaces may serve as hyperlinks, allowing access to new spaces. With virtual world interfaces, WWW sites become "places you go to" rather than simply information you download.

Although the term "three dimensional" is most commonly associated with visual media, stereo audio can also be played in a manner to convey three dimensions. Extensions to the WIRE audio web-browser system take advantage of three-dimensions to better convey web documents using audio [12]. For example, if a document is being played at one location in space, and a hyperlink is encountered, the title of the linked document (pre-fetched from the Web) can be played at another location in space. In this way, the user understands clearly that the reference is in a different context than the current document.

Whether or not the "spaces" metaphor gains as much acceptance as the document metaphor, or even replaces it, depends mainly on what additional utility it can provide. The challenge for user-interface designers, information managers, and artists, is to take advantage of the rich metaphor of "space" to help organize WWW content, make it more easily accessible, and perhaps create entirely new ways of delivering and navigating through rich multimedia information.

3.5 UNIVERSAL MESSAGING SYSTEMS

One by-product of the recent advances in telecommunications is that electronic messages now take many different forms. Many professionals are accustomed to sending and receiving FAXes, voicemail, and e-mail containing a variety of document types and media. As FAX and voice services become more common over the Internet, it will be natural to move toward a *universal mailbox*, a single repository for voice, image, and text data, and whatever other media become popular. Such a mailbox will not only offer the convenience of centralized message retrieval, it will also allow retrieval of messages from many different types of access stations. Text-to-speech synthesis will allow telephone access to text e-mail, and FAX-back interfaces will allow access to image data in the absence of a monitor. Siemens Corporate Research developed a prototype system which allows this functionality, as well as a novel phone/FAX interface for browsing long documents, structured documents and even video messages, without the use of a computer monitor [50]. This type of functionality will lead to a more complete blending of media and merging of information devices.

Another form of messaging which multimedia and the Internet allow is the *replayable workspace* [16,25], in which a user records a session in their workspace, including voice and mouse gestures. Once recorded, the session becomes an animated presentation that can be delivered asynchronously via e-mail or the WWW. Such presentations are particularly useful for tutorials and online help systems, where a demonstration can be significantly more descriptive than a series of instructions.

4. CHALLENGES AND VISIONS

Before the applications described in section 3 can be realized there are a number of challenges which must be addressed. In this section we present some of the issues which we think are more unique to multimedia applications on the Internet, rather than to Internet applications as a whole. For some of these challenges we present our vision of how they may be overcome in the future.

4.1 THE DEVELOPER'S TALE: MISSING AUTHORING FEATURES

The tools available for authoring multimedia on the Internet are primarily the same tools available for authoring multimedia CD-ROMs. This arrangement has the advantage of jump-starting Internet multimedia with the richness of these existing tools, but it also means that some features that are desirable in Internet environments may not be well supported.

4.1.1 Authoring in the Large

One problem that the Internet brings to hypermedia is what might be called *authoring in the large*. Without the size restrictions which are found in CD-ROM based multimedia, Internet authors can now tackle problems of multimedia presentations involving very large collections of documents or objects. Large databases or collections of existing documents should be structured, linked, and made available on the WWW. If the collections are large enough, automated tools are required, both to make the project feasible and to maintain its consistency.

At Siemens Corporate Research, several tools have been developed to help in this process. Given a database of objects and documents, the *Automated Document Composition Tool* [23] automatically extracts the relevant content, generates a web of hyperlinks within it, and builds a consistent structured multimedia presentation suitable for WWW distribution. For managing video data, their *Video Logging and Archiving Tool* facilitates the segmenting, logging, archiving and efficient retrieval of large quantities of video data, and makes it available from a central server.

4.1.2 Content-Based Links

Hypermedia on the WWW differs from multimedia on CD-ROMs in that there is much more reuse of media objects. Multimedia CD-ROMs typically carry stand-alone presentations that are not meant to be reconfigured. WWW hypermedia, on the other hand, consists of a collection of media objects that can be reused many times in many different presentations. Such reuse is much less common in pure hypertext, since the semantics of a text passage is much less context-sensitive.

The potential for media reuse in hypermedia emphasizes the distinction between *structural hyperlinks* and *content-based hyperlinks* [71]. The links supported in HTML are structural links; an HTML document describes a presentation of several media objects, and the links are specific to the particular document. Content-based links are links that are specific to a particular media object rather than to a particular document. For example, an image of a famous personality might be linked to a text biography, additional images, or an audio clip of a famous statement. Such links might be useful in many presentations of the original image. To properly support content-based links, links such as these should be "attached" to the object rather than the document. Any document that included the object would inherit its content-based links. We might call a link that travels with a media object a *sticky link*.

Content-based links represent knowledge about an object; they show context-independent relationships that are known about the object. Since information management of multimedia data is one of the difficult problems on the Internet, the omission of sticky links seems to be a significant loss. Not only would sticky links allow the knowledge inherent in content-based links to be shared widely, but following content-based links would yield a much more productive path for automated search engine robots.

4.1.3 Degradation of Service

Another flexibility missing from Internet multimedia authoring systems is a way to specify how a presentation should degrade when degradation is necessary. When bandwidth is insufficient, most available streaming protocols make a best effort attempt to meet the need anyway. Often, however, the semantics of the presentation dictate that some information is critical in delivery while other is less important [53]. Faced with insufficient bandwidth, it makes more sense to drop or degrade the less significant data and try to maintain the critical data. Moreover, the manner in which a stream should be degraded also varies depending on the presentation. A video stream might be degraded by dropping frames, losing resolution, or reducing the frame rate. Each of those techniques may be appropriate to different types of presentation.

Since the semantics of the presentation are completely unknown to the underlying protocol, that protocol cannot make appropriate decisions about how degradation should take place. The content developer, whose message is to be delivered by the presentation, can best describe the relative importance of the parts of the message, and how they can best be rendered in sub-optimal conditions. Thus the developer should have the opportunity to specify these concerns.

The emerging MPEG-4 standard for audio and video data [20] offers support for user/ decoder control of presentation quality. The implication is that the developer may have some choice over which degradation techniques might be available to the user/decoder, but the developers' role in this process is not discussed specifically.

4.1.4 Varied Playback Environments

Another challenge that faces Internet multimedia developers is that the environment in which different users view a presentation is extremely varied. Even among typical PC-based systems, variation is found in the processor speed, available memory, display size, color capability, audio capability, and network connection speed. Even different browsers offer support for different data formats, or render them somewhat differently. Increasingly, non-PC browsing environments such as television-based browsers, palmtop computers, telephones, and automobile terminals, provide even more extreme variation. More than most computing applications, multimedia presentations tend to be system-dependent, and so this variation presents particular problems for multimedia developers.

The simplest variation is in the power of the target machine. Multimedia playback is taxing on a system's processing and memory capabilities; a 100 MB Shockwave presentation with video clips and tightly synchronized animations performs differently on a 486-based machine with 16MB RAM than on a Pentium III with 512MB. This problem will always exist, as use of resources in multimedia presentations grows to fill the capabilities of the newest high-end systems.

More fundamental problems arise if a system lacks an entire service, for example a system with no audio card or a text-only terminal. At first glance, we may be tempted to dismiss such problems; after all, in a few years will we not be rid of such anachronisms? It is possible, however, that lack-of-service problems will not disappear so easily. As Internet access becomes increasingly significant in people's lives, we can expect an increase in the number of places and times when people will require access. They will require access stations in more varied locations. If only for reasons of cost, many of these ubiquitous access stations will provide stripped down services. In some environments it may be *desirable* to leave out some services, such as audio playback in public areas, or visual playback in automobiles. Access stations for the disabled may present similar restrictions.

CD-ROM-based multimedia typically comes with a recommended minimum configuration, and WWW based multimedia developers may adopt a similar policy as they build more demanding presentations. In this way, WWW multimedia may differ from the mainly text-based WWW information found so far, which, with some exceptions, has generally been available to any user who could manage an Internet connection. To a certain extent this is unavoidable: a system without audio capability is simply not going to be able to produce audio playback.

A more interesting option would be to allow developers to specify alternative presentations for clients that are unable to render certain media or certain combinations of media. HTML's image tag already allows an alternative text description to be specified, for use by clients that cannot render images. This arrangement puts the burden of choice on the browser, freeing the developer from specifying the conditions under which to show one alternative or the other. A more general way of specifying alternatives may go a long way to mitigating the problem of varied playback environments.

A third possibility is to develop media conversion techniques, so that presentations authored in one medium might be made available in another. An example of such a technique is the WIRE system [70]. WIRE allows a user to browse traditional HTML web documents without a visual interface by creating an audio-based rendering for the document. Although WIRE does not currently attempt to render raster image data with audio, there has been research in this area as well (for example, [26]). Systems like these have the advantage that they do not require extra work from the author, but the drawback that the presentation may not be exactly as the author intended.

4.2 THE CONTENT PROVIDER'S TALE: MULTIMEDIA INFORMATION MANAGEMENT ON THE WEB

One of the most challenging problems in traditional multimedia systems is the management of multimedia information. Non-text information is decidedly difficult to index in any automated manner, and manual indexing is not only time-consuming, it is often incomplete. On the Internet, the sheer volume of media available compounds this problem, and the heterogeneous organization makes many conventional search strategies useless.

The spectacular amount of image and audio data available on the Internet is a gold mine for multimedia developers, especially for those who do not have the facilities to digitize their own content. More importantly, if the use of raster images, audio, and video is ever to become commonplace in the communications of ordinary people, they will first require a vast source of such material to draw upon. The Internet promises to be such a source. In order for the Internet to serve this purpose, however, there must be some way to find an appropriate media object somewhere on the Web.

Right now, that is problematic. Most commercial WWW search engines are indexed entirely by keywords, and thus there is no possibility to query by likeness, or by sketch, or by some other form of example. Moreover, the techniques used in building their databases are indexed around the textual information on the page. This means that many non-text objects that could potentially be identified by keyword tags cannot be discovered using these systems.

Several groups are working to bring Query-by-Example-like interfaces to the Web for image data [18,61]. Related techniques have even been developed for audio data [11]. More research in these areas is needed, however, in both indexing and interface techniques. Even if effective indexing techniques can be developed, tools will be needed either to do automated indexing across the vastness of the Web, or to help WWW authors index their own content.

In the state of the art, searching for information on the Web is difficult for two reasons. The first is that information is distributed fairly randomly around the thousands of web servers. The second is that the information is itself unstructured, and can generally be indexed only by free-text techniques. A separate problem is that non-text media on the Web is not indexed at all, forcing a reliance on indexes of nearby text.

One remedy to these problems is to build structure into the Web itself. This cannot be achieved very easily by organizing existing information in a top down manner. A better approach is to have WWW authors build the necessary structure directly into their content. Such an approach may be acceptable to WWW authors whose main motivation of putting content on the WWW is to make it available to the widest possible audience. As authors generally want people to find their content as easily as possible, they may be willing to invest some effort in generating the information needed to allow some indexing of the WWW.

But in order for author-generated information to be useful, there must be a standard way of describing the contents of a page or site. The standard must be sufficiently easy to generate so that authors will follow it, and rich enough to allow an improvement in the quality of searches which can be made on the Web. Moreover, it should provide help in finding non-text information as well as text.

One proposed technique involves *channels*, such as Microsoft's Channel Definition Format (see Section 2.3). The idea is that a WWW author can cluster related content into logical units called channels. Indexing systems could probably exploit this additional structure. Unfortunately, to this point channels have been used mainly for optimizing information updates rather than for information discovery.

Another way to provide structured information is to assign scores to each page in a set of different categories. A set of scores forms a *description vector* for each page that can support many search styles and activities. Searches can be declared over a subset of the available categories, or which assign weights to the different categories. Results of searches, including traditional keyword searches, can be presented visually by using page score profiles to generate icons or relative positions in a result map.

Another information management problem is how to protect intellectual property. The personal computer revolution of the seventies and eighties created all manner of new questions regarding intellectual property, but most of these involved the new medium of software. The emergence of the Internet has brought a whole new round of questions, but perhaps surprisingly, many of these questions center on very traditional media like images and audio.

Although it may be difficult enough just to determine what types of media should be copyrightable [15], perhaps the most important issue is how we can protect copyrights that exist. In an environment where duplication is instantaneous, copyright is the only protection most content authors have. If one considers that the purpose of copyrights is not to prevent access, but to recover royalties from use, it seems clear that some pay-per-use model must be developed for digital media. Until such a system is in place, artists will be loath to make their work too widely available.

4.3 THE NETWORK'S TALE: NETWORK DELAY

One difficulty with transferring multimedia over the Internet is the large amount of delay experienced. This causes two problems, the infamous "World Wide Wait" experienced by users waiting for their non-text media to load, and latency in client-server interaction which make some applications impractical.

The first problem is that it simply takes a long time to download large files over the Internet. For an extreme example, consider a typical user who connects to the net over a 56.6 Kbps line. A multimedia presentation distributed on CD-ROM can be as large as 660 MB. If the user were to download this presentation in one chunk, it would take about 26 hours! This problem will ease somewhat in the future, but not entirely. If the user upgrades their service to a 128 Kbps DSL line, the transmission would still require more than eleven hours at sustained peak throughput. Available bandwidth continues to improve; the transmission described would take only about 9 minutes on a 10 Mbps ATM line. Unfortunately, the bandwidth requirement of content tends to increase along with bandwidth available. As ATM or cable modems become more commonplace, content developers will likely increase the size of their creations.

The above example is extreme because a multimedia presentation can often be downloaded piecemeal, with each media object being fetched on demand. HTML documents, for example, are downloaded one file at a time, allowing the document to be rendered incrementally. HTML is not sufficient, however, for highly dynamic or interactive presentations, and the piecemeal approach is not available with all types of presentation. Applets, for example, are downloaded completely before they are available for use. Similarly, the Shockwave plugin for WWW browsers allows streaming of a presentation's audio or video track, but otherwise requires that the entire presentation be downloaded before playback can commence. Thus a multimedia presentation designed as an applet or Shockwave file could require a significant loading time. As multimedia developers attempt to provide CD-ROM quality multimedia on the Web, either some piecemeal scheme must be developed for non-HTML presentations, or extreme downloading times must be endured.

The ultimate form of piecemeal downloading is streaming, in which the server sends data continuously and only slightly before it is needed by the client. Streaming makes sense for continuous media such as audio or video in which one can usually predict which units the client will need next. Streaming is not particularly useful for highly interactive presentations, however, since the server will not know which unit to send until the user's input is recorded.

This broaches the second delay problem, which arises in interactive applications. The problem is that there is a delay between the time the user issues a command, and the time which the client receives a response from the server. This delay is *latency* in the traditional sense, and is basically independent of transfer rate; faster modems will not improve the performance much. In an application like a video game, where fine-grained interactivity is critical, such latency is unacceptable. The current solution to the problem of highly interactive presentations is to download the entire presentation initially, but this leads back to the problem described above. Moreover, it eliminates the chance to interact with a server-side database when deciding the result of the user's action.

4.4 THE USER'S TALE: MULTIMEDIA BROWSING

The browsing metaphor used on the WWW of jumping from page to page works well for text, but begins to break down somewhat with other media. Two particular problems are with dynamic media, like video, or in very large images, like schematic drawings. In media such as these, browsing is possible *within an object*, as well as from object to object, due in one case to the temporal dimension and in the other case to the extended spatial dimension of the media. Similarly, hyperlinks may be targeted to (or from) particular places within these media.

At Siemens Corporate Research, several tools have been developed to help address these problems. The *Video Browser* automatically breaks a long video sequence up into meaningful segments based on scene changes and represented by key frames (Figure 2).

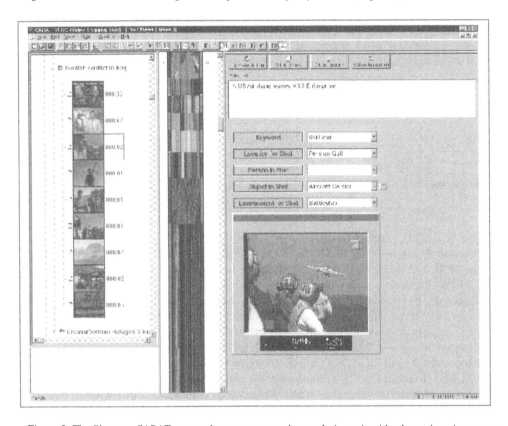

Figure 2. The Siemens *CARAT* system demonstrates modern techniques in video browsing. A user can quickly browse to any part of a video that they want to see.

Browsing through the video is facilitated by direct and hierarchical access to the content. The *Content-Based Video Player* allows video segments to be played back *intelligently*, with variable speed depending on the context of the events within the video. Browsing is facilitated by providing a more efficient scanning mode [3]. The *Schematic Viewer* facilitates browsing of large images by providing automatic feature location, and supporting hyperlinks to (as well as from) particular regions of an image [23].

5. CONCLUSION

The synergy between new digital multimedia technologies and the Internet's World Wide Web is undeniable. Not only are both individually enhanced by the presence of the other, but entirely new modes of communication, new delivery mechanisms, and new types of applications are developing from their union.

The first wave of research and application development has been focused on the more technical challenges, and we are still faced with perhaps the harder problem of how best to use our new tools. What new metaphors for publishing and mass media can better reach and involve their audiences? What new information structures can allow users better access to the Web's wealth of multimedia information? What new communication paradigms can add efficiency to our ever more distributed businesses? Our vision of a more deeply structured World Wide Web, and of a close integration between the Web and mass media, hints at answers to these questions, but the door is wide open for investigation and experimentation. The technologies and standards that are developed in the next few years will have a profound impact on everyday habits of many people for many years to come.

References

1. Aas, R., "DVD," http://www.unik.no/~robert/hifi/dvd.
2. Ahanger, G., Benson, D., and Little, T.D.C., "Video Query Formulation," Proceedings of the SPIE, Vol. 2420: Storage and Retrieval for Image and Video Databases III; 1995, pp. 280-291; http://www.scr.siemens.com/ps/spie95_1.ps.
3. Arman, F., Depommier, R., Hsu, A., and Chiu, M.-Y., "Content-based browsing of video sequences," Proceedings of the 1994 ACM Multimedia Conference, ACM: New York, pp.97-103; http://www.scr.siemens.com/ps/acm94_1.ps.
4. Blaxxun interactive, "blaxxun interactive," http://www.blaxxun.com.
5. Borenstein, N. and Freed, N., "MIME (Multipurpose Internet Mail Extensions)," Network Working Group RFC 1521-2, http://www.oac.uci.edu/indiv/ehood/MIME/ MIME.html.
6. Braden, B., and Erstin, D., "RSVP-ReSerVation Protocol," http://www.isi.edu/div7/ rsvp/rsvp.html.
7. Connectix Corporation, "Connectix VideoPhone,"http://www.connectix.com/html/ videophone.html.
8. Cover, R., "The SGML/XML Webpage," http://www.sil.org/sgml/sgml.html.
9. Ellerman, C., "Channel Definition Format," http://www.w3.org/TR/NOTE-CDFsubmit. html.
10. GEO Publishing Inc., "Emblaze Technology by GEO," http://www.emblaze.com/atomic/ home_.htm.
11. Ghias, A., Logan, J., Chamberlin, D., and Smith, B., "Query By Humming - Large Musical Information Retrieval in An Audio Database," Proceedings of the 1995 ACM International Conference on Multimedia, pp. 231-236, http://cs.cornell.edu/Info/Faculty/ bsmith/query-by-humming.html.
12. Goose, S. and Moeller, C., "A 3D Audio Only Interactive Web Browser: Using Spatialization to Convey Hypermedia Document Structure," Proceedings of the 1999

ACM International Conference on Multimedia, http://www.kom.e-technik.tu-darmstadt.de/acmmm99 /ep/goose/index.html.

13. Beatnik Inc., "Beatnik Sonify the Web," http://www.beatnik.com/index.html?authoring /products/player/player.html .

14. Hemphill, C., and Thrift, P., "Surfing the Web by Voice," Proceedings of the 1995 ACM Multimedia Conference, pp.215-222.

15. Higgs, S., "MIDI Files and Copyrights," International MIDI Association Bulletin, Spring 1993, http://www.simon.higgs.com/midi/ima-copyright.html.

16. Hou, T.Y, Hsu, A. and Chiu, M.Y., "An Active Multimedia System for Delayed Conferencing," SPIE Proceedings on High-Speed Networking and Multimedia Computing, February 1994, pp. 97-104, http://www.scr.siemens.com/ps/spie94_1.ps.

17. Hou, T.Y., et. al. "A content-based indexing technique using relative geometry features," Proceedings of SPIE/IS&T Symposium on Electronic Imaging Science and Technology, San Jose, CA, 1992, pp. 59-68.

18. IBM Corporation, "QBIC project," http://wwwqbic.almaden.ibm.com/.

19. IEEE Computer Society, "Trends & Controversies," http://computer.org/intelligent/ ex1998/html/x3010.htm/

20. International Organization for Standardization, ISO/IEC JTC1/SC29/WG11, "Coding of Moving Pictures and Audio," http://drogo.cselt.stet.it/mpeg/standards/mpeg-4.htm.

21. Internet Engineering Task Force, "Real Time Streaming Protocol," Internet Draft, http://www1.real.com/devzone/sdks/rmsdk/guide/doc/rtsp.txt.

22. Java Soft, "The Java Platform," http://www.javasoft.com/aboutJava/index.html.

23. Liu, P., Hampel, K., and Hsu, A., "Towards automating the creation of hypermedia service manuals by compiling specifications," Proceedings of the International Conference on Multimedia Computing and Systems, 1994, pp. 203-212, http://www.scr. siemens.com/ps/ieee94_2.ps

24. Macromedia Inc., "Macromedia Shockwave, Animation and Entertainment on the Web," http://www.macromedia.com/shockwave.

25. Manohar, N.R. and Prakash, A., "A Flexible Architecture for Heterogeneous Replayable Workspaces," Proceedings of the Third IEEE International Conference on Multimedia Computing and Systems, June 1996, pp. 274-278. http://www.eecs.umich.edu/~nelsonr/ online-docs/ieeemm96/all.html

26. Martins, A. and Rangayyan, R. "Experimental Evaluation of Auditory Display and Sonification of Textured Images," Proceedings of the International Conference on Auditory Display, Palo Alto, CA, 1997. http://www.santafe.edu/~kramer/icad/ websiteV2.0/Conferences/ICAD97/icad97.html

27. Microsoft Corporation, "Microsoft DirectAnimation," http://www.microsoft.com/directx /dxm/help/da/c-frame.htm?default.htm.

28. Microsoft Corporation, "Internet Server API Support Home Page," http://www. microsoft.com/support/isapi/.

29. Microsoft Corporation, "NetMeeting Home," http://www.microsoft.com/windows/ netmeeting/.

30. Microsoft Corporation, "Microsoft NetShow Version 1.0 Features," http://www. microsoft.com/syspro/technet/boes/bo/iiserver/prodfact/netfeatr.htm.

31. Microsoft Corporation, "MSDN Online Web Workshop - DHTML, HTML & CSS Home," http://msdn.microsoft.com/workshop/author.

32. Microsoft Corporation, "Microsoft Scripting Technologies," http://msdn.microsoft. com/scripting/.

33. Miller, K., Robertson, K., Tweedly, A., and White M., "Starburst Multicast File Transfer Protocol (MFTP) Specification," IETF Internet Draft, ftp://ietf.org/internet-drafts/draft-miller-mftp-spec-02.txt.

34. MIT Research Program on Communications Policy, "Internet Telephony Software," http://itel.mit.edu/itel/software.html.

35. Motorola, "Welcome to the NEW Motorola VoxML Developer Site!," http://www.voxml.com/voxml.html.

36. Murray-Rust, P., "The Chemical Mark-Up Language," http://www.venus.co.uk/omf.cml/

37. National Center for Super Computing Applications HTTPd Development Team, "WAIS and HTTP Integration," http://hoohoo.ncsa.uiuc.edu/docs/tutorials/wais.html.

38. National Center for Supercomputing Applications at the University of Illinois at Urbana-Champaign, "Common Gateway Interface," http://hoohoo.ncsa.uiuc.edu/ cgi/intro.html.

39. NCSA at University of Illinois in Urbana-Champaign, "NCSA Mosaic," http://www.ncsa.uiuc.edu/SDG/Software/Mosaic.

40. Negroponte, N., "Object Oriented Television," Wired, July 1996, pp. 188.

41. NetPhonic Communications Inc., "WebOnCall Product Info," http://www.netphonic.com/product/woc/wocprod.htm.

42. Netscape Communications Corporation, "CoolTalk," http://home.netscape.com/comprod/products/navigator/version_3.0/communication/cooltalk/index.html.

43. Netscape Communications Corporation, "Dynamic HTML," http://search.netscape.com/communicator/features/Dynamic_HTML.html.

44. Netscape Communications Corporation, "JavaScript Authoring Guide," http://home.netscape.com/eng/mozilla/Gold/handbook/javascript/index.html.

45. Netscape Communications Corporation, "The Netscape Server API," http://home.netscape.com/newsref/std/server_api.html.

46. Netscape Communications Corporation, "Using LiveConnect," http://home.netscape.com/navigator/v3.0/liveconnectsyntax.html.

47. Nielsen H. and Gettys, J., "HTTP - Hypertext Transfer Protocol," http://www.w3.org/Protocols/.

48. O'Sullivan, B., "The Internet Multicast Backbone," http://ganges.cs.tcd.ie/4ba2/multicast/bryan/index.html.

49. Parallel Graphics, "Welcome to Parallel Graphics," http://www.parallelgraphics.com/.

50. Pizano, A. and Hou, T.-Y., "Integrated Multimedia Messaging Concepts and Applications," Workshop on Multimedia Applications, 24th ACM CSC Conference, February 1996, http://www.scr.siemens.com/ps/acm96_wk.ps.

51. Real Networks Corporation, "RealMedia Architecture," http://www.real.com/realmedia/index.html.

52. Say NO to Third Voice!, "Say NO to Third Voice!" http://saynotothirdvoice.com/.

53. Schloss, G. and Wynblatt, M, "Presentation Layer Primitives for the Layered Multimedia Data Model," Proceedings of the IEEE International Conference on Multimedia Communications and Systems, May 1995, http://www.cs.sunysb.edu/~wynblatt/icmcs95.ps.

54. Sherman, C., "Web Graffiti - Web Search - 09-14-99," http://websearch.about.com/internet/websearch/library/weekly/aa091499.htm?iam=mt.

55. Spero, S., "Binary Gateway Interface - An API for Dynamically Extensible HTTP Servers," http://sunsite.unc.edu/mdma-release/BGI-spec.txt.

56. Sun Microsystems, "Java Media Framework API," http://java.sun.com/products/java-media/jmf/.

57. Sun Microsystems, "WebNFS: The Filesystem for the World Wide Web," http://www.sun.com/960710/feature2/index.html.

58. Thau, R., "Design Considerations for the Apache Server API", Fifth International World Wide Web Conference, May 1996, Paris, France, http://www5conf.inria.fr/fich_html/papers/P20/Overview.html.

59. Third Voice, "Third Voice Inc.." http://www.thirdvoice.com/.

60. University of Kansas Academic Computing Services, "About Lynx," http://www.ukans.edu/about_lynx/about_lynx.html.

61. Virage Inc., "Virage Information Retrieval," http://www.virage.com/online/.

62. VocalTec, "Internet Conference," http://www.vocaltec.com/products/atrium/icp_intro.htm.

63. The VRML Architecture Group, "The VRML Architecture Group," http://www.meshmart.org/vrmlup.htm.

64. WebTV Networks Inc., "About WebTV", http://www.webtv.net/HTML/home.about.html

65. World Wide Web Consortium, "Annotation," http://www.bilkent.edu.tr/pub/WWW/Collaboration/Overview.html#annotation.

66. World Wide Web Consortium, "Document Object Model (DOM)," http://www.w3.org/DOM/.

67. World Wide Web Consortium, "Extensible Markup Language (XML)," http://www.w3.org/XML/.

68. World Wide Web Consortium, "HyperText Markup Language (HTML)," http://www.w3.org/pub/WWW/MarkUp/.

69. Worlds Inc. http://www.worlds.net.

70. Wynblatt, M., Benson, D., and Hsu, A., "Browsing the World Wide Web in a Non-Visual Environment," Proceedings of the International Conference on Auditory Display, Palo Alto, CA, 1997, http://www.santafe.edu/~kramer/icad/websiteV2.0/Conferences/ICAD97/icad97.html.

71. Wynblatt, M. and Schloss, G., "Control Layer Primitives for the Layered Multimedia Data Model," Proceedings of 1995 ACM Multimedia Conference, pp. 167-178. http://www.cs.sunysb.edu/~wynblatt/acm95.ps.

72. Yahoo!, "Yahoo! Broadcast [Radio Station Home Page]," http://www.broadcast.com/radio.

73. Yahoo!, "Yahoo! Broadcast Television," http://www.broadcast.com/television/.

74. Yahoo!, http://www.yahoo.com.

Chapter 15

MULTIMEDIA BROADCASTING OVER THE INTERNET

Borko Furht, Raymond Westwater, and Jeffrey Ice

Abstract

This chapter presents several techniques for broadcasting multimedia data (audio and video) over the Internet. Internet broadcasting (also called webcasting) techniques have become very important in applications such as Internet (or Web) radio and television, real-time broadcasting of critical data (such as stock prices), distance learning, videoconferencing, and many others. We describe the current Internet broadcasting techniques including IP Unicast and IP Multicast, and we introduce a new technique IP Simulcast. The IP Simulcast approach is based on the hierarchical, binary structure of receivers, which at the same time become data senders or repeaters.

1. INTRODUCTION

Internet broadcasting, referred as *webcasting*, is coming of age. Now, in addition to reprocessed audio or video that is transferred from radio or TV to the Internet, webcasting also means broadcasting new, original content, sometimes live, on the Web. Taking advantage of streaming audio and video technology, site producers can bring real-time sound and vision to the Web. With the present technology, to squeeze it through a 28.8 Kbps modem line, audio and video must be compressed almost to the breaking point, and that means plenty of people will find it's not worth hearing or viewing.

However, the problems have not stopped millions of people from downloading viewers and seeking out the webcasts. Listening to music or watching video straight off the Internet (Web) still creates a strong enough buzz that people overlook shortcomings like crackly audio, slow download times, and grainy pictures. As a consequence, a number of Internet radio stations have been created, which offer programs of commercial appeal to an international audience.

The Internet protocols used to transmit this data require individual connections to be formed between servers (or senders) and their clients (receivers). The proliferation of such connections is quite expensive, because it consumes both a very high network bandwidth and processing power at the server. Well-known Internet radio stations have developed their solutions around networks of expensive servers at ever-escalating expense.

And, although we are still in the early stages of webcasting, one can already foresee what the Internet will offer a few years down the line: clear, crisp, audio and full-screen, high-quality, on-demand video. Pipe Dream, Inc. has developed a revolutionary technology, which will provide all these required features for Internet webcasting. This innovative technology consists of

- IP Simulcast – a new Internet broadcast protocol, which provides inexpensive, efficient, and reliable audio and video broadcasting,

- New audio and video compression algorithms, which allow real-time audio and video transmission of data at very low bit rates (1/3 of the modem bit rate) and with high quality.

2. PRESENT APPROACHES IN DATA BROADCASTING OVER THE INTERNET

There are three fundamental types for transmitting data on the Internet, as illustrated in Figure 1.

- IP Unicast
- IP Broadcast
- IP Multicast

IP Unicast transmission is designed to transmit data (or a packet) from a sender to a single receiver, as shown in Figure 1a. *IP Broadcast* transmission is used to send data from a sender to an entire subnetwork, as illustrated in Figure 1b. *IP Multicast* transmission is designed to enable the delivery of data from a sender to a set of receivers that have been configured as members of a multicast group in various scattered subnetworks, as shown in Figure 1c.

For radio and television broadcast applications, *a one-to-many data distribution model* is required. In the one-to-many data distribution model, the data flow is from a single sender to many receivers simultaneously, but not the whole subnetwork. Therefore, present audio and television broadcast applications typically use IP Unicast transmission, or they may also use IP Multicast transmission.

2.1 IP UNICAST

Many current radio and television Internet broadcast applications use unicast data transmission for data distribution. In this case, connection-oriented stream transports are used to distribute data to each receiver individually. These applications duplicate the data they send to each receiver and use unicast transmission to each receiver. As a result of this duplication, these applications are far from optimal due to the following reasons:

(a) Network bandwidth is wasted,

(b) They cannot scale to service increasing numbers of receivers,

(c) They cannot distribute data in a timely manner, since the delivery to each host has to be serialized.

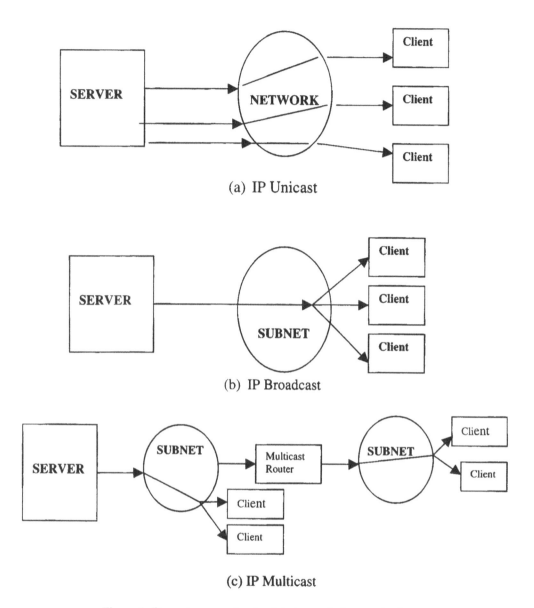

Figure 1. Present approaches in data transmission on the Internet.
(a) IP Unicast, (b) IP Broadcast, (c) IP Multicast.

2.2 IP MULTICAST

IP Multicast transmission provides sending the data from a sender to multiple receivers, but unlike IP Unicast, the number of identical copies that are sent is minimized. All receivers are configured as members of the same multicast group. The sender sends an IP packet to a multicast address, and lets the network forward a copy of the packet to each group of hosts. Multicast is not connection oriented; the sender sends data to multiple receivers over UDP (User Data Protocol). The UDP protocol, unlike TCP, makes only a "best effort" to deliver data. If a transmission error occurs, the packet is discarded [1,2,3].

The IP Multicast protocol is implemented in the routers of a network, rather than in the server. The routers in the network automatically make a copy of the multicast packet for each destination receiver. In this way, the number of excess copies transmitted to any particular subnet is minimized and, therefore, IP Multicast is much more efficient than IP Unicast, requiring much smaller server bandwidth.

The basic service of IP Multicast is unreliable unicast transmission of datagrams, which is suitable only for applications geared toward performance rather than reliability [1]. Error recovery can be done by sending requests to the server (sender). This will require a more complex scheme and a higher network bandwidth.

In addition, IP Multicast routing requires special IP Multicast routers. All intermediate routers between the sender and receivers must be IP Multicast capable, as illustrated in Figure 2.

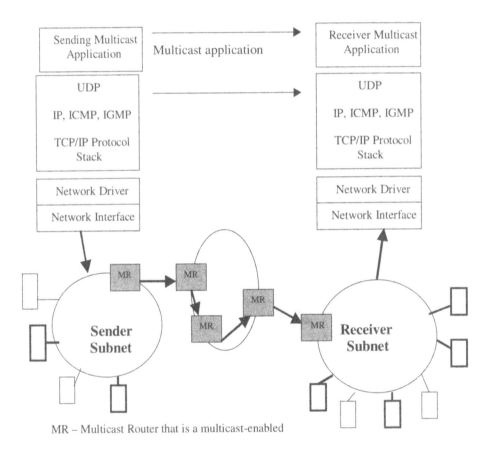

Figure 2. The network with IP Multicast-enabled components.

In many cases, firewalls in the network may need to be reconfigured to permit IP Multicast traffic.

At the receiver (client) node, a number of requirements exist in order to receive IP Multicast protocol, such as

- Support for IP Multicast transmission and reception in the TCP/IP protocol stack,

- Software that support IGMP to communicate requests to join a multicast network traffic, and

- Network interface card, which efficiently filter for LAN data link layer addresses mapped from n addresses.

2.2.1 Multicast Routing

Routing of multicast traffic is a complex problem, because a multicast address identifies a particular transmission session, rather than a specific physical destination. Some new techniques have been developed to address the problem of efficiently routing multicast traffic [7]. Since the number of receivers for a multicast session can potentially be quite large, the source should not need to know all the relevant addresses. Instead the network routers must somehow be able to translate multicast addresses into host addresses. To avoid duplication of effort, a single router is selected as the designated router for each physical network. For efficient transmission, designated routers construct a spanning tree that connects all members of an IP Multicast group, as illustrated in Figure 3. A spanning tree has just enough connectivity so that there is only one path between every pair of routers.

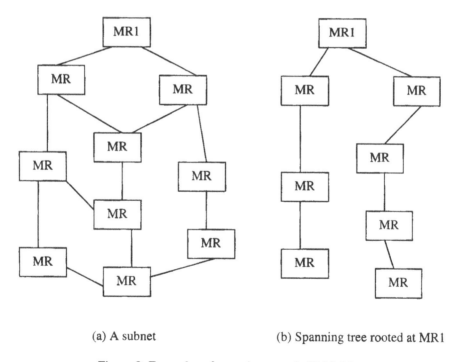

(a) A subnet   (b) Spanning tree rooted at MR1

Figure 3. Examples of spanning trees in IP Multicast.

IP Multicast routing algorithms and protocols use two approaches.

Dense-mode routing protocol assumes that the multicast group members are densely distributed throughout the network. It relies on periodic flooding of the network with multicast traffic to set up and maintain the spanning tree.

Sparse-mode routing protocol assumes that the multicast group members are sparsely distributed throughout the network. In this case, flooding would waste network bandwidth and hence could cause serious performance problems. Therefore, it uses more selective techniques to set up and maintain multicast trees.

In summary, IP Multicast provides much more efficient one-to-many data distribution than IP Unicast, but there are a number of yet unsolved issues.

1. Network issues related to all intermediate routers that must be IP Multicast-enabled and the reconfiguration of the firewall.

2. Issues related to the reliability and error control.

3. Requirements related to receivers, which need a special network card and software that supports IP Multicast.

3. INTERNET BROADCAST BASED ON IP SIMULCAST

Pipe Dream has invented a new technique, referred to as IP Simulcast, for transmitting data over the Internet from a sender simultaneously to multiple receivers. In this section, we describe basic principles of IP Simulcast as well as technical details of the IP Simulcast protocol. We also compare IP Simulcast with the other approaches including IP Unicast and IP Multicast.

3.1 BASIC PRINCIPLES OF IP SIMULCAST

IP Simulcast is an innovative solution for Internet broadcasting, which shows significant advantages over the existing techniques, including IP Unicast and IP Multicast. It resolves all the issues and problems involved in the implementation of the IP Multicast, discussed in the previous paragraph.

Similar to IP Multicast, IP Simulcast reduces the server (or sender) overhead by distributing the load to each client (receiver). Each receiver becomes a repeater, which rebroadcasts its received content to two child receivers (repeaters), forming a broadcast pyramid, as illustrated in Figure 4.

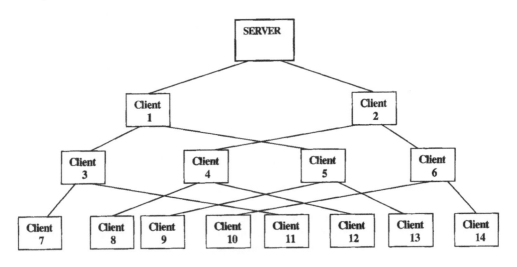

Figure 4. Broadcast pyramid applied in IP Simulcast.

In this way, the needed network bandwidth for the server/sender is significantly reduced, because the server sends just one copy of the data, which is then further rebroadcast by the receivers/repeaters. Thus, the cost of service provision is borne by the receivers (rather than the sender), who have typically paid for the fixed bandwidth that is often not used.

In this way, the IP Simulcast concept provides broadcast functionality at a lower cost than IP Multicast. Unlike IP Multicast, which requires special routers for its implementation as well as several additional requirements, IP Simulcast does not require any special requirements for its implementation.

The number of clients in the IP Simulcast pyramid grows as a binary tree. For a pyramid with 1 tree level, the number of clients is 2, for a pyramid with 2 levels, the number of clients is 6, and so on. The number of clients in the nth level is 2^n. For example, for a broadcast system with 10 levels, the number of clients in the last level is $2^{10} = 1,024$, and the total number of clients in the pyramid is then $1024 + 1022 = 2,046$.

The repeater/receiver performs conventional client functions, including error recovery and detection of the loss connection. As a consequence, IP Simulcast provides guaranteed delivery of packets, which is not the case of IP Multicast. As we mentioned in the previous paragraph, IP Multicast services make no provision for error recovery. The lost packets must be either ignored, or recovered from the server at the cost of the increased server bandwidth.

IP Simulcast uses a radically different model of digital broadcast, referred to as *repeater-server model*. In the repeater-server model, the server manages and controls the interconnection of repeaters. While the server may be fairly similar to a conventional server, the repeater contains server functions in addition to conventional client functions. In essence, each repeater not only plays the data stream back to its audience, but also transmits the data stream to two other repeaters (see Figure 4).

The fundamental part of the IP Simulcast protocol is its specification of the repeater-server relationship. The IP Simulcast server/sender performs two fundamental functions, as any conventional server.

- Transmission of the broadcast stream.
- Forming connections, which interconnects repeaters/receivers and maintains the Simulcast pyramid.

Repeaters are composed of two subsystems.

1. Repeater-client subsystem, and
2. Repeater-sender subsystem.

The repeater-client subsystem receives a broadcast stream and interactively plays back the stream to its audience. In addition, the repeater-client subsystem performs traditional client functions including connection, receipt of data, and buffer management, decompression of multimedia data, error recovery, and detection of the loss connection.

The repeater-sender subsystem rebroadcasts the data that the repeater-sender subsystem has received. It also performs error retransmission.

3.2 THE IP SIMULCAST PROTOCOL

As illustrated in Figure 4, IP Simulcast is based on the new repeater-server model. The server sends the data only to two repeaters/receivers, and then the packets are rebroadcast by each level of repeaters to the next level. In this way, a pyramid network is built, which is managed and controlled by the server. In addition, in order to assure a reliable data transmission, retransmission of lost packets or packets with errors is requested through secondary feeds (dashed lines in Figure 5).

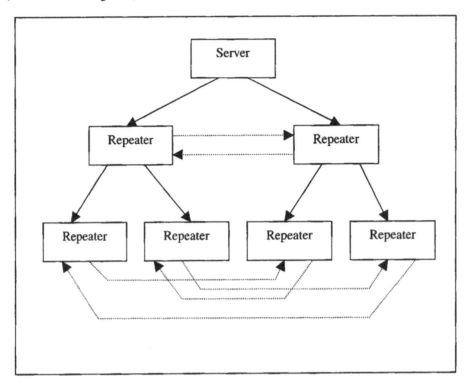

Figure 5. IP Simulcast repeater-server relationship.
Retransmission of packets is requested through secondary feeds (dashed lines).

The server functions include

- *Digitization of the program source.* A typical source program might include analog audio and analog video. These analog program sources are digitized into streams of time-varying data.

- *Synchronization of the digital source.* Streams of time-varying data may come from various sources: digitization of analog sources, stored compressed data on disk, digital data from animation programs, authoring programs, or other sources. Source programs may be interrupted, overlaid, or otherwise synchronized with advertising spots, source programs may be scheduled throughout the day, etc. The various sources of digital data must be synchronized and time stamped for playback.

- *Compression of the source.* Each stream of time-varying digital data may be compressed to reduce its size and transmission time. The compression technique is a trade-off among various factors including compression ratio, perceived quality, complexity of compression and decompression, scalability, and noise immunity.

- *Collection of the compressed source into transmission packets.* IP transmission is a packet-based protocol. The data is collected into IP packets in preparation for transmission. Compressed data may be represented by several alternative packetization schemes to adapt to different speed transmission lines or computers of different power. Each of these packetization schemes could be used to feed an alternate pyramid of repeaters.

- *Transmission of compressed source transmission packets.* Two feeds are supported, each to be received and retransmitted by its destination repeater.

- *Connection of repeaters.* Each repeater sends a request to the server asking to be serviced with the transmission stream. The server responds by selecting an available repeater to be the requesting repeater's source. The transmission stream is then fed to the requesting repeater. The server also selects a secondary feed for the requesting repeater. Error-free retransmission is accomplished over this secondary feed.

- *Collection of statistics.* The server monitors the construction and breaking of connections.

Each repeater-client has responsibility for collecting the transmitted data streams and playing them back to its audience. The repeater-clients' functions include

- *Establishment of connections.* The repeater-client issues a connection request to the server. The server will establish an individual connection to the repeater-client.

- *Reconnection.* The client must determine if a connection is broken, and attempt reconnection.

- *Caching of packets.* Received packets must be sequenced and cached in order to locate missing packets.

- *Retransmission requests.* Requests are issued to the repeater-client's secondary feed to request retransmission of missing packets.

- *Error recovery.* In the case that a packet cannot be recovered, the repeater-client must perform some recovery action (play silence, replay the last packet, degrade quality, etc.).

- *Decompression of received data stream.* The received data is decompressed in anticipation of playback.

- *Playback of data streams.* The decompressed data is played back to the repeater-client's audience.

- *Synchronization with the server.* The playback rate must match the server's capture rate to avoid overflow or starvation of the repeater-client's buffers. The repeater-client must be able to adapt to the small differences in playback rate that are bound to exist.

The repeater-transmitter performs some conventional server functions.

- *Transmission of compressed source transmission packets.* Two feeds are supported, each to be received and retransmitted by its destination repeater.

- *Retransmission of error packets.* A secondary feed is supported by each repeater-transmitter. Upon request, a missed packet is retransmitted to the destination of the secondary feed.

The broadcast system is subdivided into fractional streams for transmission purposes. Repeaters for each fractional stream are organized into a binary tree, propagating the fractional stream through all repeaters. Fractional streams are collected into a single stream by each repeater. The collection of these fractional streams causes a superposition of the binary tree into a single "bush" that represents the transmission of the full system. The topology of the superposition is chosen such that the two levels of a fractional tree are separated by one-half the width of the stage in the tree. This topology ensures that no repeater is starved by the failure of a single feeding repeater. Figure 6 shows feeding a stage of length 8 with two fractional streams.

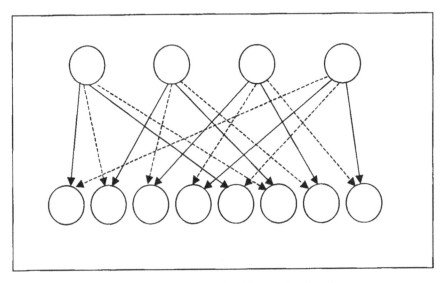

Figure 6. Feeding a stage of length 8 with two fractional streams.

Each repeater collects packets into a buffer. The buffer is used to compensate jitter delays. Additional buffering is introduced to perform error recovery. After the jitter and error delay has played out, the received packets are broadcast to the next level.

Error recovery is composed of two distinct phases: error recovery and retry service. During the error recovery interval, queries are made in the round-robin fashion to repeaters in the previous stage. During the retry service period, retry requests from the subsequent stage are serviced. Figure 7 illustrates the timing for the received packets, which are buffered for error recovery and playback.

Transmitted samples are placed in a playback buffer. Playback is synchronized to the rate at which packets are received to avoid playback buffer overflow and underflow.

An unassigned repeater issues a connection request to the server-administrator to join the broadcast. The server-administrator acknowledges the request and queues the repeater for connection. If the repeater has not been connected by the time its queue entry times out, the server-administrator issues fractional feed requests to the last complete stage, starting a feed to the repeater.

When a repeater/receiver wants to leave the broadcast, it issues a disconnection request to the server. If the queue of the repeaters waiting for connection is not empty, a repeater is selected from the queue, and the server issues fractional feed requests to the parents of the terminating repeater. On the other hand, if the repeater connection queue is empty, the oldest node on the bottom stage is used as the replacement node. In the event of node failure, the children of the node report the failure to the server.

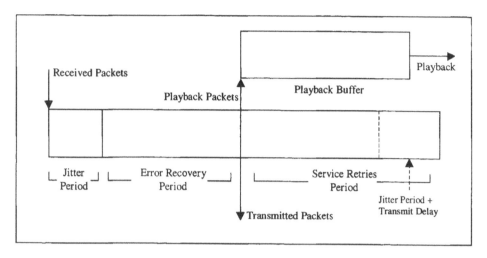

Figure 7. Timing diagram – received packets are buffered for error recovery and playback.

3.3 ANALYSIS OF THE IP SIMULCAST ALGORITHM

In this section we present a mathematical analysis of the IP Simulcast algorithm in order to get the quantitative values for the buffers in receivers/repeaters nodes needed

(a) to reduce the effect of jitter delay, and
(b) to minimize the number of lost packets.

We begin with the assumption that the stream traffic is broadcast to all nodes of the tree. Transmission packets are equal in size and require time τ to transmit. The packet transmission rate is p packets per second. Transit time T from node to node has the same mean time μ_T irrespective of the node pairs. Jitter time (J_T) is the variation in transit times from the mean and is simplistically modeled as packet interarrival time, Poisson distributed with packet arrival rate $p=1/\sigma_T$. The probability density function for jitter time J_T can be expressed as

$$f_J(t)= pe^{-pt}$$

The probability that transit time lies in the interval (t0, t1) is then

$$P[t0<t<t1]= \mu_T -\sigma_T + \int_{t0-\mu_T+\sigma_T}^{t1-\mu_T+\sigma_T} pe^{-pt}dt$$

Transmission error is modeled as dropped packets occurring at random periods, Poisson distributed, with packet dropping rate $p_d = 1/\sigma_T$. The probability density function for transmission error is given as

$$f_E(t)= p_d e^{-p_d t}$$

3.3.1 Jitter Buffering
Jitter buffering is used to reduce the effect of jitter delay. Jitter buffers are chosen sufficiently large to give desired confidence that a missing packet has been lost, and is not simply delayed. The probability that the packet interarrival time does not exceed jitter buffer time I (i.e., the confidence that the packet has been lost to error) is

$$P[t < I] = \int_0^I pe^{-pt} dt$$

Solving for I (jitter buffer time) gives

$$I = -\sigma_T \ln(1 - P[t < I])$$
$$= 1 - e^{-pI}$$

Jitter increases as packets propagate down the pyramid. A pyramid of N nodes has $n = \log_2(N)$ levels, and the PDF for jitter delay at the nth stage is

$$f_{J_n}(t) = npe^{-npt}$$

Choice of I_n, the amount of jitter buffer time needed to develop the confidence level $P[t<I_n]$ that a packet has been lost is

$$I = -n\sigma_T \ln(1 - P[t < I_n])$$

The required jitter buffer size grows linearly with the depth of the tree, as illustrated in Figure 8.

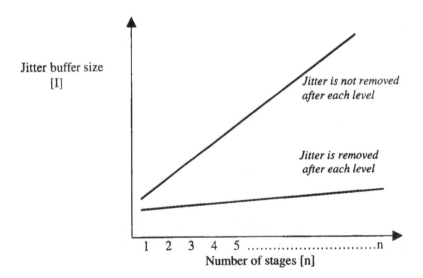

Figure 8. Jitter buffer size as a function of number of stages in the tree.

An alternative formulation is derived by assuming that transmission to the next level takes place after jitter buffering; i.e., jitter is removed at each level by introducing buffered delay in retransmission. If the desired jitter buffering confidence level at stage n is C,

$$C = P[t < I]^n = \left(1 - e^{-pI}\right)^n$$

Solving for I gives

$$I = -\sigma_T \ln\left(1 - \sqrt[n]{C}\right)$$

In this case the required buffering at the next stage slightly increases with the depth of the tree, as shown in Figure 8.

3.3.2 Retry Buffering

Retry buffering is used to minimize the number of lost packets. Lost packets are recovered by issuing retry commands to the transmitter. This is done after the jitter buffer period, and the packet should be received after round-trip transmission time plus round-trip jitter buffering. This process may be repeated until a desired confidence level of packet receipt is assured. Let the desired buffer length be B. Then, the probability that the packet arrival time does not exceed retry buffer time is given as

$$P[t < nB] = \left[\int_0^B \sigma_E e^{-\sigma_E t}\right]^n dt = 1 - e^{-\sigma_E nB}$$

where $\sigma_E = 1/p_E$, where p_E is the error packet rate.

Solving for n gives

$$n = {-\ln\left(1 - P[t < nB]\right)} \Big/ {\sigma_E B}$$

We can conclude that transmission errors accumulate at each stage, but the accumulation at each stage has a second-order dependency on the stage before.

The probability that a packet is not received at the first stage after m retry periods is

$$P[t < T] = \left[\int_0^T \sigma_E e^{-\sigma_E t} dt\right] \prod_2^m [\int_0^T 2\sigma_E e^{-2\sigma_E t} dt]$$

where the factor of 2 is introduced to account for errors in transmitting the retry request. The probability that a packet is not received at the nth stage is

$$P[t < T] = \left[\int_0^T n\sigma_E e^{-n\sigma_E t} dt \right] \prod_2^m \{ \int_0^T (n+1)\sigma_E e^{-(n+1)\sigma_E t} dt \}$$

$$= \left[1 - e^{-n\sigma_E T} \right] \left[1 - e^{-(n+1)\sigma_E T} \right]^{m-1} \approx \left[1 - e^{-n\sigma_E T} \right]^m$$

Solving for m (retry periods) gives

$$m = \frac{\ln(P[t,T])}{\ln[1 - e^{-n\sigma_E T}]}$$

Figure 9 shows the packet drop rate as a function of number of levels in the Simulcast pyramid for various number of retries (0 to 4). The system packet drop rate in this experiment is 25%, which means that at the first level 75% of packets will be received correctly, and 25% will be dropped due to transmission errors. As we can see from Figure 9, with several retries the transmission becomes much more reliable, so that in the case of 4 retries the packet drop rate at high levels is very low.

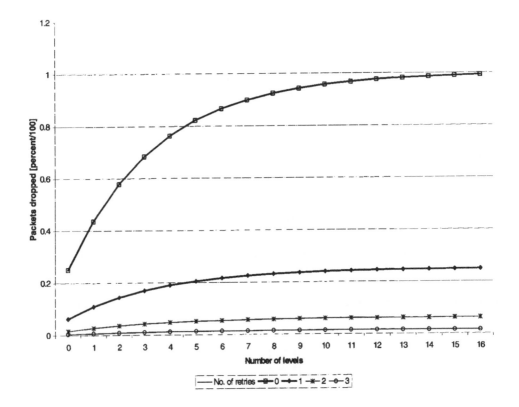

Figure 9. The packet drop rate as a function of number of levels in the IP Simulcast pyramid.

4. COMPARISON WITH OTHER APPROACHES

In this section we compare the IP Simulcast approach for audio broadcasting with the UP Unicast and UP Multicast systems. We assume an audio broadcast system, which continuously broadcast 16 Kbps to a maximum of 10,000 clients/receivers.

For the comparison, we used the following assumptions:

- When calculating the server bandwidth, we assumed 1% error retransmission and we ignored control overhead. The server bandwidth for IP Multicast reflects error retransmission from the server.
- Bandwidth cost is calculated assuming $1,000 per T1 connection per month (1.5 Mbps).
- In the case of IP Simulcast, only one server is used to manage and control the broadcasting pyramid and to compress audio. The server cost is $5,000.
- In the case of IP Unicast, 16 servers are used, each at cost of $3,000.
- In the case of IP Multicast, one server is used to support transmission to the network and one to service error retry requests (total cost $8,000).

Table 1 compares these three approaches.

Table 1. Comparison of Features of Various Techniques for Audio Broadcasting

FEATURES	IP UNICAST	IP MULTICAST	IP SIMULCAST
Server Bandwidth	162 Mbps	1.62 Mbps	16.2 Kbps
Bandwidth Cost	$100,000 per month	$20,000 per month	$100 per month
Error Recovery	By server	By server	By client
Initial Server Cost	$53,000	$8,000	$5,000
Client Reachability	Any IP address	Only clients in proprietary network	Any IP address
Implementation Issues	Cannot scale to serve increasing number of clients	Requires all intermediate IP Multicast routers Requires special network card and software which support IP Multicast	Easy to implement Does not require any special cards or routers

In summary, IP Simulcast-based solution for Internet broadcasting provides a number of advantages compared to existing technologies including IP Unicast and IP Multicast. These advantages can be summarized as follows:

- *Lower cost*. Due to inexpensive server and network requirements, IP Simulcast-based solution offers much lower price than the other solutions.

- *Better flexibility*. IP Simulcast-based solution provides a general solution and its broadcasts are received regardless of the physical solution, medium, noise of the connection, or network provider of the receiver.

- *Higher quality*. Pipe Dream's solution is designed to function in the unreliable Internet environment, and provides built-in error recovery and quality control, while the other solutions are not reliable.

5. POTENTIAL APPLICATIONS

Due to its simplicity, easy to implement, efficiency, and inexpensive initial cost for the server and network bandwidth, IP Simulcast is a very efficient and inexpensive solution for many current and potential webcast-based applications. IP Simulcast is well suited for *radio and television broadcasting*, and these are the first two applications created by Pipe Dream, Inc.

However, the other potential applications include

- Distance learning
- Electronic software distribution including software update
- Real-time broadcasting of critical data (like stock prices)
- Database replication and file transfer
- Videoconferencing and many others

We will briefly analyze the market for radio broadcasting on the Internet. The radio on the Internet application offers very attractive features to the audience, such as scheduled programs, supplementary data on the scheduled programs, as well as interactive services. Thus, more than 27% of America's 11,000 radio stations already have Web sites.

The number of radio stations offering on-line radio programs has also increased in the last several years, from 50 (in 1995) to 741 (end of 1997), of which 341 are in U.S. In 1998, the number of stations which webcasted their programs reached 2000.

The following elements comprise the attraction of live radio or video broadcast:

- The Internet is the only medium that enables a radio broadcast to be audible worldwide. The prospect of global recognition is a highly motivating element.

- The access to an innovative transmission channel will improve the coverage of their audience. Indeed, 60% of on-line radio listeners live in the radio's emission zone. Thus, employees can now listen to their radio in the workplace, a phenomenon that is developing in the U.S.

- The increase in the audience size and the increase in their listening times will increase the advertisement prices.

- The addition of real-time broadcasting radio to the Web site will also increase the number of connections to the Internet site and, consequently, the advertising income linked to it.

We developed several applications based on INP Simulcast and innovative audio and video compression technologies. They are described next.

SimulSays is the application that uses IP Simulcast protocol to allow radio broadcasters to broadcast (webcast) radio programs to an unlimited number of clients using a simple and inexpensive server and a small server bandwidth. Thus, the broadcaster needs a very low initial cost in order to begin broadcasting radio programs. Besides the IP Simulcast protocol, SimulSays applies an innovative audio compression technique, which is capable of compressing audio while maintaining its high quality. SimulSays also includes the banner function. The banner allows broadcasting advertising messages as well as transmission and display of supplementary data, such as maps, telephone numbers, election graphs, dates for various events, and many others.

Radio Player and Radio Guide, which can be downloaded from the Internet, are shown in Figure 10.

SimulSays with chat function is an upgraded SimulSays application, which provides interactivity among the receivers/clients via a chatboard. This application will enrich radio transmission and make it very attractive due to interactivity. The clients, who are involved in listening to radio programs, can interactively exchange messages among themselves.

SimulSees is also using IP Simulcast protocol to provide television broadcasters with an efficient and inexpensive solution for broadcasting (webcasting) television programs to a large number of clients. Similarly, the initial cost for broadcasters includes a simple and inexpensive server and a small network bandwidth. Besides IP Simulcast technology, SimulSays uses a new real-time video compression algorithm, which enables live video webcasting at low bit rates.

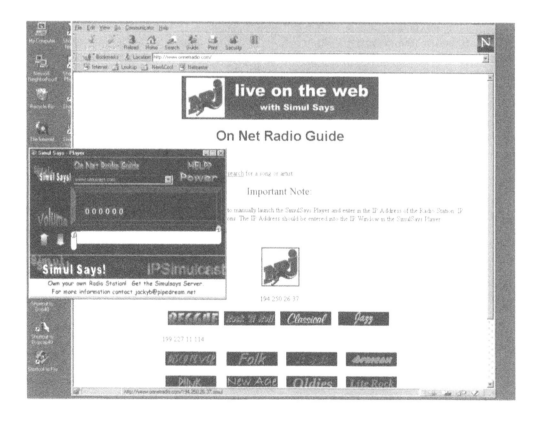

Figure 10. Radio Player and Radio Guide
that use the IP Simulcast broadcasting technique.

6. SUMMARY

In this chapter we presented several techniques for multimedia broadcasting over the Internet: IP Unicast, IP Multicast, and the new technique, IP Simulcast. In summary, the IP Simulcast protocol is the superior technique for real-time data broadcasting on the Internet. It enables an efficient coverage of "big events" on the Web, without additional investment to the server and network bandwidth. The number of connections on the Internet, covered by IP Simulcast, is practically unlimited. Coupled with efficient audio and video compression techniques, IP Simulcast offers an attractive solution for a number of broadcast applications on the Internet including radio and television broadcast, real-time broadcasting of critical data, distance learning, and many others.

References

1. C. Semeria and T. Maufer, "Introduction to IP Multicast Routing," September 1996. http://www.ipmulticast.com/community/semeria.html.
2. C. Huitema, *Routing in the Internet*, Prentice Hall, Inc., Englewood Cliffs, New Jersey, 1995.
3. "Writing IP Multicast-Enabled Applications," Stardust Technologies, http://www.ipmulticast.com/community/whitepapers/ipmcapps.html.
4. W. Bremser, "Pump Up the Volume," *Computerlife*, January 1998, p. 91.
5. M. R. Macedonia and D. P. Brutzman, "MBone Provides Audio and Video Across the Internet," *IEEE Computer*, April 1994, pp. 30-36.
6. V. Kumar, "MBONE: Interactive Media and the Internet," New Riden, 1996.
7. V. Johnson and M. Johnson, "How IP Multicast Work," Stardust Technologies, http://www.ipmulticast.com/community/whitepapers/howipmcworks.html
8. V. Johnson, M. Johnson, and K. Miller, "Implementing IP Multicast in Different Network Infrastructures," Stardust Technologies, http://www.ipmulticast.com/community/whitepapers/netinfra.html.
9. J. Ice, "Method for Connecting Systems Into a Broadcast Network," U.S. patent approved, 1998.
10. J. Ice and R. Westwater, "System and Method for Improved Quality Compression and Decompression of Speech Signals," patent pending.
11. R. Westwater and B. Furht, "The XYZ Algorithm for Real-Time Compression of Full-Motion Video," *Journal of Real-Time Imaging*, Vol. 2, No. 1, February 1996, pp. 19-34.
12. V. Hardman, M. A. Sasse, and I. Kouvelas, "Successful Multiparty Audio Communication," *Communications of the ACM*, Vol. 41, No. 5, May 1998, pp. 74-80.

Chapter 16

INTERNET-BASED UNIFIED MESSAGING SYSTEMS

Borko Furht

Abstract

In this chapter we present unified messaging systems, their evolution, architectures, enabling technologies, standards, and commercial systems and products. Unified messaging systems provide a single mailbox for all messages including voice, fax, e-mail, data, and video. Benefits of unified messaging systems are tremendous – they provide improved productivity and much more efficient communications then conventional messaging systems, and bring a positive cultural change among their users. In addition, Internet-based unified messaging systems use the Internet telephony instead of long distance for sending and retrieving voice and fax messages. We describe key technologies and various architectural approaches to unified messaging. Case studies of two commercial unified messaging systems are presented as well.

1. INTRODUCTION TO UNIFIED MESSAGING

1.1 HISTORY

Today, messaging is a strategic and mission critical necessity. Messaging has truly become an infrastructure upon many future applications will be built.

Traditionally, telephone networks, with voice and fax messages, have been most popular ways to communicate. However, recently Internet based technologies, including e-mail messages and World Wide Web, have introduced a new way to communicate, create, and exchange messages. According to the Electronic Messaging Association (EMA) study, the number of active e-mail users is expected to grow from 54 million in 1996 to 108 million in the year 2000. Clearly, electronic messaging has followed the path of the telephone and the fax machine in changing from a rudimentary tool for exchanging information among a selected group of researchers into an indispensable component of every day life. Electronic messaging is now an integral part of the worldwide information infrastructure, with applications in business, education, commerce, and interpersonal communications.

In a traditional company, these three different messaging methods (voice, fax, and e-mail) are independent. Faxes are typically sent and received via fax machines, while voice messaging resides on a voice mail system, which has no connectivity to other systems. E-mail messaging system is the part of computer and communication system and typically consists of text messages.

The main drawback of this "unconnected" messaging approach is that it requires three separate user interfaces. This approach also requires separate administrative and support functions, and consequently is of a higher cost.

Once upon a time, for communication purposes and exchange of messages everyone had two phone numbers (home and business) and a mailing address. Today, corporate America has been arming employees with cellular phones, pagers, e-mail, Internet access, and other communication tools so they can stay closer to customers and effectively communicate and exchange messages. According to the recent study, the average Fortune 1000 worker now uses an average of six communication tools [9].

Today, electronic messaging industry consists of five different segments: (1) electronic mail, (2) voice processing, (3) paging, (4) computer-based faxing, and (5) electronic data interchange.

Electronic mail is the largest segment, and according to EMA's market research survey, accounts for about 50% of total electronic messaging. Voice processing, the second largest segment, comprises of voice mail systems, voice response systems, automatic call distributors, and other voice processing systems. Service providers typically supply voice processing technology to subscribers through a private network.

The paging industry includes subscriber-based paging services and paging equipment. Computer-based faxing consists of facsimiles sent and received through a personal computer bypassing a stand-alone fax machine. This industry segment includes fax-capable modems, fax boards and chips, and fax software. Electronic data interchange (EDI) allows companies to electronically exchange business documents, purchase orders, and invoices.

Technological breakthroughs over the last decade have made electronic messaging both feasible and affordable, thereby allowing for the rapid expansion of the industry. The impact of the Internet and related technologies on electronic messaging has been tremendous. Internet technologies have provided new links between different messaging technologies.

In order to resolve the problems which have occurred due to this dramatic growth of different messaging technologies, a new approach referred to as unified messaging has emerged. The basic idea behind unified messaging is to allow users to receive and retrieve different messages (e.g. voice mail, fax, and e-mail) from one interface device, such as a PC or phone. The unified messaging can be achieved by integrating two worlds, the world of computers with the world of phones, as illustrated in Figure 1. The phone network deals with phone calls, faxes, and voice mail. It usually uses proprietary voice systems, which are not flexible and expensive. The computer world deals with e-mail messages, World Wide Web, and Intranet. It is typically based on open computer architecture.

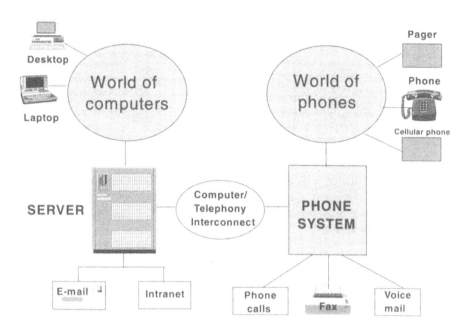

Figure 1. The foundation of unified messaging: integration of
the computer world with the phone world.

By integrating these two worlds, the user can receive and send all messages either via his/her
PC or portable computer, or via phone, cellular phone, or pager.

1.2. MESSAGE STATISTICS

In this section we present message statistics, reported by the Institute for the Future/Gallop
Organization in the article published in April 8, 1997. These statistics illustrate the
exponential growth of messages that an average business user must handle per day.

Table 1 shows an average size of e-mail, voice mail and fax messages and required storage.
Table 2 shows typical statistics for an average business user.

Table 1. Average Size of Messages
(Source: Institute for Future/Gallop Organization, article WSJ April 8, 1997).

MEDIA UNIT STORAGE	SIZE/UNIT [KB]	AVERAGE NUMBER OF UNITS	AVERAGE SIZE [KB]
E-mail (message)	24	1	25
Voice mail (sec)	5	45	226
Fax (page)	35	2.5	88.5

Table 2. Message Statistics for an Average Business User
(Source: Institute for Future/Gallop Organization, article WSJ April 8, 1997).

MESSAGE TYPE	MESSAGES PER DAY	NEW MESSAGE STORAGE [MB]	NUMBER OF ARCHIVED MESSAGES	ARCHIVED STORAGE [MB]
E-mail	13.6	0.33	100	2.44
Voice mail	11.2	2.47	15	3.31
Fax	8.8	0.76	30	2.59
TOTAL	33.6	3.56	145	8.34

From the presented statistics, which are from 1997, it is obvious that the large number of various messages arrived every day (total 33.6 per an average business user) makes the message management and manipulation a complex task. Unified messaging is the only answer to efficiently handle all messages.

1.3 DEFINITIONS

Unified Messaging (UM) is a new, hot concept and for various people means different. In order to better understand unified messaging, let us analyze the evolution of messaging from segregated to unified messaging [32].

The first generation of messaging systems, referred to as *segregated messaging*, is shown in Figure 2a. Voice and fax messages are received through the telephone network and a PBX exchange, while e-mail messages are received via a computer network. Voice messages are retrieved using a touch-tone phone, and faxes are stored and printed when desired. Email messages are sent and received through an e-mail server using an e-mail client.

In the second generation of messaging systems, referred to as *integrated messaging*, voice, fax, and e-mail messages can be retrieved through the e-mail client, as illustrated in Figure 2b. The three different messages are managed and administrated separately. The flexibility of integrated messaging is limited.

Finally, the third generation of messaging systems, referred to as *unified messaging*, assumes that there is a single mailbox for all messages, as illustrated in Figure 2c. The unified messaging allows local and remote access to voice mail, faxes, and e-mail through the e-mail client, phone, or a Web browser. There is a central management and administration of all messages regardless of their type.

According to the [47], the following definition of the unified messaging system can be used:

A Unified Messaging System (UMS) provides a single, multimedia mailbox for all messages: voice, e-mail, fax, data, and video. This mailbox is accessible from a PC, phone, or laptop computer. In addition the UMS enables the originator to easily create and send a message of any type and provides intelligence for managing messages.

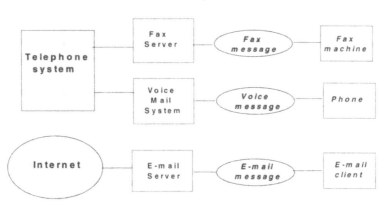

(a) Segregated messaging

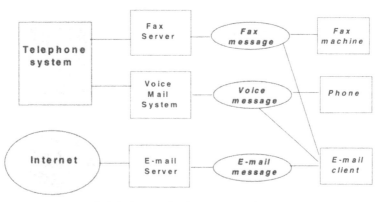

(b) Integrated messaging

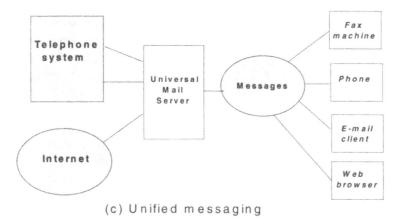

(c) Unified messaging

Figure 2. Evolution of messaging systems: from (a) segregated messaging systems to (b) integrated messaging systems, and (c) unified messaging systems.

1.4 BENEFITS OF UNIFIED MESSAGING

Today, with a growing number of professionals working from home or on the road, e-mail and voice mail have become the standard modes of communication. In traditional systems, users must use a variety of devices – phone, facsimile, and computer – to receive or send all their messages. In addition, the number of received and sent messages is growing rapidly. A Gallup poll from 1997 [10] reported that an average office worker gets 178 messages a day. Today, this number must be much higher.

Unified messaging systems are designed to solve this problem, both in small and large organizations. They provide a new approach in storing, managing, retrieving, and distributing messages. Each subscriber has only one mailbox for all his/her messages. Messages in the mailbox can be viewed, listened to, stored, and retrieved by a personal computer, the telephone, or a pager, regardless of the form in which they were created. In addition, unified messaging services provide subscribers with an intelligent control over the reception and processing of the incoming messages. Figure 3 illustrates how messages can be sent and collected from the single mailbox in an advanced UM system.

In an UM system, the users can view documents or faxes, listen to voice messages, create new messages, and manage information in the way that works most productively for them. Therefore, one of the most important benefits of unified messaging is ***improved productivity***.

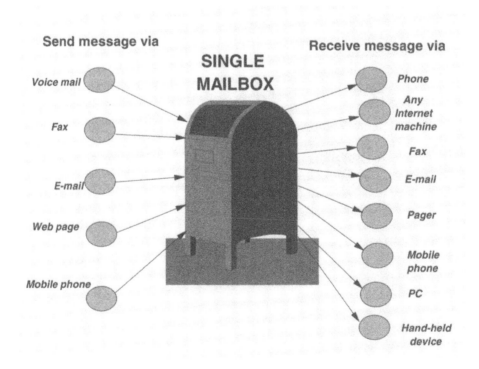

Figure 3. Single mailbox is the heart of unified messaging systems.
Methods how to send and receive messages.

Figure 4 illustrates the screen from Lucent's Octel Unified Messenger, on which different type of messages (e-mail, voice, and fax) are presented to the user on a single screen.

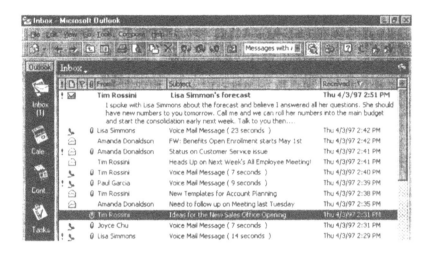

Figure 4. User's screen – example from Lucent's Octel Unified Messenger.

According to the Report from Lucent-Microsoft roundtable on unified messaging, held in Boston on September 9, 1998, the customer organizations that have deployed UM felt that the key benefit is that employees are better connected and comfortable with the UMS. These companies also indicated that UM has brought a positive change in culture within their organizations. In addition, unified messaging has improved internal and external communications among employees.

A study performed by PulsePoint Communications indicates that the most direct unified messaging saving derives from *use of the Internet telephony* instead of long distance for sending and retrieving voice and fax messages [9]. In addition, UM eliminates extra phone lines for fax or answering voice messages.

For the whole enterprise, a unified messaging system allows the company to *streamline communication administration, maintain security of company's messaging directories, simplify networking connections, and reduce communication and administration costs.* Network administrators can also work from a single screen – setting up e-mail, voice, and fax messaging capabilities.

The unified messaging systems also break the geographical chains. They assign an address to a person, not a location like in conventional telephone systems. As a consequence, the message can be routed to the subscriber regardless of his/her location.

In summary, the benefits of unified messaging systems are tremendous and it is obvious that over the next several years a number of large enterprises and medium- and small-size corporations will upgrade their traditional systems to unified messaging systems.

2. TECHNOLOGIES FOR UNIFIED MESSAGING

2.1 KEY COMPONENTS OF UM SYSTEMS

The unified messaging system is based on a single universal mailbox (UMB) for all messages. The universal mailbox (or universal message box, or universal in-box) is the heart and the main component of an UM system. However, according to Zimmer [12], there are the other three key components of future, advanced UM systems: intelligent post office, intelligent network, and intelligent services, as shown in Figure 5.

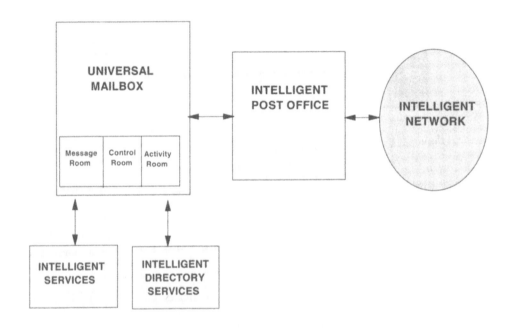

Figure 5. Key components of an advanced UM system [12].

The universal mailbox allows the user to receive all messages of different types from one location. A variety of interface devices can be connected to the single UMB (as illustrated in Figure 4), such as telephone, fax machine, PC, pager, mobile phone, or hand-held device. The single access interface provides additional functionality in creating new messages, referred to as *cross messaging*. Cross-messaging enables a message created by the originator in one medium to be converted to another medium. For example, an e-mail text message can be retrieved from a phone using text-to-speech conversion. Or, text from a fax letter can be converted to speech using optical character reader technology.

In addition, a multimedia message may contain attachments in other media. For example, text e-mail could have video, voice, data, or fax files attached; a voice mail could arrive bundled with a fax message.

According to Zimmer, the universal mailbox can be broken into three sub-components, or three rooms: the message room, the control room, and the activity room. The message room handles all the messaging needs for the users. It stores the incoming messages and notifies the user of new messages. The message room handles all types of communication: voice, fax, e-mail, video, sound, and others.

The control room is comprised of controls that help the user in managing messages. The control room deals with personal directories, security and privacy of messages, and provides the user with other services such as news, stock, weather, information services, etc.

The activity room handles interactive services, such as access to public directories, various information services, such as on-line searches, on-line magazines, Internet and Web, and others.

Intelligent post office provides routing capabilities for messages. For example, according to the user's request, some messages can be routed directly to the user, while some other, less important messages, can be directed to an assistant.

Intelligent network has the main function to locate subscribers as they travel. For this purpose, it provides a single address for each subscriber for all communications.

Intelligent services are to be built on the top of unified messaging systems. First generation of services includes business-to-business activities and consumer services, such as customized newspapers, electronic shopping, and others.

2.2 ARCHITECTURAL APPROACHES TO UNIFIED MESSAGING

As we discussed in Section 1, there are two main approaches in implementing unified messaging: integrated messaging and true unified messaging. In integrated messaging, a single logical mailbox is presented to the user, however in reality there are multiple mailboxes on one or several servers. In true unified messaging, all messages are stored in a single mailbox.

From the user's point of view, these two approaches may look similar. However, there are significant differences that affect the design and operation of the system.

From the commercial point of view, integrated messaging approach looks more appealing, because of the needs to preserve existing infrastructure – large number of e-mail and voice mail systems are already installed. The unified messaging approach usually requires a new infrastructure, but, on the other hand, it is more flexible and easier to design and operate.

There are several architectural approaches in designing integrated and unified messaging systems [9, 26]:

- Separate clients/separate servers architecture
- Single proprietary client/separate servers architecture
- Universal access messaging
- Integrated messaging architecture
- Unified messaging architecture

Separate clients/separate servers architecture, shown in Figure 6a, allows visual access for voice and fax messages on the user's PC. This approach is proposed by voice mail vendors several years ago to give users a way to easily view their voice and fax messages using a PC-based graphical interface similar to interfaces used to view and menage e-mail messages. This architecture is also referred to as *integrated desktop architecture*.

This approach allows a low cost upgrade to an existing voice mail system, however it does not unify e-mail and voice mail into a single architecture. As a consequence, multiple systems must be managed and administrated separately. Most voice mail vendors today offer a product built on this approach.

Single proprietary client/separate servers architecture, comprises a single client that integrates all media, but the servers are separated, as illustrated in Figure 6b. There is no interaction between the message store servers, since the integration is done at the client level. The PC client is connected to both servers, and appears to the user that there is a single mailbox. This approach, supported by PBX companies, relies on a specialized PC application that controls the desktop telephone and displays voice mail and e-mail messages in a single application. For the user, this approach offers a single view of all messages as well as the ability to access advanced PBX features, such as transferring and forwarding calls. However, this approach does not unify e-mail and voice mail systems. It requires separate systems, separate directories, and separate administration. This approach is sometimes referred as to *integrated client architecture* and is supported by PBX vendors, such as Nortel.

Universal access messaging architecture is based on "one access" rather than "one mailbox" approach, as illustrated in Figure 6c. This approach assumes multiple mailboxes for each type of messages, however the user can access all mailboxes with a single device – this is why this architecture is referred to as one access messaging. This approach does not require changes in the existing message infrastructure. Logica supports this approach, and the device that provides universal access to various mailboxes could be a digital mobile phone.

Integrated messaging architecture consists of separate voice and e-mail networks, but provides a bridge between the two networks. It appears to the user as one mailbox. The voice mail system is connected to the LAN, and specialized synchronization software, which runs on each e-mail server, routes and controls message traffic between these two messaging systems, as illustrated in Figure 6d. The message systems are separate

Integrated messaging architecture uses the e-mail interface to display all messages – voice, fax, and e-mail. However, the messages continue to be stored in separate voice and e-mail systems. System administrators continue to support and maintain two different networks, mailboxes, and directories. Forwarding messages back and forth across the LAN may generate a significant amount of background traffic on the network. Active Voice and AVT support this approach.

Unified messaging architecture, shown in Figure 6e, uses a single, unified mailbox and a single directory for all messages. The voice/fax messages are taken from the voice mail server and moved to the common server, which holds e-mail messages. The user can receive the messages using computer or phone. System administration tasks are significantly reduced, because there is only need to support, configure, and maintain one messaging system. Lucent's Octel Unified Messenger supports this approach.

2.3 TECHNICAL CHARACTERISTICS OF UM SYSTEMS

There are a number of technical issues to be considered when evaluating technical characteristics of commercial UM systems. These issues, listed in Table 3, are discussed next.

2.3.1 Centralized Versus Distributed UM Architecture
A very important architectural issue in designing or implementing a unified messaging system is choice between centralized and distributed server architecture.

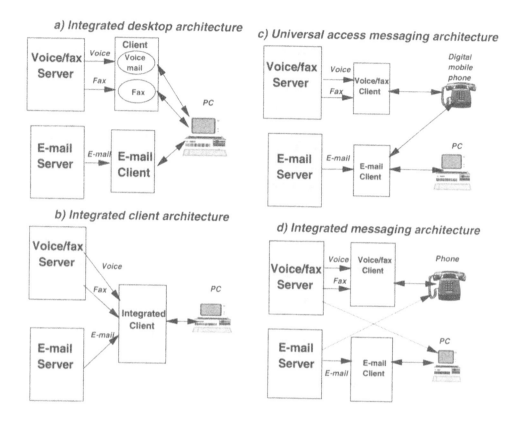

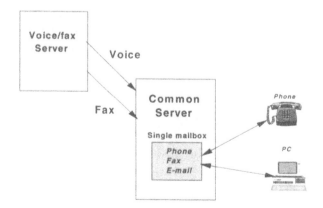

Figure 6. Various architectural approaches in integrated and unified messaging.

In a centralized architecture, a single server is used to store all messages of different media types. The centralized architecture provides simple administration, and there is no issues related to replicating and synchronizing information on different servers. However, the centralized system, based on one server, may cause a complete communication blackout if a hardware problem occurs. Lucent's Octel Unified Messenger, described in detail in Section 4, applies centralized server architecture.

Table 3. Technical Issues in Designing and Implementing
Unified Messaging Systems

TECHNICAL ISSUES
Distributed versus centralized architecture
Open versus proprietary systems
System scalability
IP-based versus PSTN-based systems
Fault-tolerant UM systems
UM systems for different size networks
Ability to integrate the system with existing messaging systems

The distributed architecture is based on separate servers each handling a particular type of media. In such system, if one of the system fails (for example voice mail system), the user can still receive other media types – in this case faxes and e-mail. Nortel's Symposium Messenger uses a distributed server architecture.

2.3.2 Open UM Systems versus Proprietary UM Systems
All participants in our survey have agreed that the standards play a crucial role in selecting and implementing UM systems. An open UM architecture is built on industry standards and facilitates the integration of components from a variety of vendors. In contrast, proprietary systems require purchases from specific vendors and don't allow the flexibility to swap components based on economic factors.

One of the main issues in implementing UM systems is the integration of existing e-mail and voice mail systems. For a service provider offering unified services, the coexistence and interoperation of a variety of telephony and computer systems is necessity. An e-mail message may consist of a number of different types of messages (text, voice, and video), and therefore it heavily depends on standards, such as SMTP and MIME (see Section 3). These standards assure the interoperability among different components of the e-mail message.

However, commercial voice message systems are usually proprietary – they use proprietary hardware, protocols, and data formats and they are designed to interact only with the same type of systems.

Therefore, the developers and integrators of UM systems must include formats and media conversation facilities to ensure proper handling and interoperability of all messages [7]. For example, a voice message must be converted in the appropriate audio format in order to be presented in an e-mail client. In addition, complex synchronization mechanisms are needed to ensure the consistency of the various mailboxes involved.

In order to resolve these interoperability problems, the Electronic Message Association has launched VPIM initiative – the Voice Presence for Internet Mail [8]. The issues addressed by VPIM include the use of SMTP and MIME to transport messages across systems and the ability to exchange messages with e-mail systems. VPIM also addresses issues related to integration of voice and non-voice mail systems.

In summary, open UM systems are based on industry standards and an open API (Application Programming Interface) for interconnections. Proprietary UM systems use proprietary hardware and are not based on standards.

2.3.3 IP-Based Versus PSTN-Based UM Systems

In a typical unified messaging system both worlds, the telephone word and the computer world, are connected. The voice messages and the faxes are sent and received through the conventional phone long distance network, sometimes referred to as Public Switched Telephone Network (PSTN). All messages (voice messages, faxes, and e-email messages) are then collected on a single unified messaging server. The UM server contains a voice board that translates analog to digital voice messages and vice versa. This system, shown in Figure 7, is referred to as the PSTN-based UM system.

All members of the expert panel agreed that the Internet is getting more and more important for unified messaging. Possible benefits of the Internet for the UM systems include:

- The Internet can be used as a universal interface
- The Internet can be used for message retrieval via Web browsers
- The Internet can be used for quickly subscribing for the unified messaging service through the Web.

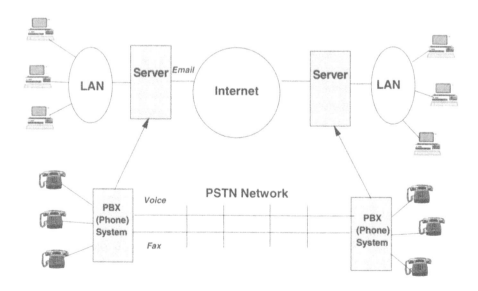

Figure 7. The PSTN-based UM system. The phone network is used for sending voice messages and faxes, while the Internet is used for sending e-mail messages.

The UM systems may use the Internet not only for sending e-mail messages, but also for voice messages and faxes – the Internet becomes a universal interface for all messages. In such system, referred as the Internet-based UM system, the Internet telephony is used instead of long distance phone network for sending and retrieving voice messages and faxes. Besides saving in long distance charges, this approach eliminates additional phone lines for fax and answering voice messages.

In an Internet-based system, shown in Figure 8, telephone messages and faxes are sent from one UM server to another over the Internet. An example of commercial system that uses this approach is CallWare's Viewpoint UM system.

The Internet has another important function in UM systems. It can provide remote access to the UM server and to all messages stored in the user's mailbox. A Web browser provides the access to the messages. This functionality can be very beneficial for mobile users, who can retrieve and send their messages from the hotel or airport using a public computer, a laptop, or a hand-held device.

Finally, the Internet can be used for quickly subscribing for the UM services through the Web.

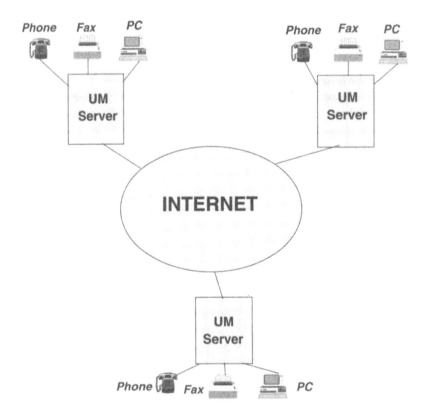

Figure 8. The Internet-based UM system.
The voice messages and faxes are sent over the Internet.

2.3.4. Fault Tolerance Issues in UM Systems

An important issue in true unified messaging systems is fault tolerance. A non-fault tolerant UM system is based on one server with a single mailbox. In this centralized-managed system, voice messages and incoming faxes are stored directly into the server's message database – a single mailbox, as illustrated in Figure 9a. In this system, if the server goes down, the complete communication system will crash. The faxes will get lost and the callers will not be able to leave voice messages.

Therefore, contemporary UM systems must embed fault tolerance in their designs. One of the possible solutions, applied by Interactive Intelligence (see Section 4), is based on a connector process, as shown in Figure 9b [32]. The connector process resides between the main server and the processes that collect and send voice messages and faxes. The connector process creates copies of all voice messages and faxes, creates and manages the queuing of incoming voice messages and faxes, and sends them to the server's message store. In order to provide full fault tolerance, the connector process must run on a separate machine.

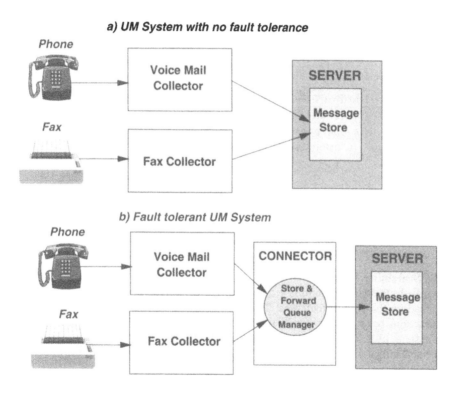

Figure 9. (a) The UM system with no fault tolerance. If the server goes down, all voice messages and faxes will be lost. (b) The fault tolerant UM system. Connecting process, which runs on a separate machine, receives and collects voice messages and faxes.

In this fault-tolerant UM system, if the main message server goes down, the connector process will continue receiving and collecting the voice messages and faxes. When the message server comes back up, the queued voice messages and faxes will be sent to the server's message store, and therefore it will be no data loss.

This approach provides a high degree of fault tolerance. It also allows greater scalability, since the rate at which new voice messages and faxes arrive is no longer depend on the rate at which the server can receive them.

When designing or purchasing a contemporary UM system, the goal should be to eliminate any hardware related single point of failure as well as provide a manageable, well performing, supportable, and reliable software system [34].

Hardware related single point of failure can be eliminated by incorporating (a) RAID disks, (b) hot swap power supplies, (c) clustered servers, (d) dual networks, and (e) multiple Internet service providers and switch links, as illustrated in Table 4.

Reliable and manageable software can be achieved by using (a) active system monitors, (such as HP OpenView, Java or SNMP monitors), (b) redundant processes, (c) autostart and scaleable process within a single server and across multiple servers, (d) performance monitoring capabilities for optimum performance tuning, and (e) lodging capabilities for security.

Table 4. Hardware and Software Techniques to Achieve Reliable,
Fault Tolerant UM Systems

Hardware Techniques	Software Techniques
RAID disks	Active system monitors
Hot swap power supplies	Redundant processes
Clustered servers	Austostart and scalable process within a single server and across multiple servers
Dual networks	Performance monitoring capabilities
Multiple Internet service providers and switch links	Lodging capabilities for security

2.3.5 Scalability Issues
A unified messaging system is scalable, if it is capable to continue performing adequately as the load on the system increases. The most common measures of load are: (a) data size, (b) transactions per second, (c) calls processed per second, and (d) the number of active users in the system. [30]. The main question is when the system bottleneck is reached, does the system have scalability beyond this point? These bottlenecks can occur at three places: (a) network (Internet or internal network), (b) processing (voice, fax, and data processing boards or system processors), and (c) storage.

Scalability is a very critical issue, because software systems that work at one level of demand or size may not work equally well as that demand or size increases. For a service provider, this may mean having to limit the number of users in the system, perform expensive upgrades to expand proprietary systems, or let the quality of the services they provide deteriorate.

Unix systems can use cluster systems that provide failover and in some cases load sharing capabilities. Unix-based UM systems can take advantage of scaleable servers that employ symmetrical multiprocessors and multiple memory backplanes.

2.4 ENABLING TECHNOLOGIES FOR UM SYSTEMS

The main technological component of a unified messaging system is a Universal Communication Server (UCS). The USC provides and manage live communications (such as phone calls, phone conferences, Internet access, Internet calls and conferences), as well as all messages including voice mail, e-mail, and faxes, as described in [33].

The USC is typically located at the edge where the Internet and telephone networks come together, as illustrated in Figure 10. When located at the edge, the UCS can provide both telephone and Internet based services, and seamlessly connect these services together. The basic requirements of an UCS can be divided into the following groups: (a) media connectivity and conversion, (b) application services, (c) storage and indexing, (d) scalability and reliability, and (e) configuration and management [33].

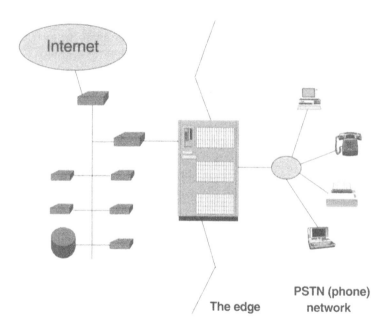

Figure 10. The Universal Communication Sever is located at the edge between the Internet and telephone networks.

Regarding to media connectivity and conversion, a contemporary UCS typically provides the following ports: ISDN digital phone ports, Ethernet IP ports, and WAN IP ports, as well as provides support for voice, fax and modem calls, and voice, image, and fax conversion.

Application services of the UCS include telephony, e-mail, and Web-based services. Storage and indexing functions include message storage and indexing, account information, and directory and PIM data access.

Regarding to scalability and reliability requirements, the UCS provides modular distribution, performs load balancing, and supports automatic fail over and self-healing functions.

Configuration and management functions of the UCS include IP configuration, PSTN configuration, application configuration, account configuration, and universal system management.

The current technology assumes that the UCS is designed based entirely on Internet standards and that should include SNMP and Java-based management tools. It should integrate with existing mail servers, telephony gateways, and networks. It should support traditional voice and fax, IP voice and fax, paging, and V.34/V.80 modem connectivity.

The USC should also allow software-based DSP function modules to be added at any time in order to support new connection or conversion types. The USC should allow software-based service modules from different vendors to run on the same hardware at the same time, receiving incoming calls, e-mail and Web requests as appropriate. The USC should be scalable from dozens to tens of thousands of ports.

One of the main requirements for the unified messaging to become effective and accepted by the users is the ability to perform content conversation from one medium to another medium – this is referred to as cross-messaging [10]. With content conversation, the users using a phone to access their mailboxes can read e-mail messages via text-to-speech conversation, or can send them via fax to a fax machine.

The current content conversation technologies allow the originator to create the message in one medium, and this message can be later converted to another medium. The following content conversation functions are feasible today and are implemented in some commercial UM systems:

- E-mail text message converted to voice in order to be retrieved by a phone
- Text from fax read by an optical character reader and converted to text or speech
- Voice mail converted to text
- Speech recognition
- Various media to fax conversation.

All these enabling technologies are available today and related products are offered by a number of companies.

With the speech recognition facilities the user can remotely over the phone manipulate and manage his/her messages. The typical voice commands include: Read, Repeat, Save, File, Acknowledge, or Forward any message received.

At the Lucent-Microsoft executive roundtable on unified messaging [29], those users who already used text-to-speech retrieval UM systems indicated that there are still problems with this technology, particularly in the following areas:

- Poor voice quality of the text to speech conversation,
- Difficulty of having to step sequentially through messages, and
- Difficulties in dealing with messages that have attachments.

2.5 ACCESS TECHNOLOGIES TO UNIFIED MESSAGING

From user's point of view, the main goal of unified messaging systems is to simplify the process of generating, accessing, and managing messages. There are four types of accesses associated with unified messaging systems: (a) desktop access, (b) phone/fax access, (c) Internet access, and (d) wireless access.

Desktop access allows access to unified messages (voice, fax, and e-mail) from desktop computers using enhanced e-mail clients. Message filtering, sorting, and prioritization are important features for desktop access.

Phone/fax access allows remote access in situations when computers are not available. Users have the ability to review a message list and select specific messages for playback from a remote phone. Voice mail messages are played back exactly as they were recorded, while e-mail messages can be played back using a text-to-speech conversion system. Besides message review, users may have limited message management options. They may remove messages from the mailbox or reply to e-mail messages with voice messages that are delivered as e-mail.

Internet access allows mobile users with a laptop or with access to a public computer (in a hotel or airport) to review and manipulate messages in their mailboxes through a Web browser. The functionality provided by Web-based clients includes the ability to retrieve, review, delete, and forward messages.

Wireless access allows mobile users with hand-held devices and cellular phones to access and manipulate their messages. Speech recognition technology plays a crucial role in wireless access allowing hands free operation.

2.6 OTHER FEATURES OF UM SYSTEMS

There are a number of other appealing features of UM systems, listed in Table 5. Some of these features are described next.

Table 5. Other Appealing Features of UM Systems

OTHER FEATURES OF UM SYSTEMS
Real-time features
Cross-messaging features
Confidentiality of fax messages
The ability to save and archive all messages
The ability to redirect all messages with a single mouse click
The ability to process messages
The ability to be notified
Intelligent agents for UM systems

Real-time features of UM systems include:

- Real time conformation of fax delivery
- Real time confirmation of email delivery
- Notification of incoming calls with caller ID
- Notification of incoming calls with caller profile

Cross-messaging enables a message created by the originator in one medium to be converted to another medium. Cross-messaging technologies have become more and more sophisticated and are presently important components of many commercial UM systems.

An important future trend is to integrate *intelligent agents* in UM systems. These intelligent agents will allow new, intelligent functions and enhanced services. They can be classified into the following groups [35]:

- Intelligent categorization of mail
- Intelligent notification process
- Automated mail routing
- Automated response management
- Automated broadcasting of messages

Intelligent categorization of mail can include a variety of criteria for categorization specified by the user. These criteria can be based on source, subject, size, content, and priority.

Intelligent notification process can include selected mail and the user can select the notification path. In addition, a number of different notification devices can be selected, such as pages, cellular phones, home/office phones, and desktop computers.

Automated mail routing can be based on source, subject, size, content, and priority. *Automated response management* includes automated greetings, which can be based on source, subject, size, content, and priority. Finally, *automated broadcasting of messages* can be based on source, destination, and subject of the messages.

In summary, the additional features preferred by the expert panel include: (i) the ability to be notified through a wireless device when important messages arrive, (ii) the ability to save and archive all messages, and (iii) the ability to process messages, e.g. reply as soon as they arrive instead of waiting to go back to the office or home.

3. STANDARDS FOR UNIFIED MESSAGING

Standards are clearly very important to customers, however, in the case of unified messaging the technology is still so relatively new that customers really don't know what standards to ask for and what they need fur future interoperability [29]. Vendors of unified messaging products and services are still free to test and experiment with new features and options, and they are not tied to any particular model of implementation including standards.

However, as the use of unified messaging becomes more pervasive, vendors will be increasingly pressured to demonstrate to customers that their products can inter-operate with a large variety of products and technologies on the market, which also means that they confirm with industry standards. According to the expert panel survey (see Appendix A), standards will play a big role in selecting UM systems.

According to [33], both service providers and customers need unified messaging standards. Service providers need unified messaging standards to:

- Allow new products and services to integrate with old ones,
- Allow all services to me managed with the same tools, and
- Make services more attractive to customers.

Customers need unified messaging standards to:

- Allow new products and services to integrate with old ones, including products and services from different vendors and providers,
- Use their personal favorite clients with new services, and

• Use new services without installing new clients.

Standards are mostly needed between building blocks of a unified messaging system. The building blocks of unified messaging systems include client software (in e-mail clients, Internet clients, and Web browsers) and various servers in the system (edge, application, and back-end servers).

In this section, we briefly introduce a variety of standards, which, in our opinion, will play important role in unified messaging systems. We also describe in detail a few standards, which according to our expert panel, will be crucial for the future of unified messaging. We also introduce Microsoft Exchange Server, which has become the server of choice for a number of unified messaging systems – therefore it has been de facto standard for UM servers.

Table 6 gives an overview of a variety of standards that can be applied in unified messaging.

Table 6. Standards for Unified Messaging

STANDARD	TYPE OF INTERFACE	BRIEF DESCRIPTION
POP3	Client-server	Used to retrieve messages from the application or back server
IMAP	Client-server	Used to retrieve, move, search, and flag messages
ESMTP	Client-server	Used to send voice, fax, and video
SMTP	Server-server	Defines the exchange of information among a large class of e-mail servers
MIME	Server-server	Defines the exchange messages, which are non-textual objects
VPIM	Client-server	Defines the exchange of voice and fax messages between voice mail systems
LDAP	Application	Standard directory access protocol
ACAP	Application	Standard user account and configuration protocol
H.323	Multimedia communications	Defines multimedia communications services in a packet-switched network (LANs, WANs, Internet)
MAPI	Internet fax client	Used to send fax as e-mail message

3.1 MICROSOFT EXCHANGE SERVER

An e-mail server is the central component of a unified messaging system. It contains unified mailboxes and supports basic administration functions. All messages, including voice mail, fax, and e-mail, are all stored as e-mail messages. An e-mail server must support POP3 and/or IMAP4 standards.

Today, 96% of Fortune 50 corporations have already standardized on one e-mail system, versus only 4% that are either currently evaluating message platforms or have chosen a platform, but have not started the deployment phase (Source: Microsoft Exchange Server).

Microsoft Exchange Server has emerged as the leading messaging platform within Fortune 50 corporations - 52% of Fortune 50 have already standardized to Microsoft Exchange. Lotus

Notes is the second most popular platform with 24% of the Fortune 50 choosing is as the preferred messaging system. The other messaging systems include HP OpenMail, Netscape, and others, as illustrated in Figure 11.

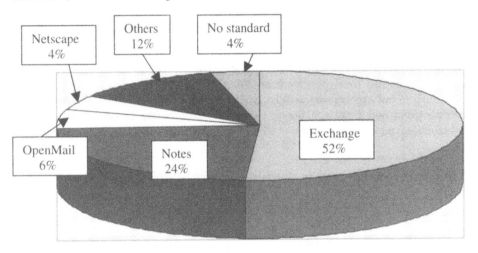

Figure 11. Most popular messaging systems within Fortune 50 corporations.

The Microsoft Exchange Server, used by several UM vendors including Lucent Technologies Octel Unified Messenger, was designed for both voice and data. It features high scalability to support thousands of users per server and tens of thousands of users in a single enterprise. It provides very high performance and implements Internet standards.

The Microsoft Exchange Server also provides high availability and fault tolerance through supporting clustering approach. It also provides high reliability with transaction-based store to ensure message delivery. Finally, it also features high security assured by single Exchange and Windows NT logon, password expiration, and support for the latest encryption standards.

The Microsoft Exchange Server supports a number of standards, such as SMTP, POP3, IMAP, LDAP, and HTTP.

3.2 CLIENT-SERVER INTERFACE STANDARDS

This section briefly presents two standard protocols for client-server exchange of messages: POP3 and IMAP.

3.2.1 POP3
The Post Office Protocol – Version 3 (POP3) is supported by a majority of present commercial e-mail servers. The goals of POP3 are:

1. To minimize resource requirements on the server by supplying only very simple access methods to messages stored in the user's mailbox.
2. To minimize implementation complexity on the client by supplying only the smallest sufficient functionality for the majority of environments.

It is designed as an asynchronous (off-line) remote message access and manipulation mechanism [7]. The user maintains a mailbox in a remote server that provides the store-and-forward capabilities needed to send and receive messages. At the request of the user, a Pop3-enabled e-mail reader connects to the POP3 server, identifies the users, and copies messages to the local machine. Once in the local machine, messages are processed and manipulated only by the e-mail client.

POP3 operates over TCP connections. A POP session consists of three parts:

- Authorization
- Transaction
- Release and update.

The server receives the commands from the clients, which consist of a keyword and zero or more arguments. During the authorization state, the server validates the user's identity via USER and PASS commands. If the authorization is successful, the session continues with the transaction state, during which any combination of commands can be issued. The following list comprises possible commands:

STAT – list the number of messages in the mailbox
LIST n – provides information about n-th message
RETR n – retrieves the n-th message
DELE n – marks the n-th message as deleted
NOOP – has no actions (used to verify the state of the server)
RSET n – marks the n-th message as unread
QUIT – ends the session.

Following the QUIT command, the server enters the update state, where it removes all messages marked as read, releases the mailbox lock, and releases the TCP connection.

POP3 has several drawbacks that typically fall into two areas:

- Inefficient use of the network
- Inability to support decentralized operations.

Although POP3 is highly optimized for efficient implementations on host systems, its use of the network is not optimal with respect to latency. The typical POP session consists of at least 4+2N round-trip interactions, where N is the number of messages retrieved. This includes three round-trips to exchange greetings, one round-trip interaction to release the session, and two round-trips for each message [1].

POP3 also limits access to a single mailbox during any given session. However, some users may decide to utilize multiple machines to process their mail. POP model of centralized operations, in which all processing is done on a single client, is not adequate for these operations.

Additional drawback is that POP3 clients must download messages to the local machine before they are available for reading. In addition, POP3 does not recognize differences in the structure of the messages. In particular, it does not provide information on whether a particular message contains attachments or not.

3.2.2 IMAP
The Internet Message Access Protocol (IMAP) is more advanced than POP3 as a client-server interface protocol. The key feature of the current version of IMAP protocol, called IMAP4, is the ability to manipulate messages stored in a remote e-mail server. Like POP3, IMAP4 can

operate in off-line mode, in which e-mail client connects to the server and copies the messages to the local machine. However, it also supports on-line and disconnected modes.

In on-line mode, messages remain stored in the server and can be accessed from multiple e-mail readers. For example, a user can read the same mailbox from the office, home, or a remote Web browser without worrying about leaving messages copies in the server and the local machines.

Other features of IMAP4 include its ability to allow concurrent access to a mailbox, support multiple mailboxes, and use system-defined and user-defined flags.

IMAP session consists of four parts:

1. Exchange greetings
2. Select and manage a mailbox
3. Manage and process messages
4. Release the session.

IMAP has a considerably richer command set than POP.

3.3 INTERNET STANDARDS

The Internet is definitely becoming more and more important for unified messaging. Two established Internet standards that allow exchange information among e-mail servers are SMTP and MIME. VPIM initiative is a new effort to establish an Internet standard for exchanging voice mail and fax messages between e-mail servers.

3.3.1 SMTP
The Simple Mail Transfer Protocol (SMTP) defines the specification for establishing connections and messages exchange among e-mail servers on the Internet. It operates over TCP connections and it is strictly mail transport protocol that does not describe the structure of the mailboxes.

SMTP is characterized by a set of text commands interpreted by the e-mail servers involved in a transaction. A single SMTP transaction consists of three steps:

1. First, the sending host issues a MAIL command that includes the identity of the sender and the reverse path that is used to report errors.
2. Then, a series of RCPT commands are sent, each of which identifies a message recipient.
3. Transaction begins with a DATA command, followed by one or more fixed-length text lines containing the message.

The SMTP is limited for exchanging textual information.

3.3.2 MIME
The Multipurpose Internet Mail Extensions (MIME) standard was designed to overcome the limitation of SMTP and to enable the exchange of non-textual objects including:

- Textual message bodies in character sets other than ASCII,
- An extensible set of different formats for non-textual message bodies,
- Multi-part message bodies, and
- Textual header information in character sets other than ASCII.

The basic idea in MIME is the structuring of the message into multiple components and parts, each of which can be encoded and processed separately. MIME protocol includes type descriptors, which define media type and subtype identifiers. Type descriptors define the general class of data, such as text, image, audio, video, etc.), while subtype identifier specifies the characteristics of the media, typically its format (JPEG, GIF, MPEG, AVI, etc.).

3.3.3 VPIM

The Voice Presence for Internet Mail (VPIM) is the initiative, launched by the Electronic Messaging Association, with the goal to establish a standard for the exchange of voice and fax messages between voice mail systems over the Internet [8]. The VPIM specification [28] is a proposed standard and has been submitted to the Internet Engineering Task Force (IETF), which is the governing body for Internet standards.

VPIM includes basic messaging capabilities of creating, forwarding, and replying to voice and fax messages over any TCP/IP network. VPIM is strictly a server-to-server protocol that does not include the interaction between voice mail systems and their clients. It includes the use of SMTP and MIME to transport messages across systems. VPIM also provides the exchange of messages with e-mail systems. This is enabled through format transformation functions and advanced directory servers that provide the address lookup and routing services needed to deliver the message to the appropriate mailbox.

The deployment of VPIM is likely to be gradual. According to Elliot [8], the companies will first use VPIM gateways to connect existing internal voice mail systems together, then perhaps to link them more tightly with remote sites, mobile workers, and trading partners.

Figure 12 illustrates how existing voice mail systems and networks will connect to TCP/IP Intranets or to the Internet via VPIM gateways on SMTP hosts. These gateways consist of software modules or adjunct standalone systems. Figure 12 also shows new voice messaging systems, which will include native VPIM and SMTP routing of VPIM messages, and will support directory address lookup. E-mail and other client-server applications can support VPIM-based MIME constructs in the same way they currently support other MIME parts.

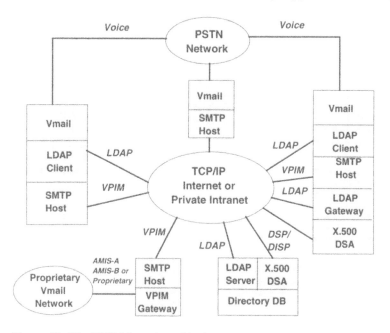

Figure 12. The VPIM-based world of voice mail systems and networks.

Nearly all major messaging vendors are supporting the VPIM standard. Many UM vendors Nortel, Lucent, Centigram, AVT and others, have committed to developing VPIM compliant networking products.

Because VPIM uses the Internet as the backbone for transmission of the voice and fax messages, this has strong benefits in the area of cost savings. By using the Internet for the routing of the network traffic, separate and dedicated digital lines between systems do not need to be purchased, installed, and managed. In this case, the Internet provides the pipe, and VPIM defines the communication structure for the networked messages.

4. UNIFIED MESSAGING VENDORS AND PRODUCTS

There are many vendors who offer unified messaging products and services. Table 7 presents the selected ten UM vendors and their basic products and characteristics.

Table 7. Overview of UM Vendors and Their Products.

VENDOR	UM PRODUCT	BASIC CHARACTERISTICS
Lucent Technologies	Octel Unified Messenger	• Based on Microsoft Exchange client/server architecture • Single mailbox for all messages
Interactive Intelligence	Enterprise Interaction Center	• Distributed client/server architecture running on Windows NT servers
Mediagate	iPOST	• Distributed architecture based on three communication servers • Single mailbox for all messages
Big Sky	Unified Messaging Assistant	• Supports Internet-based and Notes-based architectures • Voice server for Windows NT
Applied Voice Technology (AVT)	CallXpress	• Runs on Windows NT server
Amteva	Unified Messaging Plus	• Internet-based architecture • Based on an access server and Unix systems
Active Voice	ViewMail	• Runs on Microsoft Exchange server • Uses voice server for voice messages
Centigram	OneView	• Runs on PC Window desktop
CallWare	CallWare Unified Messenger	• Runs on Novel GroupWise and Microsoft Exchange • Based on either Netware or NT server
Ericsson	UMS 8000	• Wireless UM system • Based on Unix and Windows NT operating environments

In this section we present two unified messaging vendors and their products and services – Octel Unified Messenger and Interactive Intelligence Unified Messaging system.

4.1 OCTEL UNIFIED MESSENGER

Lucent Technologies Octel Unified Messenger is currently the most popular UM product on the market. It runs on the Microsoft client/server messaging system, Microsoft Exchange

Server, described in Section 3.1. It is based on a scalable, open architecture and can support thousands of users.

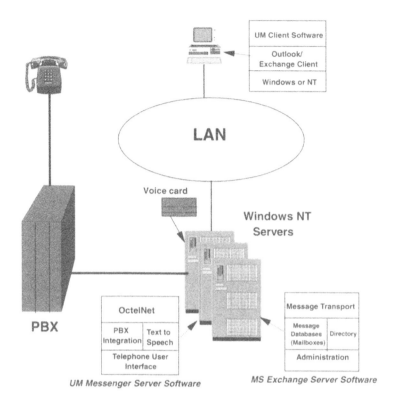

Figure 13. The architecture of the Lucent Technologies'
Octel unified messaging system.

The UM system consists of the following components, as shown in Figure 13 [26]:

- The Microsoft Exchange server,
- The Unified Message server,
- LAN and PBX components,
- Personal computer clients, and
- Exchange-compatible fax servers and gateways to outside networks and the Internet.

The Microsoft Exchange Server is a powerful, high-performance e-mail system that serves as the repository for all user messages (see Figure 14).

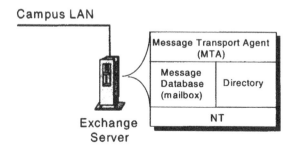

Figure 14. Microsoft Exchange Server and its software components.

Each Exchange server is also a high-performance LAN server. While a single Exchange server may contain the entire collection of Unified Messenger mailboxes in a workgroup, it typically acts as one of many Exchange servers and communicates with other Exchange servers on the local area network, on remote networks via WANs, and with other e-mail environments via the Internet. The Exchange Server contains the following components:

All user universal mailboxes.

Contents of all mailboxes. The contents consists of voice messages, e-mail messages, faxes, and other documents stored in the universal mailbox.

Directory. The Exchange directory manages addressing for the Exchange and the Unified Messenger system. Directory can also accommodate addressing for external destinations including fax numbers and e-mail addresses.

Message Transfer Agent (MTA). The MTA is the Exchange software that is used to transport messages between mailboxes and Exchange servers. It also replicates and replicates directories.

The Unified Message server software (Figure 15) runs on the Microsoft Windows NT server operating system. It serves as the integral connection between the LAN and the telephone network.

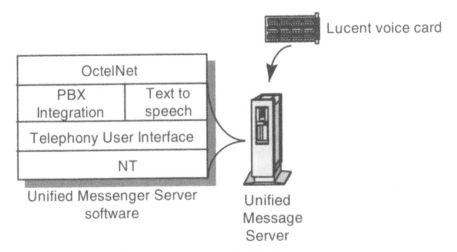

Figure 15. Software components of the Unified Message server.

The functions of the Unified Message server are to:

- Play and record voice messages
- Provide telephone answering services for individual users
- Compress audio messages in real time for storage on the Exchange server
- Retrieve audio messages from the Exchange server, decompress and play them in real time
- Interpret DTMF for mailbox manipulation and control
- Perform text-to-speech conversion for audio playback on text such as e-mail
- Exchange messages with users on existing Octel systems
- Forward incoming fax calls to an Exchange-compatible fax server
- Forward faxes and e-mail messages to an Exchange-compatible fax server for printing.

Figure 16 shows a typical user screen in the Lucent Unified Messenger system. Voice messages, stored on the Exchange Server, are available to any Exchange client software, such as Outlook. By clicking on the voice message icon, the message is retrieved from the user's mailbox on the Exchange server and staged for playback, as illustrated in Figure 17.

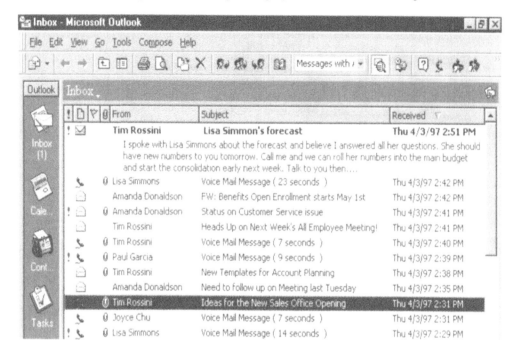

Figure 16. A typical screen of the Octel Unified Messenger.

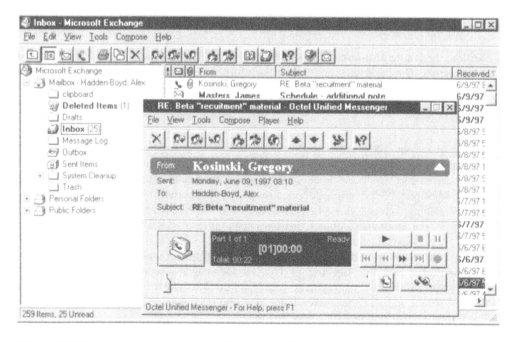

Figure 17. Voice messages are selected from the mailbox in the same way as e-mail messages.

Similarly, fax messages can be retrieved and presented on the screen, as illustrated in Figure 18.

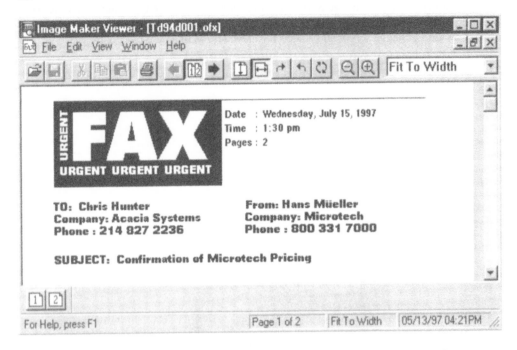

Figure 18. Fax messages are selected from the mailbox and presented on the PC screen.

Unified Messenger connections include both LAN interfaces and PBX integration. Exchange servers and Unified Message servers are high-end PC servers running Microsoft Windows NT and supporting standard LAN connections. Lucent voice processing cards, that contain digital signal processors (DSPs) to capture and compress voice data as well as to detect DTMF input, are located in the Unified Message server, as shown in Figure 15.

In addition, the Unified Message server includes a specialized connection to the PBX, called PBX integration. The PBX integration provides information about the calls as they are routed to the Unified Message server. The information includes who the call is originally intended for (called party), who placed the call (calling party), and what caused the call to be routed (no answer, busy).

According to Lucent study, the impact of the Unified Messenger on network traffic is not significant. Unified Messenger has an encoding rate of 32 Kbps, so for a 10 Mbps Ethernet LAN, one active port would use up about 0.4% of the bandwidth. This number is obtained by adding 32 Kbps plus 25% overhead divided by 10 Mbps. Similarly, 24 simultaneously active ports, all streaming data across the LAN, will use about 10% of the bandwidth capacity (24 x 0.4% = 9.6%). For more than 24 ports, there is a need for faster LAN of 100 Mbps.

The Octel UM system provides the interoperability with other Octel servers and systems as well as non-Octel systems. Because of Unified Messenger's support of OctelNet, Octel message server users can interoperate with Unified Messenger users. When a Unified Messenger system and an Octel server share the same telephone switch, some users want to configure their networking in such a way that the Unified Messenger system and Octel server operate like a single voice system. This can be achieved by using automatic mailbox forwarding, as illustrated in Figure 19.

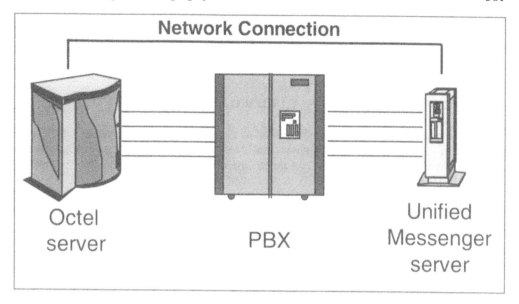

Figure 19. Messages received in the original mailbox on the Octel server are automatically forwarded to the mailbox on Unified Messenger over the network connection.

Unified Messenger users are notified of new messages through their PC client software.

With automatic mailbox forwarding, Octel message server users can continue to address messages to users on the Unified Messenger system the same way they address messages to the Octel server.

The interoperability with non-Octel users is achieved by implementing industry standards (see Section 3), including VPIM, SMTP and MIME.

The clients in the Octel UM system can be PCs or telephones. Client software resides on each client PC and it facilitates the sending and receiving of data between the client PC and the Exchange server. It also menages the display of all messages contained in the user's mailbox.

The telephone client can be used to record and listen to voice and e-mail messages. It also serves as an input device allowing the user to act on messages – reply to, forward, store, delete, print a fax, or request that an e-mail be faxed. E-mail messages are converted to speech through the text-to-speech feature. E-mail messages and attachments can also be converted to faxes for easy viewing.

In summary, Octel Unified Messenger is based on the Microsoft Exchange Server, which provides high scalability, high performance, high availability, high reliability, and high security. The UM system provides a single mailbox for all messages, including voice mail, e-mail, and fax. It allows users to access and manage all their messages from either a phone or a PC, anytime and from any place.

The system enables the reply to be in any medium of choice (voice, e-mail, or fax) regardless of the medium of the original message. The system allows users to store and organize voice and fax messages along with e-mail messages. E-mail and fax messages can be redirected from a phone or PC to any local printer or fax machine for printing.

For administration purposes, the Unified Messenger provides single point of administration and reduces cost by combining the administrative functions for voice and e-mail. In addition, centralized management allows administration from any Exchange site for the entire enterprise. Scalable architecture can support small and large sites and enables organizations to grow to hundred of thousands of users. The UM system can be integrated with most major PBX systems.

4.2 INTERACTIVE INTELLIGENCE UNIFIED MESSAGING SYSTEM

Interactive Intelligence created Interaction Mail as the unified messaging system, which is the part of their Enterprise Interaction Center (EIC) software product running on Windows NT servers. The EIC is a distributed client-server application designed to integrate seamlessly with the Internet and World Wide Web, as illustrated in Figure 20.

The Internet capabilities of the EIC include (Source: Technical Overview of EIC [46]):

- The ability to remotely retrieve all messages, including e-mail, voice mail, and faxes.
- The ability to remotely administer, configure, and monitor the EIC.
- The ability to remotely supervise business interactions.
- The ability to remotely run and view reports
- The ability to make long-distance calls over the Internet and to hold, transfer, and conference these calls just like regular long-distance calls.
- The ability to route faxes over the Internet.

The heart of EIC is multi-threaded event-processing engine capable of handling many different types of communication events – incoming and outgoing telephone calls, e-mail messages, faxes, digital and alphanumerical pages, etc, as shown in Figure 21.

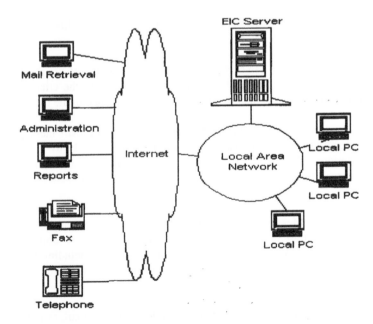

Figure 20. The Interactive Intelligence's unified messaging system is based on the EAC distributed client-server architecture.

The EIC can easily interface with popular e-mail systems, such as Microsoft Exchange and Lotus Notes, Web servers, such as Microsoft IIS, Netscape, and Apache, and database servers, including SQL Server, Oracle, Sybase, and Informix, on a corporate network. The EIC can also interface to PBX systems or communicate directly with the telephone network via analog, T1, and ISDN PRI trunks. Configuration of the system for unified messaging based on the EIC server is shown in Figure 22.

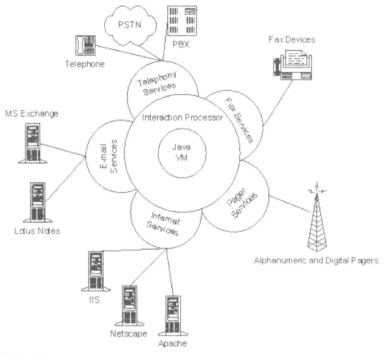

Figure 21. The EIC's Interaction Processor provides a single point of control for all communication events.

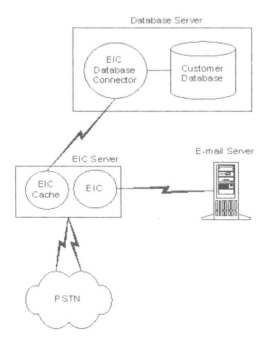

Figure 22. Configuration of unified messaging system based on the EIC server.

The system in Figure 22 consists of customer database, EIC database connector object, EIC cache object, and EIC server.

Customer database is a relational database stored on a high-capacity database server running one of the popular relational database systems (such as SQL Server, Oracle, Sybase, or Informix).

EIC database connector object (in the Microsoft DCOM format), located on the database server, handles communication with the customer database.

EIC cache object (also in Microsoft DCOM format), located on the EIC server, is used to cache information about a group of customers (e.g. 1-10,000 customers) for the unified messaging services to be provided to them.

EIC server is the server for the EIC applications and the EIC cache object. Incoming calls are routed to this server.

Microsoft Exchange or Lotus Notes mail server is where voice mail and faxes are stored. This makes it possible to provide access to these messages, as well as to e-mail messages, from a standard e-mail client (such as Microsoft Exchange or Outlook), or from a Web browser (e.g. Internet Explorer or Navigator).

PSTN trunks. Generally, several T1, E1, or ISDN PRI trunks are used to connect to the PSTN network. In some environments, it may be a PBX, which is located between the PSTN and the EIC server.

Interaction Mail is the software application for unified messaging, which allows users to access all their messages (e-mail messages, voice messages, and faxes) from a single mailbox (called "universal in-box) on their desktop PC. The screen capture in Figure 23 shows how Interaction Mail enables user's access to all types of messages.

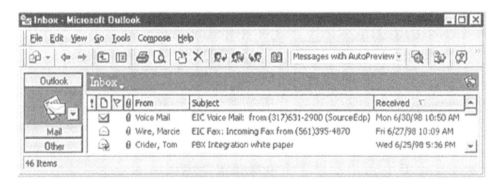

Figure 23. Interaction Mail allows users to retrieve all types of messages
(e-mail, voice, and faxes) from a universal in-box.

How the system works
In the following hypothetical example we will assume that a service provider offers unified messaging to 100,000 customers. The provider maintains a large database in which it keeps all its customer information. The system consists of ten EIC servers and five servers running Microsoft Exchange. Each EIC server is configured to handle 10,000 different customers. When EIC server 31 initializes, it downloads all the information it needs about customers 1-10,000 and keeps that information in its cache object. EIC server #2 does the same thing for

customers 10,001-20,000, and so on. Routing from the telephone company is set up so that the personal 800 numbers for customers 1-10,000 arrive on a set of twelve T1s, which are connected to EIC server #1. The personal 800 numbers for customers 10,001-20,000 arrive on a second set of twelve T1s, which are connected to EIC server #2, and so on.

When the call arrives from the PSTN over one of the twelve T1s connected to one of the EIC servers, the corresponding server answers the call and uses the dialed number to quickly look up customer information within the EIC cache object. It then plays the appropriate greeting and records the message from the caller. After compressing the message to 1K bytes per second, the appropriate EIC server sends it as an e-mail attachment into the pool of Microsoft Exchange servers where it is stored in the customer's mailbox.

If another caller sends a fax to the customer's personal 800 number, that call is too routed to the same EIC server, which recognizes the fax tones, captures the fax, and sends it to the Exchange server.

Sometime later, this customer calls in to retrieve his/her messages. He/she can either dial a special number or simply dial his/her personal 800 number. The EIC server can require the customer to enter a pass code or can be configured to recognize the number from which he/she is calling and drop him/her directly into the message retrieval part of the system. The system presents to the customer a menu of different options, which allows him/her to playback his/her voice mail messages or have his/her fax forwarded to his/her hotel. He/she can listen to e-mail messages using the system's text-to-speech capabilities.

EIC also offers a set of fax services for sending, receiving, viewing, and manipulating faxes without having to use a fax machine. The EIC server uses one or more Dialogic Gammalink fax boards for these applications. Users can access their faxes from an e-mail client, as illustrated in Figure 24. Users can also retrieve their faxes by phone and have them forwarded to a fax machine at a given phone number. The user can read a fax by using an optical character reader (OCR) or be converted to voice by text-to-speech conversation system.

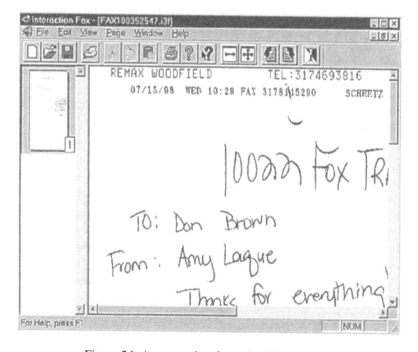

Figure 24. A screen shot from the EIC fax viewer.

Interaction mail uses a fault-tolerant approach by using a connector process. This process is located between Microsoft Exchange and the Interaction Mail processes, as presented in Figure 25. In order to provide full fault tolerance, it must run on a different machine than the one on which the Exchange Server runs. The functions of the connector processor are to creates local copies of voice messages and faxes, to handles the queuing of incoming voice messages and faxes, and to send queued messages into the Exchange message store.

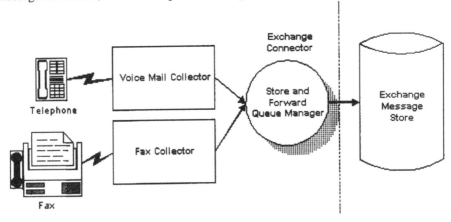

Figure 25. Exchange connector process, which runs on a different machine, provides fault tolerance.

If Exchange goes down, incoming voice messages and faxes are collected and queued. When Exchange comes back up, the queued voice messages and faxes are sent into the Exchange message store with no loss of data. Interaction mail can be integrated with most popular PBX systems (e.g. PBXs from Lucent, Nortel, Siemens, NEC, Mitel, and Ericsson). This is accomplished by using the Simplified Message Desk Interface (SMDI) protocol, as illustrated in Figure 26.

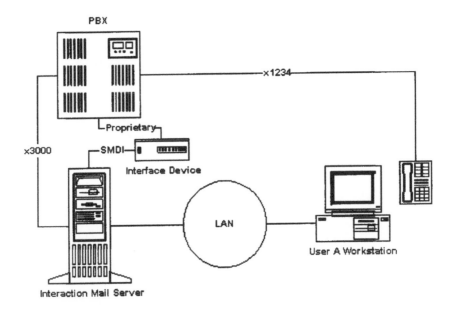

Figure 26. Integration of the EMS with popular PBX systems via SMDI protocol.

Interaction Mail can provide PBX users with integrated voice mail features without requiring any changes to the user's desktop. It provides cost-effective introduction of unified messaging into a legacy PBX environment.

5. CONCLUSIONS

Unified messaging is still in its infancy phase, but it is obvious that it will very soon enter the life of both consumer and business users. Unified messaging offers such a unique opportunity for improved productivity and long-term cost savings that it will definitely become a winning technology.

Generally, the electronic messaging perspective in the next Millenium [15]:

♦ Electronic messaging will continue to grow at phenomenal rates, as well as the Internet.
♦ Security will remain a very important issue. Digital signatures will become more prevalent.
♦ Messaging will become more sophisticated, and as such will become more of a business tool.
♦ Messaging management will become more important.
♦ Groupware or collaborative computing will be the next real infrastructure built on the messaging infrastructure.

The messaging industry started with *Call Answering*, and has moved to *Voice Messaging*, and it is currently moving to *Unified Messaging*. Many subscribers are using e-mail as a mainstream form of communication. They also use voice mail from their wireless service providers. Unified messaging provides users with access to respond to messages from a variety of networks from a single mailbox using any device.

What is the next step? One of the future trends is to provide users with flexibility to message however they like – to make messages configurable and highly personalized. This system incorporates the e-mail solution complemented with targeted telephony and Web user interfaces. This new concept is supported by PulsePoint Communications.

The vision of future unified messaging systems is that they will include a comprehensive solution, which will combine unified messaging services with other enhanced services. Such enhanced services may include call-initiation, access-control services, content and information services, and personal, time, and organization services [10]. Each new service should enhance and reinforce the benefits of other services.

There are several reasons these additional services will be necessary. The most important of these reasons is increased competition, which will increase the pressure to service providers to deliver more value to the customers. The enhanced mailbox and related services is one way to add value and differentiate one's service.

Another reason to focus on enhanced services is that public networks are converging.. Due to the growing demand for greater bandwidth, the public switched telephone network (PSTN) and packet networks are combining, making enhanced mailbox services easier to build. Finally, client devices are becoming more intelligent. Personal computers provide great power for telephony communications and even wireless handset and telephone devices are beginning to have intelligence built in [10].

In summary, unified messaging and the universal mailbox will evolve to become the primary relationship driver between service providers and subscribers [10]. The universal mailbox will become the centralized network account where all services are delivered and managed. These services will include:

♦ Message management
♦ Incoming call management
♦ Billing
♦ E-mail
♦ Information services
♦ Fax services
♦ Personal assistant services,
♦ and much more.

The universal mailbox will be accessible from any chosen device – from wireless and wireline telephones to fax machines and personal computers. The computer telephone integration will provide true communication independence enabling subscribers to access and manage all their communications and information from anywhere at any time.

The adoption of UM systems have already began. Many companies, specifically small and medium-size, have successfully deployed unified messaging systems. However, the major deployment of UM systems is expected in the beginning of the next decade (from year 2000 to 2003).

Many companies indicated that they may take as long as 2 to 3 years to migrate to the UM system. Clearly, the migration process is typically longer for large-size companies. Therefore, it is important that vendors offer the right level of business planning and technical support along with UM products and services in order to enable the successful planning and implementation of the new system (conclusion from Lucent-Microsoft Executive Roundtable).

As the use of unified messaging becomes more pervasive, vendors will be increasingly pressured to demonstrate to customers that their products can inter-operate seamlessly with a large variety of products and technologies on the market. As a consequence, unified messaging standards will play a critical role in selecting a unified messaging system.

In order to be effective, a unified messaging solution should satisfy three key requirements [10]:

♦ Message access must be device-independent. A single mailbox should store messages of different types: e-mail, voice, and fax messages. The UM system should provide access to these messages from a variety of devices include wireline and wireless telephones, personal computers, and other devices.

♦ Unified messaging system should have an ability to perform content conversion, which is essential to satisfy the requirement of device independence. With content conversion, users can access their e-mail messages using a telephone (voice recognition and text-to-speech conversion), or they can send voice mail via fax (speech-to-text conversion).

♦ Unified messaging requires server-based storage and administration of all messages. This requirement has been a major challenge for service providers and UM vendors.

In our final analysis, the following conclusions can be made:

User's Perspective
♦ The main benefits of unified messaging are improved productivity, time saving, and improved accessibility.
♦ The recommended migration path is from traditional messaging systems directly to unified messaging systems.
♦ CLECs and Internet service providers should be selected for outsourcing UM services to users.

Vendor's Perspective
♦ Current target markets for unified messaging are SOHOs, small-size and medium-size companies.
♦ Early users of unified messaging are mobile professionals and home office people.
♦ Users are typically not aware of unified messaging technologies.
♦ Unified messaging will take off in the period 2000 to 2003.
♦ The expected revenues in year 2003 from unified messaging products and services are in the range $1-$10 billions and the number of UM mailboxes is between 5 and 100 millions.
♦ The most important characteristics of UM vendors are technical features of their products and their support systems.
♦ The Internet is becoming more and more important for unified messaging.
♦ Standards play a big role in selecting unified messaging systems. Important UM standards are VPIM, IMAP, and SMTP.

Unified Messaging Products and Services
♦ The most important technical features of UM systems are that the system is using open protocols and standards, system scalability, and that the system is Internet-based.
♦ Cross messaging is important for unified messaging. The most important cross-messaging technology is text-to-speech conversation, which enables e-mail messages to be retrieved by phone.
♦ Fault-tolerant solutions are important for unified messaging.
♦ Wireless access to the unified mailbox through digital telephones and pagers is important for unified messaging.

References

1. M.T. Rose and D. Strom, *"Internet Messaging; From the Desktop to the Enterprise,"* Prentice Hall PTR, Upper Saddle River, NJ, 1998.
2. N.A. Cox, *"Handbook of Electronic Messaging,"* CRC Press, Boca Raton, FL, 1998.
3. *"The Internet and Telecommunications: Architectures, Technologies, and Business Development,"* International Engineering Consortium, Chicago, IL, 1998.
4. B. Furht, *"Handbook of Internet and Multimedia Systems and Applications,"* CRC Press, Boca Raton, FL, 1999.
5. E.C. Anderl, C.S. Batzel, G.S. Lamba, J.M. Leikness, and B.N. Sanakkayala, "An Enhanced Message Networking Topology: Multimedia Messaging with the Intuity Interchange Server," *Bell Labs Technical Journal,* Vol. 3, No. 2, April-June 1998, pp. 124-135.

6. T-Y. Hou, A. Pizano, and A. Hsu, "Multimedia Messaging Systems," chapter in the book Multimedia Tools and Application edited by B. Furht, *Kluwer Academic Publishers*, Norwell, MA, 1996.

7. A. Pizano and W.K. V. Su, "Multimedia Messaging Systems," chapter in the Handbook of Internet and Multimedia Systems and Applications, editor-in-chief B. Furht, *CRC Press*, Boca Raton, FL, 1999.

8. B. Elliot, "Unified Messaging: The VPIM Initiative," Business Communications Review, Vol. 27, No. 5, May 1997.

9. R. Grigonis, "Search of Unified Messaging," *Computer Telephony*, August 1998, pp. 44-79.

10. J. Schlueter, "Evolution of the Mailbox," in The Internet and Telecommunications: Architectures, Technologies, and Business Development, *International Engineering Consortium*, Chicago, IL, 1998, pp. 227-231.

11. R. Sum, "Unified Messaging," in The Internet and Telecommunications: Architectures, Technologies, and Business Development, *International Engineering Consortium*, Chicago, IL, 1998, pp. 223-225.

12. D.A. Zimmer, "Universal Message Services," American Eagle white paper, 1998, also Chapter 27 in "Handbook of Electronic Messaging," by N.A. Cox, *CRC Press*, Boca Raton, FL, 1998.

13. S. Dusse and T. Matthews, "S/MIME: Anatomy of a Secure E-mail Standard," *Messaging Magazine*, 1998.

14. V.G. Cerf, "Integrated Messaging Meets the Internet," *Messaging Magazine*, November/December 1997.

15. M. Rubenstein, "Messaging in the Millennium: What Will It All Mean?" *Messaging Magazine*, January/February 1998.

16. J. Rafferty, "Messaging Integration: Better Connections for Fax, Voice and E-Mail Messages," Messaging Magazine, January/February 1998.

17. J. Rafferty, "Messaging Integration," *Messaging Magazine*, November/ December 1997.

18. A.M. Rosenberg, "Getting Ready for Unified Personalized Telecommunications," *Messaging Magazine*, November/ December 1997.

19. J. Schwartz, "Where is Messaging Technology Headed in the Next Century?" *Messaging Magazine*, March/April 1998.

20. V.C. Wheatman, "Sorting Through the Secure Messaging Maze," *Messaging Magazine*, March/April 1998.

21. D.A. Zimmer, "Universal Message Services: Your Electronic Future," *Messaging Magazine*, 1998.

22. "ViewMail for Microsoft Messaging," Training Guide, 1998.

23. D. Nanneman, "Unified Messaging: A Progress Report," *Telecommunication Online*, March 1997.

24. J. Piggott, "Unified Messaging: far Cry or Boom Market?" *Telecommunication Online*, July 1997.

25. D. Kopf, "The Reincarnation of Unified Messaging," *America's Network*, November 15, 1998.

26. *"Octel Unified Messenger for Microsoft Exchange,"* Lucent Technologies white paper, January 1998.

27. *"Octel Unified Messenger Interoperability,"* Lucent Technologies white paper, January 1998.

28. *The Internet-draft VPIM Specification* (Version 2), ftp://ds.internic.net/ internet-drafts/draft-ema-vpim-04.txt

29. *"Lucent-Microsoft Executive Roundtable on Unified Messaging,"* Report, Boston, MA, September 9, 1998.

30. *"Carrier Class Unified Services,"* Amteva Technologies white paper, 1998.

31. M. Crispin, *"Internet Message Access Protocol – Version 4,"* Network Working Group, December 1996.

32. M. Taylor, *"Truly Unified Messaging,"* Interactive Intelligence white paper, June 1997.
33. J. Taylor, *"Universal Communications Servers,"* Mediagate's presentation.
34. D. Rush, *"Telinet Technologies – MediaMail,"* Telinet's presentation.
35. A. Belfer, *"Value of Enhanced Services to UM Service Package,"* CallWare Technologies presentation.
36. A.M. Rosenberg, *"Unified Messaging and Enhanced Telecommunications Services,"* TeleMessaging Communications presentation.
37. J. Taylor, "Unified Messaging Standards," MediaGate's presentation.
38. M. Ozur, *"Next-Gen Messaging for Enterprise Storms Onto the Scene,"* Internet Telephony, March 1999, pp. 68-72.
39. W.D. Livingston, *"Beyond Unified Messaging: Voicing Control Over Remote Applications,"* Internet Telephony, March 1999, pp. 74-76.
40. J. Pitcher, "Japanese Unified Messaging Seminar," Presentation, December 1998.
41. *"CallXpress for Windows NT Product Definition,"* AVT's White paper, 1999.
42. *"Computer Telephony and the Internet: An AVT Perspective,"* AVT's White Paper, 1999.
43. L. Oleson, *"Unified Messaging and the Convergence of the Voice and Data Worlds,"* Amteva Technologies White Paper, 1999.
44. *"Collaborative and Intranet Computing,"* International Data Corporation, Framingham, MA, Vol. 1, May 1998.
45. *"Total Cost of Ownership,"* Lucent Technologies, white paper, 1998.
46. *"Technical Overview of EIC,"* Interactive Intelligence, 1998.
47. B. Furht, "The Future of Unified Messaging," Research Report, International Engineering Consortium, Chicago, IL, 2000.

Chapter 17

DISTRIBUTED GEOGRAPHIC INFORMATION SYSTEMS ON THE WEB

Fangju Wang

Abstract

In recent years, Web site based geographic information systems (GISs) have been developed to facilitate geospatial data sharing. Currently, most of the systems are stand-alone. For an application that requires multiple data sets distributed at multiple sites, the user has to physically visit all the sites.

The technique reported in this chapter is aimed at integrating a collection of Web GISs into a system, which may provide more transparent and more efficient access. When visiting a participating site, the user can access the data stored at any of the participating sites as if all the data are provided by one site. The user does not need to access the data site by site. The technique is based on CORBA (Common Object Request Broker Architecture) and Java. The core component of the technique includes an ORB (Object Request Broker) and a set of service objects and application objects, which are implemented using Java applets and servlets. For a request for geospatial data, they decide where and how to obtain the data, and make the data available to the user.

1. INTRODUCTION

Geographic information systems (GISs) are a type of multimedia systems. A GIS stores raster and vector digital maps, and satellite and aerial images. It provides functions for retrieving, analyzing, manipulating, and displaying the data. A distributed GIS is a collection of sites connected with a data communication network. Each site is an autonomous GIS that has data and processing functions. A distributed GIS may present a single database image to the user and provides transparent data access. Data distribution and connection paths are hidden. To the user, the system can be accessed as if all the data and functions are provided by one site.

A distributed GIS has advantages in data sharing, reliability, and system growth. In the past decade, distributed GISs have attracted increasing interests. Research has been conducted for developing distributed GISs, for example, by Edmondson (1992), Bernath (1992), and Laurini

(1993). The more recent work includes the Alberta Land Related Information System (Goodman, 1994), the DGIS project in Australia (Hawick et al, 1997), the DISGIS project in Norway (Norwegian Mapping Authority, 1997), the geodata modeling technique for distributed GISs at Berkeley (Gardels, 1997), the virtual GIS (Abel et al, 1998), and the integration of spatial databases (Devogele et al, 1998).

To facilitate geographic data sharing and interoperability, international and national standards have been developed, Including the Open Geodata Interoperability Specification (OGIS) (Buehler and McKee, 1998), and the Spatial Archive and Interchange Format (SAIF) (British Columbia Survey and Resource Mapping Branch, 1994). The University Consortium for Geographic Information Science has included distributed computing and interoperability in its research priorities (UCGIS, 1996). A wide range of research activities have been conducted to overcome challenges to GIS interoperability (e.g. Bishr, 1998).

The technique reported in this chapter is aimed at developing Web based distributed GISs that integrate data and function components from existing Web sites, in order that the distributed system may provide more transparent and more efficient access. Since 1995, Web server-based GISs (Web GISs) have been developed for geospatial data sharing, for example, the Alexandria Digital Library (ADL) (Smith et al, 1996), and many commercial and non-commercial systems (Plewe, 1997). Using a Web browser, a user may access digital maps and images stored at a remote Web GIS.

A current Web GIS allows the user to access a digital map or an image at a time. (In the rest of this chapter, we use *data set* to refer to all the data that form a map or an image.) The services provided by the Web GISs include:

• The user may use a Web browser to display a data set (that is usually in a raster format);
• The user may download a data set and use other software to display or analyze it; or
• The user may use a Web browser with Java applets downloaded with a data set for better graphic display and analysis. (The use of applets will be discussed in the next section.)

Currently, most of the Web GISs are stand-alone. A major limitation of those Web GISs is that when visiting a site, the user can access the data stored at that site only. This limitation leads to difficulties in data access, especially for applications involving multivariate data analysis. Such applications may require access to multiple databases that are distributed at multiple Web sites. Presently, to obtain data distributed at multiple sites, the user has to physically visit all the sites one by one. This is often tedious work even though there may be some clickable hypertext links to facilitate the visit. Our technique can be used to integrate a collection of existing Web GISs into a system. The system may provide more transparent and more efficient access. When visiting a site, the user can query any of the data sets stored at any of the participating sites. To the user, the system can be accessed as if all the data are provided by one site. The user needs to tell the system *what* data are required only. The system can decide *where* and *how* to obtain the data and then make the data available to the user. In the rest of this chapter, we will call such a system a "Web distributed GIS".

There has been numerous research work conducted in integrating Web sites. Researchers have developed effective techniques for modeling the Web, querying multiple sites, integrating and extracting information, and optimizing queries (Florescu, 1998). Of the research projects for integrating multiple Web sites into a *Web data integration system*, the TSIMMIS system is a representative, in which an intelligent mediator is used to provide tools for accessing multiple heterogeneous information sources (Hammer et al, 1995; Li et al, 1998). However, little has been reported in integrating multiple Web GISs.

Our technique is based on CORBA (Common Object Request Broker Architecture) (Siegel, 1996) and Java's applet and servlet technologies. In addition, this technique makes use of the new security model that has been recently supported by Java and Web browsers. This technique has been implemented into an experimental system.

2. CORBA AND JAVA FOR DISTRIBUTED GIS'S

The CORBA framework was developed by the Object Management Group (OMG) whose mission is to bring about agreement on standards of object-oriented technology and then promulgate those standards to both vendors and consumers of the technology. OMG is now a consortium of more than 800 companies. CORBA has been widely accepted by many software developers as a standard for developing distributed object systems.

The architecture consists of five main parts:

1. An *Object Request Broker (ORB)* that is the software bus for distributed objects to transparently make requests to - and to receive responses from - other objects located locally or remotely,
2. *Common Object Services* that are collections of system-level services for extending the capabilities of ORB,
3. *Common Facilities* that provide application-specific services of direct use to application objects,
4. An *Interface Definition Language* that provides a language-neutral way to define how a service is implemented, and
5. *Application Objects* that are components implementing end-user applications.

Everything in CORBA is an object. The Common Object Services and Common Facilities are provided by a group of objects on the ORB (Orfali et al, 1996).

Java is a programming language very suitable for Internet computing and multimedia applications. There are three types of Java programs: applets, servlets, and application programs. An *applet* is a compiled Java program that is intended to be embedded into an HTML document, transported across a network, and executed at the machine that downloads it. A *servlet* is a compiled Java program that works with a server to enhance the server's functionality. An *application program* is a stand-alone program that can be executed using a Java interpreter.

Java may make a Web GIS more powerful. Currently, a large percentage of digital maps in ordinary (non-Web) GISs contains vector graphics data and has complex data structures. A Web browser alone is not able to handle those data well. The technique of Java applets may help bridge the gap between Web GISs and non-Web GISs. A well developed applet can display vector and raster maps in a way that cannot be done by using a Web browser alone. It can also interact with the user at the client (downloading) machine, and extract information from the data to answer the user's questions. The Open GIS Consortium has included Java-based technology as one of the pillars in the architecture specification for open distributed processing (Strand, 1996). The applet technology of Java has been applied in developing Web GISs, including the interactive Atlas of MapQuest, ArcJ of Eurocom, and Internet Map Server of ESRI (Plewe, 1997).

A combination of the technologies of CORBA and Java may enable us to create better distributed systems: The ORB can serve as a middleware to coordinate Java objects in applets, servlets and application programs, on both server and client machines. ORB and service objects have been defined as Java classes by software producers and used in many non-Web applications (Vogal and Duddy, 1997). In Java 2, ORB and some classes for the Common Services have been included as library classes (Heller and Roberts, 1999).

The great potential of combining CORBA and Java for GIS development has been realized by the GIS community (Strand, 1996). However, little has been reported in combining the two technologies to develop distributed Web GISs. The slow progress may be due to the technical problems in integrating data and function components from Web GISs, as well as the old security restrictions of Java and Web browsers.

In our research, we have developed a technique that can be used to integrate a collection of (existing) stand-alone Web GISs into a system. This technique is based on a CORBA-Java structure. In integrating multiple Web GISs, heterogeneity may exist in data models, processing procedures, projection systems, formats, and so on. Many services from CORBA are necessary in dealing with the heterogeneity. We use some Java facilities to implement the services. Compared with the existing work using CORBA and Java for GIS development, in this technique, the new Java security model and Java servlets were for the first time applied to GISs. The security model has made the applets in the system much more active so that existing computing resources could be better used. The servlets enhance the servers' functionality in a more efficient way. In addition, a query optimization algorithm has been developed, which is suitable for an environment involving both Web and GIS.

In the following sections, the system architecture, each of the major components, the overall query algorithm, and the query optimization procedure are described. Besides, the security model, the handling of heterogeneity and some implementation issues are presented as well.

3. THE APPROACH AND SYSTEM ARCHITECTURE

In the following discussion, a Web site that is integrated into the system is referred to as a *participating site*.

To achieve more transparent access, we install an additional system component at each participating site. The component is developed based on the CORBA model. It consists of an ORB, a set of service objects and application objects. When a user makes a data request from a client machine, the ORB, the service objects and application objects are invoked. They decide where and how the data can be obtained. They then arrange the data to be available to the client machine.

The ORB provides the mechanisms for inter- and intra-site object communications. Currently, we include three groups of service objects in the experimental system: the *Naming Service* objects that can be used to locate named objects -- digital maps and images, the *Persistent Object Service* object that provides a uniform, object-oriented interface for the data persistently stored in databases, and the *Query Service* objects that support query operations.

There were two approaches for us to choose in developing this component. One approach is to code the ORB, the services and application modules as CGI (Common Gateway Interface) programs (Brown et al, 1996). Using this method, when a data request arrives, the CGI programs are executed on the server machine. A major problem with this approach is the heavy workload at the server site for executing the CGI programs. When a server accesses a CGI program, it must first create a new process for the program and then the program can perform its operations. Doing so for every request requires considerable time and computer resources on the server machine. The workload may cause the server to slowdown, especially when it is a busy server with many CGI programs. This approach may also limit the number of requests a server can handle concurrently.

Another approach is to code the component into Java applets and servlets. Java servlets are the first standard extension to Java (Hunter and Crawford, 1998). Servlets are developed to enhance the functionality of servers, for example HTTP servers. At the server site, compiled servlet classes are placed in the standard location for servlets in the file system. When a servlet is accessed, it is loaded and invoked at the server site. For example, we can include the name of a compiled Java servlet class in an HTML page. When the HTML page is accessed, the servlet is loaded and invoked. A Java servlet may function as a CGI program. However, it requires much less computing time and system resources. Unlike CGI programs, servlets are all handled by separate *threads* within the server process. For more information about Java servlets, please see Appendix I of this chapter.

In our approach, at each participating site we install an applet and a servlet. The applet includes an ORB, Naming Service and Query Service objects, and a set of application objects. The servlet includes an ORB, and Query Service and Persistent Service objects. The Persistent Service object and the HTTP server co-manage the local database. In this way, at each participating site we have an ORB that is contained in an applet and an ORB that is contained in a servlet. We call the former an *applet ORB* and the latter a *servlet ORB*. The applet ORB is ready to be shipped to and to run on client machines. The servlet ORB stays at the participating site.

When a user visits a participating site, an applet is transported to, and then executed on the client machine, where the applet creates an ORB, the service objects, and the application objects. The objects created on the client machine contact the server sites where the required data are stored. When the server sites are contacted, servlets are loaded and invoked. The ORB, service objects, and application objects at the client and server machines work together to enable the user to query all the data distributed at the participating sites, optimize and execute the query, and present the query results.

The system components added to the participating sites have identical structures in the sense that each site has an applet ORB class, a servlet ORB class, several service object classes and a set of application class. The architecture of a participating site is illustrated in Figure 1.

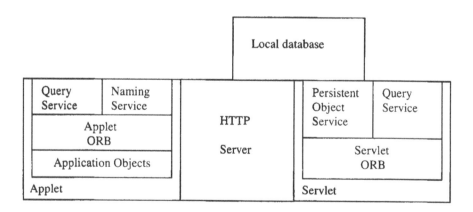

Figure 1. Architecture of a participating site.
(From Wang, Fangju and Jusoh, Shaidah, Integrating multiple Web-based Geographic Information Systems, IEEE Multimedia, 6,1,1999. With permission.)

Each participating site can still be visited as a stand-alone, autonomous Web site. When visiting a site, the user is given two choices: visiting the site as a standard-alone Web site or visiting a Web distributed GIS that comprises several sites. If the user chooses the latter, the applet containing the applet ORB, the service objects and the application objects is shipped to the client machine.

In the next section, the classes we developed for each of the Common Services, their methods and their functionality are described. The application objects and ORB are discussed as well.

4. SERVICE OBJECTS, APPLICATION OBJECTS AND ORB

4.1 THE PERSISTENT OBJECT SERVICE

The data objects persistently stored in a database are referred to as *persistent objects* in the object technology. The CORBA Persistent Object Service provides a single "object-oriented" interface for all the data persistently stored in different local databases. In our implementation, the Persistent Object Service has one class **Datastore**. (In the rest of this paper, we use bold face words for service and application object class names and plain text words for their methods. We may omit the word "object" after a class name when confusion is unlikely.)

For each local database, we install a **Datastore** (object) to provide an object interface. The **Datastore** presents the data stored in the database as objects. In other words, the **Datastore** "wraps" the local database so that the database has an appearance of an object database. This idea is also illustrated in Figure 1.

A **Datastore** has five methods: add_object for storing an object into the local database, retrieve_object for restoring an object from the database, delete_object for removing an object from the database, execute_query for executing a query against the database, and data_contents for listing the data contents in the database.

4.2 THE NAMING SERVICE

The Naming Service is used to locate data objects by name. Each data object, for example, a digital map or a remote-sensing image, has a human recognizable name. This is the name used in queries. The Naming Service maps the name into the address and the reference of the object.

We use two classes for the Naming Service: **Naming** and **BindingIterator**. **Naming** has four methods: bind creates associations between names and net addresses and object references; The unbind method removes the associations; and The resolve method finds the address and reference of a named object; and the list method iterates through all the name-object associations. When method list is called, **Naming** creates a **BindingIterator**, which has two methods: next_one and next_n.

When a user visits a participating site, the definitions of the two classes are shipped within the applet to the client machine. A **Naming** object is then created by the applet. When it is created, it does not contain any information. The information about data, addresses, and references is fetched from **Datastores** and then provided to the **Naming**. This approach may avoid possible inconsistency between the information provided by a **Naming** and the actual data sets. It also simplifies the process of updating databases. Updating a database does not require updating anything like lookup tables. The information provided by the **Datastore** that manages the database is always consistent with the database's contents.

4.3 THE QUERY SERVICE

This set includes four classes: **QueryManager**, **Query**, **QueryableCollection**, and **Iterator**. **QueryManager** has a method `create` for creating **Query** objects. **Query** has four methods: `prepare`, `execute`, `get_status`, and `get_result`. The `prepare` method is used to prepare an executable query based on the parameters passed to it. The `execute` method is called to execute the query. When method `get_status` is called, it reports the current status of executing the query: ongoing, successive, or failed. When method `get_result` is called, it creates a **QueryableCollection** and places the result of the query into it. **QueryableCollection** has methods for placing and removing objects. It has another method `create_iterator` to create a movable pointer to navigate the collection. **Iterator** provides mechanisms for traversing a collection. It has three methods: `reset`, `next`, and `more`.

Of the four objects, **QueryManager** is created when an applet is executed at a client machine or a servlet is invoked. After created, it waits for requests. A **Query** is created to handle a query. A **QueryableCollection** and an **Iterator** are created to handle a data set in the query result.

The following are the steps involved in conducting a query.
1. The client calls `create` on **QueryManager**, which then creates a new **Query**. The **Query**'s reference is passed to the client.
2. The client calls `prepare` on the **Query** with a query expression as a parameter.
3. The client calls `execute` on the **Query** to execute the query.
4. The client calls `get_status` on the **Query** to check the execution status.
5. If the query succeeds, the client calls `get_result` on the **Query**, which creates a **QueryableCollection** and places the result in it.
6. The client calls `create_iterator` on the **QueryableCollection** to create an **Iterator**.
7. The client calls the **Iterator** to get elements in the collection.

4.4 THE APPLICATION OBJECTS

We have developed three application objects **Starter**, **QueryProcessor**, and **Requester.** They are carried by the applet to a client machine.

The **Starter** starts a data request session. After a session is started, it first obtains the information about all the data sets available throughout the Web distributed GIS and displays the information for the user to request data. It then creates a **Requester** for each of the user queries.

A **Requester** is responsible for executing a query on behalf of the user. It invokes the services from **QueryProcessor** to process and optimize the query and then deals with a **Query** to have the query executed. When the result is obtained, based on the user's requirement the **Requester** may start the Web browser to display it, start the browser to run the applet associated with the data, or simply notify the user the success of downloading the data. It finishes when all the jobs are done, or an exception occurs (e.g. data retrieval at a site is unsuccessful) and the exception has been reported.

4.5 THE ORB

An ORB is an object. An ORB provides communication mechanisms for service and application objects. For each *class* of objects, the ORB has a set of interface methods, each of which corresponds to a method of the class. For example, there is an ORB interface method that corresponds to the method `execute` on **Query** class. When a client wants to invoke a method on an object, it goes to the ORB, and calls the corresponding interface method, which then handles the invocation.

As described before, a servlet ORB can be created at each participating server site and an applet ORB is created at a client machine where a visit is initiated. When two objects on different machines communicate, the ORBs on the two machines act together as a middleware to handle the communication. The ORBs take care of all the tedious tasks of locating the server object, establishing a connection, invoking the method that provides the service, getting the result, and closing the communication session.

5. THE OVERALL QUERY ALGORITHM

When visiting a participating site, the user may enter one or more queries to request the distributed data. The following is the steps involved in a data request session. The steps are also illustrated in Figure 2.
1. When the user chooses to visit the integration GIS, for example, by clicking a button on an HTML page, a Java applet containing the classes of applet ORB, service objects and application objects is transported to the client machine.
2. The applet runs on the client machine. It creates an ORB, a **Naming**, a **QueryManager**, a **Starter**, and a **QueryProcessor**.
3. The **Starter** contacts the **Datastore** at each participating site to obtain information about the available data sets, including names, addresses, object references, meta data and statistics. (In Figure 2, only one participating site is illustrated.)
4. The **Starter** calls the `bind` method of the **Naming** to create the associations between the data sets and their site addresses and object references. It then presents all the available data sets and prompts the user to query.
5. For each user query, the **Starter** creates a **Requester**, which is responsible for having the query optimized and executed, and presenting the result to the user.
6. The **Requester** calls services from **QueryProcessor**.
7. The **QueryProcessor** processes and optimizes the query, creates a query strategy that consists of a number of subqueries, and returns the strategy to the **Requester**. (The optimization algorithm will be discussed in the section of "Query Optimization".)
8. The **Requester** talks to the **QueryManager** in the Query Service. The latter creates a **Query** and passes the reference of the **Query** to the **Requester**.
9. The **Requester** calls the methods on the **Query** to have the query strategy executed.
10. To execute the query, the **Query** may call the query service objects at remote sites. (More details about the execution and synchronization of a query strategy will be discussed in the section of "Synchronization and Execution of Subqueries".)
11. Upon obtaining the query result, the **Query** creates a **QueryableCollection** and places the data in it. The **Query** passes the **QueryableCollection** to the **Requester**.

All the communications between objects go through ORBs. When a client object wants to talk to a server object, it calls an interface method on the local ORB. If the server object is at the same site, the ORB calls the server. If the server is at a remote site, the local ORB calls the remote ORB, the latter then forwards the request to the server object.

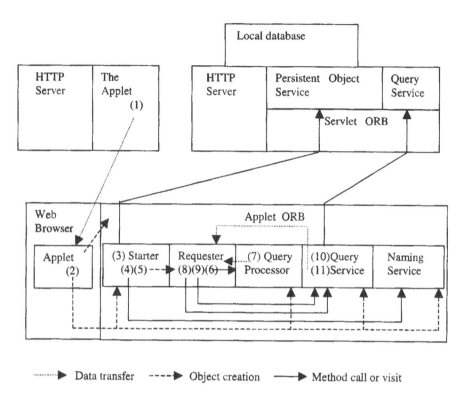

Figure 2. Steps in a data request session.
(From Wang, Fangju and Jusoh, Shaidah, Integrating multiple Web-based Geographic
Information Systems, IEEE Multimedia, 6,1,1999. With permission.)

6. QUERY EXPRESSION

User queries are expressed in the *SQL for multimedia applications* (*SQL/MM*) (ISO/IEC,
1999b), which is based on SQL:1999 (ISO/IEC, 1999a). SQL:1999 supports the *object-relational model*. It allows *user defined types* (*UDTs*) that are quite similar to object classes.
In the object-relational model, a UDT can be used as the type of a relation attribute (table
column). In an object-relational database, values in a table column can be instances of a UDT
that may have a complex structure.

In Part 3 of the SQL/MM standard, a set of *spatial UDTs* are defined for constructing digital
maps, including spatial UDTs for point, line and polygon map features. In SQL/MM, a digital
map can be logically represented as a table with its map features (spatial objects) represented
as one or more columns. One of the spatial UDTs is ST_Geometry. It is the supertype of all
the other spatial UDTs. A set of methods for spatial operations are defined on ST_Geometry,
including those evaluating spatial relationships. Since SQL/MM will be one of the most
important standards in GIS industry, we use it to express queries in this research. For more
information about the spatial UDTs and the methods in SQL/MM, please see Appendix II.

A query in SQL/MM is of the form of **select-from-where**. The **where** clause is used to
express the query condition. A query condition may consist of one or more Boolean
predicates. A predicate may be a conventional "variable-operator-constant" predicate, or a
"variable-operator-variable" predicate, where "variable" is a column name and "operator" is a

comparison operator. The two kinds of predicates express the conventional relational selection and join operations. A predicate may also be a Boolean method defined on ST_Geometry. The following is an example query in SQL/MM, in which upper case words are used for table (including map) names and lower case words for column names:

select SOIL.soil_type
from   SOIL, FARMLAND, OWNER
where OWNER.name = 'Smith' **and**
         OWNER.id = FARMLAND.owner_id **and**
         SOIL.polygon.Overlaps(FARMLAND.polygon)

This query can be used to find the soil types of the farmland owned by Smith. It has all the three kinds of predicates in its query condition.

7. QUERY OPTIMIZATION

7.1 QUERY OPTIMIZATION FOR A DISTRIBUTED GIS

A query in SQL/MM is declarative. A declarative query can usually be executed by using several different strategies, especially when multiple Web sites are involved. The difference in response time may be as large as several orders of magnitude.

In many aspects, queries in a Web distributed GIS are different from those in a non-spatial Web data integration system. So is the query optimization procedure. The current optimization techniques for a non-spatial Web data integration system include minimizing the set of Web sources to access, and minimizing the query that needs to be sent to each one (Florescu et al, 1998). When optimizing a query in a Web distributed GIS, another important factor must be taken into account, that is, the sizes of the data to be processed and transmitted. Queries in a Web GIS may involve conducting many costly spatial operations on geospatial data, and transmitting geospatial data across a network. Geospatial data (e.g. digital maps and satellite images) may have very large sizes. Reducing the sizes of the data to be processed or transmitted may significantly improve a query's efficiency.

In this research, a query optimization algorithm has been developed. The objective of the algorithm is to achieve short response time. The approaches used in this algorithm include minimizing the set of Web sources, as well as minimizing the sizes of the data to be processed and transmitted. This algorithm is aimed at finding an efficient (not necessarily the best) strategy for each query.

7.2 THE QUERY OPTIMIZATION ALGORITHM

This optimization algorithm combines the heuristic technique and the statistical technique. Two sets of heuristic rules and a cost model are used. The algorithm comprises four steps. The first step conducts query decomposition. In the second and third step, the rules are applied in generating strategy alternatives. In the fourth step, the cost model is used to select the best from alternatives.

A. Query decomposition

In this step, a query is decomposed into a number of subqueries, each of which will be distributed to a participating site to execute. (A "subquery" here refers to an ordinary query that is decomposed from a user query. It is different from a subquery defined in the SQL standards.) Query decomposition is conducted in four steps.

1. Normalize the predicate in the **where** clause into a conjunctive normal form.
2. Create a subquery for each conjunctive term. The **from** clause of the subquery includes the maps involved in the term. For example, using term P_i we create

select   ...

from $\{M\}_i$

where $P_i(\{M\}_i)$

where $\{M\}_i$ is the set of maps involved in P_i.

3. Create a "*collecting*" subquery that will be executed on the client machine for gathering intermediate results and displaying the final results.
4. Merge the subqueries that have the identical **from** clauses.

B. Query graph generation

In this step, data transmissions between subqueries are identified. The directions of the transmissions are determined in order to reduce network traffic volumes and to avoid deadlocks. The operations are represented using a directed *query graph* (Q,T) where $Q = \{q_1,...,q_m\}$ is a set of nodes representing the subqueries decomposed in the previous step, and T is a set of edges representing data transmissions between subqueries. $t_{ij}^M \in T$ denotes transmitting data set M from q_i to q_j. The following is the procedure for query graph generation:

1. For each subquery, create a $q \in Q$.
2. Let $\{M\}_i$ and $\{M\}_j$ be map sets in the **from** clauses of q_i to q_j respectively $(1 \leq i, j \leq m$ and $i \neq j)$. For each $M \in \{M\}_i \cap \{M\}_j$, create a temporary edge e_{ij}^M between q_i and q_j that represents data sharing on map M between q_i and q_j. Note that edge e_{ij}^M has no direction.
3. Determine the directions of data transmissions and convert each e_{ij}^M into t_{ij}^M or t_{ji}^M. The directions are determined using the first set of optimization rules. The following is one of the rules: "If M appears in a Boolean spatial method in q_i, and appears in a 'variable-operator-constant' predicate in q_j, turn e_{ij}^M into t_{ji}^M ". The rule can be justified by the fact that when some objects in M are used in q_i to evaluate spatial relationships, in most cases it is more efficient if they can be first selected in q_j using the 'variable-operator-constant' predicate.

C. Strategy generation

In this step, alternative strategies are generated from query graph (Q,T). A strategy is generated by assigning subqueries to sites. Minimizing the set of Web sources and reducing network traffic volumes are the objectives in assigning subqueries. A strategy is represented as a directed graph (Q^N,T) where $Q^N = \{ q_1^{n_1}, ..., q_m^{n_m} \}$ is a collection of subqueries which have been assigned to sites and T is the same as the T in the query graph. $q_i^{n_i} \in Q^N$ indicates that subquery q_i is assigned to the n_i th sites for execution.

A strategy is generated from a query graph using the second set of optimization rules based on the information of locations and sizes of data. The following is an example of the rules: "If subquery q_i has M_1, M_2, ..., M_n in its **from** clause, assign q_i to the site that has the maximum number of the data sets".

Quite often, an optimization rule may lead to more than one assignment for a subquery. Therefore, from a query graph, more than one strategy may be generated. We need to select the most efficient one to execute.

D. Strategy selection

In this final step, a cost model is applied with data statistics to estimate the response time for each alternative strategy and the best one is selected. In the cases that the required data statistics are not available, this step is not conducted and a strategy is arbitrarily selected from the alternatives.

The cost model consists of cost functions. Each spatial operation is associated with a selectivity function and a cost function. In the following, the cost model is informally described. In the expressions, τ denotes time, subscripts q and t denote "query" and "transmission" respectively, and superscripts s, e, p, and t denote "starting", "ending", "processing" and "transmitting" respectively. Note in the following discussion the superscript n_i of $q_i^{n_i}$ is omitted.

1. Identify the *starting subqueries*. $q_i \in Q^N$ is a starting query if there is no $t_{ji}^M \in T$.
2. For each subquery, estimate its starting time and ending time.
    If q_i is a starting subquery, we have $\tau_{q_i}^s = 0$ otherwise

    $$\tau_{q_i}^s = \max_j (\tau_{t_{ji}^M}^e)$$

    The ending time is estimated as

    $$\tau_{q_i}^e = \tau_{q_i}^s + \tau_{q_i}^p$$

    $\tau_{q_i}^p$ is estimated by using the cost functions of the operations in q_i.
    More details about the cost functions are described in a separate paper (Wang, 1999).

3. For each transmission, estimate its starting time and ending time. We have

    $$\tau_{t_{ij}^M}^s = \tau_{q_i}^e$$

    and

    $$\tau_{t_{ij}^M}^e = \tau_{t_{ij}^M}^s + \tau_{t_{ij}^M}^t$$

    $\tau_{t_{ij}^M}^t$ is estimated based on the size of M and the network speed.

4. The response time of a strategy is estimated as the ending time of the collecting subquery.

8. SYNCHRONIZATION AND EXECUTION OF SUBQUERIES

In a query strategy, if there is an $t_{ij}^{M} \in T$, subquery q_j cannot be started until the data from q_i are available, and q_j should be started as soon as the data are available. Synchronization of subqueries is an important task for correct and efficient execution of a strategy. In the following, we describe the synchronization mechanism developed for the experimental system. We call q_i a *supplier* subquery of q_j if q_j is dependent upon q_i for data. For simplicity, we leave out the **Datastore** service objects in the description.

After the best strategy is selected, the **Requester** calls the local **QueryManager** to create a **Query**. The **Requester** calls prepare on the **Query,** and passes the collecting subquery along with all of its direct and indirect suppliers. The **Query** prepares an executable version of the collecting subquery. Meanwhile, for each direct supplier, the **Query** calls the **QueryManager** of the remote site to which the supplier is assigned. The remote **QueryManager** creates a **Query** for the supplier subquery if it has not been created. The **Query** is referred to as the server **Query**. The client **Query** calls prepare on the server **Query** and also transmit the supplier subquery along with supplier's suppliers to the server **Query**. The server **Query** prepares an executable version of the supplier subquery and sends out the subquery's suppliers if there are any. In general, a **Query** prepares an executable version of the subquery that it is responsible for executing, and transmits the subquery's suppliers to the sites to which they are assigned.

After the preparation of the collecting subquery completes, the **Requester** calls execute on the **Query** at the client machine. It then keeps calling get_status on the **Query** to check the execution status. The **Query** at the client machine calls execute of its server **Queries**. For each supplier subquery, the **Query** at the client machine keeps calling get_status of the corresponding server **Query**. Once a supplier completes, the **Query** at the client machine gets the result and stores the data onto the disk for the collecting subquery to use. When all the suppliers complete, the collecting subquery is executed. After the collecting subquery completes, the **Query** tells the **Requester** about the completion. In general, if a **Query** depends upon a server **Query** for data, it keeps checking the server's execution status. It starts to execute its subquery when all the servers succeed. It reports a failure to its client if its own subquery fails or one of its servers reports a failure. This approach does not require any extra system components for subquery synchronization. By using the method on **Queries**, inter-object communication is minimized.

In Figure 3, an example is used to illustrate the synchronization mechanism. It is assumed that q_1, q_2 and q_3 are three subqueries that are assigned to Site 1, Site 2 and Site 3 respectively. q_3 is the collecting subquery. q_1 is a supplier of q_2, and q_2 is a supplier of q_3.

9. THE SECURITY ISSUE

As can be seen in the previous section that an object downloaded with the applet from a participating site may start a communication channel with a site other than its originating site, receives data from remote sites, writes the data onto the hard disk on the client machine, and executes a program on the client machine to display query results. It is the new Java security model that makes all these possible. Generally, an applet is only allowed to show images and play sounds, get keystrokes and mouse clicks from the user, and send user input back to the originating site. An applet is not allowed to run any local executable program, communicate with any site other than the originating site, read or write to the local file system, and find information about the local machine. Before an applet is executed, Java's *security manager* checks its code for the operations that are not allowed. Once an unallowable operation is identified, a security exception is thrown. The restrictions may prevent any malicious applets from threatening the security of a local machine. However, for many situations the restrictions are too strong. To a large extent, Java's power derives from the ability of delivering executable applets over the Internet. The strong restrictions had weakened Java. To loosen the security boundaries, a more flexible security model is needed.

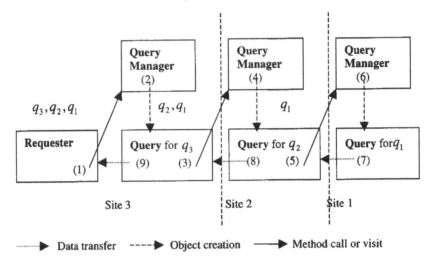

Figure 3. Execution of three subqueries.

Java 1.1 and above support a configurable security model and provide the *javakey* facility (Horstmann and Cornell, 1998). A core component of the new model is the *signed applets* from an *applet signer*. A signed applet carries with it a digital signature that indicates where the applet comes from and ensures that the applet and the embedding HTML document has not been changed after they are signed. The new versions of Web browsers have corresponding customizable security facilities. In a word, the user can configure a browser so that it may allow applets from certain sites to conduct certain sets of operations. A more detailed description about the new security model can be found in Appendix III.

In developing our experimental system, we first create the Web distributed GIS as an applet signer and have its certificate signed by a certificate signer that is accepted by Netscape Navigator. When a client visits the Web distributed GIS for the first time, the security issue is explained to the user. With the user's consent, the certificate of the Web distributed GIS is sent to the client machine and is used by javakey to create the Web distributed GIS as a trusted applet signer. After this step, the applets containing the ORB, service objects, and application object can be executed on the client machine.

10. HANDLING HETEROGENEITY

Geospatial data at different sites may be stored using different software systems, including DBMSs, GIS packages, home-developed Java programs, and so on. Each software system is usually based on a data model, for example, the relational model, the object model, and the object-relational model. A data set stored in such a software system is structured based on the model. When visiting a Web distributed GIS, a user may enter a query that involves data sets in different models. The difference in data models may create difficulties in processing the data sets together.

In addition to the heterogeneity in data models, geospatial data may be generated using different projection systems, may be in different formats (vector and raster) and may have different scales and resolutions. Heterogeneity presents a major challenge in building a Web distributed GIS. Essentially, before the heterogeneous data sets can be processed together, they must be made compatible to each other in terms of data models, projection systems, formats, scales and so on.

As described before, an important mission of the CORBA Persistent Object Services is to provide uniformity and homogeneity. In our experimental system, we are adding data conversion functions to the **Datastore** class. Presently, we are dealing with the heterogeneity problem in data models. Other heterogeneity problems will be addressed later. The following is our approach.

The mechanisms we use to handle the heterogeneity include a *common database schema* of the distributed system, an *internal query expression*, and the CORBA common services. The common database schema is similar to the "federated schema" in the federated database technique (Sheth and Larson, 1990).

The common database schema includes definitions of all the features and feature collections accessible to the user. The common schema is based on the object model and specified in the CORBA IDL. All the features and maps in the system are represented as objects in the schema. The schema is understandable to all the objects in the system. The object specifications in the **Naming** services are based on the common schema.

The internal expression of a query may have three major components: an input list, an output list, and a search condition. A user query in SQL/MM can be directly converted into the internal expression. For transmitting subqueries between sites, we use a class of objects that implement the internal query expression. A query expression object has attributes for the three components and also has a list of pointers to its direct suppliers. When subqueries are created the maps and features referenced in them are expressed using the definitions in the common schema. Then subqueries are converted into query expression objects and transmitted. After a **Query** receives a query expression object, its `prepare` method converts the expression into a query executable to the local database. In preparing a subquery, the **Query** calls `schema_mapping` on **Datastore** to translate specifications of the features and feature collections in the expression into the local scheme.

Any data transmitted between two sites are organized based on the common schema. More accurately, data moving between any pair of **Datastores** are structured as objects defined in the common schema. When a set of data is transmitted between two sites, it undergoes two conversion steps: converted into the common schema, and then converted into the local schema of the destination site. A conversion step mainly involves inserting or deleting some delimiters and sometimes changing the order of some parts of the data stream. The conversion protocols are encoded into methods on **Datastores**. A **Datastore** is responsible for the conversions between the common schema and the local schema.

A major advantage of this approach is easy implementation. The programs for conversion are easy to develop. Each of the programs has a single conversion task. For example, the `prepare` on **Query** is for query conversion only. A conversion program is "bilingual", not "multilingual".

11. SOME IMPLEMENTATION ISSUES

11.1 INTER-SYSTEM COMMUNICATIONS

In a CORBA based system, objects communicate through the ORB. As described before, in our system when two objects on different machines communicate with each other, the ORBs on the two machines work together to form the communicate channel. Communications involving servlets have special features. For example, a servlet must be "activated" before it can accept a request. Because of the features, the current CORBA classes included in Java are not suitable for our application. We developed our own ORB as well as Common Service classes.

In developing the ORB class, the key issue is the communication between two ORB objects running on two different machines. In Java, there are three major approaches that can be used to implement the communication. They are *HTTP communication*, *socket communication*, and *RMI (remote method invocation) communication* (Harold, 1997; Hunter and Crawford, 1998). Each approach has advantages and disadvantages. In our experimental system, we use a hybrid approach.

Java provides the classes of **URL** and **URLConnection** to implement HTTP communication. In HTTP communication, when communicating with the server object, the client acts like a Web browser and requests an HTML page, parsing the response. In a communication session, the client object creates a **URL** that refers to the server object by passing the server's address, port and name to the **URL** constructor. The method `openConnection` on **URL** can be used to open a connection between the **URL** and the server object. The connection is an object of **URLConnection**, which can be used to send the request. An advantage of this approach is that most firewalls allow HTTP connections. A major disadvantage is that the client and server objects cannot communicate interactively. In our implementation, this approach is used when a servlet (containing the server ORB) must be activated, for example, when **Starter** contacts **Datastores** to get the data contents of the participating sites.

Java provides two socket classes: **Socket** and **ServerSocket**. A **Socket** is a regular socket that is used by a client object to initiate a connection to a server object, and when the connection is established, it is used to transmit data. A **ServerSocket** is used by a server object to wait for connection requests from clients and, when a request arrives, to set up the connection. Once the **ServerSocket** has set up the connection, a regular **Socket** is used to send data. A major advantage of the socket approach is bi-directional communication. The client and server objects can use the same socket to communicate interactively. A major problem with this approach is that most firewalls do not allow socket connections.

The Java **RMI** interface allows Java objects on different machines to invoke each other's methods. A remote object may implement a remote interface that specifies which of its methods can be invoked by clients. Clients can invoke the methods of the remote object almost as they invoke methods on the local objects. In the RMI approach, a request can be conducted by invoking a method, and the response can be passed as the values returned by the method. RMI allows a server object to make callbacks to the methods on the client. It can work through firewalls. A major problem is it is slower than socket communication.

In our system, in addition to getting the information about the database contents of participating sites, inter-system communications are required when a client **Query** requests a server **Query** to execute a supplier subquery. The former sends the expression of the subquery to the latter and the latter returns the subquery results (as described in the section of "Synchronization and Execution of Subqueries"). When supporting this type of communication, the ORBs may use sockets or RMI, depending on the system environment, for example, the existence of firewalls. When socket communication is used, both query expressions and results are transmitted through sockets, and when RMI is used, query expressions are passed as method parameters and results are transmitted as the values returned by the methods.

11.2 MULTITHREADING

A user may enter more than one query in a data request session. For example, when a user wants to download a number of maps, he/she may enter a query for each map. In such a situation, multiple **Requesters** should be created at the same time and work concurrently. This manner is more efficient than creating a **Requester** after another one has completed its jobs. We use Java's multithreading technique to achieve the concurrency.

Multithreading is the ability of a single process to spawn multiple, simultaneous execution paths. With multithreading, all execution contexts share the CPU time and the same memory. In our experimental system, when multiple **Requesters** are needed, they are created as **Thread** objects and put into a "running" status. At the same time, each **Requester** thread starts to call the **QueryProcessor** and the **QueryManager** and then deals with the **Query**. Once the **Query** starts to execute the query, the **Requester** gives up the use of the CPU and goes to "sleep". Periodically, it wakes up and checks the **Query** for the execution status of the query. Once the query is successful, it comes back to a "running" status and conducts the rest of its duties. Upon having finishing all the jobs, the **Requester** thread "stops". Figure 4 shows how the approach of multithreading is used when two **Requester** threads are created to evaluate two queries.

The multithreading technique is also applied to **Starters**. A **Starter** duplicates itself when contacting multiple remote sites to get the information about the data available. Multithreading may enable us to make better use of the CPU time and further improve system performance.

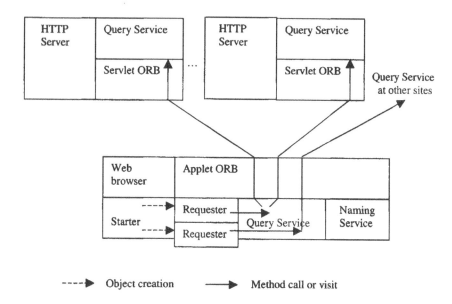

----▶ Object creation   ───▶ Method call or visit

Figure 4. Use of multithreads to execute two queries.
(From Wang, Fangju and Jusoh, Shaidah, Integrating multiple Web-based Geographic Information Systems, <u>IEEE Multimedia</u>, 6,1,1999. With permission.)

12. IMPLEMENTATION, EXPERIMENTS AND CONCLUSION

The system components are developed in Java 2. The implementation includes developing two Java programs and storing them in the file system of each participating site. The programs are the applet and the servlet. The applet contains the applet ORB class, the Naming and Query service object classes, and the three application object classes. The servlet contains the servlet ORB class, and the Query and the Persistent service object classes.

The experimental system consists of five participating sites on the Internet, running UNIX or Windows NT. Each site has an HTTP server and the ORB-Services component. About 30 digital maps and images are distributed at the sites with some duplicates. The sizes of the data sets range from 1Mb to 18Mb. The experimental system can be accessed from any machines on the Internet. Experiments were conducted to access the data sets distributed at the participating sites. To obtain data, the user needs to visit only one of the sites and then enters one or more queries. Most of the tedious work is conducted by the ORB-services component. After waiting for a certain period of time, the user may be presented the results, or notified about the success of downloading the requested data sets. To the user, all the participating sites can be accessed as if he/she is dealing with one site.

The length of waiting time depends on the number and the sizes of the data sets, the operations in a query, network traffic, as well as data distribution. When the data sets involved in a query are evenly distributed at multiple sites, the time required by the experimental system is about 1/5 - 1/4 of the time required by "manually" downloading the data in a one-by-one fashion. When all the data requested are stored at one site, the time required is still shorter than the time required by manual downloading. In the latter situation, there is no significant efficiency improvement, however, the user has been spared most of the tedious work.

The experiments have shown that the technique has basically achieved its objective of integrating stand-alone Web sites for more transparent and more efficient access. Data sharing becomes much easier and more efficient.

This research has contributed a practical technique for integrating existing Web sites. The current stand-alone Web GISs are rich resources of geographic data. By combining stand-alone Web GISs into a Web distributed GIS, this technique may dramatically improve accessibility of the data. This technique may have a considerable impact to the GIS technology specifically and the distributed object technology generally. Technically, this technique has the advantages of high efficiency and easy implementation. The high efficiency is achieved by concurrent execution of programs on both the client machine and the server machines. To integrate a Web site into the system, the only changes are the installation of the ORB-services component and modifying two or three HTML pages.

Acknowledgments

This research is supported by the Natural Sciences and Engineering Research Council (NSERC) of Canada. Ms. Shaidah Jusoh's MSc thesis project in the Department of Computing and Information Science, University of Guelph served as the initial stage of this research.

APPENDIX I - Java Servlets

Java servlets are the first standard extension to Java. A servlet is a compiled program that conforms to a specific interface that can be plugged into a Java-based server. Servlets may considerably enhance a server's functionality (Hunter and Crawford, 1998).

A servlet can perform most of the operations that a Java application program can conduct, including disk read/write, data processing, and network communication. Differing from a Java application program, a servlet does not have a "main" method. It cannot be executed by using the Java interpreter. Differing from a Java applet, a servlet is not to be shipped to client machines. While an applet works at the client side, a servlet stays with a server and works at the server-side. A servlet has certain special methods that can be called by the server in the process of handling requests.

An important type of Java servlets is HTTP servlets, which are used with HTTP servers. The name of a compiled HTTP servlet can be included in an HTML page with special tags. When the HTML page is accessed, the servlet is loaded and invoked. An HTTP servlet can also be invoked by entering its name in the "Location" field of a Web browser.

Every servlet must implement the *javax.servlet.Servlet* interface. Most servlets implement it by extending one of two special classes: *javax.servlet.GenericServlet* or *javax.servlet.http.HTTPServlet*, which are for generic servlets and HTTP servlets respectively. The two classes are included in packages *javax.servlet* and *javax.servlet.http*. The classes are bundled with the Java Servlet Development Kit (JSDK) for used with the Java Development Kit (JDK) version 1.1 and above. The JSDK is available for download from *http://java.sun.com/products/servlet/*.

APPENDIX II - SQL/MM Spatial Data Types and Type Methods

In SQL/MM, the following spatial user defined types (UDTs) are supported: ST_Geometry, ST_Point, ST_Curve, ST_LineString, ST_CircularString, ST_CompoundCurve, ST_Surface, ST_CurvePolygon, ST_Polygon, ST_GeomCollection, ST_MultiPoint, ST_MultiCurve, ST_MultiLineString, ST_MultiSurface, and ST_MultiPolygon.

ST_Geometry is the supertype of ST_Point, ST_Curve, ST_Surface, and ST_GeomCollection. ST_Curve is the supertype of ST_LineString, ST_CircularString, and ST_CompoundCurve. ST_Surface is the supertype of ST_CurvePolygon, which is the supertype of ST_Polygon. ST_GeomCollection is the supertype of ST_MultiPoint, ST_MultiCurve, ST_MultiLineString, ST_MultiSurface, and ST_MultiPolygon.

In addition to the relationships in the type hierarchy as described above, two types may also have the relationship of "a part of". That is, a type can be the type of a component of another type. For example, ST_Point is the type of the point array of ST_LineString, and ST_Curve is the type of the exterior ring and interior rings of ST_CurvePolygon.

For evaluating spatial relationships between spatial objects, a set of Boolean methods are defined on ST_Geometry. Since ST_Geometry is the supertype of all the other types in the hierarchy, any type can inherit the methods. Let ST_XXX represent a spatial relationship method. It is invoked as
a.ST_XXX(b)

where *a* and *b* are values of the same of different types. The method returns TRUE if *a* and *b* have the spatial relationship for which it is defined to evaluate, and returns FALSE if they do not have the relationship. The following are the methods and their return values:

a.ST_Disjoint(*b*)	TRUE if *a* is spatially disjoint from *b*
a.ST_Intersects(*b*)	TRUE if *a* spatially intersects *b*
a.ST_Touches(*b*)	TRUE if *a* spatially touches *b*
a.ST_Crosses(*b*)	TRUE if *a* spatially crosses *b*
a.ST_Within(*b*)	TRUE if *a* is spatially within *b*
a.ST_Contains(*b*)	TRUE if *a* spatially contains *b*
a.ST_Overlaps(*b*)	TRUE if *a* spatially overlaps *b*

APPENDIX III - The New Java Security Model

In the new Java security model, a machine may allow *trusted applets* to conduct operations that were not allowed before, including accessing the local file system and communicating with a site other than the originating site. A trusted applet is one signed by a "trusted" server (of an organization or a person).

To be able to sign applets that are trusted by client machines, a server must first become an applet signer. *Javakey* is the facility used to create signers. It generates certificates and keys. When creating a signer, Javakey generates a public key and a private key for the signer. Javakey then generates a certificate for the signer that includes information about the signer as well as the public key. The signer must have the certificate signed by a *certificate signer*. The applet signer then sends the signed certificate to the machines where signed applets will be executed. A Web browser has a list of *accepted certificate signers*. If the one who signed the certificate is on the list, the applet signer is accepted by the browser as a trusted signer and the applets signed by the signer will be treated as trusted applets.

Java applies a technique of public key cryptography that prevents a signature from being forged and the signed code from being changed. The signer uses the private key to sign an applet and the embedding HTML document. After the applet and the HTML document are downloaded by a client who already accepts the server as a trusted signer, the client uses the public key (included in the signer's certificate) to verify the signature and ensure that the code has not been changed after it is signed.

References

1. D. Abel, E. C. Ooi, K. Tan, and S. H. Tan, "Towards Integrated Geographic Information Processing," *International Journal of Geographic Information Science*, Vol. 12, No. 4, pp. 353-371, 1998.
2. T. Bernath, "Distributed GIS Visualization System," *Proceedings of GIS/LIS'92*, Vol. 1, pp. 51-57, San Jose, Calif., 1992.
3. Y. Bishr, "Overcoming the Semantic and Other Barriers to GIS Interoperability," *International Journal of Geographic Information Science*, Vol. 12, No. 4, pp. 299-314, 1998.
4. British Columbia Survey and Resource Mapping Branch, S*patial Archive and Interchange Format: Formal Definition Release 3.1*, Province of British Columbia, 1994.
5. K. Buehler and L. McKee, *The OpenGIS Guide*, Wayland, Massachusetts: Open GIS Consortium, Inc., 1996.

6. T. Devogele, C. Parent, and S. Spaccapietra, "On Spatial Database Integration," *International Journal of Geographic Information Science*, Vol. 12, No. 4, pp. 335-352, 1998.

7. P. H. Edmondson, "Managing the Distributed GIS Infrastructure - An Organizational Perspective," *Proceedings of GIS/LIS'92*, Vol. 1, pp. 196-207, San Jose, Calif., 1992.

8. D. Florescu, A. Levy, and A. Mendelzon, "Database Techniques for the World Wide Web: A Survey," *ACM SIGMOD Record*, Vol. 27, No. 3, pp. 59-74, 1998.

9. K. Gardels, "A Comprehensive Data Model for Distributed, Heterogeneous Geographic Information," http://regis.berkeley.edu/gardels, *1997*.

10. J. N. Goodman, J. N., "Alberta Land Related Information System, a Federated Database System Case Study," *URISA 1994 Annual Conference Proceedings*, Washington D.C.: Urban and Regional Information Systems Association, Vol. 1, pp. 421-431, 1994.

11. J. Hammer, H. Garcia-Molina, K. Ireland, Y. Papakonstantinou, J. Ullman, and J. Widom, "Information Translation, Mediation, and Mosaic-Based Browsing in the TSIMMIS System'," *ACM SIGMOD Record*, Vol. 24, No. 2, pp. 483, 1995.

12. E. R. Harold, *Java Network Programming*, Sebastopal, CA: O'Reilly & Associates, Inc., 1997.

13. K. A. Hawick, H. A. James, S. J. Maciunas, F. A. Vaughan, A. L. Wendelborn, M. Buchhorn, M. Rezny, S. R. Taylor, and M. D. Wilson, "Geographic Information Systems Applications on an ATM-based Distributed High-Performance Computing System," *Proceedings of the International Conference on High-Performance Computing and Networking*, pp. 1035-1037, Vienna, Austria, 1997.

14. P. Heller and S. Roberts, *Java 1.2 Developer's Handbook*, Alameda, CA: SYBEX Inc., 1999.

15. C. S. Horstmann and G. Cornell, *Core Java*, Polo Alto, CA: Sun Microsystems Press, Prentice Hall Title, 1998.

16. J. Hunter and W. Crawford, *Java Servlet Programming*, Sebastopal, CA: O'Reilly & Associates, Inc., 1998.

17. ISO/IEC, *Database Language SQL -- Part 2: SQL Foundation (Approval version)*, The International Organization for Standardization, 1999a.

18. ISO/IEC, *Information Technology -- Database Languages -- SQL Multimedia and Application Packages -- Part 3: Spatial (Approval version)* The International Organization for Standardization, 1999b.

19. R. Laurini, "Sharing Geographic Information in Distributed Databases," *Proceedings of the 16th Urban Data Management Symposium*, Vienna, Austria, pp. 26-41, 1993.

20. C. Li, R. Yerneni, V. Vassalos, H. Garcia-Molina, Y. Papakonstantinou, J. Ullman, and M. Valiverti, "Capability Based Mediation in TSIMMIS," *ACM SIGMOD Record*, Vol. 27, No. 2, pp. 564-566, 1998.

21. M. Morrison, *Java 1.1 Unleashed* (the third edition), Indianapolis, IN, Sams Net, 1997.

22. Norwegian Mapping authority, 1997, "Project Summary", http://www.statkart.no/disgis.

23. R. Orfali, D. Harkey, and J. Edwards, *The Essential Distributed Objects Survival Guide*, New York: John Wiley & Sons, Inc., 1996.

24. B. Plewe, *GIS Online: Information Retrieval, Mapping, and the Internet*, Santa Fe, NM, On Word Press, 1997.

25. J. Siegel, *CORBA Fundamentals and Programming*, New York: John Wiley & Sons, Inc., 1996.

26. T. R. Smith, D. Andresen, L. Carver, R. Dolin, C. Fischer, J. Frew, M. Goodchild, O. Ibarra, R. B. Kemp, R. Kothuri, M. Larsgaard, B. S. Manjunath, D. Nebert, J. Simpson, A. Wells, T. Yang, and Q. Zheng, "The Alexandria Digital Library: Overview and WWW Prototype," *IEEE Computer*, Vol. 29, No. 5, pp. 54-60, May 1996.

27. E.J. Strand, "Java is Hot for Distributed Computing," *GIS World*, No. 5, pp. 28-29, 1996.

28. UCGIS (University Consortium for Geographic Information Science), "Research Priorities for Geographic Information Science", *Cartography and Geographic Information Systems*, Vol. 23, No. 3, 1996.

29. K. Vogal and K. Duddy, *Java Programming with CORBA*, New York: John Wiley & Sons, Inc., 1997.
30. F. Wang, "Query Optimization for a Distributed Geographic Information System," *Photogrammetric Engineering and Remote Sensing*, 1999.

Chapter 18

DESIGN AND IMPLEMENTATION OF DIGITAL LIBRARIES

Xiuqi Li and Borko Furht

Abstract

As the Internet and the World Wide Web expanded so fast, digital libraries have become a very hot topic. Since 1992 a lot of studies have been done and some achievements have been made. This chapter is a survey of these studies. We first discuss designing digital libraries, including definition of digital libraries, infrastructure requirements for digital libraries, research issues related to digital libraries, and the architecture of digital libraries. Then a project, Digital Library Initiative, is introduced as an example of implementing digital libraries.

1. INTRODUCTION

Because of World Wide Web, access to the Internet has become part of our daily life. A huge number of people search the Internet every day. More and more people need to search indexed collections. But the commercial technology for searching large collections, developed in the US government sponsored research projects in 1960s, has not changed much. A new revolution in information retrieval technology has been spurred by this public awareness of the net as a critical infrastructure in 1990s. [1]

Many people believe that a Net Millennium, where the Net forms the basic infrastructure of everyday life, is coming. "For this transformation to actually occur, however, the functionality of the Net must be boosted beyond providing mere access, to one that supports truly effective searches"[1]. All kinds of collections must be indexed and searched effectively, including those for small communities and large disciplines, for formal and informal communications, for text, image and video repositories, and those across languages and cultures. A fundamentally new technology is needed to support this new search and indexing functionality – this is "digital libraries."

Basically the purpose of digital libraries is to bring the efficient and effective search to the Net. However, in a real digital library, searching is not enough. The main activities of users can be classified into five categories: locating and selecting among relevant sources, retrieving information from them, interpreting what was retrieved, managing the filtered-out information locally, and sharing results with others. "These activities are not necessarily sequential, but are repeated and interleaved" [2].

There is no single definition for digital libraries. And as times goes by, we know more and more about digital libraries, the definition evolves. From information management point of view, digital libraries are systems that combine the machinery of digital computing, storage and communication, the content, and software needed to reproduce, emulate, and extend the services of collecting, cataloging, finding and disseminating information offered by traditional libraries based on paper and other materials. From the user point of view, digital libraries are systems that provide a community of users with coherent access to a large, organized repository of information and knowledge.

When designing and implementing digital libraries, there are several aspects to consider [3]:

- Interoperability: how to confederate heterogeneous and autonomous digital libraries to provide users with a coherent view of the various resources in these digital libraries
- Description of objects and repositories: describe digital objects and collections to facilitate the use of mechanisms such as protocols that support distributed search and retrieval and provide the foundation for effective interoperability
- Collection management and organization: incorporating information resources on the network into managed collections, rights management, payment and control, non-textual and multimedia information capture, organization, storage, indexing and retrieval
- User interfaces and human-computer interaction: user behavior modeling, display of information, visualization and navigation of large information collections, linkage to information manipulation/analysis tools, adaptability to variations in user workstations and network bandwidth
- Economic, social and legal issues: rights management, economic models for the use of electronic information, and billing systems to support these economic models, user privacy

Since 1992, when digital libraries emerged as a research area, there has been a lot of work done. Some achievement has been made, especially in description of objects and repositories, collection organization, and user interfaces. And a lot of digital libraries have been developed, in U.S.A, European, Australia and Asia.

United States is the leader of digital library research area. National Science Foundation (NSF), Advanced Research Projects Agency (ARPA), and National Aeronautics and Space Administration (NASA) jointly funded a digital library research project called Digital Library Initiative (DLI). It is divided into two phases, which are called NLI I and NLI II, respectively. NLI I began in 1994 and ended in 1998. The total budge was US$ 25M. It focused on dramatically advancing the means to collect, store, and organize information in digital forms, and making it available in user-friendly ways for searching, retrieval and processing through communication networks. Six universities participated in this initiative. They are Carnegie Mellon University, Stanford University, University of California at Berkley, University of California at Santa Barbara, University of Illinois at Urbana-Champaign, and University of Michigan. Each university focused on a specific area. Carnegie Mellon University focused on interactive on-line digital video library system, University of California, Berkeley on environmental and geographic information, University of Michigan on earth and space sciences, University of California, Santa Barbara on spatially referenced map information, Stanford University on interoperation mechanisms among heterogeneous services, and University of Illinois at Urbana-Champaign on federating repositories of scientific literature. Compared to DLI I, DLI II is a broader and larger effort. Besides NASA, ARPA and NSF, National Library of Medicine (NLM), Library of Congress (LOC), National Endowment for the Humanities (NEH) and Federal Bureau of Investigation (FBI) also sponsored this project. There are 24 projects approved. Based on NLI I, NLI II will emphasize on human-centered research, content and collections-based research, system-centered research, development of digital libraries testbed for technology testing, demonstration and validation, and as prototype resources for technical and non-technical domain communities and will plan testbeds and applications for undergraduate education [4].

2. DESIGN OF DIGITAL LIBRARIES

When designing digital libraries, first we need to answer these questions:

1. What is Digital Library? How is a Digital Library different from an information repository or from World Wide Web? How many Digital Libraries will there be and how they will inter-link? How might this look to users [5]?

2. What will be the infrastructure for Digital Library? What is the context of a Digital Library? What is the relationship between a Digital Library and intellectual property management including publisher concern?

3. How can a Digital Library be evaluated?

The third question is the most difficult to answer. Although metrics for traditional libraries such as precision and recall can be directly applicable to some aspects of a digital library and have been widely accepted, the digital library is much more complex and there is much more to be considered. "Metrics are required to deal with issues such as the distributed nature of the digital library, the importance of user interfaces to the system, and the need for systems approaches to deal with heterogeneity among the various components and content of the digital library" [5]. There is a group working on this issue, called D-Lib Working Group on Digital Library Metrics.

There are mainly four kinds of research issues in digital libraries: interoperability, description of objects and repositories, collection management and organization, and user interfaces and human-computer interaction. We present these issues in detail in Section 2.3.

As for the architecture of digital libraries, different researchers gave different solutions. We will introduce a commonly accepted architecture, which is described in Section 2.4.

Since video has its special characteristics that are quite different from text, additional issues need be addressed in a digital video library system than a text-only digital library. These issues include video storage, video compression, video indexing, and video retrieval. We discuss these issues in Section 2.5.

2.1 DEFINITION OF DIGITAL LIBRARIES

Before defining Digital Libraries, we introduce several fundamental assumptions:

• The digital libraries are not a bounded, uniform collection of information.
• There will be increasing diversity of information and service providers.
• There is more than just searching in digital libraries.

Especially we should notice the last point. As shown in Figure 1, the main activities of users can be classified into five categories: locating and selecting among relevant sources, retrieving information from them, interpreting what was retrieved, managing the filtered-out information locally, and sharing results with others. These activities are not necessarily sequential, but are repeated and interleaved [2]. Users can move freely in the circle to get their work done. In general, users will be involved in multiple tasks at the same time. They will need to move back and forth among these tasks and among the five areas of activity. They need to find, analyze, and understand information of varying genres. They need to re-organize the information to use it in multiple contexts, and to manipulate it in collaboration with colleagues of different backgrounds and focus of interest.

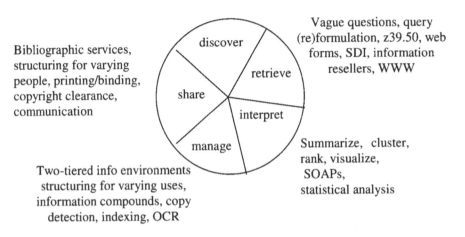

Combining use of online and human sources, metaindex, source taxonomies

Vague questions, query (re)formulation, z39.50, web forms, SDI, information resellers, WWW

Bibliographic services, structuring for varying people, printing/binding, copyright clearance, communication

Summarize, cluster, rank, visualize, SOAPs, statistical analysis

Two-tiered info environments structuring for varying uses, information compounds, copy detection, indexing, OCR

Figure 1. The main activities of digital library users.

There is no single definition for Digital Libraries. The definition evolves as research progresses and we learn more about digital libraries. Some of the current definitions are:

- Digital libraries are systems that combine the machinery of digital computing, storage and communication, the content, and software needed to reproduce, emulate, and extend the services of collecting, cataloging, finding and disseminating information offered by traditional libraries based on paper and other materials. A full service digital library must not only fulfill all essential services provided by traditional libraries but also make good use of the advantages of digital technology.

- Digital libraries are viewed as systems providing a community of users with coherent access to a large, organized repository of information and knowledge. This organization of information is characterized by the absence of prior detailed knowledge of the uses of the information. The ability of the user to access, reorganize, and utilize this repository is enriched by the capabilities of digital technologies [3].

- The concept of a "digital library" is not merely equivalent to a digitized collection with information management tools. It is rather an environment to bring together collections, services, and people in support of the full life cycle of creation, dissemination, use, and preservation of data, information, and knowledge [6].

From the definitions above, it can be concluded that researchers have stretched the definition of digital libraries. More people are recognizing that digital library is not a topic only in computer and information science, but advances in digital library also depend on efforts from legal community.

Digital libraries are libraries extended and enhanced through digital technology. Important aspects of a library that may be extended and enhanced include:

- the collection of the library
- the organization and management of the collections
- access to library items and the processing of the information contained in the items
- the communication of information about the items.

The purposes of digital libraries are:

- to speed up the systematic development of the means to collect, store, and organize information and knowledge in digital form, and of digital library collections,
- to promote the economical and efficient delivery of information to all parts of society,
- to encourage co-operative efforts which leverage the considerable investment in research resources, computing and communications network,
- to strengthen communication and collaboration between and among the research, business, government and educational communities,
- to contribute to the lifelong learning opportunities of all people.

Figure 2 shows a digital library service model. Digital libraries distribute a rich and coherent set of information services (including selection, organization, access, distribution, and persistence) to users reliably and economically. These services are enabled by a suite of tools that operates on objects consisting of content packages, related metadata, service methods, and means of management.

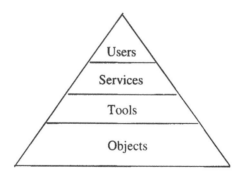

Figure 2. Digital libraries service model.

As for the relationship between digital libraries and NII, digital libraries provide the critical information management technology for the NII, and at the same time represent its primary information and knowledge repositories. In other words, digital library is the core of the NII. The information services, search facilities, and multimedia technologies constitute the digital libraries technologies. Like other NII technologies, they must provide for dependability, manageability, ease of use, interoperability, and security and privacy [3].

Notice in most cases, we use the plural term "digital libraries" meaning that we do not expect to see a single digital library. Each information repository is managed separately, possibly with different technologies, and hence each constitutes a digital library [3]. However we should integrate "virtually" separate libraries into a single one.

2.2 INFRASTRUCTURE REQUIREMENTS FOR DIGITAL LIBRARIES

Each single organization can create its own digital library. To share information across these libraries, it is necessary and important to have a common infrastructure facilitating such sharing. The same infrastructure can also be supportive to sharing of technologies used to build the digital libraries.

The infrastructure for digital libraries should include the following components:

- Shared information representation models, service representation models, and access protocols. These will facilitate the sharing of information and services across digital libraries [3].
- Information "content" sharing agreements. This will take the form of communities of organizations that agree to share their collections. Initially, the sharing may be free, but eventually the community will institute common charging schemes. The communities will also provide rules for having additional members join [3].
- Resource directories. The infrastructure should describe available information resources and relative models and protocol and characterize the contents.
- Coordination forum. The goal of this forum is to coordinate national research and development activities [3].

Among these components, to establish common schemes for the naming of digital objects, and the linking of these schemes to protocols for object transmission, metadata, and object type classifications is the most urgent need. Naming schemes for digital objects that allow global unique reference is the basis for facilitating resource sharing, linkages, and interoperation among digital library systems and for facilitating scale-up of digital library prototypes.

Another essential requirement is a public key cryptosystem infrastructure, including the development of a system of key servers and the definition of standards and protocols. This is necessary to support digital library needs in areas such as security and authentication, privacy, rights management, and payments for the use of intellectual property [3]. Only after these problems are addressed, is it possible for commercial publishers and other information suppliers to make large amounts of high-value copyrighted information broadly available to digital library users. This in turn will restrict the development of research prototypes and may be a distorting factor in studies of user behavior.

2.3 RESEARCH ISSUES IN DIGITAL LIBRARIES

There are five key research issues in digital libraries. They are (i) interoperability, (ii) description of objects and repositories, (iii) collection management and organization, (iv) user interfaces and human-computer interaction, and (v) economic, social, and legal issues.

1.   Interoperability

The more technical interoperability research involves protocol design that supports a broad range of interaction types, inter-repository protocols, distributed search protocols and technologies (including the ability to search across heterogeneous databases with some level of semantic consistency), and object interchange protocols [3]. The various services provided by digital libraries must be interoperable. Existing Internet protocols are obviously inadequate for this. New protocols and systems are needed. This incurs the question of how to deploy prototype systems and how to make the tradeoffs between advanced capabilities and ubiquity of access. Managing this contradiction will have a critical influence in the development of digital libraries.

2. Description of Objects and Repositories

Description of objects and repositories are necessary to provide users with a coherent view of information in various digital libraries. Objects and repositories must be described in a consistent fashion to facilitate distributed search and retrieval of diverse sources. Interoperability at the level of deep semantics will require breakthroughs in description as well as retrieval, objects interchange, and object retrieval protocols [3].

Issues here include the definition and use of metadata and its capture or computation from objects, the use of computed descriptions of objects, federation and integration of heterogeneous repositories with disparate semantics, clustering and automatic hierarchical organization of information, and algorithms for automatic rating, ranking and evaluation of information quality, genre, and other properties [3]. Knowledge representation and interchange, the definition and interchange of ontologies for information context, and the appropriate roles of human librarians and subject expert in the digital library context are also important.

3. Collection Management and Organization

The central problems here are policies and methods for incorporating information resources on the networked into managed collections, rights management, payment, and control. The relationship between replication and caching of information and collection management in a distributed environment, the authority and quality of content in digital libraries, ensuring and identifying the attributes of contents, enhanced support of textual information and support of nontextual and multimedia information capture, organization, storage and retrieval all call for research. The preservation of digital content for long periods of time, across multiple generation of hardware and software technologies and standards is essential in the creation of effective digital libraries and needs careful examination.

4. User Interfaces and Human-Computer Interaction

Among many issues in user interfaces and human-computer interaction, some are central problems. These issues include: display of information, visualization and navigation of large information collections, and linkages to information manipulation/analysis tools, the use of more sophisticated models of user behavior and needs in long-term interactions with digital libraries, more comprehensive understanding of user needs, objectives, and behavior in employing digital library systems, and adapting to variations in the capabilities of user workstations and network connections in presenting appropriate user interfaces.

5. Economic, Social and Legal Issues

Digital libraries are not simply technological constructs; they exist within a rich legal, social, and economic context, and will succeed only to the extent that they meet these broader needs. Rights management, economic models for the use of electronic information, and billing systems to support these economic models will be needed [3]. User privacy and complex policy issues concerning collection development and management, and preservation and archiving are also needed. Existing library practices may be helpful in solving these problems. We need to better understand the social context of digital documents, including authorship, ownership, the act of publication, versions, authenticity, and integrity.

2.4 ARCHITECTURE FOR INFORMATION IN DIGITAL LIBRARIES

In this section we discuss architecture for information presentation in Digital Libraries. We first present two solutions for the architecture, and then examine the core that supports infrastructure of one of these solutions.

2.4.1 Architecture of Digital Library Systems

According to [7], the key components in a digital library system are user interfaces, repositories, and handle system and search system, as shown in Figure 3.

User Interfaces

Each user interface has two parts. One is for the actual interactions with users. The other is **client services** that allow users to decide where to search and what to retrieve, interpret information structured as digital objects, negotiate terms and conditions, manage relationships between digital objects, remember the state of the interaction, and convert the protocols used by the various part of the system.

Repository

"Repositories store and manage digital objects and other information." A digital object is a data structure whose principal components are digital materials, or **data**, and **key-metadata**. The key-metadata includes a globally unique identifier for this digital object, called a **handle**; it may also include other metadata. The data can be elements or other digital objects [8]. There may be many repositories of various types, like modern repositories, legacy databases, and Web servers, in a large digital library. **Repository Access Protocol (RAP)** is the interface to this repository. Features of RAP include: (i) explicit recognition of rights and permissions that need to be satisfied before a client can access a digital object, (ii) support for a very general range of dissemination of digital objects, and (iii) an open architecture with well defined interfaces [7].

Handle System

Handles are general-purpose identifiers that can be used to identify Internet resources, such as digital objects, over long periods of time and to manage materials stored in any repository or database.

Search System

When a digital library system is designed, it is assumed that there will be many indexes and a catalog that can be searched to discover information before retrieving it from a repository. These indexes may be independently managed and support a wide range of protocols [7].

Based on the work in [7,10], services offered by digital libraries are divided into four parts: collection service, naming service, repository service, and indexing service. Repository service provides from simple deposit and access to digital objects to sophisticated management, aggregation and marshaling of the information stored in the repository [10]. With the index service, digital objects that may be distributed across multiple repository servers are discovered via query. The index service also provides metadata, which is used by other services, and the capabilities of its query mechanisms. The collection service provides the means for aggregation of sets of digital objects into meaningful collection [10]. Collections are created by a collection server by reading its metadata and applying its collection definition criteria to define which objects belong to these collections. A user interface gateway offers searching for and access to objects within local collections and make query routing decisions with collection service and index service together based on factors such as content, cost, performance and the like. This decomposition facilitates the extensibility of digital libraries. New services can be easily added as a component.

Handle system, digital object, and the common repository access interface (RAP) forms the core infrastructure of a digital library [10].

It should be noticed that digital library is a distributed system; the four components in Figure 3 may be physically located in many places.

An agent-based architecture for digital libraries is presented in [9]. It is presented in Section 3.1.3.

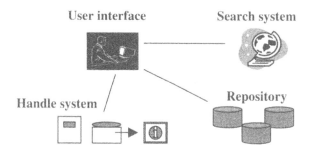

Figure 3. Major components of a digital library system.

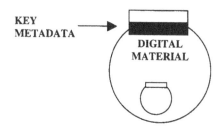

Figure 4. A digital object.

2.4.2 Digital Objects

The digital object
A digital object is a fundamental unit of the digital library architecture [7]. It consists of two components: key-metadata and digital material, as illustrated in Figure 4.

Key-metadata
The key-metadata is the information stored in the digital object that is needed to manage the digital object in a networked environment – for example to store, replicate, or transmit the object without providing access to the content. It includes a handle, an identifier globally unique to the digital object, terms and conditions, and other optional metadata.

Digital material
The digital material (or **data**) can be a set of sequences of bits or other digital objects. It is used to store digital library materials. For instance, a digital object may store a text with SGML mark-up.

Note that because of the characteristics of information, a digital object could be embedded into another digital object, which is called **MetaObject** like Metadata for digital objects.

2.4.3 Handle and the Handle System
In digital libraries, there are various items, such as people, computers, networks, repositories, databases, search systems, Web servers, digital objects, and many more. To keep track of these items, a systematic approach to identification is needed.

Handles are a set of general purpose identifies. In the digital library system, handles are used to identify digital objects and repositories. However handles can also be used to identify almost any Internet resource. A **handle system** is a distributed system that stores handles and associated data that is used to locate or access the item named by the handle.

Handles are different from the widely used Uniform Resource Location (URL) in that they identify resources by name, while URLs identify Internet resources by location.

Handles are names that persist for long periods of time, but the resource that they identify may change its form, may be stored in many locations, move its location, or otherwise be altered with time [7].

cnri.dlib/february96-arms	URL	http://www.dlib.org/dlib/februrary96/02arms.html
	RAP	repository.dlib.org

Figure 5. A handle record.

An illustrative example of handles is given in Figure 5. The handle is "cnri.dlib/july96-arms", identifying an article in D-Lib Magazine. Two fields of handle data stored in the handle system for this item indicates that this article can be found in two locations. Each data field contains two parts, a data type and the data. The first data field is of type "URL"; the associated data is a conventional URL. The second is of type "RAP", indicating that the item can be accessed using the protocol known as RAP; the data is the address of the repository in which the item is stored [7].

Note that the handle for this article remains the same forever. But the handle data may change with time. If this article is moved or duplicated in another repository, the data part of the handle recorded will be changed. The handle itself, however, will remain unchanged.

Resolving a handle is presenting a handle to the handle system and receiving as a reply information about the item identified. Usually users send a name (handle) to the handle system to find the location or locations of the digital object with that name.

Naming Authorities

Handles are created by naming authorities, administrative units that are authorized to create and edit handles [7]. A naming authority's name is composed of one or more strings separated by periods. For example,

cnri.dlib
loc.ndlp.amrlp
10.12345

In the handle system, there are two mechanisms to control that have permission to create naming authorities and create and edit handles: individual administrators and administrative groups. The latter are considered more flexible and convenient.

"Each naming authority has at least one administrator or administrative group with full privileges for that naming authority, including permission to create a sub-naming authority. The administrator creates permissions for administration of handles within that naming authority, and can also create new naming authorities. Administrators can delegate privileges to other administrators, including the privilege of creating sub-naming authorities."[7] Naming authorities are created hierarchically.

2.4.4 The Repository

A **repository** is a network-accessible storage system in which digital objects may be stored for possible subsequent access or retrieval. The repository has mechanisms for adding new digital objects to its collection (**depositing**) and for making them available (**accessing**), using, at a minimum, the **repository access protocol**. The repository may contain other related information, services and management systems.

Repositories have official, unique names, assigned or approved to assure uniqueness by a global naming authority. A repository name is not necessarily the name of a particular host. It may correspond to a set of hosts at different physical locations.

Each repository agrees on a protocol, called **Repository Access Protocol,** allowing deposits and access of digital objects or information about digital objects from that repository. RAP is used to provide only the most basic capabilities. It may change over time. Repositories may support other more powerful query languages allowing users to access objects that meet meaningful criteria.

(i) Access to a digital object (ACCESS_DO)

Access to a digital object will generally invoke a service program that performs stated operations on the digital object or its metadata depending on the parameters supplied with the service request [8]. There are three service requests, **metadata, key-metadata** or the whole **digital object**.

When a user accesses a digital object through **ACCESS_DO,** he receives a **dissemination,** the result of the service request, and information such as the key-metadata of the digital object, the identity of the repository, the service request that produced the result, the method of communication (if appropriate) and a transaction string corresponding to an entry in the transaction record. The transaction string is distinctive to the repository. In addition, the dissemination may contain an appropriately authenticated version of some portion of the properties record for that object, including the specific terms and conditions that apply to this use of the digital object and the materials contained therein.

(ii) Deposit of a digital object (DEPOSIT_DO)

There are several forms of DEPOSIT_DO. It could be taking data, a handle, and perhaps other metadata as arguments, and producing a stored digital object and properties record from these arguments." Or it may take a digital object as argument, probably with additional metadata, and simply deposit it. Also it possibly will take only data and certain non-key-metadata, automatically request a handle from a handle server, and then simultaneously store the object and register the handle.

The DEPOSIT_DO command could be used to replicate an existing digital object at additional repositories, or to directly modify an existing mutable digital object.

(iii) Access to reference services (ACCESS_REF)

This command provides a uniform and understood way to identify alternate means of accessing a specified repository and/or information about objects in that repository. Two possible responses are (i) No information, and (ii) a list of servers, protocol-name pairs, with the interpretation that each server, speaking the named protocol, will provide information about the contents of the repository [8].

2.5 DESIGN OF DIGITAL VIDEO LIBRARY SYSTEM

Video poses unique problems because of the difficulties in representing its contents. It is well known that image takes up much more space than the representation of the original text. Video is not only imagery but consists of 30 images per second [11].

Besides this, there are also other problems caused by introducing video into a digital library. In this section we will address these problems and overview the general architecture of a digital video library.

2.5.1 Research Issues in a Digital Video Library

Video compression
Video is quite different from text. From a presentation point of view, video data is huge and involves time dependent characteristics that must be adhered to for coherent viewing. Because of the storage and network limitation, before video is presented to users, it has to be compressed.

Video indexing
There have been sophisticated parsing and indexing technologies for text processing in various structured forms, from ASCII to PostScript to SGML and HTML. Video contains abundant information, conveyed in both the video signal (camera motion, scene changes, colors) and the audio signal (noises, silence, dialogue). But this information for indexing is inaccessible to the primarily text-based information retrieval mechanism. A common practice today is to log or tag the video with keywords and other forms of structured text to identify its content [11].

Video Segmentation
Since the time to scan a video cannot be dramatically shorter than the real time of the video, a digital video library must be efficient at giving users the material they need. To make the retrieval of bits faster, and to enable faster viewing or information assimilation, the digital video library will need to support partitioning video into small-sized clips and alternate representations of the video [11].

One of the issues relates to the implementation of the partitioning. In text documents, there are chapters, sections, subheadings, and similar conventions. Analogously, video data have scenes, shots, camera motions, and transitions. Manually describing this structure in a machine-readable form is obviously tedious and infeasible.

In addition to trying to size the video clips appropriately, the digital video library can provide the users alternate representations for the video, or layers of information. Users could then cheaply (in terms of data transfer time, possible economic cost, and user viewing time) review a given layer of information before deciding upon whether to incur the cost of richer layers of information or the complete video clip. For example, a given half hour video may have a text title, a text abstract, a full text transcript, a representative single image, and a representative one minute "skim" video, all in addition to the full video itself. The user could quickly review the title and perhaps the representative image, decide on whether to view the abstract and perhaps full transcript, and finally make the decision on whether to retrieve and view the full video [11].

Video Retrieving and Browsing
The basic service, offered by the digital video library, is easy and efficient information searching and retrieval. The two current standard measures of performance in information retrieval are *recall* and *precision*. Recall is the proportion of relevant documents that are actually retrieved, and precision is the proportion of retrieved documents that are actually relevant. These two measures may be traded off one for the other, i.e., returning one document that is a known match to a query guarantees 100% precision, but fails at recall if a number of other documents were relevant as well, or returning all of the library's contents for a query guarantees 100% recall, but fails miserably at precision and filtering the information [11]. The goal of video retrieval is to get the most out of both recall and precision.

It is possible that when a general-purpose digital video library is created, precision has to be sacrificed to ensure that the material the user is interested in will be recalled in the result set. Then the result set probably becomes fairly large, so the user may need to filter the set and decide what is important. Three principle issues with respect to searching for information are:

- How to let the user quickly skim the video objects to locate sections of interest
- How to let the user adjust the size of the video objects returned
- How to aid users in the identification of desired video when multiple objects are returned [11].

2.5.2 Architecture of a Digital Video Library System
The Digital Video Library System is a complex system composed of the software components shown in Figure 6. These components are described below.

Video Storage System (VSS)
The Video Storage System stores video segments for processing and retrieving purposes. In order to provide intelligent access to portions of a video, the Video Storage System must be able to deliver numerous short video segments simultaneously.

Video Processing System (VPS)
The Video Processing System consists of video processing programs to manipulate, compress, compact, and analyze the video and audio components of a video segment. It also contains a component to recognize keywords from the sound track of video segments.

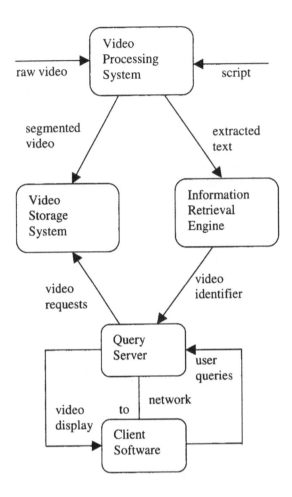

Figure 6. Software components of a digital video library.

Information Retrieval Engine (IRE)
The Information Retrieval Engine is used to store indices extracted from video segments and other information about the video segments, such as sources, copyright, and authorization. The Information Retrieval Engine can support both free-text and Boolean queries.

Client
The client is a graphical user interface residing on the user's computer. It includes interfaces for conducting structured and free text searching, hypertext browsing and a simple video editor.

Query Server (QS)
The Query Server processes video queries from the remote client and communicates with the Information Retrieval Engine and Video Storage System to enable users to extract video data and create multimedia representations of the information of interest.

As seen in the Figure 6, these components are tightly interrelated and support three very different Digital Video Library System functions:

- The creation of the Digital Video Library System archive.
- The processing of video in the Digital Video System to build automatic indices.
- The access of the Digital Video Library System by users.

The system architecture of a digital video library is shown in Figure 7.

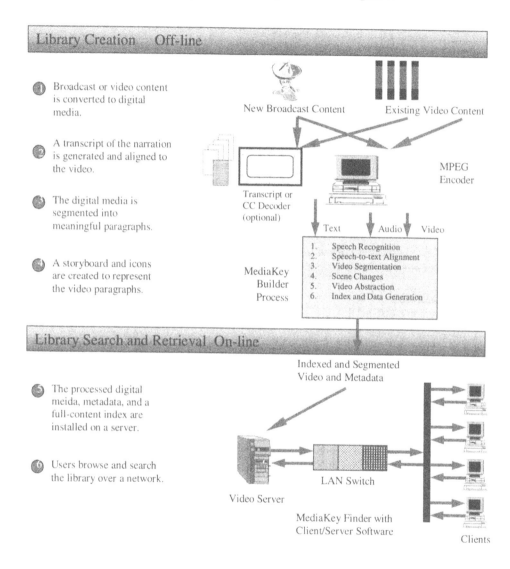

Figure 7. System architecture of a digital video library.

3. DIGITAL LIBRARIES INITIATIVE PROJECT

Since 1994, six research projects developing new methodologies or technologies to support digital library have been funded through a joint initiative of the National Science Foundation (NSF), the Department of Defense Advanced Research Projects Agency (ARPA), and the National Aeronautics and Space Administration (NASA). These are collectively referred to as the Digital Library Initiative I and the total budget was US$ 25 M. Since then, digital libraries research has been regarded as a national challenge in the United States which is similar to the High Performance Computing and Communications Program (HPCC). Digital Library Initiative I ended at the end of 1998 and Digital Library Initiative II has begun this summer.

3.1 DIGITAL LIBRARIES INITIATIVE PROJECT --- PHASE I (DLI I)

The focus of Initiative I is to dramatically advance the means to collect, store, and organize information in digital forms, and make it available for searching, retrieval and processing via communication networks – all in user-friendly ways. Six universities were involved in the Initiative I. Each university is specialized in one specific topic.

Carnegie Mellon University
http://informedia.cs.cmu.edu

The Informedia interactive on-line digital video library system created by Carnegie Mellon University and WQED/Pittsburgh enable users to access, explore and retrieve science and mathematics materials from video archives.

University of California, Berkeley
http://elib.cs.berkeley.edu

This project produced a prototype digital library with a focus on environmental information. The library collected diverse information about the environment to be used for the preparation and evaluation of environmental data, impact reports and related materials.

University of Michigan
http://www.si.umich.edu/UMDL

This project conducted coordinated research and development to create, operate, use and evaluate a test bed of a large-scale, continually evolving multimedia digital library. The content focus of the library was earth and space sciences.

University of California, Santa Barbara
http://alexandria.sdc.ucsb.edu

Project Alexandria developed a digital library providing easy access to large and diverse collections of maps, images and pictorial materials as well as a full range of new electronic library services.

Stanford University
http://www-digilib.stanford.edu

The Stanford Integrated Digital Library Project developed the enabling technologies for a single, integrated "virtual" library that will provide uniform access to the large number of emerging networked information sources and collections--both on-line versions of pre-existing works and new works that will become available in the future.

University of Illinois in Urbana-Champaign
http://dli.grainger.uiuc.edu/national.htm

This project draws on the new Grainger Engineering Library Information Center at the University of Illinois in Urbana-Champaign and the Artificial Intelligence Research Lab at the University of Arizona, http://ai.bpa.arizona.edu. This project is entered around journals and magazines in the engineering and science literature. The initial prototype system includes a user interface based on a customized version of Mosaic, software developed at the university under NSF sponsorship to help users navigate on the World Wide Web.

3.1.1 Carnegie Mellon University Informedia Digital Library Project

The Informedia Digital Video Library Project at Carnegie Mellon University is a large digital library of text, images, videos and audio data available for full content retrieval. It integrates natural language understanding, image processing, speech recognition, and video compression. The Informedia System allows a user to explore multimedia data in depth as well as in breadth.

Figure 8 is an example of how these components are combined in the Informedia user interface. An overview of the structure of the Informedia system is shown in Figure 9.

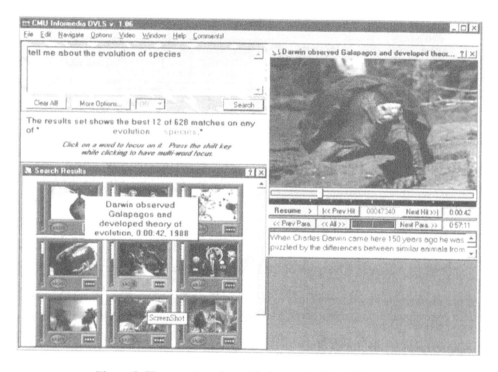

Figure 8. The user interface of Informedia digital library.

The Informedia Library project is primarily used in education and training. Besides this, another application is News-on-Demand. News-on-demand monitors the evening news from the major networks and allows the user to retrieve stories in which they are interested. The News-on-demand application focuses on the limits of what can be done automatically and in limited time [17]. While other informedia prototypes are designed to be educational test beds, the News-on-Demand system is fully automated.

Currently, the Informedia collection contains approximately 1.5 terabytes of data, which is 2,400 hours of video encoded in the MPEG 1 format. Around 2,000 hours of CNN news broadcasts beginning in 1996 forms that the main body of the content. The remaining result from PBS broadcast documentaries produced by WQED, Pittsburgh, and documentaries for distance education produced by the BBC for the British Open University. The subject of the majority of these documentaries is mathematics and science. Besides these, there is also a small quantity of public domain videos, typically from government agency sources.

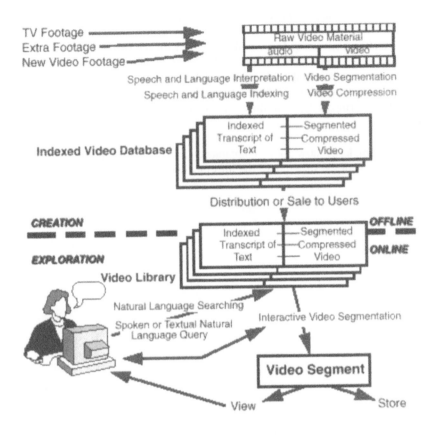

Figure 9. Overview of the Informedia Digital Video Library.

The metadata created by Informedia is extensive and automatically derived. It is an important resource for digital library researchers. Metadata for the Informedia collection includes:

1. **Transcripts** - textual forms of the audio tracks derived from:

- Closed captioning for the CNN data.
- Manual transcripts for the documentary material.
- Automatically derived transcripts from the Sphinx II speech recognizer for all of the data.

2. **Transcript alignment** - Sphinx II derived transcript to video time alignment for all three forms of transcription.

3. **Video OCR** - text regions identified and extracted from video imagery, converted to text via OCR.

4. **Face Descriptions** - human faces detected in video, described by Eigen Face representations.

5. **Geocodes** - latitude and longitude associated with video segments, derived from place names identified in the transcript and Video OCR data, computed from a gazetteer of world locations.

6. **Stills** - representative bit map or JPEG images selected from every automatically identified shot break (change of camera view).

7. **Segments** - video sequences representing single topic stories.

8. **Filmstrips** - collections of stills representing a segment.

9. **Topics** - automatically identified subjects of segments.

10. **Skims** - automatically created video abstracts comprised of concatenated sub-sections of segments creating a shortened version of the video for previewing [17].

3.1.2 University of California Berkley SunSITE Digital Library Project
This SunSITE testbed provides public access to important datasets pertaining to the environment, including environmental documents and reports, image collections, maps, sensor data and other collections [18]. At the mean time, this testbed serves as the foundation for research efforts in computer vision, database management, document analysis, natural language processing, and storage management. It is also used in School of Information Management and Systems of UC Berkeley for user assessment and evaluation and for information retrieval research. Researchers in College of Environmental Design of UC Berkeley use the testbed for Geographic Information Systems (GIS) experiments.

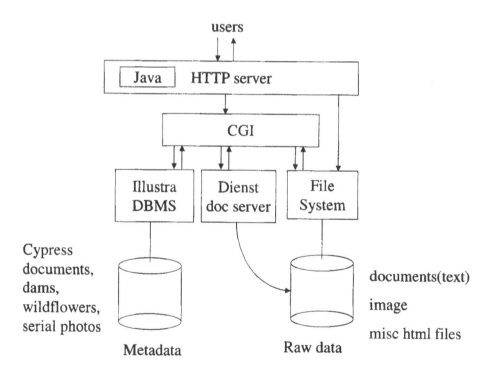

Figure 10. SunSITE digital library architecture: data access.

Software System Architecture

All access to the testbed is provided via the HTTP protocol for public and project members [18]. As shown in Figure 10, the interaction between WWW clients and other software systems is provided through the Common Gateway Interface (CGI) mechanism. Foremost among these systems is the relational database server, enabling forms-based access to nearly all data in the Berkeley Digital Library Project. Other methods besides forms are available for accessing the data, such as clickable maps and sorted lists. These and many others are available via the Access Matrix, which provides a top-level access point to all the data in the testbed.

Collections in the Testbed Database

The collection began as a testbed for research in computer science and information technology; it has since become a valuable repository of environmental and biological information. As of early 1999, the collection represents about a half terabyte of data, including over 70,000 digital images, nearly 300,000 pages of environmental documents, and over a million records in geographical and botanical databases. All of these data are accessible in online searchable databases; they are also freely available for the purpose of research and experimentation. An example is shown in Figure 11.

Figure 12 is an example of content-based searching. In this example, user can search for any picture based on specified colors.

3.1.3 University of Michigan Digital Library Project

As a large-scale effort, the University of Michigan Digital Library (UMDL) provides information services for research and education, in university and high school environments. The wide range of users and uses incurred scale and heterogeneity problem. These issues are addressed in the UMDL by designing an open, distributed system architecture where interacting software agents cooperate and compete to provide library services. The distributed architecture promotes modularity, flexibility, and incremental development, and accommodates diversity in current and future library environments. However, distribution also presents difficult problems in interoperability, coordination, search, and resource allocation. The activities are coordinated in the UMDL by dynamically forming agent teams to perform complex library tasks [19].

Agents

The architecture of UMDL, shown in Figure 13, is based on the concept of a software agent. An agent represents an element of the digital library (collection or service), and is a highly encapsulated piece of software that has the following special properties:

- **Autonomy**: the agent represents both the capabilities (ability to compute something) and the preferences over how that capability is used. Thus, agents have the ability to reason about how they use their resources. In other words, an agent not have to fulfill every request for service, only those consistent with its preferences. A traditional computer program does not have this reasoning ability.

- **Negotiation**: since the agents are autonomous, they must negotiate with other agents to gain access to other resources or capabilities. The process of negotiation can be, but is not required to be, stateful and will often consist of a "conversation sequence", where multiple messages are exchanged according to some prescribed protocol, which itself can be negotiated [9].

- **Botanical Data**

The **CalFlora Database** contains taxonomical and distribution information for the 8000+ native California plants. The **Occurrence Database** includes over 300,000 records of California plant sighting from many federal, state, and private sources. The botanical databases are linked to our CalPhotos collection of California plants, and are also linked to external collections of data, maps, and photos.

Geographical Data

Much of the geographical data in our collection is being used to develop our web-based **GIS Viewer**. The **Street Finder** uses 500,000 Tiger records of S.F. Bay Area streets along with the 70,000-record USGS GNIS database. **California Dams** is a database of information about the 1395 dams under state jurisdiction. An additional 11 GB of geographical data represents maps and imagery that have been processed for inclusion as layers in our GIS Viewer. This includes Digital Ortho Quads and DRG maps for the S.F. Bay Area.

Documents

Most of the 300,000 pages of digital documents are environmental reports and plans that were provided by California State agencies. The most frequently accessed documents include **County General Plans** for every California county and a survey **of 125 Sacramento Delta fish species**. In addition to providing online access to important environmental documents, the document collection is the testbed for the **Multivalent Document research**.

Photographs

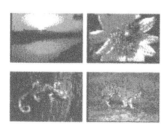

The photo collection includes 17,000 images of **California natural resources** from the state Department of Water Resources, several hundred **aerial photos**, 17,000 photos of **California native plants** from St. Mary's College, the California Academy of Science, and others, a small collection of **California animals**, and 40,000 **Corel stock photos**. These images are used within the project for **computer vision research**

Figure 11. An example of the repository of environmental and biological data.

CalPhotos
California Plants & Habitats

This form can be used to look for pictures from more than 20,000 images of California plants (native and naturalized) as well as habitats. **More information** about the collections, photographers, the system, and this query form.

To look for pictures, choose **any** of the options below. Then click "Search".

Search   Reset

Name   Enter all of part of a common name or scientific name (case unimportant)
Browse scientific names: A|B|C|D|E|F|G|H|I|J|K|L|M|N|O|P|Q|R|S|T|U|V|W|X|Y|Z
Browse common names: A|B|C|D|E|F|G|H|I|J|K|L|M|N|O|P|Q|R|S|T|U|V|W|X|Y|Z

Location   **County** any

Type of picture   ☑ any ☐ habitats ☐ wildflowers & other plants ☐ trees ☐ trees/shrubs ☐ vines ☐ fungi
☐ algae

Collection   ☑ any ☐ Brousseau ☐ California Academy of Sciences ☐ Private Collectors
☐ State & Local Agencies

Photographer   any

Color

Picture's ID   equals

Search   Reset

Number of matches: 164
next 16

Search for: blobs like "%org%"

Click on the image to see an enlargement, where available

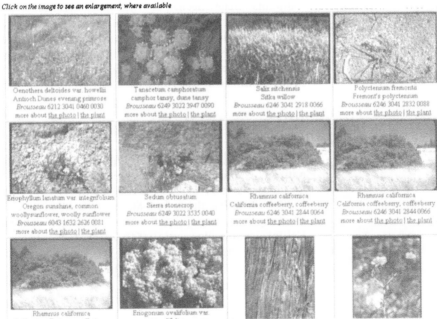

Figure 12. An example of content-based search and results of search.

Autonomy, implying local or decentralized control, is critical to scalability of UMDL. Negotiation is complementary to autonomy, in that autonomous agents must be capable of making binding commitments for the system to work.

There are three types of agents:

- **UIAs (User Interface Agents)** provide a communication wrapper around a user interface. This wrapper performs two functions. First, it encapsulates user queries in the proper form for the UMDL protocols. Second, it publishes a profile of the user to appropriate agents, which is used by mediator agents to guide the search process [9].

- **Mediator agents**, there are many types of mediator agents, performing all tasks that are required to pass on a query from a UIA to a collection, monitor the progress of a query, transmit the results of a query, and perform all ways of translation and bookkeeping. Currently, there are two classes of mediators in UMDL. "Registry agents capture the address and contents of each collection. Query-planning agents receive queries and route them to collections, possibly consulting other sources of information to establish the route."[9] Another special type of mediators, facilitators, mediates negotiation among agents.

- **CIAs (Collection Interface Agents)** provide a communication wrapper for a collection of information. CIAs perform translation tasks similar to those performed by the UIA for a user interface, and publish the contents and capabilities of a collection in the conspectus language. The conspectus is a normalized description of content. It provides interoperability for various search and retrieval methods through a common representation over collections. It is written in a language defined by UM, which is called UCL (UMDL Conspectus Language) [9].

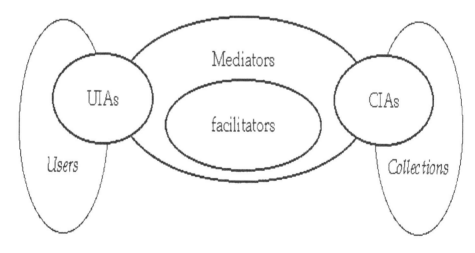

Figure 13. UMDL architecture.

Agent Teams

Complex UMDL tasks require the coordination of multiple specialized agents working together on behalf of users and collection providers [20]. While the scope and nature of the desired tasks will continually evolve, a fundamental requirement of agents is that they can form teams. Agents must therefore be capable of describing their capabilities in a way that other agents understand, and communicating these descriptions to other agents.

UMDL agents communicate at three distinctive levels of abstraction. At the lowest level, agents utilize network protocols like TCP/IP to transport messages among themselves. The interpretation and processing of these messages is dictated by task-specific protocols. At the second level, agents communicate in more widely accepted language such as Z39.50. The capabilities of a specialized agent will remain untapped unless the agent can make its abilities and location known, and participate in the team-formation process. We thus define special protocols, shared by all UMDL agents, for the team formation and negotiation tasks. These UMDL protocols represent the third level of abstraction in agent communication.

The UMDL protocols are designed to allow agents to advertise them and find each other based on capabilities. A special agent **called Registry Agent** maintains a database that contains information about all the agents in UMDL, including their respective content and capability descriptions.

Figure 14 shows the interaction between agents when there is a search by author.

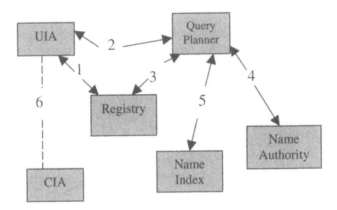

Figure 14. Interaction among agents when searching by author.

The main part of the testbed collections of UMDL is earth and space science. Commercial content focuses on timely journal literature and reference resources. These resources include:

- Encyclopedia of Science and Technology (McGraw Hill)
- 200 core and popular journals (UMI)
- Encyclopedia American (Grolier's)
- 50 scientific journals (Elsevier)
- Encyclopedia Britannica

The main tasks supported by UMDL user interface Artemis/Recommendation System are:

- Generalized "Subject Area" searches
- "Keyword" searches
- Recommendation of other web sites

The special function of Artemis is that users can make comments on the page and give it a rating.

A searching example is illustrated in Figure. In this example, the search for gemstones was created in Figure 15a and obtained results are shown in Figure 15b.

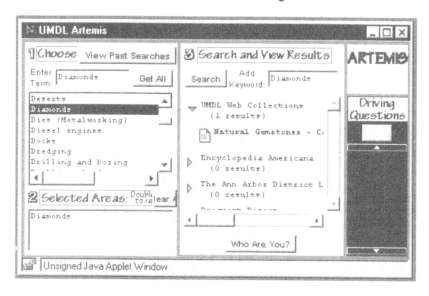

Figure 15. (a) Searching for gemstones, (b) Results of search.

3.1.4 University of California Santa Barbara Digital Library Project

The Alexandria Project's goal is to build a distributed digital library for materials that are referenced in geographic terms, such as by the names of communities or the types of geological features found in the material.

Figure 16 illustrates the basic ADL (Alexandria Digital Library) architecture, which derives a traditional library's four major components.

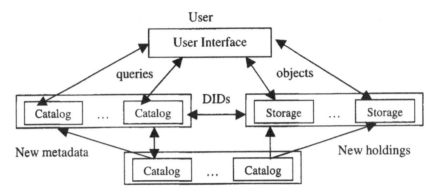

Figure 16. Architecture of ADL.

The **storage** component maintains and serves up the digital holdings of the library. These correspond to the "stacks" of physical holdings (books, journals, etc.) in a traditional library. The **catalog** component manages, and facilitates searches of, the metadata describing the holdings, analogous to a traditional library card catalog. Catalog metadata are associated with storage objects by unique object identifiers, analogous to traditional library call numbers. The **ingest** component comprises the mechanisms by which librarians and other authorized users populate the catalog and storage components. Finally, The **user interface** component is the collection of mechanisms by which one interacts with the catalog (to conduct a search) or the storage (to retrieve objects corresponding to search results).

The Web prototype architecture is shown in Figure 17.

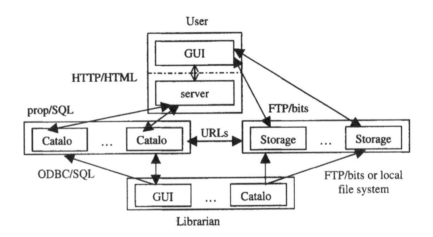

Figure 17. ADL Web prototype architecture.

ADL uses wavelets for image processing and texture for content-based retrieval. Besides, ADL also investigated parallel computation to address various performance issues, including multiprocessor servers, parallel I/O, and parallel wavelet transforms, both forward (for image ingest) and inverse (for efficient multi-scale image browsing).

Based on a traditional map library housed in the Map and Imagery Laboratory (MIL) in the Davidson Library at UCSB, ADL's holdings focus on collections of geographically referenced materials, including maps, satellite images, digitized aerial photographs, specialized textual material (such as gazetteers), and their associated metadata.

The user interface of ADL consists of several components. The major components are map browser, search options, workspace and metadata browser. Their screens are shown in Figures 18-21.

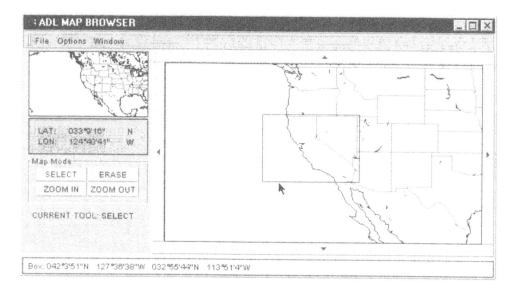

Figure 18. ADL map browser.

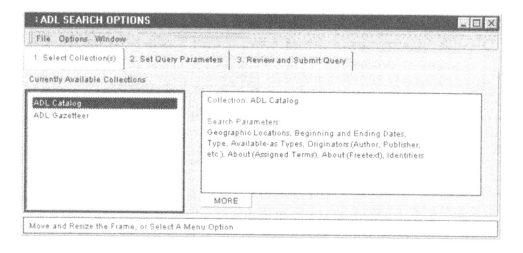

Figure 19. ADL search options.

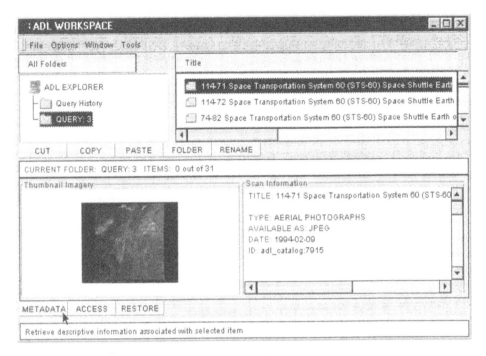

Figure 20. ADL workspace.

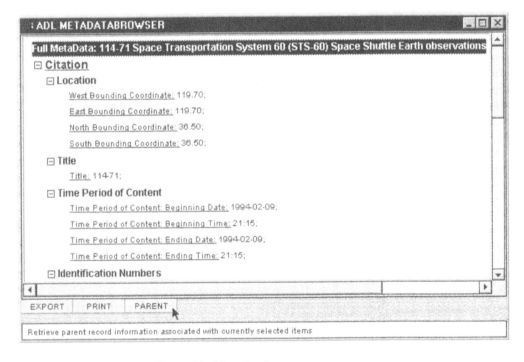

Figure 21. Metadata browser.

3.1.5 Stanford University Digital Library Project

Stanford digital library project focuses on **interoperability**. They developed the "**InfoBus**" protocol – **Digital Library InterOperating Protocol (DLIOP)**, which provides a uniform way to access a variety of services and information sources through "proxies" acting as interpreters between the InfoBus protocol and the native protocol. The InfoBus is implemented on top of a CORBA-based architecture using Inprise's Visibroker and Xerox' ILU. The second area is the legal and economic issue of a networked environment.

Figure 22 shows an example of three protocol domains. The first one is the local domain, which is a local network used by an information-services provider such as a company, a university, or even an individual. The second one is Telnet service domain, where clients log in to remote machines. The third one is HTTP, the protocol used for the WWW [21].

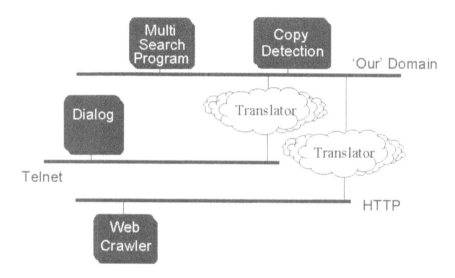

Figure 22. Interoperation across protocol domains.

The services in all the domains are accessible through their respective protocols. The service-interaction protocols in the local domain are locally controlled. The Dialog information service is an example of a Telnet-based information provider. The WebCrawler, a search engine that indexes documents on the WWW and returns their URL in response to queries, is an example of an HTTP-based service.

Dialog presents a teletype interface, through which the user first follows a standard login sequence (`Please logon:`), then selects one of the many databases offered through Dialog (`begin 245`). Users search the database through a proprietary query language (`select Library/ti`), then examine the results, and last terminate the sessions (`logout`). One possible abstraction of this process is that an open session operation is followed by open database, search, and quit operations. This abstraction can also be applied to WebCrawler, as shown in Figure 23.

The basic idea of Stanford InfoBus is Library Service Proxy. **Library-Service Proxy (LSP)** objects are created. Method calls on an LSP object invoke each interface element (`open session`, `open database`, and so on), and the method performs the appropriate operation on the corresponding service [21]. Figure 24 shows how LSPs can be used as the building blocks for the translators in Figure 23. The translator clouds are full of LSPs, each representing one service. A common interface thus makes two quite different services accessible from the local domain.

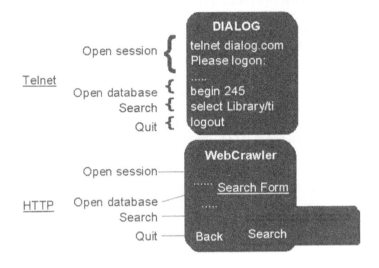

Figure 23. Glue for service access.

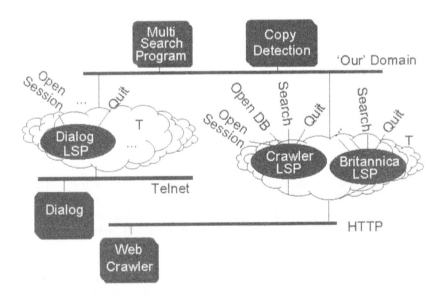

Figure 24. InfoBus idea—library service proxy.

There are many projects in Stanford digital library related to InfoBus. The collection of Stanford Digital Library is primarily computing literature. However, it has a strong focus on networked information sources, meaning that the vast arrays of topics found on the WWW are accessible through this project. The user interface DLITE is illustrated in Figure 25. It runs next to a Netscape browser.

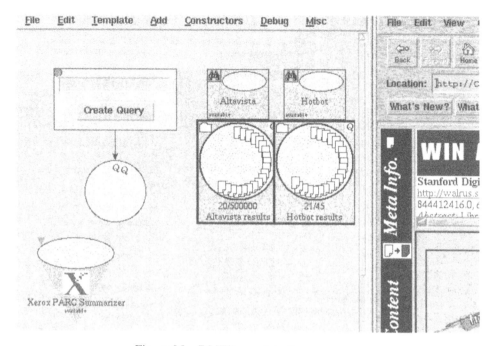

Figure 25. DLITE user interface.

3.1.6 University of Illinois in Urban-Champaign DeLiver Digital Library Project

The UIUC Digital library research effort was centered on building an experimental testbed containing tens of thousands of full-text journal articles from physics, engineering, and computer science and make them accessible over the WWW, often before they are available in print. The UIUC DLI Testbed, DeLiver, emphasized using the document structure to provide federated search across publisher collections. The sociology research included the evaluation of its effectiveness under use by over one thousand UIUC faculty and students, a user community an order of magnitude bigger than the last generation of research projects centered on search of scientific literature [22]. The technology research investigated indexing the contents of text documents to enable federated search across multiple sources, and testing this on millions of documents for semantic federation.

The structures of documents in the testbed are specified by Standard Generalized Markup Language (SGML). Their research efforts extract semantics from documents using the scalable technology of concept spaces based on context frequency. Then these efforts were merged with traditional library indexing to provide a single Internet interface to indexes of multiple repositories.

They developed a **Distributed Repository Model**, which is shown in Figure 26.

The UIUC Testbed (DeLIver) provides enhanced access over the Internet to the full text of selected engineering journals, using SGML document structure to facilitate search. Access to these materials is currently limited to UIUC faculty, students, and staff. The Testbed collection gathers articles directly from publishers in SGML format. These articles include texts and all figures, tables, images, and mathematical equations. The testbed collection presently comprises around 40,000 articles from journals in electrical engineering, physics and civil engineering.

Testbed Technologies for the Distributed Repository Model

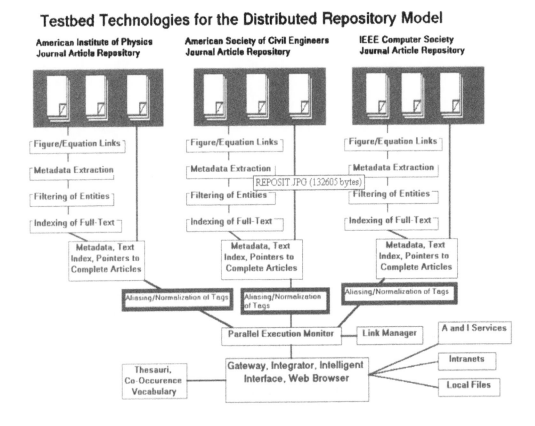

Figure 26. Testbed distributed repository model.

3.2 DIGITAL LIBRARIES INITIATIVE PROJECT -- PHASE II (DLI II)

The Digital Libraries Initiative - Phase 2 is an interagency program sponsored by the:

- National Science Foundation (NSF)
- Defense Advanced Research Projects Agency (DARPA)
- National Library of Medicine (NLM)
- Library of Congress (LOC)
- National Endowment for the Humanities (NEH)
- National Aeronautics & Space Administration (NASA)
- Federal Bureau of Investigation (FBI)

in partnership with:

- Institute of Museum and Library Services (IMLS)
- Smithsonian Institution (SI)
- National Archives and Records Administration (NARA)

The primary purposes of this initiative are to provide leadership in research fundamental to the development of the next generation of digital libraries, to advance the use and usability of globally distributed, networked information resources, and to encourage existing and new communities to focus on innovative applications areas. Since digital libraries can serve as intellectual infrastructure, this Initiative looks to stimulate partnering arrangements necessary to create next-generation operational systems in such areas as education, engineering and design, earth and space sciences, biosciences, geography, economics, and the arts and humanities. It will address the digital libraries life cycle from information creation, access and use, to archiving and preservation. Research to gain a better understanding of the long term social, behavioral and economic implications of and effects of new digital libraries capabilities in such areas of human activity as research, education, commerce, defense, health services and recreation is an important part of this initiative.

The special interests in this initiative are:

Research in the following areas:

- *Human-Centered Research*
Human-centered digital libraries research seeks to further understanding of the impacts and potential of digital libraries to enhance human activities in creating, seeking, and using information and to promote technical research designed to achieve these goals.

- *Content And Collections-Based Research*
Content and collection-centered digital library research focuses on better understanding of and advancing access to novel digital content and collections.

- *Systems-Centered Research*
Systems-centered digital libraries research focuses on component technologies and integration to realize information environments that are dynamic and flexible; responsive at the level of individual, group, and institution; and capable of adapting large, amorphous, continually growing bodies of data to user-defined structure and scale.

Testbeds and Applications
This focuses on development of digital library testbeds for technology testing, demonstration and validation, and as prototype resources for domain communities - technical and non-technical. Applications projects are expected to result in enduring information environments for research, learning, and advancing public use in creative ways.

Planning Testbeds and Applications for Undergraduate Education

Projects funded to date under DLI2 include the ones listed below. As more projects are funded, they will be added to the list below:

- **A Patient Care Digital Library**: Personalized Search and Summarization over Multimedia Information, Columbia University

- **Informedia-II**: Integrated Video Information Extraction and Synthesis for Adaptive Presentation and Summarization from Distributed Libraries, Carnegie Mellon University

- **The Alexandria Digital Earth Prototype (ADEPT)**, University of California at Santa Barbara

- **Stanford Digital Libraries Technologies**, University of California at Berkeley, the University of California at Santa Barbara, and Stanford University

- **Re-inventing Scholarly Information Dissemination and Use**, University of California at Berkeley, the University of California at Santa Barbara, and Stanford University

- **An Operational Social Science Digital Data Library**, Harvard University

- **Security and Reliability in Component-based Digital Libraries**, Cornell University

- **Founding a National Gallery of the Spoken Word**, Michigan State University

- **A Digital Library for the Humanities**, Tufts University

- **A Software and Data Library for Experiments, Simulations and Archiving**, University of South Carolina

- **Digital Workflow Management**: Lester S. Levy Collection of Sheet Music, Johns Hopkins University

- **A Multi-tiered Extensible Digital Archive of Folk Literature**, University of California at Davis

- **The Digital Athenaeum**: New techniques for restoring, searching, and editing humanities collections University of Kentucky

- **Data Provenance, University of Pennsylvania DL of Vertebrate Morphology using a new High Resolution X-ray CT Scanning facility**, University of Texas at Austin

- **Using the Informedia Digital Video Library to Author Multimedia Material**, Carnegie Mellon University

- **High-Performance Digital Library Classification Systems: From Information Retrieval to Knowledge Management**, University of Arizona

- **A Distributed Information Filtering System for Digital Libraries**, Indiana University Bloomington

- **Automatic Reference Librarians for the World Wide Web**, University of Washington

- **Tracking Footprints through a Medical Information Space: Computer Scientist-Physician Collaborative Study of Document Selection by Expert Problem Solvers**, Oregon Health Sciences University and Oregon Graduate Institute of Science and Technology

- **Image Filtering for Secure Distribution of Medical Information**, Stanford University

- **Using the National Engineering Education Delivery System as the Foundation for Building a Test-Bed Digital Library for Science, Mathematics, Engineering and Technology Education**, University of California, Berkeley

- **Planning Grant for the Use of Digital Libraries in Undergraduate Learning in Science**, Old Dominion University

- **Virtual Skeletons in 3 Dimensions: The Digital Library as a Platform for Studying Web-Anatomical Form and Function**, University of Texas at Austin

4. CONCLUSIONS

In this chapter we examined the design and implementation of digital libraries. There is no single definition for digital libraries and the definition evolves as the research goes on. The common consensus is that they provide their users with a coherent view of heterogeneous autonomously managed resources. There are a lot of research issues waiting for resolution. These issues are classified as five major kinds, namely interoperability, description of objects and repositories, collection management and organization and user interface and human-computer interaction and economic, social and legal issues.

A commonly accepted architecture of digital library is based on digital objects and handle system and common repository access interface (RAP). Handle is a general-purpose unique identifier for Internet resources, including digital objects. Handle system is a distributed system that manages handles. Access and deposit of digital objects is conducted according to Repository Access Protocol (RAP).

When designing a digital video library system, we have to consider special issues related to characteristics of video such as video compression, video indexing, video segmentation and video retrieval.

Digital Library Initiative is one of the earliest efforts in digital library research in digital library area. It consists of two phases. DLI I just ended last year. It focused on the basic issues of digital library, particularly efficient searching technical documents on the Internet. Each participant was concentrated on one specific research areas, created its own testbed and tested the ideas on the testbed. Based on Phase I, Phase II will be a broader effort and will emphasize research and practices on human-centered system. So far there have been 24 funded projects going on.

We have made some progress, especially in areas such as description of objects and repositories, user interface and interoperability. But digital libraries are very complicated systems. The problem is international. It is not a topic only in computer and information science; it involves many communities, including social, legal and political communities. Joint efforts are necessary for solutions to safeguarding digital contents and users and providing users convenient services at the same time. There is still a long way to go to maturity and commercial products.

References

1. B. Schatz and H. Chen, "Digital Libraries: Technological Advances and Social Impacts," *Computer*, Vol. 32, February 1999.
2. A. Paepcke, "Digital Libraries: Searching Is Not Enough – What We Learned On-Site," *D-Lib Magazine*, Vol. 2, No. 2, May 1996.
3. C. Lynch and H. Garcia-Molina, "Interoperability, Scaling, and the Digital Libraries Research Agenda: A Report on the May 18-19, 1995," *IITA Digital Libraries Workshop*, August 1995.
4. NSF Announcement, "Digital Libraries Initiative – Phase 2," Announcement Number NSF 98-63,1998.
5. B. M. Leiner, "From the Editor: Metrics and the Digital Library," *D-Lib Magazine*, Vol. 4, No. 7/8, July/August 1998.
6. S. M. Griffin, "NSF/DARPA/NASA Digital Libraries Initiative: A Program Manager's Perspective," *D-Lib Magazine*, Vol. 4, No. 7/8, July/August 1998.

7. W.Y. Arms, E. A. Overly, M. Restoj, and C. Blanchi, "An Architecture for Information in Digital Libraries," *D-Lib Magazine*, Vol. 3, No. 2, February 1997.

8. R. Kahn and R.Wilensky, "A Framework for Distributed Digital Object Services," *D-Lib Magazine*, Vol. 1, No. 5, May 1995.

9. W.P. Birmingham, "An Agent-Based Architecture for Digital Libraries", *D-Lib Magazine*, Vol. 1, No.7, July 1995.

10. B. M. Leiner, "The NCSTRL Approach to Open Architecture for the Confederated Digital Library," *D-Lib Magazine*, Vol. 4, No. 12, December 1998.

11. M. Christel, S. Stevens, T. Kanade, M. Mauldin, R. Reddy, and H. Wactlar, "Techniques for the Creation and Exploration of Digital Video Libraries", Chapter in the book Multimedia Tools and Applications, Ed. B. Furht, Kluwer Academic Publishers, Norwell, MA, 1996.

12. B. Scheatz and H. Chen, "Building Large-Scale Digital Libraries," *Computer*, Vol.29, May 1996.

13. V. Ogle and R. Wilensky, "Testbed Development for the Berkley Digital Library Project," *D-Lib Magazine*, Vol. 2, No. 8, August 1996.

14. Alexandria Digital Library User Interface Tutorial.

15. J. Frew, M. Freeston, R. B. Kemp, et al., "The Alexandria Digital Library Testbed," *D-Lib Magazine*, Vol. 2, No. 8, August 1996.

16. C. Lichti, C. Falousos, H. Wactlar, M. Christel, and A. Hauptmann, "Informedia: Lessons from a Terabyte+, Operational, Digital Video Database System," *Proc. of Very Large Database Conference*, New York, August 1998.

17. Scott Stevens, "Carnegie Mellon University: The Informedia Digital Video and Spoken Language Document Testbed," *D-Lib Magazine*, Vol. 5, No. 2, February 1996.

18. V. Ogle and R. Wilensky, "Testbed Development for the Berkeley Digital Library Project," *D-Lib Magazine*, Vol. 2, No. 7/8, 1996.

19. D. E. Atkins, W. P. Birmingham, E. H. Durfee, E. Glover, T. Mullen, E. A. Rundenstteiner, E. Soloway, J. M. Vidal, R. Wallace, and M. P. Wellman, "Building the University of Michigan Digital Library: Interacting Software Agents in Support of Inquiry-Based Education," http://ai.eecs.umich.edu/people/wellman/pubs/Building-UMDL.html, 1999.

20. D. E. Atkins, W. P. Birmingham, E. H. Durfee, E. J. Glover, T. Mullen, E.A. Rundensteiner, E. Soloway, J. M. Vidal, R. Wallace, and M. P. Wellman, "Toward Inquiry-Based Education Through Interacting Software Agents," *Computer*, Vol. 29, May 1996.

21. A. Paepcke, S. B. Cousins, H. Garcia-Molina, S. W. Hassan, S. P. Ketchpel, M. Roscheisen, and T. Winograd, "Using Distributed Objects for Digital Library Interoperability," *Computer*, Vol. 29, May 1996.

22. http://dli.grainger.uiuc.edu.

Chapter 19

VIDEOCONFERENCING SYSTEMS AND APPLICATIONS

Sandra Brey and Borko Furht

Abstract

In this chapter we present an overview of videoconferencing technologies, systems, standards, applications, and commercial products with an emphasis on Internet-based video-conferencing. We begin with the history of videoconferencing and then we introduce fundamentals of audio and video technologies for videoconferencing. The videoconferencing standards, such as H320, H.321, H.323, and H.324, are described next. We discuss networks for videoconferencing and evaluate IP-based and ATM-based videoconferencing systems. Various videoconferencing applications are briefly described as well as a variety of commercial videoconferencing products and systems.

1. INTRODUCTION

Videoconferencing is the transmission of live video images and audio between two or more disparate participants. Once merely a figment of science fiction writers' imaginations, it is now used for both business and personal use, on a variety of different types of network media and with varying degrees of quality.

Conversations may be one to one (point-to-point) or one-to-many (multipoint), in simplex (one-way only), half-duplex (one way at a time, taking turns) or full-duplex (all parties are seen and heard simultaneously). A range of products is offered, which span a wide spectrum of applications from group (or room) based systems, to desktop videoconferencing systems, to less expensive (and lower quality) personal conferencing/videophone systems. Products are available which can convert a multimedia PC, or even a television set, into a videoconferencing workstation.

Networks used include ISDN, IP packet-data LANs, ATM networks, analog phone lines, and even the Internet. Of course, the quality of the video and audio obtainable depends in large part on the characteristics of the network used. Factors such as data throughput rate, delay, and delay variation, differ widely based on the type of network used. Several different standards have been developed which are optimized for use on each of the different network types.

Taken together, these segments add up to a huge, rapidly growing business. This is partly due to the explosion of videoconferencing via personal computer and the Internet. The videoconferencing market is expected to exceed 3 billion dollars annually by 2001, as illustrated in Figure 1.

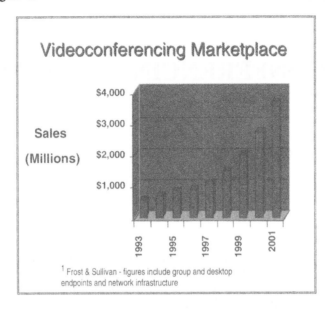

Figure 1. Projected growth in videoconferencing sales.

2. HISTORY OF VIDEOCONFERENCING

The first demonstrations of videoconferencing in the United States occurred in the 1920s. Other experiments were done in Europe in the 1930s. Put on hold during World War II, research began again in the mid 40s. However, it wasn't until 1964, at the World's Fair in New York, that Bell Labs presented the Picturephone, shown in Figure 2, to the world.

Figure 2. Advertisement for 1960's Picturephone.

This device compressed a video signal such that it could be carried over the digital equivalent of 100 telephone lines. It was designed to be a personal conferencing tool, used in conjunction with the telephone.

Nippon Electric Corporation and British Telecom developed group videoconferencing systems in the 70's. These early systems worked with analog signals, because networks deployed at that time could not provide the required bandwidth to transmit video signals in digital form.

In the early 70's and into the 80's, expensive room-based videoconferencing tools were the norm. The price of only the "codec" (coder/decoder) was $250,000. The additional costs for cameras, speakers, lighting equipment, microphones and other required equipment put videoconferencing out of the reach of all but the wealthiest companies.

The VLSI (Very Large Scale Integration) circuit technology breakthroughs made in the 80's had a major impact on the videoconferencing industry. The availability of cheap memory and powerful microprocessors allowed images to be stored and processed, steps necessary for data rate compression. This made it possible to reduce the bandwidth of the video signal to the point where it was able to be transported over available networks.

For years the videoconferencing market was plagued by high costs, low quality, and the inability of different products to work together. Due to innovations in networking and computer technologies, the quality has improved while the prices have continued to drop.

Videoconferencing was a tool used primarily by the upper echelons of the business world until 1990. Also, it was virtually unavailable on the desktop until 1994. VTEL, founded in 1985, offered the first PC-based system.

Two other pioneering companies in the field of video compression were Compression Labs Incorporated, founded in 1976, and PictureTel, established in 1984. PictureTel developed the first software based videoconferencing system to become commercially available. It required a mere 224 Kbps bandwidth, revolutionary at the time.

In December of 1990 an interoperability videoconferencing standard was accepted by CCITT (now ITU). This allowed compatibility of products among different vendors. It was designed mainly for the group-based systems.

Before standardization, all parties involved would have to be using the same manufacturer's product, on a similar network. Clearly, this was not compatible with the idea of videoconferencing between people from different organizations, such as for a sales presentation. Only those closely affiliated could be included. The adoption of standards has been a stimulus to the videoconferencing market, as the opportunities for and rewards of true interconnectivity become apparent. Today, people are able to videoconference over different network configurations, using different, standard compliant products.

The cost of videoconferencing tools continues to plummet. Indeed, some vendors have software products that can be downloaded for free from the Internet. This, coupled with the availability, and popularity of multimedia-enabled PCs with fast processors and plentiful memory, is pushing the videoconferencing market to the desktop, supplanting the room-based systems. One can find the rudimentary personal conferencing capabilities bundled with the operating system, preinstalled on the consumer personal computer.

More inclusive standards were ratified by the International Telecommunication Union's Telecommunications Standardization Sector (ITU-T) in 1996, providing for interoperability among devices operating over various networks. One of these standards, H.324, defines videoconferencing over standard phone lines (POTS). H.323 addresses the requirements of videoconferencing communications over local area networks (LANs) and the Internet. The adoption of these standards has set the stage for a skyrocketing PC-based personal conferencing market.

3. AUDIO AND VIDEO FUNDAMENTALS

The bandwidth requirements of uncompressed video data are immense; therefore it is necessary to perform compression prior to transmission over communication channels. The compression must occur in real-time to satisfy the strict timing constraints of the videoconferencing session.

The audio and video signals must be converted from analog form to digital form and stored digitally to be manipulated by the computer. The codec (COder/DECoder), the centerpiece of any videoconferencing system, performs the function of coding, decoding, compressing, and decompressing the video and audio.

3.1 HARDWARE vs. SOFTWARE CODECS

Codecs may be implemented in either hardware or software. Deploying hardware codecs on a network requires disassembly of each computer which becomes tedious when working with a large system of many computers.

A software codec is usually easier to deploy, but puts a burden on the host's CPU, potentially making it problematic to concurrently run other applications. Hardware codecs have their own processors, allowing them to relieve the host processor of such duties as call setup, compression and decompression, and echo-cancellation. Clearly, there are other factors to consider when determining which to use, such as RAM, the speed of the network, the quality of the video capture card, among others. For example, if the networking environment is a 28.8 POTS connection, a hardware codec won't offer any improvement.

Software codecs are far less expensive than hardware codecs. In fact, both Microsoft and Intel have versions, albeit minimally equipped, that can be downloaded free from the Internet. The hardware variety comes in a wide range of prices.

3.2 AUDIO CODING AND COMPRESSION

3.2.1 Pulse Code Modulation

Digitizing an analog audio signal is done through a process called Pulse Code Modulation (PCM). The sampling rate and the number of bits per sample are defined parameters of the process. The sampling rate is the number of samples per second. Bits per sample is the number of bits used to represent each sample value. Additionally, the number of channels can be one for monaural, two for stereo, and so on.

Digitizing the audio signal requires the analog audio signal to be passed through several stages. First, the signal is low-pass filtered to remove high frequencies. Any audio signals present, which have frequencies above 1/2 of the sample rate, will be "aliased", or translated to lower frequencies, and result in a distorted reproduction of the original sound. Due to the finite rolloff of analog filters, it is a practical necessity to sample at more than twice the maximum audio frequency of interest. Although humans can perceive sound frequencies between 20 Hz and 20 kHz, videoconferencing systems are typically designed to handle speech quality audio which encompasses a much smaller range of frequencies. Telephone quality audio extends from about 300 to 3300 kHz.

After filtering, the signal is sampled. The amplitude values of an analog audio signal, representing the loudness of the signal, are continuously varying in time. To encode this signal digitally, the amplitude value of the signal is measured (sampled) at regular intervals. According to the Nyquist Theorem, to have lossless digital representation of the analog signal, the sampling rate must be at least twice that of the highest frequency present in the analog waveform. This is termed the "Nyquist rate".

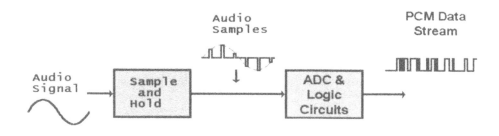

Figure 3. PCM encoder simplified block diagram.

The sampled value is then quantized. This requires the value to be mapped into one of a set of fixed values, which are binary coded for transmission. See Figure 3 for a diagram of the encoding process.

The errors, which result from this mapping of analog values to quantized levels, result in "quantization noise". It follows that the level of quantization noise drops as the quantization levels become closer together. Therefore, more bits of quantizer resolution translate to less quantizer noise, and hence greater dynamic range.

Some implementations have a linear quantization. Other approaches may use a logarithmic quantization, which results in a type of audio compression, reducing quantization noise during quiet intervals without wasting bits at higher signal levels.

The total bit rate for a monaural PCM signal can be found by multiplying the sample rate by the number of bits/sample. A stereo signal would require twice the bit rate, etc.

Because of the fact that telephone quality voice transmission requires about 3 kHz of audio bandwidth and 256 quantum levels, a sample rate of 8 kHz and 8 bits per sample are commonly used, resulting in the 64 kbps channels used for ISDN and other phone applications.

3.2.2 ADPCM

Adaptive Differential Pulse Code Modulation is a compressed version of PCM, which requires a lower bit rate than standard PCM to transmit the same voice information.

In DPCM, previous PCM samples are used to predict the value of the current sample. It is possible to do this because of the patterns present in speech samples. This prediction algorithm is performed at both the transmitting and receiving end. The transmitter compares the actual sample to its predicted value, and computes the error. Because the error signal will have a lower variance than the original speech samples, it can be quantized with fewer bits than the original speech signal. This error signal is then transmitted.

Because the prediction algorithm is performed at the receiving end as well, the receiver knows what the predicted value is. It uses the error signal to correct the predicted value and reproduce the original sample. This predict-compare-adjust process is repeated for each input sample, reproducing the original PCM samples at the output.

The system is called "adaptive" because the prediction parameters and the quantization levels of the error signal can change dynamically depending on the rate of change of the sample values (i.e. signal level).

Many ITU-T videoconferencing recommendations include ADPCM encoding methods. Different flavors of ADPCM encoder/decoders vary in the way the predicted value is calculated and how the predictor or quantizer adapts to signal characteristics. This results in various levels of compression. Standards include G.721, G.722, G.723, G.726, and G.729. Various characteristics of these standards are summarized in Table 1.

Higher quality speech (50 Hz -7 kHz, 14 bit resolution) may be encoded by dividing the audio spectrum into two subbands and performing separate ADPCM coding on each. The technique is covered in G.722 and is called "Sub-Band ADPCM". G.722 specifies three modes of operation: 64, 56 and 48 kbps.

3.2.3 LPC/CELP/ACELP

LPC (Linear Predictive Coding) is used to compress audio at 16 Kbps and below. An LPC encoder fits speech signals to a simple analytic model of the vocal tract. The signal is broken into frames, usually tens of milliseconds long, and best fit parameters for each frame are transmitted and used by the decoder to generate synthetic speech that is similar to the original. The result is intelligible but artificial sounding.

Plain LPC is not included in videoconferencing standards, but is the basis for CELP (Code Excited Linear Prediction) which is important for obtaining high audio compression rates in videoconferencing. CELP is quite similar to LPC. The CELP encoder does the same frame-based LPC modeling but then computes the errors between the original speech and the synthetic model and transmits both model parameters and the errors. The error signal actually represents indices in a "codebook" of "excitation vectors" shared by the encoders and decoder. Thus the error signal is very much compressed. It follows that the computational complexity and speech quality of the coder depend upon the search sizes of the code books, which can be reduced at the expense of sound quality.

CELP makes possible much higher quality speech at very low data rates. ITU-T Recommendation G.728 uses a variation of CELP, LD-CELP (Low Delay CELP). The compressed audio requires a bandwidth of only 16 kbps, but the encoder and decoder are quite computationally complex, requiring special hardware.

Table 1. Audio Standards G Family

ITU STANDARD	YEAR APPROVED	ALGORITHM USED	BIT RATE	BANDWIDTH [KHZ]	TYPICAL END-TO-END DELAY [MS]	APPLICATION
G.711	1977	PCM	48,56,64	3	<<1	GSTN telephony, H323 & H320 videoconf.
G.723	1995	MPE/ACELP	53,6.3	3	67-97	GSTN videotelephony H.323 telephony
G.728	1992	LD-CELP	16	3	<<2	GSTN, H320 videoconf.
G.729	1995	ACELP	8	3	25-35	GSTN telephony, Modem H.324, GSTN videoph.
G.722	1988	Subband ADPCM	48,56,64	7	<2	ISDN videoconf.

3.3 VIDEO COMPRESSION

Since network bandwidth is in limited quantity, and video is inherently bandwidth thirsty, the choice of video compression technique takes on great importance.

Video is composed of a sequence of still images, called frames. The sequence of frames is presented at a rate that makes the motion of the depicted video scene appear fluid. The frame rate for television in the United States is 30 frames per second. The frame rate in a business quality videoconferencing session should be at least 15 frames per second. At lower rates the video will appear jerky.

Each frame of the video is digitally represented as a two dimensional matrix of pixels. Color images are composed of three image frames, one for each color component.

Video compression is typically lossy, meaning some of the information is lost during the compression step. The compression process takes advantage of the functioning of human vision, discarding information that is not perceptible. Further compression can be achieved, further reducing the required bandwidth, but at the sacrifice of quality. The required level of quality will depend on the application.

Color space sampling and redundancy reduction is techniques common to most video codecs. Color space sampling is a technique used to reduce the amount of data that needs to be encoded. Because the human eye is less sensitive to chrominance information, an image encoded in YUV space can have the U and V components subsampled. In this way, these components will require one half, or less, of the bits required to encode the more important Y component. Redundancy reduction is also used to decrease the amount of encoded information. Intraframe encoding achieves compression by reducing the spatial redundancy within a picture. This technique takes advantage of the fact that neighboring pixels in an image are usually similar.

Further compression is achieved through interframe encoding, which uses the fact that neighboring frames in a sequence of images are usually similar, by reducing the temporal redundancy between frames.

3.3.1 Discrete Cosine Transform
Discrete Cosine Transform is a video compression technique that forms the basis for the two important video compression standards, H.261 and H.263. This compression algorithm is

also used by the Joint Photographic Experts Group (JPEG) standard for still-image compression. DCT is an intraframe spatial compression technique that converts pixel values into their frequency-based equivalents.

The first part of the algorithm transforms the pixel value information into values in the frequency domain. The encoding process then codes the higher frequency components with less fidelity than the lower ones, since the human eye is more responsive to low frequencies than to high ones.

The DCT algorithm begins by dividing a frame into eight-by-eight blocks of pixels. The DC coefficient is the first value produced by the transform. Its value represents the average luminance for the entire block. The remaining 63 coefficients, called AC coefficients, are calculated, concentrating the low-frequency components in the upper left corner, and the high-frequency components in the lower right corner. The low frequency components describe detail shifts in the image such as edges and color changes, while the higher frequencies describe larger areas of uniform color. No information is lost during the DCT step of the algorithm; the data could be recovered by performing an inverse DCT.

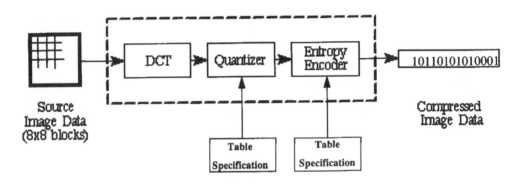

Figure 4. DCT encoder block diagram.

3.3.2 Quantization
The next step is quantization; it is the lossy step of the encoding process. First, an 8x8-quantization matrix is generated. The values in this matrix are calculated from a user defined quality factor. Each coefficient is divided by its corresponding value of the quantization matrix. The purpose of quantizing is to reduce the amplitude of the coefficients and to increase the number of zero value coefficients. The quantization matrix is designed so that the values increase diagonally right. This is so that the value of more of the higher frequency AC components, which are less visually significant, will go to zero.

3.3.3 Run-length and Entropy Encoding
This bit stream undergoes further compression through runlength and entropy coding. The run-length encoding removes long runs of zero valued coefficients. The entropy encoding process encodes the information efficiently based on statistical characteristics. Patterns that are statistically more likely to occur are encoded with less bits. Huffman entropy encoding is used in the H.261 and H.263 standard codecs.

The DC component undergoes differential encoding. It is encoded as the difference between the current DC coefficient and the DC coefficient of the previous block. Next, the AC coefficients are encoded in a zigzag sequence from the upper left of the block to the bottom right. The AC coefficients are then run-length encoded and entropy encoded to produce a binary coded stream. Figure 4 shows a block diagram of the DCT encoding process.

At the receiving end the decoder will reverse the encoding process. The decoder will be provided the same quantization and entropy tables that were used to encode the data.

This type of intraframe compression can achieve compression on the order of 15:1, with excellent quality. As compression increases, the quality of the image decreases.

3.3.4 Motion Compensation

A sequence of frames from a video is full of redundancy; there is little noticeable difference between subsequent frames. The purpose of interframe coding is to remove this temporal redundancy, and vastly improve the compression ratio. Motion Compensation is an interframe coding technique that involves working with 16 by 16 macroblocks to identify a group in the previous frame that best matches a group on the current frame. This difference between the frames is coded along with a vector that describes the offset of that group. This data is then entropy coded, to achieve yet further compression.

3.4 ITU-T VIDEO COMPRESSION STANDARDS

3.4.1 ITU-T Standard H.261

The H.261 is a video codec for audiovisual services at p x 64 kbps (p=1,2,3...30), and uses a DCT based codec. H.261 supports two image formats, Common Interchange Format (CIF), and quarter CIF (QCIF). CIF is 352 by 288 pixels; QCIF is 176 by 144 pixels. Support of QCIF is mandatory, and support of CIF is optional.

The standard does not define a required frame rate for compression, however for a codec to be H.261 compliant, it must decode up to and including 30 frames per second. The DCT algorithm is used for intraframe coding, but only certain frames of the video sequence are fully encoded in this way. For interframe coding, the H.261 standard calls for coding only the difference between a frame and the previous frame.

The more complex and processing-intensive motion compensation interframe coding is only optional for H.261 coders, however the H.261 decoder must be able to decode motion compensation information. DCT intraframe coding is mandatory for both the coder and decoder.

Typical compression ratios are around 80 to 100:1. However, compression ratios can go as high as 500:1, depending on the video.

3.4.2 ITU-T Standard H.263

The H.263 is a video codec for narrow telecommunications channels (less than 64 Kbps). The formal name of H.263 is "Video Coding for Low Bit Rate Communication." It is a backward compatible refinement of the H.261 standard, adding many performance and error recovery improvements.

Like H.261 the support of the QCIF format is mandatory. H.263 also optionally supports several other formats. Sub Quarter Common Intermediate Format (sub-QCIF) is supported for very low-resolution images. Also supported are 4CIF, which has four times the resolution as CIF, and 16CIF, which has sixteen times the resolution of CIF. Table 2 presents a summary of the video picture formats.

Table 2. Video Picture Formats.

Picture Format	Number of Luminance Lines	Number of Luminance Pixels	Number of Chrominance Lines	Number of Chrominance Pixels	Supported in H.261	Supported in H.263
sub-QCIF	96	128	48	64	not supported	optional
QCIF	144	176	72	88	optional	mandatory
CIF	288	352	144	176	mandatory	mandatory
4CIF	576	704	288	352	not supported	optional
16CIF	1152	1408	576	704	not supported	optional

Where the H.261 standard was limited to full pixel precision for motion compensation, H.263 has required support of half-pixel precision. The half-pixel refinement greatly improves the picture quality, particularly in low-resolution video.

New to the H.263 standard are negotiable coding options offering improved performance. One of these options is the support of P-B frames used in interframe encoding. This is a technique that is also used in MPEG video. Although it is computationally more expensive, it allows for much higher compression, and therefore a potentially higher frame rate.

4. COMPONENTS AND FUNCTIONS OF A VIDEOCONFERENCING SYSTEM

A typical videoconferencing system and its components are shown in Figure 5. Videoconferencing stations are equipped with video and audio capture and compress subsystems, and decompress and display subsystems. The communication media can be POTS (Plain Old Telephone System), LANs, or WAN.

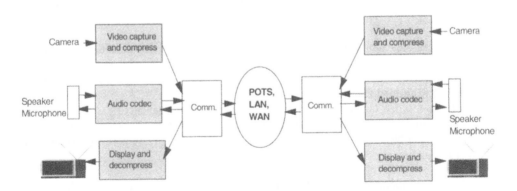

Figure 5. Components of a videoconferencing system.

The common software architecture of a videoconferencing system, shown in Figure 6, consists of videoconferencing application, middleware, video and audio codec and data, stream multiplexer and demultiplexer, and line drivers.

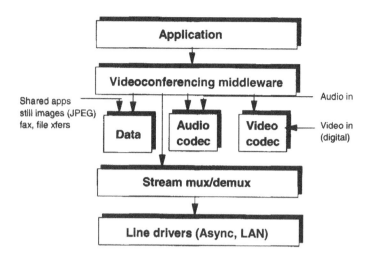

Figure 6. Common software architecture of a videoconferencing system.

Videoconferencing systems support a number of functions including:

Multipoint connection set up. The system should be able to negotiate for network resources and end-to-end conference capabilities.

Dynamic session control. The system should have an ability to add and delete participant to/from an existing videoconference. Such a change may require modification of the underlying network configuration.

Conference directory. The system should provide a conference directory service that will support conference registration, announcement, and query. The directory should contain various information such as: the title and the brief description of the conference, a list of participants, start and end time for the conference, audio and video coding schemes, their protocols and QOS requirements, and shared working space.

Automatic conference scheduling and recording. The conference scheduling function combined with resource reservation mechanisms will allow planning of network resources. Automatic conference recording is a useful function that does recording of conference sessions in a form of multimedia documents.

Conference termination. The system should be capable to release all reserved resources when the conference is complete.

5. VIDEOCONFERENCING STANDARDS AND NETWORKS

5.1 VIDEOCONFERENCING STANDARDS

The original, widely accepted videoconferencing standard was H.320, which defines a methodology for transporting videoconferencing traffic over ISDN. However, in 1996, additional standards for videoconferencing emerged - H.323, H.321, and H.324. These standards define methodologies for videoconferencing over other various networks such as POTS, IP networks such as LANs and the Internet, and ATM networks. Each of these standards brings with it certain capabilities and quality levels, illustrated in Figure 7. Each has advantages and disadvantages in videoconferencing transmission.   The various characteristics of these standards are summarized is Table 3, and discussed in the following sections.

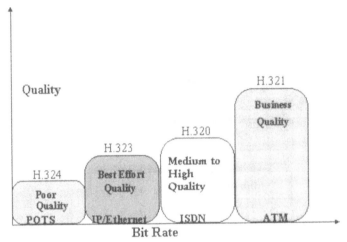

Figure 7. Quality of videoconferencing standards.

Videoconferencing involves the transmission of video, audio, and data. Data can be in the form of whiteboard data or shared application data, used in a collaborative conference. These different types of information have different reliability and delay variation requirements of the networks over which they are being transmitted.

Table 3. Characteristics of Various Videoconferencing Standards

	H.320	H.321	H.323	H.324
Approval Date	1990	1995	1996/1998	1996
Network	Narrowband Switched digital ISDN	Broadband ISDN ATM LAN	Non-guaranteed bandwidth packet switched networks	POTS, the analog phone system
Video	H.261 H.263	H.261 H.263	H.261 H.263	H.261 H.263
Audio	G.711 G.722 G.728	G.711 G.722 G.728	G.711 G.722 G.728 G.723 G.729	G.723
Multiplexing	H.221	H.221	H.225.0	H.223
Control	H.230	H.242	H.242 H.230	H.245
Multipoint	H.231 H.243	H.231 H.243	H.323	
Data	T.120	T.120	T.120	T.120
Communication Interface	I.400	AAL I.363 AJM I.361 PHY I.400	TCP/IP	V.34 Modem

Video and audio data are delay sensitive; they can't tolerate much deviation. They need to arrive at a constant rate with little variance to be presentable and intelligible. Large delays, known as jitter, will cause the picture to appear "jerky". The audio will sound unnatural if it encounters network delays. Video and audio are less sensitive to reliability.

Uncompressed video can tolerate some lost or corrupt frames without severely affecting the quality of the presentation. A corrupt frame will simply be replaced by the next frame of the video.

Compressed video may suffer from unreliable transmission. This is because in interframe encoding, a video compression technique, redundant information has been removed and just the differences between the frames are transmitted. This interdependency could cause problems in an unreliable transmission environment. However, video compression techniques have been designed to work around this problem. This can be compensated for by periodically sending complete information about a frame, even if the data in these blocks has not changed.

Conversely, general data is not sensitive to delay but is sensitive to reliability. An example is a data file that is sent over a network. Since it doesn't have the same strict timing constraints of the audio and video, it doesn't matter how long the file takes to get to its destination. But the data information in the file needs to be correct, as any transmission errors may render it useless.

5.2 NETWORK CONFIGURATIONS FOR MULTIMEDIA CONFERENCING

Several network configurations are used for multimedia conferencing (Figure 8):

- Fully distributed (mesh) network,
- Centralized (star) network,
- Double-star network, and
- Hierarchical network.

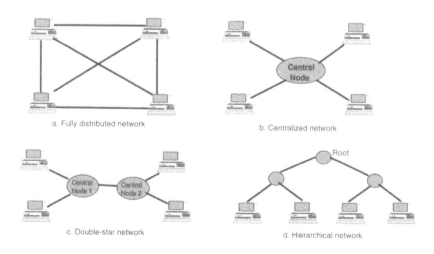

Figure 8. Network configurations for videoconferencing: (a) distributed network (mesh), (b) centralized network (star), (c) double-star network, and (d) hierarchical network.

The fully distributed network is based on multiple point-to-point links, and connects each participant with each other. Each participant sends the media directly to every other participant. The processing and mixing media is done at each individual participant's location. This configuration uses the highest network bandwidth and duplicates the work involved in mixing data at every participant's location. On the other hand, this system gives the best (shortest) delay time when considering media transmission and mixing. Its major disadvantage is that with increased number of conference participants, the point-to-point connections increase rapidly.

The centralized network consists of a central node connected to every participant of the conference. The central node acts as intermediate processor and performs media mixing. It received multimedia data from participants, mixes or processes the media, and then broadcasts the media back to participants. The centralized system has an advantage that the mixing and processing of media is only done once within the system. The disadvantage of the system is an increased delay time when transmitting composite media from one to another conference participant, since the intermediate processor must wait until all media is received before it begins media mixing and broadcasting.

The double-star network is extension of the centralized network. In this system, a central node from one star network is connected to another central node of another star network. The central node is used as a concentrator for several sites communicating via a single bi-directional link with several sites connected to a second central node.

The hierarchical network is another extension of the centralized network. The system consists of a series of intermediate nodes, with one root node and other as internal nodes in a tree structure. All intermediate nodes are capable of performing mixing and processing of data, while leaves in the tree are the conference participants. The multimedia data is sent up to the tree for mixing and processing. A mixer receives the media from multiple leaves or mixers below it, and then transmits the mixed media to the mixer above. The completely mixed data is generated by the root node and then broadcasted directly from the root to the leaves of the tree involved in the conference. This configuration reduces the network traffic, and therefore the system is capable of handling larger number of conference participants than either centralized or distributed networks.

Videoconferencing poses very strict timing requirements. The one-way end-to-end delay is defined from the time when the conference participant moves or speaks until the time the motion or sound is perceived by the other participants. This time should be less than 150 milliseconds, which gives the total round trip delay less than 300 milliseconds for maintaining conversation "face-to-face".

The total one-way time delay comprises of four major components: sending workstation operation, sending workstation transmission time, network delay, and receiving workstation, as illustrated in Figure 9.

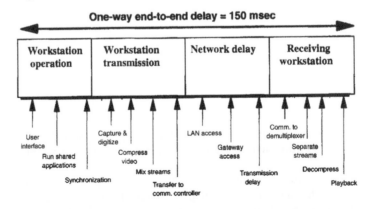

Figure 9. The one-way end-to-end delay in videoconferencing.

The delay between audio and video is very critical and limited to 20 to 40 milliseconds in order to provide good lip synchronization.

5.3 CIRCUIT SWITCHING vs. PACKET SWITCHING NETWORKS

Circuit-switched communication is a manner of data transmission where the communication path is established and reserved for the duration of the session. The bandwidth allocated for a session is used exclusively by it alone. The resources used by the session are freed, and available for other calls, at the end of the session. The dedicated bandwidth is an advantage for videoconferencing, providing predictable delays. However, circuit-switching transmission underutilizes network resources, as the dedicated bandwidth can go unused at times of limited activity.

Unlike circuit-switched transmission, a packet-switching environment has no dedicated bandwidth circuit set up; the bandwidth is shared with other network users. The information is divided into packets, and each packet is routed individually through the network. Since the packets may take different routes, they may arrive at their destination at different times and out-of-order. This variable delay in the delivery of information can cause problems in the quality of videoconferencing applications. Video packets received out-of-order may have to be discarded. Various protocols have been developed to try to overcome these inherent problems associated with packet switching such as RSVP, and RTP. These attempt to provide some quality of service over this type of transmission, and are discussed in later sections.

5.4 ISDN VIDEOCONFERENCING

Integrated Services Digital Network, ISDN, is a circuit switched end-to-end digital service. ISDN was designed to support the transmission of a wide variety of services, including voice, data, and video at high speeds over the public switched telephone network (PSTN). ISDN relies on 64 kbps channels, originally chosen to support digitized voice traffic.

Two access rates are defined for ISDN: Basic Rate Interface (BRI) and Primary Rate Interface (PRI). The user information is carried over bearer channels, known as B channels, each having a capacity of 64 kbps. The Basic Rate Interface provides 2 B-channels, while the Primary Rate Interface provides 23 B channels, in North America and Japan, and 30 B channels in Europe. A separate channel, the D-channel, is used for signaling. The D-channel has a data rate of 16 kbps in the BRI and 64 kbps in the PRI.

While a single BRI service is not sufficient to support a business quality videoconference with a frame rate of 15 frames per second, this service does satisfy requirements for many videoconferencing applications, such as desktop videoconferencing. A business quality videoconference will require at least 6 B channels with a data rate of 384 kbps (6 x 64). This setup is normally only seen in group based systems. In the past, ISDN videoconferences were just point-to-point connections. However, today it used for multipoint as well, by using a Multipoint Control Unit (MCU). Figure 10 illustrates a typical ISDN videoconferencing session.

Despite its reputation for difficult installation, lack of availability, and expense, many videoconferencing products on the market utilize ISDN. One of the main reasons for ISDN videoconferencing's broad acceptance is the timely emergence of ITU standards supporting it in 1990. The standards for other communication networks were not seen until 1996. However, with so many changes taking place, and the ratification of further standards for videoconferencing over such diverse networks as POTS, and IP based networks such as LANs and the Internet, ISDN's days as the dominant videoconferencing communications medium are over. While ISDN will continue to provide the quality required for business applications, POTS and Internet products have become more widespread among home and less serious users.

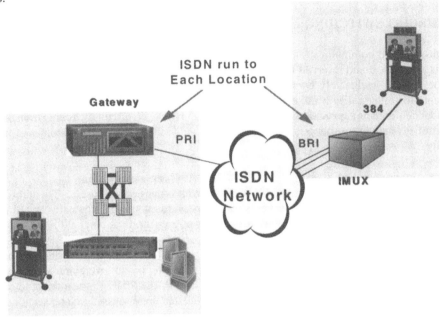

Figure 10. Example of an ISDN videoconference connection.

ITU-T Standard H.320

ITU-T's ratification of standard H.320, titled "Narrow-Band Visual Telephone Systems and Terminal Equipment", in December 1990, gave the videoconferencing industry a much needed jump-start. This standard was optimized for popular circuit-switched media such as ISDN. For the first time, a standard existed that made it possible to link equipment from different vendors in the same conference.

H.320 is an umbrella standard. It contains other standards concerning audio and video encoding and compressing, specifications for how calls are negotiated, how the data is multiplexed and framed, multipoint conferencing, data transmission, and communication interfaces.

5.5 PLAIN OLD TELEPHONE SERVICE (POTS) VIDEOCONFERENCING

The telephone system gradually began converting its internal connections, once purely an analog system, to a packet-based, digital switching system in the 1960s. Today, nearly all voice switching in the US is digital within the telephone network. However, the final link from the local central office to the customer site remains primarily an analog line, although it too is being replaced. This connection is often called Plain-Old Telephone Service (POTS).

The standard telephone system is the most widely pervasive network in existence. The availability of this existing infrastructure, combined with the latest CPU's, compression techniques, and advanced modem technologies, has brought videoconferencing to the home consumer. In May of 1996 the ITU-T ratified the H.324 standard for videoconferencing, which defines a methodology for transporting videoconferencing across POTS.

POTS videoconferencing has been technically difficult because of the low bandwidth of audio phone lines. However, with improved coding methods, there is sufficient bandwidth available to support audio, video and data sharing with this media. And the equipment is inexpensive and easily installed, relative to other existing methods.

Although most Pentium PC's can digitize local video at 15 fps and higher with little problem, quality suffers because the POTS modems cannot transmit the data fast enough to maintain the same frame rate. This typically restricts POTS-based videoconferencing to just a few frames per second. Thus, POTS videoconferencing does not approach the levels of quality required for even the most casual of business needs, and is better suited for home and recreational uses.

A POTS connection can be established either modem-to-modem, or over the Internet.
An Internet POTS connection requires the user to first establish a dial-up connection to the Internet. A call is then made to someone else on the Internet, who is also probably using a modem. The quality of the connection varies, as Internet traffic can severely compromise the quality of the videoconference. A typical frame rate is 2 to 5 frames per second, and basically looks like a series of stills. The advantage to this method is that a call can be made to anyone in the world for the price of accessing the Internet. A modem-to-modem connection can achieve frame rates of 5 to 10 frames per second, because the Internet traffic is avoided. But, long distance phone charges will apply if calling out of area.

POTS videoconferencing is finding acceptance in the consumer marketplace, due to the ubiquitous nature of the phone system. Also, recreational videoconferences do not require the same quality level of a live business meeting or a training class. Furthermore, today's PCs come multimedia equipped, with modems, are inexpensive, and readily available.

ITU-T Standard H.324

The H.324 ITU standard, titled "Multimedia Terminal for Low Bitrate Visual Telephone services over the GSTN", was the first standard to support point-to-point video and audio compression over analog POTS lines. Specifically, H.324 is designed to optimize videoconferencing quality over the low-speed links associated with the POTS system, typically operating at the speeds of modems - 28.8 kbps - 56 kbps. This standard allows users to interoperate across diverse endpoint such as ISDN, ATM, POTS, or mobile devices, and makes it possible to hold modem-based, POTS video calls that connect equipment made by different vendors. H.324 terminals may carry real-time voice, data, and video, or any combination, including videotelephony.

H.324 is an umbrella recommendation with a similar structure to H.320, its ISDN counterpart. See Section 4.7, Summary of Standards, for specifics on the various standards that H.324 supports.

5.6 IP-BASED VIDEOCONFERENCING

Networks are a fundamental part of today's information systems. They form the backbone for information sharing in enterprises, governmental and scientific groups. This shared information comes in a variety of forms such as e-mail and documents, files sent to colleagues, and real-time applications such as videoconferencing.

Local Area Networks (LANs) are commonly used on campuses and in companies to connect desktop computers together. At the physical layer, LAN's are frame-based and usually consist of 10 Mbps Ethernet, 16 Mbps Token Ring segments, or ever 100 Mbps Fast or Switched Ethernet.

Ethernet and Token Ring networks differ in the way that clients gain access to the transmission medium. Ethernet is a *Carrier Sense Multiple Access with Collision Detection* (CSMA/CD) network where clients transmit data and listen to detect collisions. If a collision occurs, the client must wait a random amount of time before transmitting again. Token Ring is a network where a token is passed around and clients must gain access to the token before transmitting.

Internetworking is the process of connecting various networks together. These different networks may have different network technologies and different network protocols. In the 70's, the development of technologies and protocols for internetworking were initiated by the US Defense Advanced Research Projects Agency (DARPA). The communications protocol developed under this project, called the IP (Internet Protocol), allow applications the ability to talk to other applications, regardless of the underlying network technology. IP is actually a suite, or stack, of protocols. These standards have been adopted as the standard protocols for internetworking.

The *Internet* resulted as new wide area networks were created in the US and the rest of the world and became interconnected using the IP stack of protocols. The Internet (with a capital I) refers to a worldwide set of interconnected networks. The Internet is the most widely used universal information network.

Two different transport layer protocols were developed for use with IP. TCP (Transmission Control Protocol) will be familiar to most readers and is the protocol commonly used for Email, FTP, and Web Surfing. TCP/IP is capable of transporting large amounts of data between computers, with 100 percent accuracy, but can delay transmission and reduce throughput, as error checking occurs at every node in the transmission path. Any corrupt or lost packets are retransmitted, and if congestion is encountered, the packets are rerouted. Because TCP/IP has variable length packets, each device along the network needs to determine the length of each packet, it copies the whole packet into memory before forwarding it, slowing transmission.

Although these attributes are critical for effective data transmission, the are not conducive to the real time video and audio streams needed for videoconferencing, where data must arrive consecutively and in a timely manner, or it's useless. If lost packets were retransmitted, they would arrive too late to be of any use.

In addition to TCP, the IP allows for a second mode of data transfer, specified by the UDP (User Datagram Protocol). In contrast to TCP, UDP offers no guarantee of packet delivery, and packets can be dropped when the network is busy, with no way for any network element to ask for retransmission. It promises only "best effort" service quality. For video, it is preferable to miss a frame in order to maintain the overall flow.

There is, in essence, a tradeoff between reliability and timeliness; timeliness must win for IP videoconferencing, which abandons TCP for audio and video and instead specifies the UDP. However, TCP is used for data transfer, the control channel and the call signaling channel.

5.6.1 Disadvantages of Using IP for Videoconferencing
IP networks do not have an underlying QoS architecture on which to base video transport. Even switched Ethernet infrastructures are quite unpredictable in nature, especially on network trunk links and through routed backbones, and this leads to increased delay and jitter, greatly decreasing picture quality. This effect is most visible when using the Internet.

Video on Ethernet infrastructures also has the unfortunate side effect of permitting interaction between the data and the video traffic. The bandwidth requirements of the video traffic slow down the data traffic on the network, the best effort nature of the transmission may impact the quality of the communication. Management of network resources becomes a key element of IP videoconferencing standards, as bandwidth may be reserved for videoconferences or, in fact, held from them so that other network applications may still function.

Expensive, high-bandwidth networks must be obtained to reduce the likelihood of latencies and bottlenecks. Currently, the Internet simply does not offer the performance required for high quality videoconferencing. Often, video over the Internet looks more like a still picture, has little or no motion and broken audio, and is pretty much a useless business tool. However, for personal use, or more informal business uses, Internet videoconferencing apparently does have a place, because its popularity is growing to the point that it may make POTS-based standards irrelevant.

5.6.2 Requirements for IP Videoconferencing

IP videoconferencing can make sense as a corporate solution if the network is sufficient. The first consideration is available bandwidth because this determines audio and video quality. 10 Mbps Ethernet LANs are the minimum used in most companies today, and these have enough bandwidth to support desktop conferences. Multiple simultaneous calls require more bandwidth, and a 100Base-T backbone is the minimum requirement for handling many simultaneous calls. Larger organizations may require even more than 100M bit/sec backbone.

With a LAN offering significantly more bandwidth than ISDN, the video quality within a conference can be potentially much higher and can approach that of television. Communications advancements such as Fast Ethernet (100 Mbps) and ATM (155 Mbps) have increased available bandwidth, and Multicast technology has reduced network loading in conferences involving more than two participants.

However, as IP videoconferencing becomes more popular, existing networks may become bogged down with its traffic, degrading the quality of the video and audio, but also slowing other network applications such as web browsing. Most organizations have less bandwidth over the wide area network as compared to the LAN, so this problem will be grow especially acute if simultaneous multiple "external" videoconferences are required.

One alternative for communicating with distant locations is through ISDN gateways. These devices can convert LAN systems to H.320 ISDN and call out to circuit-switched locations. This gives users the flexibility of H.320 compatibility as well as the option of dial-up access to remote locations.

Despite the disadvantages of implementing videoconferencing over IP networks, the ready accessibility and low cost have moved the market in this direction.

5.6.3 RSVP

Ethernet's inherent lack of Quality of Service has prompted the designers of this network transport system to go back to the design board and attempt to retrofit Ethernet with QoS capabilities. This new protocol, called the Resource Reservation Protocol (RSVP), is a signaling system designed to enable the end points of a network transaction to request network bandwidth for particular communication streams and receive a reply indicating whether the request has been granted. Many IP-based videoconferencing products support RSVP, which is likely to become a widely accepted method of enabling existing network infrastructures to deliver some QoS- like capabilities.

However, RSVP cannot solve the fundamental QoS issues of frame based networks. Because it operates in the Ethernet environment, RSVP must deal with variable length frames. It is probable that small 'latency sensitive' frames carrying videoconferencing could easily be stuck in a buffer behind much larger 'data' frames. This is the case for 10Base-T, 100Base-X and Gigabit Ethernet.

RSVP is a simple signaling system, where every hop-by-hop link must be negotiated separately. There is still no end-to-end guarantee of a minimum service level. ATM, on the other hand, sets up an end-to-end connection with a specific QoS class that commences at call set-up and ends at call teardown.

5.6.4 RTP

In conferences with multiple audio and video streams, unreliable transport via UDP uses IP Multicast and the Real-Time Protocol (RTP) developed by the Internet Engineering Task Force (IETF) to handle streaming audio and video. IP Multicast is a protocol for unreliable multicast transmission in UDP. RTP works on top of IP Multicast, and was designed to handle the requirements of streaming audio and video over the Internet. A header containing a time-stamp and a sequence number is added to each UDP packet.

With appropriate buffering at the receiving station, timing and sequence information allows the application to eliminate duplicate packets; reorder out-of-sequence packets; synchronize sound, video and data and achieve continuous playback in spite of varying latencies. RTP needs to be supported by Terminals, Gateways, and MCUs with Multipoint Processors.

5.6.5 RTCP

The Real-Time Control Protocol (RTCP) is used for the control of RTP. RTCP monitors the quality of service, conveys information about the session participants, and periodically distributes control packets containing quality information to all session participants through the same distribution mechanisms as the data packets.

5.6.6 Multicast

In some videoconferencing applications it is necessary to send the same real-time video and/or audio streams to multiple destinations throughout the global Internet. Typically this would be accomplished by sending multiple streams of redundant packets, one for each destination. This can be very inefficient and slow.

RTP-based applications can use "IP multicast" capabilities in conjunction with the MBONE (Multicast BackBONE), a virtual network designed to facilitate the efficient transmission of video and audio signals simultaneously over the Internet. The network is composed of "islands", Internet sites supporting multicast and linked by virtual point-to-point links called "tunnels". The IP multicast packets are encapsulated for transmission through the tunnels, so that they look like normal unicast datagrams to intervening routers and subnets. Once they reach the destination island, they are copied and forwarded to destinations as required.

5.6.7 ITU-T Standard H.323

In 1996, the ITU ratified the H.323 standard for videoconferencing over packet-switched networks, such as Ethernet and Token-Ring, and ultimately the Internet. The standard is platform independent and runs on top of common network architectures.

To ensure that critical network traffic will not be disrupted by videoconferencing traffic, the standard includes network traffic management capabilities and supports multicast transport in multipoint conferences.

H.323 defines four major components for a network-based communications system: Terminals, Gateways, Gatekeepers, and Multipoint Control Units, shown in Figure 11.

Terminals are the client endpoints on the LAN that provide the user interface. All terminals must support voice communications; video and data are optional. Also required of H.323 terminals is support of H.245, for negotiation of channel usage and capabilities, Q.931 for call signaling and call setup, Registration/Admission/Status (RAS), a protocol used to communicate with a Gatekeeper; and support for RTP/RTCP.

Gateways provide translation between H.323 conferencing endpoints and other terminal types, such as H.320 and H.324. Gateways are not required if connections to other networks are not needed, since endpoints may directly communicate with other endpoints on the same LAN. Terminals communicate with Gateways using the H.245 and Q.931 protocols.

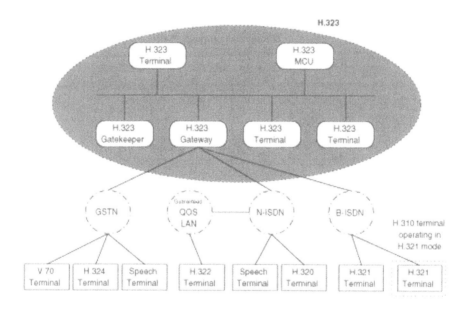

Figure 11. H.323 network and interfaces.

The **Gatekeeper** acts as the central point for all calls within its zone and provides call control services to registered endpoints. It translates addresses from LAN aliases for terminals and gateways to IP or IPX addresses, as defined in the RAS specification, and manages bandwidth. While a gatekeeper is an optional part of an H.323 system, all compliant terminals must support its use.

The **Multipoint Control Unit** (MCU) supports conferences between three or more endpoints, handling negotiations between all terminals to determine common capabilities for audio and video processing, and controlling multicast.

5.7 ATM-BASED VIDEOCONFERENCING

Unlike many specialized networks used in the past, Asynchronous Transfer Mode, ATM, is a networking technology that was designed at the outset to be service independent. The flexibility of ATM allows it to support a variety of services with different bit rates, burstiness, and acceptable delay characteristics. The bit rate can be constant for the whole transmission, or it can be variable over time. ATM satisfies all the various types of data, each with unique service requirements, found in videoconferencing such as video, audio and data.

ATM was designed to be efficient in the use of its available resources. All available resources are shared between all services, such that the optimal statistical sharing of the resources is achieved.

5.7.1 Basic Principles of ATM

ATM is based on the concept of asynchronous data transfer. It combines the best qualities of circuit-switched and packet-switched communication. ATM does not use fixed bandwidths as in circuit switching techniques such as ISDN. It is implemented by using virtual circuit packet switching technology with fixed sized packets, called cells. In the virtual circuit technique all the cells in a call follow the same route, and arrive in the correct sequence.

Each cell is 53 bytes in length, 48 bytes for the information field and 5 bytes for the header. To guarantee a fast processing in the network, the ATM header has very limited function. Its main function is the identification of the virtual connection by an identifier, which is selected at call set up and guarantees a proper routing of each packet. The information field length is relatively small, reducing the network queuing delays. This in turn leads to small delays and a small delay jitter as required by real-time applications such as videoconferencing. No processing is performed on information field of the cells inside the network, further reducing delays.

ATM is connection oriented. Before information is transferred from the terminal to the network, a logical/virtual connection is set. When a user requests a connection, it provides information to the network about its requirements such as peak cell rate, acceptable cell delay variation, sustainable cell rate, and its highest expected cell burst. If the network can support this connection without jeopardizing the promised quality of service for the existing connections, the connection is accepted. On admission into the ATM network, a virtual channel is set up between the end users, through the network.

ATM provides a Quality of Service (QoS) system that is vastly more sophisticated than that found in IP networks. While IP networks attempt to provide quality with protocols such as RSVP and RTP, it is not guaranteed. A constant good quality videoconferencing application with a fixed frame rate, no audio gaps, and lip synchrony, can only be guaranteed on a network with a guaranteed QoS. Although possible on dedicated LANs or unoccupied high-speed links, in general it requires ATM or ISDN connections, with guaranteed QoS.

5.7.2 ITU-T Standard H.321

H.321 is the ITU-T's standard defining the implementation of videoconferencing over ATM. It is an enhancement of the ISDN standard H.320, and is fully compatible with existing H.320 systems. Like ISDN, H.321 is implemented at transmission rates, which are multiples of 128 kbps (128 Kbps, 384 Kbps, 768 Kbps, etc.). The standard was designed to take advantage of the inherent QoS capabilities of ATM, delivering the highest quality videoconferencing.

Implementing an H.321 ATM-based videoconferencing is less costly and less complex than ISDN, for several reasons. ATM switches are significantly cheaper than ISDN switches. Also, in an ATM implementation, single gateways give centralized access to other networks, where an ISDN implementation requires separate IMUXs for each end-point ISDN user. Not only does this extra cabling required in ISDN implementations increase costs, it also makes the installation more complex.

H.321 is claimed to deliver high-quality videoconferencing at significantly lower costs and with greater flexibility than with ISDN based standards, yet to provide significantly higher quality levels than IP-based implementations. ATM's unique suitability to the transport of video, as well as voice and data, is making it the network of choice for many videoconferencing applications.

5.8 ITU-T STANDARD T.120 FOR DATA

ITU-T Recommendation T.120 is specified as the standard for data transfer for many different videoconferencing standards. The specification defines protocols and services for multipoint data conferencing, and enables participants to share data during a conference. This data could be whiteboard data or another type of data such as a binary file. T.120 is actually a series of recommendations listed below.

T.121: Generic Application Template (GAT). Defines a template as a guide for developers in managing T.120 resources.

T.122: Defines Multipoint Communication Services (MCS) available to developers.

T.123: Defines low-level of protocol stack for audiographics & audiovisual conferencing for various types of networks (including POTS, ISDN, and LANs).

T.124: Defines Generic Conference Control (GCC), the mechanism to set up and manage conferences mandatory for 'group' conferences.

T.125: Defines MCS data transmission protocol.

T.126: Multipoint Still Image and Annotation protocol (also known as T.SI). Defines the protocol used to provide interoperability with graphics data in applications such as whiteboarding, annotated image exchange, screen sharing and remote apps control.

T.127: Multipoint Binary File Transfer protocol (also known as T.MBFT). Defines the protocol used to support binary file transfer within a conference.

T.128: Defines Multipoint Application Sharing protocol (also known as T.SHARE).

T.134: Defines Multimedia Application Text Conversation protocol (also known as T.CHAT).

T.135: Defines how to achieve secure T.120 conferencing.

6. APPLICATIONS

Once used only for high profile, executive, business oriented room-based conferences, videoconferencing is now being used or has shown great promise to be beneficial in a variety of areas of human activity.

6.1 PERSONAL CONFERENCING

In the business community, users are using videoconferencing for spontaneous video-enhanced telephone-like communications from desktop to desktop. Some businesses even have "open camera" policies in the workspace. This makes it possible to see if another worker is in his cubicle and therefore (maybe unfortunately for him if he seeks to get any work done) available.

As the Internet becomes more and more ubiquitous, videoconferencing is sure to follow the trends in Internet telephony. Although the quality of video will be low (at least for the time being) it will not be long before many on-line users will commonly place a video call to their friends and loved-ones on-line, seen in Figure 12.

Figure 12. Example of personal videoconferencing session.

6.2 BANKING AND FINANCIAL SERVICES

Video conferencing technology is becoming a large part of their overall long-term company strategies for many banks and financial service providers, who are using it in areas such as home banking, customer kiosks, automated teller machines (ATMs), video tellers, video call centers, and in conjunction with on-line Internet banking services. Through the use of face-to-face video conferencing capabilities, banks are able to handle more business while improving convenience and flexibility for their customers, without losing the personal contact which their customers value. Customers gain the ability to speak face-to-face with specialists who can assist them in opening accounts, pre-qualifying for mortgages and automobile loans, and obtaining investment advice, even from their desktop.

6.3 DISTANCE LEARNING

Videoconferencing is becoming a key element of *distance learning* programs at many schools, and allows educators to create a seamless and real-time interactive learning environment, which can bridge vast distances and include multiple sites. It is used from kindergarten to graduate school.

In public schools, "virtual field trip" programs like the "Jason Project", created by Dr. Robert Ballard (the man who found the *Titanic*), promise to bring the excitement of live scientific exploration to millions of schoolchildren who could otherwise not participate. Ballard has taken his audience to the Rainforests of South America and deep into the sea. As schools are wired for Internet, this type of program may become commonplace. An example of a virtual field trip is seen in Figure 13.

Over 30% of the 3500+ higher education institutions in the US already use videoconferencing to deliver part of their course curriculum. The goals and benefits of implementing videoconferencing in a distance learning setting include increasing school enrollment, creating new revenue streams by reaching out to non-traditional and previously inaccessible student populations, and cutting delivery costs.

For the traditional classroom, videoconferencing enables institutions to import global expertise. It may also provide an effective way for teachers, administrators and students from different institutions to collaborate by sharing resources and information.

Figure 13. A virtual field trip using videoconferencing.

6.4 DISTANCE TRAINING

Most large corporations have determined that it is in their critical business interest for their workers to have access to the educational opportunities that will help them increase their knowledge level and skill sets. They know this is necessary to compete, and accordingly are investing large sums of money in workforce training and education. Today over $50 billion is spent annually on corporate training, and over $6 billion is spent annually on the purchase and maintenance of facilities and equipment for this purpose.

Videoconferencing is quickly becoming part of many companies' overall employee training programs, because it provides a way to offer high-quality training while cutting course delivery costs. Because employees do not have to leave their offices for extended periods of time, disruptions are minimized and short-term productivity is not sacrificed.

6.5 PERSONNEL RECRUITMENT

Videoconferencing can be used as a screening tool for corporate personnel departments. It allows face-to-face interviews to occur without the expense of flying each potential candidate to the job location.

6.6 HEALTH CARE

Videoconferencing is used in numerous clinical applications. The most common application is in radiology, but it is also used for cardiology, dermatology, psychiatry, emergency medicine, home health care, pathology, and oncology.

The healthcare industry is a rapidly growing and evolving market. As healthcare corporations merge and form huge networks, successful organizations will be those that can leverage the medical expertise and resources of their member institutions across multiple sites.

The use of videoconferencing increases operational efficiency through better use of staff resources, provides rapid information transfer, achieves better physician collaboration, and facilitates medical education, as illustrated in Figure 14.

Figure 14. A remote consultation.   Figure 15. MedLink bedside terminal.

Uses include patient interviews, remote medical examinations using remote sensors, medical education via "interactive rounds", remote consultation with a specialist, and even such mundane uses as enabling hospital administration to negotiate medical supply contracts.

Videoconferencing is used in some hospitals to facilitate the care of newborns in the neonatal intensive care unit (NICU). These babies may be hospitalized for the first several months of their lives, see Figure 16. Videoconferencing systems are installed in the NICU, as well as the homes of families with newborns in the unit, enabling family members to see and talk to their babies and review their progress with doctors, all from their homes.

Once the baby is sent home with his or her nervous parents, the hospital staff use the system to monitor the progress of the baby and provide comfort and support to the parents. By using videoconferencing, the hospital can smooth the transitions of NICU babies from the hospital to their homes, while reducing overall costs.

Figure 16. Baby in NICU.

Psychiatrists can us videoconferencing technology to monitor their patients such as those with severe mental illnesses, personality disorders, and adjustment problems. For example, a psychiatrist employed at a state hospital may have patients who live over a wide area and who are unable to travel. Even hearing- or speech-impaired patients may be reached in this way, provided that the doctor knows sign language.

One example of videoconferencing used by the medical industry is the *MedLink* Mobile Videoconferencing Unit (by PictureTel), designed to operate at the patient's bedside and allow him to speak with a remote specialist face-to-face. This system is shown in Figure 15. The MedLink delivers separate or simultaneous medical data along with videoconferencing to any of PictureTel's other products. It is based on the Venue 2000 Model 50 platform and is network independent. The network link can range from simple ISDN through T-1/E-1 or the unit can be attached to the local area network to take advantage of existing topologies.

6.7 LAW ENFORCEMENT AND SURVEILLANCE

Videoconferencing technology is used for remote video monitoring of secured locations, as well as for replacing human operators at monitoring locations, such as at drawbridges, which must be raised and lowered based on boat and car traffic. Figure 17 illustrates TeleEye, a remote videoconferencing surveillance system.

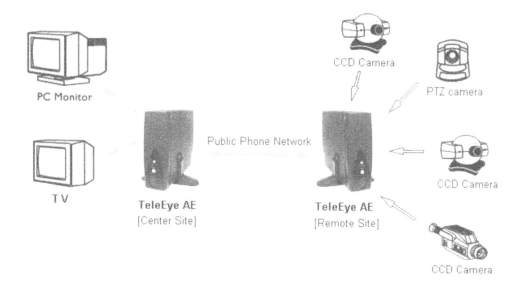

Fgure 17. TeleEye videoconferencing surveillance system.

6.8 TELECOMMUTING

Some companies use videoconferencing to allow employees to work out of their homes. This is part of a trend termed telecommuting.

For example, IBM has put 95% of their US marketing and services personnel into telecommuting. They have been able to close or reducing the size of the field sales offices accordingly, and claim a 15% gain in productivity and a 40-60% savings in real estate per location. One benefit of the system is that it allows cheap customer follow-up "video visits", which be cost-prohibitive if carried out in person.

6.9 LAW AND CRIMINAL JUSTICE

Many state and federal courts now use videoconferencing to arraign criminals, for appeals and parole hearings, and to provide telemedicine to inmates.

Lawyers use desktop system to hold meetings with their clients and to gather data from expert witnesses without incurring large expenses.

6.10 PRODUCT DEVELOPMENT AND MANUFACTURING

In today's global economy, it is not unusual for products to be developed at multiple locations. For example, a complex consumer electronics item may have the software developed overseas, the electronics developed at one location and manufactured at still another, all while the overall project is being managed at the company's home office.

In order for such a project to be completed while its market window is still open, communications and teamwork between the disparate design teams is critical. Videoconferencing allows team members to interact as though they were co-located, sharing ideas, drawing pictures, and generally becoming comfortable with each other, while saving millions of dollars in travel expenses and lost travel time. Design and engineering teams can then conduct design reviews at a distance with full audio-visual support.

Once the product moves to manufacturing, complex mechanical problems can be communicated to remotely located experts, who can solve the problem quickly and get the production line up and running as soon as possible. This is critical, as factory downtime translates to dumping money in the trash

6.11 GOVERNMENT

State, local governments, and municipalities commonly use videoconferencing for conducting daily business such as meetings, interviews, public hearings, training, and press conferences. A cost benefit analysis conducted by the state of Utah showed it achieved a 69 percent cost savings in travel expenses for events in which videoconferencing was used. In Oregon, the state reported that it realized up to a 90 percent cost savings through the implementation of teleconferencing events versus face-to-face events. As taxpayers demand more performance for less money, videoconferencing is sure to become even more important to government function.

7. VIDEOCONFERENCING PRODUCTS

Videoconferencing is a many-tiered market. There are basically three classes of products available: group (or room) based systems, desktop videoconferencing systems, and the lower-end personal conferencing/videophone systems.

7.1 GROUP-BASED VIDEOCONFERENCING

The group-based systems, generally operating over ISDN networks, were the first to enjoy widespread market acceptance, and for years were the mainstay of the videoconferencing market. Today, however, the market for desktop and personal videoconferencing products is exploding, and overtaking the group-based market.

The group-based systems require the users to convene to a conference room equipped with videoconferencing equipment, as illustrated in Figure 18. The session may be multicast, and users at the other end may be either at group-based sites or desktop. The system can be enclosed in one cabinet with a monitor and camera on top. Alternatively, the products such as the codec, cameras, projection equipment, audio equipment, and lighting can be purchased separately to achieve the desired presentation quality. Figure 19 shows an example of group-based videoconferencing equipment.

Figure 18. Group-based Videoconferencing.   Figure 19. Group-based equipment.

Table 4 summarizes group-based videoconferencing manufacturers, products and equipment included, as well as the standards under which they operate.

Table 4. Group-Based Videoconferencing Products.

Manufacturer	Product	Product Description	Camera	Mic	H.320	H.323	T.120
Intel	TeamStation System	Conference room workstation videoconferencing system, includes add-in card	✓	✓	✓	✓	✓
NEC	VisualLink 384	Set-top device	✓	✓	✓		
PictureTel	SwiftSite II	Portable, set-top group videoconferencing system	✓	✓	✓		✓
Sony	TriniCom Digital Meeting System	Parallel-port peripheral	✓	✓	✓		✓
VTEL	WG500 WorkGroup	Includes PC	✓	✓	✓	✓	✓

7.2 DESKTOP VIDEOCONFERENCING

Because of the universal accessibility of the PC, desktop conferencing is appealing to a much broader customer base than the traditional group systems. Desktop systems are installed on workstations or PCs and connect over standard LANs, and operate under the H.323 standards. These systems take advantage of several features found in today's widely available multimedia PC, such as high-resolution monitors, powerful processors with MMX technology, speakers, and microphones. Videoconferencing packages are available that augment the multimedia PC with a camera and software. Figure 20 shows typical desktop videoconferencing equipment and Figure 21 shows a desktop videoconferencing session. Table 5 summarizes desktop videoconferencing manufacturers, products and equipment included, and the standards under which they operate.

Figure 20. Desktop   Figure 21. A desktop videoconferencing session.
videoconferencing equipment.

Table 5. Desktop Videoconferencing Products.

Manufacturer	Product	Product Description	Camera	Mic	H.320	H.323	T.120
Intel	ProShare Video System 500	Computer Add-in Card	✓	✓	✓	✓	✓
PictureTel	Live200	Computer Add-in Card	✓	✓	✓		✓
PictureTel	LiveLAN	Computer Add-in Card	✓	✓		✓	✓
VTEL	SmartStation Desktop 384	2 Computer Add-in Cards	✓	✓	✓	✓	✓
Zydacron	OnWAN350	Computer Add-in Card	✓	✓	✓		✓

7.3 PERSONAL VIDEOCONFERENCING WITH VIDEOPHONES

Videophones are also considered a personal conferencing tool, but are generally of lower quality than the desktop-to-desktop variety, and appeal to a different market segment. Videophones may be special telephones that include a small video screen, set-top boxes operating with the user's TV, but are most often implemented as software running on the PC. They communicate via POTS analog phone lines, and conform to the ITU-T's H.324 standards.

The dedicated telephone with integrated video screen, known as a desktop videophone, shown in Figure 22, is the most expensive option in the videophone arena, however installation and operation is simple. These devices simply plug into any analog telephone outlet and are ready to make a video call. Depending on the vendor, features such as adjustable picture quality, size and frame speed, electronic pan, tilt, zoom, snapshot, caller ID, and auto answer can be found. There is no software to install, or special wiring involved. These videophones are designed to work with other H.324-compatible videophones including computer-based videophones.

8X8 VC150   MM220 Videophone

Figure 22. Desktop videophones.

Figure 23. Comtrad C-Phone system.   Figure 24. Set-top videophone system.

The next, slightly less expensive, option is the set-top box device, shown in Figures 23 and 24. This device is about the size and shape of a cable TV converter box, and hooks up to the TV just like a VCR. It may be operated via remote control. The product includes a camera, a modem, and an H.324 industry standard videoconferencing codec. The system uses a television set to present the audio and video of the person being called, thereby making this solution more economical.

Figure 25. Videophone kit.   Figure 26. Intel videophone.

A third option available for videophone conferencing is available in the form of software that is installed on the user's PC. These products are similar to the desktop videoconferencing systems, except that these systems are operating over POTS. Table 6 shows a list of videophone manufacturers and products. This solution takes advantage of the existing capabilities of today's multimedia PC, making this it by far the most economical solution available. In fact, new PCs, with an Intel® Pentium® III processors, come preinstalled with the latest Intel® Video Phone software, shown in Figure 24. All that is required is a camera.

Most videoconferencing vendors provide the products as a kit, which includes the software, video capture board (optional), and a camera.

The user can choose to make video phone calls over regular telephone lines or through the Internet. When used over regular telephone lines, the audio and video quality is much better than that of video phone calls made through the Internet. The quality of an Internet videophone call will vary depending on Internet traffic at the time of the call.

Many of these products support both H.323 and H.324 standards, and support a variety of broadband Internet connections, including cable modems, DSL, ADSL and LAN.

Table 6. H.324 Videophone Products.

Manufacturer	Product Number	Product Description
8x8	VC150	ViaTV Desktop Videophone
8x8	VC105	ViaTV Set-Top Videophone W/Camera
Winnov	Videum Conference Pro	Videoconferencing Kit
Winnov	VideumCam	Videoconferencing Kit
Panasonic	Eggcam	Desktop Video Camera w/Cu-Seeme
3Com	Bigpicture VideoPhone	PC Videoconferencing Kit, includes video capture card
Intel	Create and Share	PC Videoconferencing Kit

References

1. E. Brown, "Videoconferencing Systems," *New Media*, December 1998.
2. K. Nisenson, "Tune in to IP Videoconferencing," *Network World*, September 1998.
3. W. Wong, "Video Conferencing for the Enterprise," *Network Magazine*, April 1998.
4. T. Trowt-Bayard and Jim R. Wilcox, "Video Conferencing and Interactive Multimedia: The Whole Picture", Flatiron Publishing, March 1997.
5. M. Herman, "The Fundamentals of H.324 Desktop Videoconferencing," *Electronic Design*, October 1996.
6. C. Tristram, "Video Conferencing: A Work in Progress," *Network Magazine*, April 1998.
7. S. J. Bigelow, "The Many Faces of Videoconferencing," *Bay Area Computer Currents*, October 1998.
8. K. Cholewka, "IP VideoConferencing: Beat the Clock," July 1997, http://www.data.com/tutorials/video.html.

9. DataBeam Corp, "A Primer on the H.323 Series Standard, Version 2.0," http://www.databeam.com/h323/h323primer.html.

10. CMU Artificial Intelligence Repository, "CELP: FS-1016 Code Excited Linear Prediction Coder," http://www.cs.cmu.edu/afs/cs/project/airepository/ai/areas/speech/systems/celp/0.html.

11. Coding and Compression, http://www.cs.ucl.ac.uk/staff/J.Crowcroft/mmbook/book/node91.html.

12. FVC.COM, "Videoconferencing Standards," December 1997, http://www.fvc.com/whitepapers/standards.html.

13. Cisco Systems, "Packet Voice Primer," http://www.cisco.com/warp/public/cc/sol/mkt/ent/gen/packv_in.htm.

14. T. Needleman, "A Videoconference on Every POTS," http://www.zdnet.com/pcmag/features/vidconf/pots.htm.

15. TeamSolutions (UK) Limited, "Video Standards and Terminology," January 29, 1999, http://www.teamsolutions.co.uk/tsstds.html.

Chapter 20

INTERNET-BASED DISTANCE LEARNING

Sam Hsu, Nalin Sharda, and Oge Marques

Abstract

Distance learning utilizing the Internet as a transport structure to deliver instructions has been a popular issue in recent years. Education institutions, business circles and government agencies as well are welcoming the Internet era with active efforts to find ways of conducting education, training, and business electronically and cost-effectively. In this chapter, instead of a general introduction to the topic of distance learning, while publications of this nature are widely available, we report three case studies related to Internet-based distance learning conducted at Florida Atlantic University recently. The first case is pertinent to a virtual classroom model that features controlled approaches to avoid unauthorized netsurfing and to maintain an orderly audio conferencing during a class session [1]. The second case reports a collaborative project concerning synchronous distance education between Florida Atlantic University in US and Victoria University in Australia [2]. The third case is related to conducting virtual office hours to enhance the interaction between the instructor and students [3].

1. VIRTUAL CLASSROOMS WITH CONTROLLED APPROACHES

1.1 INTRODUCTION

The purpose of this project was to develop a virtual classroom model that features a controlled approach for synchronizing student activities and regulating group interactions in real-time.

Along with the fast-growing of the Internet we have seen in recent years a booming of virtual classrooms that are taking the advantage of the worldwide networking infrastructure to conduct education electronically. Various virtual classroom systems have been developed so far [4, 5]. Examples of representative virtual classroom systems include Virtual Classroom at New Jersey Institute of Technology [6], Virtual Classroom at Cornell University [7], Saddle Project at Boston University [8], Collaboratories at the US Department of Energy [9], Albatross Project at National Chiao Tung University, Taiwan [10], and Interactive Remote Instruction System at Old Dominion University [11]. Each system may have its own features differing from others. In essence, they all have one common goal – to educate students who are motivated to learn but are blocked by their geographical locations and/or working schedules. However, two areas that face almost all virtual classroom systems that provide real-time interactivity with students over the Internet but have not been given due attention are a) controlled activities for students who are out of the reach of direct supervision from the instructor, and b) coordinated interaction among participants while using audio tools for interactive dialogs. We have therefore developed a virtual classroom model that features a centralized mouse control mechanism to provide the instructor with the capability to call remote students' attention to class and to synchronize class activities, and a First-Come First-Serve (FCFS) floor control to regulate participants engaged in audio conferencing in an orderly fashion. The model is named VCOIN, acronym for *Vi*rtual *C*lassroom *O*ver the *In*ternet [12].

1.2 VCOIN FEATURES

The major features of VCOIN include the following:

- Uses the Internet as its networking infrastructure for information distribution.
- Uses existing video/audio conferencing tools for interactive real-time communication.
- Uses standard web browsers for graphical user interfaces.
- Employs a mouse control technique to prevent students from conducting unauthorized surfing in cyberspace.
- Employs a floor control algorithm that allows the instructor centralized floor control while students are allowed to access the floor in an FCFS fashion.
- Introduces the concept of virtual experimenter.
- Provides a chat tool to enable interactive text-based communications between the instructor and the students.

1.3 A VCOIN PROTOTYPE

A prototype of VCOIN has been implemented using various programming tools such as HTML, Java, JavaScript, Perl, and C. Several VCOIN trial sessions have been conducted using multiple computer labs that are interconnected via a 100 Mbps Ethernet-type campus backbone. Figure 1 shows a screen capture of the instructor's interface. VCOIN uses Netscape Navigator for its user interface. Features shown on this screen include a course outline, centralized mouse control, floor control and chat board. Each is housed in a separate frame on the screen.

1.4 CENTRALIZED MOUSE CONTROL USING MOUSE DETECT

In a conventional classroom, the instructor can actually oversee student activities. This situation is quite different in a virtual classroom. A student can be temporarily absent or engaged in netsurfing on a totally unrelated Web site in the case of an Internet-based virtual classroom setting. VCOIN builds into itself a unique feature of checking and controlling the student activities at a remote place. This feature is called *Mouse Detect*. Consider a scenario in which the instructor expects all students to pay attention to what he/she is demonstrating. The instructor will then request the students to place their mouse in a specific area on their screen. VCOIN will detect these activities and notify the instructor of the students' current status.

Figure 2 shows two screen captures regarding centralized mouse control. The instructor's interface, Figure 2(a), has a list of participants, shown by student names, and their current status. The status of 'Active' indicates that the student has placed his/her mouse in the designated area. This is interpreted as the student is paying attention to the instructor since it prevents him/her from netsurfing the Web or performing other tasks on that computer. When a student has moved his/her mouse pointer outside the specified region, shown in Figure 2(b), the corresponding entry on the instructor's interface will be changed from 'Active' to

'Inactive' immediately. The instructor can then notify the student (e.g. via an audio tool) for not paying attention.

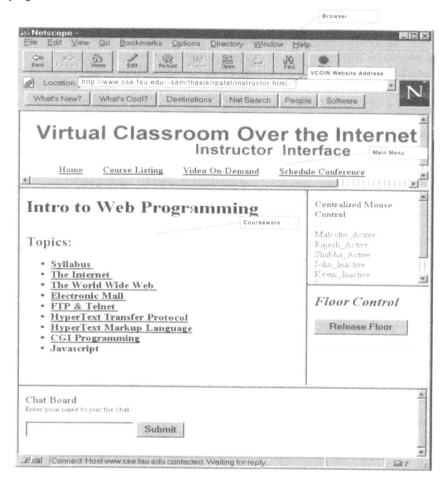

Figure 1. A screen capture of VCOIN instructor interface.

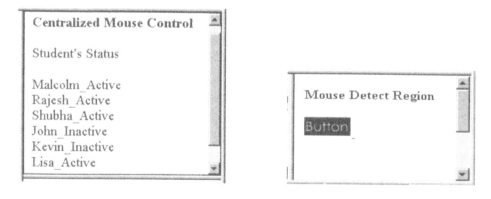

(a) Instructor's frame

(b) Student's frame

Figure 2. Screen frames for centralized mouse control.

1.5 FLOOR CONTROL

Floor control is a mechanism that allows the proper use of a shared resource. These shared objects may include video conferencing, audio conferencing, or whiteboard type of applications where more than one participant can have access at a time. Floor control can be implemented using many different algorithms. In VCOIN, a combination of a centralized control (for instructor) and an FCFS (for students) is employed. The instructor always has the authority to speak. A student user is allowed to speak only when he/she is given the permission of floor control by the instructor. This type of control is necessary to avoid chaos and confusion in a conferencing environment and it helps to structure the interaction and reduce the bandwidth requirement.

The floor control algorithm used in VCOIN is an FCFS algorithm for students and centralized control for the instructor. To request the floor control, a student has to submit the request from his/her VCOIN interface. On the other hand, if the instructor would like to release the floor control from a student who currently has it, he/she would have to click on "Release floor" button on the VCOIN interface. The following diagram, Figure 3, shows the two different interfaces.

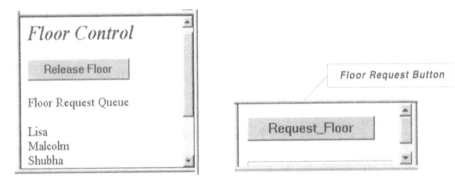

(a) Instructor's floor control frame   (b) Student's floor control frame

Figure 3. Frame layouts of floor control.

The algorithm for implementing floor control is shown in Figure 4. The users who wish to take the floor control submit their request to the controller. The controller puts the request of each user into the FIFO queue. Because the conferencing application is used in a virtual classroom environment, initially the instructor must be having the floor control. Users have three options:
- Request floor control
- Release floor control
- Quit conference

If a user requests for floor control, his/her UserID is added to the FIFO queue only if it is not in the queue. When the user having the floor control requests for release of floor, the controller pops the first element off the FIFO queue and give the floor control to it. The conference application will then allow that user to access the shared resource. If a user requests to quit the conference, the floor control mechanism would remove the corresponding UserID from the current user list.

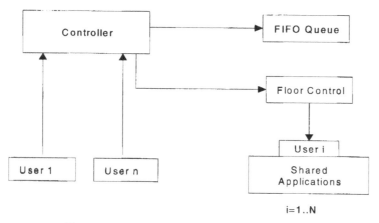

Figure 4. Block diagram of a FIFO floor control.

1.6 VIRTUAL EXPERIMENTER

This feature is used to provide hands-on experience with the material covered in class. It is implemented as a Java applet that can run on any Java-enabled system. Figure 5 shows an example of using it. Figure 6 shows an overview of its implementation

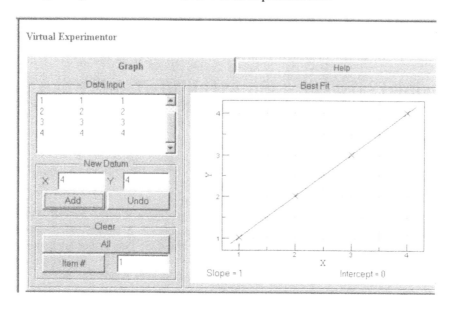

Figure 5. Virtual experimenter in use.

1.7 CONCLUSION

We have discussed various features of VCOIN, a virtual classroom model that can take advantage of a worldwide networking infrastructure of the Internet to conduct education electronically. In addition to having features that are common in most concurrent internet-based virtual classroom systems, we have also focused on two features that are, in general, overlooked in most systems: a) A centralized Mouse Detect feature for monitoring and controlling student activities at a remote place b) A combination of centralized and FCFS floor control for regulation of audio/video communications of student groups. A prototype has been developed. The practicality of the VCOIN model was successfully validated during pilot runs by a group of instructors and students using multiple computer labs. Several screen captures are provided to illustrate the performance of the prototype during these pilot runs.

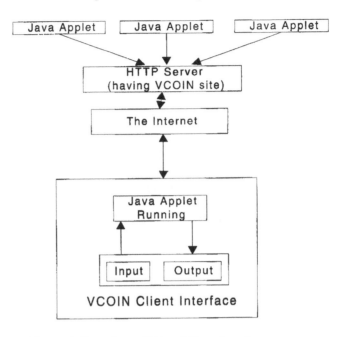

Figure 6. Overview of Virtual Experimenter.

2. VIDEO CONFERENCING EXPERIMENTS BETWEEN FAU AND VU FOR DISTANCE LEARNING USING CLASSPOINT SOFTWARE

2.1 INTRODUCTION

The objective of this project was to investigate the suitability of Internet-based videoconferencing systems to synchronous distance education.

Synchronous distance education uses tools that allow the instructor and the student(s) to log on at the same time, and have virtual face-to-face contact. A simple videoconferencing tool allows transmission of only audio and video information. This is not adequate for distance education. Application-sharing and whiteboard facilities in conjunction with videoconferencing provide a richer environment for distance education. Some of the software tools used for synchronous distance education today include Microsoft's NetMeeting, White Pine's ClassPoint, and PictureTel's Liveshare. Our aim is to investigate the suitability of Internet-based videoconferencing systems to synchronous distance education. We investigated a number of videoconferencing tools aimed at distance learning. We found the ClassPoint system of White Pine Software [13] one of the most promising tools. We chose this software also because of a special offer made by White Pine to educational institutions in 1998.

Background of the people involved in these experiments is as follows. Nalin Sharda and Sam Hsu are academics at Victoria University (VU) and Florida Atlantic University (FAU) respectively. Satish Gangisetty and Krishna Adusumilli are graduate students at VU and FAU respectively. During the first half of 1998 initial work started at VU and FAU in parallel, almost independently. During the second half of 1998 Nalin Sharda spent a semester at FAU on a visiting position. The inter-university experiments started during this period. Further experiments were conducted in the beginning of 1999.

2.2 CLASSPOINT SOFTWARE

ClassPoint is an instructor-controlled learning environment that can use the Internet for communication and a Web browser as the user interface. It supports multi-point video and audio conferencing, Web tours, class setup and scheduling. It includes shared whiteboard and some other useful features. ClassPoint uses the client-server model [14] shown in Figure 7.

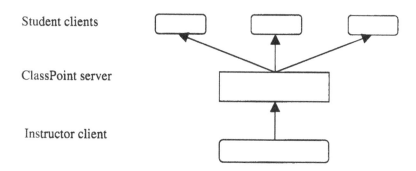

Student clients

ClassPoint server

Instructor client

Figure 7. ClassPoint's Client/Server model.

ClassPoint operation is built upon White Pine's CU-SeeMe videoconferencing software and MeetingPoint [15] conference server software. MeetingPoint is the server that provides a complete multimedia conference environment with features such as:

- H.323 compliant audio and video conferencing.
- Data sharing with T.120 standard.
- Security features to control access.
- Billing and tracking support.
- Bandwidth management function.

The main components of the ClassPoint software are:

- Planning Center software.
- Instructor software.
- Student software.

Planning Center Software: The course administrator and the instructor use the ClassPoint Planning Center to create and manage new classrooms. Administrator can create classes and assign students / instructors to these. Each student is assigned a user name and a password. If required, the administrator can also create a group user name and password for general login. It also enables the administrator to keep track of late students. Users enter classes (i.e. login from their workstation) that are currently in session on the ClassPoint Server, using the Planning Center. When a user enters a class the Class Point Student or Instructor application is launched and connected to the specified class. Once a user is connected to the class, (s)he can have a multimedia conference with other users in the same class. ClassPoint Planning Center software requires Windows NT workstation version 4.0 or server with Microsoft Service Pack 3 with a 166 MHz Pentium processor. A minimum of 64 MB RAM and 23 MB of hard disk space is required. TCP/IP networking software and MeetingPoint Conference Server software version 3.051 are required.

Instructor Software: ClassPoint Instructor is the client component through which the instructors can login from a remote site and conduct a class. The instructor manages student participation and interaction in the classroom. The instructor has full control over the students' privilege to participate in the class. The instructor can communicate with the students using audio and/or video, chat, and whiteboard [16,17,18] tool. The instructor also has the ability to conduct Web tour(s) for the class.

Student Software: ClassPoint Student is the client component through which the students can join and participate in the online classes. With the help of this software, students can view class materials before the class or after the class through the ClassPoint server. A student can request the instructor to grant spotlight. Once the spotlight is granted, the entire class can see and hear the student with the spotlight. A student can conduct public or private chat with other students or the instructor.

System Requirements: ClassPoint Instructor and Student require a minimum of 100 MHz Pentium processor with Windows 95 or Windows NT 4.0. The RAM should be at least 32 MB and the hard disk space of 12 MB is required. TCP/IP network connection, video camera, and headphones are essential. The speed of the Network connection should be at least 33.6 Kbps.

2.3 EXPERIMENT SETUP

We conducted a series of distance education experiments between Victoria University (VU) and Florida Atlantic University (FAU). Figure 8 depicts the logical connection between the various clients and the server in the ClassPoint / MeetingPoint system.

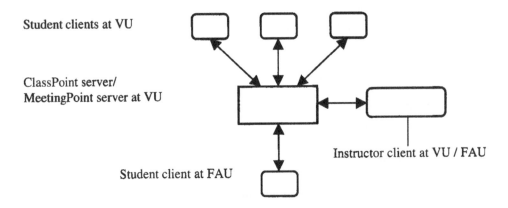

Figure 8. Experiments setup.

The ClassPoint server makes use of the MeetingPoint server. This server was setup at VU. Instructor and Student client software was installed at both FAU and VU.

Specifications of the LAN system, the client workstation, and the server are as follows.

Client workstation used at FAU:

- CPU: Pentium-II, 120 MHz.
- Memory: 64MB RAM.
- Operating System: Windows NT4.0 workstation.
- LAN connection: 10 Mbps Switched Ethernet.
- Internet connection to the LAN: T1 leased line.

Client workstation used at VU:

- CPU: Pentium Pro, 200 MHz.

- Memory: 32 MB RAM.
- Operating System: Windows95.
- LAN connection: 10 Mbps Switched Ethernet.

Server used at VU:
- CPU: Pentium Pro, 200 MHz.
- Memory: 64 MB RAM.
- Operating System: Windows NT4.0 server.
- LAN connection: 100 Mbps Switched Ethernet.
- Internet connection: 36 Mbps ATM Microwave link.

2.4 EXPERIMENTS AND QUALITATIVE RESULTS

The main aim of our experiments was to get a clear understanding of the capabilities of the ClassPoint software and its operation over the Intranet and the Internet environments. First, by running the Instructor client at FAU and Student clients at VU, some qualitative testing was performed. Nalin Sharda logged in as the instructor from FAU and conducted a distance education class for a group of students logged in from VU. We observed that simplex (one way) communication worked reasonably well. However, the turnaround time for half-duplex (two-way, one direction at a time) communication was too long, to consider the videoconference equivalent to a virtual face-to-face contact. For quantitative testing, Satish logged in as the Instructor client from VU, Krishna logged in as a Student client from FAU, and some other student clients logged in from VU. During these experiments quantitative measurements were made using the NetMedic tool installed on the clients at VU.

2.4.1 Experimentation over the Intranet
Experimentation over the Intranet involved installation of Instructor clients and the Student clients on user workstations, configuring them for optimum performance, and making appropriate measurements with the NetMedic tool while a videoconference session was in progress.

Audio and Video Conference: To observe the effect of additional students on the classroom operation in a simple videoconference, three sets of experiments were performed, with one, two and three students. Before starting the experiments ClassPoint Setup Assistant software was run on the clients to properly adjust the various settings like audio, video and microphone. Parameters such as Receive Rate, Send Rate, and CPU load were measured using NetMedic.

Whiteboard and Application-sharing: For this experiment, the instructor enabled the whiteboard and application-sharing feature of ClassPoint in his Instructor panel. Students were asked to join in collaborative data conferencing using the whiteboard. While the Instructor and Student clients were engaged in a conference the data rates and CPU load were noted using NetMedic. Next, the students were asked to share an application – such as, Microsoft Word or Power Point – with the instructor.

2.4.2 Experiments Performed on the Internet
Experiments performed on the Internet were almost similar to the experiments performed on the Intranet. However, the traffic conditions on the Internet were quite different. Network congestion and delays introduced due to the various components of the communication path, and geographical separation were some of the problems that affected the video quality on the Internet.

Audio and Video Conference: In the experiments performed on the Internet, the number of clients that can be introduced in the ClassPoint session were fewer as compared to those on the Intranet. Before establishing a videoconference between the Instructor and the Student clients the Setup assistant was run to fine-tune the audio and video devices. The size of the ClassPoint windows and the Student and Instructor panels were adjusted for good picture quality. While the videoconference session was in progress, data rates such as Receive Rate, Send Rate and the CPU load were measured using the NetMedic tool. In contrast to the experiments performed on the Intranet, the success rate of the experiments performed over the Internet was not good. While the Student client in Florida heard the Instructor client clearly, the Student client could not be heard properly in Melbourne. Audio was frequently breaking and the video streams were very slow. Sometimes the video froze completely. The Frame Rate was very low with little lip-synchronization. The experience on the Internet was a bit frustrating.

Whiteboard and Application Sharing: Experiments were performed with whiteboard and application sharing. The collaborative features worked satisfactorily. Some animation files were played at the Instructor client while the students were collaborating with the instructor. While audio and video communication over the Internet was of poor quality, collaborative tools worked well.

Distance Education Class: Nalin Sharda conducted a synchronous distance education class for his students at VU. Only one Student client was logged in from VU due to throughput limitations of the Internet. Nalin logged in as the Instructor client from FAU and Satish logged in as the Student client from VU. The computer screen of the Student client was projected on a large screen for the entire class to see. A half-hour lecture was conducted for the students of "Networked Multimedia" subject. The topic of the lecture was, "Distance Education Over the Internet". Following the lecture, we had a question answer session. Students came to the Student client workstation, one at a time.

For the lecture, transmission was purely simplex. The quality of audio and video during the lecture was reasonably good; i.e. the students could understand the lecture content clearly. The question answer session used half-duplex communication. The turn-around time of the half-duplex communication was significant. This reduced the effectiveness of the virtual face-to-face contact. Figure 9 shows a couple of (digital) photographs taken while the actual videoconference session took place between Melbourne and Florida.

2.5 QUANTITATIVE RESULTS

In this section we present quantitative results obtained from the experiments described in the previous section.

Data, such as throughput measured at each client, can be useful in determining the network load and may be used for network capacity planning. This information can also help in setting appropriate limits on the maximum number of participants allowed on the server simultaneously. We used the bit rate measured at each client to calculate the burstiness of the data streams. Burstiness is the ratio of the Peak Bit Rate (PBR) to the Mean Bit Rate (MBR). This Information can be used to understand the data transmission requirements at particular nodes, and help in planning and designing networks for distance education.

Nalin Sharda and Satish Gangisetty   Sam Hsu and Satish Gangisetty

Figure 9. Videoconferencing between VU and FAU.

2.5.1 NetMedic.

NetMedic tool was used for measuring various parameters. This tool works well in the Windows and the Internet environments. It can be used to measure the Receive Rate, Send Rate, and CPU load (i.e. utilization). This tool can also be used to generate traffic reports, trace frequently visited sites, number of hops between the client and the server, slowest sites and also to keep track of the health of the computer. Although NetMedic provides a wide range of measurement techniques, only three of these were used in our experiments.

2.5.2 Data Rates and CPU Utilization.

Three experiments were performed on the Intranet, namely, Instructor client with one, two, and three Student clients. Figures 10 through 12 are the graphs of the data for the experiment with one Student client. These graphs depict the variations of Receive Rate, Send Rate and CPU utilization respectively, for the Instructor client.

Figure 10 shows how the Receive Rate (in Kbps) varied with time (in seconds). Over this period the Least Bit Rate (LBR) is 59 Kbps, Peak Bit Rate (PBR) is 108 Kbps, and Mean Bit Rate (MBR) is 71.8 Kbps. Burstiness of the Receive Rate is 1.5.

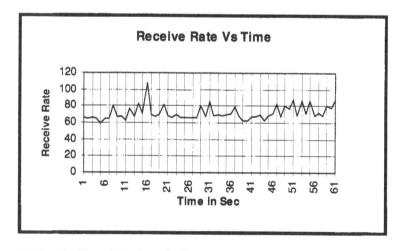

Figure 10. Receive Rate (Kbps) on the Instructor client connected to one Student client.

Figure 11 shows how the Send Rate varies with Time. LBR = 50 Kbps, PBR = 118 Kbps, MBR = 84 Kbps and burstiness = 1.4.

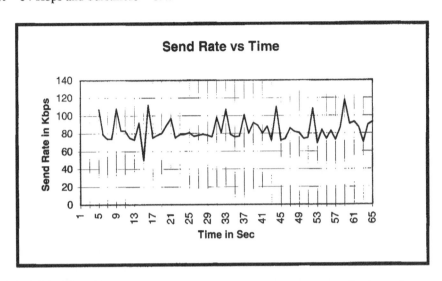

Figure 11. Send Rate on the Instructor client connected to one Student client.

Figure 12 shows CPU utilization variation with Time. It can be seen from the graph that CPU utilization varied between 30% and 79% with an average value of 48.5%, and burstiness of 1.63.

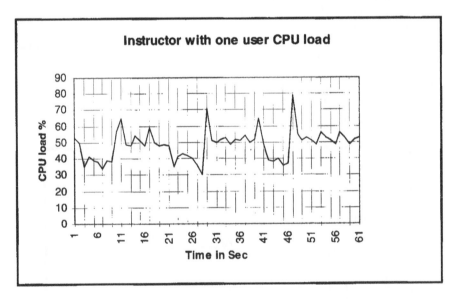

Figure 12. CPU Utilization on the Instructor client connected to one Student client.

Data Summary: Graphs of the data for two and three student experiments are not given, to avoid repetitious presentation. A summary of the results for the experiments performed on the Intranet is given in Table 1.

Table 1. Summary of Data Rates and CPU Utilization for Experiments over the Intranet

Parameter	1 Student	2 Students	3 Students
Receive Rate			
Least	59 Kbps	82 Kbps	89 Kbps
Peak	108 Kbps	122 Kbps	172 Kbps
Mean	71.8 Kbps	96.5 Kbps	126.8 Kbps
Burstiness	1.5	1.26	1.36
Send Rate			
Least	50 Kbps	70 Kbps	67 Kbps
Peak	118 Kbps	382 Kbps	114 Kbps
Mean	84 Kbps	87.8 Kbps	86.3 Kbps
Burstiness	1.4	4.35	1.32
CPU Load			
Least	30 %	39 %	36 %
Peak	79 %	83 %	90 %
Mean	48.5 %	59.8 %	60.4 %
Burstiness	1.63	1.39	1.4

Similar data for the experiments performed on the Internet are given in Table 2. In the Internet experiment only one Student client was logged on with one Instructor client. Two experiments (Ex-1, Ex-2) were performed. Data recorded for the Instructor and the Student clients and their average (Av.) values are given in Table 2.

Table 2. Summary of Data Rates and CPU Utilization for Experiments over the Internet

Parameter	Instructor Client			Student client		
	Ex-1	Ex-2	Average	Ex-1	Ex-2	Av.
Receive Rate	Kbps	Kbps	Kbps	Kbps	Kbps	Kbps
Least	81	87	**84**	85	84	**84.5**
Peak	126	134	**130**	122	120	**121**
Mean	101	97	**99**	98	97	**97.5**
Burstiness	1.24	1.38	**1.31**	1.24	1.23	**1.23**
Send Rate						
Least	1	68	**34.5**	33	69	**51**
Peak	103	112	**107**	92	99	**95**
Mean	86	80	**83**	72	78	**75**
Burstiness	1.2	1.39	**1.29**	1.27	1.27	**1.27**
CPU Load	%	%	%	%	%	%
Least	53	79	**66**	100	100	**100**
Peak	96	90	**93**	100	100	**100**
Mean	85	85	**85**	100	100	**100**
Burstiness	1.1	1.05	**1.07**	1	1	**1**

Data Analysis - Intranet Experiments: With three observation points, we can stipulate some conclusions. The main observations that we can make from the data presented in Table 1 are as follows.

All types of Receive Rates (least, peak, and mean) increase with the number of student clients. Though the increase is not proportional to the number of Student clients. Burstiness of the traffic, on the other hand, decreases with increasing number of Student clients. This implies that a high-speed connection will be better utilized with more students in a distance education class. In other words, the communication infrastructure cost can be amortized over a larger number of students lowering the per student cost.

The data for the Send Rate has similar characteristics, but for the anomalous jump in the traffic values for the two-student experiment. This could be due to higher level of movement in the picture frame.

Similarly, increase in the CPU utilization is apparent with increase in the number of students. Peak utilization for three-student experiment was 90%. This suggests that the CPU will get saturated if more students are added to the videoconference. In fact, we did observe that for four or more Student clients, the screen of the Instructor client froze every now and then. We attribute this to saturation of the CPU's processing power. Practical implication of this point is that the instructor must use a high powered CPU to have effective videoconference as the number of students increases.

Data Analysis - Internet Experiments: For experiments on the Internet we were restricted to only one Student client communicating with the Instructor client. With more than one Student client in the virtual classroom the system did not work properly. Therefore, we did not consider it worthwhile noting down traffic data. By comparing Tables 1 and 2 we can see that data rates obtained in the Internet experiment are of similar magnitude as those in the Intranet experiments. But the CPU utilization is much higher, especially for the Student client, which is 100%. A fully saturated CPU will lead to increased delay in processing and transmitting the data.

2.5.3 Transmission Delay

Good quality audio and video communications require low latency (accumulated delay) between the sender and the receiver. This is because audio and video loose relevance if they are not delivered in a timely manner. For a good quality audio and video the delay should not be more than 400 milliseconds (ms) [17]. The sender, the networking devices, and the receiver together introduce delays along the communication path [18].

Delay in audio and video transmission encountered over the Internet connection was measured. This delay dictates if the videoconference works well as virtual face-to-face contact, or not. The CPU load was also measured to identify situations where the bottleneck was the processing power of the CPU, and not the network.

Audio Delay Measurement: A simple experiment was performed in order to measure the delay in audio transmission. An agreed upon text trigger (TT) (e.g. Go) was typed in the chat window by the instructor. The student spoke a pre-decided audio trigger (AT) (e.g. "Hello") on receiving the TT in his chat window. An electronic stopwatch was started at the very instant the TT was transmitted. When the instructor heard the AT, the stopwatch was stopped. The delay in transmitting the TT was considered negligible. Therefore the time on the stopwatch was noted as the delay in audio transmission. Delay was measured for three minutes over fifteen trials. Audio delay data is given in Figure 13.

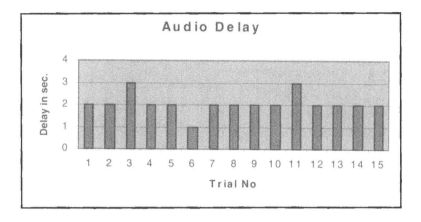

Figure 13. Transmission delay for audio.

Video Delay Measurement: Delay in video transmission was measured by a similar procedure. The instructor in Melbourne, transmitted a TT to the student in Florida. The student at Florida was asked to send a visual trigger (VT) (e.g. raise his forefinger) on receiving the TT. As the time delay in transmitting the TT was neglected, the time between sending the TT and receiving the VT was noted as the delay in video transmission. This delay was measured for four minutes, over twenty trials, as shown in Figure 14.

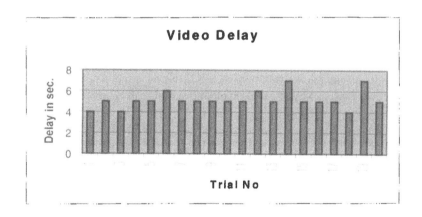

Figure 14. Transmission delay for video.

Delay Data Analysis: From Figure 13 we can see that the audio delay varied from 1 to 3 seconds. For most of the trials the audio delay was 2 sec. This is much greater than the acceptable value of 400 ms. We can see the variation in the video delay in Figure 14; it varied from 4 to 7 sec. For most of the trials the video delay was 5 sec. Not only is the video delay more than the acceptable value, but also more than twice the audio delay. This mismatch in audio and video delays led to severe lack of lip-synchronization.

One of the main reasons for these excessive delays is the lack of adequate bandwidth on many of the Internet connections. Moreover, the Internet is a public domain information network [18]. An end-to-end connection on the Internet passes through many intermediate links and nodes. Individual users do not have the ability to reserve service aspects, such as bandwidth and buffer space on these intermediate links and nodes. The TCP/IP suites of protocols used on the Internet were not designed to carry real-time audio and video data. Multimedia information networking systems [18] currently under development will alleviate some of these problems in the near future. Internet2 [19] is an effort aimed at developing an information superhighway for universities and research organizations. Such application specific information networks will also help in providing low delay connections over the Internet.

2.6 CONCLUSIONS

From our experiments we conclude that the videoconferencing tools such as ClassPoint provide excellent feature for synchronous distance education. It will be possible to use these tools for virtual classroom creation in the near future. But, at this point in time their suitability must be evaluated for specific environments. Operation of these tools is more successful on the Intranet environment; but that is not what distance education required. Operation of these tools over the Internet is far from satisfactory. Enhancements such as Internet2 will improve the situation. Further experiments are required to build a thorough understanding of the impediments in the deployment of videoconferencing for synchronous distance education.

3. VIRTUAL OFFICE HOURS USING NETMEETING

3.1 INTRODUCTION

The purpose of this project was to assess the feasibility of using off-the-shelf collaboration tools to implement the concept of virtual office hours.

The use of the Internet to enable communication between instructors and remote students in a format similar to that used for office hours is one of the features of many Web-based distance education systems. Virtual office hours (VOH) via the Internet can be established by using simple asynchronous tools such as e-mail or discussion lists. The interaction between instructor and students can be significantly improved by using synchronous, real-time tools. An easy and inexpensive way to enable such interactions can be obtained by using an off-the-shelf collaboration software.

We have assessed the usefulness and suitability of a specific software package, Microsoft® NetMeeting™, for the implementation of virtual office hours. The product's main features, some of its pros and cons, the experiments performed to evaluate its use for virtual office hours and corresponding results and lessons learned are described next.

3.2 WHY VIRTUAL OFFICE HOURS

The use of the Web for distance education has grown exponentially in the past few years. An ever-growing number of Web-based courses in virtually any field of knowledge are now available worldwide. Moreover, conventional, live courses are also incorporating Internet-based features, such as compilation of relevant course information into HTML pages, electronic submission of assignments, and e-mail communication between students and instructors.

One of the most important features of any distance education system is the ability to allow remote students to reach their instructors and interact with them in a format similar to the well-known concept of office hours. The simplest way of implementing the VOH concept is to enable e-mail communication between students and instructor. An alternative option consists of offering the students the possibility of formulating their questions using a Web-based form, such as in [20]. A natural extension of the concept is the use of discussion lists, where students can benefit from other students' questions and previous discussions on the subject. All these methods of communication between students and instructors are asynchronous by nature, and their effectiveness will depend strongly on how promptly the questions get answered.

The VOH concept was made popular by the Department of Chemistry and Biochemistry at UCLA [21] and was later extended to many other colleges and universities, such as the Santa Monica College [22]. Their VOH project has got a very high approval rate from students [21][23] who appreciate the availability of course material in electronic format as well as the possibility of interacting with instructors out of class or office hours. At a larger scale, students in many other colleges and universities are having access to similar systems and their response has been consistently positive [24].

We believe that virtual office hours should go beyond asynchronous interaction and decided to test possible tools and techniques to implement real-time, synchronous interaction between students and instructors using a commercial (off-the-shelf) collaboration tool.

3.3 WHY NETMEETING

There are many conferencing tools available, such as White Pine's CU-SeeMe, PictureTel's LiveShare Plus, or Microsoft NetMeeting. Some of them, e.g. White Pine's ClassPoint, specifically target the distance education market. These tools usually provide highly interactive, synchronous, bi- or multidirectional features, e.g. audio and video conferencing, and multipoint data conferencing using tools such as chat rooms, shared clipboard, whiteboard, and file transfer capabilities. We decided to use Microsoft NetMeeting for a number of reasons described later in this chapter. At the same time, we carried out experiments using White Pine's ClassPoint (see Section 2 of this Chapter) and continued developing our own Web-based collaboration tools [1] [25].

Microsoft NetMeeting can be briefly described as a collaboration tool that combines voice and data communications, video, real-time application sharing, file transfer, a full-featured shared whiteboard, and text-based chat [26]. NetMeeting is targeted at home users, as well as small and large organizations and claims to allow users to "take full advantage of the global reach of the Internet or corporate intranet for real-time communications and collaboration."[27] Connecting to other NetMeeting users is made easy with the Microsoft Internet Locator Server (ILS), enabling participants to call each other from a dynamic directory within NetMeeting or from a Web page. Connections can also be established by calling the other party's IP address. While connected on the Internet or corporate intranet, participants can communicate with audio and video, work together on virtually any 32-bit Windows-based application, exchange or mark-up graphics on an electronic whiteboard, transfer files, or use the text-based chat program.

Some of the most prominent features of NetMeeting 2.1 are [27]:

- **Internet phone/H.323 standards-based audio support**: real-time, point-to-point audio conferencing over the Internet or corporate Intranet. Half-duplex and full-duplex audio support for real-time conversations, automatic microphone sensitivity level setting, and microphone muting, which lets users control the audio signal sent during a call. This audio conferencing supports network TCP/IP connections. Support for the H.323 protocol [28][29] enables interoperability between NetMeeting and other H.323-compatible audio clients.

- **H.323 standards-based video conferencing** including the following features:

   (a) Participants can switch audio and video to another person during a meeting. This feature compensates for the impossibility of multipoint audio and video conferencing.
   (b) Users can dynamically adjust the video image quality and change the size of the video window, balancing the need for higher quality or faster performance.
   (c) In the NetMeeting main window, the video preview and receive windows are integrated on the Current Call window. Users can view these video windows from Current Call, or drag them to a different location on the desktop.
   (d) Users can choose whether or not to transmit video immediately when a call starts. Also, they can pause or resume sending or receiving video by pressing a button in the video window frame.
   (e) NetMeeting automatically balances the performance and quality of video during a meeting based on the speed of the network connection, providing the highest quality, lowest bandwidth video capabilities.
   (f) Administrators can control access to video features using NetMeeting custom settings.
   (g) On MMX-enabled computers, NetMeeting uses the MMX-enabled video codecs to improved performance for video compression and decompression algorithms.
   (h) Support for H.323 conference servers and gateways (currently being developed by leading vendors) will enable NetMeeting users to participate in meetings with multiple audio and video connections.
   (i) H.323 standard-based video technology is also compliant with the H.261 [30] and H.263 [31] video codecs.

- **Intelligent Audio/Video Stream Control**, which automatically balances the load for network bandwidth, CPU use, and memory use. This intelligent stream control ensures that audio, video, and data are prioritized properly, so that NetMeeting maintains high-quality audio while transmitting and receiving data and video during a call.

- **Multipoint data conferencing**: Two or more users can communicate and collaborate as a group in real time. Participants can share applications, exchange information through a shared clipboard, transfer files, collaborate on a shared whiteboard, and use a text-based chat feature. Also, support for the T.120 data conferencing standard enables interoperability with other T.120-based products and services. The multipoint data conferencing features are listed in Table 3.

NetMeeting provides a broad support of international standards, to ensure interoperability among solutions from different vendors.

3.3.1   NetMeeting pros and cons
The following *pros* and *cons* are compiled based on data from comparative reviews, threaded discussions, relevant Web pages and the authors' experience using NetMeeting in their classes.

Pros
- NetMeeting users can talk, send video, type text and share applications all at the same time [26].
- The main tool as well as its Software Development Kit (SDK) and Resource Kit (for Network Administrators) are free and can be downloaded from Microsoft Web site [32].
- NetMeeting is continuously being improved and its basic architecture is being widely supported.
- NetMeeting can be expanded / integrated with other applications using its SDK.

- Broad support of international standards for easy interoperability with solutions from different vendors.
- NetMeeting provides a good degree of privacy during a call (using the "do not disturb" option).
- NetMeeting supports application sharing in multiparty calls. Any collaborating participant can assume mouse control and work in the shared application while others watch. Application sharing has proven to be NetMeeting's "killer feature" [26].

Table 3. Features of Multipoint Data Conferencing

Application sharing	A user can share a program running on one computer with other participants in the conference. Participants can review the same data or information, and see the actions as the person sharing the application works on the program.
Shared clipboard	The shared clipboard enables a user to exchange its contents with other participants in a conference using familiar cut, copy, and paste operations.
File transfer	Users can send a file in the background to one or all of the conference participants. When one user drags a file into the main window, the file is automatically sent to each person in the conference, who can then accept or decline receipt. This file transfer capability is fully compliant with the T.127 standard.
Whiteboard	Multiple users can simultaneously collaborate using the whiteboard to review, create, and update graphic information. The whiteboard is object-oriented (as opposed to pixel-oriented), enabling participants to manipulate the contents by clicking and dragging with the mouse. In addition, they can use a remote pointer or highlighting tool to point out specific contents or sections of shared pages.
Chat	A user can type text messages to share common ideas or topics with other conference participants, or record meeting notes and action items as part of a collaborative process. Also, participants in a conference can use chat to communicate in the absence of audio support.

Cons

- NetMeeting's audio and video features work only between two participants, so a three-way call cannot be established.
- NetMeeting is very CPU intensive and requires a powerful machine, especially for audio and video conferencing. The recommended hardware includes a Pentium-MMX 200 MHz or better, at least 32 MB of RAM, 40 MB of free disk space, and good quality peripherals (sound card, video card, microphone or headset, camera, and modem) [26].
- Audio pauses, delays, and momentary loss of full-duplex capabilities are frequent. Moreover, delays, variable latency (jitter) and uneven packet transmission rates (common to any IP-based transmission) may cause deterioration of audio, video, and whiteboard actions.
- Video frame size is too small and frame rate is too low to make video communication a fully enjoyable experience.
- Problems using NetMeeting in intranets protected by firewalls have been reported [33]. Directions of how to get around with this problem can be found at [34] and in chapter 11 of [26].
- NetMeeting has shown security leaks, which can pose great risk to users' data and privacy. An example of a problem in this category is the so-called "Speed Dial" issue [35].

- NetMeeting 2.1 contains a useful whiteboard module that does not comply with T.126, the object-exchange standard under T.120. However, Databeam has produced a tool called MeetingTools [36], which installs on top of NetMeeting and enhances NetMeeting calls. With MeetingTools, NetMeeting users can drive "massive-point" conferences, where hundreds of simultaneous users view the activity from their Web browsers.
- NetMeeting setup is time-consuming and non-technical users can easily get frustrated.
- NetMeeting can be seen as part of the Microsoft monopolizing strategy, and its seamless integration with other Microsoft products (particularly Internet Explorer, Outlook, Windows Explorer, and Exchange) is controversial. Along the same reasoning, one may wonder how long will the product still be offered free of charge.

3.4 EXPERIMENTS

NetMeeting has been used by the authors to implement the concept of virtual office hours. Our aim is to extend to distant students via the network the one-to-one interaction of typical office hours meetings. To evaluate the usefulness of specific NetMeeting features for the purpose of distance education, particularly for virtual office hours, students from two sections of the "Introduction to Microprocessor Systems (CDA3331)" course, offered by one of the authors during the Spring'99 semester have been selected to participate in evaluating those aspects.

It is expected that the level of interaction (e.g., text only, one- or two-way audio/video) be limited mainly by the students' hardware and networking capabilities. However, to what extent the impact that different hardware, software, and especially the quality of the networking connection would have on the overall effectiveness of the approach has remained as an open question that has motivated the authors to design and carry out actual experiments. So far, eight separate experiments in rather different environments, ranging from low-speed modem dial-up connection from students' homes to LAN-based connection with two-way audio and video capabilities between one of our computing laboratories and the instructor's office have been conducted. All experiments have been carried out on a one-to-one and student-to-instructor basis.

In each experiment, a student initiated a dialog by calling the instructor's office using NetMeeting (dialing the instructor's network IP address) in a way similar to a phone call. After connection was made, efforts would be directed at attempting to use all possible features of NetMeeting initially. Whenever a specific feature would exhibit problems (e.g. two-way audio), we would fall back to the minimal interaction, i.e. text-based chat, and agree on using whatever tools were available to achieve a satisfactory two-way communication. The subject of the conversations was always related to the course, simulating a live office hour meeting, lasting between 10 to 30 minutes.

3.5 RESULTS

The results detailed below refer to a universe of eight experiments, each involving one student and one instructor in a one-to-one and real time interaction. A total of eight different students participated in the experiments. Since this number may not represent a significant sample space of the total student population, we emphasize their importance in a qualitative, rather than quantitative way.

- **Connection**: we managed to achieve a good mix of different connection conditions: half the students used the department LAN, calling the instructor's office from one of our labs. The other half was equally spread between modem, cable modem, and T1 (enterprise) Internet connections.

- **NetMeeting's features**: students evaluated eight features for their quality and usefulness for the VOH concept using a 0-3 scale (0 = very bad; 3 = very good). The distribution of grades for each feature is summarized in Figure 15. From that diagram several conclusions can be drawn:
  (i)   The most consistent feature (which was always available, regardless of technical difficulties) was the text-based chat. All students used it and graded it "very good".
  (ii) The shared whiteboard (see Figure 16 for an example of whiteboard contents saved into a file for possible reuse) got a very positive response from all students who used it.
  (iii) The file transfer feature got positive evaluations from the few students who used it.
  (iv) The application-sharing feature was highly appreciated by the few students who tried it.
  (v)   Audio and video capabilities got all possible grades, showing a high dependence on the quality of the equipment and the network connection.

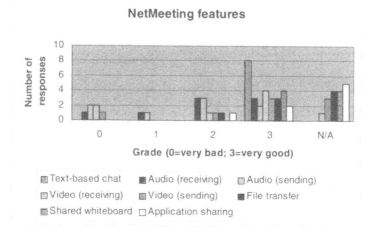

Figure 15. Summary of evaluation of NetMeeting's features.

- **General evaluation**: 75% of the students considered NetMeeting a suitable tool to implement the VOH concept. All but one rated the tool as "very useful" to help in distance learning, in general. Overall, three quarters of the students considered the VOH concept (very) useful.

3.6. LESSONS LEARNED, CONCLUSIONS, AND RECOMMENDATIONS

The VOH experiments have been evaluated to be satisfactory both from the instructor's as well as the students' perspectives. Some of the lessons we have learned are:

- NetMeeting setup can be time-consuming and many students got discouraged after a few unsuccessful attempts.
- Students (particularly Computer Science and Engineering students) are always supportive to the introduction of new technology into the educational process and eager to use it to its maximum possible extent. One clear example is the preference for NetMeeting calls over telephone calls to the instructor's office, despite all the technical difficulties with two-way audio connection over the Internet.
- There is a clear and strong dependence between the quality of the connection and the overall satisfaction with the tool. Students who tried it from one of the labs during Spring Break (network traffic was low those days in contrast to car traffic by the beach) had a

completely different experience than those who attempted to use NetMeeting from home, in the middle of a busy working day.

• For the purposes of VOH, NetMeeting features can be divided into essential, extremely useful, and accessory. In the first group we'd include text-based chat and two-way audio. In the second group, shared whiteboard and application sharing. File transfer and video communication would belong to the last group.

We believe the overall results of our first experiments were very positive and encouraging. They have confirmed our expectations as to whether NetMeeting could be used to implement the VOH concept. We plan to extend the use of NetMeeting for virtual office hours during the upcoming semester and will keep an eye on possible third-party products that can make the experience even more enjoyable.

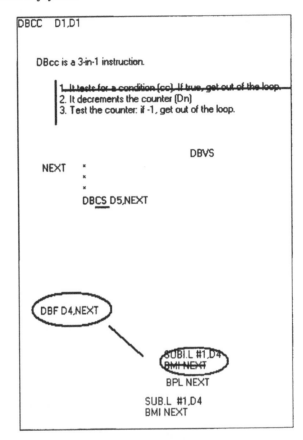

Figure 16. Whiteboard contents.

References

1. S. Hsu, A. Pandya, and R. Patel, "Yet Another Virtual Classroom Over the Internet," *Proc. of 1998 ASEE/IEEE Frontiers in Education Conference (FIE '98)*, November 1998, Tempe, Arizona, pp. 717-721.
2. Sharda, S. Gangisetty, K. Adusumilli, and S. Hsu, "Application of Video Conferencing to Distance Education: A Case Study with the ClassPoint Software," *Proc. of SCI'99, World Multi-conference on Systems, Cybernetics and Informatics*, August 1999, Orlando, Florida.

3. O. Marques, S. Hsu, and N. Sharda, "Virtual Office Hours Using NetMeeting," *Proc. of SCI'99, World Multi-conference on Systems, Cybernetics and Informatics*, August 1-5, 1999, Orlando, Florida.

4. Yahoo!-Education:Distance Learning: Colleges and Universities, http://www.yahoo.com/Education/Distance_learning /Colleges_and_Universities/.

5. ICDL ONLINE, http://www-icdl.open.ac.uk/ index.htm.

6. M. Turoff, "Designing a Virtual Classroom," *Proc. of 1995 International Conference on Computer Assisted Instruction ICCAI '95*, March 1995, Hsinchu, Taiwan.http://www.njit.edu/CCCC/VC/Papers/ Design.html.

7. D. Dwyer, K. Barbieri, and H.M. Doerr, "Creating a Virtual Classroom for Interactive Education on the Web," *Proc. of 3rd International WWW Conference*, Darmstadt, Germany, April 10-14, 1995, http://www.tc.cornell.edu/~dwyer/Overheads/Virtual.Classroom/ctc.virtual.class.html.

8. T.D.C. Little and D. Venkatesh, "The Use of Multimedia Technology in Distance Learning," *Proc. IEEE Intl. Conf. on Multimedia and Networking*, September 1995, pp. 3-17.

9. R.T. Kouzes, J.D. Myers, and W.A. Wulf, "Collaboratories: Doing Science on the Internet," *IEEE Computer*, Aug. 1996, pp. 40-46.

10. M-C Lai, B-H Chen, and S-M Yuan, "Toward a New Educational Environment," *Proc. 4th International WWW Conference*, Boston, Massachusetts, December 1995. http://www.w3j. com/1/lai.238/paper/238.html.

11. K. Maly, H. Abdel-Wahab, C. Overstreet, J. Wild, A. Gupta, A. Youssef, E. Stoica, and E. Al-Shaer, "Interactive Distance Learning over Intranets," *IEEE Internet Computing*, Vol. 1, No. 2, Jan/Feb 1997, pp. 60-71.

12. R. Patel, "VCOIN: Virtual Classroom Over the Internet," Master's thesis, Florida Atlantic University, April 1998.

13. http://www.wpine.com/Products/ClassPoint/index.html.

14. G. Gagliardi, *"Client / Server Computing,"* New Jersey: Prentice Hall, 1994.

15. http://www.wpine.com/Products/MeetingPoint/index.html.

16. B. O. Szuprowicz, *"Multimedia Networking,"* McGraw-Hill, 1995.

17. F. Fluckiger, *"Understanding Networked Multimedia: Applications and Technology"* New Jersey: Prentice Hall, 1995.

18. N. K. Sharda, *"Multimedia Information Networking,"* New Jersey: Prentice-Hall, 1999.

19. http://www.internet2.edu.

20. Virtual Office Hours Page http://www.isop.ucla.edu/ids/mailform/mailform.htm.

21. Virtual Office Hours, White Page http://xenon.chem.ucla.edu/uclavoh/docs/white-page.html.

22. SMC Virtual Office Hours, http://voh.smc.edu/.

23. J. M. Chen, "Virtual office hours connect professors, students," http://www.dailybruin.ucla.edu/DB/Issues/96/2.23/news.virtual.html.

24. G. Landgraf, "Virtual office hours," http://www.student.com/article/emaileducation.

25. S. Hsu and K. K. Adusumilli, "Softboard - An Online Blackboard", *Proc. AACE/WebNet '98*, November 1998, Orlando, Florida, Session 829.

26. B. Summers, *"Official Microsoft NetMeeting Book,"* Redmond, WA: Microsoft Press, 1998.

27. NetMeeting Resource Kit, http://www.microsoft.com/netmeeting/reskit/.

28. Draft ITU-T Recommendation H.323V2 (1997): "Line Transmission of Non-Telephone Signals."

29. A Primer on the H.323 Series Standard http://www.databeam.com/h323/h323 primer.html.

30. ITU-T Recommendation H.261 (1993): "Video Codec for audiovisual services at pX64 kbit/s."

31. ITU-T Recommendation H.263 (1995): "Video Codec for narrow telecom-munications channels at < 64 kbit/s."

32. NetMeeting Home, http://www.microsoft.com/netmeeting.
33. WWWDEV Archived Mailing List: Net-Meeting - Discussion thread starting at: http://leahi.kcc.hawaii.edu/org/wwwdev/logs/0811.html.
34. How to Establish NetMeeting Connections Through a Firewall, http://support.microsoft.com/support/kb/articles/q158/6/23.asp.
35. NetMeeting Speed Dial issue, April 21, 1998, http://www.microsoft.com/windows/ie/security/ netmbuff.asp.
36. DataBeam MeetingTools, http://www.databeam.com/meetingtools/.

Chapter 21

MULTIMEDIA NEWS SYSTEMS

Benjamin Falchuk and Ahmed Karmouch

Abstract

In this chapter we discuss a multimedia news system that we have developed in the Multimedia Information Research Laboratory at the University of Ottawa and beyond. The system consists of a production server for document authoring, a conferencing system for collaborative news article creation, a news database server with aging and archiving, and user sites. All components of the system communicate via OCRInet, an ATM network in the Ottawa region. We provide an overview of the components of the system and how they achieve synchronization, as well as discuss the news and video browsers to facilitate browsing, searching, and extracting media from the news database. In particular, we focus on the representation and browsing of news video objects. Finally, we discuss the Internet and its role in future multimedia news systems.

1. INTRODUCTION

There is currently a great deal of research in multimedia as it relates to the areas of authoring, databases, and applications such as multimedia news. Our research laboratory has developed the following components of a multimedia communications and information system called MEDIABASE: a document model, a data model, a database architecture, a storage subsystem, a multimedia file system, communications protocols, and a media player [3]. MEDIADOC, the document model, includes both logical and layout structures and integrates information and script structures to capture synchronization information within the document hierarchy. It allows authors to create multimedia scenarios, for example, news documents, and specify the temporal and layout relations between all objects [4]. MEDIASTORE and MEDIAFILE, the storage and file system components, provide the low level storage and database functionality of the system as well as handling synchronization, querying, and meeting real-time constraints [3]. A multimedia news application [19,20] runs on top of the MEDIABASE platform.

Other research projects relating to on-demand multimedia news and supporting architectures exist. Lippman et al. have proposed Newspeek, an intelligent application which gathers and presents daily news information from remote sites based on reader profiles and presentation preferences [6]. Touch screens and gesture-based inputs drive browsing in Newspeek. Miller et al. describe a news system involving Dow Jones and NYNEX over broadband networks consisting of a production center, a media service center, and user sites, featuring news alerts, updates, aging, archiving, profiles, and distribution control [10]. Hoffert et al. describe

EDUCOM's on-line news system which features hypertext-type navigational functionality [2]. Ohkubo et al. describe a system which presents a large amount of information using a newspaper-type metaphor and features increased browsing capabilities [12]. Koons et al. have created an information system using elements from computers, televisions, and printed documents to form a new communications medium [5].

This chapter is organized as follows: in Section 2 we detail the platform and components that enable the multimedia news application, in Section 3 we describe the application, in Section 4 we describe a video representation and browsing tool for news videos, and in Section 5 we comment on how Internet technologies relate to news services. In Section 6, conclusions are drawn and the chapter is summarized.

2. MULTIMEDIA NEWS SYSTEM PLATFORM

There is currently a need to create applications that exploit the capabilities of broadband information networks such as ATM. In coordination with the Ottawa Carleton Research Institute (OCRI), the Communications Research Center (CRC), the Ottawa Citizen, and Algonquin College (all in the Ottawa region), we have developed a distributed multimedia news system. Our goal was to implement a far-reaching news system involving: (i) a main production center, (ii) a news content server and database from which production may draw during document creation, (iii) a news database for completed documents encompassing all aspects of document aging, archive management, etc., communications protocols, and (iv) user sites distributed over OCRInet (see Figures 1 and 2). The remainder of this section describes in more detail the architecture of our multimedia news system.

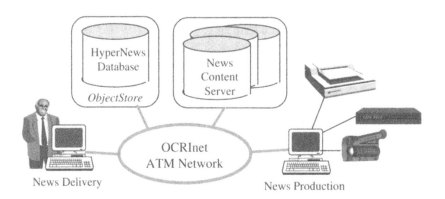

Figure 1. The generic architecture of the system

2.1 NEWS PRODUCTION

The backbone of the production center is the production server. It is the source of all the data needed for creation of a multimedia document. Attached to it, in hardware, are video and audio capturing devices, which allow for the capture and editing of these data types on a per-sample basis. Support for the editing of graphic and text objects is also provided. Files required at the production server are transferred on demand over the network from their source.

The server caters to the stations participating in production which range from microcomputers to DEC Alpha stations. Also at the disposal of the producers are scanners, video cameras, microphones, and PC-VCRs (VCRs controllable by PC software). Production is greatly enhanced by the existence of network groupware and collaborative software so that news stories may be authored jointly in a distributed fashion. For instance, two journalists and an editor may collaborate on a story using shared applications (e.g., whiteboards and word processors) and video conferencing, as in Figure 3.

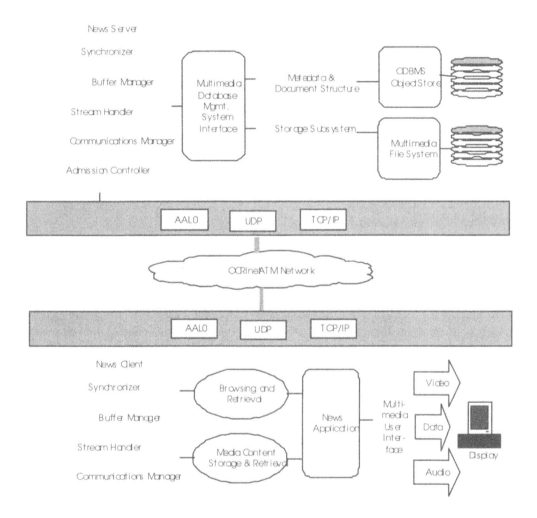

Figure 2. News production, sharing, access, and retrieval.

The news content server is related to the production center. The content server runs on a DEC Alpha station and provides production with a large repository of media objects which are then available to authors. For example, if an author requires a short video clip of the Prime Minister of Canada, he/she could query the content server for all clips having "Jean Chretien" or "prime minister" and "Canada" in the keyword description.

News production is done mainly at two sites; the Ottawa Citizen and Algonquin College (a technical College with special courses in computer programming and New Media design). The Citizen provides the editorial expertise in the creation of the text and content of the news documents. They also have the photographers and VTR operators who gather news on location. Algonquin College has the technical expertise in multimedia production; audio and video editing or photograph scanning can be done at the college. Computer animations can also be produced using SGI machines and sophisticated software. Files are exchanged freely between the two sites via OCRInet, arranged by editors into documents using scenario editors, and then stored in the multimedia database for future reference. Group video-conferencing sessions between remote editors, journalists, and artists are used to create news documents (see Figure 3).

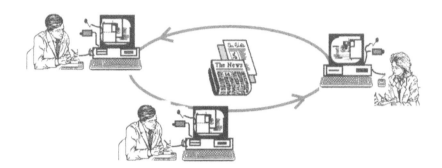

Figure 3. Groupware-based news production.

2.2 MULTIMEDIA DATABASE

The news database is a large, distributed, object-oriented, multimedia database. Currently we use the commercial product *ObjectStore* to implement the object-oriented schema that we designed, and Sun Sparc-10 stations function as database servers. We have developed high-level multimedia communication protocols within the OSI framework to support efficient transmission of media over networks. These protocols must address issues such as media-dependent bit rates, synchronization, and timing-constraints. The data model allows the representation and manipulation of multimedia documents. The document architecture [4] supports the division and subdivision of documents into objects that have semantic meaning. These objects may be general items like chapters, sections, or paragraphs, or items specific to particular document types such as scenes, sub-scenes, etc.

The database supports navigation and querying of multimedia objects. *Collections* contain links to all the documents in a database that follow the semantic information associated with the collection (i.e., keywords). When documents are created, its link is automatically inserted into the appropriate collection(s). Media objects are decomposed into segments that represent either video frames, segments of frames, segments of audio, or portions of text.

The architecture of the database is three-tiered, consisting of the external level, the conceptual level, and the physical level (see Figure 4). The physical level consists of an object database and storage system, the conceptual level is the set of classes and methods defined to support all media types, and the external level is the application view and client system. Data is stored in both high-speed active storage devices and tertiary storage devices. The database system must handle document aging – for example, a news article may go through several "editions" as a story evolves; each should be available. It must also handle frequent updates of volatile information such as stock prices and sports scores.

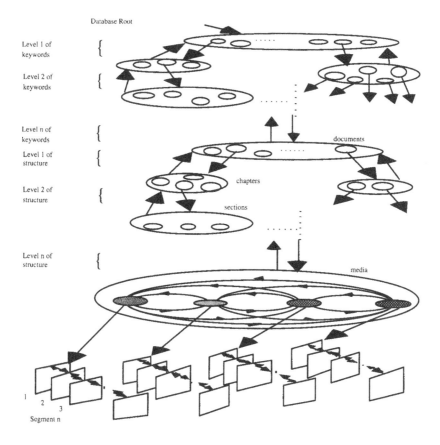

Figure 4. News document representation on the ObjectStore OODBMS.

2.3 CLIENT SERVER COMMUNICATIONS MODEL

The news application is currently operational on OCRInet ATM network. OCRInet is the world's first metropolitan area research network driven by asynchronous transfer mode technology. OCRInet, which employs fiber optic cables to link more than twenty nodes, connects technology companies, telephone companies, government laboratories, and educational institutions. OCRInet commenced network operations in January 1994 and is a partnership between industry, government, and educational institutions. It includes both service and equipment providers as well as the user community in its membership.

Communications over the network are achieved using the client server architecture. This communication architecture is designed to ensure transparency in the interchange of information to screen end-users from the underlying architecture of the application. Distributed applications complying to the model may actually consist of a number of independent programs running on remote hosts scattered over the network, without the users' knowledge.

The *multimedia database server* waits and listens to any service request from a client. It accepts the request if it can cater to this new client. It acts on the request to create, remove, update, or retrieve a document, part of a document, or an object. It then establishes parallel connections to the client depending upon the media type to be sent and the schedules of the synchronized data transfer. The *admission controller* accepts or rejects the request based on resource availability. The *communications manager* establishes new connections and sends and retrieves data streams. The *stream handler* parses the incoming data stream and formats the outgoing stream with a header. The *buffer manager* in the server buffers the data to have an optimum flow control between the database and the communications channel while the buffer manager in the client presents information. The *synchronizer* in the server facilitates concurrent retrieval of multimedia objects with temporal links from the database, and the one in the client dispatches the different multimedia objects to the presentation agent for concurrent display or playback.

2.4 COMMUNICATION AND PRESENTATION

There are two types of integration required by Distributed Multimedia Information Systems, spatial and temporal. In this section, we will discuss temporal integration, or synchronization as it applies to transport and presentation levels. We also discuss the design of a multimedia presentation agent.

2.4.1 Independent Synchronized Entity (ISE)

The MEDIADOC model provides a framework to represent and manipulate complex intermedia relationships within a single multimedia document. The document synchronization is represented by a scenario structure, which defines the set of temporal relationships between the media objects. The scenario adds a temporal dimension to the document architecture, thereby creating a document model capable of representing and manipulating its own presentation flow. MEDIABASE uses a progressive document retrieval strategy [3]. This strategy consists in retrieving, transferring, and displaying Independent Synchronized Entities (ISEs). An ISE is a sub-tree element, which can be synchronized independently of any other sub-tree element of the multimedia document. Figure 5 gives an example of an ISE. The "movies" article is independent of any other article or section of the multimedia newspaper, but its media objects are interdependent for their presentations.

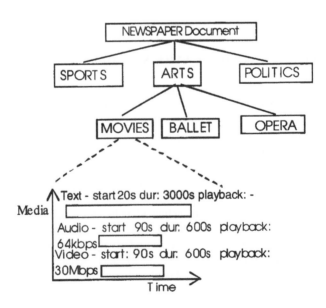

Figure 5. Example of ISEs in a document

The progressive document retrieval method allows us to display one ISE while its successor is being retrieved over the network. This method does not overburden the storage capacity of the local workstation, but it does require a continuous flow of information from the source, through the transport and into the presentation synchronizer of the Distributed Multimedia

Information Systems. Therefore, there are three different synchronization levels that must be achieved during the playback of a multimedia document: Presentation, Transport, and Database synchronization.

Presentation synchronization handles the rendering of the multimedia document at the local workstation. Rendering the document at this level is a two-step process. First, the *presentation synchronizer* requests the MEDIADOC document from the remote database without the contents of the document. This allows the presentation synchronizer to scan the scenario of the document and order the ISEs for sequential rendering. When rendering an ISE, the presentation synchronizer creates a *rendering process* for each media object within the ISE. These rendering processes are responsible for the synchronized playback of the media object. The synchronizer controls the playback rate of the media object by suspending and resuming its presentation process. The presentation synchronizer negotiates, for each media, a data delivery rate from the transport synchronizer via a dynamic quality of service (DQoS) parameter.

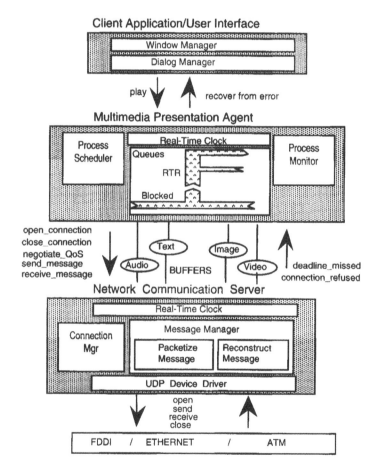

Figure 6. Multimedia presentation agent architecture.

Transport synchronization handles the network communication aspect of the Distributed Multimedia Information Systems and therefore must deal with the problems associated with network communications [21]. The *transport synchronizer* creates communication channels for each rendering process initiated by the presentation synchronizer. Dynamic media objects like audio and video will require throughputs, which are dependent on their capture rates. The transfer over the network of each media object is controlled by a dynamic quality of service

(DQoS) parameter that is exchanged between the transport synchronizer and the presentation or database synchronizer.

2.4.2 Presentation Agent

The Architecture of the Multimedia Presentation Agent (MPA) is shown in Figure 6. The agent is a client of the network communication manager and services the requests of the user-interface application. The primitives offered by the MPA are play, pause, stop, rewind, forward, and scan. The functionality of the main components follows.

The client application invokes document rendering via the play primitive of the MPA server. This primitive passes the MEDIADOC document to the *process scheduler*, which schedules the ISEs for playback. When a rendering process is initiated for a media object, the MPA requests a communication channel from the *network server*. If the connection is refused, the MPA can abort the transfer or renegotiate the connection using the media object's DQoS parameter. If the connection is accepted, the *process scheduler* of the MPA puts the process on the blocked queue where it waits for the media object's start time (see Figure 7).

The *process monitor* supervises the execution of all playback processes and manages both the ready to run (RTR) and the blocked queues. Once the start time of a blocked process has been reached, the process monitor moves the process from the blocked queue to the RTR queue where it waits for its time slice.

An executing *playback process* first attempts to fetch its content part from the remote database. If the process has to wait for the data to be produced by the network server, the process is removed from the monitor and put on the blocked queue. This process will be awakened by either receiving the data it is waiting for, or by a time out. The time out is set to the maximum delay time a process is willing to wait for its next data segment. In the case of NTSC video, the time out is set to the interframe arrival time of 33ms. If the process was awakened by a time out, the MPA informs the network manager of the missed deadline and renegotiates the transfer parameters by the *negotiate_QoS* primitive. If the negotiation fails, the transfer is aborted.

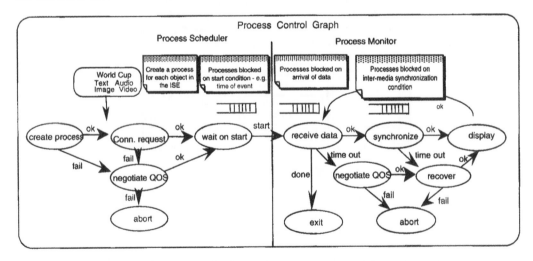

Figure 7. Presentation scheduler and monitor.

If a process is awakened because the data has arrived, the process will attempt to "rendezvous" with any other processes (media) to which it is synchronized. The process will exit the rendezvous on two conditions: time out and failure. The time out condition is used to enforce a constant playback rate for the media object. On time out, the data will be displayed by the client application. The failure condition informs the client application that the media are out of synchronization. The client application makes use of the media object's DQoS to recover from this error. For example, if a video frame failed to synchronize with its corresponding audio track, the client application could ignore this error and allow the process to continue. By setting a bound on the number of failures, the process will be able to continue in a loosely synchronized fashion.

The client application uses the MPA's pause and stop primitives to suspend or abort the presentation of the multimedia document. The forward and rewind primitives are used to relocate the relative temporal position of the multimedia document. The scan primitive permits the client application to render the document (forward or backward) at an accelerated rate. It accomplishes this by skipping ISEs, media objects, or data segments, i.e., display every 10th frame of the video object, depending on the default skip size defined by the client application.

2.5 ACCESS AND RETRIEVAL

User sites are distributed over the ATM network. Ideally, they consist of hardware and software capable of displaying multimedia data, but the system is flexible enough not to send types of data that the user cannot handle. User sites all have client routines installed in software so that searches and queries (undirected searches) on the database, using the client-server model, may be performed. The *Netscape Navigator* browser is typically used to display hypermedia news; some documents can therefore be created using the Hypertext Markup Language (HTML). By nature, Navigator cannot display true synchronized multimedia and thus we have developed a hybrid system for ATM that incorporates the features of Navigator and HTML as well as a true multimedia player. We have distributed the client software and player and an extended (using CGI and Java) Navigator player (see Figure 8).

3. NEWS SERVICE FUNCTIONALITY

Previous attempts at on-demand news systems have revealed several of the key aspects of architecture and functionality that should be integrated into the system; we provide these features as well some unique ones. Since the objective of the system is to provide daily information in a user-friendly way, the application running at the user site should be a unique blend of user-friendly screens and powerful search, query, and browsing mechanisms while maintaining the transparency of data distribution. Also, it should offer novel features that will facilitate users in the context of multimedia news. Note that video presents particular challenges in this area and current research is striving to solve these challenges. In this section we discuss some of the features present at the user sites and in the next section we present the idea of "video-tiles," a graphical way of representing and browsing video objects. The remainder of this section describes the key features that are available to the users of our multimedia news.

• *Security:* Before a user may receive the orientation screen, which can be used to either begin browsing or perform some specialized function, he/she must provide a password. The need for security becomes apparent when we discuss personal profiles and scrapbooks.

• *User Interface and Navigation:* We have selected a *sections metaphor* for presentation of news stories. Buttons at the bottom of the screen and pull-down menus provide the functions. The screen itself contains several pushable icons corresponding to sections of a newspaper – sports, business, etc. (Figure 8). Using a familiar metaphor reduces cognitive load for users. After selecting a section, the user is presented with a number of stories; a selection on a story "plays" the story on a media-player. Returning to the section index and front page, index is accomplished with a selection at any time. This helps to ensure that the user never becomes "lost in the hyperspace" of the multimedia news.

• *Follow-Ups:* Through the use of keywords, the reader may *follow-up* any article or media object just viewed. By a single click (backed up by a distributed query on the database servers) he/she will be presented with related articles and media objects.

• *User Profiling:* A subtly different yet more interesting way of presenting information is to do so by *user profile* or preference. We believe that each user should have his/her own customizable profile file. To create, edit, or remove a profile, the user selects a button at the bottom of the screen. In creation, the user is presented with a number of keywords from a fixed "news vocabulary;" for instance, cinema, sports, hockey, business, stocks, columnist names, etc. Each word can be added to the profile. The user is also given the option to add his/her own words to the profile. These keywords act as filters to the vast information source – by selecting the special section "By Profile," the user receives only stories whose keywords match the selected keywords. Premade profiles are also available for copying. Other prototype news systems have used the concept of *intelligent* user profiles [6,10]. They differ from the previously described profiles in that they "evolve" over time by "watching" what types of articles the user likes to read. For instance, if a user continually reads articles relating to "automobiles," the intelligent profile will add this keyword to itself (if it is not already there) so that in the future these types of articles will be automatically presented to the user.

A problem with any type of news filter like profiles is that if the user is continually presented with the same type of stories, he/she may miss pertinent information from other areas. We propose to "spice up" filtered news with random stories from a variety of fields and so the user may stumble upon otherwise missed information.

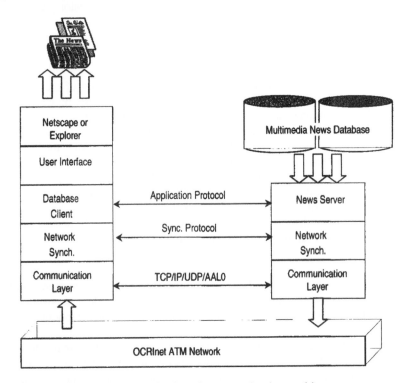

Figure 8. The playback and communication architecture.

• *Intelligent Agent:* At our laboratory, we are performing on-going research in the growing area of *intelligent agents*. An agent performs some action or makes some decision on behalf of its user. It makes this decision or action either because it was supplied with a rule by the user, which prompted it, or it has a knowledge base from which it deduced that the action was appropriate. Agents can also learn by watching their users use application programs and by examining user satisfaction with the choices or actions they have made. In general, there are two main issues, *competence* and *trust*. Competence addresses how the agent acquires and uses salient information, and trust addresses the level of faith the user has in his/her agent to make decisions and actions on his/her behalf [7].

We believe the concept of agents is of great interest within a news context; users may not have time to read *all* the news that is presented. We want them to be able to dispatch *software robots* to scout the database servers, communicate with other users' agents, and search for particular products and events in the news. For instance, a user could tell his/her agent to "be on the lookout" for 1985-1989 Toyota Corolla automobiles for sale and when one is found, to alert the user. This shows the need for user *alerts*. When stock prices change, or when a product is found, the user needs to be informed as soon as possible. A user's session may be interrupted (with his/her permission) at any time by a critical event requiring an alert.

• *Aging:* News stories go through an *aging* process as they develop. These aging stages should be available to the user so that, if desired, a story's development may be reviewed. The documents that include these stories are themselves archived so that old news editions are available to the user for browsing and searching.

• *Proxies:* We believe that *proxies* should also be incorporated into the news context. Proxies are a way to quickly scan a large amount of information. We have a special section called "Headlines and Bulletins" which is a kind of news-proxy. Selecting this section will provide only top stories in each of the other sections – this is news-at-a-glance. We are also investigating "video-proxies" and "news-proxies" where a multimedia news document is played in a compressed, rapid manner, but at a rate slow enough for a user to "get the drift of it."

• *Querying and Searching:* Querying and searching are important in the system. Together, they should support a user who wishes to search for an article or media object relating to something *specific* – for instance, a video clip of Madonna and Michael Jackson together – or something *general* – for instance, a video clip about war. Our first prototype uses keyword searching, but we are also investigating more complex search mechanisms such as color and object querying. Queries and searches will be available within media objects (for example, search for "bicycle" in this text object), articles (for example, search all media in this article) and the database (i.e., search the entire archive). Ultimately we want to realize *multimedia perception* – a multimedia query specification language with a seamless interface.

• *Multimedia Scrapbooks:* Another feature that we feel is interesting enough to include at the user sites is the idea of *multimedia scrapbooks*. That is, with certain arrangements, a user can be allocated a certain portion of the archive for his/her own use. Then, at any point during browsing, if an article is of particular interest, the user may arrange to have the media objects included in his/her personal scrapbook where personal annotations or custom documents may be created. A student doing a project on Canadian fisheries, for example, could build up a scrapbook of related media objects and from this put together a custom multimedia presentation on the subject. Consider the ramifications of giving other users (particularly students) read access to these scrapbooks. Students could *share their views* on areas of interest – there are educational benefits to viewing information from a different perspective; this is, in fact, the concept of hypertext and hypermedia. We could create an interactive, collaborative, educational media-space.

• *Advertising:* Finally, what would a newspaper be without *advertising?* Multimedia advertising is an issue that has some interesting questions. In an interactive multimedia news system, should advertisements be intrusive or should the user be able to avoid them? We feel that advertisement is best handled with profiles and intelligent agents – that is, give the user control over what he/she must view. The profile should serve as a filter to eliminate advertisements, which are of no interest, and the agents can be directed to search for advertisements (including multimedia classifieds) which may be of interest.

Advertisements may be linked to editorial content. For instance, a product review article could be linked to appropriate advertisements. In an even better scenario, imagine a video clip of a new movie by Sylvester Stallone in which he portrays a motor-bike racer. It could be very lucrative for retailers to associate themselves with the clip. For instance, a local motorcycle dealership that carries that same line of bikes that we saw in the clip, or a boot store that carries the same boots that the actor was wearing may want to do this. Direct links to advertisers are available and users may eventually be able to order products over the OCRInet. An index of advertisers is also present in that day's edition for users whose primary goal is to browse merchandise.

4. THE NEWS VIDEO BROWSER

It is clear that news stories, clips, and highlights in digital video form will be available to news-on-demand users. Video is appearing more and more in other applications, too; video-conferencing, video-on-demand, video-editing, interactive encyclopedias, and multimedia mail, to name just a few. We are interested in studying further the areas of video-on-demand and interactive video, to discover new ways to represent, browse, and manipulate video that map well into the news context. We are primarily concerned with video objects that are stored in some large repository (e.g., a multimedia database), but live video from broadcast centers is also of interest to us. There are two main issues when dealing with video repositories; (i) representing the stored videos as a whole to the user, and (ii) support for browsing through individual videos. This section first discusses other research done relating to video representations and video browsing techniques, and then proposes a video browser for the news application.

4.1 VISUAL INDICES TO VIDEOS

Representing a video by using a textual name (e.g., "concert") does not provide much information about the content or length of the video. This is the problem with *textual* indices in a *visual and temporal* medium. The alternative is to provide some kind of graphical index (or icon). However, providing a single icon to represent the video provides little information about the content of the video and almost nothing of the temporal nature of the video. Some related work is now discussed.

Zhang et al. have developed algorithms to automatically parse television news and create 3D visual indices often called "micons" [16] (also proposed by Mackay et al. [8]). Micons are iconic cubes with 3 faces. The front face shows a key frame or the current frame, and the top and side faces are striped in different colors representing the presence of camera breaks in the video. The depth of the micon is proportional to the relative length of the video. Alternatively, in Zhang et al. [17], the top and edge faces consist of the pixels from the top and right edges of each of the frames in the video, thus creating a stack effect and providing what they call the "visual rhythm" of the video. The micon conveys content *and* temporal information. Ueda et al. use an array of micons to represent video structure in a video editing context thereby creating a more informative clip window [15]. A different approach is taken by Teodosio et al. [13]. By preprocessing videos and using image processing algorithms, they create what they call "salient stills" (single frames) as indices to videos. The salient still reflects temporal changes that occurred in the video and preserves critical aspects of the content. It may feature any or all of the variable resolution patches, composited objects from the scene, or a field of view greater than that of any single frame in the video. Finally, Tonomura et al. developed the "VideoSpaceIcon" to represent spatial and temporal aspects of video [14]. By first detecting the camera operations in a video segment using image processing, the VideoSpaceIcon can be built, allowing viewers to grasp the physical space of the segment at a glance. "X-Ray" images are incorporated as well and camera movements are made apparent through icon shape.

4.2 SUPPORT FOR VIDEO BROWSING

Let us say that a user wishes to browse a video and assume that the video has been indexed at some granularity. Browsing means intelligently interacting with the video, whereas watching the video means passively viewing the content from start to finish. The VCR can be a model for the minimum amount of interaction that a user must be given (play, stop, rewind, fast-forward, and pause modes) but users should be able to do more; for instance, replay video, browse scenes, play at variable speeds and directions, and have quick, easy, random access to the smallest granularity of video that is indexed – i.e., scenes or frames.

The micon may actually be used for browsing through video content. An interactive micon can be equipped with a cursor bar which moves along the side face (backwards and forwards in time). In an approach used in [17], frames or camera shots, depending on the type of micon, may be selected and played by moving the cursor bar to them and clicking. However, once the shot is selected there is no iteration and the process does not repeat on the selected shot itself. Mills et al. solved this problem with their "video magnifier" tool [11]. The video magnifier allows the user to recursively magnify the resolution of a video while preserving a global context. By global context we mean the answer to the question, "what am I looking at with respect to the video as a whole?" Earlier work by Furnas addressed this problem with fish-eye views of data [1], as has recent work by Mackinlay et al. who present data graphically on a long folded "wall" using perspective transformations [9], and in a companion paper, present hierarchic information graphically in 3D trees of cones called "cone-trees." The video magnifier produces a hierarchic view of the video with smaller and smaller levels of granularity. Also, the upper levels of the hierarchy remain displayed while browsing at a lower level. This allows the user to visualize his/her current position in the video with respect to the video as a whole, thus preserving global context.

4.3 NEWS VIDEOS – TEMPORAL STRUCTURE AND KEY-FRAME SELECTION

In the context of multimedia news, we expect that television news stories will be an important component of media content and video reports and clips from TV news will be media objects within multimedia news articles. By video reports, or news video stories, we mean the kind of news story filed by, for example, a foreign correspondent or a CNN reporter. What is the structure of these video reports and will they map well into our video browser? We believe that they will, based on their innate temporal structure. By watching a number of these reports, it is easy to find a generic temporal structure into which most fall. In [16], the temporal structure of a news broadcast is illustrated as a series of anchor-person shots, commercial shots, etc. Figure 9 illustrates the temporal structure of *news-shots* (as opposed to entire news broadcasts). A news-shot is an independent news story, filed on video, which describes the complete story.

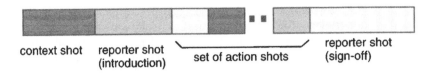

context shot   reporter shot   reporter shot
                   (introduction)   set of action shots   (sign-off)

Figure 9. Temporal structure of a news video story.

The first shot of such a video is usually a context shot with the reporter's voice-over. It sets the scene for the story and may consist of several camera shots. Next we see the reporter as she tells us the story. Then, again with voice-over, a series of action shots. Finally, we see the reporter again as she summarizes and signs off (e.g., "Sue Smith, CNN News, Budapest"). It is not hard to see that by simply taking the first frames of all the camera cuts, the news video story is represented compactly and in a very informative way. We are interested more in news video stories rather than news broadcasts for the following reason: the multimedia news system will already contain the in-depth type of news reporting found in newspapers and will rely on news video stories to complete the story and fill in gaps. We have no immediate plans to introduce *entire news broadcasts* into our system, preferring to simply playback the video stories on demand.

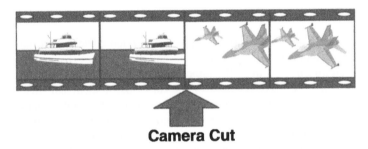

Camera Cut

Choose the next frame as a representative icon
Figure 10. Choosing frames for the video browser - frames following camera cuts
are selected as indices.

In some video tools, such as the hierarchic video browser, representative frames are selected from the stream because of their position in the stream. For example, they are chosen because they are the 100th, 200th, 300th, etc. frames. In other systems, such as ours, frames are chosen because they represent camera transitions or breaks. We chose to use camera breaks since, in the news context, they segment the streams into more meaningful sub-streams, or groups. Figure 10 illustrates the frame selection procedure.

Discovering camera operations after-the-fact is crucial to video tools, which offer a basic browsing unit that depends upon camera-cuts. Any system which can offer scene browsing or shot browsing needs to be able to first detect these scenes and shots. See [19] for details of our research into this area. The basic premise of segmenting video streams into cuts is that frames on opposite sides of a camera-break have radically different content (based on some appropriate metric). Detecting the cuts is a matter of comparing adjacent frames for significant content changes. One way of doing this is by making pair-wise comparisons of pixel intensity values where two pixels' intensity is said to be different if their difference exceeds some threshold. Adjacent frames are said to be different if the number of pixels that are deemed different also exceeds some threshold. A second way of detecting cuts is to compare intensity or color histograms. Making cut detection more difficult is the possible presence of special effects serving as transitions. These include fade-ins and outs, wipes, and dissolves [15-17].

Determining camera operations such as pans and zooms is accomplished in similar ways; one finds motion vectors, which reveal these operations. For instance, by examining blocks of pixels in groups of frames it is possible to compute a vector indicating how the positions of the blocks changed through the group. Using suitable thresholds, it can be concluded that, in general, camera pans are revealed as horizontal vectors, camera zooms are revealed as radial vectors, and so on [15-17,19].

4.4 THE VIDEO-TILES TOOL FOR NEWS VIDEOS

Work in our lab has shown that a graphical tool for video browsing that we call "video-tiles," is very effective. Video-tiles are both a way of representing the video in a single graphical entity and an interactive tool for browsing through the video. They are a visual way of representing and browsing videos, interactive, scalable, and recursive. Video-tiles are not media players per se. We assume however, that the media player can be spawned at any time during browsing (e.g., to view or edit a video segment).

The basic premise of video-tiles is to allow hierarchic browsing through various levels of granularity in a fashion similar to that of the video magnifier. The shape of a video-tile is rectangular and is composed of processed frames of video of varying size. In the center of the tile is a video keyframe, which represents the whole video. Initially this could be the median frame, the first frame, or even a salient still of the video — we will call this level 1 and it is actual size — has the same resolution as the video — say, 320x240 pixels. Level 1 can also be thought of as the current frame. Along the perimeter outside of this center frame (in contact with its edges) there is a "ring" of level 2 frames each of whose length and width is half that of the center frame (one quarter of the area). This level has 12 frames, which represent a finer grain view of the video. Where the video was represented by a single frame at level 1, it is represented by 12 frames at level 2. Similarly, level 3 is a ring of 36 frames surrounding level 2, of half the size of those at level 2. We have seen that even up to level 5 (length dimensions one sixteenth of the size of the level 1 frame) that the frames show enough colors or shapes to convey *some* meaningful contextual information. Note that at level 5 the video (or segment of the video) is represented by 180 evenly spaced frames. Accompanying the tile will be a video bar that indicates where in the video segment the current frame is located. This provides some temporal information.

The video-tile is interactive. That is, by selecting any one of the frames in the tile, a new tile is produced. The new tile now features the selected frame as the level 1 frame. If we assume that the first video-tile drawn has a domain of frames equal to the number of frames in the video, then the second tile drawn (after the first click) will have a domain equal to some subset of previous domain, say one half of it. The median fame of this new domain is the selected frame and outer rings of the tile span only the new domain. Thus the user continually zooms into the video and, as new tiles are drawn, previous ones remain on the screen; global context is therefore preserved.

Special inputs, such as double clicks, are reserved for starting the media player. That is, if rather than browsing to a lower level the user wishes to play the video commencing at a particular frame in the tile (in either standard or proxy mode), then a double click on that frame will start the player. The player must be equipped with at least basic VCR functions as well as some of the features mentioned in the previous section. Furthermore, the number of levels in the tile may be changed at any time and so the user can "grow" or "shrink" the tile to see a greater or fewer number of representative frames per iteration.

The idea of "video-proxies" is incorporated into our player. Proxies are small, low-resolution, or intermittent representations of videos. Rather than playing a full size 5-minute video, a user might want to view a small, low-resolution version of the movie, which played only every 10 frames. In this way, the 5-minute video can be previewed in 30 seconds (or less). In effect, the single frame in the tile's center is the ultimate proxy – one frame. The outer levels are better and better proxies which, if played back (with appropriate delays), give a brief overview of the clip.

The browser will track the user's journey through the video and will be able to reproduce the "video-footprints" the user made in the video so that his/her steps may be retraced, rebrowsed, or even sent to another user. Consider merging the ideas of salient stills and video-footprints. After browsing through (and possibly "marking" certain frames) a video clip, a salient still can be produced *on only those frames which are marked* – a user's entire browsing *experience* (with that clip) is represented by a single image.

4.4.1 Example Scenario

Figures 11 through 13 illustrate a browsing session in which a user zooms into a particular spot of an animated cartoon. For this test case, the basic browsing unit is *not* the camera cut but rather groups of frames which need not have camera cuts at both ends (although every camera cut belongs to a group).

Figure 11. Initial tile – the focus is on the first frame but the entire story is represented as sub-tiles at level two and ordered in a clockwise fashion from the NW corner.

Note that in the first tile the cartoon is represented by twelve sub-tiles at level 2 and the focus is at the first frame which happens to be the title of the cartoon. These level 2 sub-tiles tell the complete story in a condensed visual way. Note how the sliding scales at the bottom of the tool effectively display both the current focus frame and the current frame range at any given iteration. The video-tiles tool has proven to be very effective for news story videos, particularly since the temporal format of such short videos may often be parameterized to a greater or lesser extent.

Figure 12. Focusing on the part of the story where the cat is blown out of the hatch. The user has selected sub-tile 6 (ordered clockwise from the NW corner) from Figure 11.

Figure 13. Zooming further into this part of the story by reducing the scope of frames being viewed.

5. INTERNET-BASED NEWS SERVICES – PUSHING DATA

Internet connectivity is currently high and increasing and there are alternative news applications emerging that work strictly on TCP/IP. Many of these applications are based on push technology on the World Wide Web, a delivery model in which updates and newly created articles are sent from servers to the clients' desktops asynchronously (e.g., as they are published). This reduces the latency between the time that the article is published on the Web and the time that the user is aware of it and able to read it. Servers can also create user-awareness of new data in more clumsy ways including posting "what's new" pages, sending E-mails to clients, or installing bookmark-managing software on the client side. Pushing data to the desktop, however, is currently seen as the most attractive and effective fashion to deliver news on the Internet. Some commercial products are BackWeb, iFusion, PointCast, Marimba, and Intermind (see [18] for detailed product reviews).

The push technology works in subtly different ways, depending on the product that the client is using. Generally speaking, the model is similar to a broadcast model; *transmitters* serve content, *tuners* accept content, and *channels* carry content. When there is data to be viewed, the user must be notified. The news client talks to the end-user through the screen-saver or desktop. In this sense the screen-saver is a "live" entity. The screen-saver informs the user of new content, or displays short notifications (e.g., "new data at CNN relating to O.J.Simpson"). Alternatively, the server-side may bypass the desktop and send an E-mail notification to the end-user. Typically, notifications are small and may be Universal Resource Locators (URLs) or simply notifications of change. In a few systems notifications may be content itself (e.g., an HTML document with images). For proprietary desktop screen-saver applications, notifications may be in the form of active links (not URLs) that load content. In general, the OCRI-net based system that we have described has advantages over push technology. It is more customizable with profiles and is intended for high-speed networks. However, the Web is becoming a high-stakes medium for commercial products that deliver timely information, and push technology will remain a large part of this. Future Web-based news applications will likely develop features that equal and surpass those that we have described.

6. CONCLUSIONS

We have described a multimedia news-on-demand system that is an informative and educational tool for a variety of types of users with varying needs. We continue to test our user interface and refine it in accordance to user-comments and surveys. A complex platform called MEDIABASE provides the storage, transport, and synchronization of multimedia news articles. A unique nonlinear video-browsing tool is provided to scan video content of news videos, which frequently appear in, or are linked to news documents. Further readings detailing this application are available [19,20]. We are currently studying how to further automate and facilitate news access and retrieval using the mobile agent paradigm over the MEDIABASE platform [23]. We maintain a Web page [22] that details our current research program and other related publications.

References

1. Furnas, G., "Generalized Fisheye Views," *Proc. of CHI'86 Human Factors in Computing Systems*, ACM, 1986.
2. Hoffert, E. and Gretsch, G., "The Digital News System at EDUCOM: A Convergence of Interactive Computing, Newspapers, Television and High-Speed Networks," *Comm. of the ACM*, Vol. 35, No. 4, April 1991.

3. Karmouch, A., "A Multimedia Information and Communications System: MEDIABASE," *Proc. Multimedia Comm.'93*, Banff, April, 1993.

4. Karmouch, A. and Emery, J., "A Multimedia Document Architecture and Rendering Synchronization Scheme," *Proc. Second Intl. Conf. on Broadband Islands*, Athens, 1993.

5. Koons, W., O'Dell, A., Frishberg, N., and Laff, M., "The Computer Sciences Electronic Magazine: Translating from Paper to Multimedia," *Proc. of CHI'92*, May 3-7, 1992.

6. Lippman, A. and Bender, W., "News and Movies in the 50 Megabit Living Room," IEEE, *Globecom*, Tokyo, November, 1987.

7. Maes, P., "Agents that Reduce Work and Information Overload," *Comm. of the ACM*, 37(7), July, 1994.

8. Mackay, E. and Davenport, G., "Virtual Video Editing in Interactive Multimedia Applications," *Comm. of the ACM*, 32(7), July, 1989.

9. Mackinlay, J., Robertson G., and Card S., "Perspective Wall: Detail and Context Smoothly Integrated," *Proc. of CHI'91 Human Factors in Computing Systems*, ACM, 1991.

10. Miller, G., Baber, G., and Gilliland, M., "News On-Demand for Multimedia Networks," *Proc. ACM Multimedia 93*, June 6, 1993.

11. Mills, M., Cohen, J., and Wong, Y., "A Magnifier Tool for Video Data," *Proc. of CHI'92*, May3-7, 1992.

12. Ohkubo. M., Kobayashi. N., and Nakagawa. T., "Design of an Information Skimming Space," *Proc. ACM Multimedia 93*, June 6, 1993.

13. Tesodosio, L. and Bender, W., "Salient Video Stills: Content and Context Preserved," *Proc. ACM Multimedia 93*, June 6, 1993.

14. Tonomura, Y., Akutsu, A., Otsuji, K., and Sadakata, T., "VideoMAP and VideoSpaceIcon: Tools for Annotating Video Content," *Proc. of INTERCHI'93*, April 1993.

15. Ueda, U., Miyatake, T., Sumino, S., and Nagasaka, A., "Automatic Structure Visualization for Video Editing," *Proc. of INTERCHI'93*, April 1993.

16. Zhang, H., Gong, Y., Smoliar, S., and Tan, S., "Automatic Parsing of News Video," *Int. Conf. on Multimedia Computing and Systems*, IEEE, 1994.

17. Zhang, H. and Smoliar, S., "Developing Power Tools for Indexing and Retrieval," *S.P.I.E.*,Vol 2185, 1994.

18. PC Magazine on-line, Push Technology, http://www.zdnet.com/pcmag/features/push.

19. Falchuk, B. and Karmouch, A., "An Interactive Multimedia News Service over an ATM Network," in *Multimedia Tools and Applications*, B.Furht (Ed.), Kluwer Academic Publishers, MA, 1996, pp. 155-184.

20. Falchuk, B. and Karmouch, A., "A Multimedia News Delivery System over an ATM Network," *Proc. Int'l. Conf. Multimedia Computing and Systems*, pp. 56-63, Washington, D.C., May 1995.

21. Li, L., Karmouch, A., and Georganas, N.D., "Performance Modeling of Distributed Integration in Real-Time Multimedia Scenarios," *Proc. Multimedia Communications*, Banff, April 13-16, 1993.

22. Multimedia Information Research Laboratory, University of Ottawa, Dept. Electrical Engineering, A.Karmouch (director), http://deneb.genie.uottawa.ca.

23. Falchuk, B. and Karmouch, A., "A Mobile Agent Prototype for Autonomous Multimedia Information Access, Interaction and Retrieval," *Proc. MMM'97*, Singapore, Nov. 1997.

INDEX

Printed and bound by CPI Group (UK) Ltd, Croydon, CR0 4YY

22/10/2024

01777630-0015